The Wiley Blackwell
Handbook of Mindfulness

The Wiley Blackwell Handbook of Mindfulness

Volume I

Edited by

Amanda Ie
Christelle T. Ngnoumen
Ellen J. Langer

WILEY Blackwell

This edition first published 2014
© 2014 John Wiley & Sons, Ltd.

Registered Office
John Wiley & Sons Ltd, The Atrium, Southern Gate, Chichester, West Sussex, PO19 8SQ, UK

Editorial Offices
350 Main Street, Malden, MA 02148-5020, USA
9600 Garsington Road, Oxford, OX4 2DQ, UK
The Atrium, Southern Gate, Chichester, West Sussex, PO19 8SQ, UK

For details of our global editorial offices, for customer services, and for information about how to apply for permission to reuse the copyright material in this book please see our website at www.wiley.com/wiley-blackwell.

The right of Amanda Ie, and Christelle T. Ngnoumen, and Ellen J. Langer to be identified as the authors of the editorial material in this work has been asserted in accordance with the UK Copyright, Designs and Patents Act 1988.

Wiley also publishes its books in a variety of electronic formats. Some content that appears in print may not be available in electronic books.

Designations used by companies to distinguish their products are often claimed as trademarks. All brand names and product names used in this book are trade names, service marks, trademarks or registered trademarks of their respective owners. The publisher is not associated with any product or vendor mentioned in this book.

Limit of Liability/Disclaimer of Warranty: While the publisher and authors have used their best efforts in preparing this book, they make no representations or warranties with respect to the accuracy or completeness of the contents of this book and specifically disclaim any implied warranties of merchantability or fitness for a particular purpose. It is sold on the understanding that the publisher is not engaged in rendering professional services and neither the publisher nor the author shall be liable for damages arising herefrom. If professional advice or other expert assistance is required, the services of a competent professional should be sought.

Library of Congress Cataloging-in-Publication Data

The Wiley Blackwell handbook of mindfulness / edited by Amanda Ie, Christelle T. Ngnoumen, and Ellen J. Langer.
      pages cm
   Includes bibliographical references and index.
   ISBN 978-1-118-29487-1 (cloth)
   1. Attention.   2. Consciousness.   3. Leadership–Psychological aspects.   I. Ie, Amanda, editor of compilation.
   BF321.W5495 2014
   158–dc23

                                                                                          2013041266

A catalogue record for this book is available from the British Library.

Cover image: © Ellen Langer
Cover design by Cyan Design

Set in 10/12.5pt Galliard by Aptara Inc., New Delhi, India
Printed in Malaysia by Ho Printing (M) Sdn Bhd

1   2014

Contents

Notes on Editors

Amanda Ie is a researcher in the Department of Psychology at Harvard University (Ph.D. from Harvard University; B.Sc. from Brown University). Her research interests include thought suppression, intrusive thought contents, mindfulness, and multitasking.

Christelle T. Ngnoumen is a doctoral student and researcher in the Department of Psychology at Harvard University (B.A. Brown University). Her research explores the mindlessness of stereotyping, implicit social cognition, and face perception.

Ellen J. Langer is Professor of Psychology at Harvard University and widely considered to be the "mother" of mindfulness. She is the recipient of four distinguished scientist awards, a Guggenheim Fellowship, among a host of other honors, and has authored over 200 research articles on mindfulness and topics such as perceived control, aging, learning, and decision-making. She is the author of 11 books, including *Mindfulness* (1990); *The Power of Mindful Learning* (1997); *On Becoming an Artist: Reinventing Yourself Through Mindful Creativity* (2007); and, most recently, *Counterclockwise: Mindful Health and the Power of Possibility* (2009).

Notes on Contributors

Susan Albers is a clinical psychologist at the Cleveland Clinic. She graduated from the University of Denver and did her predoctoral internship at the University of Notre Dame. Dr. Albers completed her post doctoral work at Stanford University. Dr. Albers has written six books on the topic of mindful eating including *Eat.Q.*, *Eating Mindfully*, *Eat, Drink & Be Mindful*, *Mindful Eating 101*, *50 Ways to Soothe Yourself Without Food*, and *But I Deserve This Chocolate*. Dr. Albers was awarded the University of Denver, Master Scholar Award. She conducts mindful eating workshops internationally (www.eatingmindfully.com).

Stuart Albert is an Associate Professor at the Curtis L. Carlson School of Management at the University of Minnesota. He received his Ph.D. from The Ohio State in social psychology, and has been a visiting scholar both at Harvard and MIT. His new book, entitled: *WHEN: the Art of Perfect Timing* (Jossey-Bass, 2013), summarizes 20 years of research into the question of when to act so as not to be too early or too late, as well as how to identify timing-related risks, an environment or context that changes overnight, for example.

Ronald A. Alexander, licensed psychotherapist, leadership consultant, clinical trainer, is the executive director of the Open Mind Training® Institute in Santa Monica. A pioneer in Somatic Psychotherapy, Holistic Psychology, Mindfulness, and Leadership Coaching, he was one of the early practitioners to apply Buddhist psychology and mindfulness to Western mental health. Alexander conducts professional and personal trainings nationally and internationally. He is a long time extension faculty member of UCLA. Alexander is the author of *Wise Mind Open Mind: Finding Purpose and Meaning in Times of Crisis, Loss and Change* (New Harbinger, 2009). www.openmindtraining.com (longer bio in Dropbox folder).

Wyatt C. Anderson is a doctoral student in Social Psychology at the University of Georgia. He is broadly interested in the perception of meaning in life and how people cope with uncertain experiences.

Diane B. Arnkoff is a faculty member in the Department of Psychology at The Catholic University of America. She was Director of Clinical Training for 10 years and is now Professor Emerita. Her research areas include anxiety in nonclinical populations. Recently, she and her colleagues have been studying how mindfulness and related constructs play a role in anxiety and how mindfulness may improve the outcomes in intervention programs for social anxiety and stress. She also researches psychotherapy from the perspective of psychotherapy integration, focusing on the treatment decisions made by eclectic and integrative therapists.

Emily Balcetis is an Assistant Professor of Social Psychology at New York University. Her research interests fall at the intersection of social and cognitive psychology. Specifically, she investigates what and how motivations influence visual perception, social judgment, and decision-making. She earned her Ph.D. in Social and Personality Psychology from Cornell University, where she held a Sage Fellowship and earned the Society of Experimental Social Psychology 2006 Dissertation Award for her research on motivated visual perception.

David Black is Assistant Professor of Preventive Medicine at the University of Southern California Keck School of Medicine. His research program centers on the delivery and evaluation of mind-body intervention modalities—specifically mindfulness training—to alleviate mental and physical symptoms associated with health and disease states. He is the author of more than 25 peer-reviewed publications, including articles in leading journals such as *JAMA Pediatrics, Journal of Adolescent Health, Pediatrics,* and *Psychoneuroendocrinology.* He is the Editor of *Mindfulness Research Monthly* (www.mindfulexperience.org), a web-based dissemination bulletin informing the latest advances in mindfulness research. His current objective is to delineate biophysiological mechanisms underlying integrative health interventions.

Pablo Briñol is Associate Professor of social psychology at the Universidad Autónoma de Madrid (Spain), and visiting scholar at Ohio State University. His research interest focuses on the study of the psychological mechanisms underlying attitudes and persuasion, with emphasis on metacognitive processes and measures of change. Dr. Briñol has published several books in the domain of persuasion, and more than 100 publications. His research has appeared in top journals of the field, including Psychological Bulletin, Advances in Experimental Social Psychology, *Journal of Personality and Social Psychology,* and *Psychological Science.*

James M. Broadway earned his Ph.D. in Psychology (Cognition and Brain Science) from Georgia Institute of Technology in 2012. His research interests include understanding how the brain performs attention, working memory, time perception, and other mental functions. He is working with Jonathan Schooler to investigate psychophysiological correlates of mind-wandering.

Lori A. Brotto has a Ph.D. in clinical psychology and is an Associate Professor in the UBC Department of Obstetrics and Gynaecology, and Head of the Division of Gynaecologic Specialties, as well as a registered psychologist in Vancouver, Canada. She is the director of the UBC Sexual Health Laboratory where research primarily focuses on developing mindfulness-based interventions for women with sexual desire and arousal difficulties, and women with chronic genital pain. Other major lines of research include exploring sexuality and reproductive health in ethnic-minority women, studying the intracrinology of androgen metabolites in women's desire, asexuality, and sexuality after cancer. Dr. Brotto is the Associate Editor for *Archives of Sexual Behavior* and *Sexual and Relationship Therapy*, and has over 80 peer-reviewed publications.

LeeAnn Cardaciotto is Associate Professor of Psychology at La Salle University in Philadelphia, PA. Her research interests focus on the study of mindfulness and related constructs including self-compassion. Her work in this area began with the development of the Philadelphia Mindfulness Scale (PHLMS) to assess mindfulness as a bi-dimensional construct, and has continued to examine this model in a variety of contexts including social anxiety disorder. She also incorporates mindfulness- and acceptance-based approaches in her teaching of master's-level counseling students.

James Carmody is an Associate Professor of Medicine at University of Massachusetts Medical School. He is interested in the qualities of attending to experience that are associated with well-being, particularly those associated with mindfulness practice. His research is in the psychological and neural mechanisms of mind–body processes related to mindfulness practice, and he is PI on several NIH-funded mindfulness trials. Jim studied and practiced in Zen, Tibetan, Theravada, and Advaita traditions in a number of countries for 40 years. He leads courses for clinicians with the goal of making the conceptualization and experience of mindfulness straightforward, jargon-free, and accessible for patients. His work has been featured in numerous media including the *New York Times* and *NPR*.

Shelley Carson received her Ph.D. in psychology from Harvard University, where she continues to teach and conduct research in the areas of creativity, resilience, and psychopathology. Her work has been published widely in national and international scientific journals and featured on the Discovery Channel, CNN, and NPR. She has won multiple teaching awards for her popular course *Creativity: Madmen, Geniuses, and Harvard Students*. She is the author of the award-winning book *Your Creative Brain: Seven Steps to Maximize Imagination, Productivity, and Innovation in Your Life* (Jossey-Bass, 2010), and coauthor of *Almost Depressed: Is My (or My Loved One's) Unhappiness a Problem?* (Hazelden, 2013).

Jason Clower is Associate Professor of Comparative Religion and Asian Studies at California State University, Chico. He studies Buddhist and Confucian philosophy and Asian-inspired spiritual movements in California.

Shana Cole is a social psychology Ph.D. candidate at New York University. Her research broadly explores the ways in which visual perception informs, guides, and serves successful self-regulation. She studies this within a wide variety of domains, including health, culture, relationships, politics, and emotion regulation. Her dissertation work focuses on the role of visual perception in self-control conflicts, detailing visual biases that emerge as people struggle to remain committed to long-term goals in the face of temptation.

Alia Crum is an Adjunct Professor of Management and Postdoctoral Scholar at Columbia Business School. Dr. Crum received her Ph.D. from Yale University and B.A. degree from Harvard University. Her research examines the effect of mindsets— the lenses through which information is perceived, organized, and interpreted—on important outcomes such as work performance, interpersonal behavior, and physiological health.

Jack Demick, a clinical and developmental psychologist, currently teaches courses in human development at Brown University. Previously, he has held positions at Clark University, Harvard University, and the University of Massachusetts Medical School. He has published numerous journal articles and book chapters, has coedited eight volumes, and serves as the editor of the *Journal of Adult Development*. His representative research interests include cognitive development (e.g., cognitive style, environmental cognition) and social development (e.g., adaptation of families to infant and child adoption, other life transitions) across the life span.

Sona Dimidjian joined the faculty at the University of Colorado, Boulder in 2006 and is an Associate Professor in the Department of Psychology and Neuroscience. Her research addresses the treatment and prevention of depression, particularly among women during pregnancy and postpartum. She is a leading expert in cognitive and behavioral approaches to depression and the clinical application of contemplative practices, such as meditation and yoga. She has a longstanding interest in the dissemination of evidence-based treatment, both nationally and internationally.

Maja Djikic is a Senior Research Associate and the Director of Self-Development Lab at Rotman School of Management, University of Toronto. She is a psychologist specializing in the field of personality development. She has been a postdoctoral fellow with Desautels Centre for Integrative Thinking (Rotman School of Management) and Psychology Department at Harvard University. She has published more than 20 articles and book chapters in the area of personality development. Her research has been published in *Journal of Research in Personality*, *Psychological Science*, *Creativity Research Journal*, *New Ideas in Psychology*, *Journal of Adult Development*, and others.

Elissa Epel is an Associate Professor at the UCSF Department of Psychiatry. She examines how stress processes lead to early disease precursors, focusing on overeating, abdominal obesity, and immune cell aging, and whether interventions can reverse stress-related tendencies and damage. Epel studied psychology and psychobiology at Stanford University (B.A., 1990), and clinical and health psychology at Yale University (Ph.D., 1998). Epel has received research awards from APA (e.g., the APA Early Career Award, Academy of Behavioral Medicine Research Neal Miller Young Investigator Award).

Ronald M. Epstein is Professor of Family Medicine, Psychiatry and Oncology at the University of Rochester Medical Center, where he practices family medicine and palliative medicine and directs the Center for Communication and Disparities Research. His research on improving patient–physician communication focuses on marginalized populations, stigmatized conditions such as depression and HIV, and end-of-life care. He has written extensively about and developed innovative educational programs in mindful practice, communication skills, physician self-awareness, and assessment of professional competence. He is a graduate of Wesleyan University and Harvard Medical School, and has authored over 200 articles and book chapters.

Emily B. Falk is an assistant professor within the Annenberg School for Communication at the University of Pennsylvania. Dr. Falk's research integrates methods from cognitive neuroscience, social psychology, and communication studies to understand media effects at the individual, group, and population levels. Falk's lab has conducted studies examining neural precursors of the spread of messages, and ongoing work examines neural processes relevant to understanding social norms, social influence, and effective communication. She received her bachelor's degree in neuroscience from Brown University, and her Ph.D. in psychology from the University of California, Los Angeles (UCLA). See http://cn.asc.upenn.edu for more information.

Sayyed Mohsen Fatemi (Ph.D., University of British Columbia, 2003, Post Doctorate, Harvard University, 2009–2013) has done his postdoctoral studies in the Department of Psychology at Harvard University in areas of social, clinical, health, and cross-cultural psychology with a focus on Mindfulness. He is an Associate and a Teaching Fellow in the Department of Psychology at Harvard University and works in areas of social and cross-cultural psychology. Dr. Fatemi is a frequently published author and poet, and has been the keynote speaker of a number of international conferences. Dr. Fatemi teaches in the department of psychology at Harvard University, University of Massachusetts in Boston, Western Washington University, and Boston Graduate School of Psychoanalysis. He has also taught at the University of Toronto and the University of British Columbia. Dr. Fatemi is a registered psychologist and has worked on the implications of mindfulness for anxiety attack, personality disorders, family and spousal issues, relationship management, psychology of negotiations, psychology of mass media, and political psychology. He is a popular guest of multiple television and radio programs, and has offered training and coaching programs all across the world in areas such as negotiation and intercultural skills, creative thinking, leadership skills, emotional intelligence, and conflict resolution.

Jennifer N. Felder is a doctoral candidate in the clinical psychology program at the University of Colorado, Boulder Department of Psychology and Neuroscience. She is the project coordinator of the "Increasing Access to Depressive Relapse Prophylaxis with Web-Based MBCT" project (PIs: Zindel Segal and Sona Dimidjian). She is broadly interested in treatment and prevention of depression among pregnant and postpartum women, and pragmatic and stigma barriers to mental-health care.

Michael S. Franklin received his Ph.D. from the University of Michigan, Ann Arbor in the area of cognition and perception. He researched memory for order information, as well as musical training and its relation to cognitive skill. He is currently involved in research projects focused on both mind-wandering and anomalous cognition.

Brett Froeliger is an Assistant Professor in the Department of Neurosciences and member of the Hollings Cancer Center at the Medical University of South Carolina. Dr. Froeliger directs the Translational Research of Addiction and Integrative Neuroscience (TRAIN) Laboratory. The primary objective of the TRAIN lab is to investigate novel therapeutic strategies for treating drug addiction and psychiatric illness.

Ana P. Gantman is a social psychology Ph.D. candidate at New York University whose work broadly focuses on the processes involved in both conscious and nonconscious goal pursuit, intentionality, and folk theories of free will.

Frank L. Gardner is Professor, Chair, and Director of the PsyD Program in School and Clinical Psychology at Kean University in New Jersey. He earned his Ph.D. in

Clinical and School Psychology from Hofstra University, and is board certified in clinical psychology. With over 30 years of experience as a practicing clinical psychologist, Frank's specialties include the evidence-based psychological treatment of anger and violence, mood disorders, anxiety disorders, and interventions for performance enhancement. He is codeveloper of the Mindfulness-Acceptance-Commitment (MAC) approach to performance enhancement and psychosocial well-being, and is the founding Editor-in-Chief of the *Journal of Clinical Sport Psychology.*

Eric L. Garland is Associate Director of Integrative Medicine in the Supportive Oncology and Survivorship Program at Huntsman Cancer Institute and an Associate Professor at the University of Utah College of Social Work. His biobehavioral research agenda is focused on translating findings from cognitive and affective neuroscience into treatments for stress-related conditions. Dr. Garland is the developer of Mindfulness-Oriented Recovery Enhancement (MORE), a multimodal intervention designed to ameliorate transdiagnostic mechanisms underpinning stress, addiction, emotion dysregulation, and chronic pain. He has received funding from the National Institutes of Health to conduct clinical trials of MORE as a treatment for alcohol dependence, prescription opioid misuse, and chronic pain. Complementing his expertise in clinical research, Dr. Garland is a licensed clinical social worker with over a decade of experience providing cognitive-behavioral and mindfulness-based therapies for persons suffering from addictive behaviors, psychological distress, and chronic pain conditions.

Carol R. Glass is Professor of Psychology and Undergraduate Program Director at The Catholic University of America. She specializes in CBT for anxiety disorders, as well as mindfulness-based interventions, and has over 30 years of experience as a licensed clinical psychologist. Her research interests include the role of cognition in anxiety and mindfulness-based approaches to reduce stress and promote peak performance. Dr. Glass is a codeveloper of Mindful Sport Performance Enhancement and has co-led evaluations of MSPE with athletes. She is a Fellow of the American Psychological Association and on the Board of Directors of the Society for the Exploration of Psychotherapy Integration.

Elisha Goldstein is a clinical psychologist with a private practice in Los Angeles and an international speaker on the intersection of mindfulness and psychotherapy. He is author of multiple titles including *The Now Effect, Mindfulness Meditations for the Anxious Traveler*, and the upcoming book *Breaking the Depression Code: 7 Steps to an Anti-Depressant Brain*, and coauthor of *A Mindfulness-Based Stress Reduction Workbook*. He is also author of the *Mindful Solutions* audio series, and the Mindfulness at Work® program currently being adopted in multiple multinational corporations. He lives in Santa Monica with his wife and two boys. His website can be found at www.ElishaGoldstein.com

Peter M. Gollwitzer has developed various models of action control throughout his academic career: the Theory of Symbolic Self-Completion (with Robert A. Wicklund), the Rubicon Model of Action Phases (with Heinz Heckhausen), the Auto-Motive Model of Automatic Goal Striving (with John A. Bargh), the Mindset Model of Action Phases, and the Theory of Implementation Intentions. The latter theory explains how people can automate the initiation of goal-directed responses by making if–then plans. In all of the theories named above, various mechanisms of action control are delineated, and respective moderators and mediators are distilled.

Jeremy R. Gray is an Associate Professor in the Department of Psychology at Michigan State University. His research program is concerned with understanding individual differences in self-regulation, as manifested in behavior and brain activity. Specific lines of research include emotion–cognition interactions, meditation, intelligence, and creativity. He has received grant funding from both NSF and NIH, and an NSF Career Award in 2007 (on research integrating affect, self-control, and intelligence). Before studying cognitive neuroscience, he practiced Zen meditation in the Soto tradition for two years at the San Francisco Zen Center.

Jeffrey Greeson is an Assistant Professor of Psychiatry & Behavioral Sciences at Duke University Medical Center. Dr. Greeson earned his doctorate in Clinical Health Psychology from the University of Miami and his master's degree in Biomedical Chemistry from Thomas Jefferson University. At Duke Integrative Medicine, his research on the outcomes and mechanisms of Mindfulness-Based Stress Reduction and other mindfulness-based interventions has been supported by the National Center for Complementary & Alternative Medicine (NCCAM) and the National Heart, Lung, and Blood Institute (NHLBI) of the National Institutes of Health (NIH). Dr. Greeson has practiced and researched mindfulness meditation for 15 years.

Cynthia R. Gross is a professor of Pharmacy and Nursing and faculty in the Center for Spirituality & Healing, University of Minnesota. Her research focuses on how mindfulness training affects symptoms and quality of life. She led the MVP #1 trial which compared mindfulness training to Lunesta® for chronic insomnia, and demonstrated comparable benefit without side effects. The MVP#1 publication (PMC3077056) is summarized in *Best of Sleep Medicine 2012*. She coauthored a 2013 systematic review of mindfulness measures (doi:10.1007/s11136-013-0395-8). She is currently conducting an active-controlled, NIH-funded trial of telephone-adapted MBSR for anxiety in kidney-transplant candidates.

June Gruber is an Assistant Professor of Psychology at Yale University. Dr. Gruber also holds a secondary appointment in the Department of Psychiatry and is an Affiliated Faculty Member in Cognitive Science and the Interdepartmental Neuroscience Program. She received her Ph.D. in Clinical Psychology and B.A in Psychology from the University of California, Berkeley. Dr. Gruber's research examines how positive emotions relate to psychological disturbance among people at risk for, and diagnosed with, bipolar disorder as a prime candidate to study positive emotion disturbance, as well as healthy community samples focusing on understanding the normative function of positive emotion states.

Lene Handberg is Educational Director, Tarab Institute International, with branches in Germany, Finland, France, Great Britain, Sweden, Slovakia, Holland, and India, and President of Tarab Ling Association in Dehradun, India. Ms. Handberg was assisting Lharampa Geshe Tarab Tulku XI, who developed a complete Modern Education called Unity in Duality® (Inner Science, Personal-Development, Art-of-Relating and Psychotherapeutic and Spiritual Application), by extracting the universalities, beyond culture and faith. Ms. Handberg, whom Tarab Tulku designated as his successor in 2004, holds a Semrig Thablam Rabjam degree (S.T.R./Ph.D.) and is teaching this approach around the world, including India and United States. www.tarab -institute.org

Craig Hassed's teaching, research, and clinical interests include mindfulness-based stress management, mind–body medicine, health promotion, integrative medicine, and medical ethics. Craig is regularly invited to speak and run courses in Australia and overseas, and was the founding president of the Australian Teachers of Meditation Association. He is a regular media commentator, writes regularly for medical journals, and has published six books including *Know Thyself* on mindfulness-based stress management, *The Essence of Health* on the lifestyle approach to health and chronic illness, a textbook co authored with Kerryn Phelps, *General Practice: The Integrative Approach*, and, most recently, *Mindfulness for Life*, coauthored with Stephen McKenzie. His seventh book on the role of mindfulness in education is due for release early in 2014.

Whitney L. Heppner is an Assistant Professor of Psychological Science at Georgia College & State University. She received her Ph.D. in Social Psychology from the University of Georgia, and she was a postdoctoral fellow in the Cancer Prevention Research Training Program in Health Disparities Research at M.D. Anderson Cancer Center. Dr. Heppner's research explores the role of trait mindfulness and induced states of mindfulness in cognitive functioning, psychological well-being, and the pursuit of health goals such as smoking cessation.

Wray Herbert is writer-in-residence at the Association for Psychological Science, where he writes the "We're Only Human" and "Full Frontal Psychology" blogs. He is a regular contributor to The Huffington Post and other national publications, and author of the book On Second Thought. He was a Washington, DC-based journalist for three decades, specializing in psychological science and mental health. He was behavioral science editor for *Science News*, editor-in-chief of *Psychology Today*, assistant managing editor at *US News & World Report*, and also a regular columnist for *Newsweek* and *Scientific American Mind*, and a mental-health journalism fellow at The Carter Center. He lives with his wife on Cornfield Creek, in Maryland.

Robert K. Hindman is a postdoctoral fellow at the Beck Institute for Cognitive Behavior Therapy. He received his Ph.D. in clinical psychology from The Catholic University of America as a member of the Anxiety, Mindfulness, and Psychotherapy Integration Research Lab. His research interests include anxiety and mindfulness-based interventions. For his dissertation, Dr. Hindman developed and compared mindfulness-based interventions for stress reduction in university students in order to determine the most effective method of mindfulness instruction. He completed his predoctoral internship at the Coatesville VA Medical Center.

Michael Hogan is a researcher and lecturer at NUI, Galway, whose research foci include: systems science and integral frameworks; behavioral and electrophysiological aspects of executive control, learning and memory; physical activity and cognitive performance; personality and cognition in younger and older adults; emotion and cardiovascular responding; the cerebellum and aging cognition; positive psychology; critical thinking and education; chronic pain; spirituality; and mindfulness. Michael's first book, *The Culture of our Thinking in Relation to Spirituality*, examines the problems faced by scientists as they attempt to understand spirituality. The book considers the way different worldviews and philosophical perspectives can influence the models of spirituality we build. Michael worked on the design of the collective intelligence stakeholder engagement methodology used in the SeaforSociety project (2012–2014). He is Irish member representative of the European Science Foundation (ESF) Steering Committee for European Research Network for Investigating Human Sensorimotor Function in Health and Disease (ERNI-HSF). He is a Director of the Structured Ph.D. in Perception, Cognition and Action; Director of the Structured Ph.D. in Learning Sciences; and coleader of the Health and Well-Being theme at the Whitaker Institute for Innovation and Social Change, NUI, Galway. He publishes widely in international peer-reviewed publications.

Idar Alfred Johannessen is Associate Professor of Organization Studies at Stord Haugesund University College, Norway. He received his cand. polit. degree in Sociology from the University of Bergen in 1980. Since then, he has specialized in Action Science, the approach to individual and organizational learning developed by Chris Argyris and his colleagues. Idar worked as an interventionist and trainer before returning to academia. In recent years, his research has focused on leadership in complex operations in Norway's off-shore industry, in particular how mindful improvisation takes place in contexts with rigorous procedures.

Silvia Jordan is Assistant Professor at the Department of Organization and Learning at the University of Innsbruck. She received her Ph.D. in Business Studies and her diploma in Psychology from the University of Innsbruck, and has been a Fellow at the Department of Accounting at London School of Economics and Political Science. Her research focuses on the areas of management accounting, risk and regulation, and organizational learning. She is particularly interested in the ways in which people and organizations, through various representational practices such as setting of performance targets and standards of "good practice," forecasting and risk mapping, make up, intervene in, and are affected by uncertainties related to complex interactions, high hazards, crises and organizational and societal change.

Yoona Kang is a postdoctoral researcher at Annenberg School for Communication in University of Pennsylvania. In her research, she utilizes contemplative practices to identify and characterize neurocognitive mechanisms of attitude change and well-being. Yoona's current research focuses on the role of contemplative practices on systematic shifts in self-referential processes and their subsequent effects on attitude and behavior change. She investigates convergent evidence from behavioral and neural outcomes to test these questions using various methods including response-latency techniques and fMRI. Yoona received her B.A. in Psychology from University of California, Los Angeles, and Ph.D. in Cognitive Psychology from Yale University. While in graduate school, she was also a visiting researcher at Brown University and coordinated an NIH-funded clinical trial that examined the effect of mindfulness-based interventions on depression and anxiety.

Keith A. Kaufman is a licensed clinical psychologist working in the Washington, DC area. He codeveloped Mindful Sport Performance Enhancement (MSPE) for his dissertation at The Catholic University of America, and has remained at that university as a Research Associate, teaching undergraduate Sport Psychology and coleading a sport psychology lab that has continued research on MSPE. Dr. Kaufman also operates a private psychotherapy practice that specializes in sport and exercise psychology. He received the 2002 Patrick F. Earey Award from UNC-Chapel Hill, and a special commendation from the American College Counseling Association for meritorious service following the Virginia Tech shootings.

Jean L. Kristeller is Professor Emeritus of Psychology at Indiana State University and Founding Director and current President of The Center for Mindful Eating. She received her doctorate in clinical and health psychology from Yale University in 1983, with previous faculty appointments at Harvard Medical School and the University of Massachusetts Medical School. She has conducted research on the psychology of food-intake regulation and on meditation for over 25 years, with NIH-funding investigating the value of Mindfulness-Based Eating Awareness Training (MB-EAT) on binge-eating disorder, obesity, and diabetes in collaboration with Duke University, UC-San Francisco, and Ohio State University.

Jon A. Krosnick is the Frederic O. Glover Professor in Humanities and Social Sciences at Stanford University, Stanford, CA and a University Fellow at Resources for the Future.

Amey Kulkarni is a doctoral student in Social Psychology at the University of Georgia. His primary research interests include flow, mindfulness, and meaning. He is also interested in examining social psychology phenomena from an anthropological perspective, more specifically through the lens of I-D Compensation theory.

Tuuli Lehti has a Bachelor of Science (Tech) degree from Aalto University in Espoo, Finland, where she is currently finishing her master's degree in biomedical engineering. In addition, she is pursuing a medical degree at the University of Helsinki, Finland. While she continues to deepen her understanding of mindfulness, she takes great interest in integrative medicine that takes into account the interrelatedness of the body and the mind. Besides academic life, Tuuli enjoys French cuisine and Spanish flamenco.

Andrew Luttrell is a currently a doctoral student in the department of psychology at the Ohio State University. He holds an M.A. degree in social psychology also from the Ohio State University. His research focuses on attitude strength processes and persuasion with a particular emphasis on the role of attitude certainty.

Christopher Lyddy is a doctoral candidate in Organizational Behavior at Case Western Reserve University. He studies Eastern mindfulness' workplace integration and performance impacts. He received a MCP at the Massachusetts Institute of Technology and a B.A. at the University of Michigan. He has worked as a researcher at the Brookings Institution and Sloan School of Management at MIT.

Leonard L. Martin received his Ph.D. in social psychology from the University of North Carolina at Greensboro. After that, he spent two years in a postdoctoral position at the University of Illinois studying social cognition. He then took a position at the

University of Georgia where he has been since with the exception of a 5-month stay at the Max Planck Institute in Munich. He sharpened his interest in hunter-gatherers when he studied Anthropology for a year as part of UGA's Program for Study in a Second Discipline.

Donald McCown is Assistant Professor of Integrative Health and Director of the Center for Contemplative Studies at West Chester University of Pennsylvania, and has held positions as Lecturer at Thomas Jefferson University and Director of Mindfulness at Work programs at Jefferson's Mindfulness Institute. He holds a Ph.D. from Tilburg University, a Master of Social Service from Bryn Mawr College, and a Master of Applied Meditation Studies from the Won Institute of Graduate Studies. He has completed the advanced Mindfulness-Based Stress Reduction (MBSR) trainings through the Center for Mindfulness at the University of Massachusetts Medical School. He is the primary author of *Teaching Mindfulness: A Practical Guide for Clinicians and Educators* and *New World Mindfulness: From the Founding Fathers, Emerson, and Thoreau to Your Personal Practice*, and author of *The Ethical Space of Mindfulness in Clinical Practice*.

Lance M. McCracken is Professor of Behavioural Medicine at King's College London. He is also a Consultant Clinical Psychologist and the Psychology Lead at the INPUT pain-management centre at St Thomas' Hospital in London. He is on the editorial board of a number of journals, including *Health Psychology*, *Journal of Behavioral Medicine*, *European Journal of Pain*, Pain Management, *The Journal of Pain*, *BMC Musculoskeletal Disorders*, *Cognitive Therapy and Research*, and *British Journal of Pain*. His primary research interests are in Acceptance and Commitment Therapy (ACT), psychological flexibility, treatment provider behavior, and chronic-pain treatment development.

Benjamin W. Mooneyham earned his B.S. in Physics and B.A. in Psychology from Washington & Lee University in 2010. His research investigates distortions in the subjective experience of time and the resulting perceptual consequences.

Zella E. Moore is an Associate Professor of Psychology at Manhattan College in New York. She received her PsyD in Clinical Psychology from La Salle University. Zella is codeveloper of the Mindfulness-Acceptance-Commitment (MAC) approach for enhancing human performance and psychosocial well-being and is the founding Senior Associate Editor of the *Journal of Clinical Sport Psychology*. From a clinical perspective, Zella has worked with individuals with depressive disorders, anxiety disorders, and schizoaffective disorder, and specializes in the treatment of anger dyscontrol and its behavioral manifestations. Finally, Zella is most dedicated to teaching and mentoring undergraduate psychology students at Manhattan College.

Michael D. Mrazek earned his B.A. at Rice University in 2006 and his Ph.D. from the University of California Santa Barbara in 2013. His research focuses on the opposing constructs of mind-wandering and mindfulness, with an emphasis on how cultivating a capacity for nondistraction can impact educational and professional performance.

Carin Muhr is an associate professor of Neurology at the Department of Neuroscience, Uppsala University, Sweden and President of Tarab Institute International and Tarab Institute Sweden, and has studied Buddhist Psychology, within Unity in

Duality® in India. Dr. Muhr's research encompasses mainly headache and neuroen-docrinology with extensive PET studies in pituitary tumors. Dr. Muhr has for several years engaged in international research and pedagogical projects addressing human rights and gender issues in medicine and bioethics, in India, in Grenada, St George's University, and in Peru, Universidad St Martin de Porres, Lima, where she also is an Honorary Professor.

Kristina Niedderer is Reader in Design and Applied Arts at the University of Wolver-hampton. She leads the "Material and Theoretical Practice" research group as well as Contextual Studies for the M.A. Design and Applied Arts. She was originally appren-ticed, and worked as a goldsmith and silversmith in Germany. She then trained as a designer and design researcher in the UK. A practitioner and researcher, Kristina exhibits and publishes her work regularly at international level. She has been a keynote speaker and has lectured at universities worldwide on research topics including con-ceptual and technical issues in craft and design, mindful design for behavior change, and principles and practices of using creative practice within (doctoral) research. Info: www.niedderer.org

Gabriele Oettingen explores how conscious and nonconscious processes interact in controlling thought, emotion, and behavior. She distinguishes future thought involv-ing fantasies versus expectations and their impact on information processing, effort, and performance. Her model of mental contrasting specifies how future thought can create and dissolve goal pursuit, and how it can lead to successful plans and goal attainment.

Andrew Olendzki is the senior scholar at the Barre Center for Buddhist Studies, an educational center dedicated to the integration of scholarly understanding with med-itative insight, and a senior scholar at the Mind and Life Institute. He is a former director of the Insight Meditation Society in Barre, Massachusetts, and has taught at several New England colleges (including Harvard, Brandeis, Smith, Amherst, Hamp-shire and Lesley). He is the author of *Unlimiting Mind: The Radically Experiential Psychology of Buddhism* (Wisdom, 2010), and writes the column Thus Have I Heard for Tricycle: The Buddhist Review.

Francesco Pagnini is Assistant Professor at the Catholic University of Milan and col-laborates as postdoctoral fellow with Harvard University. He has completed his Ph.D. in Clinical Psychology from the University of Bergamo. His primary interest is focused on the improvement of psychological well-being of people with chronic disease, in particular with interventions that improve mindfulness. He is currently carrying out research on mindfulness both in Milan, in collaboration with Niguarda Ca' Granda Hospital, and in Cambridge, MA, working with Professor Ellen Langer and Dr. Deb-orah Phillips. He is currently Associate Editor for the journals *Frontiers in Psychology for Clinical Settings* and *BMC Psychology*.

Tracy Peng received her M.D. from the Keck School of Medicine at the Univer-sity of Southern California and completed psychiatry residency at California Pacific Medical Center. She is also a graduate of the End-of-Life Counselor Training offered through Zen Hospice Project (now offered by the Metta Institute). Having practiced psychiatry for over a decade, she now focuses on clinical care and training residents as integrative psychiatrist at the Osher Center for Integrative Medicine at UCSF.

Richard E. Petty received his B.A. from the University of Virginia and his Ph.D. from Ohio State. His research, focused on the conscious and unconscious factors responsible for changes in attitudes and behaviors, has resulted in eight books and over 300 articles and chapters. Honors include fellow status in the American Academy of Arts and Sciences, the American Association for the Advancement of Science, APA, and APS. He received the Distinguished Scientific Contribution Awards from the Societies for Personality and Social Psychology (SPSP) and Consumer Psychology. He was President of SPSP and Editor of the Personality and Social Psychology Bulletin.

Dawa T. Phillips received his B.A. Hons (2001) and M.A. Hons from A.H.E.T. in France in 2004. His research focuses on the cognitive and behavioral impact of mindfulness, contemplative practices, and mindfulness-based interventions, with an emphasis on the impact of enhanced mindful awareness on academic and professional performance in children, youth, and leaders.

Deborah Phillips is a postdoctoral fellow in psychology at Harvard University. After receiving her Ph.D. at MIT, she focused her career in human-resources strategy and planning, returning to academia in 2010. Her research in maximizing sociocognitive mindfulness developed by Ellen Langer follows from early doctoral work on employment for the disabled, and worker productivity in the private and foundation sectors. She currently focuses on improving productivity and well-being through mindfulness interventions in employment, aging, and chronic disease with Dr. Langer and colleague Dr. Francesco Pagnini.

Timothy R. Pineau is a 6th-year Ph.D. candidate in Clinical Psychology at The Catholic University of America. In addition to more than a decade of competitive rowing and coaching experience, Timothy's graduate research has focused on the role of mindfulness in sport performance. For his recently completed dissertation research, Timothy helped develop an updated and expanded version of Mindful Sport Performance Enhancement (MSPE) and studied this approach with long-distance runners. Timothy has coauthored one journal article and seven posters on his work with mindfulness in sports and is a member of the American Psychological Association and the Association for Applied Sport Psychology.

Michael Pirson is the director of the Center for Humanistic Management and Associate Professor for Global Sustainability and Social Entrepreneurship at Fordham University, New York. He is a research fellow at Harvard University and a Partner of the Humanistic Management Network. His work focuses on trust and well-being in organizational contexts, exploring mindfulness as a lever to enhance both.

Rolf Reber received his doctoral degree at the University of Bern, Switzerland, and is currently professor at the Department of Psychology at the University of Oslo and adjunct professor at the Department of Education at the University of Bergen, Norway. With his colleagues, he examined effects of metacognitive experiences on evaluative judgments that led to processing fluency accounts of aesthetic pleasure, mathematical intuition, the "Aha"-experience, and paradoxes in Confucian thought. Moreover, he developed Example Choice, a new teaching method to increase student interest at school. He is an award-winning teacher and author of two popular psychology books in German.

Diane K. Reibel is the Director of the Mindfulness Institute at Jefferson-Myrna Brind Center of Integrative Medicine and Clinical Associate Professor in the Department of Emergency Medicine at Jefferson Medical College. She is a certified mindfulness-based stress reduction (MBSR) teacher and has been teaching MBSR for over 18 years to patients, medical students, and healthcare professionals. In addition to her passion for teaching mindfulness she studies the physiologic effects and health outcomes of mindfulness training, and her research is published and widely cited in both scientific journals and the popular press. Dr. Reibel is coauthor of the book *Teaching Mindfulness: A Practical Guide for Clinicians and Educators.*

C. Scott Rigby received his Ph.D. in clinical psychology from the University of Rochester, focusing on applications of Self-Determination Theory in a variety of contexts, including education, religious beliefs, and interactive technology. He is the author of the book *Glued to Games: How Video Games Draw Us In and Hold Us Spellbound* (2011), along with his coauthor, Richard Ryan. He is the founder and president of Immersyve, Inc.—a company dedicated to applying principles of motivation and behavior change to create meaningful experiences in areas ranging from health care to video games. He resides in Celebration, Florida.

Leonard L. Riskin is Chesterfield Smith Professor of Law at the University of Florida Levin College of Law and Visiting Professor at Northwestern University School of Law. He studied law at N.Y.U. (J.D.) and Yale (LL.M.) law schools. His scholarship and teaching focus on negotiation and mediation and the role of mindfulness in helping law students, lawyers, judges, and mediators feel and perform better (which covers a lot of ground). He has conducted training programs around the world and has published several books, numerous articles in professional journals, and essays in popular publications such as the *New York Times Magazine* and *The Atlantic.*

James L. Ritchie-Dunham is the author of *Ecosynomics: The Science of Abundance* (ecosynomics.com). Jim is president of the Institute for Strategic Clarity, a researcher in Langer's Mindfulness Lab, adjunct professor of strategy at the EGADE Business School (Mexico), and founder of Vibrancy Ins., a publishing, consulting, and conferencing company. Previously, he was managing partner of a strategy consultancy, a visiting scholar at MIT's Sloan School, a professor at the ITAM (Mexico), and a petroleum engineer at ConocoPhillips. He has a Ph.D. in Decision Sciences from UT Austin, two masters in international management from Thunderbird and ESADE, and a BSPE from the University of Tulsa.

Scott L. Rogers is founder and director of the Institute for Mindfulness Studies, the University of Miami School of Law's Mindfulness in Law Program, and codirector of the University of Miami's Mindfulness Research and Practice Initiative. He is creator of Jurisight®, one of the first programs in the country to integrate mindfulness and the law, and he has authored books on mindfulness for law students, lawyers, law faculty, and parents. Scott has spoken at law and scientific conferences, appeared on television and National Public Radio, and been interviewed in newspapers and magazines for his work on mindfulness. He lives in Miami Beach with his wife and two children. To learn more about Scott and his work, visit www.scottrogers.com, www.mindfulliving.net, and www.miamimindfulness.org

Richard M. Ryan is a codeveloper of Self-Determination Theory, an internationally researched theory of human motivation and personality development that has been applied in schools, clinics, sport teams, and work organizations around the world. Ryan is a Fellow of several professional organizations, and an Honorary Member of the German Psychological Society. He has received career awards from several societies, and fellowships from the Cattell and Leverhulme foundations. Ryan has also been a Visiting Professor at the Max Planck Institute, the University of Bath, and Nanyang Technical University. He is currently Director of Clinical Training at the University of Rochester.

Esa Saarinen is Professor of Applied Philosophy in the Department of Industrial Engineering and Management at Aalto University, Espoo, Finland. His work lies at the intersection of systems intelligence and positive philosophical practice. As a "philosopher of the everyday," a celebrated lecturer, and a well-known media figure in Finland, he is deeply committed to understanding and promoting human flourishing on the individual, group, and organizational levels. Over the course of nearly 40 years, Saarinen has published widely for both academic and popular audiences about a variety of topics, including media philosophy, systems intelligence, positive philosophical practice, and leadership.

Gavriel Salomon received his Ph.D. in educational psychology and communication from Stanford (1968), received the Israel National Award for research in education (2001), received an honorary doctorate from the Catholic University of Leuven, Belgium, and is a fellow of a number of international organizations. He was dean of the Faculty of Education at the University of Haifa, served as the head of the Center for Research on Peace Education at the university, and serves as the cochair of Sikkuy. Salomon has written and edited a number of books and more than 120 articles and book chapters in the fields of cognition, technology in education, and peace education.

Matthew A. Sanders received his Ph.D. in Social Psychology from the University of Georgia. He is currently working as a postdoctoral researcher at the University of Oklahoma studying the ways in which political orientation affects Americans' views of other nations. His work is focused more generally on the way in which political orientation affects goals and information processing.

Jonathan W. Schooler is a Professor of Psychological and Brain Sciences at the University of California Santa Barbara. A former holder of a Tier 1 Canada Research Chair, he is a fellow of a variety of scientific organizations, on the editorial board of a number of psychology journals, and the recipient of major grants from both the United States and Canadian governments as well as several private foundations. His research and comments are frequently featured in major media outlets such as *The New York Times*, *The New Yorker*, and *Nature Magazine*.

Howard Schubiner, MD, is the director of the Mind-Body Medicine Center at Providence Hospital and a Clinical Professor of Internal Medicine at Wayne State University School of Medicine in Detroit, MI. He has published studies of an innovative psychophysiological model for the treatment of chronic pain and is conducting an NIH-funded trial using an emotional expressive therapy for fibromyalgia. Dr. Schubiner is a senior mindfulness teacher and the author of *Unlearn Your Pain* (2010) and *Unlearn Your Anxiety and Depression* (2014).

Patricia P. Schultz is a doctoral clinical psychology student at the University of Rochester under the mentorship of Professor Richard M. Ryan (Ph.D.). She is interested in human motivation, mindfulness, and well-being (psychological and physical), particularly in educational, health care, and work contexts.

Zindel Segal is Distinguished Professor of Psychology in Mood Disorders at the University of Toronto—Scarborough. He is also the Director of Clinical Training in the Psychology Department's Graduate Program in Psychological Clinical Science. Dr. Segal's publications include *Interpersonal Process in Cognitive Therapy* (1990), *Vulnerability to Depression* (2011) and *The Mindful Way Through Depression* (2007). He is a Founding Fellow of the Academy of Cognitive Therapy and advocates for the relevance of mindfulness-based clinical care in psychiatry and mental health.

Sana Sherali earned her bachelor's degree from the University of Miami in Florida in psychology. She has conducted research on healthy behaviors, body-image disorders, and self-regulation, and combines approaches drawing from clinical psychology and social cognition. She now holds the position of Social Media Coordinator for the Tyra Banks Company.

Daniel J. Siegel is an author, educator, and founding editor of the *Norton Professional Series on Interpersonal Neurobiology*. He is Clinical Professor of Psychiatry at the School of Medicine of the University of California, Los Angeles, where he serves as Codirector of the Mindful Awareness Research Center. He is also the Executive Director of the Mindsight Institute, an educational center devoted to promoting insight, compassion, and empathy in individuals, families, organizations, and communities. Dr. Siegel's books include *Mindsight, Pocket Guide to Interpersonal Neurobiology, The Developing Mind, The Mindful Therapist, The Mindful Brain, Parenting from the Inside Out, The Whole-Brain Child*, and *Brainstorm*.

Madeleine W. Siegel is an undergraduate at the University of California, Berkeley. She has worked as a coinstructor in mindfulness training for children, a teaching assistant in human development courses, and a cotherapist for adolescents in group therapy. She is currently a student in the College of Natural Resources.

Kelly B. Smith has a Ph.D. in Clinical Psychology and is currently a Post Doctoral Fellow in the UBC Department of Obstetrics & Gynaecology under the mentorship of Dr. Lori Brotto. Dr. Smith's research focuses primarily on chronic genital pain in women. She has received several research awards and is currently supported by Post

Doctoral Fellowship Awards from the Michael Smith Foundation for Health Research and the Canadian Pain Society. Dr. Smith currently serves on the Editorial Board for the *Archives of Sexual Behavior*.

Elizabeth A. Stanley is associate professor of security studies at Georgetown University and the founder of the nonprofit Mind Fitness Training Institute. She served as a U.S. Army military intelligence officer in Korea and Germany, and on deployments in the Balkans. She has spoken and published widely on topics related to mind fitness, resilience, military effectiveness and innovation, and national security. Creator of Mindfulness-based Mind Fitness Training (MMFT)®, she has taught MMFT to troops before combat and others in high-stress environments to build resilience and optimize performance, and has participated in four Department of Defense-funded studies to examine MMFT's effectiveness.

Alexander I. Stingl teaches in Medical Humanities, Science and Technology Studies, and Critical Thinking. He is an affiliated research faculty at the STS Center at Drexel University, a collaborating researcher at the University of Kassel, Germany, CLWF Vrije University Brussels, Belgium, and a contract lecturer at Leuphana University, Lüneburg, Germany. His current research includes: Semantic agency theory (SAT) and interrelations between the body, the State, scientific communities, their publics, and the political imagination. He has written articles on ADHD, medical imaging, nomadic statehood, among others; books on the Enlightenment idea in Adorno/Horkheimer and Foucault, and on the coevolution of biology, philosophy, and sociology; and with Sabrina M. Weiss, he has forthcoming articles and chapters. Along with Sal Restivo, they cowrote *Worlds of ScienceCraft: New Horizons for the Philosophy of Science Studies* (Ashgate).

Kathleen M. Sutcliffe is the Gilbert and Ruth Whitaker Professor of Business Administration and Professor of Management and Organizations at the Stephen M. Ross School of Business at the University of Michigan. Her research is aimed at understanding how organizations and their members cope with ambiguity and unexpected events, processes of mindful organizing, and how complex organizations can be designed to be more reliable and resilient. A recent book includes *Managing the Unexpected: Resilient Performance in an Age of Uncertainty*, 2nd ed. (coauthored with Karl E. Weick, Jossey-Bass, 2007).

Carla Treloar is Professor and Deputy Director of the Centre for Social Research in Health at the University of New South Wales, Australia, and a member of numerous advisory committees for government, health agencies, and nongovernment organizations. Her research encompasses the social aspects of drug use in relation to prevention of drug-related harms (particularly hepatitis C), engagement of people who use drugs in health and other services, and critical analysis of the structure and operation of services for people who use drugs. Carla is committed to the effective translation of research into policy and practice and to ethical and respectful conduct of research in close collaboration with affected communities.

David L. Vannette is a Ph.D. Candidate in the Department of Communication at Stanford University, Stanford, CA.

Timothy J. Vogus, Associate Professor, Owen Graduate School of Management, Vanderbilt University (timothy.vogus@owen.vanderbilt.edu) received his Ph.D. from the University of Michigan. His research focuses on the cognitive, cultural, and emotional processes through which individuals and workgroups enact highly reliable performance. More specifically, his research specifies the mechanisms through which collectives create and sustain a culture of safety as well as how they detect and correct errors and unexpected events through mindful organizing. He is especially interested in these dynamics in healthcare organizations. His research has been published in leading management and health-services outlets including *Academy of Management Review, Annual Review of Public Health, Journal of Organizational Behavior*, and *Medical Care*.

Helané Wahbeh is an Assistant Professor at Oregon Health & Science University in the Department of Neurology. She is a naturopathic physician and clinician researcher focused on mind–body medicine research. She is the principal investigator of VET MIND, a clinical research study funded by National Institute of Health National Center for Complementary and Alternative Medicine. VET MIND examines the mechanistic pathways of mindfulness meditation in combat veterans with PTSD. Dr. Wahbeh serves as Institutional Review Board cochair and mentor for Masters of Integrative Medicine students at the National College for Natural Medicine. She has completed the Mindfulness-Based Stress Reduction Teacher Training, a four-year Corelight Meditation Teacher Training, and has a 12-year daily meditation practice.

Katherine Weare is known internationally for her work on children's mental health and well-being, and social and emotional learning. She trained as a teacher of adult mindfulness at the University of Exeter in the UK and has expanded her work to include mindfulness for children and young people. Her publications include overviews and reviews of the evidence base. She is currently working closely with the UK's Mindfulness in Schools project and the Wake Up Schools initiative founded by Zen Master Thich Nhat Hanh, and is a member of the core group of the Mind and Life school's initiative.

Sabrina M. Weiss is a Visiting Assistant Professor in the STS Department, Rochester Institute of Technology. She specializes in interdisciplinary ethical application of philosophical and ecological concepts of embodiment to technoscientific and technosocial knowledge production. She also holds an M.S. in Bioethics from Albany Medical College and B.S. in STS from Stanford University.

Christopher Willard is a psychologist, psychotherapist, and educational consultant in the Boston area specializing in mindfulness-based work with adolescents and young adults in private practice and at Tufts University. He has been practicing meditation for over 15 years, leading workshops locally and internationally on the topic of mindfulness with young people. He currently serves on the board of directors at the Institute for Meditation and Psychotherapy, where he teaches in the core faculty. His thoughts on mental health have been featured in *The New York Times*, cnn.com, and elsewhere.

He is most recently the author of *Child's Mind*, a book on teaching mindfulness practices to children and adolescents, which has now been translated into multiple languages. He is currently completing two more books about bringing mindfulness to youth.

Emily J. Winch is a Psy.D. student at La Salle University in Philadelphia, PA. She is currently completing an internship at the Philadelphia VA Medical Center. Her areas of interest include the use of contextual behavior therapies, the role of compassion in psychological well-being and therapeutic change, and the treatment of anxiety and mood disorders.

Scott C. Woodruff is completing his Ph.D. in clinical psychology from the Catholic University of America and is currently on predoctoral internship at the Philadelphia VA Medical Center. His research interests include anxiety, mindfulness, and self-compassion, as well as the similarities and differences between traditional cognitive-behavioral and mindfulness-based therapies. Scott meditates regularly and has traveled to multiple countries with a prominent Buddhist influence, including Bhutan, Thailand, Cambodia, and Vietnam. Prior to moving into psychology, he worked in the film business for several years and earned an MBA at NYU's Stern School of Business.

Timothy W. Wright is a Psy.D. Clinical Psychology graduate student at La Salle University, Philadelphia, and is currently completing a Psychology Internship at VA Maine Healthcare System. He also received his M.S. in Occupational Psychology from University of London. Clinically, he specializes in contextual cognitive behavioral therapies and health psychology. His research interests lie in treatment processes, the integration of Buddhist psychology and therapeutic mindfulness, and the promotion of health-behavior change.

Sigal Zilcha-Mano is a clinical psychologist who integrates clinical practice, teaching, and research. Her research focuses on the study of outcomes and process of various psychotherapies and interventions aimed at improving well-being. She is particularly interested in how mindfulness, a variety of meditative practices, psychodynamic psychotherapies, cognitive behavioral psychotherapies, and animal-assisted therapies affect mental health and quality of life. She received her Ph.D. from Bar-Ilan University in Israel, where she was awarded a President's Grant for Special Distinction. She has completed two postdoc research fellowships, one at Harvard University and one at Adelphi University through a Fulbright scholarship.

General Introduction

There currently exist two dominant mindfulness camps. The Western camp involves social psychological approaches to mindfulness, as exemplified by the work of Ellen Langer. Langer's approach is sometimes referred to as "mindfulness without meditation." The nature of its practices is highly psychological, and very little to no emphasis is placed on meditation. The Western camp contrasts with more Eastern approaches to mindfulness, which are rooted in Buddhist philosophy and are more contemplative and based on meditation. A dominant branch of the Eastern camp is approaches to mindfulness that incorporate both psychological and meditative elements. These Eastern-derived models borrow forms of meditation from the Eastern camp and empirically apply them in Western settings. The Western and Eastern models propose different and unique theoretical principles, but they also share significant similarities. Most important, both approaches aim to cultivate a present-oriented mind, thereby permitting individuals to increase health and well-being. This handbook compares and contrasts Western and Eastern mindfulness camps with the aim of transforming their seemingly oppositional relationship into a complementary one. The chapters included in this handbook have been specifically selected because they adequately represent the ways in which mindfulness has been applied in various fields and settings, including medicine, mental health, education, organizations, and sports. Mindfulness has also proved to have a powerful influence on cognition, attitudes, and interpersonal relationships.

Part I
Origins and Theory

The concept of mindfulness originates from ancient Buddhist, Hindu, and Chinese philosophies. These more Eastern approaches to mindfulness are meditative in their nature and emphasize nonreactive awareness and concentration of one's self and experiences (e.g., viewing the body in and of itself; feelings in and of themselves; mind in and of itself; and mental qualities in and of themselves; Thanissaro Bhikkhu, 2007). The role of such mindfulness practices is to keep the mind properly grounded in the present moment and to decrease reactivity to what happens in the moment. It is a way of relating to all experience—positive, negative, and neutral—such that overall levels of suffering are reduced, and sense of well-being increases (Germer, Siegel, & Fulton, 2005).

Today, there are a variety of definitions of mindfulness within both Eastern and Western approaches. The Eastern approach to mindfulness has undergone several transformations following its introduction into Western culture and contemporary psychology. Basic definitions of mindfulness include "moment-by-moment aware-ness" (Germer et al., 2005), "keeping one's consciousness alive to the present reality" (Hanh, 1976), "attentional control" (Teasdale, Segal, & Williams, 1995), "a form of self-regulation of attention" (Hassed, 2013), "paying attention with purpose, non-judgmentally, and while in the present moment" (Kabat-Zinn, 1994, 2005), "the bringing of one's awareness to current experiences through observing and attending to the changing field of thoughts, feelings, and sensations from moment to moment" (Bishop et al., 2004), and "complete attention to one's experience on a moment-to-moment basis" (Marlatt & Kristeller, 1999).

Western conceptions of mindfulness emerged around the 1970s. The Western camp was heavily influenced by Ellen Langer's pioneering work on mindlessness and choice (Alexander, Langer, Newman, Chandler, & Davies, 1989; Langer, 1992; Langer, Beck, Janoff-Bulman, & Timko, 1984; Langer, Blank, & Chanowitz, 1978; Langer & Moldoveanu, 2000). Langer's work originated independently of any reference to

The Wiley Blackwell Handbook of Mindfulness, First Edition.
Edited by Amanda Ie, Christelle T. Ngnoumen, and Ellen J. Langer.
© 2014 John Wiley & Sons, Ltd. Published 2014 by John Wiley & Sons, Ltd.

Eastern contemplative traditions. Her concept of mindfulness originates from a social psychological approach, and emphasizes actively drawing novel distinctions. Her early research focused on mindlessness and its prevalence in daily life, after which she began to explore the other side of the coin—mindfulness—and its potential benefits in areas such as aging, mental and physical health, behavioral regulation, interpersonal relationships, creativity, and the workplace.

Toward the 1980s, a unique conceptualization of mindfulness branched off the Eastern camp. This Eastern-derived approach to mindfulness integrates both psychological and meditative elements. Increasingly more empirical work examining the health outcomes of cultivating mindfulness through the practice of meditation has stemmed from this branch. Eastern-derived approaches to mindfulness were spearheaded by Jon Kabat-Zinn's work on the clinical applications of mindfulness (Kabat-Zinn, 2003, 1990, 1994; Ludwig & Kabat-Zinn, 2008). According to Kabat-Zinn (2005), mindfulness practice promotes full awareness of the present moment, with the intention of embodying an orientation of calmness and equanimity to the best of one's ability.

The role that meditation plays in the process of cultivating mindfulness differs in Langer's and Kabat-Zinn's conceptualizations of mindfulness and is perhaps a distinguishing factor for the two approaches. Langer characterizes mindfulness as a universal human capacity that need not be enhanced through the practice of meditation. Rather, mindfulness is gained by maintaining an orientation in the present, openness to novelty, alertness to distinctions, sensitivity to different contexts, and an awareness of multiple perspectives (Langer, 1990). In Langer's model, mindfulness is also enhanced through attending to the variability of one's mental and physical states.

Kabat-Zinn's conception of mindfulness is similar to Langer's in its focus on moment-to-moment awareness. The process by which mindfulness is attained, however, differs from Langer's in its emphasis on meditation. Kabat-Zinn addresses noticing new things in a manner more akin to many Eastern meditative practices. His mindfulness-based stress reduction (MBSR) program involves techniques designed to promote relaxation such as the following of one's breath, Hatha yoga, and breathing exercises to ameliorate various symptoms associated with chronic pain, stress, anxiety, depression, irritable bowel syndrome, psoriasis, eating disorders, and other chronic conditions.

Two other early contributors to the burgeoning of Eastern-derived, mindfulness-based approaches to medicine include Herbert Benson and Richard Davidson. Benson's greatest contribution is his demonstration of how meditation can ameliorate stress responses and thereby prevent the subsequent series of negative physiological reactions normally associated with stress. According to Benson (1975), the mind and body are one system, with the experiences of the latter capable of being regulated by the qualities of the former. Many Western and Eastern-derived approaches similarly subscribe to such mind–body monism. Langer's approach to improving physical and psychological health is guided by the perspective that the mind and body comprise a single system, and that every change in the human being is simultaneously a change at the level of the mind (e.g., cognitive changes) as well as the body (e.g., cellular, hormonal, neural changes).

Using modern techniques from neuroscience, Davidson demonstrated that the very qualities of the mind and its contents (e.g., happiness) can be learned, much in the same way that most skills are acquired. Some of Davidson's latest research suggests that meditation can be used to train minds into becoming happier and generally more positive (Davidson & Scherer, 2001). Langer et al. assessed the mindfulness levels of 300 people in China and discovered a positive association between mindfulness and happiness. These results are in line with Davidson's proposal and demonstrate how a mindful outlook (which can be trained and learned) could potentially contribute to increased positive qualities and experiences.

While Eastern (including Eastern-derived) and Western conceptions of mindfulness are similar in their health and quality-of-life outcomes, the processes by which these effects are obtained are qualitatively different. While the former emphasize practices rooted in meditation, the latter foster a heightened sense of awareness through maintaining an open awareness of novel information and forming new categories out of one's experience. While there surely are noticeable differences between Eastern and Western approaches to mindfulness, the degree of similarities between the two significantly outweighs their differences.

Eastern and Western conceptions of mindfulness are similar in their fundamental view of the relationship between the mind and the body as a dynamic one whereby human behavioral experiences and personal qualities can be moderated through systematic mental practice. Both camps have enriched the field, and generated greater awareness and appreciation for the wealth of benefits gained from the remarkably simple process of acknowledging novel experiences. Despite the multiple working definitions that exist for mindfulness, the element of appreciating novelty is reinforced in both Eastern and Western camps, perhaps highlighting its essentiality.

The first section of the handbook explores the historical origins of the mindfulness concept. Langer's chapter encapsulates over 35 years of her research on mindfulness. She develops the construct of mindfulness through putting it into practice across a variety of experimental and clinical settings and across a variety of populations. Her work demonstrates the powerful role of mindfulness in extending the limits of human functioning, and in improving health and promoting longevity.

Siegel and Siegel reveal the benefits associated with both contemplative and creative forms of mindfulness. More specifically, they present the positive changes associated with maintaining open awareness and learning from an open and engaged stance. They propose that "presence" is a state of mind that incorporates both contemplative and creative forms of mindfulness. Furthermore, it enables individuals to thrive amidst uncertainty.

Carmody explores the commonalities and differences between Western and Eastern (including both Eastern-derived) conceptions of mindfulness. All approaches similarly view experience as shaped by perception, particularly with regard to awareness. Additionally, they all foster improvements in well-being. While the Eastern approach focuses more on both the senses—unfiltered by any conceptual categories—and intellect, Western practices directly address cognitive realms.

Olendzki traces the progression of mindfulness from its early Buddhist origins through its integration into psychological science. According to Olendzki, mindfulness is a much-needed tool in today's externally oriented societies. Mindfulness's goal of allowing individuals to access their emotions would likely provide them with a greater understanding of their internal experiences, which are often overlooked amidst preoccupations with the material world.

Muhr and Handberg review the main theorems that underlie traditional mindfulness training (e.g., the distinctions between mind–body and subject–object). Their chapter explores the Four Mindfulness practices and their relevance to personal development and psychological health. They also discuss the similarities and differences between traditional mindfulness meditation and the mindfulness techniques applied in modern therapeutic settings.

Fatemi discusses the nature of paradigmatic shifts in the field of psychology, and elaborates upon the kinds of conditions under which such shifts are either well received or faced with hesitations. He demonstrates how Langer's (2009) work on mindfulness questions mainstream psychology's reliance on positivism and rationality and challenges the certainty of knowing. More specifically, he argues that Langer's work advocates a tilt in mainstream psychology's position of positivist knowing towards a stance of not knowing, the latter stance being one that affords the exploration of an expansive array of epistemologies and unlocks the search for predetermined knowledge fostered by the positivist position.

Djikic highlights factors that distinguish Eastern and Western conceptions of mindfulness, including a cultural divide between being and doing, respectively. This divide is apparent in more Eastern approaches' emphases on internal attitudes and ways of being as the targets of self-development, while more Western approaches focus more on action as the fuel of transformation and developmental change. Djikic further elucidates on the distinctions between Eastern and Western approaches through a discussion of how they conceptualize the nature of problems, their causes, and their solutions.

References

Alexander, C., Langer, E., Newman, R., Chandler, H., & Davies, J. (1989). Aging, mindfulness and meditation. *Journal of Personality and Social Psychology, 57,* 950–964.

Benson, H. (1975). *The relaxation response.* New York, NY: HarperCollins.

Bishop, S. R., Lau, M., Shapiro, S., Carlson, L., Anderson, N. D., Carmody, J., ... & Devins, G. (2004). Mindfulness: A proposed operational definition. *Clinical Psychology: Science and Practice, 11*(3), 230–241.

Davidson, R. J., & Scherer, K. R. (2001). Editorial. *Emotion, 1,* 3–4.

Germer, C. K., Siegel, R. D., & Fulton, P. R. (Eds.). (2005). *Mindfulness and psychotherapy.* New York, NY: Guilford Press.

Hassed, C. (2013). Mind–body therapies: Use in chronic pain management. *Australian Family Physician, 42*(3), 112–117.

Hanh, T. N. (1976). *The miracle of mindfulness: A manual for meditation.* Boston, MA: Beacon.

Kabat-Zinn, J. (1990). *Full catastrophe living: Using the wisdom of your body and mind to face stress, pain, and illness.* New York, NY: Dell.

Kabat-Zinn, J. (1994). *Wherever you go, there you are: Mindfulness meditation in everyday life.* New York, NY: Hyperion.

Kabat-Zinn, J. (2003). Mindfulness-based interventions in context: Past, present, and future. *Clinical Psychology: Science and Practice, 10,* 144–156.

Kabat-Zinn, J. (2005). *Coming to our senses.* New York, NY: Hyperion.

Langer, E. J. (1990). *Mindfulness.* Cambridge, MA: Da Capo Press.

Langer, E. (1992). Interpersonal mindlessness and language. *Communication Monographs, 59,* 324–327.

Langer, E., Beck, P., Janoff-Bulman, R., & Timko, C. (1984). The relationship between cognitive deprivation and longevity in senile and non-senile elderly populations. *Academic Psychology Bulletin, 6,* 211–226.

Langer, E., Blank, A., & Chanowitz, B. (1978). The mindlessness of ostensibly thoughtful action: The role of "placebic" information in interpersonal interaction. *Journal of Personality and Social Psychology, 36,* 635–642.

Langer, E., & Moldoveanu, M. (Eds.). (2000). *Journal of social issues: Mindfulness theory and social issues.* New York, NY: Society for the Psychological Study of Social Issues.

Langer, E. J. (2009). *Counter clockwise: Mindful health and the power of possibility.* New York, NY: Ballantine Books.

Ludwig, D. S., & Kabat-Zinn, J. (2008). Mindfulness in medicine. *Journal of the American Medical Association, 300,* 1350–1352.

Marlatt, G. A., & Kristeller, J. L. (1999). Mindfulness and meditation. In W. R. Miller (Ed.), *Integrating spirituality in treatment* (pp. 67–84). Washington, DC: American Psychological Association Books.

Teasdale, J. D., Segal, Z. V., & Williams, J. M. (1995). How does cognitive therapy prevent depressive relapse and why should attentional control (mindfulness) training help? *Behaviour Research and Therapy, 33,* 25–39.

Thanissaro Bhikkhu (2007, June 5). Strength training for the mind. *Access to Insight.* Retrieved from http://www.accesstoinsight.org/lib/authors/thanissaro/strengthtraining.html

1

Mindfulness Forward and Back

Ellen J. Langer

During the 1970s, the cognitive revolution was well under way, and social psychologists were busy researching attribution theory, the dominant concern of the time (see Harvey, Ickes, & Kidd, 1978). Although I, too, was considered a social cognition researcher, I suggested that before we concern ourselves with what people were thinking, we should consider questioning whether they were thinking at all. In 1978, we conducted one of our first studies to explicitly suggest that much of the time, people were mindless (Langer, Blank, & Chanowitz, 1978). For example, in one of these studies, people were interrupted while about to use a Xerox machine with a request that made little sense. In one condition, the experimenter asked, "Can I use the Xerox machine *because I want to make copies?*" People were more likely to comply when a reason was given than when one was not, regardless of whether the reason was informative.

Several earlier studies we conducted already suggested the absence of deep processing. In one of these studies, a request for help was made where the words spoken were identical but were spoken in a different but still sensible order (Langer & Abelson, 1972). If subjects processed the whole request, there should not be a difference in compliance. The opening words ("My knee is killing me, would you do me a favor" vs. "Would you do me a favor, my knee is killing me"), however, primed a different behavioral response. Although it was years in coming, there is now a vast literature on priming, showing that much of our behavior is controlled by primes rather than under our immediate control. Before addressing some of this work, it may be useful to consider our other early priming studies.

Early Studies on Mindless Priming

Robert Abelson and I (Langer & Abelson, 1974) had therapists watch a video of a person being interviewed. Half of the time, the person was labeled "patient," and half

The Wiley Blackwell Handbook of Mindfulness, First Edition.
Edited by Amanda Ie, Christelle T. Ngnoumen, and Ellen J. Langer.
© 2014 John Wiley & Sons, Ltd. Published 2014 by John Wiley & Sons, Ltd.

of the time, he was called a "job applicant." Despite the fact that these were highly educated therapists trained to be careful observers of behavior who watched the very same video, the label primed the way the person would be seen. The "patient" was in need of therapy while the "job applicant" was fairly well adjusted. This work demonstrated the illusory correlation effect and the pervasiveness of mindlessness. Study after study would eventually show that people engage in hypothesis confirming data searches, ignoring all other information (Chapman & Chapman, 1967; Hamilton & Gifford, 1976).

Also in the 1970s, I proposed a theory about the illusion of control (Langer, 1975). These studies can be understood as priming studies as well. When elements of a skill situation, such as choice, stimulus familiarity, practice, and competition, are introduced into a chance situation, they prime a skill orientation, and thus people respond in a way more sensible to situations where their behavior can affect the outcome. Choosing a lottery ticket, for example, makes the ticket more valuable to people. An extension of this finding later became known as the endowment effect (Thaler, 1980), another much researched topic suggesting once again that mindlessness is pervasive.

Social psychologists were now starting to question whether phenomena like attitude formation/change were as had been previously understood or whether they were instantiations of mindlessness. For example, Shelley Chaiken (1980) distinguished between heuristic and systematic processing, and Cacioppo and Petty (1979) discussed central and peripheral processing, where heuristic and peripheral were essentially mindless. When the source of the message was seen as credible, when the way the argument was presented was reasonable (familiar), when the source was attractive, or when the message was given in a catchy slogan, mindlessness prevailed.

When information is given by an authority, seems irrelevant, or is given in absolute language, people take in the information without questioning it and become trapped by the substantive implications of that information in the future should that information become relevant and where a deeper understanding would be helpful (Chanowitz & Langer, 1981). I would submit that most of what we learn, we learn in this absolute way. Most of our education, indeed, is geared to the giving of absolute facts, irrespective of context, and thus promotes mindlessness. How often have we been told to learn something so well that it becomes second nature? This, too, is an instruction that promotes mindlessness. We learn how to do the task and now don't have to think about it when such thought could yield superior performance (see Langer, 1997).

The evidence that mindlessness is pervasive was mounting. Numerous studies showed that people respond passively to cues in the environment rather than actively make choices. For example, (1) affective priming asserts that affective reactions can be evoked with minimal stimulus input and virtually no cognitive processing (Zajonc, 1980); (2) intentions and goals can be activated nonconsciously by the environmental context (Bargh & Chartrand, 1999); (3) the chameleon effect (Chartrand & Bargh, 1999) demonstrates that people unwittingly mimic others so that their motor behavior unintentionally matches that of strangers with whom they worked together on a task; and (4) the vast literature on stereotyping shows that single cues like gender or race can overshadow an enormous amount of countervailing information and be automatically activated (Blair & Banaji, 1996). Each of these and more speak to the mindlessness of everyday behavior.

In one study, for example, Bargh, Chen, and Burrows (1996) found that simply cuing old age led subjects to walk more slowly. In an extension of that work, we had people categorize photos by age, thereby priming old age for young subjects, or we had them categorize the same photos along several dimensions. This mindfulness treatment erased the mindless effect of priming (Djikic, Langer, & Stapleton, 2008).

Most recently we have studied the mindlessness that results from reliance on GPS systems. To do this, Jaewoo Chung and I (Chung & Langer, 2013) developed a mindful indoor navigation system that provides choice to users. Choice promotes mindfulness. It is through noticing differences among alternatives that one arrives at a decision. We found that the mindful GPS system increased perceived control; decreased travel time, errors, and confusion; and increased the number of landmarks noticed.

Even multitasking looks different through the mindlessness/mindfulness lens. The mindless use of so many electronic gadgets now available has been shown to result in decrements in performance. Nevertheless, we found that people with higher trait mindfulness scores on the Langer Mindfulness Scale (LMS; Langer, 2004) are better able to multitask (Ie, Haller, Langer, & Courvoisier, 2012).

From Mindlessness to Mindfulness

Some argue that there is a place for mindlessness. I believe mindlessness is reasonable only when two conditions are met: when we have found the very best way of doing something, and when nothing changes. Clearly, from Heisenberg forward we know that everything is always changing. I further have argued that not only is everything changing but also at any one time things look different from different perspectives. Most typically, we're unaware of subtle changes because we confuse the stability of our mindsets with the stability of the underlying phenomenon. By freezing our understanding, we forfeit the possibility of choosing to act differently. The counterargument is usually that mindfulness takes more time than mindlessness and is more effortful. I'm not sure that is so, but even if true, the difference is only milliseconds and rarely does that small time difference truly matter. In making this argument, someone once created the condition where a child is about to walk into oncoming traffic. The person thought that mindlessly pulling the child to safety would be best done mindlessly. I countered that if the adult had been mindful, the child wouldn't have gotten to the curb in the first place. Moreover, there may be some advantage in mindfully scanning the driver's behavior to see which way would actually be safest to take the child. When we are mindless, we give up the option to make that choice. To see mindfulness as being more effortful is to confuse it with controlled processing as discussed below.

My original research on mindlessness gave way to questions about the other side of the coin, mindfulness. My particular approach to mindfulness grew out of our early work on choice. In the illusion of control studies, it was clear that choice was important—so important that even in situations that were deemed chance-determined, choice mattered to people. The most telling study on the topic was the research Judith Rodin and I were to conduct with elderly nursing home adults

(Langer & Rodin, 1976; Rodin & Langer, 1977). The experimental group was given choices to make (e.g., a plant to take care of) and a pep talk encouraging them to make the choices they used to make when they were younger. To control for all of the content provided, comparison subjects were given tender loving care and were told the nurses would help them care for the plants. Our follow-up study revealed that twice as many people in the group given choices to make were still alive 18 months later, compared to the control group. What was it about making choices that produced such extreme effects?

To actively make a choice, we notice aspects of the alternatives. If these aspects are novel, we may be led to choose other than our habitual choice. To always select the same alternative may seem like a choice from the observer's perspective, but for the actor it may be a habitual response. As such, it requires very little from us and may seem almost a nonevent. If everyday I have orange juice without considering whether today I might prefer grapefruit juice, no choice is being made. To make a choice, there has to be a consideration of one or more of the options not taken. Thus, actively drawing novel distinctions was taken to be the crucial element of the nursing-home findings. To test this idea, we gave nursing-home residents instructions in mindful distinction drawing and replicated the longevity findings (Alexander, Langer, Newman, Chandler, & Davies, 1989; Langer, Beck, Janoff-Bulman, & Timko, 1984).

In one of these studies (Alexander et al., 1989) we compared mindful-noticing subjects and transcendental meditators to relaxation control subjects. The procedure was tailored to meditation (i.e., sitting still with one's eyes closed) so not the best way of testing mindfulness as we study it. Still, the results for the mindful-noticing group were clearly superior to the control group, as was the Transcendental Meditation treatment. Meditators and mindful-noticing subjects demonstrated improvements on measures of cognitive flexibility; paired associates learning; word fluency; mental health; systolic blood pressure; treatment efficacy; ratings of behavioral flexibility and perceived control; aging; and higher survival rate. The process of meditation helps loosen the grip of categories over us; meditation results in postmeditative mindfulness. Mindfully noticing different aspects of these categories similarly—and perhaps more directly—loosens their grip.

Over the last 40 years, in study after study, we increase novel distinction-drawing—mindfulness—and find significant improvements in psychological and physical functioning (see Langer, 1989, 1997, 2005, 2009, for reviews). It is not incompatible with meditation. It is a different way to get to essentially the same place. When we actively draw distinctions, we come to see that context and perspective matter, we see we didn't know it as well as we thought we did, and this uncertainty keeps our attention on the topic. We see that our evaluations change depending on the context, and thus we become less evaluative (e.g., rigid from one perspective is consistent from another). And all of these years of study suggest that mindfulness is literally and figuratively enlivening.

In a very different arena, we asked whether aspects of childbirth were mindless (Zilcha-Mano & Langer, 2013). In this instance, we operationalized mindfulness as attention to variability—the essence of which, again, is noticing novelty—to examine whether mindfulness would result in better health outcomes for mother and infant. At week 25–30 of pregnancy, participants were given instructions to attend to the variability of their sensations (positive/negative). The LMS was used to assess trait mindfulness and to see its relationship with health outcomes (see Chapter 45). The mindfulness training resulted in better health for both mother and infant. In addition, trait mindfulness predicted the well-being of the expectant mother and better neonatal outcomes. Our newest work is aimed at testing the effects of attention to variability on disorders such as depression, multiple sclerosis, amyotrophic lateral sclerosis, and cancer.

There are numerous other findings regarding the LMS. Most recently, we found a strong correlation between the scale and measures of subjective well-being in participants in mainland China, replicating the work in the US. Indeed, in study after study, we've found that both trait and state mindfulness are strongly related to happiness.

Mindfulness: What It Is and What It Isn't

More formally, mindfulness is defined as an active state of mind characterized by novel distinction-drawing that results in being (1) situated in the present; (2) sensitive to context and perspective; and (3) guided (but not governed) by rules and routines. The phenomenological experience of mindfulness is the felt experience of engagement. Noticing/creating novelty reveals inherent uncertainty. When we recognize that we don't know the person, object, or situation as well as we thought we did, our attention naturally goes to the target. By attending to variability, the hallmark of mindfulness, eventually we stop confusing the stability of our mindsets with the stability of the underlying phenomena.

Mindlessness, by contrast, is defined as an inactive state of mind characterized by reliance on distinctions/categories drawn in the past. Here (1) the past overdetermines the present; (2) we are trapped in a single perspective but oblivious to that entrapment; (3) we're insensitive to context; and (4) rules and routines govern rather than guide our behavior. Moreover, mindlessness typically comes about by default not by design. When we accept information as if unconditionally true, we become trapped by the substantive implications of the information. Even if it is to our advantage in the future to question the information, if we mindlessly processed it, it will not occur to us to do so (Chanowitz & Langer, 1981). The same rigid relationship results from mindless repetition (Langer & Imber, 1979, 1980).

Because my work on mindfulness began during the "cognitive revolution," it was cast in cognitive terms. It was never meant to describe a cold cognitive process. Indeed, as the mind/body discussion below makes clear, the dualism distinction is questionable at best. Nevertheless, we recently set out to test the effects of mindfulness without meditation on our senses. Participants were given instructions and practice in noticing novelty regarding vision or touch. Relative to control groups, these participants showed enhanced functioning. That is, mindful instructions improved both vision and kinesthetic senses (Langer, Reece, & Rood, 2013).

The many health-related experiments we have conducted make clear that our mindfulness treatments result in better health and increased longevity (Langer, 2009). For medical conditions in general, there is a mindless illusion of stability, where people often implicitly expect their condition to either stay the same or get worse if it is chronic. Although nothing stays the same, minor positive fluctuations may be over-looked. It is in noticing these minor changes that control over the disease may lie. Several things follow from this attention to symptom variability: (1) we come to see that we don't have the problem all of the time; (2) if sometimes it is better than other times, we may ask why; (3) after asking why, we generate answers and may be able to solve the problem; and (4) even if we don't find a solution, the mindfulness that the search entails is good for our health. Thus, noticing novelty has a direct effect on health and an indirect effect (i.e., considering potential solutions); the more mindful we are, the more likely we will avert the health danger before it has arisen.

The Mind/Body "Problem" Reconsidered

The age-old mind/body problem (i.e., how can something nonmaterial, a thought, affect the material body?) continues to challenge philosophers and scientists alike. The implicit assumption—that mind and body are separate entities—may be the problem, however, that needs to be addressed. From Plotinus to Nagarjuna to Spinoza, a long line of thinkers through the ages have proposed that mind and body are but two sides of the same coin. That many such thinkers were often dwelling over concerns of philosophy or religion when they developed this idea may unfortunately have caused this insight to be met with suspicion, even outright derision, by the modern scientific academe. Current findings from fields as diverse as social psychology, neurobiology, and cognitive science, however, indicate that the tides of popular sentiment may once again be turning.

The Langer and Rodin (1976) study discussed above indicated that merely changing the content of one's thinking could indeed generate significant effects in the body and that mind and body were not as divorced from one another as the dominant scientific paradigm at that time had theretofore assumed. Now, it is more or less taken for granted that mind affects body, although the pathways are still unknown.

My newest work proposes a reworking of our understanding of the relationship between mind and body where the search for pathways from one to the other may be misguided, and do so from the perspective of mindfulness theory. It begins with the view that mind and body are just concepts. We have accepted them mindlessly as if they are more than a particular way to organize information.

Mindful Choice: Questioning the Basic Assumptions

Mindfulness allows for doubt and that allows for choice. When mindless, by contrast, our behavior is predetermined by the past, closing us off to choice and new possi-bilities. We live in a world governed by the principles of science. The precision with which we can now measure the world in and around us is, however, only as useful as the degree of mindfulness we employ to analyze it. Science becomes mindless when we automatically begin to conflate *precision* with *certainty*. Certainties lead to mind-lessness; when we think we know, there is no reason to find out. Too often, scientists observe a phenomenon, create a theory to explain it, and then collect data to prove their theory. Not surprisingly, confirmation is found. Theory is supposed to be understood as possibility, but at least in the social sciences, it most often is taken as absolute fact leaving little experienced difference between laws and theories. These theories build upon each other with the result of a series of concatenated probabilities making it harder and harder to question the basic assumptions of the original proposition. Scientific evidence can only yield probabilities, but science in use takes these probabilities and converts them into absolutes.

Take medicine, for example. Many diseases are labeled chronic. Chronic is understood as uncontrollable. If something is understood to be uncontrollable, we would be foolish to try and control it. Yet no science can prove uncontrollability. All science can prove is that something is possible, or it is indeterminate. Indeterminate is very different from uncontrollable. Moreover, by generalizing the findings to the population because of methodological considerations like random assignment without due regard to the subject population actually used (e.g., all of those people who self heal are missing from the medical database), we are discouraged from trying to self heal. In any experiment, the researcher has to make many hidden decisions regarding the parameters of the study (e.g., who the subjects actually are, the time and circumstances in which they'll be tested, the amount of the independent variable to administer). With these dimensions out of mind, findings seem more stable than they might otherwise seem. Couple this with the mistaken tendency of people to seek certainty and confuse the stability of their mindsets with the stability of the underlying phenomena, and we end up with an illusion of knowing and unnecessary limits to what we might otherwise find out.

This illusory sense of knowing is pervasive, extending even to the point where we misconstrue the nature of our own mental processes. What are we actually doing when we hold a certain concept in our mind's eye? Picture a car, for example. Now, start taking away individual elements that seem essential to the "car-ness" of it all, and ask yourself if you'd still know it's a car. A car without wheels? Still a car. Minus a steering wheel, or a bumper or an engine? Still seen as a car (albeit perhaps not one you'd want as yours). A Jeep and a station wagon and a Smartcar all somehow fit into this same category of "car," despite their clear diversity in features and appearance. Wittgenstein (Mora, 1953) famously performed a similar dissection of conceptual categories, effectively demonstrating (in his case, with the concept of "game") the inherent illusion that our mental categories for things are actually based upon some identifiable set of core features. So, what is it that makes a car a car? Not much, as it turns out.

Recent findings in the field of cognitive neuropsychology have begun to indicate that this assertion—that conceptual categories lack inherent unifying features—is backed by more than just sound logic. Barsalou (2009) and Wilson-Mendenhall, Barrett, Simmons, and Barsalou (2011) have established that the brain doesn't actually use a set of core concepts to define mental categories of objects and phenomena. Rather, our thought processes remain in a perpetual state of collection, assessment, and reaction to incoming information. It is only at the point of higher-level cognitive processes that we begin to grow lazy and assume that all examples of cars have some inherent "car-ness" about them. (Or, for that matter, that all instances of fear, or anger, or pride, must necessarily be connected by some unifying element.) In reality, the idea of "car" (or "fear," or any other concept) is actually represented in our brains as a loose amalgam of instances (this morning on the way to work in traffic, on a showroom floor, in a junkyard), specific examples (a Smartcar, a station wagon, a Jeep), functions (creating momentum, providing shelter, controlling climate), and other characteristics of certain objects that we learn at some point to clump together. In short, there's no core element that makes a car a car every time, all of the time. Mindfulness requires that we engage the world with this same degree of dynamism and flexibility.

Reuniting the Mind and Body

No matter what we are doing, we are doing it mindlessly or mindfully, and the consequences of being in one state or the other are enormous. Research described in over 150 research papers and four books on the topic of mindfulness reveals that the simple process of creating/noticing novelty is literally and figuratively enlivening. We've found increases in well-being, health, competence, relationship satisfaction, effective leadership, and creativity to name a few of the many findings. Perhaps the most startling findings are the most recent. In one study (Langer, Russel, & Eisenkraft, 2009), we instructed symphony musicians to play a familiar piece of music and either make it new in very subtle ways that only each musician would individually know or recall a performance of the music that they were very pleased with and replicate it. We taped the performances and played them for audiences, blind to our instruction, and they overwhelmingly preferred the mindfully played piece. The musicians showed a similar preference. An interesting aspect to this work is that rather than cacophony, when each individual "did it their own way," superior coordinated performance resulted. In other work we also showed that mindfulness seems to leave its imprint in the products of our labor (Langer, 2005).

More important to the present discussion is recent work that follows up on research originally conducted in 1981. The idea was and is deceptively simple. Mind and body are just words, concepts to which we rigidly adhere. What would happen, we asked, if we got rid of the distinction between mind and body? If we put the mind and body back together so to speak, then wherever the mind is, so too would be the body. Within this understanding, there is no reason to search for mediating mechanisms. Whatever is going on at the level of the brain is happening simultaneously with the thought and is just another level of analysis. With this view in mind, we conducted a series of investigations where we put minds in healthy places and took physical measurements.

In the first of these studies (see Langer et al., 1990), elderly men were taken to a timeless retreat retrofitted to 20 years earlier. To firmly anchor their minds in that earlier time, they would speak for the week in the present tense about the past for the full week they spent there. A comparison group of men lived the week at the retreat reminiscing about the past. For them, their minds were firmly in the present. The results were notable, especially considering that the study was conducted back in 1981 before there was any mind/body research and before 80 became the new 60. Despite how enfeebled these men in their 80s were at the start of the study, both groups improved significantly from where they started. Hearing, vision, memory, and grip strength were significantly different after the week. The experimental group showed further improvement differing significantly from the comparison group with respect to manual dexterity; digit–symbol substitution scores (63% of the experimental group improved compared to 44% of the control group); height; gait; posture; joint flexibility; and diminished symptoms of arthritis. We photographed everyone before and after the week and found that all of the experimental participants looked noticeably younger at the end of the study.

In my view, it was the change in mindset, much the same way a placebo works, that accounted for the difference between the two groups. By priming a time when they were vital, their mindsets of old age as a time of debilitation became irrelevant. (Of course, over the week, many things could have varied that we couldn't possibly control in such an ambitious undertaking. We were, however, able to use tighter controls in more recent investigations.) Two things should be addressed regardless of the explanation for the findings one may choose. The first is the widespread belief that elders are not supposed to improve their hearing and vision—or indeed improve on any of the measures we took. Below I'll return to this in a discussion of science. The second issue to consider is that the idea of mind/body unity led to these findings, and thus at the least the theory serves a heuristic purpose.

Alia Crum and I (Crum and Langer, 2007) tested this mind/body hypothesis in a very different setting with chambermaids. We started by inquiring about how much exercise they thought they got in a typical week. Surprisingly, they thought they didn't get exercise, despite the fact that their work is exercise. Exercise, they thought, was what one did after work. If exercise is good for our health, and they get more than the surgeon general recommends, then we should expect that they would be healthier than socioeconomically equivalent others who do not exercise as much or as consistently. Interestingly, they were less healthy. While noteworthy, this was not the focus of the study. We randomly divided the participants into two groups and taught one group to change their mindset to view their work as exercise. We took as many measures as we could think of regarding food eaten in the course of the month between tests, exercise intensity at work, and exercise outside of work. We found no differences between the two groups on any of these measures. Nevertheless, the two groups significantly differed on measures of waist to hip ratio, weight loss, body mass index, and blood pressure. We attribute these improvements for the experimental group to the change in mindset.

We tested this mind/body hypothesis in another series of experiments (Langer, Djikic, Pirson, Madenci, & Donohue, 2010). Here we focused on vision. The standard Snellen eye chart has letters that get progressively smaller as one reads down the chart. Implicitly this creates the expectation that soon we will not be able to see. In one study, we reversed the eye chart so that the letters get progressively larger, thereby creating the mindset that soon we will be able to see. With the change in mindset, participants were able to see what they "couldn't" see before. With the standard eye chart, there is also an expectation that we will start to have difficultly around two-thirds of the way down the chart. Accordingly, we adapted the standard eye chart such that it began a third of the way down the standard chart. Again, participants could see what they couldn't see before. In yet another study, we took advantage of the mindset that pilots have excellent vision. We had men don the clothes of air force pilots and fly a flight simulator. Control participants simulated flying the simulator. Vision improved for those embodying the mindset of pilot.

Finally, we wanted to see if we could condition improved vision (Pirson, Ie, & Langer, 2012). Participants in two experimental groups read a chapter of one of my books where the font of either the letter "a" or the letter "e" was much smaller than other letters (e.g., can, take, many) while participants in the control group read the chapter in a standard font size. Over time, those in the experimental groups would of course come to know what the smaller letter represented. After reading the chapter, participants' visual acuity was assessed. Regardless of the specific letter that was manipulated, results across three experiments showed that participants in the experimental groups scored higher on visual acuity than the control group, once again demonstrating the malleability of visual acuity.

Our accepted theories and mindsets tell us that vision is not supposed to improve. But from where do these mindsets come? We accept negative mindsets (e.g., vision will necessarily worsen over time) and we create theories of the eye to show why this must be. The expectation becomes self-fulfilling, further validating the original supposition. Yet with this simple understanding that our own minds create our seeming limitations, we may come to be more than alternative mind/body views currently enable.

Support for this view comes from recent work on embodied cognition. While our research has focused on measuring mind changes on the body, this work focuses on body changes affecting the mind. The idea is the same. Put the body in a particular position, and the entire individual is in that mode. For example, stand tall, and we become more confident (Carney, Cuddy, & Yap, 2010); think about the future or the past, and we lean forward or back (Miles, Nind, & Macrae, 2010); squeeze something soft/hard, and we perceive gender ambiguous faces as female/male (Slepian, Weisbuch, Rule, & Ambady, 2011).

As work on embodied cognition reveals, social psychologists are beginning to circumvent presumed limits that result from dualist thinking. I think the entire research enterprise would prosper from consideration that virtually all of our findings are only part of the picture. When, in a typical experiment, the researcher puts in some strong cue that people follow, yielding significant results, we might consider that our subjects do so mindlessly. As Helen Newman and I argued, the typical social psychological experiment might be an exercise in testing mindlessness. Those who do not give us what we expect are part of the variability. This variability, however, might be understood as mindful responses. In that study (Langer & Newman, 1979), we used the popular Kelley (1950) paradigm where participants were led to believe that the speaker they would soon hear was personally warm/cold. Those who confirmed the experimenter's hypothesis were reasonably oblivious to what was said.

Consider some of our field's most important research. Findings from research on "thin-slices" of behavior (Ambady & Rosenthal, 1993) may rely on mindlessness. If we were mindful, our tendency to make dispositional attributions might change since the situation would no longer be ignored, and so the effect might disappear. Similarly, priming and the chameleon effect rely on mindlessness, so these findings would also look very different if mindfulness prevailed.

Conclusions

Is mindfulness more effortful? At least up to some point, mindfulness is energy begetting not consuming. Part of the reason people think of mindfulness as effortful is because it is confused with worry. It is not thinking novel thoughts about a problem that is effortful. It is worrying that the answer will be wrong that takes effort. In general, controlled processing is confused with mindfulness. Controlled processing is the operation of overlearned thought to a problem. Adding or multiplying numbers for example without regard to choosing different number systems on which to base one's answer is effortful. Moreover, play and enjoying humor are not effortful, and both rely on novelty. Recognizing that evaluations are in our minds and not in events leaves us less stressed and less reactive, both of which are energy consuming.

Because this work began with the cognitive revolution, it did not seem important then to stress that mindfulness—West or East—is not solely a cognitive process. Indeed, the idea of cognition as being separate from other ways of responding runs counter to my research but follows from mind/body dualism.

Just as psychologists are becoming increasingly aware of mind/body unity and what it promises for our well-being, the culture at large may also be in the midst of an evolution in consciousness. When we become mindful, either in our waking state by allowing and encouraging all of our senses to notice novelty or through meditation, the outcome is the same. These are two roads to the same place. They are neither mutually exclusive nor at odds with each other. There are contexts where one or the other may be preferable. Those who want a major life change, for example, may find meditation to be the path to take. Those who find meditation difficult or too unfamiliar, mindfulness as I study it may be more appropriate. Until schools and organizations provide opportunities or encourage students and employees to meditate, it may be worth while to recognize that mindfulness without meditation can be easily accommodated into present organizational structures. As all of us come to see that mindfulness is effortless and always available, and results in better health, effectiveness, and happiness, it is likely to become the preferred choice to the currently more normative version of being sealed in unlived mindless lives.

References

Alexander, C. N., Langer, E. J., Newman, R. I., Chandler, H. M., & Davies, J. L. (1989). Transcendental meditation, mindfulness, and longevity: An experimental study with the elderly. *Journal of Personality and Social Psychology, 57*(6), 950–964. doi:10.1037/0022-3514.57.6.950

Ambady, N., & Rosenthal, R. (1993). Half a minute: Predicting teacher evaluations from thin slices of nonverbal behavior and physical attractiveness. *Journal of Personality and Social Psychology, 64*, 431–431. doi:10.1037/0022-3514.64.3.431

Bargh, J. A., & Chartrand, T. L. (1999). The unbearable automaticity of being. *American Psychologist, 54*(7), 462–479.

Bargh, J. A., Chen, M., & Burrows, L. (1996). Automaticity of social behavior: Direct effects of trait construct and stereotype activation on action. *Journal of Personality and Social Psychology, 71*, 230–244. doi:10.1037/0022-3514.71.2.230

Barsalou, L. W. (2009). Simulation, situated conceptualization, and prediction. *Philosophical Transactions of the Royal Society of London: Biological Sciences, 364*, 1281–1289. doi:10.1098/rstb.2008.0319

Blair, I. V., & Banaji, M. R. (1996). Automatic and controlled processes in stereotype priming. *Journal of Personality and Social Psychology, 70*, 1142–1163. doi:10.1037/0022-3514.70.6.1142

Cacioppo, J. T., & Petty, R. E. (1979). Neuromuscular circuits in affect-laden information processing. *The Pavlovian Journal of Biological Science: The Official Journal of the Pavlovian, 14*(3), 177–185. doi:10.1007/BF03001979

Carney, D. R., Cuddy, A. J. C., & Yap, A. J. (2010). Power posing brief nonverbal displays affect neuroendocrine levels and risk tolerance. *Psychological Science, 21*(10), 1363–1368. doi:10.1177/0956797610383437

Chaiken, S. (1980). Heuristic versus systematic information processing and the use of source versus message cues in persuasion. *Journal of Personality and Social Psychology, 39*(5), 752–766. doi:10.1037/0022-3514.39.5.752

Chanowitz, B., & Langer, E. J. (1981). Premature cognitive commitment. *Journal of Personality and Social Psychology, 41*(6), 1051–1063. doi:10.1037/0022-3514.41.6.1051

Chapman, L. J., & Chapman, J. P. (1967). Genesis of popular but erroneous psycho-diagnostic observations. *Journal of Abnormal Psychology, 72*(3), 193–204. doi:10.1037/h0024670

Chartrand, T. L., & Bargh, J. A. (1999). The chameleon effect: The perception–behavior link and social interaction. *Journal of Personality and Social Psychology, 76*, 893–910.

Chung, J., & Langer, E. (2013) *Mindful navigation*. Cambridge, MA: Harvard University.

Crum, A. J., & Langer, E. J. (2007). Mind-set matters: Exercise and the placebo effect. *Psychological Science, 18*(2), 165–171. doi:10.1111/j.1467-9280.2007.01867.x

Djikic, M., Langer, E. J., & Stapleton, S. F. (2008). Reducing stereotyping through mindfulness: Effects on automatic stereotype-activated behaviors. *Journal of Adult Development, 15*(2), 106–111. doi:10.1007/s10804-008-9040-0

Hamilton, D. L., & Gifford, R. K. (1976). Illusory correlation in interpersonal perception: A cognitive basis of stereotypic judgments. *Journal of Experimental Social Psychology, 12*(4), 392–407. doi:10.1016/S0022-1031(76)80006-6

Harvey, J. H., Ickes, W. J., & Kidd, R. F. (1978). *New directions in attribution research*. Hillsdale, NJ: Lawrence Erlbaum.

Ie, A., Haller, C. S., Langer, E. J., & Courvoisier, D. S. (2012). Mindful multitasking: The relationship between mindful flexibility and media multitasking. *Computers in Human Behavior, 28*, 1526–1532. doi:10.1016/j.chb.2012.03.022

Kelley, H. H. (1950). The warm-cold variable in first impressions of persons. *Journal of Personality, 18*(4), 431–439.

Langer, E. J. (1975). The illusion of control. *Journal of Personality and Social Psychology, 32*(2), 311–328. doi:10.1037/0022-3514.32.2.311

Langer, E. J. (1989). *Mindfulness*. Reading, MA: Addison-Wesley.

Langer, E. J. (1997). *The power of mindful learning*. Reading, MA: Addison-Wesley.

Langer, E. J. (2004). *Langer mindfulness scale user guide and technical manual*. Worthington, OH: IDS Publishing Corporation.

Langer, E. J. (2005). *On becoming an artist: Reinventing yourself through mindful creativity*. New York, NY: Ballantine Books.

Langer, E. J. (2009). *Counterclockwise: Mindful health and the power of possibility.* New York, NY: Ballantine Books.

Langer, E. J., & Abelson, R. P. (1972). The semantics of asking a favor: How to succeed in getting help without really dying. *Journal of Personality and Social Psychology, 24*(1), 26–32. doi:10.1037/h0033379

Langer, E. J., & Abelson, R. P. (1974). A patient by any other name....: Clinician group difference in labeling bias. *Journal of Consulting and Clinical Psychology, 42*(1), 4–9. doi:10.1037/h0036054

Langer, E. J., Beck, P., Janoff-Bulman, R., & Timko, C. (1984). An exploration of relationships among mindfulness, longevity, and senility. *Academic Psychology Bulletin, 6*(2), 211–226.

Langer, E. J., Blank, A., & Chanowitz, B. (1978). The mindlessness of ostensibly thoughtful action: The role of "placebic" information in interpersonal interaction. *Journal of Personality and Social Psychology, 36*(6), 635–642. doi:10.1037/0022-3514.36.6.635

Langer, E. J., Chanowitz, B., Palmerino, M., Jacobs, S., Rhodes, M., & Thayer, P. (1990). Nonsequential development and aging. In C. N. Alexander & E. J. Langer (Eds.), *Higher stages of human development: Perspectives on adult growth* (pp. 114–136). New York, NY: Oxford University Press.

Langer, E. J., Djikic, M., Pirson, M., Madenci, A., & Donohue, R. (2010). Believing is seeing: Using mindlessness (mindfully) to improve visual acuity. *Psychological Science, 21*(5), 661–666. doi:10.1177/0956797610366543

Langer, E., & Imber, L. (1979). When practice makes imperfect: the debilitating effects of overlearning. *Journal of Personality and Social Psychology, 37*, 2014–2025.

Langer, E. J., & Imber, L. (1980). Role of mindlessness in the perception of deviance. *Journal of Personality and Social Psychology, 39*(3), 360–367. doi:10.1037/0022-3514.39.3.360

Langer, E. J., & Newman, H. M. (1979). The role of mindlessness in a typical social psychological experiment. *Personality and Social Psychology Bulletin, 5*(3), 295–298.

Langer, E. J., Reece, A., & Rood, D. (2013). *Mindful sensation enhancement.* Manuscript in preparation.

Langer, E. J., & Rodin, J. (1976). The effects of choice and enhanced personal responsibility for the aged: A field experiment in an institutional setting. *Journal of Personality and Social Psychology, 34*(2), 191–198.

Langer, E., Russel, T., & Eisenkraft, N. (2009). Orchestral performance and the footprint of mindfulness. *Psychology of Music, 37*(2), 125–136. doi:10.1177/0305735607086053

Miles, L. K., Nind, L. K., & Macrae, C. N. (2010). Moving through time. *Psychological Science, 21*(2), 222–223. doi:10.1177/0956797609359333

Mora, J. F. (1953). Wittgenstein, a symbol of troubled times. *Philosophy and Phenomenological Research, 14*(1), 89–96.

Pirson, M., Ie, A., & Langer, E. (2012). Seeing what we know, knowing what we see: Challenging the limits of visual acuity. *Journal of Adult Development, 19*, 59–65. doi:10.1007/s10804-011-9132-0

Rodin, J., & Langer, E. J. (1977). Long-term effects of a control-relevant intervention with the institutionalized aged. *Journal of Personality and Social Psychology, 35*(12), 897–902. doi:10.1037/0022-3514.35.12.897

Slepian, M. L., Weisbuch, M., Rule, N. O., & Ambady, N. (2011). Tough and tender: Embodied categorization of gender. *Psychological Science, 22*(1), 26–28. doi:10.1177/0956797610390388

Thaler, R. (1980). Toward a positive theory of consumer choice. *Journal of Economic Behavior & Organization, 1*(1), 39–60. doi:10.1016/0167-2681(80)90051-7

Wilson-Mendenhall, C. D., Barrett, L. F., Simmons, W. K., & Barsalou, L. W. (2011). Grounding emotion in situated conceptualization. *Neuropsychologia, 49*(5), 1105–1127. doi:10.1016/j.neuropsychologia.2010.12.032

Zajonc, R. B. (1980). Feeling and thinking: Preferences need no inferences. *American Psychologist, 35*(2), 151. doi:10.1037/0003-066X.35.2.151

Zilcha-Mano, S., & Langer, E. J. (2013). *Mindful attention to variability and successful child birth.* Manuscript submitted for publication.

Further Reading

Hsu, L. M., Chung, J., & Langer, E. J. (2010). The influence of age-related cues on health and longevity. *Perspectives on Psychological Science, 5*(6), 632–648. doi:10.1177/1745691610388762

2

Thriving With Uncertainty

Opening the Mind and Cultivating Inner Well-Being Through Contemplative and Creative Mindfulness

Daniel J. Siegel and Madeleine W. Siegel

Introduction

Recent studies of the state of "being present" for experience, being aware of what is happening moment by moment, suggests that "presence" is a key component to well-being (Parker, Nelson, Epel, & Siegel, in press). Presence is measured in research protocols by the absence of "mind-wandering" in which a personal present focus of attention is not including present activities (Hasenkamp, Wilson-Mendenhall, Duncan, & Barsalou, 2012; Kane et al., 2007; Killingsworth & Gilbert, 2010; Mrazek, Smallwood, & Schooler, 2012; Smallwood & O'Connor, 2011). This unintentional distraction from the moment, distinct from intentional free-associative explorations of active, purposeful imagination, has been associated with the negative health finding of decreased lengths of telomeres—the ends of chromosomes that are needed to maintain cellular life and health (Epel et al., in press). Negative life events are also associated with decreased telomere length (Tyrka et al., 2010), whereas positive life events are associated with enhanced telomere length (Carrol, Diez Roux, Fitzpatrick, & Seeman, 2012). Presence is associated with increases in the enzyme telomerase that maintains and even repairs telomeres (Blackburn & Epel, 2012; Epel et al., in press). Recent studies of contemplative mindfulness practice suggest that increasing the capacity to be aware of moment by moment experience with the suspension of judgment (Kabat-Zinn, 2006)—to be "mindful"—is associated with increases in telomerase as well (Epel, Daubenmier, Moskowitz, Folkman, & Blackburn, 2009; Jacobs et al., 2010).

Other studies of mindfulness training (Davidson et al., 2003; Davidson & Begley, 2012) reveal several health-promoting changes in the physiology and psychology of individuals learning to focus attention on what is happening in the present moment without being swept up by judgmental thinking and imprisoned by prior expectations. These enhancements of health include improved immune function, increased sense

The Wiley Blackwell Handbook of Mindfulness, First Edition.
Edited by Amanda Ie, Christelle T. Ngnoumen, and Ellen J. Langer.
© 2014 John Wiley & Sons, Ltd. Published 2014 by John Wiley & Sons, Ltd.

of well-being, and a "left-shift" in baseline neural activity indicating the capacity to approach, rather than withdraw, from challenging internal or external stimuli.

Being "creatively mindful" has also been associated with positive changes in physiology and in psychological well-being (Langer, 1989, 2009; Langer & Moldoveanu, 2000). By experiencing learning from an open and engaged stance, being presented with material that does not prematurely close perception and understanding through constrictive categories and by involving the learner actively in the educational process, creative mindfulness can be viewed as also increasing the individual's way of "bring present" with the learning experience (Siegel, 2007a).

In these ways, we can see that both creative and contemplative mindfulness produce positive effects on health and well-being and also enhance the general sense of presence in an individual's life. What might be the underlying shared mechanisms of these two distinct approaches to being mindful that might explain their similar outcomes? To address this question, we will offer a fundamental proposal and discuss several possible shared mechanisms that might underlie their commonalities. Our goal is not to review the exciting and growing research on empirical studies of mindfulness, but rather to explore the important concepts and their interrelatedness in fundamental ways that may inform future investigations and the creations of practical applications.

Our proposal is that presence, the experience of open awareness we are suggesting is within both contemplative and creative forms of mindfulness, is a state of mind in which an individual learns to live with uncertainty. Beyond merely *tolerating* a state of not knowing the outcome of thought or action, we are proposing that *thriving* with uncertainty becomes a way of being for individuals who experience the different approaches to being mindful. While this hypothesis will need focused empirical research to support its possible validity, we hope that by offering this detailed conceptual discussion, future investigations may illuminate the core processes connecting contemplative and creative mindfulness with well-being.

To attempt to illuminate the possible mechanisms underlying how we cultivate a mental state in which we thrive with uncertainty, we need to first explore the concept of the mind itself.

Mind, Brain, and Relationships

To understand how being mindful creatively or contemplatively might influence our physiological, psychological, and relational well-being, we will first explore a way of defining what the mind is, and then discuss how it relates to health in the body as well as in our social lives. The fundamental question we begin with is, "What is the connection among body, mind, and relationships?" What might these three seemingly distinct aspects of human life share in common? What actually links them to one another?

The body is composed of molecules that are assembled into cells that form systems that are differentiated and linked to one another to enable physiological processes to emerge and life to be stabilized and maintained (homeostasis), changes across time to be adapted to (allostasis), and reproduction to be possible. Allostasis can be thought of as the way we maintain stability (homeostasis) through the experience of change across time with an adjustment of multiple physiological regulatory systems to the demands posed by the environment (see McEwen, 2000; Sterling & Eyer, 1988). Within each cell is a nucleus with genetic material, surrounded by the cell body with various organelles subsuming a range of functions each helping subcomponents function together as a larger whole. Cells link within organs, organs interact within bodily systems, and the whole body maintains a coordination and balance of homeostasis in the moment, and of allostasis over changes occurring across time.

From the time of conception, cells form the basis of life. The single-celled conceptus differentiates into two, four, eight, 16, 32 cells, with more and more divisions of cells until trillions of cells differentiate to form our various systems. Of note is that the collection of cells that form the outer layer of the conceptus, the ectoderm that will form our skin, partly folds inwardly to create the origin of our nervous system. The neural tube is formed with the growth and migration of the basic cells, the neurons, extending our neural system from head to toe. It is this origin of the nervous system from the ectoderm, as it is with the skin itself, which makes our nervous system function to link the inner and outer worlds. Part of this migration of neurons is to the head where an extensive organization of neurons and their supportive glial cells, the astrocytes and oligodendrocytes, form our brainstem, cerebellum, limbic region, and neocortex. Part of neural differentiation is to the far reaches of our limbs and to the extensive innervation of our internal organs—our heart and intestines—that, like the brain in the head, are constructed into interconnecting spider-web-like systems.

The parallel distributed processing of our extensive neural networks forms a system in which it is believed that information can be processed (McClelland & Rogers, 2003; Raffone & Van Leeuwen, 2001; Rogers & McClelland, 2008). Examination of the fundamental ways in which neurons communicate with one another suggests that ion flow down the axonal length of the membrane, called the action potential, serves as a means of electrical transmission of the equivalent of the flow of current down to the end of the neuron. Chemical release at the junction between two neurons in the form of various neurotransmitters into the synaptic cleft produces changes in the downstream or postsynaptic neuron. These changes either facilitate or inhibit the instantiation of an action potential in this neuron. In sum, the process of "neural firing" involves the *electrochemical flow of energy* between and among neurons distributed both in the head and throughout the body.

Recent explorations of how the brain functions reveal the profoundly social nature of our neural lives. As vertebrates, we have an extensive central nervous system that helps regulate our bodily physiology, to create allostasis. As mammals, we are creatures that live and regulate ourselves through interactions with others of our species, key interactions that enable us to maintain our bodily equilibrium. As humans, we have an extensive set of social interactions, beginning at birth, that influence both how the nervous system develops and how it functions in the moment and across the lifespan. These early social interactions shape not only neural connections, but even the epigenetic molecules that control gene expression in neural regions that regulate our internal state (Roth & Sweatt, 2011). It may be for this reason that the most robust predictor of medical health, mental health, longevity, and even "happiness" is the presence of supportive and close relationships in a person's life (see Barnes, Brown,

Krusemark, Campbell, & Rogge, 2007; Fagundes, Bennett, Derry, & Kiecolt-Glaser, 2011; see also Rakel et al., 2009; Siegel, 2012a; Tronick, 2004). If relationships are so important in our health, what exactly defines a relationship?

A relationship can be defined as the patterns of how energy and information are shared between two or more people. Energy is the capacity to do something; information is a pattern of energy that has symbolic value or meaning beyond simply the pattern of neural firing. Flow is the change of something across time. And so the basic unit of a relationship is the flow of energy and information, and how this flow is shared between two or more people and the environment. Whether we examine the close attachment between infant and caregiver, the intimate communication of romance, the emotional connections in friendship, or the larger ways in which we live within families, affiliate with groups, or live within communities and embedded in our larger culture, our relationships interact with our nervous systems to shape who we are (see Siegel, 2012a). Naturally, our genetics shape how we develop as well, including how the epigenetic regulation of gene expression is shaped by experience, but we are "hard-wired"—that is, we have inherited the need—to connect with each other in ways that promote health and longevity.

So, we have defined one aspect of the body, the nervous system, as an *embodied mechanism* of energy and information flow. We have further defined relationships as the *sharing* of energy and information flow between and among people. What, then, is the "mind"?

Though mind is rarely defined and even called a "vague term" in the *Oxford Companion to the Mind* (Gregory, 2004), there is some general consensus that components of the mind, the many elements that comprise our mental life, include our feelings, thoughts, memories, perceptions, hopes, dreams, beliefs, and attitudes. Mental life also includes, but is not limited to, awareness, or the experience of being conscious. And mind also refers to our subjective experience, the felt texture of our inner lives, the mental "sea inside." We can also have a mind, but not have "theory of mind" or "mentalization" that would allow us to know that we have a mind—in ourselves or in others.

In the interdisciplinary field called *interpersonal neurobiology* (Siegel, 2012b) we attempt to combine a wide range of sciences into one consilient (Wilson, 1998) approach that suggests that we can offer not just a description of what comprises mind, but actually a working definition. In this definition, we see the fundamental process of energy and information flow as our unit of analysis: Energy and information are the "stuff" of the system we are examining. The "embodied nervous system" we are calling simply the brain is the *bodily mechanism* of that flow; relationships are the *sharing* of that flow; and mind is defined as an emergent self-organizing, embodied, and relational process that arises from and also regulates the flow of energy and information. In simple terms, beyond awareness and subjective experience, this third aspect of the mind can be defined as *an embodied and relational process that regulates the flow of energy and information.*

Within this definition, we can see that what occurs experientially within an individual's flow of energy and information and how that flow occurs between people gives rise to mental life. This embodied mechanism and this sharing of energy and information can occur within us, between ourselves and another individual, and among several people in a family or classroom or group, or among widely distributed clusters of people within communities, societies, and the larger culture (see Kitayama & Uskul, 2011; LeVine, 2010; Szyf, McGowan, Turecki, & Meaney, 2010). In this way, disciplines from neuroscience and psychology to sociology and anthropology can find a way of communicating with one another using this proposed definition illuminating one aspect of mind. From this window, we can see how patterns of energy and information flow are shaped by neural structure and by the many forms of relationships we have in our lives.

We can also see that this definition of mind helps us to step into the question of how mindfulness changes our relational and our bodily well-being. How we focus attention within the experience of creative or contemplative mindfulness can now be viewed in terms of how we regulate the flow of energy and information. Attention is a term used to designate the process of how information flow is directed, and information is created and transformed by way of the change in energy patterns across time. Certain swirls of energy, like sounds or sights, contain patterns with symbolic value that we call information. And attention directs this movement of energy and information across time, but within us (our nervous system) and between us (our relationships).

With this definition, we are not attempting to explain what subjective experience is, nor are we offering to step into the exciting but complex set of discussions about what consciousness is, or how it may arise from neural firing patterns, if it indeed does in such a simple, unidirectional way as we'll discuss later in the chapter. Here we are suggesting that this third aspect of mind—its regulatory function as an emergent, embodied and relational self-organizing process—will be of potential help in illuminating the nature of the various forms of mindfulness. Self-organization is an innate property of complex systems—collections of elements that are open to influences outside of themselves and that are capable of becoming chaotic. As an emergent process, self-organization both arises from and also regulates the interactions of elements of the complex system (Kröger, 2007; Kauffman, 1996). In this case, the complex system in question is energy and information flow within an individual and between an individual and the environment, including our social environment. Our minds are both embodied and socially embedded. Our proposal is that both creative and contemplative approaches to being mindful involve our minds, and how the mind regulates energy and information flow in a specific manner. We will turn know to how relationships and the embodied brain interact to shape the experience of mindfulness in its contemplative and creative forms.

Four Hunches

Four different avenues of explanation will be offered here to invite further explorations of how the mind, brain, and relationships contribute to the health-promoting aspects of being present within contemplative and creative ways of being mindful. These avenues may at first be considered metaphors, stories that reveal possible mechanisms that may, or may not, shed some new light on this topic. These metaphoric stories are inspired by scientific studies of actual mechanisms, but we are not claiming that there is enough empirically derived, objective data at this point to assert these

Layer	Top-down	Top-down dominance	Top-down
1	⇓	⇓⇓⇓	⇓
2	⇓	⇓⇓⇓	⇓
3	⇓	⇓⇓⇓	⇓
Awareness	⇒→⇒→	→⇒⇒⇒	⇒→→→→→
4	↑	↑	↑↑↑↑↑
5	↑	↑	↑↑↑↑↑
6	↑	↑	↑↑↑↑↑
	Bottom-up	Bottom-up	Bottom-up dominance

Figure 2.1   A metaphoric map or schematic proposal of top-down and bottom-up processing and the six-layered cortical columns. The information from sensation flows "bottom-up" from the lower layers of the column streaming from layers 6 to 5 to 4. Information from prior learning, called "top-down," streams from layers 1 to 2 to 3. Awareness is thought to emerge by the commingling of these two streams. In the first condition, bottom-up and top-down are balanced, and the resultant awareness blends the two streams. In the second condition, top-down input is dominant, and prior expectations and categorizations overshadow incoming sensory streams within awareness. In the third condition, sensory input in the here and now is dominant and awareness reflects a predominance of input from this sensory flow. Mindfulness may enable layers 3 and 4 to be disentangled by at first practicing enhancement of the bottom-up flow of present sensory experience. Used with permission. Copyright © 2010 by Mind Your Brain, Inc. Daniel J. Siegel, M.D., *The Mindful Therapist* (2010).

ideas as proven, but rather as valid notions, as possibly helpful concepts. With this in mind, we invite you to have "the willing suspension of disbelief" and consider if these metaphors work for your own interests and understanding. If they meet this first criterion, of their potential heuristic usefulness from the personal, subjective reality of your own experience, then perhaps further investigation may be warranted to move from proposed metaphoric hunch to a mechanistic hypothesis inspiring possible future study and the development of potential application.

Hunch 1: Cortical columns and top-down versus bottom-up processing

Our first hunch relates to the architecture of the neocortex. The cortex is generally structured as six cellular layers, or cortical columns. Columns are associated with one another within regions that function to mediate a given modality, such as hearing or sight. Although controversial, one idea is that information is created by patterns of neural firing that has a proposed bidirectional flow (Lubke & Feldmeyer, 2007; Sporns, 2011; Supp, Schlögl, Trujillo-Barreto, Müller, & Gruber, 2007). As revealed in the schematic of Figure 2.1, one way of conceptualizing this bidirectional flow is to view how neural firing patterns that are initiated by stimuli coming into the cortex (such as sight, sound, or bodily sensation) move from "bottom-up" as they pass first to the lowest layers of the column (layers six, five, and four) and up to the highest layers (three, two, and one). In contrast, *prior learning* shapes how the higher layers will respond following the initial input of a bottom-up flow. In other words, prior experience, embedded in synaptic connections that help shape memory storage, will serve as a "filter" that makes incoming streams of bottom-up data shaped, molded, and categorized. This can be called "top-down," using this term specifically to refer to how prior learning shapes the processing of information (patterns of energy flow) emerging from the bottom-up input to that cortical column. Simply put, there is no such thing as "immaculate perception"—we are structured to filter present experience through the lens of past events and how we have processed them.

For example, if I observe a flower with my eyes, the photons stimulating my retina will send streams of energy flow (neural firing patterns) through my optical nerve and then through my thalamus and on to the back of my cortex where the columns in the occipital lobe will become active. If I've seen that kind of flower before—and if I use a linguistic symbol, a word, to name it—then that top-down process will alter how I ultimately receive the bottom-up input into awareness. Across a possible range of interacting columns (not necessarily within a single column), top-down flow will "crash" into and mingle with bottom-up flow, and the result will influence my subjective experience within awareness of the flower in that moment. In other words, prior learning will shape present perception.

This first hunch is about the idea that the brain is an anticipation machine, shaping what it experiences now by what it experienced before in order to get ready for what might happen in the immediate next of now. In getting ready for the horizon of the present moment, we are actively constructing an anticipated map of what is likely to happen next. This mapping of reality is simply what the cortex does, and it is, in some way not yet understood, how our mental experience of both awareness and inner, subjective experience is shaped. This anticipatory quality of cortical mapping has been called dynamic representations (Freyd, 1987). Patterns learned from the past shape perceptions in the present.

Here is the proposal: Mindfulness may involve a suspension or minimization of the influence of top-down on bottom-up experience. Within creative mindfulness, this would involve letting go of fixed categories and names. Within contemplative mindfulness, this would be seen as the route to being curious, open, and accepting of whatever is present in the moment. Letting go of judgments and expectations would occur by inhibiting top-down flow from imprisoning the presence that emerges with bottom-up. In both creative and contemplative mindfulness, enhancing bottom-up and downregulating top-down would be the shared mechanism that permits a form of "presence" to arise for the individual, a presence that promotes a clarity of awareness and physiological as well as interpersonal benefits.

Hunch 2: Experiencing versus observing

Our second hunch may be related in part to the first proposal. Recent neuroimaging studies affirm the neural nature of what contemplative mindfulness practitioners have described for centuries: There is a distinct experiencing mode and a distinct observing mode in how we experience perception and awareness. In the brain, the regions with activities that correlate with these mental experiences are an observing circuit that has been identified as more midline, whereas the experiencing circuits are more lateralized (see Farb et al., 2007). We can observe experience from afar, noting things within a "witnessing" observer function or experience this directly. Even the way we remember autobiographical events can be through this "experiencer" (through our own glasses) or "witnessing" lens (from a corner of the ceiling). In many ways, contemplative mindfulness can be seen as a way of differentiating and then linking these two circuits of the brain (see Siegel, 2007a, 2007b).

Observational processing offers a witness function, one that is not directly in the experience but takes note, observes, and even narrates ongoing experience. In this way, observational circuitry overlaps with the notion of mental time travel (Tulving, 2005) and a default mode of resting cortical processing (see Zhang & Raichle, 2010) in which the prefrontal cortex mediates the ability to link present experience with events from the past and plans for the future. It is important to note that this planning for the future is different from anticipating the "immediate next of now" that happens automatically (without effort or intention), apparently throughout the cortex, as a function of our cortical columnar architecture.

The brain is an anticipation machine as a whole; the midline observing prefrontal cortex specifically involves itself with, among many other executive functions, planning for the future and a sense of self. Basic learning involves the top-down influence on present perception so that action can be the most adaptive to the environmental demands. This is the inherent anticipatory quality of neural learning. Our first hunch addresses this function and how it may shape—that is, inhibit—the ability to be "fully present" for what is unfolding as it is happening. This second hunch extends this temporal challenge to being mindful into a broader time frame, revealing how the midline observing circuitry (involving but not limited to the prefrontal regions) is creating autobiographical and factual accounts of the past, actively relating them to the present, and then helping either document events in constructed historical accounting or actively creating the unfolding narrative of a person's life.

This narrative function (see Bruner, 2003) makes our experience within awareness shaped by an "inner voice" or "inner observer" that may comment on ongoing events, make suggestions about what is going on, and actively alter what we do and how we interpret the meaning of present, past, and anticipated future events. Because such a narrative process is greatly aided by language, some authors suggest (see Gazzaniga, 1998) that our narrative observing function is dominant on the left side of the brain. Iain McGilchrist (2009) furthers this notion by noting the left hemisphere's use of denotative and abstract language versus the right's more contextual and metaphoric use of language.

Before we take on in more depth our third hunch, which will address laterality issues, here let us say that both contemplative and creative mindfulness would emphasize honoring the primary sensory data of the experiencing circuit and urge (create the conditions enabling) the observing circuit to take a break from its at times incessant narrating activity that distances an individual from primary sensation and being fully present for what is happening as it is happening.

In fact, recent studies of the default mode of brain function, the resting state of the brain when not given a specific task to carry out, reveals a robust set of midline firing patterns that we have that have been indicative of states of wellness or states of nonwellness. When not integrated well, such default mode processes correlate with mental illness (Zhang & Raichle, 2010). Studies of contemplative mindfulness have even revealed that mindfulness training increases the integrative capacity of the default mode circuits, overlapping with the midline observational regions.

Creative mindfulness might ingeniously be setting up learners and teachers alike to let go of fixed ideas and constricting language that could be considered aspects of the processes for the observing circuit. In contrast, the experiencing circuit is a bottom-up dominant passage of energy and information that is about being with what is, as it is happening, without narrative distortions. It would be a possible research project to explore how mindful learning might enhance the integrative default mode state.

Narrative and observation have an important role to play in how we approach and appreciate life. Narrative enables us to reflect on what has happened, connect this to what is happening now in our experience, and then plan for the future. This mental time travel ability is both beautiful and a burden. The beauty of narration is that it gives us a four-dimensional (across space, across time) sense of ourselves, empowers us to actively take our reflective awareness and shape our ongoing lives in narrative enactment, and offers us the opportunity to articulate and experience a deep gratitude for our lives. Pennebaker's studies of narration reveal its health-promoting effects (Ramirez-Esparza & Pennebaker, 2006). The burden of narration is that it can distance us from the vitality of lived, primary experience. The benefits of narration are that they integrate memory and emotion, helping us make sense of our lives across time and contexts. But excessive narrativizing in life can give us a dulling of the fresh, spontaneous emergence of living in which we are simply categorizing all events into clusters related to prior experience. Our narrative themes may also distort what we experience to conform to what we know so that we gain a sense of mastery in our lives. Narratives can make us feel certain in the face of the anxiety that may emerge in the face of uncertainty. And so narration is a mixed blessing. When it is integrated with direct experience, the outcome can be health promoting. And as we'll see in our future discussions, integration is the coordination and balance of aspects of a system created by way of the linkage of differentiated parts. Integration can be seen as the fundamental mechanism of well-being—and here we can see the differentiation of observation from experience and their appropriate coordination and balancing in life would be at the heart of both creative and contemplative mindfulness.

Coordinating and balancing both the bottom-up and top-down (Hunch 1) cortical layers' streaming and the activity of the experiencing and observing circuits (Hunch 2) are two proposed ways in which mindfulness is mediated in the brain. Top-down and observation are both aspects of neural functioning that may be involved in how our mental life wrestles with unfolding experience to achieve a sense of predictability, of finding certainty in a world filled with uncertainty.

And so, with these first two hunches, we come to address how uncertainty, for the brain, is a two-edged sword. For a brain that needs to anticipate the immediate next of now so that it can avoid danger and be prepared to act effectively and efficiently, uncertainty is not welcome. Certainty enhances survival. This is the value of top-down and observation—they allow us to anticipate and to plan for experience, and therefore to control uncertainty, or at least prepare for it. And for a narrating brain, too, making sense of the world brings a comfort with knowing and a top-down framework into which one can enfold all perceived, lived events. Narrating allows us to plan for the future, to deal with uncertainty by making a schedule, by organizing our mental calendar, so that we know now what will happen in the future and that we can actually enact that plan to literally shape our present based on our plans—our narrative themes that then mutually reinforce themselves.

When we experience life, present events can be immediately placed within our narrative schemata—the mental models that shape our narrative themes. We then continue with our self-reinforcing, antiuncertainty life by continually re-enacting these themes and categorizing experience into thematic chapters over and over again. Our perceptions of the world are folded into narrative perspectives as we filter what we see based on what we expect, discarding what does not fit in a form of selective perceptual neglect. Trauma, in fact, can be defined by how an experience cannot be neatly placed into the structure of our life narrative (see Siegel, 2010). In many ways, traumatic events assault our drive for certainty.

And so we can see that uncertainty is a threat both from the bottom-up/top-down cortical column perspective and from the experiencing/observing sensed versus narrating life domain. With top-down, we handle uncertainty with learned filters of anticipation. With observation, we deal with uncertainty with thematic filters, narrative enactments, and planning.

But uncertainty is not always a source of anxiety or danger. In fact, learning to live comfortably with uncertainty can be a source of emergent vitality in these arenas. Sensing the aroma of a flower can be immensely rewarding, before and beneath any words that might name that plant a "rose" or narrate that event as "just another walk in the park to get exercise." When we see with fresh eyes, we are honoring the novelty of bottom-up and the purity of the experiencer. When we expand our narrative stance to embrace uncertainty, we come to open our minds to new and enriching ways of being. Uncertainty does not need to be an enemy. But active efforts to release the pull of certainty to enhance survival within top-down and observation in the forms of creative and contemplative mindfulness approaches may be necessary as we grow past childhood into the adolescent and adult years as life unfolds and the brain matures. What Hunches 1 and 2 suggest is that there is a vulnerability in our survival-oriented evolved neural systems that make the drive for certainty innate. Mindfulness approaches may be a direct educational approach and training of the mind to liberate the vigilance and perceptual filtering controls that such certainty circuits create. With such integration of the fullness of bottom-up and direct experience, the mind can feel the freedom to be fully present for life.

Hunch 3: Cortical asymmetry and neural integration

Our third hunch builds on the finding that the two sides of the brain, especially in the limbic areas and the higher cortical regions, are asymmetric in both function and structure (see McGilchrist, 2009). Modern neuroscientists often downplay the significance of this "laterality," but it is clear from an enormous amount of carefully collected studies in our and other species that the nervous system has been asymmetric for millions of years. One basic idea about this asymmetry is that when areas are differentiated and then they become linked, we can achieve more complex functions. But how is the right side of the brain different from the left? Colwyn Trevarthen (2009) and Iain McGilchrist's (2009) reviews of the extensive science exploring this issue suggest the following notions. Streams of information within the form of neural electrochemical energy flow within the embryonic brain travel upward from the right and left limbic area in distinct streams. This differentiated flow upward stimulates the growth of the right and the left cortex in distinct ways. In general, the right is more active after birth and grows more in the first few years than the left. The cortical columns in the right hemisphere have more intercolumn connections than the left, making the information created by these connections more cross-modal. In other words, the differentiated regions of the right are more interconnected to one another enabling the neural clustering of information processing to be more "contextual" and involving a range of modalities within a given information flow. In contrast, the left is thought to have more closely associated columns that are more isolated in their distinct clusters, enabling a deeply focused form of information processing. On the left, then, information processing is more "in-depth" and specialized for a given modality, and so it can be thought of as "decontextualized" and "analytic" as it "breaks down" elements into isolated components rather than "seeing the whole" within the accumulation of parts as the right may be more likely to do (see McGilchrist, 2009, for a thorough review).

The two hemispheres often work together, and each contributes to many of the processes that have been popularly thought of as distinct: reasoning and language, for example, have processes on both sides of the brain. Yet inhibition is also a dominant process, with activity in one hemisphere downregulating the activity in the other. Anatomically, the right hemisphere has a more prominent size of its prefrontal area, whereas the left is more expanded in the back, in the occipital region. The right hemisphere receives more direct input from, and sends more direct output to, the lower regions of the brain and the body itself, and hence some have called the right a more "emotional" and "somatic" side of the brain (see Devinsky, 2000).

The two sides of the brain focus attention in distinct ways. The right side mediates a form of sustained, broad, open, and vigilant attention, whereas the left side processes more of a sharply focused attention that narrowly directs the flow of energy and information. Not only are the ways of focusing attention distinct, but also the way we sense the world is different on each side. The ways of being mediated by each side, rather than actually what they "do," is perhaps a more accurate way of sensing their differences. McGilchrist's (2009) analysis of these distinctions urges us to consider the right as a mediator of an individualistic, sensory, living, context-perceiving and relational way of experiencing the world. For the right hemisphere, things are seen as unique, and we sense the living nature of our ways of belonging and connecting. The world is seen within a relational whole. The right, then, embeds a sense of being within a part of a larger, interconnected whole. Even the right's way of knowing is within an acknowledged limited perspective, with an awareness that there is a larger context into which the self as a part may fit.

The left, in contrast, uses denotative language and abstraction to create a definitive vision of the world that is known, fixed, decontextualized, static, and disembodied. The left creates a sense of the conceptual and generalized but is "ultimately lifeless" and not even aware of its own limited way of perceiving reality. The argument that

McGilchrist makes is that the challenge is that modern culture drives an overemphasis on left-sided ways of perceiving and being in the world. The cultural processes of rules and digital abstractions, of the virtual realities that fill our technical involvements, reinforce the left hemisphere.

The challenges to finding integration across the hemispheres are that the left hemisphere has a logical, linguistic "voice" that cogently argues its own point of view, while the right hemisphere's contribution to reasoning and language is not as forthright. In fact, we can simply state that the logical use of linguistic language to assert its own view of reality makes the left side often more persuasive in the reality of its ways of being and perceiving the world. For the left, the right-sided way of being is invalid; for the right, the left side's particular patterns are possible in that it is open to the limitations of its own perceptions and beliefs. Furthermore, much of the interaction between the two sides of the brain is based on inhibition—activity in the right shuts down activity on the left, and vice versa. And so how can the two sides of the brain come to coordinate and balance their differentiated functions into a linked and integrated system?

Our suggestion is that both creative and contemplative mindfulness may promote integration across the hemispheres. How does mindfulness relate to this asymmetry across the hemispheres? One could correctly infer that right-sided functions may be seen to facilitate our embracing of the unknown, enabling uncertainty to be a part of the world-view of that form of "right-sided" consciousness. However, contemplative mindfulness studies (Davidson et al., 2003) reveal the empirical finding of a "left shift" in which there is an increase in left frontal activity supportive of an "approach-mode" of neural functioning. In other words, contemplative mindfulness training enables a person to be more likely to approach, rather than withdraw, from challenging stimuli (Urry et al., 2004). This finding does not mean that other aspects of right-hemisphere processes are not actively at work, but imaging studies do not provide empirical support for the view that contemplative mindfulness is a "right-sided function."

However, contemplative mindfulness does involve the fundamental process of interoception—the awareness of the sensory input of the body. This process is dominant on the right side of the brain, involving right anterior insula and right anterior cingulate regions of the brain (Craig, 2009; Critchley, 2009). These interoceptive inputs are in turn followed by right medial prefrontal and right orbitofrontal cortical activations that are associated with both insight and empathy. As contemplative mindfulness studies support improvements in both self-awareness and empathy, associated also with improved self- and other-directed compassion, we can see that these right-sided dominant processes do in fact support the intuitive notion that mindfulness may involve, in part, the activation of right-sided functions.

Research not only studies the practice of contemplative mindfulness, as in meditation effects, but also investigates innate traits of being mindful. For mindfulness personality traits, Baer, Smith, Hopkins, Krietemeyer and Toney (2006) have determined these five factors with the propensity to: be aware of what is happening as it is happening; be nonjudgmental (letting go of expectations and criticisms); be nonreactive (coming back to emotional equilibrium readily after perturbations); be able to name and describe the internal world; and be able to have self-observation (observing the self from a bit of a mental distance).

Here are some theoretical notions about the hunch that the brain's asymmetry may play a role in the differentiated aspects of being mindful—as general traits of our personality or as states of mind created in the moment. Given our earlier discussions, we can see how an observing self may have somewhat of a left-sided dominance when narrative language use is involved, as would the capacity to use words to label the internal world. In contrast, emotional regulation (being nonreactive) may have a right-sided dominance, with right prefrontal areas playing a more direct role in effortful control of emotion (Lewis & Stieben, 2004; Wager et al., 2008).

One might also propose that being nonjudgmental would involve some right-sided inhibition of left-sided, language-dominant categorical expectations. Relevant here, the left hemisphere is sometimes called "the digital processor" in which it tends to categorize things into binary clusters: black or white, right or wrong, up or down, left or right, correct or incorrect, good or bad. In contrast, the right side is sometimes called the "analogic processor" in that it sees the shades of gray between black and white, assesses the context between right and wrong, and sees from many points of view. Words in the right can be used within metaphors, embracing the multiplicity of meanings rather than a strict adherence to a limiting, singular definition of a term. In this way, the right is said to see between the lines, the left reads the lines. The right senses the spirit of the law, whereas the left is the letter of the law. Right views context, whereas left reads text. With this background, where would being aware of what is happening as it is happening fit in? How would creative mindful approaches of "if" within the languaging of learning fit into this asymmetry?

Some everyday impressions about mindfulness and laterality might suggest that the right is about "being in the world" whereas the left is about "doing things in the world." This overly simplistic view may seem quite limiting, yet it may not only be empirically supported, but also have some merit worth exploring in mindfulness studies. Is there a "doing" versus "being" set of circuits? However and wherever such ways of being versus doing may or may not be ultimately discovered, in everyday life there does seem to be a subjective distinction between entering a "being-mode" versus engaging a "doing-mode" in our inner lives and in our relationships. Imagine times when you want a friend to "just listen" to what you are saying, to just bear witness to your story, rather than having you "do something" to solve the problem.

If this is true, then perhaps both creative mindfulness, with its focus on expanding a sense of understanding beyond categories and a sense of "right or wrong," is engaging our "being with" the material mode rather than a "doing mode of getting it right." Creative mindful learning would invite a way of being with the material, of empowering the student to make this new knowledge their own, rather than simply to memorize a "to-do" specific languaging of prescribed action. Being with the educational experience makes the internal subjective texture of learning quite distinct from the constraints of conventional educational dialogue. And within contemplative mindfulness, the curiosity, openness, and acceptance that are the core of being mindful are in their essence ways of being, not so much ways of doing. And so for each form of mindfulness, being rather than specific doing may be the key to what "being mindful" entails.

If left-sided cortical columns are more top-down in their clustered processing than the right's (a possibility needing more empirical validation), then we can see that just "being with" experience might have a right-sided dominance. Michael Gazzaniga once stated that the "purpose of the right side of the brain is to simply see things as they are" (Gazzaniga, February 1996, Keynote Address, American Association of Directors of Psychiatry Residency Training Programs, San Francisco), whereas the left functions to conceptualize and categorize experience. These latter top-down processes, perhaps dominant on the left, can then keep us from just "being with" experience as it is happening. We "do" something with our moment-by-moment experience within the categorizing, analyzing columns of the left side of the brain. Such processing may be the root of the narrative functions being dominant on the left side, as suggested by Gazzaniga (1998). We move into cortically created representations distant from direct experience, make abstractions, and replace the right side's broad, open, vigilant attention with the sharply focused attention of the left. Here is the proposal we are making: The left constructs its perceptions of the world with a "doing mode" that is an active top-down, narrating process.

But this is only part of the story. Further in opposition to the intuitive sense that many have that mindfulness may be more of a right-sided dominant affair, we can also argue elements of a different, counterintuitive strategy for laterality: that mindfulness does not involve a favoring of one side over the other but rather cultivates an integration across the hemispheres.

Integration is the linkage of differentiated parts. And integration can be proposed to cultivate harmonious functioning, as it is based on the coordination and balance of different aspects of a system (Siegel, 2012b). So, we now move to this fundamental idea explored in the field of interpersonal neurobiology: *mindfulness may create well-being by promoting integration*. This proposal is supported by a collection of recent studies that reveal that the integrative fibers of the brain are those that are both activated and apparently stimulated to grow in contemplative mindfulness training (Luders, Toga, Lepore, & Gaser, 2009; Lazar et al., 2005). Such fibers include regions of the prefrontal cortex and hippocampus that link widely separated areas to each other. Such permits the coordination and balance of functions in the body as a whole. This is internal, neural integration. And mindfulness supports closer and more rewarding interpersonal relationships; enabling people to be present with one another as they honor each other's differences while promoting compassionate linkages (see Parker, Nelson, Epel, & Siegel, in press). This is interpersonal integration.

Internal and interpersonal integration may be the fundamental ways in which mindfulness and presence promote well-being (Siegel, 2009). And so here is the summary of our third hunch. Both contemplative and creative mindfulness promote bilateral integration in the brain, supporting internal and interpersonal integration and health in a person's life.

Hunch 4: Energy and information as transformations of probability between uncertainty and certainty

In both creative and contemplative forms of mindfulness, we can propose that awareness in these states involves a way of channeling energy and information flow—of paying attention in the present—in a particular manner. Mindful awareness is at the heart of being mindful, of mindfully paying attention. But what exactly is "awareness"? And what does "attention" really involve? How does being mindful shape our thoughts and feelings—and what is a thought or a feeling, really? To explore these essential and fundamental questions, we will now come to our fourth hunch and attempt to address directly what it means to say that the mind is "an embodied and relational process that regulates the flow of energy and information." This hunch states that mindfulness involves a unique and specific way of shaping how energy is transformed in our brains and in our relationships.

Though descriptions of mental life exist within a range of fields from psychology to anthropology, a formal definition of "mind" is not available, even in the field of "mental health" (Siegel, 2012a, 2012b). In interpersonal neurobiology, as discussed above, we take a consilient view, drawing on a wide range of disciplines to try to identify a universal set of principles shared across these separate fields of study. In this interdisciplinary approach, a definition of mind is offered that states that one aspect of mind is the embodied and relational process that regulates the flow of energy and information. This view of mind sees energy and information flow as the essence of the complex system that gives rise to the emergent, self-organizing process we are defining as "mind." Energy does not just flow within the skull, but is within the whole body. And so we can use the term "embodied brain" to indicate the extended nervous system that is a part of the whole body through which electrochemical energy flows. Certain patterns of flow contain symbolic value, and we call this "information." All information rides along changes in energy movement across time. Flow means changes across time. And so we have the first part of the origin of mind emerging from this embodied mechanism. This is the embodied mind, and it is an emergent property that arises from and also regulates the electrochemical energy transformations in the body. We are not separating mind from brain, but rather seeing these as aspects of one system, the system of energy and information flow within us and between us.

And so fundamental to our definition is that the mind is not only embodied but also relational. This is a part of the definition that often gets the most heated discussion and debate. "Don't I own my own mind?" is often the concerned question, and this stance is quite understandable. But as any social psychologist, sociologist, anthropologist, teacher, parent, or friend knows, our relationships directly shape how we feel and think. Our beliefs, hopes, dreams, memories, and life stories are directly shaped by our relationships. And so the life of the mind is deeply influenced, indeed created by, our communication and connections with others. And so what are a commonly held set of features that describe the life of the mind—from feelings and thoughts to memories and beliefs—are directly shaped by how we relate to one another. How can this be if we "own" our own mind? If the mind is our own, doesn't it just reflect the activity of the brain? Here we see that viewing the mind as relational, not only embodied, opens our field of study to embrace the powerful findings of social psychology, sociology, and anthropology. Relationships and culture each shape mind as much as physiology and synaptic connections. We can see mind from synapse to society because our unit of study is energy and information flow. And this flow occurs as much within us as it does between us.

Our relationships themselves are characterized by the patterns of how we share energy and information flow. Whether we are studying parent–child relationships, romance, friendships, schools, communities, and societies, we are examining the ways in which energy and information are exchanged. These patterns of communication, within culture and within homes, among many people or between two individuals, are always mediated by a flow of information that rides upon shifts in energy. Even the study of one's relationship within oneself, the inner nature of our subjective lives and how we focus attention, how our observing self accepts our experiencing self, can be seen as a pattern of energy flow that enables information to be created. And so a first impression is that contemplative mindfulness may evoke an "integrated relationship" internally—one that is based on internal attunement that enables an observing self and an experiencing self to be differentiated and linked, to be integrated. And creative mindfulness may be created interpersonally as the teacher provides an educational experience that promotes the integration of bottom-up and top-down, of experiencing and observing. The student can have a relationship with the material that is integrative as it arises from mindful instruction that sets the stage for such integration as discussed in our earlier hunches.

As we've stated, information can be seen as a pattern of energy that has symbolic value or meaning. Some energy, like a blast of sound, may be "pure energy" without symbolic value. This pattern of sound just is what it is. In contrast, if we hear the sound "Golden Gate Bridge" we are having energy waves (air molecules' movement creating pressure on our ear drum) induce electrochemical changes in our acoustic nerve. Ensuing cascades of electrochemical transformations in the head streaming through the brain somehow, in ways no one knows, become associated with the subjective sense of that phrase, and the subjective experience of seeing that bridge over the San Francisco Bay in our "mind's eye."

This is an important point: No one knows how subjective experience (as in the internal seeing of the bridge in one's memory or imagination) and neural firing (ions flowing in and out of membranes and the release of neurotransmitters within the synapse linking neurons to each other) mutually create each other. It is simple, and quite common, to say that neural firing creates subjective experience. When certain regions of the brain become active, as in the occipital cortex for visual imagination, memory, or perception, we "see something." But we also know that imagining something, like playing the piano keys of a scale, can also make changes in the brain's firing and ultimately the very structures that are associated with that process (Pascual-Leone, Amedi, Fregni, & Merabet, 2005; also see Doidge, 2007, for an overview). In fact, mindfulness meditation is the use of subjective experience and the focus of attention to intentionally create a mindful state that shapes neural firing and creates long-lasting neural growth (Davidson & Begley, 2012; Lazar et al., 2005; Luders et al., 2009). Naturally, we could approach this in a simple and unidirectional way and state that we are simply making parts of the brain fire and that brain activity always "creates the mind." And this indeed may be true. But let's take a more open-minded position at first and see where this goes. Let's in fact be creatively mindful and avoid the premature closure of possibility, the premature hardening of the categories (Cozolino, 2003).

Descriptions of mental functions exist, naturally. But amazingly we do not have a straightforward statement of what the "mind" actually is beyond some views that state mind is "simply brain firing." While action potentials and chemical release (brain firing) is one aspect of the story, it is not the "same aspect" as having a thought or feeling. Just as an apple has skin and seeds, the whole apple is not one or the other. We don't say the skin is the seed. They are two aspects of one thing—of the whole apple. Similarly, mind and brain are not the same. They are two aspects of one thing, and that thing we are suggesting is energy and information flow.

We actually don't know what a thought or a feeling really "is." We simply do not know what awareness or consciousness and subjective mental experience actually "are." And so to say that our inner mental lives are "simply a product of brain firing" is actually not founded in science. After all, neural firing is not the same as being aware or having the subjective experience of, say, feeling curiosity or love or fear or joy. Yes, brain injuries in specific regions can impair specific mental functions. But this longstanding finding demonstrates an association, not necessarily causality. The skin and the seed are both part of the same apple, but they are two distinct but interdependent aspects of the whole. When certain parts of the brain are damaged, certain mental functions cannot occur. With a stroke, for example, we may lose the ability to feel fear or think empathically or see visually. Our mental processes may depend completely upon neural processes, just as the survival of the apple's seeds may depend on the intactness of the skin. The mind does need the brain to create itself. But, thinking mindfully, perhaps the mind uses the brain to create itself. And when certain neural or certain relational processes do not occur, the mind also may be constrained. The mind uses both the brain and relationships to create itself. We are stating that the mind is not limited to the boundaries of the skin, and that as a self-organizing process, it arises from that which it will also regulate. This recursive property is simply the mathematics of complex systems. Complex systems have emergent properties that are recursive. And this emergence, we are proposing, is a process of both our embodied brains and of our interactions with other. The mind is both embodied and relational.

To understand how the mind becomes mindful, creatively or contemplatively, taking on these issues straight on is important, if not essential. We will move beyond these very controversial issues to a proposal that comes from direct observation of inner mental life, from the first-person accounts reported by hundreds of individuals in a wide variety of cultures to one of us (DJS). While they cannot be quantified as statistical analysis requires, science also emerges from careful observation. And when it comes to the mind, to our subjective inner life, careful observation may be essential to explore, systematically, what "mind" actually is. We will combine these observational narrative reports with an interpretation of the science of energy from the field of physics.

Knowing that for many in academic psychology and psychiatry, attempting to link the findings of physics to the study of the mind is often discouraged, we nevertheless will explore this fourth hunch about our discussion of mind and how this may pertain to the various aspects of mindfulness. We feel that inviting ourselves to link this working definition of mind as an embodied and relational process that regulates energy and information flow to the field of mindful awareness can reveal possibilities that may be of value for both future research and direct practical applications. We ask you to consider choosing to be open to the possibility that what follows may be useful, even if it is quite unconventional.

Energy is the focus of study of the field of physics. In classical physics, a Newtonian view of the world examines forces that operate on large-scale clusters of matter, studying motion and gravity. When subatomic particles are studied, however, classical laws of physics do not generally apply. Instead, modern physics (from the last 100 years) has examined the study of quantum mechanics in order to help make sense of empirical findings. In the study of light, for example, photons have been revealed to have both wave and particle properties, and as movement of energy across time, light offers a fundamental way of studying how aspects of our universe works. In quantum physics, what has been discovered are a set of principles that appear to apply not only to the microscopic world, where they can be measured readily because of their small dimensions, but also to all of matter, no matter the size. In a quantum view, energy is measured as degrees of probability along a spectrum from open possibility to fixed certainty. There are many fascinating aspects of this field of study, including the finding that measuring a photon, for example, makes it collapse its wave function (across a spectrum of possible values) and be measured with certainty as a particle (with a certainty of its location at a point in time). There is also the intriguing "entanglement" implication of quantum mechanics suggesting that movements of particles, their spins and probabilities, have influences from particles not in physical proximity to them. Quantum equations that are created to explain empirical findings require these "at a distance" factors. Recent discoveries of the Higgs boson, the theoretical but empirically predicted particle that could explain the nature of matter as accumulations of particles to create mass, reveal how deep quantum analysis may offer new insights into the mysteries of our universe.

Why would our mental lives live in a different plane of reality than the rest of the world as some assert (Wallace, 2010)? We are suggesting that judicial explorations of the nature of energy may offer us at least empirically inspired though theoretically constructed ideas that might help us to see mental life in a new light. We understand that the following interpretation of the lessons from physics needs empirical validation and may not be initially embraced, but attempting to find a link between possible meanings of energy principles with observations of mental life may prove fruitful. These quantum ideas have intriguing possibilities about the universe, and about our own mental lives. While there may be many aspects of quantum physics that ultimately shed some new light on our mental explorations, here we will focus on the fundamental view that energy is measured in degrees of probabilities.

When spending a week with over 100 physicists, one of us (DJS) was able to informally ask innumerable academicians to define what energy is. The overall statements from these dedicated scientists was that while we really don't know what these various forms of energy "are," the physicists uniformly stated that "energy" is a term generally signifying the capacity to do something. As one professor stated it, energy is the "capacity to do stuff." Energy takes many forms, from kinetic energy of the movement of particles of matter to light energy. But as a general aspect of our physical universe, this capacity to do something is measured as degrees of probability. Energy moves along "an energy-probability curve" that spans from certainty (100% probability) to uncertainty (near 0% probability). If a state of energy is highly likely, it moves toward 100% probability. If a state of energy is highly unlikely, it moves toward 0% probability. This range of the energy-probability curve from uncertainty to certainty will be the focus of our discussion.

We are presuming that there is one domain of reality and that it is logical inference, then, to assume that mind lives within that reality. If this is indeed true, the natural

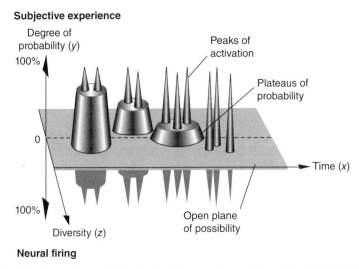

Subjective experience

Degree of probability (*y*)
100%

Peaks of activation

Plateaus of probability

0

Time (*x*)

100%

Diversity (*z*)

Open plane of possibility

Neural firing

Figure 2.2 The plane of possibility. Used with permission. Copyright © 2010 by Mind Your Brain, Inc. Daniel J. Siegel, M.D., *The Mindful Therapist* (2010).

extension of this thinking is to state that if the mind is a process that regulates energy flow within and between us, that it is embodied and relational, then applying the laws of quantum physics—our most thorough and contemporary study of energy—is a natural, logical next step to deepening our understanding of mind.

And so here is our unconventional proposal. We are suggesting that the term, "energy flow," means that "probability shifting" is how energy changes "across time" (flow). Notice that flow does not require movement across space. As we explore mental life, we may come to see that our subjective experience does not reside in a particular three-dimensional spatial location, but it does exist within a certain "probability space"—where a degree of certainty exists at a given moment of time. Figure 2.2 is a drawing offering one metaphoric way of illustrating what this probability space might look like. At the top of the graph is our mental life; at the bottom is our neural firing. Note that these may be completely overlapping across time, cosynchronous, so that neural firing and mental life happen at the same time. But this may not always be true. One process may slightly precede the other, and "drag the other forward." This is highly controversial but in fact may explain certain subjective ways we use the mind to actually change the function and structure of the brain. The seed can influence the skin just as the skin can influence the seed of the apple. The key is to be open-minded about which process drives the other forward.

The next aspect of Figure 2.2 to focus upon is what gives this figure its name, "The Plane of Possibility." Here, let's focus on the top part of this graph, our mental life. The range of probability, from zero to 100, is depicted on the *y* (vertical) axis. Time is mapped out on the *x* (horizontal) axis. As time moves forward, the probability value can shift from within the plane (near a zero probability), where open possibility is present, to other values along the energy-probability curve. Above the plane, the probability curve shifts from near zero toward 100% certainty.

For the mind, we can propose this idea: Awareness is a state of energy probability near zero. Awareness has at least two components: A sense of knowing, and that which is known. The sense-of-knowing aspect of awareness arises from an energy-probability curve of uncertainty. What is the "known" of awareness under usual circumstances is the focus on the energy curve above uncertainty—toward higher degrees of probability. A sampling process, akin to the 40 cycle per second oscillations of the thalamo-cortical circuits in the brain (see Llinas, 2008), may occur whereby the subjective experience of awareness oscillates between the open plane (the sense of knowing) and the plateaus and peaks of elevated probability (that which is known).

With some exercises, individuals can actually focus a spoke of attention of the "wheel of awareness" practice linking the hub (sense of knowing) with the rim (that which is known). The findings from this practice correspond to the spatial plane of possibility in that the rim comprises peaks and plateaus, the spoke is attention (shaping the direction of energy and information flow), and the hub is the metaphoric symbol for open awareness, a sense of knowing found in the plane of possibility. In some practices, individuals are given the opportunity to "bend the spoke around" and focus attention directly on awareness itself. People describe this aspect of the exercise of focusing directly on this plane of possibility as "openness; wide-as-the-sky; deep as the ocean; at home; expansiveness; and having a sense of deep peace." As this exercise of "the wheel of awareness" unfolds, they experience the plateaus of elevated probability and the peaks of certainty as feelings or moods or intentions, and then as specific thoughts, images or emotions, respectively. In this proposal, the sense of knowing within awareness is an energy curve that has moved to the open plane, a mood or intention is a plateau of elevated probability, and a specific thought, image, memory, or emotion is a peak of certainty.

In this hunch, we are offering the idea that if the mind is indeed a process that regulates energy, then it can be seen as an active way of modulating energy-probability curves that define what "energy flow" really means. Mindfulness, we are suggesting, strengthens the ability of the mind to move the energy-probability curve more fully into the plane of possibility. The oscillatory sampling would then have a fuller representation with this end of the curve. So, rather than being swept up in a specific term (a restrictive peak), mindful learning would create more dominance of the plane of possibility in the representation of that learned element. Mindful learning, then, we propose involves enhancement of the plane of possibility. From the wheel terminology, mindful learning would harness the hub. Creative mindfulness uses relationships of an individual to others and to their environment to foster this movement into the open plane.

We further suggest that contemplative mindfulness uses inner attention to train the mind to move energy curves toward the open plane by way of focusing attention on intention and placing awareness on awareness. These processes build on the executive, integrative circuits in the brain that permit neural processing to achieve more flexibility, to pause before enacting impulses or engrained, habitual patterns of response. From the plane of possibility perspective, contemplative mindfulness can be seen to build the capacity of the individual's mind to move the energy curve into the open plane and loosen the grip of the top-down influences of previously engrained expectations and judgments, represented in high peaks and restrictive plateaus.

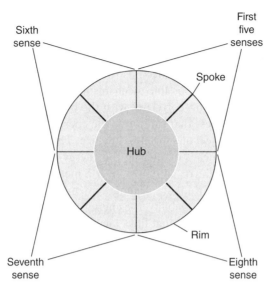

Figure 2.3 The wheel of awareness. The hub represents the experience of knowing within awareness; the spokes are focused attention; the rim is the known of awareness including our sensations and other mental processes. The sectors of the rim are as follows: first five (outer world), sixth (body), seventh (mental activity), and eighth (relationships) senses. Used with permission. Copyright © 2007 by Mind Your Brain, Inc. Daniel J. Siegel, M.D., *The Mindful Brain* (2007).

In creative mindfulness, we can further suggest, presenting educational material with words that have broad rather than highly constrained meaning (Langer, 1989, 1997, and this volume) can be seen to pull the peaks of certain definitions down to plateaus and ultimately into the plane that enables alternative meanings of the word to be considered. In the mind, this would be experienced as a feeling of inner freedom and vitality. In the brain, we can suggest, this might be revealed as more widely distributed neural activation patterns that would deepen memory profiles and make access to encoded experience more robust and connections among learned items more intricate and therefore activating a more widely distributed set of neural representations.

Contemplative mindfulness enables the practitioner to repeatedly enter a state of being aware of awareness. While the wheel of awareness exercise was developed as a technique to integrate consciousness (Siegel, 2007a, 2012b), differentiating the known from the sense of knowing, it also meets the criteria for a mindfulness practice. The visual image of a wheel helps to focus attention as a moving spoke along the rim which represents anything one might be aware of, from sights and sounds to thoughts and feelings (see Figure 2.3). Awareness can be seen as composed of the known (the rim) and the knowing (the hub). Here, the hub represents what it means to "know" within awareness itself. Within the wheel of awareness practice, the subjective texture of pure awareness is experienced directly as a way of sensing the feeling of directing attention to the hub itself. The participant in the exercise does not focus the spoke on the rim, as in the prior part of the practice, but now bends the spoke to focus attention on awareness itself.

Across cultures and across educational backgrounds, the descriptions have been universally similar, as described above. The awareness of awareness ("the hub on hub" part of the wheel practice) is experienced as the state of deep openness. The plane of possibility diagram offers one possible mechanism to explain the subjective mental experience descriptions. The hub correlates with the plane, and the rim includes the plateaus and peaks. The process that can move the energy curves is attention, represented by the spoke in the wheel of awareness practice. The mind is that process which "regulates energy flow" by means of altering the energy-probability curve in a range from certainty (as in a thought or an emotion or a memory), to less certain but to various degrees of probability (thinking, feeling, remembering), and then to the sense of knowing within the plane of possibility, the energy curve at the point of uncertainty. This model offers one possible view that links mental processes—such as thought and emotion and memory—with the experience of consciousness (see Siegel, 2012b, for an in-depth discussion of this proposal).

In this perspective, mindfulness strengthens the capacity of an individual to move into the plane of possibility with more ease. If an oscillating sampling process is involved in everyday experience of being aware, one in which we dip from plane to plateau and peak in order to be aware of our five senses, our bodies, and our mental activities such as thoughts and feelings, then we can propose that mindfulness might increase the frequency of "being in the plane" during that sampling process. Such a sampling appears to be a fundamental part of the neural correlates of consciousness (see Llinas, 2008; Edelman & Tononi, 2000a, 2000b). We can be aware of a thought, but not mindfully aware of it. We can learn a fact, but not mindfully learn that fact. These would be how we can go "on automatic pilot" and become imprisoned by top-down patterns of restrictive language, perceptual distortions, and even emotional response. Being in the plane would be seen in the wheel of awareness practice as "strengthening our hub" so that we experience life from a place of openness to new possibilities.

Our fourth hunch proposes that both creative mindfulness and contemplative mindfulness strengthen the hub of the mind, enhancing the ability of the individual to use attention to move the energy curves that arise in everyday life and learning toward the open plane of possibility. It is from this hub of the mind, this plane of possibility, that the capacity to be present arises.

Conclusion: A Possible Way of Putting the Pieces Together

Creative and contemplative mindfulness may share in common the strengthening of the ability of an individual to be present in life, to be aware of what is happening in a direct and vital way. This presence could enable individuals to thrive with uncertainty: To live fuller and more robust lives because they are able to be present with what is. We have suggested that this ability to live well with uncertainty may occur by way of four possible but interacting mechanisms in need of further empirical study. Our first hunch is that mindfulness enables the enhancement of bottom-up ways of perceiving the world. The release from top-down constraints that create anticipatory states of mind based on what has been learned in the past would provide a direct way of "seeing life clearly" by minimizing these automatic restrictions on living.

Second, we've explored the possibility that mindfulness enhances our experiencing circuitry so that we balance our tendency as we age to observe and narrate with a renaissance of our capacity to live life directly. We come to see with child's eyes, making the ordinary once again extraordinary. Mindfulness would not only be about "being in the flow" without narration but also involve a balance in the two and permit choice of which circuits to engage in particular lived moments.

Third, we are suggesting that an integration of the two hemispheres may be how mindfulness creates an openness to both be with and understand experience as the right and left hemispheres come to coordinate and balance their differentiated functions. Such bilateral integration may permit a more flexible and adaptive way of being in the world than either hemisphere alone could create.

Finally, we've stepped gingerly into the world of physics and energy studies to propose that mindfulness strengthens our mental and physiological lives by creating a stronger capacity of the mind to create the openness of possibility contained within mindful awareness. This openness can be seen as the movement of an energy-probability curve from restricted but important zones of certainty and probability down into an "open plane of possibility" in which awareness emerges. Both contemplative and creative approaches to mindfulness may cultivate their health-mediating effects by strengthening the capacity to move more freely among these zones of the probability curve from certainty to openness. In this view, thriving with uncertainty is created by this strengthening of the mind's ability to regulate energy and move it freely into this plane of open possibility.

Mindfulness in its creative and contemplative forms enables us individually to create more vital and open states of mind, ways of being, ways of living. Mindfulness collectively can help us sense the ways in which we are profoundly interconnected to one another, and to our home, this planet we call Earth. By underscoring the ways in which mindfulness enables us to thrive with uncertainty, our hope is that as we approach the uncertainties of life on our planet, we will perhaps become better able to help one another develop the resilience that will support our approaching, rather than withdrawing from, the challenges we face in our very fragile and rapidly changing world.

References

Baer, R. A., Smith, G. T., Hopkins, J., Krietemeyer, J., & Toney, L. (2006). Using self-report assessment methods to explore facets of mindfulness. *Assessment, 13*(I), 27–45.

Barnes, S., Brown, K. W., Krusemark, E., Campbell, W. K., & Rogge, R. D. (2007). The role of mindfulness in romantic relationship satisfaction and responses to relationship stress. *Journal of marital and family therapy, 33*(4), 482–500.

Blackburn, E., & Epel, E. S. (2012). Psychological stress and telomere length. *Nature*, in press.

Bruner, J. S. (2003). *Making stories: Law, literature, life*. New York, NY: Harvard University Press.

Carroll, J. E., Diez Roux, A. V., Fitzpatrick, A., & Seeman, T. (2012). *Emotional social support is positively associated with late life telomere length: The multi-ethnic study of atherosclerosis.* The 70th Annual Meeting of the American Psychosomatic Society, Athens, Greece.

Cozolino, L. (2003). *The neuroscience of psychotherapy.* New York, NY: WW Norton.

Craig, A. D. (2009). How do you feel—now? The anterior insula and human awareness. *Nature Reviews Neuroscience, 10,* 59–70.

Critchley, H. D. (2009). Psychophysiology of neural, cognitive, and affective integration: fMRI and autonomic indicants. *International Journal of Psychophysiology, 73*(2), 88–94.

Davidson, R. J., & Begley, S. (2012). *The emotional life of your brain: How its unique patterns affect the way think, feel, and live—and how you can change them.* New York, NY: Penguin Group/Hudson Street Press.

Davidson, R. J., Kabat-Zinn, J., Schumacher, J., Rosenkranz, M., Muller, D., Santorelli, S. F., … Sheridan, J. F. (2003). Alterations in brain and immune function produced by mindfulness meditation. *Psychosomatic Medicine, 65*(4), 564–570.

Devinsky, O. (2000). Right cerebral hemisphere dominance for a sense of corporeal and emotional self. *Epilepsy & Behavior, 1*(1), 60–73.

Doidge, N. (2007). *The brain that changes itself: Stories of personal triumph from the frontiers of brain science.* New York, NY: Penguin.

Edelman, G. M., & Tononi, G. (2000a). Reentry and the dynamic core: Neural correlates of conscious experience. In T. Mezinger (Ed.), *Neural correlates of consciousness: Empirical and conceptual questions* (pp. 139–151). Cambridge, MA: The MIT Press.

Edelman, G. M., & Tononi, G. (2000b). *A universe of consciousness: How matter becomes imagination.* New York, NY: Basic Books.

Epel, E., Puterman, E., Lin, J., Blackburn, E., Lazaro, A., & Mendes, W. (in press). Wandering minds and aging cells. *Clinical Psychological Science.*

Epel, E., Daubenmier, J., Moskowitz, J. T., Folkman, S., & Blackburn, E. (2009). Can meditation slow rate of cellular aging? Cognitive stress, mindfulness, and telomeres. *Annals of the New York Academy of Sciences, 1172,* 34–53.

Fagundes, C. P., Bennett, J. M., Derry, H. M., & Kiecolt-Glaser, J. K. (2011). Relationships and inflammation across the lifespan: Social developmental pathways to disease. *Social and Personality Psychology Compass, 5*(11), 891–903.

Farb, N. A. S., Segal, Z. V., Mayberg, H., Bean, J., McKeon, D., Fatima, Z., & Anderson, A. K. (2007). Attending to the present: Mindfulness meditation reveals distinct neural modes of self-reference. *Social Cognitive and Affective Neuroscience, 2*(4), 313–322.

Freyd, J. J. (1987). Dynamic mental representations. *Psychological Review, 94*(4), 427–438.

Gazzaniga, M. S. (1998). *The mind's past.* Berkeley, CA: University of California Press

Gregory, R. L. (2004). *Oxford companion to the mind* (2nd ed.). Oxford, UK: Oxford University Press.

Hasenkamp, W., Wilson-Mendenhall, C., Duncan, E., & Barsalou, L. (2012). Mind wandering and attention during focused meditation: A fine-grained temporal analysis of fluctuating cognitive states. *NeuroImage, 59,* 750–760.

Jacobs, T. L., Epel, E. S., Lin, J., Blackburn, E. H., Wolkowitz, O. M., Bridwell, D. A., … Saron, C. D. (2010). Intensive meditation training, immune cell telomerase activity, and psychological mediators. *Psychoneuroendocrinology, 36*(5), 664–681.

Kabat-Zinn, J. (2006). *Coming to our senses: Healing ourselves and the world through mindfulness.* New York, NY: Hyperion.

Kane, M. J., Brown, L. H., McVay, J. C., Silvia, P. J., Myin-Germeys, I., & Kwapil, T. R. (2007). For whom the mind wanders, and when. *Psychological Science, 18*(7), 614.

Kauffman, S. (1996). *At home in the universe: The search for the laws of self-organization and complexity.* New York, NY: Oxford University Press.

Kitayama, S., & Uskul, A. K. (2011). Culture mind and the brain: Current evidence and future directions. *Annual Review of Psychology, 62*, 419–449.

Lubke, J., & Feldmeyer, D (2007). Excitatory signal flow and connectivity in a cortical column: focus on barrel cortex. *Brain Structure and Function, 212*(1), 3–17.

Killingsworth, M. A., & Gilbert, D. T. (2010). A wandering mind is an unhappy mind. *Science, 330*(6006), 932–932.

Kröger, H. (2007). Biological and physical principles in self-organization of brain. *AIP Conference Proceedings, 905*(1), 168–174.

Langer, E. J. (1989). *Mindfulness*. Reading, MA: Addison-Wesley/Addison-Wesley Longman.

Langer, E. J. (1997). *The power of mindful learning*. Reading, MA: Addison-Wesley/Addison-Wesley Longman.

Langer, E. J. (2009). *Counterclockwise*. Reading, MA: Addison-Wesley/Addison-Wesley Longman.

Langer, E. J., & Moldoveanu, M. (2000). The construct of mindfulness. *Journal of Social Issues, 56*(1), 1–9.

Lazar, S. W., Kerr, C. E., Wasserman, R. H., Gray, J. R., Greve, D. N., Treadway, M. T., … Fischl, B. (2005). Meditation experience is associated with increased cortical thickness. *Neuroreport, 16*(17), 1893–1897.

LeVine, R. A. (2010). Plasticity and variation: Cultural influences on parenting and early child development within and across populations. In C. M. Worthman, P. M. Plotsky, D. S. Schecher, & C. A. Cummings (Eds.), *Formative experiences: The interaction of caregiving, culture, and development psychobiology* (pp. 9–11). New York, NY: Cambridge University Press.

Lewis, M. S., & Stieben, J. (2004). Emotion regulation in the brain: Conceptual issues and directions for developmental research. *Child Development, 75*(2), 371–376.

Llinas, R. (2008). Of self and self-awareness: The basic neuronal circuit in human consciousness and the generation of self. *Journal of Consciousness Studies, 15*(9), 64–74.

Luders, E., Toga, A. W., Lepore, N., & Gaser, C. (2009). The underlying anatomical correlates of long-term meditation: Larger hippocampal and frontal volumes of gray matter. *Neuroimage, 45*, 672–678.

McClelland, J., & Rogers, T. (2003). The parallel distributed processing approach to semantic cognition. *Nature Reviews Neuroscience, 4*(4), 310–322.

McEwen, B. S. (2000). The neurobiology of stress: From serendipity to clinical relevance. *Brain Research, 886*, 172–189.

McGilchrist, I. (2009). *The master and his emissary: The divided brain and the making of the western world*. New York, NY: Yale University Press.

Mrazek, M. D., Smallwood, J., & Schooler, J. W. (2012). Mindfulness and mind-wandering: Finding convergence through opposing constructs. *Emotion*.

Parker, S. C., Nelson, B. W., Epel, E., & Siegel, D. J. (in press). The science of presence: A central mediator in the interpersonal benefits of mindfulness. In K. W. Brown, J. D. Creswell, & R. M. Ryan (Eds.), *Handbook of mindfulness: Theory and research*. New York, NY: Springer.

Pascual-Leone, A., Amedi, A., Fregni, F., & Merabet, L. B. (2005). The plastic human brain cortex. *Annual Review of Neuroscience, 28*, 377–401.

Raffone, A., & Van Leeuwen, C. (2001). Activation and coherence in memory processes: Revisiting the parallel distributed processing approach to retrieval. *Connection Science, 13*(4), 349–382.

Rakel, D. P., Hoeft, T. J., Barrett, B. P., Chewning, B. A., Craig, B. M., Niu, M. (2009). Practitioner empathy and the duration of the common cold. *Family Medicine, 41*, 494–501.

Ramirez-Esparza, N., & Pennebaker, J. W. (2006). Do good stories produce good health? Exploring words, language, and culture. *Narrative Inquiry, 16*(1), 211–219.

Rogers, T., & McClelland, J. (2008). Précis of semantic cognition: A parallel distributed processing approach. *Behavioral & Brain Sciences, 31*(6), 689–749.

Roth, T. L., & Sweatt, J. D. (2011). Annual research review: Epigenetic mechanisms and environmental shaping of the brain during sensitive periods of development. *Journal of Child Psychology and Psychiatry and Allied Disciplines, 52*(4), 398–408.

Siegel, D. J. (2007a). *The mindful brain: Reflection and attunement in the cultivation of well-being.* New York, NY: W. W. Norton & Company.

Siegel, D. J. (2007b). Mindfulness training and neural integration. *Journal of Social, Cognitive, and Affective Neuroscience, 2*(4), 259–263.

Siegel, D. J. (2009). Mindful awareness, mindsight, and neural integration. *The Humanistic Psychologist, 37*(2), 137–158.

Siegel, D. J. (2010). *Mindsight: The new science of personal transformation.* New York, NY: Bantam.

Siegel, D. J. (2012a). *The developing mind, second edition: How relationships and the brain interact to shape who we are.* New York, NY: Guilford Press.

Siegel, D. J. (2012b). *Pocket guide to interpersonal neurobiology: An integrative handbook of the mind.* New York, NY: W. W. Norton & Company.

Smallwood, J., & O'Connor, R. C. (2011). Imprisoned by the past: Unhappy moods lead to a retrospective bias to mind wandering. *Cognition & Emotion, 25*(8), 1481–1490.

Sporns, O (2011). The human connectome: A complex network. *Annals of the New York Academy of Sciences, 1224,* 104–125.

Sterling, P., & Eyer, J. (1988). Allostasis: A new paradigm to explain arousal pathology. In S Fisher & J Reason, James (Eds.), *Handbook of life stress, cognition and health* (pp. 629–649). Oxford, UK: Wiley.

Supp, G. G., Schlögl, A., Trujillo-Barreto, N., Müller, M. M., & Gruber, T. (2007) Directed cortical information flow during human object recognition: Analyzing induced EEG gamma-band responses in brain's source space. *PLoS ONE, 2*(8). e684. doi:10.1371/journal.pone.0000684

Szyf, M., McGowan, P. O., Turecki, G., & Meaney, M. J. (2010). The social environment and the epigenome. In C. M. Worthman, P. M. Plotsky, & D. S. Schechter (Eds.), *Formative experiences: The interaction of caregiving, culture, and developmental psychobiology* (pp. 53–81). New York, NY: Cambridge University Press.

Tyrka, A. R., Price, L. H., Kao, H-T., Porton, B., Marsella, S. A., & Carpenter, L. L. (2010). Childhood maltreatment and telomere shortening: Preliminary support for an effect of early stress on cellular aging. *Biological Psychiatry, 67*(6), 531–534.

Wager, T. D., Davidson, M. L., Hughes, B. L., Lindquist, M. A., & Ochsner, K. N. (2008). Prefrontal–subcortical pathways mediating successful emotion regulation. *Neuron, 59*(6), 1037–1050.

Wallace, A. (2010). *Hidden dimensions: The unification of physics and consciousness.* New York, NY: Columbia University Press.

Wilson, E. O. (1998). *Consilience.* New York, NY: Random House.

Trevarthen, C. (2009). The functions of emotion in infancy: The regulation and communication of rhythm, sympathy, and meaning in human development. In D. Fosha, D. J. Siegel, & M. F. Solomon (Eds.), *The healing power of emotion.* New York, NY: W. W. Norton & Company.

Tronick, E. (2004). Why is connection with others so critical?: Dyadic meaning making, messiness and complexity governed selective processes which co-create and expand individuals' states of consciousness. In J. Nadel & D. Muir (Eds.), *Emotional development* (pp. 86–111). New York, NY: Norton & Company.

Tulving, E. (2005). Episodic memory and autonoesis: Uniquely human? In H. S. Terrace & J. Metcalfe (Eds.), *The missing link in cognition: Origins of self-reflective consciousness* (pp. 3–56). New York, NY: Oxford University Press.

Urry, H. L., Nitschke, J. B., Dolski, I., Jackson, D. C., Dalton, K. M., & Mueller, C. J., … Davidson, R. J. (2004). Making a life worth living: Neural correlates of well-being. *Psychological Science, 15*(6), 367–372.

Zhang, D., & Raichle, M. E. (2010). Disease and the brain's dark energy. *Nature Reviews Neurology, 6*(1), 15–28.

Further Reading

Brown, K. W., & Cordon, S. L. (2009). Toward a phenomenology of mindfulness: Subjective experience and emotional correlates. In F. Didonna (Ed.), *Clinical handbook of mindfulness* (pp. 59–81). New York, NY: Springer.

Epel, E. S., Blackburn, E. H., Lin, J., Dhabhar, F. S., Adler, N. E., Morrow, J. D., & Cawthon, R. M. (2004). Accelerated telomere shortening in response to life stress. *Proceedings of the National Academy of Sciences, 101*(49), 17312–17315.

Hasson, U., Ghazanfar, A. A., Galantucci, B., Garrod, S., & Keysers, C. (2012). Brain-to-brain coupling: a mechanism for creating and sharing a social world. *Trends in Cognitive Sciences, 16*(2), 114–121.

Kabat-Zinn, J. (2003). Mindfulness-based interventions in context: Past, present, and future. *Clinical Psychology: Science and Practice, 10*(2), 144–156.

Kornfield, J. (2009). *The wise heart: A guide to the universal teachings of Buddhist psychology.* New York, NY: Random House.

3

Eastern and Western Approaches to Mindfulness

Similarities, Differences, and Clinical Implications

James Carmody

As the efficacy of mindfulness training in reducing distress and increasing quality of life (QOL) has been demonstrated through well-controlled trials, an increasing number of mindfulness-based programs have sprung up designed for specific populations and circumstances. Summaries of their positive effects are covered in a number of reviews (Chiesa & Serretti, 2011; Hofmann, Sawyer, Witt, & Oh, 2010; Irving, Dobkin, & Park, 2009). While each of these programs has as its goal the reduction of mental suffering, descriptions of their training protocols reveal important divisions and variations between them in their conceptions of the construct of mindfulness and how it is best learned and taught.

The most widely studied programs are as follows:

1 The Buddhist-derived approach popularized by Kabat-Zinn in which the experience of mindfulness is to be found in the experience of meditation practice. This has found its most popular expression in mindfulness-based stress reduction (MBSR) and mindfulness-based cognitive therapy (MBCT).

2 The conception described by Hayes in acceptance and commitment therapy (ACT) and dialectical behavior therapy (DBT) in which the approach to mindfulness is based upon the psychological processes involved in the domination of the literal and evaluative functions of human language and cognition (Fletcher & Hayes, 2005). These programs also draw upon cognitive behavioral therapy but have removed mindfulness from a meditation foundation and freely adapted their training protocols to suit the circumstances of their clinical populations.

3 The approach described by Langer, which derives from social psychological principles, implicitly draws upon elements of each, but approaches mindfulness as the desired end-result of an open and curious orientation to the environment. Its training protocols, described below, focus directly upon encouraging the cultivation of such a stance to experience.

The Wiley Blackwell Handbook of Mindfulness, First Edition.
Edited by Amanda Ie, Christelle T. Ngnoumen, and Ellen J. Langer.
© 2014 John Wiley & Sons, Ltd. Published 2014 by John Wiley & Sons, Ltd.

Despite the apparent differences in their understanding and approach to mindfulness, each of these programs has been shown to improve one or more QOL-related variable. So, are these different conceptions and practices primarily semantic and merely ones of emphasis, or do they represent fundamentally different approaches to something they each call mindfulness that somehow arrive at a similar experiential end (Langer & Moldoveanu, 2000)?

The question of commonality is not without controversy. In the meeting of these approaches, discussions of mindfulness and mind–body medicine more generally become a confused and confusing interface between the parsimonious approach of science, and the narratives of religious/spiritual aspiration and meaning. For some clinicians and researchers, the clinical mindfulness training programs are an extension of their own personal commitment and identification as dharma practitioners. They would claim that the Buddhist view brings a unique and "paradigm-changing" approach to the cultivation of well-being. From this perspective, approaches to mindfulness that do not derive their foundation from Buddhist principles and trainings would be seen as superficial and, at worst, denying patients the opportunity for a richer and more penetrating experience. This belief persists despite wide differences in approach and trainings within Buddhist traditions, and debate as to whether any of these clinical approaches can be said to exemplify the construct described in the Buddhist texts (Rapgay & Bystrisky, 2009). Such particular views stand in contrast with Langer's more embracing contention that all mindfulness programs simply employ different means to get to a "there" that is the same for each (Langer, 2009). Since no universally agreed-upon criterion is on the horizon, it is unlikely that views on the "true" nature of mindfulness will be reconciled.

But focusing on the parochial question of what mindfulness is and which program most accurately reflects it does not get very far with the more essential question of how best to reduce mental suffering. Each of these programs focuses on qualities of the attending-to-experience that result in improvements in well-being. Therefore, it may be helpful to scrutinize the perceptual skills trainees are asked to cultivate in the training exercises. What is it that people are actually asked to do in the training? Comparisons of the training protocols may provide a more general knowledge of the qualities of attending to experience that facilitate well-being; knowledge that can only improve clinical efficacy, adaptability, and accessibility.

In this chapter, I discuss some issues that bear upon these qualities of attending, as well as similarities and differences between the "there" for the programs and, finally, the means by which they support getting "there." I follow Langer's lead in referring to the Buddhist-derived conceptions of mindfulness as Eastern, and the psychological understandings as Western. To provide a foundation for comparing and contrasting the approaches, I first summarize the fundamental features of the Eastern use of the term, and follow this with a description of Langer's conception, since it is the most conceptually divergent in its approach to cultivating mindfulness. I then discuss the apparent similarities and distinctions between the two approaches and suggest that the clinical goal of both approaches would be better served by shifting the focus to the generalizable attending skills developed through each. Since both conceptions of mindfulness use a phenomenological approach, I use a psychological conceptual framework throughout.

The Eastern Conception and Approach to Mindfulness

The Eastern conception of mindfulness emerges out of the primarily introspective approaches to knowledge extant in India at the time of the Buddha that had the goal of reducing mental suffering. In this view, the root problem preventing mental peace is ignorance of the momentary construction of the sense of self and ownership in the mind, and the associated craving and aversion. The term mindfulness has come to be the accepted English translation of the Pali word "sati" (sometimes translated as awareness), which is one of the mental qualities whose cultivation is considered important in a larger systematic path to dispel that ignorance and the development of mental peace. But since Pali is no longer a spoken language, and the teachings have undergone adaptations in each of the countries to which Buddhism spread, there is considerable variation in the ways different traditions approach and understand the construct described in the original texts.

As Eastern mindfulness is once again adapted, this time to Western clinical settings, the definitions and terms used to describe it have been cobbled together from traditional and contemporary constructs (Bishop et al., 2004; Brown & Ryan, 2004). And as might be expected, given its religious roots, there is ongoing debate as to where its "true" understanding is to be found (Grossman, 2011). That the word "mindful" had a pre-existing meaning in English has extended the confusion. Nevertheless, programs such as MBSR and MBCT were developed to reflect a spirit of mindfulness as it is generally taught in traditional Buddhist monastic settings. And even as they vary in detail, most definitions of mindfulness in the clinical literature center around that of Kabat-Zinn of "paying attention in a particular way: on purpose, in the present moment, and nonjudgmentally" (Kabat-Zinn, 1994; Shapiro, Carlson, Astin, & Freedman, 2006). A long list of additional descriptive expressions has also been used such as: beginner's mind, being in the moment, present-centered awareness, embodiment, being rather than doing mode, etc.

Most programs adhering to the Eastern conception first ask the beginner to cultivate the capacity to deliberately redirect attention to an arousal-neutral mind object; most often the sensations associated with breathing. Not only does this exercise develop facility in the use of attention, but directing it to this arousal-neutral object creates a relatively calm mental state that can be accessed anywhere and at all times. This mental calm can be cultivated both as an end in itself and as a mental state conducive to the process of further experiential discovery.

Beginning instruction with the realm of sensation in this way has a couple of other advantages. First, it is the realm of experience most easily recognized and perceptually distinguished from the thoughts and feelings that comprise the two other components of everyday experience (Carmody, 2009). As such, it is readily accessible to the beginner. It is also the realm in which delight is most acutely experienced. Second, it redirects attention away from the ongoing internal monologue with its judgments and their accompanying unpleasant affect and to which attention repeatedly defaults. The capacity to distinguish between sensations and cognitions in this way opens the possibility of being able to remain longer in the sensory realm before attention is once again overtaken by the cognition-based internal monologue categorizing (even in novel ways), judging and comparing the experience with imagined or remembered others.

These principles are exemplified in the use of the body scan as an initial mindfulness training exercise. Having established some facility in bringing attention to the sensations of the breathing, attention is moved in a systematic way through the entire body with the instruction to notice whatever sensations happen to be present in each part, and noticing the difference between the sensations, their associated feeling tone, and any cognitive commentary that is present. The instructions also ask participants not to try to change the sensation/thought/affect during the exercise, but simply to acknowledge and accept its presence. This process of perceptual differentiation and re-cognition of the components of experience is sometimes further supported by giving cognitive labels to them as they are noticed, such as "this is a thought," "this is a sensation," etc., or "this sensation has an unpleasant feeling associated with it ... ," or "this emotion is associated with these sensations, thoughts," etc. As facility develops, recognition of the components as such becomes increasingly immediate, and some psychological distance from the content of cognitions is cultivated.

The Western Conception of Mindfulness

The approach extensively described and studied by Langer is probably the most radical departure from the Eastern approach in that it focuses upon the lived end-point of being more mindful. This is a mode of functioning that actively engages in reconstructing the environment by continually creating new categories or distinctions and thus directing attention to new contextual cues that may be controlled or manipulated as appropriate (Langer & Moldoveanu, 2000). Mindfulness is contrasted with the mindlessness characterized by processing environmental cues in an automatic and inflexible manner, and where cognition relies on preformed environments determined by automatic categories no longer consciously available for consideration. Approaching situations with curiousity and cognitive flexibility, on the other hand, reveals their novelty, keeping us in the present and open to new information. This mindful perspective-taking increases creativity and more fruitful behavioral responses to situations and problems. The whole individual is said to be involved in this process, and the felt sense of this is one of heightened wakefulness (Carson, Shih, & Langer, 2001).

Langer and colleagues have demonstrated that interventions manipulating the environment to increase awareness of these automatic mindsets, and stimulating new more fruitful perspectives (Langer, Bashner, & Chanowitz, 1985) result in remarkable increases in creativity, attending, and learning. In a widely cited study of longevity in nursing-home residents (Alexander, Chandler, Langer, Newman, & Davies, 1989), the mindfulness intervention required them to engage in both a structured word-production task and an unstructured creative mental activity task. Subjects were required to think of a word, take its last letter, and find a new word beginning with that letter. They were not permitted to use any word more than once per session, and the level of demand of the program was continually increased to keep it novel and so more mindfulness inducing. Subjects were then instructed to produce words relating to specific categories such as animals, springtime, foods, places, etc. This task did not specify rules for thinking or particular target thoughts. Rather, the individual was asked to think about any topic in new and creative ways. Illustrations were provided such as thinking of unusual uses for common objects, or picking a controversial topic and arguing the side contrary to one's established opinion. Subjects were asked not to lapse into daydreaming but to actively direct their thinking during the process. They produced words for approximately 6 min, engaged in creative mental activity for 6 min and closed with another 6 min of word production followed by 2 min of rest.

Commonalities and Differences in These Approaches to Mindfulness

The most readily apparent principle the approaches have in common is the foundational idea that our experience of the world is shaped in large part by the way we perceive it. In the Western understanding of mindfulness, this principle emerges out of ideas from attribution theory in social psychology in which our experience of the world is reconstructed in the mind by attributing to the objects of the world those qualities detected through our senses. But Langer's work challenged the notion that people act only rationally on their beliefs, and are instead often guided by unconsciously processed information. Her mindfulness interventions encourage recognition of unconscious processes shaping inappropriate responding, replacing them with more appropriate ones. In the Eastern conception, the attribution principle is stated explicitly and radically in the Rohitassa sutra, a paraphrase of which reports the Buddha as having said: in this [fathom-long] body, with its senses and intellect, the entire cosmos is created along with the opportunity for its cessation. In this understanding, we are ignorant (unconscious) of the most fundamental processes shaping perception, and the training exercises are geared toward bringing them into awareness.

At this level, then, the two approaches have a good deal in common. In the Western conception, human suffering is created, or at least exacerbated, by people unconsciously employing outdated and inappropriate categories and mindsets in responding to everyday life situations (Langer et al., 1985). This results in lack of spontaneity and reduced awareness of the social and physical world and prevents the possibility of creative change. The training exercises to reduce this mindlessness such as the word "production" exercise or being challenged to think about a topic in a new and creative way by, for example, arguing the side contrary to one's usual opinion on a controversial topic, are designed to counteract this tendency. By intellectually challenging people to develop fresh, creative perspectives and explanations more appropriate to the situation at hand, the exercises make more apparent the automatic/unconscious categories that have been shaping responses. The language of these mindfulness instructions also reveals the influence of the classical Greek method of enquiry that it shares with cognitive therapy where solutions are sought through exposing conceptual flaws, and knowledge and happiness are furthered by creating a more rational and appropriate path. This is a training that is dynamic and values perspective taking as a way of better understanding the world.

The intellect-centered exercises, such as the word-production challenges, have features in common with exercises used in some Eastern approaches to mindfulness training. For example, one of the functions of the koans, used in some Zen traditions, is to foster curiousity about rational cognitive processes, albeit by frustrating their attempts to find a solution. Challenging the primacy they typically hold on attention exposes the perceptual filtering preventing more immediate experience of the world. The attribution principle is exemplified also in the "nine dots" puzzle, an exercise included in the MBSR class handbook and in management classes, to illustrate how the usual ways of thinking and perceiving can prevent us from recognizing that solutions to some problems emerge only when we "think outside of the box." Many MBSR programs also use the old/young woman trompe l'oeil picture from Gestalt psychology figure/ground experiments as a way of helping participants recognize the unconscious and automatic processes at work in shaping the way we typically perceive the world. Similarly, the compassion generating exercises commonly included in MBSR, MBCT, and DBT (Birnie, Speca, & Carlson, 2010; Shapiro, Brown, & Biegel, 2007; Van Dam, Sheppard, Forsyth, & Earleywine, 2011) are another way of exposing, for some, the unrecognized judgment-related categories and negative affect they may hold toward their own self, or others.

In these ways, then, the training for both approaches can be said to promote a mode of functioning characterized by curiosity, recognition of preformed categories, appreciation of the novelty of every situation, and actively engaging in reconstructing the environment and stimulating new perspectives.

However, while the Western approach is said to involve the whole individual in the process of enquiry, the training focuses primarily on constructions of the intellect; fostering an intellectual curiosity about concepts being used and whether they are appropriate to the situation and challenging trainees to create new ones. The senses are employed in the service of stimulating the intellect. In the Eastern approach, trainees are similarly encouraged to be curious about old habits of attending and aware of the concepts shaping their perception, but the training exercises are more perceptually granular and direct attention to the sensory realm as an end in itself. Cultivating awareness of bodily sensations is foundational in the Eastern approach, including physical sensations unfiltered by conceptual categories. The body scan, for example, directs curiosity and attention toward bodily sensations, as sensations, throughout the body, especially those usually missed because of their subtlety or as a result of inattention to the body parts in which they are occurring. And even though both approaches encourage trainees not to lapse into daydreaming, the Western approach to training does not appear to give particular attention to cultivating awareness of when this has occurred.

Eastern instructions for developing the capacity to become aware of bodily sensations also include facility in redirecting attention to the sensations of breathing as an effective way of reducing arousal. In this respect, it is interesting to note that in the study of the nursing-home population referred to above, no differences were found in anxiety, depression, or appreciation of self and the environment following an intervention using the Western training exercises. Reductions in anxiety and depression are, however, a usual outcome following Eastern training and are related to the emotion regulation that is associated with attentional regulation.

Mindfulness training instructions in each of the approaches can be said to provide both encouragement and the means to recognize and discern one or more of three features of everyday mental activity, and how they impact well-being (Carmody, 2009): first, by supporting recognition that the apparent seamlessness of everyday experience comprises three experiential components (thoughts/images, sensations, and their pleasant/unpleasant/neutral feeling tone) that can be perceptually discriminated and that these components form conditioned cycles of association. Second, facility in attention regulation provides the trainee the opportunity to notice which component of experience the attention is on at any moment and, if they so choose, to redirect it to a more neutral or positively valenced object. This experientially reveals to the person the principle that arousal levels follow the affective valence of the object of attention. The other option, of refraining from attempting to change what is noticed, gives the person an opportunity to develop tolerance for intense experience and emotion regulation. Third, in the process of this learning, the trainee recognizes that the three components comprising experience are events occurring in the field of awareness, bringing about a decentering or meta-awareness that creates a psychological distance from the components' content.

How recognition of these three features is best internalized so as to obtain the gains in well-being resulting from them differs in the Eastern and Western approaches. The Eastern tradition emphasizes the necessity of the meditation practice characteristic of those programs, and reductions in distress are indeed related to practice (Carmody & Baer, 2008). And there is evidence that the learning results in a lasting increase in well-being (Pbert et al., 2012). Just how much practice is required remains an open question. In contrast, the Western approach relies upon exercises that intellectually challenge existing categories or immersion in a structured environment that exposes them, and the derived benefits appear to be immediate. Proponents of meditation, however, would contend that it provides deeper insight into the process by which all mental life is constructed from moment to moment, both the functional and less than optimal; and that this is a quite different approach to change than considering just the appropriateness of a category's content, or continually coming up with new, albeit creative and novel, cognitive categories and processing solutions to an ongoing and changing situation or problem. Whether the more perceptually detailed training of the Eastern approach, and the time spent in meditation practice, results in additional benefits not immediately apparent is an empirical question deserving of study. This is important because the amount of time required to complete these programs is a significant barrier to many people, not to mention the exotic associations meditation has in many people's minds.

Perhaps, however, the most important source of misunderstanding in the "there" between Eastern and Western approaches is in the Rohitassa sutra phrase that states not only is the entire cosmos created in the body, but also it contains the *opportunity for cessation of the entire cosmos*. As the Buddhist-derived practices have been integrated into Western programs, this radical notion of cessation often stands unstated in the background of discussions of clinical mindfulness. Cessation is the ultimate goal in the Buddhist system and comes through experiential recognition of the illusion of a permanent and unchanging self—the coalescing of experiential components comprising it are recognized as occurring in a more fundamental and unchanging field. This insight results from adherence to the prescribed eightfold system in which formal mindfulness practice plays an important role linking back to the "clear seeing" referred to in the traditional roots of mindfulness (Thera, 1992).

This cessation is, however, rarely the goal of trainees in clinical settings where mindfulness is introduced. Most patients are more interested in obtaining the situational relief from anxiety and depression that comes with the relatively limited amount of mindfulness practice recommended in the programs. This is illustrated in one of the few MBSR long-term follow-up studies (Kabat-Zinn, Lipworth, Burney, & Sellers, 1987) that found that the majority of participants did not maintain a regular meditation practice; the learned technique they used most frequently and found most helpful was the simple act of redirecting attention to the sensations of breathing at times of stress.

It may be that patients of certain temperaments will find one approach more attractive than the other. No doubt some people experience delight when engaging in challenging mental/conceptual activities characterized by Langer's and colleagues' training exercises, and through them learn to increase the opportunity for greater well-being. Such people may flee from an exercise like the body scan, finding it exquisitely uncomfortable or boring. For others, it is the realm of sensation that holds most delight; a realm that often becomes neglected in the process of socialization. For them, this rediscovery is a revelation and a comfort. They may find conceptualizations boring and diminishing of their delight, and fear becoming "lost in their heads." The different types do not often understand or appreciate the other, and although they can learn to appreciate the other better, and it sometimes becomes a source of enrichment, the fundamental difference remains.

In Conclusion

Eastern and Western approaches to clinical mindfulness programs appear to vary in their understandings of the construct. Training in each, however, results in improvements in well-being. Proponents of the Western approach contend that all mindfulness programs simply employ different means to get to a "there" that is the same for each. But without an agreed-upon criterion reference, the question of the conceptual independence of each, and which is the more "true" understanding of mindfulness, is unlikely to be resolved. The more general and clinically profitable question to ask is what if any are the therapeutic properties they may have in common. And since programs ask participants to attend to their experience in particular ways, this question can be approached by examining the instructions trainees are asked to follow in their everyday lives, delineating the qualities of attending the programs share, and considering the ways each approach can complement the other. This approach can result also in a better understanding of processes that are common across many mind–body training programs.

References

Alexander, C., Chandler, H., Langer, E., Newman, R., & Davies, J. (1989). Transcendental meditation, mindfulness, and longevity: An experimental study with the elderly. *Journal of Personality and Social Psychology, 57*(6), 950–964.

Birnie, K., Speca, M., & Carlson, L. E. (2010). Exploring self-compassion and empathy in the context of mindfulness-based stress reduction (MBSR). *Stress and Health, 26*(5), 359–371.

Bishop, S., Lau, M., Shapiro, S., Carlson, L., Anderson, N. D., Carmody, J., … Devins, G. (2004). Mindfulness: A proposed operational definition. *Clinical Psychology: Science and Practice, 11*(3), 230–241.

Brown, K. W., & Ryan, R. M. (2004). Perils and promise in defining and measuring mindfulness: observations from experience. *Clinical Psychology: Science and Practice, 11*(3), 242–248.

Carmody, J. (2009). Evolving conceptions of mindfulness in clinical settings. *Journal of Cognitive Psychotherapy, 23*(3), 270–280.

Carmody, J., & Baer, R. A. (2008). Relationships between mindfulness practice and levels of mindfulness, medical and psychological symptoms and well-being in a mindfulness-based stress reduction program. *Journal of Behavioral Medicine, 31*(1), 23–33.

Carson, S., Shih, M., & Langer, E. (2001). Sit still and pay attention? *Journal of Adult Development, 8*(3), 183–188.

Chiesa, A., & Serretti, A. (2011). Mindfulness-based interventions for chronic pain: A systematic review of the evidence. *The Journal of Alternative and Complementary Medicine, 17*, 83–93.

Fletcher, L., & Hayes, S. C. (2005). Relational frame theory, acceptance and commitment therapy, and a functional analytic definition of mindfulness. *Journal of Rational-Emotive and Cognitive-Behavior Therapy, 23*(4), 315–336.

Grossman, P. (2011). Defining mindfulness by how poorly I think I pay attention during everyday awareness and other intractable problems for psychology's (re) invention of mindfulness: Comment on Brown et al. (2011). *Psychological assessment, 23*(4), 1034–1040.

Hofmann, S. G., Sawyer, A. T., Witt, A. A., & Oh, D. (2010). The effect of mindfulness-based therapy on anxiety and depression: A meta-analytic review. *Journal of Consulting and Clinical Psychology, 78*(2), 169–183.

Irving, J. A., Dobkin, P. L., & Park, J. (2009). Cultivating mindfulness in health care professionals: A review of empirical studies of mindfulness-based stress reduction (MBSR). *Complementary Therapies in Clinical Practice, 15*(2), 61–66.

Kabat-Zinn, J. (1994). *Wherever you go there you are.* New York, NY: Hyperion.

Kabat-Zinn, J., Lipworth, L., Burney, R., & Sellers, W. (1987). Four-year follow-up of a meditation-based program for the self-regulation of chronic pain: Treatment outcomes and compliance. *The Clinical Journal of Pain, 2*, 159–173.

Langer, E. J. (2009). *Counter clockwise: Mindful health and the power of possibility* (Vol. 22). New York, NY: Ballantine Books.

Langer, E. J., Bashner, R. S., & Chanowitz, B. (1985). Decreasing prejudice by increasing discrimination. *Journal of Personality and Social Psychology, 49*(1), 113.

Langer, E. J., & Moldoveanu, M. (2000). The construct of mindfulness. *Journal of Social Issues, 56*(1), 1.

Pbert, L., Madison, J. M., Druker, S., Olendzki, N., Magner, R., Reed, G., … Carmody, J. (2012). Effect of mindfulness training on asthma quality of life and lung function: a randomised controlled trial. *Thorax, 67*(9), 769–776. doi:10.1136/thoraxjnl-2011-200253

Rapgay, L., & Bystrisky, A. (2009). Classical mindfulness. *Annals of the New York Academy of Sciences, 1172*(1), 148–162.

Shapiro, S. L., Brown, K. W., & Biegel, G. M. (2007). Teaching self-care to caregivers: Effects of mindfulness-based stress reduction on the mental health of therapists in training. *Training and Education in Professional Psychology, 1*, 105–115.

Shapiro, S. L., Carlson, L. E., Astin, J. A., & Freedman, B. (2006). Mechanisms of mindfulness. *Journal of Clinical Psychology, 62*(3), 373–386.

Thera, N. (1992). *The heart of Buddhist meditation.* Kandy, Sri Lanka: Bhuddist Publication Society.

Van Dam, N. T., Sheppard, S. C., Forsyth, J. P., & Earleywine, M. (2011). Self-compassion is a better predictor than mindfulness of symptom severity and quality of life in mixed anxiety and depression. *Journal of Anxiety Disorders, 25*(1), 123–130.

4

From Early Buddhist Traditions to Western Psychological Science

Andrew Olendzki

From earliest times, human beings have inhabited two worlds, one external and material, the other internal and experiential. The first is well known, as our capacity for engaging with and changing the material world is everywhere evident, while a good accounting of the evolution of our inward-facing world is less apparent. It is written in the language of the arts: storytelling, poetry, music, dance, drama, myth, and all the many ways people have expressed what they see and think and feel inside. The history of mindfulness is one thread in this account of the human exploration of the subjective and experiential realm. Originating in the distant past as part of the contemplative practices of early Indian religiosity, mindfulness was developed by the Buddha and his followers into an effective tool for accessing, describing, understanding, and ultimately transforming the landscape of inner experience. In recent times it is having a profound impact on an array of modern and postmodern fields of inquiry, and in particular is contributing to a series of innovations in the fields of learning, health, and therapeutic psychology. At a time when our capacity for impacting our outer world is reaching unprecedented heights, mindfulness is emerging as an important tool for exploring our inner life with greater clarity and immediacy.

Ancient Origins

Consciousness itself, the ability to know or be aware of an object, is as old as the hills, in so far as the basic ability to process information can be accomplished by quite simple neural networks. Even relatively small bundles of neurons, connected to rudimentary sense receptors, are capable of "knowing" to avoid an object in one's path, that a particular sound is associated with a predator, or that a certain odor can be followed to locate food. To be conscious of that knowing, however, that is to have a sense of knowing that one knows and being able to take one's own inner experience as

The Wiley Blackwell Handbook of Mindfulness, First Edition.
Edited by Amanda Ie, Christelle T. Ngnoumen, and Ellen J. Langer.
© 2014 John Wiley & Sons, Ltd. Published 2014 by John Wiley & Sons, Ltd.

a deliberate object of awareness, is a matter of much greater complexity and may not have fully developed until the emergence of *Homo sapiens*. All early human cultures may be presumed to have explored deeply the interior dimensions of experience, for all describe rich mythic realms traveled by the shaman to gain knowledge from the inner reaches of the psyche. And while some sort of mental training would have been involved in the mastery of hunting skills, the systematic training of the mind in attention enhancement and concentration seems to have been of particular interest to the early inhabitants of the Indus and Ganges river valleys of North India.

Of the three major early civilizations that flourished 5000 years ago, along the Nile, Tigris/Euphrates, and Indus river systems, the Egyptian culture demonstrates a strong outward-facing focus. The sheer mass of stonework found in monuments, statuary, temples, and tombs is staggering, reflecting an apparent obsession with transforming and leaving a lasting mark upon the material environment. In remarkable contrast to this, the archeological remains of the Harappa civilization of the Indus watershed show very little concern for such outer changes, with uniform, utilitarian brickwork and almost no monumental structures, a corpus of terracotta goddess figurines that appear to be cobbled together for short-term use and then discarded, and an apparent lack of weaponry offset by a preponderance of toys and beads. What might account for such an apparent difference in cultural orientation? Humans appear to be equally capable worldwide, but different cultures define differently what matters are of greatest importance by inclining their attention and energy in particular ways. One hypothesis that can be offered to explain the striking differences between the material remains of these two civilizations is that perhaps early Indian culture was oriented more toward the inner dimension of human experience.

Hints that this might be the case come from both the archeological record and from a study of the unique elements of early Indian religious belief and practice. Small clay seals depict a human form seated in what to a modern observer seems a pose of yogic meditation; a lack of tombs or burial sites is consistent with a view of life recycling rather than of long-term survival after death; and the temporary nature of the goddess figurines suggests an emphasis on the experiential process of ritual rather than upon the sanctity of its representative objects. As we gain access to early Indian thought through the rich oral literature of the sixth and fifth centuries BCE, we find a whole complex of religious ideas and practices that are entirely different from what we are accustomed to seeing in the West, in so far as they emphasize the careful exploration of interior experience rather than populating the cosmos with gods. Consciousness itself is the sacred mystery, as it is directly experienced here and now. It is to be tamed by yogic disciplines, experimented upon using ascetic austerities, and observed empirically with meditation. Since none of these practices appear to have cognates from the same period in the West, it is not unwarranted to surmise they have their origins deep in the pre-Vedic indigenous Indian past (Reat, 1990).

Contemplative Practices

The Buddha, living squarely in the fifth century BCE, was already heir to a long tradition of meditation and mental training. Many of the *Upanishads* predate Buddhism, and although extant manuscripts of Yoga, Sāmkya, and Jain teachings are later, they clearly have their roots in this earlier era as well. These indigenous traditions all diverge from the Vedic orthodoxy, itself imported from the West with the Aryan migration into North India in the late second millennium BCE, in several important ways. They are more concerned with the exploration of inner landscapes than of outer realms, and thus place greater emphasis on direct experience than on ritual communication with external deities. The stress is on phenomenology rather than ontology, that is to say exploring the textures of "that which appears" in experience is more significant than discerning "the reality" of what lies behind appearances. The goal is not communication with a greater other and transcendence of the human condition but rather the integration and optimization of experience in this world, this body, this moment. The question is not "How can I escape this world for something better?" but rather "How can I attain profound well-being right here and now, regardless of the conditions I encounter in this world?" The approach to religious practice is more empirical and experimental than mythical, and in the earlier stages of all these Indian traditions, there is very little mythical content amid the rich set of experiential practices.

Foundational among these practices was *yoga*, a word meaning "discipline" or the yoking of the mind and body to the will. Quite different from its popular modern forms, early yoga involved an integrated teaching around the purification of the mind from its numerous defilements and toxins. The mind is capable of great clarity and happiness but is occluded by mental and emotional habits that obstruct access to a natural font of well-being. Training involves ethical restraint, physical disciplines such as bodily postures, breath regulation, and bodily purification, and mental disciplines such as control of the senses, the cultivation of contentment, and the development of healthy psychological habits (Eliade, 1958/1990). Pre-eminently, yogic practice involved calming, unifying, and focusing the mind. Related spiritual practices centered on many different forms of asceticism, which were seen as a way of experimenting with consciousness. Activities such as holding the breath, retaining a single posture for great lengths of time, going without food, and even the voluntary exploration of pain all served to enable the first-hand observation of cause and effect. How is the manifestation of consciousness altered in each of these circumstances? What can be learned about the conditions supporting the arising and passing away of pleasure and pain? Just as a material substance can be investigated by heating it in a crucible and observing how it breaks apart into its constituent components, so too can consciousness be empirically investigated by bringing heat (*tapas*—the Sanskrit word for both heat and asceticism) to bear upon the mind and body and watching closely what happens.

Meditation is part of this religious movement, consisting of a disciplined and repeatable protocol for the systematic exploration of consciousness. By removing oneself from the everyday duties of secular life, simplifying the elements of one's daily routine, and sitting quietly in isolation for long periods of time, the ancient yogis (those whose minds are yoked to the examination of experience) learned how to substantially amplify the power of their minds. As we have discovered independently today, by simply keeping the mind focused on a single object, for example by repeating a single word without distraction, for as little as 20 min at a time, one is able to activate the parasympathetic nervous system and elicit a profound mental and physical relaxation response that, among other things, enhances the functioning of the immune system (Benson, 1975/2001). The *shramanas*, or wanderers, of ancient India took this phenomenon a good deal further, describing extraordinary altered states of consciousness and a nuanced understanding of the moment-to-moment construction of psycho-physical experience (Hartranft, 2003).

Of particular interest was the exploration of the six different modalities of consciousness, the seeing, hearing, smelling, tasting, and touching that emerged from the interaction of the five sense organs with their corresponding sense objects, along with the experience that seemed to be independent of the senses taking place in the mind itself. They were also intrigued with the pleasure/pain reflex, and closely regarded the textures of these sensations and the conditions under which they arose or passed away. Another matter of great interest was an exploration of the range of human emotional responses, from primitive an hurtful emotions such as hatred and cruelty, to the most sublime expressions of loving kindness, compassion, and empathic joy. One important discovery was that if one is able to separate temporarily from the range of unwholesome or unhealthy emotions (i.e., those that lead to suffering), while at the same time practicing the inner technologies of concentration and single-pointed focus, the mind is capable of getting "absorbed" into concentrated states of ever-increasing levels of attenuation. These states are characterized as particularly blissful, with their pleasures getting gradually more rarefied until the pleasure evolves into a profound and imperturbable state of equanimity. Concentrating the mind even further, one is able to attain extraordinary states of awareness, experiencing such phenomena as infinite space, infinite consciousness, an apparent nothingness, and a state so subtle as to seem uncertain whether any perception whatsoever remained (Ñānamoli & Bodhi, 1995, pp. 257–259). Such attenuated states of consciousness yielded access to unusual mental and psychic abilities, were thought by many to lead after death to rebirth in heaven, and resulted in a tremendous settling of the mind and focusing of its power.

The Buddha

All this took place in the centuries before the Buddha, who was heir to the rich contemplative practices and psychological models of this tradition. The Buddha himself learned these techniques of meditation and asceticism from other teachers, having given up a comfortable life as a prince to join the movement of wandering *shramanas* and take up the quest for awakening. According to tradition he mastered both practices quickly and took each to its ultimate stage of development, but found both to be lacking in some important respect. Having learned all his meditation teachers had to offer, he turned down an invitation to lead their groups and took up a period of intensive ascetic practices. Having starved himself to within an inch of his life, he renounced asceticism too as unproductive (Ñānamoli & Bodhi, 1995, p. 336–40). Indeed, one of the unique character traits of the Buddha appears to be his ability to master things quickly, but then to turn away from them if they are not working.

The awakening experience the Buddha had under a tree in his 35th year appears to constitute a radical psychological transformation, a fundamental reordering of his psyche. As it is most simply described in the early texts, the fires of greed, hatred, and

delusion were quenched (*nirvāna*) within him, and his mind attained a state of profound peace and well-being that was independent of external conditions. The event is
depicted with ever-increasing mythic elaboration as the tradition matures, but underneath all the legendary material the earliest textual strata seems to speak of awakening
in more modest terms, as the overcoming of inner obstacles, the purification of the
mind from its psychological toxins, the healing of an illness, or the waking (*Buddha*)
from slumber. More importantly, this awakening is said to be accessible to anyone
in this lifetime who is willing and able to engage with a very demanding path of
moral behavior, mental training, and deepening understanding. The Buddha spent
the remaining 45 years of his life walking the breadth of the Ganges plain, sharing his
understanding of how suffering manifests in human experience, how it may be healed
through the cultivation of nonattachment, and inspiring a community of monks, nuns,
and laypeople along a path leading to the cessation of suffering.

There are many ways the Buddha innovated the meditation traditions he inherited,
and these have much to do with how mindfulness is understood and practiced today.
To begin with, he seems to have augmented, if not invented, the meaning of mindfulness (*sati*), to the extent it became the centerpiece of his contemplative training.
The term *sati*, which is based on a word for memory, may originally have referred
to the state of mind needed to recall from memory vast tracts of oral literature when
chanting. The mind must be concentrated, surely, but also open to the flow-through
of information. Unlike the one-pointed focus of the earlier yogic meditations, mindfulness meditation involves being attentive to the stream of consciousness as it naturally arises and passes away in the mind. The emphasis shifts from the imperturbable
depths of concentration to the agility of attending to one thing after another without
getting distracted by, absorbed into, or attached to the objects of experience. While
the ancient yogis were trying to attain altered states of mind through the attenuation of consciousness, Buddhist monks and nuns were trying to notice everything
that was happening naturally throughout the day with a heightened acuity of awareness. At its root, mindfulness means keeping things in mind, staying present to what
is happening, being able to know or be aware of one's experience with great clarity as it is happening. This requires a good deal of concentration but goes further
by putting this focus into motion, as it were, to observe everything very carefully as
it occurs.

Another way Buddha added to what he received from previous tradition was to situate mental training of all kinds between the pillars of two parallel enterprises: moral
integrity on one hand and penetrative wisdom on the other. Meditation, in the Buddha's view, is never meant to be practiced in isolation or as an end in itself, but is
imbedded in a foundation of ethical behavior and culminates with insight into knowing and seeing for oneself things as they actually are.

Mindfulness and Integrity

Early contemplative practices investigated the nature of consciousness directly and
derived their knowledge primarily from empirical observation. This being the case, it
is a remarkable insight that moral integrity is seen to be a natural property of the mind,

rather than something ancillary. The Western religious and philosophical traditions are inclined to apply the laws of nature only to the material world, and have considered questions of value and normative behavior to be best addressed in the realms of religion, where it is the free choice of an agent outside the matrix of cause and effect, or of civic culture, where it becomes a matter of personal responsibility or social duty. In Buddhism, moral quality is seen as an essential quality of every episode of consciousness, in so far as each moment of awareness is shaped by an emotional response that can be known to be either wholesome, unwholesome, or ethically neutral. The moral value of a mind moment is defined by its effect, not only upon the outer world and others, but upon one's own stream of consciousness. It is unwholesome or unhealthy when it contributes to suffering and obscures wisdom, it is wholesome or healthy when it leads away from suffering and enhances wisdom, and in some cases neither occurs, and it is merely functional. Moral value is measured at three phases of experience: in states, behaviors, and traits: *states* of mind are those volitional emotional responses that are presently arisen and active in the mind, and constitute the phenomenological content of experience; *behaviors* are how these states are acted out in thought, word, or deed; and *traits* are the more abiding underlying patterns of character and personality that have been laid down by habit, learning, or conditioning as a residue of each volitional action. These three are all inter-related aspects of the same process, called *sankhāra* in Pali, and together account for the idiosyncratic construction of personality in a psychological model that is ultimately without a self. Another word for this process in ancient India was *karma*.

One tangible effect of this ethical component of experience is that moral integrity is a precondition for the efficacy of meditation. According to the early Buddhist teachings, the mind is simply unable to become concentrated if it is permeated with such unwholesome states as sensual desire, ill-will, restlessness, sluggishness, or doubt. These act as obstacles to mental tranquility, hindering the mind's ability to become focused and alert. The mind is not a neutral tool that can be used to regard inner emotional states from an objective viewpoint, but is itself permeated by and molded by the very states it is trying to observe. Using the mind to see itself is like using a telescope or microscope—if the lenses are obscured by dust or debris, agitated by vibration, incapable of adjustment, or if there is insufficient light, then it is impossible to see accurately what is present. So, too, the mind must be cleared of its hindrances, at least temporarily, before one can hope to use it to see into itself with any clarity.

The ethical valence of states, behaviors, and traits also allows some forms of meditation to become an activity of mental hygiene. Just as one might clean off a blotch on the face before stepping into public view, one might also choose to abandon a toxic emotion that has arisen in the mind. And just as one might take care not to soil oneself anew, a person can bring a mental scrupulousness to all they think, do, and say throughout the day, guarding against the sorts of situations known to provoke or sustain unwholesome states. The same works for wholesome factors, and learning to cultivate good qualities that have not yet arisen in the mind and reinforce those that have can also be an important way of wielding the power of mindfulness to help bring about psychological transformation. There are two simple but insightful principles at work here: (1) whatever one thinks or ponders upon will become the inclination of one's mind; and (2) only one state can manifest in the stream of consciousness at a time, so when a wholesome state is present, an unwholesome state is excluded (and vice versa; Ñānamoli & Bodhi, 1995, p. 208). In pointing out this way in which our minds work, the Buddha emphasizes the extent to which we all have a good deal of influence over what sort of person we become, by choosing ethically wholesome options at every opportunity and allowing unwholesome states to atrophy. This, too, is a significant expansion of mindfulness to cover all aspects of daily life, for the householder as well as the monastic.

Mindfulness and Wisdom

Just as mindfulness is rooted in mental integrity, so also it is meant to lead the way to wisdom. While the early yogis aspired to higher states of consciousness, the Buddhist meditator was after seeing directly into (*vipassanā*) the nature of experience and understanding its characteristics. Mindfulness is a tool for seeing things with enhanced presence and steadiness of gaze, but the work done by this tool is gaining insight into the way things are. It was understood that the mind is naturally beset with a distorted view of reality, in so far as meaning is constructed internally from the importation and interpretation of a vast array of data delivered to the mind by the senses, but the elements of the construction process can be seen directly, with wisdom, as they operate. As consciousness cognizes a sensory or mental object, perception interprets it, feeling assigns a corresponding hedonic valance to it, and volitional formations respond emotionally to it based upon existing behavioral traits and learned responses. Since all this happens again and again in moments of cognition that arise and pass away in rapid succession, it is customary and adaptive for the mind to conjure up and project onto experience such things as object constancy, narrative cohesion, and a more or less coherent sense of personal identity. The world of lived experience is a virtual world, in other words, and the early Buddhists recognized this by considering much of what we know to be under the influence of delusion.

   Wisdom, which counteracts this delusion, involves overcoming the habitual misinterpretations that get us through the day, allowing our gaze to penetrate constructed appearances and see more subtle truths underlying common assumptions about ourselves and the world we inhabit. The first of these insights is into impermanence, the fact that nothing is stable, and all is fabricated. This is not questioning the stability of the external world, but refers to our own experience of the world. We are accustomed to using the word *world* to refer to what is "really out there," but Buddhists use it in the sense of us all living in the *world* of our own constructed experience, our own virtual reality. It is not an ontological question about what really exists, but an epistemological issue of how our knowledge is synthesized. Through consistent practice of mindfulness meditation, one gets beyond the mere idea that everything changes and gradually develops a direct, visceral appreciation of the radical contingency of all phenomena. This insight into experience, a sort of "phenomenological intelligence," serves to loosen attachment to what is wanted or not wanted and allows the mind to rest with equanimity in awareness of whatever is happening in the moment.

A second major breakthrough in understanding has to do with realizing the nature of suffering. Opening to what is uncomfortable, both physically and mentally, is an important first step away from the natural reflex to resist or ignore what is unpleasant and toward the acceptance without judgment of what is actually occurring in experience. With steady mindfulness, one can discern that all suffering is rooted, not in the nature of the object itself, but in our own response to the object. Just as stress is not an inherent property of anything existing in the outer world but is defined as an unhealthy internal response to an external influence (Kabat-Zinn, 1990), so also the Buddhists discriminate between pain, which is just a sensation of discomfort, and suffering as an emotional reaction to the pain. Suffering is thus something created in the mind and consists of an unskillful craving for pain to cease or for pleasure to persist. When one sees directly in one's own experience the way favoring and opposing all that is happening is itself the cause of suffering, one learns, too, that shifting or recontextualizing one's relationship to the objects of experience can result in the reduction and even cessation of suffering.

The signature Buddhist insight to which mindfulness practice leads is nonself. This is not to say that a self does not exist, but rather that it is as impermanent as everything else in nature and that its construction is rooted in the craving that causes suffering. The doctrine of nonself was a challenge to the Hindu sense of self (*ātman*), which was said to be ultimately real (*sat*), to consist of pure consciousness that needs no object (*cit*), and to be intrinsically blissful (*ānanda*). Each of these characterizations is undermined in the direct experience of moment-to-moment mindful awareness of the stream of consciousness as it unfolds in human experience. First, the substantiality of consciousness is refuted by seeing the relentless rise and fall of one moment of consciousness after another, each involving its own instantaneous birth and death. Permanence and constancy are ideas constructed as mental fictions to help bring some stability to experience, but do not hold up under direct phenomenological observation. Second, similarly, since consciousness is an emergent property dependent upon the senses and their objects rather than an independently existing entity, it is thoroughly contingent. Every moment of consciousness can be seen empirically as an event requiring the interaction of an organ (eye, ear, nose, tongue, body, mind) and a corresponding object (sights, sounds, smells, tastes, touches, thoughts). One is always aware *of* something (an object) *by means of* something (an organ), which renders consciousness itself, the six ways of knowing (seeing, hearing, smelling, tasting, touching, thinking), a naturally caused event rather than a transcendent reality. Third, the final claim of blissfulness is also more an idea than an experience, in so far as the feeling tones of pleasure and pain can be observed to arise dependent on conditions, and cease when those conditions change. When two sticks are rubbed together, heat is produced, but when the contact ceases the corresponding heat no longer occurs (Bodhi, 2000, p. 597). Sustained mindfulness practice will reveal that there is indeed a sense of self produced every moment when craving takes place, such that one has the sense of being a person who likes or does not like what is happening. But that self will vanish as soon as the moment passes away, is conditioned like everything else in the natural world, and will experience pleasure and pain in more or less equal proportions. This is a far cry from the transcendent spiritual essence the self is often assumed to be.

What Is Mindfulness?

Now that we have seen that the Buddha was heir to a rich contemplative tradition extending back centuries, and that he redirected the concentration practices of his era to be rooted in ethical integrity and to lead toward understanding experience in transformative ways, it remains to address the question of mindfulness itself. What exactly is happening in the mind of those meditators sitting immobile with legs crossed, back straight, and eyes hooded, with perhaps the hint of a smile on their faces? The Buddhist tradition possesses a sophisticated model of mind and body, and can actually answer this question with some precision (Olendzki, 2010, 2011). There are five different levels or modes of mental operation, each somewhat more complex than the previous as additional mental functions come in to play.

1 To begin with, all instances of coherent experience involve the interaction of many different systems and processes that co-occur in complex interdependence with one another. This is a model not of interconnected parts but of inter-related events. At its most basic level, all human experience is a flow of occurrences unfolding one after another with such rapidity that we normally engage with it at much higher levels of interpretation. A well-concentrated mind serves as a tool capable of zooming in below the threshold of ordinary awareness to reveal mental functioning more precisely. From this perspective, as we have seen, every moment of consciousness emerges from the interaction of a sense organ and a sense object, and involves an act of interpretive perception, a feeling tone on a spectrum between pleasure and pain, and some form of emotional and volitional response. In its simplest configuration, therefore, experience always consists of a single-pointed focus upon one of the six points of contact (five senses and the mind as sixth), along with the basic and universal mental functions of feeling, perception, intention, and attention. At this most rudimentary level of mental function, one is generally so embedded in experience that there is little or no metacognition. Although we are conscious enough to walk across a room without bumping in to anything, we are not really consciously aware of what we are doing much of the time—we just do it. This characterization of experience may well correlate with what has been identified as the default mode network of the brain (Raichle et al., 2001).

2 The sense of being consciously aware arises when additional mental systems become engaged, such as choosing where attention will be directed (as opposed to it merely responding to environmental stimuli) and choosing to hold the attention on a particular object. The ability to direct and sustain awareness on a chosen object contributes substantially to the sense of agency, and is our primary tool for problem solving and narrative construction. Conscious awareness is also augmented by qualities such as confidence, heightened energy, enthusiasm, and the initiation of bodily, verbal, or mental action. These more intentional mental functions come and go in experience depending on circumstances, interweaving with the less intentional default states, to yield a continuity of consciousness with both active and passive components. The second mode of mental functioning is this more active form when we have the sense of doing what we do deliberately, on purpose, or with conscious attention.

3 All this dynamic mental functioning is ethically neutral, but now moral valence enters the picture. According to Buddhist psychology, these mental factors are regularly augmented and modulated by either wholesome or unwholesome states of mind. When angry, hateful or greedy, for example, consciousness is colored by the additional factors of delusion and restlessness, and its inherent moral compass of conscience and respect for others is inhibited. Similar unwholesome emotional states such as conceit, avarice, envy, and cruelty take over the direction of the basic mental processes, and factors such as intention and attention are put to work causing suffering and creating harmful causes and effects (*karma*). These unhealthy states not only harm others by being enacted in behavior, but also lay down character traits in ourselves that cause difficulties downstream in the stream of consciousness as we inherit their detrimental effects in subsequent mind moments. Much of the difficulty we face as human beings, say the Buddhists, comes from this third mode of mental function, when the mind's activity is hijacked by toxic emotional patterns rooted in greed, hatred, and delusion. This is the cause of all suffering, from minor episodes of individual psychological discomfort to massive collective behaviors that destroy life and the living systems that support it. Although one can still direct attention deliberately, and one is capable of heightened concentration, there can be no true mindfulness when the mind is immersed in unwholesome states.

4 Fortunately, these unhealthy mental events are as episodic as everything else, and every ensuing mind moment holds an opportunity for change. The basic functions of the mind may also be pervaded and guided by wholesome emotional states, foremost of which is mindfulness, but loving kindness, compassion, and empathic joy are also examples of wholesome states. As an object is cognized by consciousness, it may also be regarded mindfully, which brings with it such states as confidence, equanimity, benevolence, and nonattachment, and which also preserves the full engagement with the innate ethical restraints of conscience and respect. Such moments are considered to be healthy, in the sense they contribute to clarity and point away from suffering, and skillful, in so far as they can be practiced and developed. Mindfulness is thus a mental *state* arising in the mind as a volitional attitude toward an object of experience that can be extended into *behavior* through acting, speaking, or thinking with equanimity, and can strengthen and develop as a personality *trait* through systematic practice. The reason mindfulness practice is considered so beneficial is that whenever mindfulness manifests in the mind as a state, unwholesome states are excluded from the mind stream, healthy behaviors are enacted, and wholesome traits are laid down and reinforced. The equanimity inherent in mindfulness avoids the twin errors of either reinforcing unwholesome states by embracing them and acting them out, or suppressing them with an aversive response, which may have a short-term benefit but will result in long-term difficulty. Mindfulness is a wholesome response that simply sees things as they are, without favoring or opposing, which allows for a radical nonattachment to all experience. Since craving and grasping are the primary causes of suffering, in the Buddhist analysis, learning to hold oneself in the midst of all experience with an attitude on nongrasping is inherently healing.

5   The culminating and thus optimal state of mental functioning involves the active manifestation of wisdom, by means of which one is capable of *understanding* experience rather than merely experiencing it, directing it, wielding it unskillfully, or even seeing it clearly with mindfulness. It is this fifth stage that is most transformative, in so far as the unhealthy emotions are seen to be impermanent, the cause of suffering, and ultimately without self. Seeing things in this way leads to what the Buddhists call disenchantment, emergence from the thrall of attachment and aversion, and dispassion, being able to relate to all experience with equanimity and understanding rather than with conditioned compulsion. In such states the psychological toxins find no footing and gradually dissipate, resulting in a person who not only has an ever-clearer mind and breaks the habit of taking everything personally but also acts with increasing integrity as an expression of their wisdom.

Mindfulness and the West

Twenty-five centuries lie between the time of the Buddha and the current age, centuries filled with remarkable twists and turns of Buddhist tradition. Moving northwest from their homeland in Northern India, the teachings gradually worked their way overland through Central Asia to China, Korea, Japan, and Tibet, changing and adapting to new civilizations, new languages, and new ideas as they went. More conservative traditions tried to maintain the early teachings as the movement spread southeast to Sri Lanka, Cambodia, Burma, Thailand, and the islands off the Asian mainland. The teachings on mindfulness were woven into every iteration of Buddhist thought and practice, even as the tradition diversified by incorporating new forms of philosophy, devotion, monasticism, social engagement, and the arts. Somehow the simple teaching of how to stay present to the inner life, how to be aware of what is arising and passing in immediate experience, remained at the heart of all forms of Buddhism. Whether one is chanting, studying, meditating, debating, or engaging in daily affairs, mindfulness is a crucial ingredient to the practices of a Buddhist in any of its manifestations.

Buddhist teachings entered Western experience through three main channels. First, it was transplanted by immigrant communities, primarily Chinese and Japanese workers coming to California in the 19th century, and Tibetan and Southeast Asian population displacements in the 20th century. Second, Buddhist thought gradually became known through the work of academics and intellectuals as the languages and literatures of the colonies became known to their civic administrators, as the museums of Europe filled with exotic artifacts, and as the fields of ethnography and comparative religion took shape in Western universities. Finally, mostly in the 20th century, a number of Eastern teachers came West, and Western students went East to engage directly with the practice of meditation and the experiential investigation of ancient doctrines. The early phases of this encounter were of course fraught with misunderstandings and shallow caricatures, but the depth and sophistication of mutual understanding have grown steadily. The postwar countercultural generation in particular became intrigued with the arts and sciences exploring the inner rather than outer dimensions of human experience, and meditation was found at the heart of an array of new approaches to spirituality.

Among the historical factors that helped make meditation practices accessible in the West, in addition to the dislodging of Buddhist teachers from their indigenous settings by war and invasion, were reform movements within Burma, Thailand, and Sri Lanka. In Burma, Mahāsi Sayadaw and U Ba Khin led movements to make intensive meditation retreats, which were largely the province of monks, accessible to lay householders in great numbers. Retreat centers flourished, first in Burma and then in India and other countries, and lay in the path of wandering Western youths who learned the practices of insight meditation in Bodhgaya and elsewhere in Asia and brought them back to their homelands. In Thailand, a forest practice tradition developed alongside the mainstream state religion, and teachers like Ajahn Chah and Buddhadāsa were particularly welcoming of the foreigners who were making the rounds on their spiritual journeys. Sri Lanka became home to a whole generation of British and German scholar monks such as Bhikkhus Ñānamoli and Ñānaponika, and nuns such as Ayya Khema, who turned away from the conflicts of Europe in the middle of the century and found refuge in southern monasteries. So it is that mindfulness, which is present in all Buddhist schools but is most explicitly emphasized in the Theravada Buddhism of these countries, was poised by the end of the twentieth century to have a major impact upon the mainstream cultures of North America, Europe, and Australia.

Throughout its history, as Buddhism moved from country to country, it adapted to local custom in the short run and transformed local culture in the long run. When transferred from a more developed to a less developed civilization, the importation and embrace of the tradition by the receiving culture were near total; such is the case as Buddhism moved into Sri Lanka and Tibet from India and into Korea and Japan from China. When the transition is between more equal partners, as from India to China and, one might argue, from Asia in general to the West in general, it is a more gradual process that takes much longer to have a significant impact. It was centuries before Buddhism was well understood in China, and its influence on the West is only now being strongly felt, 200 years after first significant contact. A tipping point was reached when well-educated native Chinese understood that Buddhism offered something quite different from Taoism and Confucianism, and this is when uniquely Chinese forms such as Ch'an and Pure Land Buddhism emerged and took root. We may be reaching a similar point of quickening influence in the early years of the 21st century, as Buddhism gradually comes into view as preserving a unique and valuable perspective—an inner perspective—that has little counterpart in Indo-European or Judeo-Christian tradition. The emerging global civilization is unlikely to be converted *to* Buddhism, but almost surely will become significantly transformed *by* Buddhism.

While Buddhist ideas encountered and syncretized with Bon in Tibet, Shinto in Japan, and various forms of animism throughout Southeast Asian, the native traditions it engages with in America and the West include such things as science, materialism, psychology, romanticism, commercialism, and New Age thinking. It is inevitable that contemporary Buddhist understanding would be molded by these perspectives and that it would go through various stages of development in the process. Who knows how far along we are on this continuum, but it seems significant that the traditional Buddhist notion of mindfulness is entering mainstream discourse in at least two places. One is among the scientific community, which is engaged in an important new research agenda to study and understand consciousness. The other is among psychologists, who are drawing upon the introspective practices of ancient India in their treatment of emotional suffering.

Mindfulness and Healing

Western psychology grew out of the field of natural philosophy, which only recently began incorporating Eastern perspectives into its theoretical frameworks. Early psychologists (Wundt, Titchener) used introspection as an approach to learning about the mind and behavior, but this approach was soon abandoned and replaced by behaviorism, which appeared a much more objective way of studying the mind scientifically. Behaviorists (Watson, Skinner) were famously uninterested in consciousness itself, preferring to measure input stimuli and output responses but treating the mind itself like a black box, which should not, and perhaps could not, be penetrated. Attitudes toward consciousness as a legitimate field of inquiry began to loosen up midcentury as computers came online and were used as a model for human intelligence, and changed more dramatically with the maturing of the cognitive revolution and with new directions in neuroscience around the turn of the millennium. As consciousness itself became an acceptable topic of investigation, mindfulness emerged from monasteries and spiritual retreat centers and moved into the laboratory as a tool for accessing internal states. The new scanner technologies that allowed access to mapping brain activity from a third-person perspective needed to be integrated with first-person reporting of the subject, and meditation training proved a valuable way of accessing this. Researchers were also interested in gaining a better understanding of the states of mind exhibited by all forms of meditation, and looked carefully at what neuronal mechanisms are associated with various nonordinary states of consciousness. The collaboration between traditional Buddhist meditation practices and cutting edge scientific research techniques is perhaps best symbolized by images of Buddhist monks wired up with electrodes or emerging from fMRI machines. While traditional religious views subordinated materiality to spirit, and conventional scientific assumptions reduce consciousness to materiality, there is some indication that new models for understanding the mind as a "middle way" between these two alternatives are emerging from this cooperation, promising a true integration of both objective and subjective perspectives (Thompson, 2007).

An appreciation of the value of mindfulness as a contributor to both physical and mental health has also developed over the last few decades as modern psychology, increasingly influenced by medical paradigms, concerns itself with repairing damage inflicted by trauma and restoring health compromised by illness. Buddhist sages have always been represented as profoundly peaceful and healthy, for reasons rooted in their own mental skills rather than in divine grace, and researchers became interested in investigating whether the practices of mindfulness, meditation, and inner transformation might be somehow quantifiable, repeatable, and applicable to anyone. Early projects looked at the physiological effects of Transcendental Meditation and Zen meditation, and were encouraging. The field gained momentum when Herbert Benson identified a "relaxation response" that can be induced by anyone repeating any word consistently to induce a state of concentration, and when Jon

Kabat-Zinn began introducing meditation practices into medical settings in what has come to be known as mindfulness-based stress reduction. In both cases, the calming of the mind could be seen to have a direct influence on calming the body, which measurably increased the effectiveness of the immune system and contributed to other healthy effects. Now, it seems as if there is almost no field of human endeavor that would not benefit from meditation. Mindfulness training is being introduced to a host of secular settings such as hospitals, schools, and prisons, and is being applied to a wide array of activities such as caregiving, recovery, conflict resolution, sports, and performance enhancement generally. Mindfulness also seems to be a key component in the many forms of positive psychology that are steering the field away from its medical roots and extending into an open-ended exploration of human flourishing.

As a tool for psychological healing, mindfulness has been having an impact on a number of new treatment modalities that have emerged in recent decades, such as cognitive-behavioral therapies, acceptance and commitment therapy, dialectical-behavioral therapy, and others (Germer, Siegel, & Fulton, 2005). What these approaches have in common is a tendency to view the mind as a series of interdependent processes rather than as the interaction of structures, and a belief that mental health is augmented by allowing the flow-through of experience rather than trying to inhibit, resist, or mold it in a particular way. Traditional Buddhist insights that stem from mindfulness practice, such as seeing the impermanence, the interdependence, and the impersonality of mental events, can be brought to bear on dysfunctional mental habits and disorders. For example, learning to trust that various mental states will naturally arise under certain conditions, but that they will just as naturally pass away when those conditions change, can be of immense help to those struggling with anxieties, compulsions, addictions, or related uncomfortable and unwelcome mind states. Similarly, learning to see arisen mental states as not belonging to or defining a particular construction of self can help one who is caught in identifying with their depression, is afflicted by past trauma, or is learning to cope with a new disability. Learning to face mindfully the textures of chronic pain or emotional distress rather than avoid them with fear can help one see that while pain might be an inevitable component of human existence, the suffering it gives rise to can be modulated by a range of more skillful emotional responses. In particular, understanding the self to be a contingent fabrication that takes different forms under changing circumstances, rather than being a fixed entity with fixed characteristics, can help anyone gain comfort and empowerment in any difficult situation. Mindfulness helps us release our grasp on conceptual definitions of ourselves that may have been built up over years from habit and conditioning, and open to the freedom of recreating ourselves anew each moment.

With its roots in ancient India and its branches now spreading their leaves throughout our world, it remains to be seen what fruits will ripen on this tree of mindfulness. It is remarkable that we even have access to the contemplative arts of our distant ancestors, and we owe a debt of gratitude to the many generations who have kept this lore alive over so many centuries. The inner knowledge accessed by the investigation of our own experience promises to complete us as human beings, uniting the interior and exterior aspects of our nature in ways that have not been possible until now. Our future well-being may well depend upon our ability to understand and transform ourselves at least as well as we do the world around us.

Mindfulness and Mindlessness

All that has been said so far has focused upon mindfulness as an element of the Buddhist meditation tradition. The term mindfulness has also been applied to a field of psychological and social science research that studies the beneficial effects of attention in general, and to heightened attention in particular, and applies these benefits to fields such as education. Ellen Langer has been a pioneer in this field who began by studying various forms of what she has called mindlessness (Langer, 1989). It was illuminating to reveal the extent to which normal human functioning takes place with little deliberate attention, and how much of what people do each day is governed by unconscious decision-making and the passive response to cues. A considerable body of research has documented the scope of this lack of conscious attention in numerous contexts, and points to its detrimental effects upon a range of endeavors. The reversal of this phenomenon calls for mindfulness, used in this context to indicate a state of greater consciousness, heightened awareness, and more developed powers of attention and creativity. This maps on to the five-part model described above as primarily emphasizing the differences between the first and second level of functioning, namely when we are not paying attention and when we are. When functioning within the rudimentary default mode network, much of what we think is habitual and unexamined, and most of what we do is automatic and reflexive. While calling this mindlessness might be an overstatement, we are certainly working with less than our full complement of mental faculties. When attention is deliberately aroused, directed, placed, and sustained, things are very different, and Langer and colleagues have done much to dramatically demonstrate this contrast and present the benefits of heightened awareness.

Mindfulness as a concept in social psychology differs from Buddhist mindfulness in several ways. One difference is that social scientists stay firmly in the realm of conceptual thinking, using the term mindfulness to refer to ways of sharpening and even augmenting the use of what in Buddhism are called "mental objects," while in more traditional Buddhist practices mindfulness training is more apt to pull attention away from the "mind door" and place it more fully on the data presenting at the "sense doors." While Buddhists are largely trying to neutralize the symbolic narrative of the mind, social scientists are often trying to augment and improve it. Another contrast is the ethically neutral stance of so much scientific inquiry, compared to the fundamental role of ethics in early Buddhist mental training. Mindfulness in Buddhist practice is not meant to increase the efficiency of the mind as much as to help transform its quality, and that quality is measured on a scale of ethical wholesomeness and unwholesomeness. Learning to see how much harm comes from mindless behavior is indeed beneficial, but issues of ethical integrity do not lie at the heart of the social scientific study of mindfulness as they do in the Buddhist tradition.

A third difference between the two uses of the word mindfulness has to do with the role of equanimity. As the term is defined above in the Buddhist context, the presence of equanimity as a mental state in the mind at the moment of cognizing an object is a crucial part of the definition of mindfulness. One is always attentive to something, when consciously directed attention is heightened and intentionally wielded, but it is only when coupled with equanimity—neither favoring nor opposing what one sees, hears, touches, or thinks—that attention evolves into mindfulness. This distinction is entirely lacking in the social scientific sense of the word, although the benefits of keeping an open mind and the nonattachment to pre-existing views are clearly recognized.

Despite these distinctions, there are also similarities. Both senses of the term share the goal of steering human experience in healthier directions, and both are involved with enhancing bottom-up processing in the brain. Part of what we experience comes into the mind from the senses, but this is heavily mediated and interpreted by top-down processes that impose assumptions upon incoming data and modify experience in ways that are comfortable and familiar. As Langer has demonstrated well, a person's established views and assumptions, called by her their "mindset," impose themselves upon incoming data and greatly narrow the possible range of interpretation and response. Recognizing that this is happening, and working to soften the pre-existing contexts and strengthen the freshness of new information, is something that both forms of mindfulness have in common. Both approaches, too, are working to enhance human flourishing, and thus share a natural affinity. It is likely that the two fields will continue to inform and expand one another as interest in mindfulness continues to grow.

References

Benson, H. (1975/2001). *The relaxation response.* New York, NY: HarperCollins.

Bodhi, B. (2000). *The connected discourses of the Buddha; a new translation of the Samyutta Nikāya.* Boston, MA: Wisdom.

Eliade, M. (1990). *Yoga, immortality and freedom.* Princeton, NJ: Princeton University Press. (Original work published 1958)

Germer, K., Siegel, R., & Fulton, P. (2005). *Mindfulness and psychotherapy.* New York, NY: Guilford Press.

Hartranft, C. (2003). *The yoga-sutra of Patanjali; a new translation with commentary.* Boston, MA: Shambhala Press.

Kabat-Zinn, J. (1990). *Full catastrophe living.* New York, NY: Delta.

Langer, E. J. (1989). *Mindfulness.* Reading, MA: Addison-Wesley.

Ñānamoli, B., & Bodhi, B. (1995). *The middle length discourses of the Buddha: A new translation of the Majjhima Nikāya.* Boston, MA: Wisdom.

Olendzki, A. (2010). *Unlimiting mind: The radically experiential psychology of Buddhism.* Boston, MA: Wisdom.

Olendzki, A. (2011). The construction of mindfulness. *Contemporary Buddhism, 12*(1), 55–70. doi:10.1080/14639947.2011.564817.

Raichle, M. E., MacLeod, A. M., Snyder, A. Z., Powers, W. J., Gusnard, D. A., & Shulman, G. L. (2001). Inaugural article: A default mode of brain function. *Proceedings of the National Academy of Sciences, 98*(2), 676–82. doi:10.1073/pnas.98.2.676.PMC14647.PMID11209064

Reat, N. R. (1990). *Origins of Indian psychology.* Berkeley, CA: Asian Humanities Press.

Thompson, E. (2007). *Mind in life: Biology, phenomenology, and the sciences of mind.* Cambridge, MA: Belknap Press.

5

Mindfulness Meditation from the Eastern Inner Science Tradition

Carin Muhr and Lene Handberg

Introduction

Based on the work of Buddhist scholars from Nalanda University such as Vasubandhu (fifth century AD), Kamalaśīla, (c. AD 740–796) and Atiśa (c. AD 982–1054) traditional Mindfulness training is presented herein from the point of view of the interrelatedness of phenomenal reality called Pratītyasamutpāda (Sanskrit), *tendrel* (Tibetan), or "unity in duality" (UD),[1] as taught by the Tibetan scholar, Tarab Tulku (1935–2004).[2] This view examines the interrelated nature of reality using a polar framework of "subject–object," "body–mind," and "energy–matter" that will be expounded below together with an analysis and investigation of perception on gross as well as subtle levels.

Mindfulness, as used above and when capitalized herein, refers to the Nalanda University related traditional Buddhist spiritual discipline of "the four mindfulness meditations"[3] (of body, feeling, mind, and phenomena), which is a meditative investigation into the nature of reality that helps the practitioner to realize the nature of reality and the attainment of spiritual goals. In this work, we briefly explain these traditional practices, aims, and viewpoint, and explore ways in which these methods can be applied in ordinary circumstances to improve psychological and general health.

In the first part of this chapter, we will discuss some of the main theorems underlying Eastern inner science[4] (EIS) and traditional Mindfulness training in particular. We will also define terms and discuss the distinctions made between the gross material body and the subtle body, the body–mind and subject–object poles in the context of traditional Mindfulness meditation and UD. UD, as a term used herein, is synonymous with the term "tendrel," as defined in note 1, and refers to the general view (and established education based on this view) that despite the appearance of separation, all phenomenal existents are interrelated and interdependent, and as such exist in both unity and duality.

The Wiley Blackwell Handbook of Mindfulness, First Edition.
Edited by Amanda Ie, Christelle T. Ngnoumen, and Ellen J. Langer.

In the second part, we will outline the meditative practices of Śamatha and Vipassanā, which are the foundational practices for the "four mindfulness meditations," and in a secular context discuss the relevance of all these practices to personal development and general psychological health. The discussion will continue to elucidate the underlying theoretical and analytical framework of EIS as an approach to understanding, working with, and developing the mind. However, while monastics and serious lay practitioners who engage with these spiritual practices have as their ultimate goal the attainment of a fully realized mind, this work is much more limited in its scope, discussion, and application of these methods. This is in accord with the intentions of Tarab Tulku, who studied and compiled the universalities of ancient Eastern traditions and created UD, and whose view is well represented in this work. He encouraged the use of these traditionally spiritual investigative practices, which require a high degree of meditative discipline and accomplishment, but from a less elevated level for practical applications in personal development, art-of-relating,[5] psychological health, and general well-being.

In the third part, we will discuss some of the similarities and differences between traditional Mindfulness practice and the mindfulness practices used in modern therapeutic psychology and in UD. We will also discuss the usefulness of the EIS theoretical framework in explaining the positive effects that have been demonstrated with modern mindfulness practice.

Basic Tenets, Terms, and Prerequisites for Traditional Mindfulness and UD

In this part, we review some basic tenets and define terms that are used in this work to discuss traditional Mindfulness meditation and related terms as they are used in UD.

Interrelated nature of reality and EIS

EIS traditionally includes meditative investigations and understandings of reality that are common to Buddhism, Hinduism, Jainism, and Brahmanism. Its achievements rest on insights acquired logically and empirically through meditative practices and contemplative investigations into the nature of existence and the interrelatedness of such distinctions as *body*, *mind*, and *reality*. This tradition developed sophisticated theorems of reality, which for the most part could be subsumed with the term *interrelated nature*, meaning that all of reality, everything existing, is relational, and that nothing, including the self, exists in and of itself in a static or isolated way.

According to the ontology of EIS, our entire experience of reality is interrelated with the mind. This is not a negation of the existence of external reality but merely an observation that experience is strictly a product of the mind and is limited to and shaped by the capabilities of the five senses and other mental faculties such as cognition, perception, language, and emotions. EIS holds that there are broader and subtler ranges of perception available to human experience that can be achieved through the practice of Mindfulness meditation and the contemplation and cultivation of attention on mental and sensory phenomena.

Terms of analysis 1: Subject–object, mind–body, energy–matter   Mindfulness practice utilizes a set of representative polar terms with which one can analyze the nature of experience and existence. Three polar terms are employed by Tarab Tulku to help illuminate the nature of our apprehension of reality (Tarab Tulku, 2002, 2006; Tarab Tulku & Handberg, 2005):

1 Subject–object: The subject-pole refers to the mind that perceives, and the object pole refers to the phenomena appearing to the perceiving mind. It is important to note here that the object pole does not refer to an external object but refers only to the phenomena appearing to the mind. The term also refers to the interrelation-ship between the subject–object poles, as they are mutually dependent and do not actually exist separately. On a deeper level of analysis, the subject refers to the body and mind of the perceiver, and the object is whatever actually exists and is show-ing properties or characteristics according to the way it is approached or perceived (i.e., through the body and mind). On this level of analysis, we call the object the *referential object* to refer to the nature or characteristic of the reality beyond our perception rather than the discrete object as ordinarily taken to mind through the senses and cognitive faculties. Similarly, we refer to the whole of reality (as it exists beyond our perceptive faculties) as *referential reality*. The subject and "referential object" are also interrelated, although in a different way than in ordinary percep-tion. This idea is further elucidated herein (but briefly, as it is somewhat beyond the scope of this work) and particularly in the sections on the third and fourth mindfulness meditations.
2 Body–mind: Mind and body are interdependent. Without mind, the body does not function, and vice versa. The body, and its senses in particular, limits what and how phenomena can be perceived. In this tradition, a distinction is made regarding the body where it is physical in one aspect and energy in another; for example, the *subtle body* (defined further below), like the body in our dreams, is not a physical body but functions in similar ways.
3 Energy–matter: Energy in this sense refers to the very subtle nature of reality, well beyond the perceptions of ordinary minds, which, according to EIS, is the non-substantial potential field from which reality formation occurs and exists as matter (unfolded nature). Energy is considered as the enfolded order of reality and matter as the unfolded order. EIS holds that energy and matter are interrelated and in a dynamic flux at any given moment. However, although briefly discussed in the sec-tions on the third and fourth mindfulness meditations, this polar relationship and its analytical use for radical transformation are beyond the scope of this chapter.

According to Tarab Tulku, these polarities are mutually dependent and have both dual and unified characteristics (Tarab Tulku, 2006). Because we experience the mind perceiving an object and the object as separate things, we can easily grasp the dual nature of the subject–object poles. Nevertheless, the perceiving mind and the object perceived arise in dependence upon each other and are therefore not separate entities but are essential to each other and have the same root. It is in this sense that the subject–object poles are said to exist in unity with each other. The same is applied to the body–mind and energy–matter polarities. These poles are said to be unified, because what appears to be separate is found under analysis to be inseparable and having the same root, hence the term unity in duality.

While a full discussion of the referential object (as mentioned above in item 1) is beyond the scope of this work, it is discussed in some detail in the following sections on the third and fourth mindfulness practices. One important issue with regard to the subject–object polarity and the subject–"referential object" interrelationship is that these have different bases or roots. The subject–object poles are entirely rooted in the personal sphere where the object, as experienced, is a personal formation of reality. This ordinary object appearance should not be mistaken as the referential object, which root is of the universal sphere, no matter what it is or how it truly exists. The only reality we have any say in creating, particularly in the context of mental and physical health, is that which we ordinarily take to mind through our senses and other faculties, the object poles.

Terms of analysis 2: Types of mind and body   The philosophy and practice of EIS examine reality on the basis of the interrelatedness of phenomena and the self-referential[6] nature of experience, and provide an analysis of reality in terms of phenomena and mind. Phenomena are the objects of perception appearing to the mind (i.e., the idea of a table, a feeling, the form and color of a thing, etc.), and the mind is the subject of perception. The terms *mind* or *minds* are used herein to refer to the types or character of consciousness that experience phenomena. The mind is categorized into the five *sense minds* and a *sixth mind* that includes three subcategories: the *conceptual, feeling,* and *image minds.*

The physical body with the five basic senses (taste, touch, smell, sight, and hearing) provides the basis for perception. The sense organs and sense abilities are considered as faculties of the five sense minds that directly perceive phenomena and are independent of cognitive functions (language, labels, memory, concepts, etc.).

The *sixth mind* constitutes mental factors such as feeling, thinking, image and representation, cognition, memory, and so on, and is categorized into three minds, the *conceptual, feeling,* and *image minds.* An additional category of *subtle bodies* is included in the category of the sixth mind,[7] that is, these do not belong to the category of the five sense minds.

A *subtle body* is, for instance, the body in our dreams. When dreaming, we rely on the dream body to sense the world, just as we rely on the physical body when awake, but the dream body has a greater and more subtle range of sensory capabilities and a wider range of bodily abilities (e.g., flying). EIS holds that the subtle body and subtle mind have a wider range of perception and movement than the physical body and ordinary mind.

Although we could discuss a number of levels of subtle embodiment from the ordinary body in dreams to the body used for focused imagination or visualization and onward, the terms subtle body and mind are used herein to refer to the body used by very advanced spiritual practitioners who have achieved Śamatha and Vipassanā, and are well practiced in Mindfulness. At this level, advanced practitioners train to extend their subtle body and mind in manifest referential reality. Such experiences are held to be real in the sense that they are not imagined or necessarily private.

Subtle bodies and minds of the sort discussed above are the rare result of extensive spiritually based body–mind training and proceed in stages where the practitioner gains awareness of ever-more subtle aspects of body, mind, and reality. The early stages of such training are focused on balancing and stabilizing the mind in ways and with aims that are different from, but not entirely unlike, those of modern psychology.

UD has adapted these methods of training and applies them to more ordinary aims such as personal development and psychological health. In this regard, we introduce the term *imagery-body*, which is akin to subtle body but at a much less elevated level. At the most basic level, the imagery-body is the same as that used by athletes and artists, for example when a gymnast or musician mentally rehearses the physical movements of their craft. This technique is also used in modern psychotherapy and called by different names such as guided practice, embodied imagination, and so on. But at this level, the imagery-body is still a private experience. At more advanced levels of imagery-body, we can begin to experience the commons of manifest referential reality at more subtle levels than available through the physical senses and ordinary capacities of the sixth mind. These distinctions will become clearer as we proceed.

In the remaining part of this section, we continue to use the term subtle body, but it should be considered that the term imagery-body applies generally and analogously to the discussion as well.

EIS asserts that the mind and body, experienced at any level from the gross physical to very subtle, are mutually dependent, interrelated phenomena and that the mind always has an embodiment of some kind as the basis for experience. EIS further posits the subtle body and mind as real and concurrent with subtle realities. Mindfulness training and UD cultivate awareness based on subtle embodiments, and concurrently develop more subtle mental capacities, albeit at different levels, but in the early stages they are similar. The subtle embodiments allow for a more extensive and less projective (e.g., in the sense of conceptual interpretation) experience of reality.

The ordinary activities of mind arise on a *momentary* basis and operate through the capacities of the five sense minds and/or aspects of the sixth mind[8] (conceptual, feeling, image minds, and subtle body senses). None of these minds can directly experience another mind's domain. Each sense mind's way of experiencing is unique, as are each of the aspects of the sixth mind; for example, the conceptual mind can only experience words and ideas, or *conceptual reality*, which is not accessible by any other types of mind. While functioning uniquely, all of the minds influence experience, particularly that of the three sixth minds, and more so when we are conceptually or emotionally dominated.

Normally, according to EIS, in the waking state we experience sense reality by means of the sense minds. The mind experiences phenomena through the physical body's five senses, becoming the respective five sense minds. According to EIS, no mind is waiting to experience but arises momentarily when the right conditions are present, in this case, when there are functional senses and referential object of the respective sense mind. Also that means that the individual sense mind and the referential sense object arise simultaneously.

The sixth mind has three parts, of which, one, the conceptual mind, operates through means that are *indirect* inasmuch as it abstracts and uses language as the basis for perceiving/cognizing/experiencing the object. The other parts, the feeling and image minds, provide *direct* means to experience phenomena, because they don't use abstraction and language for perception and therefore cannot add or delete anything. These three minds and the subtle bodies are outlined below. The subtle bodies are included here because their nature is not based on the physical body, and they are thus considered part of the sixth mind.

1 Sixth mind: Tarab Tulku explicitly categorizes the sixth mind into three types of mind that are important for explaining the dynamics of mind, and which he holds to be implicit in the Sutras and Tantras.[9]

2 The *conceptual mind*[10] experiences only by means of naming and language, and thereby generates a dynamic, momentary, abstract, and generalized experience of reality.

3 *Image mind* provides the three-dimensional experience of form and space. For example, visual and aural sensory information gives us mental images of the spatial characteristics of phenomena such as distance and dimension, like visual images of objects such as a chair or table, and aural images provide spatial characteristics of place and distance. The image mind operates momentarily through its perceptive capacities, giving us a dynamic field of image reality.

4 The *feeling mind*[11] provides, for instance, the basic evaluative feeling experience as supportive, neutral, or negative regarding the continuation of existence, and on this basis we conceptually make further judgments and evaluations, and take actions accordingly. Feeling in this context does not refer to the language labels we ordinarily apply to our feelings; that is the role of the conceptual mind. The feeling mind, while able to experience qualities of feeling (e.g., intuition, instinct, empathy, emotion, feeling-tone, self-referential feeling, deep meditative states), is not capable of labeling its object. In this sense, the feeling mind is characterized by touching and uniting with its object, subject and object poles being inseparably together (e.g., the feeling of the feeling mind is feeling)—it provides a unified way of experiencing. The feeling mind operates momentarily and is unique because it is the only mind that is naturally unifying.

When conceptually and emotionally dominated, the experience of the image mind is specifically responsive to what the conceptual mind names, and on this basis the feeling mind gives rise to experiences of emotions, happiness, and so on. To a high degree, our normal human experience in modern cultures is based on the perceptions of the conceptual mind, which is dependent on sense minds, which is again dependent upon the physical body's sense organs. Experience is thus strongly connected with the conceptual mind and the physical body.

The conceptual mind is by nature selective in its capacity to render phenomena empirically or experientially. Only that which is named becomes part of the conceptual reality. It is because of the abstraction, generalization, and selectivity of language that the conceptual mind enables us to compare and analyze phenomena, by naming only particulars of interest to represent the whole of an object (the rest staying conceptually unnoticed). The conceptual cognitive capacity naturally and subconsciously screens out the particulars it doesn't name. It can also add information to the perception of sense reality such as ideas about ownership, intention, causation, quality, value, and so on by force of habit, acculturation, education, and past experience, and so on. The conceptual mind can also recall the past and predict future events. Because the conceptual mind is limited to interpreting the selected sense data, rather than experiencing them directly and completely in their interrelated complexity, it has no inherent capacity to directly experience sense reality or to have any other direct experience of reality.

According to EIS, it is possible to experience phenomena without engaging the conceptual mind, in other words, without naming or thinking about that which we perceive, though this way of experiencing is very different and unconventional compared with normal conceptual experience. Where the experience of conceptual mind is considered a generalization and abstraction of sensory and other experiences, and therefore indirect, the feeling and image categories of sixth mind are seen as direct experience[12] (inasmuch as they do not use language).

The three types of sixth mind represent specific ways in which we experience reality, and two of these correspond with the sense fields. The body sense, and senses of taste and smell (subject and object poles being naturally unified), are in this manner similar to the *feeling* mind, and seeing and hearing (perceiving image, space, and dimension) are similar to the *image* mind of experiencing form and spatial relations.

Because the feeling and image minds perceive directly, their experience is contemporaneous with whatever is presented to them. Nevertheless, while the experience of the feeling and image minds may be direct and in the present moment, it should be noted that we cannot absolutely and directly experience the "referential object" with any type of mind.[13] This is because all minds have limited and specific perceptual faculties, which, in meeting with the referential object, determine the way reality appears. This counts equally for direct and indirect ways of experiencing.

Furthermore, it should be mentioned that the five sense minds (subject poles) and their respective objects (object poles) are seen as being interrelated and separate from each other, with no overlapping perception. The five sense minds and the three sixth minds all independently perceive their object. Each mind has a subject and object pole, as these are inherent in the nature of perception. These minds are interrelated, but there is no overlapping perception or sharing of one mind's object pole with another mind.

For example, the eye sense mind perceives an object, let's say the form and color of a bird, and the hearing mind perceives its object, the sound of a bird's song, at the same time. The ear and the eye senses perceive independently of each other with no overlap. Like the five sense minds, the conceptual, feeling, and image minds are respectively interrelated but with no overlapping perception. All the minds are interrelated, which may lead to the composite experience of a "beautiful singing bird," but this experience is a product of the interrelationship and cooperation of perceived phenomena.

EIS distinguishes different subtleties of body and mind. On the most apparent level, that of conceptual mind and the gross physical body, we have the least subtle and most common and dominant of all body–mind experiences. Through traditional

Mindfulness practices, a subtle body–mind basis for experience is cultivated. The subtle body and mind have the basis of the sixth mind. EIS states that with the subtle mind and body, we have the capacity to experience subtleties of referential reality. The ability to use subtle body and mind requires special training and practice, and, once accomplished, the experience of referential reality becomes deeper and more extensive. An adept experiences reality according to the subtlety of the body and mind they have engaged. Just as in ordinary dreams, although in this case the experience is veridical, the dimensions of time and space may open up (at random or upon mastering this body–mind), and aspects of body and mind such as intuition, perception, and freedom of movement are greatly enhanced.

All of the minds discussed, for those who are mindful of them, give very different experiences of reality. While we conventionally do not pay close attention to anything but the conceptual mind, with greater awareness our experience of reality could be very different and much deeper and broader than ordinarily experienced.

Traditional Mindfulness and UD Mindfulness for Physical and Mental Health and Traditional Mindfulness and UD Mindfulness for Spiritual Ends

The body–mind basis for traditional Mindfulness

The achievement of Śamatha meditation practice is a prerequisite for practice of the four Mindfulness meditations. Śamatha is a type of meditation practice that implies a shift from conceptual dominance to the dominance of the directly perceiving minds, and it also implies a shift to a more subtle body base. The practice and attainments of Śamatha are beyond the scope of this chapter; however the preliminary result of this practice is a stable and calm mind. The practitioner trains to focus on an object without effort or distraction from random thoughts, memories, disturbing emotions, sleepiness, and so on—as long as one wishes. This ability is often referred to as one-pointed concentration.

On the basis of this first part of Śamatha attainment, training in visualizing and mastery of the first level of subtle body–mind and the subtle sight mind in particular can begin. Visualization, which implies the use of the subtle body visual sense mind to see, provides a method for training in using the subtle body, for instance in connection with the Mindfulness investigations, to experiencing the nature of increasingly deeper levels of reality.

In Śamatha attainment:

1 there is the ability in particular to use the first level of the subtle body's eye-sense mind with the same acuity as that of the physical eye-sense mind resulting in very clear visualizations;
2 one-pointed concentration is the ability to stay with the visualization or feeling mind object for as long as one wishes.

These two points make the Traditional Mindfulness Meditations a "high practice."

In accordance with Vasubandhu and others, the four Traditional Mindfulness Meditations are practiced in three consecutive stages:

1 Śamatha: one-pointed meditation attainment, using subtle body;
2 Vipassanā: investigative Mindfulness meditation based on Śamatha attainment, realizing the nature of the object under investigation. (Vipassanā is explained below);
3 unity of Śamatha and Vipassanā: meditation merging with the realization of the object of investigation.

In the remaining discussion of these practices, our focus will shift from a description of the traditional application of the Mindfulness meditations and methods as a spiritual discipline to more practical applications for use in personal development and therapeutic methodology, as recommended and developed by Tarab Tulku under UD. In this framework, we refer to semi-Śamatha, semi-Vipassanā, and semi- *Unity of* Śamatha *and* Vipassanā.

Semi-Śamatha: One-pointed UD meditation attainment—using imagery-body   Since Śamatha practice is not simple, and very few people attain its goal of using the subtle body as a basis for experience, Tarab Tulku suggests that for personal development and psychotherapeutic work, one can use an embodiment "in-between" our normal physical body and a subtle body, which is called an *imagery-body*. Imagery-body is the embodiment we use when daydreaming, for improving sport performances or the kind of embodiments that are used in guided psychotherapy. Imagery-body is connected with the energy level of the physical body and can be used for practical purposes, as described later.

But what is this imagery-body? In the Abhidharmakosa, Vasubandhu differentiates between two levels of body sensation: the ordinary body sensations of temperature, pressure, pain, etc., and deeper or subtle body sensations (Abidharmakosa-bhasyam, 1988). This deeper level of body sensation is connected to and experienced as the energy basis for the physical body. When connected with the latter, one gains access to a deeper and stronger inner presence and a deeper experience with regard to "other"[14] phenomena in the perceptual field. An imagery-body, as the basis for investigation, thus provides the possibility for deeper insight into how specific, more superficial minds function and how their corresponding realities come about. This makes it more apparent to the practitioner how the mind is involved in the appearance of reality (object pole). Using imagery-body as described above, one comes to experience a deeper level of reality and, based upon directly perceiving minds, enables one to experience a larger number of particulars (object pole). It also enables one more easily to become one-pointed (i.e., not being conceptually determined).

Semi-Vipassanā: Investigative UD mindfulness meditation—based on semi-Śamatha attainment   Semi-Vipassanā meditation is the analytical investigation[15] into the nature of mind and phenomena. It requires a kind of being where the faculties of the subtle body provide the basis for the various minds being applied to the object under investigation. In this UD investigative meditation, one stays in contact with oneself and the object of investigation using feeling-mind and image-mind on the basis of the imagery-body.

Using direct (nonlanguage) experience and awareness enables one to stay in contact with the causal and ever-changing-phenomenal-nature of reality, beyond language selection and fixation, providing a complete experience with all the particulars available (within the range and limitations of the particular body basis and perceptive faculty used).

Conceptual reality doesn't follow the changing process of the "referential reality"; it is a fixated reality, as its object is of an abstracted and generalized nature. For changing ideas, we conceptually rely on changing the words one by one, making up a different conceptual reality, which again is fixating reality in a new idea—in this way, it can of course address ever-changing reality, but only in general terms. However, rather than being the dominant mode of perception, on the basis of imagery-body and directly perceiving image and feeling realities, the conceptual mind is used in cooperation with the other types of mind and becomes a more subtle[16] and very useful tool for investigation and realization, letting us stay in contact with the direct experience of the object under investigation.

Unity of semi-Śamatha and semi-Vipassanā: UD mindfulness meditation merging with the realization of the object of investigation   When, through investigative mindfulness meditation, as described above, we reach a certain level of accomplishment or realization in connection with the nature of the object under investigation, we merge or unite with this realization of the nature of the object of investigation. This is, in a sense, a collapse of the subject–object dichotomy and is accomplished using imagery-body and feeling mind experience. We stay merged with the realization of the object's nature, as long as we wish, assimilating the realization.

The four Mindfulness meditations and UD mindfulness

According to Vasubandhu, the four Mindfulness meditations are as follows:

*   Mindfulness of body;[17]
*   Mindfulness of feeling-tone;[18]
*   Mindfulness of mind;[19]
*   Mindfulness of phenomena.[20]

In the text (Abidharmakosabhasyam, 1988), it says: "You have to find the general and special characteristics of 'body,' 'feeling,' 'mind' and 'phenomena'." With "characteristics," they point to the specific nature of the subject-poles, the object-poles, and the referential object. Thus, the investigative field of the four Mindfulness practices encompasses investigation into the nature of all existence, first on the level of the conventional or ordinary experience of reality and then on deeper and more fundamental levels of reality, which is unconventional and extraordinary.

From a UD point of view, for personal growth and therapy, the most important aspects of these investigative methods pertain to developing an understanding of how we participate in the appearance of ordinary reality. This investigation and the realization that follows give us the best opportunity to deal with ourselves and our reality in regard to our health and environment. Due to the limited scope of this presentation, even though we will present the fourth mindfulness training concerning phenomena, we will not analyze the "referential object" in much detail, because it is primarily relevant to spiritual practice and much less relevant to mental and somatic health issues. The remaining portion of this section presents suggestions from a UD point of view only of the investigative part of the mindfulness meditations, as that is most relevant in this context, all of which should be done on the basis of imagery-body.

First Mindfulness: UD mindfulness on "body"[21] and corresponding "phenomena"

In traditional Mindfulness, the term "body" refers to any form or embodiment of one's entity existence that is present to the sense minds and the sixth mind, including but not limited to the physical body. However, in UD, in this context we are concerned only with the investigation of our physical human body and its five sense minds, especially the body sense.

The body sense, in this context of mindfulness, includes all of the five basic senses (touch, smell, taste, sight, and hearing), but *touch* is inadequate to describe the totality of body sense. The somatic body sense in particular is very complex, a fact that is often taken for granted, and includes touch (pressure), temperature, pain and pleasure, movement, weight, and energy, and provides a wide range of gross and subtle sensations.[22] As we discuss the body sense, it is important to keep in mind the gross and subtle levels of sensation and the great depth and range of the sense minds.

According to EIS, specifically Dignaga (AD 480–540) and later Dharmakirti (AD 600–660), the five sense minds perceive directly. They do not use language, so they have no ability to pick and choose or isolate, as we do conceptually when naming a particular aspect of the referential object in question. Since the sense minds don't use language, they can only perceive in the present moment, and naturally and indiscriminately perceive what appears to them. To quote from Dharmakirti: "When the nature of a thing is cognized in direct perception all of its aspects are cognized …" (Zwilling, 1976). "All of its aspects" refers only to the aspects that are available for the particular sense mind in a particular moment under any particular circumstance and within the range of this direct faculty, that is, the sense minds are not selective with regard to the range of sensory information acquired by them.

That the senses have a counteractive effect on emotions and other mental disturbances is well known in the West as well as in the East. Our languages are full of common expressions referring to this wisdom with sayings like "come back to your senses," "count to ten," and "take a deep breath," all of which are meant to bring us back into the present and in touch with the common ground of human experience. Coming back to the present, which is possible only with direct perception, has a calming effect on the body and mind, and is an excellent antistressing method in itself (Grossman, Niemann, Schmidt, & Walach, 2004; Kabat-Zinn, 2003). The sense experience has the power to counteract the conceptual mind's tendency to grasp and hold its perceptions by making available other particulars from the sense field that were previously excluded from the conceptual reality.

This is particularly important for personal development and psychotherapy. Vulnerable self-references like feelings of persecution, inferiority, or insecurity, and habitual fixations of conceptual reality, such as prejudices, cultural taboos, and phobias, tend to engender distressful mental experiences. These tendencies, helped by the conceptual mind, are normally mildly dissociative in the sense that they represent a disconnection from or loss of direct perception by the senses and are thereby unique to the perceiving individual. They are not generally shared by others, nor are they part of common human experience. These conceptual realities, while they appear real to the perceiver, never become reality for the senses. So, to come back to the sense experience is a great and perhaps necessary means to reconnect to reality and undercut illusory and destructive mental tendencies.

This practice of connecting to the sense minds also helps one to recover from destructive conceptual perceptions of self. Coming back to one's senses, especially at a deeper level, helps to overcome the gap between a grounded sense of self and the conceptual idea of self; it builds a sense of inner strength and self-presence, and undercuts the dissociative tendencies that naturally arise due to domination of the conceptual mind. Without these mitigating factors, the negative tendencies of the conceptual mind would cause or exacerbate stress and stress-related psychosomatic conditions. By practicing this method, one recovers a firm and stable ground of being and an increased sense of self-worth and self-confidence.

All of these mitigating factors help to reduce the experience of existential fear— fear of destruction of that which is conceptually identified as self. Such existential fear is basic to all negative emotions. Cultivating ordinary body sense and imagery-body sense and making this the self-referential basis of experience, rather than just the conceptual idea of oneself, help one to reduce and eventually eliminate the habit of engaging with destructive emotions.[23]

Western culture and philosophy have placed much emphasis on reason, rationality, and logic in investigations of reality, almost exclusively through the use of conceptual thinking and an objective analysis of external phenomena. While this approach has made significant contributions to human understanding, relatively little attention has been focused on the inner nature of mind, body, experience, and the interrelated perception of reality, which is so fundamental to the approach found in EIS and UD and which is much more common in Eastern cultures. In modern times, with the media's relentless cultural dissemination and emphasis on individualism, materialism, and consumption, many people in the West (and increasingly those in the East) have largely lost touch with the body sense as the basis for a common human experience of reality. Due to the dominance of the conceptual mind, its view of reality fails to connect with common human perception of reality or to recognize the interrelatedness of phenomena, especially that of the mind, body, and reality. Because many people in modern cultures are not being united with direct experience of body sensations, they are showing early symptoms of dissociative or more severe disorders, which cause people to become sensitive and easily vulnerable, as supported by current research in this area (D. J. Siegel, 2010a).

Since all human beings have the same kind of senses and therefore sense experience (unless these are impaired), the sense reality is our common ground of reference. Seen from a personal development or psychotherapeutic perspective, it is strongly empowering for the individual to recognize this and to develop a common referential ground using the two levels of body sense and any other type of direct sensing. By developing a stronger connection to direct sense perception, one is better able to intuit the sensations of others and in conversation to better understand what they mean, a condition that would help to prevent many misunderstandings.

In UD, it is recommended that the practice of experiencing and connecting with the ordinary somatic body sense or imagery-body sense be conducted daily through meditation and/or by being generally mindful throughout the day when doing routine activities such as exercising, bathing, martial arts, and so on. Most important is that the mind is brought back into being aware of the body sense experience, preferably many times each day (and ultimately to maintain this awareness throughout the day), which will make one feel grounded, safe, and at home within.

Points of investigation in UD mindfulness meditation on body sense mind/reality:

- Do the sense minds experience past, present, or future?
- Can we have sense experience without using language?
- Do the sense minds pick and choose what they perceive or experience, of what is reflected within their range and respective perceptual fields?
- Do the sense experiences make available a shared, cross-cultural reality?
- Could the body sense counteract dissociative tendencies?
- Can the sense minds, especially body sense, counteract a narrow conceptually named field, especially when we are emotionally distressed or just stressed, and thereby bring us into a less projective and emotionally distressful condition?
- Would grounding by means of body sensing diminish fear?
- Does body sense open intuitive feeling when in contact with others?
- Do we have a deeper level of body sense through which we can contact a deeper inner strength in ourselves?

Special points of investigation—when firmly rooted in body sense mind/reality　Normally, we consider sense reality to exist "out there," independent of the senses, but the view of UD, resting on the shoulders of EIS, tells us that this is not so. If our senses were constructed differently, our sense reality would likewise be different, as is the case for other species. On this basis, we can consider the extent to which sense experience is based on the perceptual capacity of our senses, and therefore is internally determined, rather than as a direct experience of phenomena as they conventionally appear to exist "out there."

For spiritual development, the relational nature of the sense field becomes very interesting and necessary to realize in order to go beyond the physical body and the sense realm, and to enter the deeper fields of existence, the spiritual realm.

Therefore, for advanced practitioners, who are firmly rooted in body–mind as the basis for investigation, and *for no one else*, the interrelation between the subject-pole and the object-pole of the sense realm could be investigated to determine whether the object-pole exists in and of itself on the outside.

Advantages found in UD mindfulness meditation on physical body sense mind/reality—on the basis of achieved equality between body sensing and conceptual perception:

- concordance with the common human basis (sense minds) of reality;
- connecting directly to the body sense brings awareness into the present and relieves stress;
- enhancing one's ability for clear, nonprojective communication;
- increased intuitive ability with self and others;
- decreased restlessness and existential fear;
- greater ability to deal more appropriately with difficult situations;
- reduced dissociative tendencies and related stress;
- reduction of habitual engagement with destructive emotions (fear, etc.) and related stress;
- supporting greater self-confidence and self-worth;
- increased capability for natural somatic healing.

Second Mindfulness: UD mindfulness on "feeling-tone" and corresponding "phenomena"

The next Mindfulness Meditation deals with feeling-tone.[24] According to UD, any living entity in existence has basic evaluative feeling-tone[25]—not just humans and animals, even plants—based on attraction to that which feels as though it is sustaining the continuation of the entity's existence and rejection or avoidance of that which feels that it could hinder continuation. Evaluative feeling-tone is the initial stage of our actions in life—the feeling-tone is fundamental to action. Without evaluative feeling-tone or feeling in general, there would be no incentive to act.

According to EIS, the subtle, evaluative feeling-tone is always present with any mental experience. Connecting to the feeling-tone of mind means to connect with the sixth mind on a deeper and quieter level with an expanded feeling of oneself. Through this experience, it's possible to have a basic and united feeling of body and mind as well as of subject and object and at the same time a feeling of not being so separate from others.

Based on the sensations of the body and bringing awareness to the feeling-tone of mind helps to overcome the gap between the conceptual ideas of self and simply feeling oneself from inside. There are many levels of this unification, each level bringing one into deeper and stronger contact with one's inner feeling of being present.

Points of investigation in UD mindfulness meditation on feeling-tone/reality:

- Is there something that could be recognized as feeling-tone?
- Do we have evaluative feeling-tone in connection with any perception by either of the five sense minds and sixth minds?
- Is feeling-tone basic to what we choose to name conceptually and does it therefore become an important determining factor for our formation of reality and action?

- Does contacting basic feeling-tone one-pointedly counteract fear?
- Does contacting feeling tone counteract feelings of isolation and loneliness?

Advantages found in UD mindfulness meditation on feeling-tone/phenomena   Reuniting through feeling-tone with oneself and others, counteracting the gap between the conceptual ideas of self and simply feeling oneself from inside:

- gives the individual a way to feel "at home" and safe;
- counteracts disassociation;
- gives a feeling of expansion, incorporating others, and counteracts feelings of loneliness, separation, and isolation;
- increases confidence about one's feelings making one less vulnerable to doubt and manipulation;
- counteracts the gap between the conceptual ideas of self and simply feeling oneself from inside.

Third Mindfulness: UD mindfulness of "mind"[26] and corresponding "phenomena"

In EIS, mind is categorized into the five sense minds and the sixth mind, as already mentioned. The sense minds have been discussed, so here we have three types of sixth mind according to Tarab Tulku's tripartation into conceptual mind, image mind, and feeling mind.

UD mindfulness investigation on mind—in regard to conceptual mind and corresponding conceptual phenomena/conceptual reality

EIS philosophers, realizing the interrelated nature of phenomena,[27] have not investigated mind (subject-pole) without also investigating its object (object-pole) and vice versa. And because realization of these interrelationships is valuable for health and relations with others, these are investigated here, too.

Dignaga (AD 480–540) and Dharmakirti (AD 650), the latter presenting Dignaga's Pramāña work in a more understandable way, was the first to comprise and systematize Buddhist logic, rejecting the prevailing theory by claiming that the conceptual mind cannot directly perceive sense-reality. The conceptual mind can only perceive indirectly by means of the nonaffirmative generalization,[28] literally translated as "exclusion from the other." In other words, the conceptual mind perceives by means of a "general differentiation of similars and dissimilars in one go," mirroring the naturally inherent differentiation of similars and dissimilars[29] in regard to the sense object. This means that the conceptual mind's object-pole is based only on the labels projected onto the object in question, giving an affirmative perception and thus achieving the abstraction and isolation of the perceived object. This way of perceiving is very different from that of the senses.

A consequence of the conceptual mind's unconscious screening out of everything except that which is selected and named, thereby isolating its object, is great flexibility and freedom to build conceptual reality. However, the conceptual reality seems to appear as an independent phenomenon existing "out there" in its own right, in the exact way we experience it. So apart from bringing about a way to grasp hold of and communicate about reality, the naming and language used, which is based on general differentiation of similars and dissimilars, at the same time conceals the abstract and nonaffirmative nature of the conceptual formation and all the unnamed particulars, whereby we easily mistake the conceptual object for the sense object. In other words, we incorrectly and unconsciously accept the conceptual object as one and the same as the sense object.

The way in which the conceptual mind conceals the individual nature of a phenomenon, by naming only selected aspects with labels and categories, is clearly expressed by Kamalashila, in his Tattvasangrahapanjika (Zwilling, 1976):

> Conceptual identification. … is imputed upon numerically different particulars as their common character. … conceptual cognition conceals the individual nature of those things by superimposing a unity upon them, which is its own creation. The superimposition of such a unity results in the particulars being conceived of as similar. (Zwilling, 1976)

The ability to abstract lifts the human mind out of the otherwise strong bondage to sense reality and paves the way for comparison, reasoning, and analysis, and thereby for thinking and reflection as well as for our specific human way of communication on the basis of language. Also, as already mentioned, it forms the basis for the great flexibility and freedom of mind that only humans are known to enjoy.

The ability of the conceptual mind to screen, isolate, and select aspects of observed phenomena has nothing but positive impacts, as long as there is a natural balance among the different ways of accessing reality. However, when the gross conceptual mind, with its specific conceptual reality, overly dominates, and especially if we are engaged with vulnerable self-referential feelings,[30] we create a problematic reality for ourselves. When the conceptual mind and its conceptual reality take over, there is little opportunity for direct sense experience, leaving us with nothing to counteract the deficiencies of the selected, named, and identified conceptual reality.

Abstraction by "general differentiation of similars and dissimilars in one go" as well as "naming" doesn't simply define our conceptual relationship to the outer world; it also defines our conceptual relation to self. A dominant conceptual mind narrows the experience of self in the same way it limits that of phenomena conventionally perceived as outside oneself. Our modern world culture has an alienating effect on people with regard to their perceptions of self and other, which is normalized along with the increasing dominance of the conceptual mind. Many people in modern cultures experience a distance to everything, including to themselves, which often results in an experience of loneliness and emptiness, and, in the worst cases, can lead to paranoia and other desperate dissociative conditions, at times leading to suicide or violating aggressive behavior.

Based on that which is named through this abstracting process, the conceptual mind operates with the sense that its perception of a given experience or situation is complete, regardless of how many phenomenal aspects have or haven't been conceptually addressed. Recognizing this, we are left with the conceptual freedom to create another "complete idea" based on other chosen and named points of reference. In other words, this recognition leaves us with the great prospect of a highly flexible mind that is able to counteract the closed mindedness inherent with an overly dominant conceptual mind. This knowledge is already being used to a certain degree within counseling and psychotherapy today, as within the different types of therapeutic mindfulness practices. It should be further emphasized that, in accordance with EIS and UD, the conceptual mind has no direct[31] means to distinguish between the conceptual reality and the sense reality, as the sense reality is not within its field of experience.

When the conceptual field overly dominates our sense field and thereby limits our ability to differentiate and generate a complete experience, our capacity for reality determination is severely narrowed, and this can have other important implications for how our reality formations are determined. For example, such limitation makes us much more easily manipulated, giving unnecessary influence to television, newspapers, the advertising industry, or our own preconceived ideas about who we are and what we can and cannot do, or to such vulnerable notions that other people are in some unrealistic way against us. An overly dominant conceptual mind narrows and limits our ability to perceive reality and gives too much access and power to these and other forms of reality determination.

But most importantly, while we often believe that we are using the sense minds, we are usually relying on conceptually and selectively formed descriptions of what has appeared to the senses. We thereby impair our natural ability to get our feet on the ground, to counteract or compensate the conceptual mind's natural selectivity, when things are "getting out of hand" or "driving us out of our minds," especially under emotional or mentally disturbed conditions. This is in accord with what Steven C. Hayes says in connection with training clients "not to take the map for the territory": "The point is to begin to learn how to look at thoughts rather than looking at the world through thoughts, and to learn how to detect the difference" (Hayes, Follette, & Linehan, 2004).

For better or worse, people are free to choose what the conceptual mind names and therefore what becomes the basis for a given perception of reality. Nevertheless, people have a tendency to become habituated to certain perceptions of reality and are therefore conceptually dominated in ways that are certainly selective and may appear biased or even intentional, and this can occur at various levels of human interaction.

Everyone adopts culture in a particular way according to the specific environment in which one is raised. People assimilate cultural norms and social values into a uniquely conceived and conceptually based view of reality. On this basis, we can understand some of the fundamental reasons behind misunderstandings and clashes between cultures. Language, which is foundational to culture, also carries such biases and selectiveness even within the same or similar types of cultures. At the group, family, and individual levels, various and more idiosyncratic conceptual realities will form on a wider continuum between so-called normal and pathologically structured views of reality. For those who are conceptually dominated, it is very difficult to realize that none of these conceptual realities exist by themselves but are continuously reproduced through language, which is the basis of all conceptual thinking. At an individual level, due to different experiences in life, we create different self-referential imprints,[32] for example good versus vulnerable self-referential feelings. As the conceptual mind abstracts from sense-reality and as its experience appears on the basis of just a few selected and named points of reference of an otherwise complex and interrelated reality, it is particularly receptive to the prevailing imprints of self-referential feeling.

On the basis of a relatively permanent personal crisis, determined by prevailing vulnerable self-references, the conceptual selectiveness becomes increasingly idiosyncratic and pathological in terms of its lack of reference to a commonly shared sense reality. On a more permanent basis, where, through a force of habit, individuals mistake the appearance of conceptual reality as sense reality, persons may hallucinate under certain circumstances, especially when vulnerably loaded self-referential imprints take over—similar to nightmares, but in the waking state.

None of this diminishes the importance of the conceptual mind for our thinking, reasoning, analysis, and communication; in fact, we would appreciate this ability even more if we realized its flexible nature and its inability to directly perceive the sense field and the dynamic and ever-changing field of phenomena. For this and other reasons, we should also realize that conceptual reality should not stand alone but needs to be compensated by direct types of perceptions to get a more complete "picture" of the phenomenal field all together.

Points of investigation for UD mindfulness meditation in regard to conceptual mind and corresponding phenomena:

- Are the different sense realities and conceptual reality the same or different and in which way might they be different?
- Does the conceptual mind only have the perceptual means of using language in order to grasp its object (and in that way only has indirect access to the sense reality, etc.) or are there other means open to the conceptual mind?
- Does conceptual reality exist in and of itself on the outside or is it interrelated with the subject-pole?
- Investigate whether or not conceptual reality is a generalized and abstracted reality in line with Dignaga and Dharmakirti's analysis as outlined above, and whether or not the conceptual mind screens out what it doesn't name, not knowing that it screens anything out; and whether conceptual mind therefore by nature isolates what it addresses.

Advantages found in UD mindfulness meditation—regarding conceptual mind and corresponding phenomena, on realizing that conceptual reality is not the same as sense reality and that conceptual reality doesn't exist out there in and of itself:

- provide a choice in how to build conceptual reality and change it by naming some other particulars;
- no longer determine so strongly what is mentally "seen" and felt;
- enable one to change habitual thought patterns and fixation of reality through language;
- give one the power of choosing to reproduce conceptual reality (in its cultural, social, and individual varieties);

- reduce the stress inflicted by believing in such fixations as "being difficult," "impossible," "against me," "sick," and so on;
- change the determining effect conceptual reality has on image and feeling realities, diminishing its otherwise independent role of establishing reality.

UD mindfulness investigation on mind—regarding mental-image mind and corresponding image phenomena

The image mind provides us with a sense of space, dimensionality, and form that gives us an overall sense of place and solidness in reality. We have discussed how the senses of seeing and hearing help to provide an experience of distance between subject and object, and the image mind has similar capabilities. For instance, descriptions are usually accompanied by the experience of mental images, as when reading a book and the imagination provides dimensionality to the scenes being described.

In the waking state, when mentally created images become vividly clear and dominant, overruling the sense experiences, they are imagination, visions, visualizations, hallucinations, or images accompanying conceptual description specifically in relation with emotions. The apparitions connected with emotions and hallucinations appear with such clarity, as if one had seen them by using the physical eyes. However, they are seen only by the sixth mind's eyes.

The images experienced in dreams are of the sixth mind. According to UD, the reason these images are formed is that we have mental and self-referential imprints and imprinted mental patterns, and even collective and universal imprints. The dream images can be good, bad, or neutral, and they arise in connection with particular self-referential feelings. When a self-reference is negative, we can have mental images rising in the form of nightmares, where secondary causes such as events that have occurred during the day trigger underlying self-referential imprints to arise as dreams—for example, specific fears relating to our vulnerabilities.

People in the waking state, when emotionally or mentally unbalanced and even when they are not, can see things that other people don't see. These images are also not sense images, even if we mistake them to be, but rather sixth-mind images. When people want to convince you, they often say, "I have seen it with my own eyes." Actually, we have this problem more often than we are aware. We just think we have seen it with our physical sense minds, but very often it is not true, a fact well known to police investigators when eye-witnesses report very different things, even though they all saw the exact same events. In this way, we actually see with our mental image mind, or the sixth sense eyes, more often than commonly believed.

Points of investigation in mindfulness meditation—regarding image mind and corresponding phenomena:

- Do we and other people have different types of image realities in connection with everyday experiences, such as daydreaming, imagination, and night dreams, and even extraordinary experiences, such as visions and hallucinations?
- Do these realities exist "out there" in and of themselves or are all these mental reality appearances interrelated with "image mind"?

- Are there specific embodiments as a base for these different image experiences like daydream, imagination, night dream, and so on, or do they all rely on the physical body or no embodiment?
- Could there be something to the saying that "we learn to see," so there would be cultural, social, and individual aspects to the appearances we "see" mentally?
- Are these mental "image" realities influenced by what is named, that is, conceptual reality?
- Would that mean that I could have a say in the way reality appears to me?
- Could self-references influence the way image reality appears, and if so, would that be all the time or under specific conditions?

Advantages found in UD mindfulness meditation—regarding image mind and corresponding phenomena, on realizing that mental-image reality doesn't exist "out there" in and of itself, and that it is not sense mind appearances:

- can provide important insight into the say one has over the appearance of reality, in terms of being less determined by conceptually dominated perception and therefore giving more determinative power on the subject-side;
- helps one to break the habits of conceptually dominated perception based on vulnerable self-references that otherwise could result in feelings of depression, paranoia, and victimization.

UD mindfulness investigation on mind—regarding feeling mind and corresponding phenomena

The many types and levels of feeling range from the deepest, totally uniting third meditation state, which is the deepest meditation state,[33] to the subtlety of shifting moods or the most expressive and violent emotions. However, in UD, we are mainly concerned in this context with the feeling mind (subject-pole) and the more or less normal feelings (object-pole) that we all experience in our daily lives.

We saw under "feeling-tone" that according to EIS, feeling at this level is the initial state of action, but feeling is also the result of action, and apart from that, in accordance with UD, feelings also provide deep and necessary nourishment for the body and mind. Below, we will discuss the most important aspects of the feeling mind and feeling-based reality for everyday life: *the self-referential feeling and emotions.* With the latter, we will touch upon the dynamic of mind and emotions expressed in the interrelation of conceptual mind, image mind, and feeling mind—and their corresponding realities—in the construction of the individual person's general experience of reality, as seen from the UD point of view.

UD investigation into interrelated nature of self-referential feeling and corresponding phenomena

According to Tarab Rinpoche, the self-referential feeling[34] refers to the existential center of experience. With any experience, we naturally have a self-referential feeling.

This should not be seen as a contradiction to the common notion in Eastern philosophy of "selflessness,"[35] a term often used in Buddhist literature. Selflessness, in Buddhism, actually refers to the negation of an independently existing self-entity or the independent existence of other persons or things. People normally perceive themselves as separate and apart from the phenomena they experience. In Buddhist philosophy, everything, including the self, only exists relationally or in dependence on other things, and therefore nothing has an independent existence. In Western literature, the term "selflessness" is often misleadingly interpreted as the negation of a self, giving rise to many misunderstandings, and perhaps this translation is not well chosen. Self-references exist, albeit relationally, and forms the existential core of our experience, which is often determined by our self-referential imprints.[36]

In spiritual practice, the goal is to transcend the different levels of self-reference and ultimately even any sort of self entity existence. However, this is not the goal of personal development and psychotherapy where one does not try to get rid of the experiential center of oneself, what Jung referred to as "ego." In UD, the immediate goal is to change and transform inadequate, disturbing, and rough layers of self-reference, in order to become more flexible and develop more balanced and nuanced ways of experiencing reality and also to diminish existential fear for developing a basis for a more loving and compassionate attitude.

According to UD, all beings, and especially humans, right from the time of conception have a strong drive to uphold their existence. From this early stage of life, beings form self-referential feelings and conceptual habits by continuously assimilating and accumulating what is needed, while rejecting and fighting against what seems to hinder development into a more fully formed human being. This process doesn't stop with becoming a teenager or adult, but becomes more sophisticated throughout life, developing and settling into different types of self-referential feelings and conceptual identifications. People, particularly when they are conceptually dominated, always have both of these as the central self-referential core, accompanied by certain behavioral patterns to counteract fear and gain stability.

Although people share the common capacity for self-reference at different levels in an interrelated reality, we actually create much more unique matrices of self-reference throughout our development than is commonly realized, in accordance with our personal experience. Throughout our development, such personal experiences create imprints or predispositions regarding our self-referential perceptions, which are continuously reinforced and sometimes modified through subsequent activation and experience, resulting in an increasingly complex and interrelated reality formation. It is important to note that such formations of self-referential feeling, however dynamic, are automatically predisposed and based upon existing imprints without the freedom of choice one would have if this process was not operating under the habits of a dominant conceptual mind.

With the development of language, which is inherently conceptual, we gain the capacity to have conceptually based self-referential identities. From the time of linguistic development, we have the possibility to establish an outer conceptual relation to ourselves, in other words, to cultivate the ways in which we see ourselves and are seen in the world. These sorts of outer conceptual relations are dependent on specific conventional support. For instance, the self-identification of having a certain position in society needs support from that society, and when that falls away, the status, position, and especially the identity upheld by such support fall away, too. Therefore, when people are strongly conceptual and thus have little or no direct contact with a genuine self-referential feeling based in the common ground of sensory experience, the loss of such support can easily result in a crisis of identity.

Also, if and when a person doesn't get the love and support needed during the time of their development, there is a greater possibility for establishing vulnerable self-references. Obviously, the earlier and more severe these experiences are, the more likely it becomes that vulnerable self-references may develop and impact the person's experience of reality and self. However, one cannot tell how a particular situation will affect a given person, as there is some variation from person to person in how and when a lack of support is experienced, and therefore how and when the person establishes a vulnerable self-reference. Some people even establish very good and supportive self-references under difficult circumstances. Also, one would have to take into account how many times a vulnerable self-reference has been activated due to circumstances and caused more imprints. Only the behavior of the individual in everyday life and their innate dispositions will determine the result of the circumstances under which their development is influenced.

We should also mention that an underlying UD view in connection with established vulnerable self-references is that because one has created these, they can also be undone. If recognizing that these are self-established, and if one is not satisfied with the easy "solution" of blaming others, circumstances, and so on (even though "others" and "circumstances" are always and undeniably involved), the vulnerable self-references and corresponding reality experiences can be transformed.

UD investigation into the dynamics of emotional feeling mind and corresponding phenomena

Emotional feelings are an important area of investigation because of their influence on experience and their relationship with self-referential feelings. We have already mentioned that our overall experience of a given situation is entwined with the cultural, linguistic, and individual ways of conceptually selecting and naming specific aspects of sense experience. We have also highlighted the different ways and levels at which habitually established self-references continue to develop and influence the selective process and impact the corresponding reality formations of the image and feeling minds. The momentarily active self-reference influences the conceptual experience (of self, a person, and/or a situation) by pushing through a *specific selective process*. When the conceptual mind predominates, the basis of reality formation is removed from the direct nature of the sense minds and depends largely on the predispositions of the conceptual, feeling, and image minds. The central self-referential feeling, especially in the context of conceptual domination, has a strong impact on our emotional experience of reality.

When a vulnerable self-reference is activated, we are often out of touch with direct sense experience. In other words we have a diminished or nonfunctioning compensatory mechanism that would, under different conditions, allow us to use the sense minds to achieve an expanded freedom to select and compile our conceptual reality and, thereby, our emotional responses.

In a sort of negative-feedback loop, on the basis of vulnerable self-referential feelings, we conceptually describe a more negative reality, which is then followed by, and correlated to, an experience of mental-image reality that is equally negative. This happens, because as we describe reality conceptually, our image mind sees reality accordingly. And as this mentally experienced appearance is subconsciously taken to be the sense reality, it mistakenly becomes actual reality to the person experiencing it. Once the object is thus grasped by means of both description and appearance in terms of a mental image, the experienced object becomes the only reality momentarily available to the perceiver and the feeling mind experiences accordingly. Through the feeling response, conceptual, and image-reality constructs are confirmed and support the rise of an emotional defense of the often increasingly more vulnerable self-referential feeling.

While the basic process of affirming reality formations just described is not necessarily negative, in the case of identification with vulnerable self-references and the arising of negative emotions, the process of reality formation from conceptual mind to image mind to the feeling mind has the effect of making the conceptual mind and its reality even more negatively selective. In this scenario, the vulnerable self-references have a strong negative effect on the experience of reality, and if we don't realize that we have our own say in the way reality appears to us, we may become increasingly sensitive and emotional.

As long as, and to the extent that, the conceptual mind is dominant, there is a diminished capacity to utilize the common ground of the sense minds to counteract the build up of negative conceptual, image, and feeling realities. This can result in an increasingly more private (i.e., not shared) reality that over time can bring about dissociative conditions and alienation.

In order to counteract a problematic conceptual reality, one can pay attention to the common ground of human reality, which is based in the sense minds, and bring oneself back into sense reality, or if one has the capacity, one may join a deeper or subtler embodiment (the deeper the more effective).

Through practice, one gradually realizes the interrelationship between subject and object as well as between body and mind as described above, and becomes increasingly more aware and grounded (in sense reality). This process allows one to be more present to the common ground of shared reality, and it deepens one's sense of dignity and calls for respect from others. It also undercuts the effect of vulnerable self-references as one's reality changes according to the decreased domination of the conceptual mind and the deepened level of sensory embodiment (physical or more subtle embodiments). During this process, the vulnerable self-references continue to have less and less impact on establishing reality.

If one is able to counteract the habits of dominant conceptual reality formation by getting in touch with and centering on more genuine, direct, and subtle self-references, one can determine which part of the problematic experience has to do with one's own vulnerabilities (these can be changed) and which part has to do with the other/referential object (these can also be dealt with, albeit in another manner). But if one doesn't have the ability to choose a more genuine self-reference consciously by connecting with physical or more subtle sensory embodiments, one is stuck in this unpleasant and often increasingly vulnerable self-referential feeling.

In this way, UD suggests that it is possible to take care and gain control over the self-referential feeling, putting us in command of ourselves and our reality. To take care of one's own self-referential feeling doesn't imply that we do not see what is happening on the outside and become passive, but rather the opposite: if I manage not to get into an emotional reaction—which is always connected with the condition of my present self-referential feeling either being supported or being threatened—and change the vulnerable self-referential feeling, I would not get entangled with the happenings on the outside and would be able to act appropriately in the given situation.

It should be clear from this short presentation, in accordance with UD and based on EIS, that when one is conceptually dominated, the resulting conceptual reality formation is sensitive to the self-referential feeling with which one presently identifies. It should also be clear that with further habitual description of the situation experienced, one is reinforcing and even deepening the imprinted negative self-referential patterns, making them more likely to appear again and determine future conceptual realities. Above all, it should be clear that these habits can be changed, resulting in an expanded, more positive, and balanced grasp of reality.

Points of investigation in UD mindfulness meditation in regard to ordinary feeling mind and corresponding phenomena, when joining the feeling-tone and/or deep body sensation (as dealt with above under first and second mindfulness meditations) investigate:

- whether the feeling comes from outside or is interrelated with feeling mind;
- whether the object-pole of feeling is also feeling or something else;
- the role of feeling in the way one directs one's life;
- whether we have more than one self-referential feeling;
- whether it makes sense that the self-referential feeling (subject-pole) is the primary cause of action/Karma, and that what we experience happening outside (object pole) is a secondary cause—the primary cause being essential;
- the extent to which the self-referential feeling influence conceptualization, mental-image experience, feeling, and actions/Karma;
- whether the self-referential feeling changes due to changes in external circumstances (referential object) alone, or whether the self-referential feeling changes mainly due to my specific experiences (object pole) of the outer circumstances (referential object);
- whether it is possible to gain command over the self-referential feeling (by changing or transforming it) and, in this way, gain command of how reality is perceived/experienced.

Advantages UD mindfulness meditation on mind—in regard to ordinary feeling mind and corresponding phenomena:

- realizing that feeling doesn't come from the outside, naturally diminishing outer determination and opens for possibilities to change;

- realizing that the self-referential feeling is the core around which reality unfolds places the power of change in the individual's hands;
- realizing that everyone has many self-referential feelings, not just the one identified with at any given moment, opening the possibility of changing, or transforming the disturbing self-references without encountering existential fear;
- realizing that, if the self-referential feeling is vulnerable and disturbs the ongoing experience, one has the ability to change or transform this existential center for the better, opening the prospect of gaining command of the experience (one's reality)—in fact, one might be able to realize that by taking care of the inner condition, one may always feel all right;
- mastering the self-referential feelings helps, in particular, to not get entangled with the emotions and vulnerable self-references of other people, a condition through which one could become even more helpful to others, looking past their self-referential system and corresponding reality.

Mindfulness investigative meditation of mind—finding and merging with a deep level of feeling mind and corresponding phenomena—traditional Mindfulness and UD mindfulness for spiritual ends

This last section on feeling mind and the following section on the fourth Mindfulness Meditation on Phenomena in regard to the deeper level—not already included under the first three mindfulness investigations—represents advanced stages of investigative meditation. At this level of accomplishment, the adept goes beyond ordinary self-referential perceptions based on physical body and imagery body, that is, these investigations are based on the attainment of Śamatha and Vipassanā.

In the previous sections, we have suggested methods of practice in accordance with the goals of general well-being, and mental and physical health on levels at which the ordinary self-referential mode of awareness is important and necessary. At this advanced level with such basic goals having already been met, it becomes the aim of practice to experience a mind that is without the strong dual nature of conventional self-referential experience, and thereby beyond the concerns of ordinary mental and physical health and well-being.

The goal of attaining a healthy, grounded, and balanced sixth mind, rooted in the commons of sensory reality is commensurate with spiritual practice. This is in fact a requirement for these more advanced meditations. The practitioner at the initial stage of this practice is not completely free of vulnerable self-referential imprints. However, these would be well within the range of what would be considered healthy by modern therapeutic standards and even in ancient cultures. In the context of the current discussion, this presents a point of departure from the application of these practices to conventional therapeutic methods for attaining general psychological and physical health and well-being. Therefore, subsequent sections are limited to cursory discussions of the attainments of these meditations without guidelines to engaging with them as a particular form of therapeutic practice.

In the previous investigative meditations, the practitioner engages with different types of disturbing self-references in connection with investigating the nature of conceptual mind and reality formation, through the nonconceptual nature of feeling and image minds and corresponding phenomena, realizing their interrelated natures; and into the complexly interrelated self-referential matrices of identity based on the habits, predispositions, or imprints, acting as a supporter basis to the conceptual, image, and feeling realities and vice versa, in the dynamic play of the minds and their unfoldment of reality.

In the final investigative and merging meditations on feeling mind, one naturally begins to experience the dissolution of the subject–object dichotomy, because in these subtle body–mind states, there is no longer ordinary conceptual mind activity and no image reality, that is, there is only the feeling mind/unified experience left.

Implicit with this investigative meditation on the deep level of feeling mind is the aim to attain a state of awareness that is beyond the ordinary subject–object polarity of experience inherent in the sense minds and the three categories of the sixth mind. In essence, these final meditations are directed at an experience of mind that is beyond the categorizations and framework of sense minds and normal sixth mind subject and object poles/reality formation, normal levels of self-reference, and so on that have been used to arrive at this point.

The Earlier Buddhist Schools[37] spoke about this very fundamental phenomenon of mind as "a light in a pot with holes," the holes referring to the sense minds and the different types of sixth mind; and the light in the pot referring to the most subtle nature of mind, *the mind principle*, which is the potential of the sense and sixth minds.

Mindfulness of this deeper state of feeling mind is one of the higher meditations and is related to the meditation traditions of *Mahamudra, Dzogchen, Nature of Mind, and Void*.[38] In the early stages of this practice, the practitioner may glimpse the "light in the pot," but maintaining such an unusually subtle and practically nonself referential awareness for more than a fraction of a second is quite difficult. The accomplishment of this stage of meditation is attained when the practitioner can maintain a "one-pointed" feeling awareness of uniting with the light in the pot/nature of mind/void nature/*rigpa* nature/"clear light"[39] at will for as long as desired. This type of experiential condition is only possible on the basis of the absolute, most direct, and subtle form of self-referential embodiment and awareness:

> In this most subtle state called *lungsem*, where *sem* relates to the most subtle self-referential mind nature and *lung* to movements/vibrations, the most subtle trace of body, it no longer makes sense to differentiate body and mind—they are said to be inseparable. (Tarab Tulku & Handberg, 2005)

In this way, in accordance with the EIS Tradition, the practitioner can eventually reach a "clear and uniting quality of mind and phenomena," a mind that proceeds to unify the subject and referential object (and not just the subject-pole and object-pole). This basic or fundamental mind nature or mind principle is thus necessarily both a "personal" and a "universal" phenomenon and, in accordance with Tarab Tulku,[40] reaches even a primordial level of existence.

The second objective (which is simultaneous with the former) is to gradually merge with these increasingly subtle levels of self-referential feeling and awareness, progressing to a state of universal nondual body–mind awareness with only the absolute subtlest form of embodiment that is with only a trace of self-reference and experience of subject and object unity, and even beyond that. Practitioners who have achieved this stage of meditative accomplishment have done so through either a gradual process of the meditation stages or a more direct path, both through the practice of stages of Śamatha and Vipassanā meditations and accomplishment of more and more subtle embodiments and refined sixth mind.

Even if one can intellectually understand these stages of practice, there really is no diving into the light in the pot/nature of mind/void nature/*rigpa* nature/clear light, since, without training and accomplishment, one would simply, on the basis of creating a conceptual idea about it, be imagining such direct contact with the fundamental nature of mind. In these unknown territories, it is therefore necessary to proceed with proper guidance.

Those who achieve the final or resultant stage of this meditation (sometimes referred to as the state of fearlessness) are beyond self-interest, not needing anything to uphold identity. This condition is the right and only true basis for the most appropriate action with regard to benefiting others, unconditioned compassion, action based on unconditioned love, the actual goal of all spiritual traditions. It is all in accordance with the deepening of body–mind and self-referential feeling that it is possible to approach genuine unconditional love and compassion in the first place.

Fourth Mindfulness: Mindfulness investigative meditation of phenomena[41]—merging with a deep level of referential phenomena—traditional Mindfulness and UD mindfulness for spiritual ends

The last part of the fourth Mindfulness Meditation is also a very deep and subtle investigation corresponding with the deepest level of the third Mindfulness Meditation, focusing on the nature of phenomena itself. This cursory treatment can hardly do justice to the topic, but hopefully it will shed some light on the direction and outcome of this meditative investigation. The bases for this practice are traditionally the accomplishments of Śamatha, that is, usage of subtle body beyond the imagery body, and Vipassanā and the previous mindfulness meditations. We have already been dealing with part of the nature of phenomena in connection with the mindfulness of "body" and the different types of sixth minds as the distinct object poles. These are the objects we have in our experience, whether they represent the object poles of the senses or that of the conceptual, feeling, and image minds.

While we can easily understand the interrelated nature of external things such as the causes and conditions of an ever-changing array of phenomena, it is slightly more challenging to see that all phenomena, as we experience them, are inherently interrelated with the minds, and moreover that the conceptual reality we form has its own and sometimes very personal way of experiencing—as we have already discussed above.

Even if we were adepts and had the capability to experience directly, without using the ordinary level of conceptual mind, we still would have only an experience of what the minds can provide, which is limited to a particular range of perception. The important implication of this is that because of such limitations, we do not have any truly direct means of experiencing the full nature of referential phenomena through our senses or any of our other minds. The object poles we experience, which include oneself, are as much a product of our minds as they are a mere reflection of the entire phenomenal world, referential reality.

In the previous meditations, we took phenomena as object poles in a more discrete manner than we do in the present investigative and merging meditation. Now, we investigate phenomena inclusively. In this manner, the practitioner is able to get closer to distinguish the rules of referential reality's nature.

Nevertheless, when we continuously are anchored in body sense or even cultivate subtler energy embodiments, the conceptual mind calms down, and it no longer dominates over the other sixth minds. The real challenge here—as above—is that we have to work with the conceptual mind on an increasingly subtle body basis while all the time staying in direct contact with the object under investigation through feeling and image minds.

Staying in direct and one-pointed contact with referential reality with that to which the words refer, seeing with the mind eyes and hearing with the mind ears—Śamatha attainment—and using Vipassanā as an investigative means, we can gain much more precise access to the rules of referential reality—all in accordance with the subtlety of the body–mind interrelationship we use.

In this meditation, the objective is to investigate the nature and workings of referential phenomena, that is, to discover its nature and rules. Traditionally this investigation has several parts: investigation into referential phenomena to determine whether or not anything exists in and of itself in regard to "oneself"; whether or not anything exists in and of itself in regard to "other"—everything else other than one self; whether or not referential phenomena are subjected to causal nature, moment-to-moment changing nature and composite nature as well as to interrelated natures and how these interrelations determine referential reality's unfoldment in duality.

These investigations on referential phenomena start with the investigation of conceptual reality realizing its nature, the way it functions, and its limitations and capabilities in order to let the nature and rules of the phenomenal world or referential phenomena stand out more clearly. Tarab Tulku said:

> The first part of the fourth practice of mindfulness in regard to phenomena is again connected to the conceptual reality.[42] This type of object is functional, so it exists. We can describe and work with it, and yet it's nothing solid, nothing tangible. In the exercise one should try and get an experience and realization of the particular nature of the conceptual reality. This investigation follows what in Inner Science is called "interrelated nature" and what in *Boddhisattvayana*[43] is meant by "everything is an illusion." The conceptual reality exists but there is nothing solid upholding it. When realizing the nature of conceptual reality, it's like a fantastic painting in the air one can walk straight through.[44]

Here, Tarab Tulku is talking about the nature of how the "referential object" appears to the conceptual mind, but similar investigations are carried out in relation to the other minds. In this way, we realize that everything we experience is like an apparition; it is at best only a reflection of the "referential reality" (actual reality), not the object itself, and it appears as thoughts, images, sensations, and feelings—none of these are solid things; they are all the object-poles of mind.

The second part of the Mindfulness Investigations of referential phenomena takes us into the study of the phenomena of "oneself." Traditionally, this investigation is connected with the five *Skandhas* or Heaps: body, feeling-tone, discrimination, other mental functions, and the basic nature of the mind-principle. The outcome of the investigation might be (like in EIS) the realization that there is no independent existence of oneself on the outside of the composition of the "five heaps"/five Skandhas; oneself has a compounded nature that changes from moment to moment, and none of the Skandhas exist in and of themselves either.

A further level of investigation would be to detect rules of the "referential reality" in terms of "ourselves" and "everything else." We investigate the causal, composite, and ever-changing nature of reality, as well as Nagarjuna's[45] eight interrelationships/*tendrels*: becoming and cessation, the finite and the infinite, localization, and de-localization, part and whole, which has been arranged in pairs by Tsongkhapa[46] in accordance with the nature of "individual identity," "time," "extension in space," and "conjunct nature."[47] Investigative questions could be: Are these interrelations essential or not, and why? Why are they placed in pairs and why do they relate to "individual identity," "time," etc.? Are these actual rules of the unfoldment of referential reality? Could we find any other essential rules?

A possible continuation of this investigation would be to investigate the matter–energy (potential field) interrelationship that Tarab Tulku and Handberg (2005) pointed to as essential to referential phenomena, too. Everything we experience with our senses is of "form" or matter nature.[48] However, when we go deeper into the nature of mind and phenomena, EIS holds that oneself and everything have the nature of energy, and on a deeper level, we partake in the potential field or even in unity nature of subject and referential object.

Thus, the practitioner could achieve the realization or at least get a glimpse of the emptiness or void nature of the "referential object," that is, the realization that even the referential object, all the way into its energy or even potential field, is of relational nature, devoid of inherent characteristics. These kinds of realizations are the most efficient means to undercut the attachment to self- and other-identification, that is, the fixation of self and other, which is the main hindrance for attending a deeper level of oneself and phenomena, for finally merging with the unity of both. These fixations are said to be the root cause of duality.

It is important to note that none of this is meant to say that we do not exist; it is only an investigation into how we actually exist. Tarab Rinpoche with Candrakirti (650 AD) stressed that, even though everything exists in a relational way, in a causal and moment-to-moment way, and that nothing exists in and of itself, everything still exists. Realizing this leads to the experience of "void nature" or "emptiness" of phenomenal existence, which is the way we actually exist in accordance with EIS.

Comparison Between UD and the Social Psychological Concept (SPC) and the Eastern-Derived Approach (EDA) and Transcendental Meditation (TM)

This section compares some of the essential ideas found in contemporary approaches to mindfulness. On this basis, the similarities and differences between the ideas presented by Dr. Ellen Langer, which are representative of the SPC, and those that are generally representative of an EDA and those representative of TM are discussed with specific reference to the ideas representative of UD.

Some basic tenets are presented that are essential for understanding the background of the Traditional Eastern Mindfulness and about Mindfulness from a UD view. As defined earlier, Mindfulness, as a term used herein, refers to the Buddhist practice of meditative training and investigation into the nature of reality. In this section, we want to select a few of these basic tenets to make comparisons with the SPC, represented by Dr. Ellen Langer and by the EDA, and discuss the following concepts: interrelated nature of reality; the different minds and different levels of the minds (including comments on TM); being in the now—in the present with acceptance and practices thereof; and body–mind and health perspectives.

The discussion is limited to only a few points of what is included under the different approaches to mindfulness. We restrict the discussion to some basic tenets of UD to analyze a few of the similarities and differences. In this short article we can only refer to a few of the many knowledgeable practitioners and scientists working with mindfulness in the West. The practitioners/scientists representing an EDA to mindfulness have, to a varying degree, a Buddhist influence, which in turn has been adopted into modern mindfulness practice in different ways depending on the aims for using mindfulness and the population that is addressed. We have chosen to pool the references for this part, as most of the comparison is presented to include only the main features and not the detailed perspectives.

"Interrelated nature of reality"

UD The view of UD on "interrelated nature of reality" including "the transitory nature or moment-to-moment changing nature of everything that exists," is the base for every experience and is fundamental to the UD view (see section "Interrelated nature of reality and EIS").

SPC Dr. Langer emphasizes that the person who experiences is part of and influences the experience. She states that it is important to be aware that one person's perspective is only one of many possible perspectives, and that the mindset of that person and the context will decide how reality will appear (Langer, 1979, 1989, 1997, 2009; Langer & Benevento, 1978).

We see this as one way to express interrelated nature, and it seems similar to what is theorized in social constructionism, which in turn has similarities to Buddhist theories (Gergen & Hoskin, 2006). Langer describes this in her many research publications and books, and she states that things are neither good nor bad, and nothing stands still, but everything is changing momentarily. Langer also states, with respect to this same reason, that research can only yield probabilities but is often taken for facts. This demonstrates the importance of an awareness of interrelated nature of reality— nothing existing in and of itself, but everything is by nature relational.

EDA   The concept of the "interrelated nature of reality" is prevalent in most of the work on mindfulness, and it seems that the more Buddhist-inspired mindfulness that is applied, the more the interrelated nature is emphasized. It seems clear that most researchers/practitioners share a similar perspective that the individual makes a personal interpretation of their experiences in order to construct reality and thus is responsible for creating the personal experience of reality. This interrelatedness is also described to exist on a much larger scale inasmuch as we are all interconnected and part of a larger whole. However, it is not often discussed to what degree a person can reach the "true nature" of the referenced reality. It sometimes appears like this referenced reality is described as existing "out there" in a way that is actually similar to how it is experienced and that it is possible to reach and describe reality on this basis in a more or less objective and accurate way. Also, the transitory nature of all things is often presented and discussed but with varying emphasis and views.

Comments to "Interrelated nature of reality"   In both SPC and EDA, the similarities to UD are many, although it seems, as in UD, that there is more absolute emphasis on the "interrelated nature of reality" in every experienced situation, in particular in regard to each type of mind (subject-pole) and corresponding object-pole—clearly differentiated from the referential object.

The different minds and different levels of the minds

UD   The specification of the five sense minds and the sixth mind and the latter's different aspects, and in particular the role of the conceptual mind and the different more subtle minds, is basic to understanding that the reality experienced appears according to which mind and degree of subtlety of the mind are engaged.

SPC   Dr. Langer writes that words are only concepts, that these concepts limit our thinking and our way of looking at things, that our mindset holds them still, and that we cannot even consider change until we become more flexible with regard to our conceptual structures.

EDA   The five sense minds are described, and there seems to be some agreement about the importance of using all these sense minds to enhance awareness and be in the present. The different mindfulness practices train the person to gain a deep and direct contact with the different sense minds. The sixth mind and the conceptual mind in particular are discussed in most practices, advising the practitioner to calm down the conceptual mind and not follow the thoughts that arise. However, very often, the conceptual mind and the sense minds are not separated out clearly. But mostly, the practices emphasize how different an experience will be depending on which sense mind is used. Furthermore, the guided instruction, if present, encourages the person to be in the body, not only to think (be conceptual) about it, but to really be in the body senses. It is considered that to be attuned to one's inner sensations through introspection, which is trained via mindfulness, enhances the ability to become aware of another person's internal emotional states, thus enhancing empathy.

Dr. D. Siegel describes in his book "The Mindful therapist" a model that illustrates how reality is fixated in the subjective experience that evolves from "the plane of possibility" to "the plateau of probability" and to the finally fixated stage in "the peak of activation" (D. J. Siegel, 2010a). Neural firing takes place simultaneously, and he points out that it is our experiences that shape our brain. Siegel, furthermore, also defines Mindsight as the ability to look into the inner world of our selves and emphasizes the importance of mindfulness and taking our mind into account (D. J. Siegel, 2010b).

TM Addressing the interesting question "if direct change in state of consciousness through specific mental techniques can extend human life and reverse age-related declines," Alexander, Langer, Newman, Chandler, and Davies (1989) studied a group of 73 elders (mean age 81 years). The researchers in the study were able to demonstrate clear positive health effects with also increased longevity by training elderly people in TM and Mindful training in active distinction. Furthermore, Balaji, Varne, and Ali (2012) summarized, in their review on yogic practices and TM, that they "found that there were considerable health benefits, including improved cognition, respiration, reduced cardiovascular risk, body mass index, blood pressure, and diabetes. Yoga also influenced immunity and ameliorated joint disorders." Although Ospina et al. (2007) in their meta-analyses expressed criticism with regard to the methodology used in many of the studies, they stated that 55 studies indicated that some meditation practices produced significant changes in healthy participants.

Comments on the different minds and different levels of the minds Direct and indirect perception does not seem to be analyzed in the same way with regard to the different types of minds as in UD. However, it is of vital importance to carry out analyses in this way in order to avoid being dominated by the conceptual mind, which always perceives indirectly and is focused only on the past or the future. Instead, it is important to balance this limitation of conceptual thinking with the direct perceiving capabilities of the sense minds and sixth minds, such as the body sense, which is always in the present and will thus bring the person into consensus with the basic ground of reality common to all human beings.

Although the conceptual mind and the five physical sense minds are often discussed in both SPC and EDA, the differentiation and the impact of the different minds and the more subtle body–minds as described by UD seem to be taken into account less often, and only the more general term "mind" is used. However, in SPC, Langer strongly emphasizes the importance of de-fixation of the experienced reality, by constantly considering other perspectives. Likewise, Siegel's work can be seen as demonstrating the need for an awareness of the inner world as part of the mind. With regard to the UD view, opening up to sense realm and other compensatory minds simultaneously could create a balance with respect to the conceptual mind. However, perhaps the most important issue is to reflect and take into account what role the "mind" might have in the specific situation, which certainly is not always the case in science and health care. However, one difficulty in comparing different theories is that the same term could refer to different entities or aspects of mind. For example, the modern term "sixth somatic sense," also described as a "non-worded world of sensation," is used in the West to represent body sense, but according to traditional Mindfulness and UD, body sense belongs to the five senses and is separate from the sixth sense. Also, the terms "body and mind," "body–mind," and "subtle body" are used with different meanings, for UD terminology—see section "Terms of analysis 2: Types of mind and body."

"TM: Accomplishment of the deep level of mind," would be comparable to a stage described in the section "Mindfulness investigative meditation of mind—finding and merging with a deep level of feeling mind and corresponding phenomena—traditional Mindfulness and UD mindfulness for spiritual ends" and is related to by UD and EIS as "a final level of meditation," and "mindfulness of phenomena," seems to correspond to what is described in TM as the state of a purely content-free, silent state of awareness. In accordance with UD, it becomes clear that there are many levels of the deep feeling mind or "void" nature (in some schools, they discuss 16 levels of void), beyond the sense field and conceptual field, and even beyond any image appearance, that is, reality of form manifestation.

Being in the now—in the present with acceptance and practices thereof

UD   UD asserts that the mind and body are mutually dependent and interrelated phenomena, and that any type of mind always has an embodiment of some kind. Mindfulness practice cultivates awareness based on the subtle body sensing, and concurrently develops more subtle mental capacities. UD holds that there is a broader and subtler range of perception available to human experience that is achieved through the manifold practices as a prerequisite of Traditional Mindfulness meditation and the contemplation and cultivation of attention on mental and sensory phenomena.

SPC   Dr. Langer states that, "A mindful approach to any activity has three characteristics: the continuous creation of new categories; openness to new information; and an implicit awareness to more than one perspective"; furthermore, that mindfulness is to notice new things, be in charge and be attentive and actively make choices. Langer uses the expression mindlessness as the opposite of mindfulness, and mindlessness is governed by the "autopilot." Langer says about being present that "if you are not there, there is no possibility to know that you are not there." Instead of specially assigned practices, Langer advocates a continued attitude with awareness, like a beginner's mind, a mindful curiosity, and to always be attentive and see alternatives and actively make choices, which will put you in the present; also, to always realize and have the awareness that there is never one but many perspectives in every situation and that nothing is static. To realize and maintain awareness that there are many possible perspectives relates to what is included in the UD definition of mindfulness as "investigation into the nature of reality" but in Langer's mindfulness, without meditation.

There is also a form of acceptance to this situation with the awareness that there are many possible perspectives.

EDA All mindful practice includes being in the present. This is basic to training in mindfulness and includes bringing one's complete attention to the present experience on a moment-to-moment basis with awareness of one's own inner emotions and reactions, and remaining nonjudgmental. This involves awareness of the five sense minds and focusing on what experiences can be felt through them, as well as letting thoughts (conceptual mind) come and go without placing any particular attention on them. Furthermore, the attitude towards what happens should include acceptance of the experiences; one should not try to change them. If guided, the person will be told to "be in the experience/feeling" and not just to think about being there but actually be in the body, thereby having a more direct, sense-based experience. Focusing on the breathing is often used as a means to get into body sense. Many of the practices include some form of focused attention on the different parts of the body similar to what Jon Kabat-Zinn (2003) describes as a "body scan." Typically these practices start with focusing on breathing and systematically go through the different parts of the body to get in contact with the physical senses and whatever can be experienced. There is also more formal meditation like sitting meditation with more analytical aspects to it and with the use of visualization. Most of the different kinds of sitting meditations include calming down the conceptual mind and just letting thoughts come and go without thinking about what has been going on in the past or what might happen in the future (Kornfield, 2008).

Usually, it is advisable to set aside a special time for these practices daily. The aim is that the person should remain mindful as much as possible. Different short practices are also presented in order to include the practice into daily life situations and to simplify and find time for the practice, such as "red light practice," checking one's breathing at regular intervals, mindful eating, mindful walking, and so on.

Furthermore, moving meditations like Yoga, Tai chi, Chi Gong, and similar training forms, which all can support developing a body sense, are often included in contemporary mindfulness practices. There are many workbooks with practical hands on instruction on how to apply mindfulness in everyday life.

Comments to being in the now—in the present with acceptance and practices thereof
From a UD point of view, these Mindfulness practices would bring one into the present, undercutting stress, and so on, and are very useful for their compensatory effect to the conceptual mind's unconsciously screening out what it doesn't name. And the deeper the body basis for these practices, the better, as this generates the possibility for one to realize the interrelated nature of subject-poles and object-poles, and therefore see one's own influence on the perception of reality that would otherwise be accepted as existing—objectively, as it occurs to the conceptual mind.

However, according to Traditional Mindfulness, this would be considered true mindfulness only if the investigations were done on the basis of a meditative state of mind, that is, from a subtle body base, which would give an even deeper realization of the interrelated nature of reality and the possibility for going beyond that which we ordinarily take to exist objectively.

Body–mind interrelation and health perspectives

UD   Well-being is a major goal of all activities in Buddhist traditions, as it is in UD, and not just for the individual but also from a much wider perspective. UD confirms that it is possible for the mind to influence human physiology and bodily functions, an assertion that is well confirmed by modern research. In UD, training personal development is a major aim, the latter part of which is specifically directed to the Art-of-Relating and Psychotherapy with direct therapeutic applications.

While UD primarily provides a basis for personal development and psychotherapy, it holds that there is an even broader and subtler range of perception available to human experience that is achieved through the manifold practices leading up to and including the Traditional Mindfulness meditations (see section "The four Mindfulness meditations and UD Mindfulness").

Regarding mindfulness of the body, and other embodiments, the more subtle the body the more subtle the sense capacities and the more the space and time dimensions open up.

SPC   Dr. Langer states that mind and body are "just concepts" and that mind and body are not separate but belong together; the mindset will decide what happens in the body as the mind–body is one. This is the main focus of the fascinating research by Dr. Langer, as reported in her book "Counter clockwise": "Where the mind is, the body will be." The majority of Dr. Langer's research studies clearly demonstrate how mindfulness exerts a dramatic effect on health and prolongs life (Langer, 1979, 1989, 1997, 2009; Langer & Benevento, 1978).

EDA   Mindfulness is based on an awareness of the interrelation of body and mind. It is well accepted that the mindset will change and have an effect on the physiology of the body as well as the function of the brain. Body–mind clinics focusing on this close interrelation are also gaining greater acceptance in health care. Neuroscience research has demonstrated that neuroplasticity is enhanced as a result of mindfulness practice, which again emphasizes the interconnection between the body and the mind. Mindfulness practice furthermore stimulates neural integration of different essential parts of the brain, including the middle prefrontal cortex, the region for the executive functions of the brain, that are of major importance for mental health and in turn for general well-being. Moreover, Mindsight, as defined by D. Siegel (2010b) "to see the mind—the inner world in ourselves—and shape it towards health," is one further essential step to developing the vast capacity of the "mind." This is also in line with the theory that of what all takes place in the mind, the subjective experiences are correlated with neural firing and vice versa, which is verified by research on neuroplasticity. Thus, our brain is shaped by our experiences. In connection to this, Dr. Siegel further describes a triangle of well-being and resilience that consists of the brain, the mind, and relationships. Thus, there is a structural and functional base in the brain that, in combination with the mind and relationships, can be developed to support well-being and health.

Mindfulness has most extensively been used to achieve stress reduction through the establishment of the Mindfulness Based Stress Reduction (MBSR) program at the

University of Massachusetts Medical Center by Dr. Jon Kabat-Zinn (2003) and has proven to be very effective. Mindfulness practice, on both a short- and long-term basis, has been extensively researched and shown to be effective in treating a large number of diseases, mental as well as somatic and to increase neural integration, which is considered essential for a well-functioning brain and mental health, and even to have a positive effect on the telomeres and slow down the aging process, and also to enhance empathy (Carlson, Speca, Faris, & Patel, 2007; Davidson et al., 2003; Doidge, 2007; Epstein, 1999; Goldstein, 2012; Hanson, 2009; Hölzel et al., 2011; Jacobs et al., 2011; Kabat-Zinn, 2003; Krasner et al., 2009; Lazar et al., 2000, 2005; Rakel et al., 2009; Schwartz & Begley, 2002; Segal, Williams, & Teasdale, 2002; Shealy, 2011).

Comments on body–mind interrelation and health perspectives   Body–mind and health aspects might be where the similarities are the greatest between the different approaches, perhaps because the prerequisites to realize the potential health aspects are based on a deep understanding of the interrelatedness of mind and body. The mind's ability to alter brain function and cause neuroplastic changes, which has been demonstrated through advanced scientific research, will most likely lead to increased awareness and insight in medical and other healing professions.

Concluding Remarks

It appears that, as a whole, there are many similarities between mindfulness as approached by UD, the SPC by Langer, and the EDA, all of which share the goal to increase health and well-being, and use mindfulness as a method. However, some major differences appear with regard to the differentiation of minds in UD, the different levels at which the analysis of reality takes place. Also distinct in UD is the differentiation between direct and indirect means of perception pertaining to sense minds, and feeling and image minds (direct) versus the conceptual mind (indirect) and the claim that the sense, image, and feeling minds don't use language as the basis for perception. Recent research in neuroscience and other areas has clearly demonstrated positive structural and functional effects on the brain, neuroplastic changes, and dramatic positive health effects in persons with regard to applying mindfulness as described by SPC, EDA, and UD-Buddhist approaches. Medical health care would certainly benefit by taking mindfulness into account with respect to the well-being of both patients/clients and healthcare professionals. Furthermore, research studies on epigenetics have underlined the significance of our mindset demonstrating a direct health effect by influencing the genes (Lipton, 2005).

Dr. Langer demonstrates in her research the very significant and impressive effects of being aware of one's mindset and emphasizes that there is more than one perspective in any given situation, which, when taken into consideration by the person, can have a major impact on health and well-being. Dr. Kabat-Zinn has successfully pioneered the use of mindfulness in medical practice through his MBSR program (Kabat-Zinn, 2003). Dr. D. Siegel states that "Mindsight enables us to sense and shape energy and information flow. Mindsight takes away the superficial boundaries that separate us and enables us to see that we are each part of an interconnecting flow, a wider whole" (D. J. Siegel, 2010b).

Awareness of the interrelated nature of reality with regard to the different categories of minds and degrees of subtleness opens one up to the insight that we are creators of our experienced nature of reality and thus in control of our lives, and therefore have plenty of possibilities for changing our condition and reality experience all along with becoming more aware of this very interrelated nature of being. Furthermore, there is the prospect of realizing that we are interconnected with one another leading to Tarab Tulku's words: "If we knew how interrelated we are, we would take great care of the other, as we would realize her/him to be part of myself."

Acknowledgments

We want to express our sincere thanks to Stephen Lawrence Johnson for very valuable assistance with the manuscript.

Notes

1. Sanskr. Pratityasamutpada, Tib. *Tendrel* or *tenjung* relates to the interrelation of all phenomenal existents, the cause-and-effect nature of reality, the transitory or moment-to-moment changing nature of everything, part and whole interrelation, becoming and cessation, finite and infinite, localization and delocalization, etc. Tarab Tulku emphasized in particular the interrelations of subject and object, body and mind, and energy and matter. Tarab Rinpoche expressed the meaning of *tendrel* in English as *unity in duality*, emphasizing that the interrelated nature of existence is at the same time both in unity and in duality. *Unity in Duality*® is also a trademark held by Tarab Institute Inter. that represents the overall educational view of Tarab Institutes and Tarab Ling, the educational organizations founded by Tarab Tulku. These organizations are dedicated to applying the view of tendrel/unity in duality (including mindfulness) also to more ordinary concerns such as general health and well-being rather than strictly to advanced spiritual practice.
2. Tibetan Scholar: Tarab Tulku, Lharampa Geshe/D.Phil. (1935–2004) from Drepung Monastic University, Tibet. Tarab Rinpoche was a Lecturer at Copenhagen University and Research Librarian at the Royal Library of Copenhagen.
3. This is a translation of the Tibetan term *Dran-pa nyer-bzhag bzhi* (Phon. *drenpa nyershak shi)*. These meditations are first described in the Satipatthanas in the Pali Cannon and are more commonly referred to as the Four Foundations of Mindfulness.
4. The term "Inner Science" is a translation of Tib. *Nang-don rig-pa* (Phon. *nangdön rigpa*). Here, it refers to the universalities underlying eastern traditions, in accordance with Tarab Tulku, in his extraction of the same. We have translated to the term "science" in order to draw attention to the similarities of this method to modern scientific inquiry inasmuch as Inner Science is an empirical method based on observation and verification. Specifically, Eastern Inner Science refers to ancient Indo-Tibetan theories and practices employed to investigate the nature of reality using the mind itself through various frameworks—see note 1.
5. Art-of-relating, in UD terminology, refers to a specific way of dealing with relationships based on insight into the interrelated nature of reality.

6. In ordinary perception, there is always self and an object. This is what is meant by self-referential nature of experience.

7. In Tibetan, the subtle bodies are called Yid-lus, phon. *yilü* = "(sixth-)mind-bodies."

8. In accordance with EIS, any aspect of mind that is not directly related to the senses is placed in the category of sixth mind, but the important point is that all minds are momentary and arise simultaneously with the phenomena perceived.

9. The Buddhist literature is categorized under either the Sutras or Tantras.

10. Tib. Yid-kyi rtog-pa'i rnam-shes (Phon. *yikyi togpe namshe*).

11. Tib. Yid-kyi myung-wa'i rnam-shes (Phon. *yikyi nyongwe namshe*).

12. Tib. Ngönsum (Phon. *mNgon-sum*).

13. By the later Inner Science Schools (Yogacara and Madhyamaka), it is questioned whether its possible to pinpoint anything, as nothing has characteristics that exist independently, such characteristics only exist relationally.

14. We use the term "other," implying others and everything else—except oneself. So, oneself and other comprise everything within a certain perceptive field.

15. There are different types of vipassana meditation; some are more analytical, and some are less, but in accordance with Tarab Rinpoche, all vipassana meditation uses some measure of notifying mind (i.e., conceptual mind) for its attainment.

16. In Tibetan, this subtler conceptual mind type is called Shes-rab (Phon. *sherab*).

17. Tib. Lus (Phon. *lü*).

18. Tib. Tshor-ba (Phon. *tshorwa*).

19. Tib. rNam-shes (Phon. *namshe*).

20. Tib. Chos (Phon. *chö*). Skr. *Dharma*.

21. Tib. Lus dren-pa nyer-bzhag (Phon. *lü dren pa nyershag*) relating to the first *skandha*.

22. Modern scientists have identified as many as 15 additional senses with unique sense organs buried deep within the tissues of the body called proprioceptors. There is scientific evidence that the basic senses such as sight and smell also function on subconscious levels providing very subtle levels of sensation.

23. Destructive emotions are those that have a destructive effect on oneself and others. Constructive emotions are not a problem for personal development and one's mental and somatic health—just the contrary.

24. Tib. Tshor-ba (Phon.) *tshorwa*.

25. The evaluative feeling-tone is related to the second psycho- and physical constituent, *skandha*.

26. Tib. Sems dran-pa nyer-bzhag (Phon. *sem drenpa nyerchag*).

27. Tib. rTen-drel (Phon. *tendrel*).

28. Skr. Nivirtti, Tib. lDog-pa (Phon. *dogpa*).

29. Tib. Log-pa (Phon. *logpa*).

30. See below under "Mindfulness of feeling-mind."

31. "Direct" here only implies "without use of language."

32. Tib. dBag-chags (Phon. *bagcha*). Skr. Vasana (English). These are sedimental imprints or impressions. Our experiences create "energy" imprints, which at a later time, under specific secondary conditions, can become activated and, for instance, give rise to a specific "self-reference."

33. This is a state of mind that, as is said in the Tantras, we naturally attend to in the final stages of death as well as in the deepest state of dreamless sleep—but generally unconsciously.

34. Tib. bDag-'dzin (Phon. *dagdzin*). Skr. *atmagraha*.

35. Tib. bDag-med (Phon. *dagme*). Skr. *anatman*.

36. Sanskr. Vasana; Tib. dBag-chags (Phon. *bagcha*). Skr. *vasana*.

37. Vaibhasika and Sautrantika.

38. The term Mahamudra means "great movement or position," and it relates equally to the practice and to the goal of the practice. Dzogchen derives from the Nyingma tradition/the Eldest Tibetan Buddhist School, and seems to have been brought to Tibet by Padmasambhava, a Tantrician and Magician from eighth-century India, with whose help Buddhism was introduced into Tibet. Both Mahamudra and Dzogchen are called "direct" means, as they aim in a "direct" way, without much guidance into all the intermediary stages, for the goal of mahamudra and *rigpa* respectively. At the same time, it's interesting to see that in accordance with the Tantras, the goals of *rigpa*, mahamudra, void meditation, and nature of mind meditations are all again correlated with the state we naturally enter at the time of deep dreamless sleep and the final stage of dying.

39. In accordance with Tarab Tulku's teaching material in UD Education, Module IV. The "clear light" relates to the final state of dying, and the third and final meditation state in accordance with the "Clear Light Yoga."

40. TTR Yogacara—UD Education Module 1, W3. Tarab Institute Inter. www.tarab-institute.org

41. Tib. Chos dran-pa nyer-bzhag (Phon.) *chö drenpa nyerchag*.

42. The conceptual part of the *denminduje* (Tib. *lDan-min "dus-byed*)—this category has different parts, like rules of nature or natural laws, but the most dominant part is the conceptual reality.

43. The Inner Science Schools of Buddhism can be parted into the Earlier Schools of Inner Science and the later Schools, the latter often known by the name Boddhisatvayana.

44. Tarab Tulku, sound file and transcript, Vaibhasika, Hamburg, 2003.

45. Nagarjuna (c. AD 150–200), the originator of Madhyamaka Inner Science of Mind and Phenomena, and also called the second after Buddha Sakyamuni. He is the author of basic works of the early Madhyamaka like Mula-madhyamaka-karika (Tib.) *dBu-ma rtsa-ba'i tshig-le 'ur byas-pa shes-rab ces bya-ba*, 1970, Delhi, where he presents the Eight *Tendrels*.

46. Tsongkhapa (1357–1419) (Tib.) *dBu-ma rtsa-ba'i tshig-le 'ur byas-pa shes-rab ces bya-ba'i rnam-bshad rigs-pa'i rgya-mthso*.

47. Tarab Rinpoche and Handberg (2005).

48. Tib. *zug, gZugs*, (Sanskrit) *rupa*.

References

Abidharmakosabhasyam. (1988). *The Abhidharma: The origin, growth and development of a literary tradition.* Berkeley, CA: Asian Humanities Press.

Alexander, C. N., Langer, E. J., Newman, R. I., Chandler, H. M., & Davies, J. L. (1989). Transcendental Meditation, mindfulness, and longevity: An experimental study with the elderly. *Journal of Personality and Social Psychology, 57*(6), 950–964.

Balaji, P. A., Varne, S. R., & Ali, S. S. (2012). Physiological effects of yogic practices and Transcendental Meditation in health and disease. *North American Journal of Medical Sciences, 4*(10), 442–448.

Candrakirti (approx. AD 650), *Phong-po lnga'i rab-tu 'byed-pa* (Peking ed.), p. 5267.

Carlson, L. E., Speca, M., Faris, P., & Patel, K. D. (2007). One year pre–post intervention follow-up of psychological, immune, endocrine and blood pressure outcomes of mindfulness-based stress reduction (MBSR) in breast and prostate cancer outpatients. *Brain, Behavior, and Immunity, 21*, 1038–1049.

Davidson, R. J., Kabat-Zinn, J., Schumacher, J., Rosenkranz, M., Muller, D., Santorelli, S. F., … Sheridan, J. F. (2003). Alterations in brain and immune function produced by mindfulness meditation. *Psychosomatic Medicine, 65*, 564–570.

Dharmakirti. (approx. AD 650), *Pramanavarttikam, bsTan-'gyur* (Peking ed.), p. 5717.

Doidge, N. (2007). *The brain that changes itself.* New York, NY: Penguine books.

Epstein, R. M. (1999). Mindful practice. *Journal of the American Medical Association, 282,* 833–839.

Gergen, K., & Hoskin, D. M. (2006). If you meet social construction along the road: A dialogue with Buddhism. In M. G. T. Kwee, K. J. Gergen, & F. Koshikawa (Eds.), *Horizons in Buddhist psychology practice, research & theory* (pp. 299–314). Chagrins Falls, OH: Tao Institute.

Goldstein, E. (2012). *The now effect.* New York, NY: Atria Books, Simon & Schuster.

Grossman, P., Niemann, L., Schmidt, S., & Walach, H. (2004). Mindfulness-based stress reduction and health benefits: A meta-analysis. *Journal of Psychosomatic Research, 57*(1), 35–43.

Hanson, R. (2009). *Buddha's brain—The practical neuroscience of happiness, love & wisdom.* Oakland, CA: New Harbinger.

Hayes, S. C., Follette, V. M., & Linehan, M. M. (Eds.). (2004). *Mindfulness and acceptance expanding the cognitive-behavioral tradition.* New York, NY: The Guilford Press.

Hölzel, B. K., Carmody, J., Vangel, J. M., Congleton, C., Yerramsetti, S. M., Gard, T., & Lazar, S. W. (2011) Mindfulness practice leads to increases in regional brain gray matter density. *Psychiatry Research, 191*(1), 36–43.

Jacobs, T. L., Epel, E. S., Lin, J., Blackburn, E. H., Wolkowitz, O. M., Bridwell, D. A., & Saron, C. D. (2011). Intensive meditation training, immune cell telomerase activity, and psychological mediators. *Psychoneuroendocrinology, 36*(5), 664–681.

Kabat-Zinn, J. (2003). Mindfulness-based interventions in context: Past, present, and future. *Clinical Psychology: Science and Practice, 10,* 144–156.

Kornfield, J. (2008). *The wise heart.* New York, NY: Random House.

Krasner, M. S., Epstein, R. M., Beckman, H., Suchman, A. L., Chapman, B., Mooney, C. J., & Quill, T. E. (2009). Association of an educational program in mindful communication with burnout, empathy, and attitudes among primary care physicians. *Journal of the American Medical Association, 302,* 1284–1293.

Langer, E. (1979). The illusion of incompetence. In L. C. Perlmuter & R. A. Monty (Eds.), *Choice and perceived control.* Hillsdale, NJ: Erlbaum.

Langer, E. (1989). *Mindfulness.* Reading, MA: Addison-Wesley.

Langer, E. (1997). *The power of mindful learning.* Cambridge, MA: Perseus Books.

Langer, E. (2009). *Counter clockwise, mindful health and the power of possibilities.* New York, NY: Ballantine Books.

Langer, E., & Benevento, A. (1978). Self-induced dependence. *Journal of Personality and Social Psychology, 36*(8), 886–893.

Lazar, S. W., Bush, G., Gollub, R. L., Fricchione, G. L., Khalsa, G., & Benson, H. (2000). Functional brain mapping of the relaxation response and meditation. *Neuroreport, 11*(7), 1581–1585.

Lazar, S. W., Kerr, C. E., Wasserman, R. H., Gray, J. R., Greve, D. N., Treadway, M. T., ... Fischl, B. (2005). Meditation experience is associated with increased cortical thickness. *Neuroreport, 16*(17), 1893–1897.

Lipton, B. H. (2005). *The biology of beliefs.* India: Hay House.

Ospina, M. B., Bond, K., Karkhaneh, M., Tjosvold, L., Vandermeer, B., Liang, Y., ... Klassen, T. P. (2007). Meditation practices for health: state of the research. *Evidence Report/Technology Assessment, 155,* 1–263.

Rakel, D. P., Hoeft, T. J., Barrett, B. P., Chewning, B. A., Craig, B. M., & Niu, M. (2009). Practitioner empathy and the duration of the common cold. *Family Medicine, 41*(7), 494–501.

Schwartz, J. M., & Begley, S. (2002). The mind and the brain: Neuroplasticity and the power of mental force. New York, NY: Harper Collins.

Segal, Z. V., Williams, J. M. G., & Teasdale, J. D. (2002). *Mindfulness-based cognitive therapy for depression a new approach to preventing relaps.* New York, NY: The Guilford Press.

Shealy, N. (2011). *Practical applications and scientific proof—Energy medicine.* Virginia Beach, VA: 4th Dimension Press.

Siegel, D. J. (2010a). *The mindful therapist: A clinician's guide to mindsight and neural integration.* New York, NY: W. W. Norton & Company.

Siegel, D. J. (2010b). *Mindsight: The new science of transformation.* New York, NY: Random House.

Tarab Tulku. (2002). *Einheit in der dualität/unity in duality—Einfürung anhand einer darlegung von Tendrel/Introduction through an exposition of Tendrel.* Munich, Germany: Privatinstitut Tarab Ladrang.

Tarab Tulku, & Handberg, L. (2005). *Einheit in der Vielfalt—Moderne Wissenschaft und östliche Weisheit im Dialog.* Berlin, Germany: Theseus Verlag.

Tarab Tulku XI. (2006). *"Tendrel" inner science of mind and phenomena, Tib: Nang-don rig-pa'i gzhung-las byung-ba'i sems-kyi tshan-rig rten-'brel snang-ba'i gzi-byin.* Himashal Pradesh, India: Norbu Linka. (To be published in English "Inner science of mind and reality—from the point of view of Tendrel.")

Zwilling, L. (1976). *Dharmakirti on Apoha: The ontological, epistemological and semantics of negation in the Svarthanumanapariccheda of the Pramanavarttikam.* Ann Arbor, MI: UMI Dissertation Services.

Further Reading

Siegel, R. (2010). *The mindfulness solution: Everyday practices for everyday problems.* New York, NY: Guilford.

Varela, F., Thomson, E., & Rosch, E. (1991). *The embodied mind: Cognitive science and human experience.* Boston, MA: MIT Press.

6

Exemplifying a Shift of Paradigm

Exploring the Psychology of Possibility and Embracing the Instability of Knowing

Sayyed Mohsen Fatemi

The Role of Perspectives and Paradigms in Psychology

At the center of psychological research and studies, there lies an underlying choice of perspectives in which knowing and its modes are defined. The studies, therefore, are essentially tied to their original source in that one cannot expect to see results and findings that are not compatible with their leading perspective. For instance, a Freudian perspective cannot give rise to findings that question the fundamental assumptions of Freud's views on human nature. Similarly, a humanistic psychological perspective would espouse practices and approaches that ultimately explain their sensibility within their original source. Also, a behaviorist perspective based on Skinner's law of positive reinforcement would, inevitably, search for outcomes and consequences that follow behaviors and that subsequently lead to an increase in the frequency of those behaviors.

The notions of paradigms can be explored within a perspective in that a perspective or world view can entail a series of assumptions and beliefs that tend to explain ontological and epistemological relationships: they would represent how things are, how understanding takes place, how the relationships among things are established, what knowing is all about, how we discover relationships among phenomena, etc.

Kuhn (1962) critiques the cumulative process of facts and their implications for scientific progress and questions the dependency of the scientific progress on the steady accumulation of facts indicating that the progress happens only when there is a shift in paradigm. Paradigms, Kuhn (1962) argues, can narrow one's perspective too much and prevent scientists from observing realities that fall outside of the paradigm. As Kuhn (1962) indicated, the real breakthroughs happen during paradigm shifts, when a new way of thinking replaces an older model. A new paradigm does not comply with the old one not only because the presuppositions have changed in the new paradigm but also because the entire scientific field and its relevant problems have been redefined in light of the new paradigm. Therefore, what may be considered a problem may no

The Wiley Blackwell Handbook of Mindfulness, First Edition.
Edited by Amanda Ie, Christelle T. Ngnoumen, and Ellen J. Langer.
© 2014 John Wiley & Sons, Ltd. Published 2014 by John Wiley & Sons, Ltd.

longer be a problem in view of the new paradigm, and what made sense within the old paradigm may be totally nonsensical in view of the new paradigm. For example, Fischer (2006) argued that psychological textbooks in the 1960s and 1970s defined psychology as the science that predicted and controlled behavior, and he provides a recount of the pervasive research methods based on the domination of the paradigm and indicates that

> By now, with psychology having been established as a rigorous empirical discipline, most psychologists no longer accept the "control and predict" definition and no longer cite logical positivism and related philosophical foundations, but often do count on accepted experimental procedures and statistical analysis as adequate to continue building a body of knowledge. Psychology textbooks most often define psychology as the study of human and animal behavior. (p. xx)

New paradigms are not warmly received, as they shatter the taken-for-grated assumptions. The emergence of the new paradigms is often associated with skepticism, mistrust, and disbelief: the new paradigms are unsettling, as they perturb the longstanding mindset that has already developed familiarity, comfort, and accessibility of the truth. To exemplify, those who have been recursively and extensively exposed to the hegemony of natural science as the leading master of inquiry for social science and psychology find it ineluctably hard to receive a perspective that questions the tyranny of the rational empiricism or logical positivism namely questioning the applicability and plausibility of natural science paradigms in the realm of psychology.

According to Kuhn (1962):

> The physical referents of these Einsteinian concepts [space, time, and mass] are by no means identical with those of the Newtonian concepts that bear the same name. (Newtonian mass is conserved; Einsteinian is convertible with energy. Only at low relative velocities may the two be measured in the same way, and even then they must not be conceived to be the same.) (p. 101)

Deep down a psychological perspective, one may discern an orientation that not only suggests a way of looking at the world but also highlights what is important to know. Within an August Comte's orientation, for example, one may see the emphasis on the so-called facts and causes of behavior. The assumptions within a paradigmatic analysis would espouse a set of beliefs that demonstrate how knowing is possible. Once the paradigms are recursively established, they become almost unquestionable, since they tend to show the right way of knowing, acting, and thinking. Questioning the paradigms would then require disobedience from the structurally established sovereignty of the operating set of beliefs. This would lead to exclusion from the domain of the ruling paradigm with its own practical consequences.

Describing the practical consequences of a leap beyond the established paradigms, Scileppi, Teed, & Torres (2000) indicate that

> University dissertation committees and journal editors more readily accept research supporting the dominant paradigm, and foundations and government agencies are more

likely to fund such research. The general population finds the result of research favoring the dominant paradigm to be more believable. These societal effects influence students and novice researchers to choose to investigate only phenomena that are declared valid by the dominant perspective. Thus, the dominant paradigm is unfairly supported, and other views are quickly discounted. (p.12)

One may, therefore, claim that any psychological study or perspective can reveal a bigger perspective that defines, promotes, prescribes, controls, and even proscribes practical approaches, practices, and methods.

Mindfulness and Psychological Paradigms

The dominant paradigm in the mainstream psychology including the experimental psychology is very much close to the assumptions of the natural sciences with the notion that through the use of the quantification and the use of statistics, one can know the real world. The discourse of the positivist psychology is built on a position of certainty that knowledge is indeed attainable through the specific methodological shields. The certainty is largely borrowed from empiricism where the ideas need to be subjected to empirical investigation before they can be called scientific.

Langer's (2009) work on mindfulness can be seen as a work that questions the pervasive paradigm within the mainstream psychology. Interesting enough, she moves in line with the paradigmatic pillars of experimental psychology and demonstrates the inadequacy of the mainstream psychology. Langer's work, similar to those in the camp of hermeneutic and social constructionist psychologists, advocates that knowledge is constructed through our actions and interactions. What gives further merit to her work in this regard is her substantiation of the insufficiency of the mainstream paradigm through the use of the exclusive language of the mainstream psychology. In other words, others who have challenged the dominant paradigm of the positivist psychology have often used a language that is already marginalized in the mainstream psychology. Langer's work abides by the positivist paradigm, yet it shows how our ideas without reflecting any objective reality are constructed to rationalize or justify different discourses of domination. Langer (2009, p. 18) dissociates from the tyranny of the paradigm and indicates that "a new approach to psychology and to our lives is needed." Langer's position of challenge begins from her research on mindfulness. Langer's (2009) mindfulness questions the reliance on positivism and technical rationality while challenging the certainty of knowing. Mindfulness, according to Langer (2009), entails an active state that is associated with creation of new knowledge, welcoming new horizons of information, noticing new things, and being open to the possibility of multiple perspectives. It is through an active state of mindfulness, Langer (2009) argues, that one would embrace the complexity, uncertainty, instability, and uniqueness of the phenomena. Through numerous experiments, she has demonstrated how the mere reliance on positivist-oriented knowing would lead to the monopoly of the legitimacy of one way of knowing, namely the so-called rational way of knowing over numerous other ways of knowing. Langer's (2009) mindfulness advocates a tilt towards the position of not *knowing*, since the fixed position of positivist *knowing* would hamper the exploration of an expansive array of epistemologies and locks the search for knowing in a predetermined point. The questionable knowing has its roots in positivism and enlightenment whereby rationality is defined through an access to restricted avenues of awareness mainly embodied through the linear and analytical forms of thinking. Langerian mindfulness opens up the horizon for revisiting the well-established epistemologies and argues that as much as they have contributed to expansion of our understanding, they have contained our ways of thinking. Through her research on the implications of mindlessness and mindfulness, Langer (2009) highlights the significance of the contextual components including cultural, social, economic, and political contexts, and indicates how the hegemony of positivism and its aspirations to make broad comparisons have contributed to the promotion of insensitivity towards contexts thus fostering mindlessness. Her delineation of this mindlessness would purport how the emphasis on uniformity of positivist driven methods such as questionnaire boils down to the marginalization of the contexts. In line with Bruner's (1986) distinction between the paradigmatic mode, namely the logico-scientific mode and the narrative mode, Langer (1989) recognizes narratives and presents them as an independent mode of cognition while demonstrating psychology's incarceration within natural science (logicoscientific mode) as a form of mindlessness.

Langer's work has already been inspiring in micro levels in that it has encouraged, promoted, and induced research findings and studies that demonstrate the impact and implications of mindfulness for numerous areas including health, education performance, learning, and creativity. Nonetheless, the field of psychology may prosper from a shift of paradigm through Langerian mindfulness as one may also attribute the trend of some of the already-ongoing developments in psychology to an explicit or implicit inspiration from such mindfulness. This shift is inviting, as it calls upon the exploration of a wide variety of epistemologies and even ontologies that may have been concealed to oblivion due to the hegemony of discursive manifestations of the positivist-driven paradigm.

Psychology and Acting From a Single Perspective

Mindfulness, according to Langer (2009), consists in a series of transformations in *being, thinking, feeling,* and *living.* It liberates us from getting incarcerated in the persistence of acting "from a single perspective."

An example of this persistence can be found in the positivist psychology that claims full accessibility of reality and its apprehensibility: reality can be fully understood, as it is driven by universal laws. The reality, therefore, can be defined, described, explained, predicted, and controlled.

Positivist psychology driven by logical positivism posits that empirically verified observations are the only valid data. This perspective, which goes back to 19th century, has been influenced by bigger underlying perspectives, including rationalist philosophers such as Descartes, the British empiricist philosophers such as Loke, and positivist philosophers of science like Popper.

Positivist psychology, due to its focus from a single perspective, has been mindless about the research subjects' sense of research setting. It is in line with this parochialism of positivist psychology that exclusions have superseded inclusions. As Banister, Burman, Parker, Taylor, and Tindall (1994, p. 8) indicate, "it is understandable, though not surprising, that language is absent from most studies in psychology." They proceed with the quotation from Harre and Secord (1972) and write "the pretence that people do not speak is also the core of the repression of meaning in positivist research" (p. 8 in Banister et al., 1994).

Langer (1997) encourages a mindful disengagement from remaining in a single perspective and exploring alternative ways of looking and says:

> In a mindful state, we implicitly recognize that no one perspective optimally explains a situation. Therefore, we do not seek to select the one response that corresponds to the situation, but we recognize that there is more than one perspective on the information given and we choose from among these. (p. 108)

Through a discussion of the story of the Prince and the Pauper, Langer (2009) highlights a very significant point in terms of understanding the perspective with vital implications for doing psychological research. If the one who tries to understand the perspective of the other is formidably entrenched in their own perspective and cannot by any means establish a fairly solid understanding of the other's perspective, the attempt is nothing but a pretentious gesture.

Social psychology, in its pervasive positivist version, has been mainly concerned with applying the knowledge to the problem. In applying the knowledge to the problem, the choice of applying the right technique has appeared as one of the first and foremost priorities. Ironically enough, this has been embedded in the assumption that the practical problems can be solved merely through the application of the right technique, namely reduction of practical issues to the question of applying the right technique. This has led to a high involvement on examining what is technically given to the subject or the participant of research: an engagement with tools, techniques, procedures, methods, and instruments. The procedure-stricken research has been searching for the application of the right technique to the problem; the meaning, however, as established by the other has often been neglected, ignored, or marginalized. The focus on behavior independent from the meaning as created by the other has promoted an algorithmic understanding of psychological phenomena. The research in psychology, therefore, if conducted from a single perspective, would only stabilize the position of the observer without revealing the truth of the observed. In elucidating the significance of understanding the perspective of the other, Gadamer (1988) elaborates the significance of attention towards the acknowledgment of the possibility of a perspective being different from one's own:

> To reach an understanding with one's partner in a dialogue is not merely a matter of total self-expression and the successful assertion of one's point of view, but a transformation into a communion, in which we do not remain what we were. (p. 341)

Mainstream psychology has mainly operated from an observer's perspective in which the observer is eventually entitled to conduct the observation and endorse the process of inclusion or exclusion. The legitimacy, thus, unfolds itself within the power of the observer as their observation would finally represent the amount of certainty taken from the dynamics of observation. This, in a more practical sense, would allow the observer to legitimize the responses that need to be taken vis-à-vis the observation. One may look at the mainstream positivist research or positivist therapeutic measures within psychology, for example, to see how the researcher or therapist would embark on creating a view based on their assumptions that can justify both the interpretation and the action.

Langer's (2009) work on mindfulness can be seen as a pivotal source of awareness for exploring the relationship between the underlying perspective of an observer in a psychological research and the power of the perspective in leading the direction that he/she takes in dealing with the psychological phenomena. Langer's presentation of mindfulness allows us to understand how the context that plays a huge role in the interpretive process is itself created by the one who is subsequently bound by the context. The context thus is, on the one hand, the creator of the perspective from which the action seeks its justification and, on the other hand, created by the one who opens up the relationship between the context and himself/herself. Through a mindful exploration of the Prince and the Pauper, Langerian understanding of mindfulness pinpoints how an understanding of the perspective of the other may lead us to a faulty understanding of both the context and the perspective if it is superficially taken as an experience of another perspective while essentially remaining in one's own perspective. In other words, if a researcher or a therapist pretends to be in the shoes of the client (the patient) while knowing that this being in the shoes of the client (patient) would soon be replaced by being in their own shoes as a researcher or a therapist, this not only means a distorted understanding of the perspective but also develops more gaps between the perceiver and the experience as a result of which the experience is still unknown to the pretentious knower of the experience. Conversely, the researcher or the therapist may not claim that she/he has understood the other's perspective, yet she/he can acknowledge openness towards the existence of the other perspective.

How can the researcher understand the perspective of the other if they are afraid of losing control of their own perspective in the process of the research or therapy? How can the researcher understand the perspective of the participant or the subject of the research if the researcher is recursively stalled in the language induced by their perspective?

Langerian mindfulness is not just a focus on the cognition; it is a shift of understanding: a shift from epistemology to ontology. Langerian mindfulness, in this sense, requires a change of being and not just knowing. It calls for a nonalgorithmic understanding of the perspective of the other and sensitivity to the incessantly on going process of genuine novelties that unfold themselves beyond the established contingencies. Langerian mindfulness (Langer, 1997, p. 124) reiterates that "a mindful approach does not favor the observer's over the actor's perspective."

One may see another example of psychology's mindlessness and its concentration from a single perspective in psychology's infatuation with the illness model. Psychology, one may argue, has been so mindless about the possibilities right from the beginning. It has acted in the language of Langer (1989, 1997) "from a single perspective" and has been oblivious of any shift of attention. The negative psychology itself is a salient example of mindlessness where the windows towards any opening have been fully blocked with an emphasis on negativity.

Elaborating on this negative orientation of psychology, Fineburg (2004) cites numerous examples and indicates that

> VanderStoep, Fagerlin, and Feenstra (2000) surveyed introductory psychology students to see what concepts were recalled most after taking the course. The concepts most often recalled were overwhelmingly related to negative psychology and the illness model. Students most often remembered learning about Phineas Gage and his brain injury, systematic desensitization, narcolepsy, Milgram's obedience study, attitudes influencing behavior (presented through a "controversial issue" debate), and two disorders—dissociative identity disorder and schizophrenia. The other ideas recalled—"psychic" powers, altered visual perception, neuron firing, and classical conditioning—could be considered neutral, but not specifically positive. Many introductory psychology students do not continue to higher levels of psychology, so their overall perceptions of psychology center around the disease and illness model that has dominated for the past half century. (p. 198)

In pursuit of the monolithic perspective with a concentration on negativity, psychology seems to have mostly generated a flux to corroborate the categorization of the illness model in various arenas. One may track down the ubiquitousness of this trend in plethora of research from personality to happiness where the impossibility of increasing one's happiness and the inevitability of a real transformation would call for a quintessential applicability and plausibility (see Allport, 1955; Lykken & Tellegen, 1996; McCrae & Costa, 1990; Suh, Diener, & Fujita, 1996).

Acting from a single perspective and its consequential mindlessness has been a driving force so dominantly that it has affected thinking about wellness and health. It is, then, not surprising that our understanding of wellness has been mainly embedded within an illness orientation. There seems to be scant research that has examined the concept of being well as an independent state of being without a focus on the illness models (see Medich, Stuart, & Chase, 1997; Paul & Weinert, 1999).

A Langerian perspective with mindfulness would illustrate how psychology's entrenchment within the pillars of stabilized definitions and their urge for constancy has deprived us from looking outside the preestablished borders. In identifying the underlying elements of the cling to such mindlessness and getting encapsulated in one single perspective, Horwitz (2002) writes:

> The emergence and persistence of an overly expansive disease model of mental illness was not accidental or arbitrary. The widespread creation of distinct mental diseased developed in specific historical circumstances and because of the interests of specific social groups ... By the time the DSM-III was developed in 1980, thinking of mental illness as discrete disease entities ... offered mental health professionals many social, economic and political advantages. In addition, applying disease frameworks to a wide variety of behaviors and to a large number of people benefitted a number of specific special social groups including not only clinicians but also research scientists, advocacy groups, and pharmaceutical companies, among others. The disease entities of diagnostic psychiatry arose because they were useful for the social practices of various groups, not because they provided a more accurate way of viewing mental disorders. (p. 16)

Elucidating the perniciously embedded mindlessness within the medical-oriented psychology as an example of acting from a single perspective, Langer (2009) argued that

> We can become effective health learners only by questioning the traditional ways we respond to medical information. We will be ready to seek a new way if we recognize that doctors can only know so much, that medicine is not an accumulation of absolute truths, that incurable really means indeterminate, and that our beliefs and most of the relevant external world are social constructions. (p. 29)

Langerian mindfulness, thus, highlights how the perspective can be limited and limiting and how the containment of the perspective may develop the illusion of mastery without allowing a search for alternative ways of exploring the unresolved mysteries.

It may be in line with the achievement of such a mindfulness and understanding the tyrannical subjugation of psychology's longstanding mindlessness that Seligman and Csikszentmihalyi (2000) revisit the sovereignty of medical-oriented psychology and its pervasive attachment to the illness model. They question the pathology, faults, and dysfunctions as the bare-bone essentials of human conception. The whole enterprise of positive psychology, one may suggest, demonstrates an implicit flight from mindlessness to mindfulness where, in the language of Langer (1997), "the value of uncertainty" is celebrated, as it allows one to mindfully deconstruct the assumptions that may have been considered as ineluctably solid due to their frequent and extensive exposure. Seligman (2002, p. 211) appears to be, for instance, mindful of Langerian alternative ways of looking when he indicates that "current dogma may say that negative motivation is fundamental to human nature and positive motivation merely derives from it, but I have not seen a shred of evidence that compels us to believe this." Positive psychology, albeit away from the flurry of negativity and its connectedness to psychology's main subject matter, is still steeped within the discourse of the mainstream positivist psychology with that being presented as a laudable sign of superiority to others including humanistic psychology. This might as well demonstrate how the hegemony of a paradigm would have an influence on those who even oppose the implications of the paradigms and yet reside within the same route of thinking.

Psychology seems to have been mindlessly preoccupied with acting from a single perspective that strongly stresses a focus on the illness, disorder, diagnosis, problems, and malfunction. This preoccupation has resulted in producing other perspectives that have tightened the examination of a search beyond the discourse of negativity. Maddux, Snyder, and Lopez (2004) appear to highlight the dangers of such mindlessness as they reveal a connection between the illness ideology and psychology.

They deconstruct the underlying elements of such mindlessness that has imposed its heavy implications on psychology and indicate:

> The discipline is still steeped not only in an *illness metaphor* but also an *illness ideology*— as evidenced by the fact that the language of clinical psychology remains the language of medicine and pathology. Terms such as *symptom, disorder, pathology, illness, diagnosis, treatment, doctor, patient, clinic, clinical, and clinicians* are all consistent with the ancient assumptions captured in the term *clinical psychology* and with an ideology of illness and

disease. Although the illness metaphor (also referred to as the *medical model*) prescribes a certain way of thinking about psychological problems (e.g., a psychological problem is like a biological disease), the *illness ideology* goes beyond this and tells us to what aspects of human behavior we should pay attention. Specifically, it dictates that the focus of our attention should be disorder, dysfunction, and disease rather than health. Thus, it narrows our focus on what is weak and defective about people to the exclusion of what is strong and healthy. (Maddux et al., 2004, p. 322)

A Langerian understanding of psychology illustrates the mindless entrapment by getting encircled in one single perspective and their implications. It delineates how a research, a project, and a focus can be incarcerated within the limiting tendencies of one perspective and how perspectives can constrict and contain our choices. The frequent exposure to specific pervasive perspectives in psychology and their infusing suggestions may overwhelmingly insinuate that what is out there is the mere or exclusive representation of the fact; it harbors the illusion of accessibility to a truth that can serve as a preamble for compartmentalizing the truth and falsehood.

Langer (2009) demonstrated how psychology's infatuation with the mindless pursuits of recursive conceptions within the prematurely established discourses can respectfully blindfold us and bring a seemingly decent fixation within the stable yet perturbable flux of promoted certainty. Langer (2009) indicates that "a disease's mere label has the ability to foster an illusion of control wherein immediately the expert begins to consider the disease as fixed and inert" (p. 133).

Langerian perspective on psychology displays a full engagement within the paradigm of the mainstream psychology to corroborate a solid understanding of the methodological rigor of the hegemony and substantiates the fallacies of the dominant models in action; it speaks the language and yet does not get drowned in the language; it speaks the language to show the inadequacy of the language.

One may look at the crisis in psychology in 1960s and 1970s, and the debate on the new paradigm versus the old paradigm to see the challenges of illustrating the deficiencies and inoperability of the old paradigm within the positivist framework. The endeavors to suppress the interpretation turned out to be impossible (Parker, 1989), and the old assumptions based on quantification were perturbed; the tyranny of the scientific positivism came to an end, and the quantitative worlds of facts and laws proved to be vulnerable. Langerian perspective on psychology applies a mindful understanding of the quantification and displays an interpretive shift from the positivist approach; it demonstrates that not all quantitative research is positivist.

In nullifying the all-encompassing mentality of precision within the quantitative analysis and the statistical focus on psychology, Langer (2009) argued that "numbers and the tests they represent are not useless. They are tools, and tools can be helpful if used mindfully to guide us and to give us ideas—not to govern what we do or do not do" (pp. 138–139).

A Langerian understanding of mindfulness can, thus, be well attuned to a return of meaning in research. Qualitative research might, therefore, be reminded to be more mindful of the threads that may be missing in the literature and yet can be well scrutinized within the Langerian school of mindfulness. Langerism addresses the "methodological horrors" (Woolgar, 1988). In describing these horrors, Banister et al. (1994) write:

> indexicality, in which an explanation is always tied to a particular occasion or use and will change as the occasion changes; inconcludability, in which an account can always be supplemented further and will continually mutate as more is added to it; and reflexivity, in which the way we characterize a phenomenon will change the way it operates for us and that will then change our perception of it etc. (pp. 3–4)

Langer (2009) presented a mindful understanding of the above and indicates "what can we do in the face of a culture that quantifies every thing? We can remind ourselves what these words and numbers really do and do not tell us. And we can reassert the uncertainty that they hide" (p. 140).

Psychology and Entrapment by Categories

Langerian mindfulness (1989) highlights the role of getting settled in the perfunctory repose of the categories and indicates that "mindlessness sets in when we rely too rigidly on categories and distinctions created in the past ... We build our own and our shared realities and then we become victims of them—blind to the fact that they are constructs ideas" (p. 11).

During the past 30 years, there have been more than 45,000 published articles on depression, with only 400 on joy (Hall, 1998). Psychology seems to have been largely encapsulated and entrenched within the categories created by the pervasive discourse of negativity within the bedrock of the illness model. The pervasiveness of the categorization has brought an implicitly induced mindlessness that has prevented most of the research in psychology from breaking the establishment and the tyranny of the categories. The confirmatory reference points have reclaimed their sensibility within the paradigmatic analysis of the categories, which, notwithstanding their generative power of conducting reflection on the categories, their ramifications, and their imbrications, have attested to a tacit mindlessness in which the sovereignty of the established categories has not been mindfully deconstructed.

One of the main reasons of psychology's entrapment in the illness model and its emergent categories may be examined in the contextual analysis of psychology's growth and development. Both in the United States and in Western Europe, psychology has been influenced, at least as much as the products are concerned, by the underlying social, economic, political, and even military factors. The Great Depression, the World Wars, the Cold War mentality of fear and anxiety, the probability of increasingly growing forces of harm and danger are among a few of the contextual elements that have potentially contributed to the significance of a direction towards which psychology has marshaled its forces. One may need to look at the assessment tools and their initial applications for military goals to reconnoiter how psychological tools and assessments have expedited their process of growth through a recondite emplacement within the mentality of power. The contexts, albeit varied in terms of manifestations, have strikingly impacted psychological scholarship. Darwinian theory and its operative metaphors in ruling out the possibility of a search for genuine virtues, Hobbes' epistemology of human beings' innate badness, the Soviet Union's launching of Sputnik, the first man-made space satellite, are some of the many other examples of the contextual factors that have forcibly prescribed a direction for psychology that displays its revelatory mindlessness in probing realms and perspectives beyond the formidability of the context. It seems that psychology has been extensively subjected to its contexts' oriented propensities and has been incarcerated within the definers of the contextual constraints.

On the paralyzing impact of contexts and their dictating mindlessness, Langer (1989, 1997, 2009) illustrates how contexts can induce "premature cognitive commitment" and pinpoints that "contexts can be an influence, even when we are trying to make the most precise and specific judgments" (p. 38).

In an effort to break the contexts and to promote mindfulness for revisiting what has easily been concealed to oblivion, Langer (1997) challenges the underlying contextual constriction of the notion of intelligence, its roots in the 19th century, and its overarching inundation in determining our thinking about its possessiveness of the truth.

Elucidating the perils of contextual subjugation and its debilitating effects, Langer (1997) indicates how implicit or explicit submissiveness within the contextual borders would deprive us from adopting a proactive posture or a creative approach.

Langer's points on entrapment by categories can be very helpful in understanding how psychology's incarceration within some of the preestablished categories has imposed a one-sided direction in thinking about social phenomena. Langer's illustration of mindlessness by categories would facilitate the process of looking at the psychological trends and their social implications. Once the categories have been established, they have been operative in making judgments and making decisions. If you seem to fit the categories as they have been designed, you would be automatically subjected to the defining borders of the categories. In the realm of social services, for example, one may see how this entrapment would have led to "blaming the victims for not adjusting to degrading social conditions" (Nelson & Prilleltensky, 2005). In further exemplification of such entrapments and their social implications, Nelson & Prilleltensky (2005) write:

> As an example, the field of psychology had created intelligence testing in the UK (Francis Galton) and France (Alfred Binet) and IQ tests were imported to and refined in the US during this period. Galton and other psychologists in the area of intelligence testing were proponents of Social Darwinism (Albee, 1996a), which took Darwin's concepts of natural selection and survival of the fittest and applied them to human beings and intelligence. IQ was viewed as an innate quality of individuals, and people with low IQ scores were seen as inferior and unworthy, people who should be "weeded out" of society because they weakened the genetic stock. The eugenics movement, which was prominent in the 1920s, used the philosophy of Social Darwinism to advocate for the separation of the "feeble-minded" from the rest of society into institutions, sterilization of people with low IQ, and restrictions on the immigration of people deemed to be inferior (those from eastern and southern Europe, Africa and Asia). (p. 8)

One may see further depth of such mindlessly accepted categories and their social destructive implications as Nelson & Prilleltensky (2005) highlight "chilling" quotes from Albee (1981), who presents examples with instantiation of such mindlessness:

> We face the possibility of racial admixture here that is infinitely worse than that favoured by any European country today, for we are incorporating the Negro into our racial stock while all of Europe is comparatively free from this taint … the decline of American intelligence will be more rapid … owing to the presence of the Negro. (Brigham [Princeton psychologist], 1923)

> [Massive sterilization] is a practical, merciful and inevitable solution of the whole problem can be applied to an ever widening circle of social discards, beginning always with the criminal, the diseased, and the insane and extending gradually to types which may be called weaklings rather than defectives and perhaps ultimately to worthless race types. (Grant [New York Zoological Society], 1919) (Nelson & Prilleltensky, 2005, p. 8)

Psychology and the Sovereignty of Labels

The literature in psychology is brim with examples of mindless entrapment by labels and their metaphoric implications (see Churchland, 1987). One may need to look at the research on cognition, for instance, and find out how computers and their affiliated terms and connotations gave rise to a mindless search for explorations of one of the main subject matters in psychology, namely mind. When computers occupy the zeitgeist of scholarly works for mind, they bring a series of morphologically based concepts that develop and promote their restrictive approach towards thinking about mind. Our computer-driven research of the mind would suggest that the computer and the mind would have the same attributes: the computer can be considered with the attributes of the mind including the memory, and the human mind has the characteristics of the computer such as data processing. Notions such as coding, decoding, message, information, input, output, processing, to name a few, would structure the path of thinking about the mind in a way that other possibilities would be marginalized or overshadowed. The diverse qualities of the phenomena may be accordingly suppressed in the huge priming of the established labels that prescribe the direction and the sensibility of taking a direction to approach the subject matter. The following statements by Nadeau (1991) may cast further light on our mindless entanglement:

> Human beings are programmed in a manner analogous to programming computers. The hardware that is our brain allows us to assimilate the software of language and this software becomes the basis for encoding all aspects of the elaborate software package of a transmitted culture. (p. 171)

The same can be said when the metaphors of biology marshal their forces in thinking about social phenomena. This has turned out to be a common practice, namely borrowing terms and labels from biology or natural sciences and applying them in social sciences. Among some recent examples, one may refer to Wilson's (1998) book, *Consilience*, with a biological interpretation of culture and society based on Darwinian evolutionary theory. Getting immersed in reductionism and evolutionary notions of the fittest, Wilson (1998) lays huge emphasis on the only possible way of consilience where all phenomena are "based on material processes that are ultimately reducible, however long and tortuous the sequences, to the laws of physics" (p. 297).

The created models in the heart of these metaphors would limit our thinking within the domain of the prescribed structural configuration as if there were stable qualities within the social organisms. Accordingly, our intellectual endeavors to understand the phenomena would be subscribed to a quest for stability within the form. For example, if the adaptation model stands at the apex of our thinking about social phenomena, we would automatically look for the social organism's response by focusing on the best form of adaptation. The response may be taken as an explanation of the organism's stability that would help us apprehend its progress. This entangles us on a unilateral gaze at the outcome without understanding the process in which the constantly ongoing flow of events would call for a mindful understanding of the meaning within the human interactions. A mindless indulgence on the Darwinian biology and its attributions to human phenomena in social psychology would similarly produce labels and metaphors that block our understanding of the complex interplay of diversity and its implications for understanding the meaning created by human beings in social settings. Once we create a compartmentalization and let it pervasively serve as a leading metaphor, we assign labels that can allocate the individuals to the groups of our compartmentalization. If the individual fails to fall into the created categories, it would be labeled as a mismatch of the group: it does not fit our classification and can thus be labeled as the opposite of our previously constructed labels. ADHD, learning disability, general disability, and so many other socially constructed labels within our seemingly psychological analysis move in that direction. The boundaries and limits of the frequently cited labels would induce significant consequences that impede the process of transformations as they insinuate a pseudoemplacement of truth and its associated validity and reliability within the recursive patterns of labels pervasiveness.

A Langerian approach displays how getting encircled by the labels hamper the possibility of a genuine look at what may lie beyond our assumptions. Langer (2009) indicates that:

> Labels lead us to go on hypothesis-confirming data searches. That is, we look for evidence to support the label. Since most information is ambiguous, the result is "seek and ye shall find." The label "patient" leads us to examine behavior and life circumstances through a problem-finding lens. The label "patient" also leads us and doctors to search for illness-related symptoms. In both cases, behavior and sensations from the norm are interpreted as unhealthy. Moreover, independent cues of health may be totally ignored. (p. 135)

On the social level, we may see labels and metaphors that suggest an unquestionably established relationship between technical progress and the progress of democracy, the increase in computer mediated world and the enhancement of health and security, the advancement of technology and the rise in human comfort.

Social psychology's engagements with some of the created metaphors have led to the promotion of certain structural thinking about social phenomena. For example, elaboration likelihood model presented by Petty and Cacioppo (1986a, 1986b) presented a metaphoric understanding of the persuasive process that suggests an either–or way of thinking about the persuasiveness: the central routes versus the peripheral routes. Under the conditions of high involvement, the message would be processed centrally, and accordingly the receiver of the message would be highly involved in examining the content, arguments, and ideas of the message, whereas under the conditions of low involvement, the message is processed peripherally in that the receiver of the message pays no serious and central attention to issues such as content arguments and ideas in a message; instead, the receiver, under low-involvement conditions, would pay attention to issues such as attraction, expertise, and appearance of the sender, and therefore the message is peripherally processed. In central processing of the message, ELM suggest, there would a high active participation, whereas in peripheral processing, such an active participation decreases. The model would structure our thinking about persuasiveness through the creation of a metaphoric label namely routes that suggest we think about the message either this way (peripherally) or the other way (centrally), and we cannot think simultaneously both ways or in ways different from the peripheral or central. A mindful exploration of the peripheral may suggest that a peripheral route is also tied to a central route in that one needs to be centrally involved to some extent to proceed with a peripheral route. If the factor that activates the peripheral route activation (e.g., the attractiveness of the sender of the message) does not require any thought or consideration, can it ever bring the suggestion that, since this speaker is so attractive, thus what he/she says is perhaps true? The peripheral route, hence, is dialectically tied to a central route, to use the language and metaphor of the model.

On another level, the implications of negative labels associated with despair, inadequacy, deficiency, and despondency in psychotherapy may be explored in the context of the underlying epistemological, ontological, and etiological psychological perspectives where the focus on negativity has dissipated any mindful endeavor for searching beyond the mindlessly planted assumptions. One may go through Freud's words to detect numerous examples of the monolithically mindless attention and its embedded insinuations. In one of his assertions, Freud (1918–1996) says: "I have found little that is 'good' about human beings on the whole. In my experience most of them are trash..."

The important point to note here is that through the imposition of labels and their mindless expansion, we circumscribe thinking about the psychological phenomena and limit the production of ideas, understanding, and perspectives that go beyond the limited products. The limits, therefore, identify the psychological phenomena and make it look stable and fixed. Langerian mindfulness, however, warns against the danger of this caging by the labels and argues that within these limits, the psychological phenomena and its individual or social its manifestations are open to the possibilities for change and, thereby, definition: the labels should not lead us to term them as unquestionably true.

With a focus on the practical implications of mindless entrapments by the recursive patterns of labels and their inducing assumptions, Linley and Joseph (2004) examine the relationship between the deeply embedded assumptions within any psychological practice and discuss how practitioners often mindlessly go for the implementation of the practices without mindfully excavating the recondite constituents of the implicitly established messages within their mindlessly taken-for-granted axioms. On the role of these assumptions and their implications, they write:

> Further, these assumptions are typically implicit, and therefore are often uncritically accepted by practitioners trained in a particular model and a particular way of knowing. It is precisely because these fundamental assumptions are implicit that they are so often taken for granted and unchallenged, assuming the position of the status quo. (Linley & Joseph, 2004, p. 714)

One needs to read the above-mentioned citations mindfully to realize that their words are in fact tantamount to Langerian mindfulness and its call for deconstructing the layers of the assumptions that justify one's constant positioning in a single perspective.

Langer (2009) extends this from the world of psychology to the world of medicine and challenges the consecration of the mindlessly accepted principles that seem to acknowledge the ownership of knowing and knowledge to a group:

> We would be aware that medical facts are not handed down from the heavens, but in fact are determined by people under changing, different conditions. I don't think I can say often enough that medical decisions rest on uncertainty—if there were no uncertainty, there would be no decision to be made. To reveal at least some of this uncertainty would mean that while our doctors may be knowing and caring, they cannot be all-knowing. They are subject to the same biases and value-based judgments as the rest of us. But doctors often feel they have to hide their uncertainty. (p. 136)

Maddux, Snyder, and Lopez (2004) seem to have been inspired by a mindfulness when they examine the mindless implications of psychological wellness and illness, and suggest, "We can not conduct research on the validity of a construction of psychological wellness and illness. They are social constructions grounded in values, not science, and socially constructed concepts can not be proven true or false" (p. 321).

Langerian understanding of mindfulness would help us understand how our language demonstrates our priorities and how it shapes our living and being. If the language is mindfully chosen or changes, that would bring a transformation in one's being. Once the subscription to a language is mindfully examined, the very examination can delineate the limiting conditions of the language used, and that examination would develop mindfulness in the choices that one may have.

Exemplifying the underlying elements of the use of the words "remission" and "cure," Langer (2009) indicates how our frequent exposure to the mindlessly accepted labels, names, and words would stop us from exploring our choices. She challenges the pervasive discourse of language in psychology and medicine and explains:

> The way we use language encourages people with cancer, alcoholism or depression to consider their disorders as an intractable part of who they are. Colds and headaches, by contrast, describe how we are at a particular time, not who we are. We might be able to improve "how we are" if we make decisions about what to call our ailments based on differences from one episode to the next. (pp. 129–130)

The Psychology of Possibility

The psychology of possibility is one of the conspicuous landmarks of the shift in Langerian mindfulness. The psychology of possibility offers a shift from "knowing what is" to "knowing what can be" (Langer, 2009, p. 15).

The psychology of possibility critically questions the sovereignty and subjugation of knowing; it strikingly shatters the reliance on the structural repose of habitual ways of thinking; it ruptures the dependency on the plethora of circumscribing factors including our thoughts, our experiences, our schemas, and our assimilating concepts. The psychology of possibility harbors the flight from the routinized discourse of entanglement within the prescribed signifiers to the infinite realm of becoming. The psychology of possibility is not a positivist-driven psychology with a concentration on logical positivism, linear modes of thinking, and illness models. The psychology of mindfulness is a psychology of hope, faith, and meaning making; it is a psychology of self-empowerment, self-growth, and self-consummation. The psychology of possibility does not lie in negation and disconnectedness; it is a psychology of connectedness: it illustrates the possibility of repositioning one's self through a nonevaluative process in which negativity does not stop the process of furthering one's movement. The psychology of possibility celebrates the process of becoming through a mindful examination of choices. The psychology of possibility allows one to linger in the spaces of being and becoming. The psychology of possibility highlights how our mindsets are paralyzed within the illusion of stability; the psychology of possibility enlightens the possibility of an exquisitely fresh experience with revitalizing implications. In elucidating this, Langer (2009) indicates that "we hold things still in our minds, despite the fact that all the while they are changing. If we open up our minds, a world of possibility presents itself" (p. 18).

The psychology of possibility does not look for endorsement through probabilities; it encourages thinking beyond the stability of the established patterns of thinking. In dissociating from the dependency of mindset based on a mere focus on "is" than "can be," Langer (2009) writes:

> There are many cynics out there who are entrenched in their beliefs and hold dear their view of the world as fixed and predictable. There are also people who, while not cynical, are still mindlessly accepting of these views. A new approach to psychology and to our lives is needed because the naysayers—those who demand empirical evidence are—winning. It is they who have determined what's possible and what's achievable, to our collective detriment. (p. 18)

A Langerian understanding of psychology is constantly seeking the dialectics of construction and deconstruction where the certainty of the assumptions and the hubris of knowing can be openly exposed to the manifestation of uncertainty and a quest for alternative possibilities. A Langerian understanding of psychology offers a new reference point that goes beyond the government of numbers and the illusion of precision. This new reference point propounds that one's level of *being* can be continuously heightened not through a repose in the repertoire of schemas and engagement in the cognitive process of Piagian assimilation and accommodation but through a genuine and mindful exploration of the flux of novelty and its innovative unfolding as one flexibly and yet persistently embraces the incessantly flow of presence. Although it can lead to an inclusion or a discovery of flow in Csikszentmihalyi's (1990) sense, this is different, since it serves as a springboard for fostering higher stages of *being*. In doing this, Langerian perspective offers a new paradigm.

Psychology has long been sitting on the pulpit of intercepting actualities and has thus produced the borders and the definers of the psychological products within the prescribed paradigmatic analysis of what is out there. A Langerian perspective, however, propounds a concentration on potentialities and possibilities where the innovativeness of the next moment is by no means pledged by the attractors of the sovereignty of the familiar. This moves in line with fighting for *otherwise* (Fatemi, 2009) where:

> Creativity targets the unknown, the unfamiliar, the unexplored. It searches the mystery within mastery, the opening within the blockage, the revolution within stability, the disintegration within integration, the decomposition within the composition, the indeterminacy within determinacy, and the light within the darkness. (p. 50)

A Langerian perspective on psychology is creative and creational in that it continuously and not continually encourages innovation and novelty, and induces a constant engagement with revisiting the perspective that positions the actor. This, ipso facto, brings an exquisite manifestation of the experience where the experience is not merely compartmentalized within the repetitious patterns of the priming, cultivation, or association. In delineating the function of this experience, Langer (2009) writes:

> When we learn mindlessly we look at experience and impose a contingent relationship between two things—what we or some one else did and what we think happened as a result. We interpret that experience from a single perspective oblivious to the other ways it can be seen. Mindful learning looks at experience and understands that it can be seen in countless ways, that new information is always available, and that more than one perspective is both possible and extremely valuable. It is an approach that leads us to be careful about what we "know" to be true and how we learn it. At the level of the particular experience, each event is unique. Why do we think we can learn from experience? That is, if events don't necessarily repeat themselves, what can one event teach us about a future event? (pp. 29–30)

A Langerian understanding of psychology, therefore, is not built upon a linear understanding of phenomenon and their relationship. The linear understanding allows one to search for sensibility, yet it imposes syntagmatic relations that need to be observed upon any examination. Langerian perspective on psychology challenges the Cartesian epistemology and the presumed discovery of law-like generalizations that appear as the foundation for deductive explanations and predictions. This might bring Langerian epistemology in close proximity with Heidegger (1959), where he questions Cartesian discourse and its subject–object orientation indicating that nothing new can be learned as understanding becomes tantamount to nothing but a repetition of what has already been included in the interpretive process.

Heidegger (1959, pp. 157–158) elucidates that "[Man] is always thrown back on the paths that he himself has laid out: he becomes mired in his paths, caught in the beaten track, and thus caught ... excludes himself from being. He turns round and round in own circle."

A Langerian understanding of psychology avoids such a circle and considers language as a choice; it invites mindful listening and warns against the mere presentation of a spectator, as, in the language of Heidegger (1959, p. 13), it "is in words and language that things first come into being and are." A Langerian understanding, therefore, focuses not on an already-existing understanding but on making understanding possible and initiating understanding in multifarious and polysemic levels. In doing this, Langer (2009) suggests:

> Experience can be a feeble teacher. How do we learn when we think we are learning from experience? We look back at the experience—an experience that could be understood in countless ways—and impose a relationship between two things even though many other relationships could have been constructed. Once we have the relationship in mind we look for confirmations and eliminate alternative understandings. So experience too often "teaches" us what we already know. Sometimes yesterday's progress is today's failure. We try walking on a broken leg that is healing and we're doing fine, and then we see we've pushed ourselves too far and the next day we have to take it easier. We could have understood our past experiences to lead us to give up, take it easy, or try harder. (pp. 30–31)

A Langerian understanding of psychology reproaches the scientific dogmatism and its consequential reductionism, and critiques the establishment of a determinate reality for human intellect. A Langerian perspective explicates the significance of understanding the process, and in doing this it brings into perspective James's (1971) view that life is so opulently rich. In doing this, Langerism is very much in common with James's notion of indeterminism and his illustration of the limitation of the knowing and the knower. Yet, along with James (1956), Langerism encourages the search for "real, genuine possibilities in the world," as it fosters and facilitates the process of transcending the ordinary to higher and mystical stages of consciousness or, in the language of James (1958), "from a less into a more." Thus, Langerism may serve as a preamble for a transcendental process of *being* and becoming away from the quotidian engagements that only resonate with the platitudes of the entanglement with the ordinary. In describing the possibility of such a process and its experiential understanding, James (1971) writes:

> There are possibilities [in us] that take our breath away of another kind of happiness and power based on giving up our own will and letting something higher work for us, and these seem to show a world wider than either physics or philistine ethics can imagine. Here is a world in which all is well. (p. 266)

The point here, however, is to argue for a broader demonstration of Langerian mindfulness where, in addition to its significant applications and implications, mindfulness can be taken as a foundational perspective that can serve as a leading theory.

Langerism can, then, be taken as a new reference point for psychology where the research, teaching, learning, and, more importantly, understanding can be fundamentally transformed. This transformation, besides its numerous practical benefits, can give rise to attention towards the unprivileged voices that may have been concealed to oblivion in the mindless entrapment of the discourses of power. Indicating how the mindsets on expertise would develop mindlessness, Langer (1989) explains how the hegemony of those who construct the dominant narratives in a society have the power to exclude people and groups. She elaborates the mindlessness beneath the narrative structures that turn out to be the internalized truths within a society and expounds on the society's mindlessness to abide by the standards established by the so-called experts. Langer (2009) demonstrated the impacts of the dominant discourses in suppressing marginalized voices and depicts the extension of the mindlessness to the individual level where individuals are mindlessly subscribed to the hegemony of the discourses that they search for their meaning through an automatic obedience to the norms set by the dominant discourses. As Langerism would open up numerous possibilities for exploring the significant interstices that may have been largely overlooked and their marginalizing implications, it can also be of vital importance for practitioners within the psychological field. To exemplify, some therapists may be mindlessly entrapped by the categories such as cross-generational coalitions, rigid boundaries, or self-differentiation, and accordingly may not be able to examine the dehumanizing implications of such categories. However, some therapists' mindless clinging to the scientific dogma and the persistence to reductionism may reveal the pernicious impacts and dehumanizing effects of reducing people to DSM-IV diagnoses. Langerism questions the therapists' privileged access to the truth and saliently highlights the mindful process of revisiting the assumptions and the views that, if not reexamined, can lead to insidiously paralyzing outcome and consequences. In line with this, Langerism would facilitate the process of a genuine cultural psychology where the intercultural phenomena would be studied not on the strength of the dominant positive paradigmatic analysis but by virtue of a quest for understanding while lingering in the unfamiliar paradigm. This may also suggest that truths can be institutionalized, and the process of institutionalization of the truth may hamper the process of a recondite cultural understanding. To do this, Langerism can be of great service to psychology of mass media where the social construction of reality would unfold itself.

In discussing the nature of Langerian mindfulness, Sternberg (2000) examines mindfulness in the body of psychological constructs and proposes that mindfulness would be a better fit in the realm of cognitive styles.

Coming from a mindful perspective and looking for alternative ways of interpretation, one may also suggest that mindfulness is a stage of *being*; a higher *being* that is well connected to knowing: knowing becomes *being*. Ha'iri Yazdi (1992) explores this relationship of knowing and being in the following way:

> The inquiry into the nature of the relationship between knowledge and the knower can lead to the very foundation of human intellect where the word knowing does not mean any thing other than being. In this ontological state of human consciousness the constitutive dualism of the subject–object relationship is overcome and submerged into a

unitary simplex of the reality of the self that is nothing other than self-object knowledge. From this unitary simplex, the nature of self-object consciousness can, in turn, be
derived. (p. 1)

Langerian mindfulness, therefore, presents a shift from epistemology to ontology.
It opens up a new state of *being*. Psychology, having got itself disengaged from any
ontological engagements, can view mindfulness on the strength of an epistemological position. The search for mindfulness in psychology is, thus, conducted within
the epistemological priming of the presentations that, according to the very nature
of Langerian mindfulness, may have not have been very mindful of the multiple perspectives outside the realm of the epistemological endeavors. To put it in another
way, psychology's long engagements with the quest for sensibility within the familiar
epistemological paradigms may have accentuated the process of an overindulgence in
the epistemological positioning at the cost of an ongoing mindlessness towards the
ontological engagements.

Langerian understanding of psychology develops a link between both realms,
namely epistemology and ontology, and openly embraces the possibility of an ontological influence on the epistemological realm. It could, among other potential services
for the world today, offer a more mindful understanding of the need for a solid interdependence between the two known realms that have mindlessly turned back at one
another. A Langerian understanding of psychology, hence, opens up the possibility
for a genuine interdisciplinary and multidisciplinary search with an emphasis on the
distinctions of each operating perspective.

If mindfulness is taken as *being*, a higher stage and a state of *being* at that, psychology's task would find itself inextricably tied to an etiological responsibility, namely
providing a great repertoire of mindfulness for fostering growth in both individual
and social levels. Langerian understanding of mindfulness can, therefore, be a great
tool at the service of both cultural and political psychology where the perfunctory
knowing of relations and relationship can bring detrimental implications for world
peace and security. Langerian understanding of psychology may accordingly promote
rich opportunities for affecting the quality of life with positive social, individual, and
political implications.

Langerian presentation of mindfulness, hence, brings a fundamental deconstruction
of some of the mainstream psychological assumptions that have dominated our psychological understanding. Langerian mindfulness and its consequential experiments
have brought new findings in numerous areas of psychological research including creativity, health, performance, education, learning, and decision-making. This, can be
taken as a micromanifestation of the Langerian version of mindfulness, whereas in the
macrolevel Langerian presentation of mindfulness propounds a transformative process of examination of psychological phenomena; it augurs changes in psychological
thinking while going beyond the realm of thinking. Langerian understanding of mindfulness can be interpreted as a new understanding of psychology in which the reference
points for the psychological analysis would be openly exposed to a mindful excavation
of both the perspective and the actor.

Langer may be described as the forerunner of the Western psychology of possibility.
Contrary to the mainstream psychology that legitimizes psychology's dependency on

the observer's version of understanding and their authoritative privilege in endorsing the observer-driven truth, Langerian psychology examines the hegemony of the context-oriented truth and probes the necessity for looking at the a priori assumptions that act as the driving forces of the psychological analysis. In doing this, Langerian understanding of psychology would potentially offer an in-depth look at a wide variety of psychological assumptions that are implicitly taken for granted.

References

Albee, G. W. (1981). Politics, power, prevention, and social change. In J. M. Joffee & G. W. Albee (Eds.), *Prevention through political action and social change* (pp. 5–25). Hanover, NH: University Press of New England.

Allport, G. W. (1955). *Becoming: Basic considerations for a psychology of personality*. New Haven, CT: Yale University Press.

Banister, P., Burman, E., Parker, I., Taylor. M., & Tindall, C. (1994). *Qualitative methods in psychology: a research guide*. Buckingham, UK: Open University Press.

Bruner, J. (1986). *Actual minds, possible worlds*. Cambridge, MA: Harvard University Press.

Fischer, C. T. (2006). *Qualitative research methods for psychologists: Introduction through empirical studies*. San Diego, CA: Academic Press.

Harre, R., & Secord, P. F. (1972). *The explanation of social behavior*. Oxford, UK: Basil Blackwell.

Churchland, P. (1987). *Matter and consciousness: An introduction to the philosophy of mind*. Cambridge, MA: MIT Press.

Csikszentmihalyi, M. (1990). *Flow: The psychology of optimal experience*. New York, NY: Harper-Collins.

Fatemi, S. M. (2009). *How we speak shapes how we learn: a linguistic and psychological theory of education*. New York, NY: The Edwin Mellen Press.

Fineburg, A. (2004). Introducing positive psychology to the introductory psychology student. In P. A. Linley & S. Joseph (Eds.), *Positive psychology in practice*. Hoboken, NJ: John Wiley & Sons.

Gadamer, H. (1988). *Truth and method*. New York, NY: The Crossroad Publishing Company (Original 1965, 1975 English.)

Ha'iri Yazdi, M. (1992). The principles of epistemology in Islamic philosophy. State University of New York Press.

Hall, T. (1998). Seeking a focus on joy in the field of psychology. *New York Times*, Tuesday April 28, section F, p.7.

Heidegger, M. (1959). *An introduction to metaphysics*. New Haven, CT: Yale University Press.

Horwitz, A. V. (2002). *Creating mental illness*. Chicago, IL: University of Chicago Press.

James, W. (1958). *The varieties of religious experience; A study in human nature*. New York, NY: New American Library.

James, W. (1971). A pluralistic universe. In R. B. Perry (Eds.), *Essays in radical empiricism and a pluralistic universe*. New York, NY: Dutton.

Kuhn, T. S. (1962). *The structure of scientific revolution*. Chicago, IL: The University of Chicago Press.

Langer, E. J. (1989). *Mindfulness*. Reading, MA: Addison-Wesley.

Langer, E. J. (1997). *The power of mindful learning*. Reading, MA: Addison-Wesley.

Langer, E. (2009). *Counterclockwise: mindful health and the power of possibility*. New York, NY: Ballantine Books.

Linley, P. A., & Joseph, P. (2004). Toward a theoretical foundation for positive psychology in practice. In P. A. Linley & S. Joseph (Eds.), *Positive psychology in practice*. Hoboken, NJ: John Wiley & Sons.

Lykken, D., & Tellegen, A. (1996). Happiness is a stochastic phenomenon. *Psychological Science, 7*, 186–189.

Maddux, J. E., Snyder, C. R., & Lopez, S. (2004). Towards a positive clinical psychology: Deconstructing the illness ideology and constructing an ideology of human strengths and potential. In P. A. Linley & S. Joseph (Eds.), *Positive psychology in practice*. Hoboken, NJ: John Wiley & Sons.

Medich, C., Stuart, E., & Chase, S. (1997). Healing through integration: promoting wellness in cardiac rehabilitation. *Journal of Cardiovascular Nursing, 11*(3), 66–79.

McCrae, R. R., & Costa, P. T. (1990). *Personality in adulthood*. New York, NY: Guilford Press.

Nadeau, R. (1991). *Mind, machines and human consciousness*. Chicago, IL: Contemporary Books.

Nelson, G., & Prilleltensky, I. (2005). *Community psychology: In pursuit of liberation and well-being*. New York, NY: Palgrave Macmillan.

Parker, I. (1989). *The crisis in modern social psychology, and how to end it*. London, UK: Routledge.

Paul, L., & Weinert, C. (1999). Wellness profile of midlife women with a chronic illness. *Public Health Nursing, 16*(5), 341–350.

Petty, R. E., & Cacioppo, J. T. (1986a). *Communication and persuasion: Central and peripheral routes to attitude change*. New York, NY: Springer-Verlag.

Petty, R. E., & Cacioppo, J. T. (1986b). The elaboration likelihood model of persuasion. In L. Berkowitz (Ed.), *Advances in experimental social psychology* (Vol. 19, pp. 123–205). San Diego, CA: Academic Press.

Scileppi, J. A., Teed, E. L., & Torres, R. D. (2000). *Community psychology, a common sense approach to mental health*. Upper Saddle River, NJ: Prentice-Hall.

Seligman, M. E. P. (2002). *Authentic happiness: Using the new positive psychology to realize your potential for lasting fulfillment*. New York, NY: Free Press.

Seligman, M. E. P., & Csikszentmihalyi, M. (Eds.). (2000). Positive psychology. *American Psychologist, 55*(1), 5–14.

Suh, E. M., Diener-E., & Fujita, F. (1996). Event and subjective well-being: Only recent events matter. *Journal of Personality and Social Psychology, 70*, 1091–1102.

VanderStoep, S. W., Fagerlin, A., & Feenstra, J. S. (2000). What do students remember form introductory psychology? *Teaching of Psychology, 2*, 89–92.

Wilson, E. O. (1998). *Consilience: The unity of knowledge*. London, UK: Little, Brown.

Woolgar, S. (1988). *Science: The very idea*. Chichester, UK: Ellis Horwood.

Further Reading

Baylis, N. (2004). *Teaching positive psychology*. In P. A. Linley & S. Joseph (Eds.), *Positive psychology in practice*. Hoboken, NJ: John Wiley & Sons.

Cacioppo, J. T., Petty, R. E., Kao, C. F., & Rodriguez, R. (1986). Central and peripheral routes to persuasion: An individual difference perspective. *Journal of Personality and Social Psychology, 51*, 1031–1043.

Cacioppo, J. T., Petty, R. E., & Morris, K. (1983). Effects of need for cognition on message evaluation, recall, and persuasion. *Journal of Personality and Social Psychology, 45*, 805–818.

Chaiken, S. (1980). Heuristic versus systematic information processing and the use of source versus message cues in persuasion. *Journal of Personality and Social Psychology, 39*, 752–756.

Csikszentmihalyi, M. (1997). *Finding flow: The psychology of engagement with every day life.* New York, NY: Plenum Press.

Darley, J. M. (1991). Altruism and prosocial behavior research: Reflections and prospects. In M. S. Clark (Ed.), *Prosocial behavior* (pp. 312–327). Newbury Park, CA: Sage.

Egan, G., & Schroeder, W. (2009). *The skilled helper: A problem-management and opportunity development approach to helping.* Toronto, Canada: Nelson.

Ellis, A. (1984). Must most psychotherapists remain as incompetent as they are now? In J. Hairman (Ed.), *Does psychotherapy really help people?* Springfield, IL: Charles C. Thomas.

Epstein, S. (1998). *Constructive thinking: the key to emotional intelligence.* Westport, CT: Praeger.

Epstein, S., & Meier, P. (1989). Constructive thinking: A broad coping variable with specific coping components. *Journal of Personality and Social Psychology, 57*, 332–350.

Folkman, S., & Moskowitz, J. T. (2000). Positive affect and the other side of coping. *American Psychologist, 55*, 647–664.

Freud, S. (1996). NUMBER: 23091. In R. Andrews, M. Biggs, & M. Seidel (Eds.), *Columbia world of quotations* (letter dated October 9, 1918, "Psychoanalysis and faith: The letters of Sigmund Freud and Oskar Pfister," no. 59 from the International Psycho-Analytical Library in 1963, New York, NY: Columbia University Press).

Gerbner, G., Gross, L., Morgan, M., & Signorielli, N. (1994). Growing up with television: The cultivation perspective. In J. Bryant & D. Zillmann (Eds.), *Media effects: Advances in theory and research* (pp. 17–41). Hillsdale, NJ: Lawrence Erlbaum Associates.

Heath, R. L., & Bryant, J. (1992). *Human communication theory and research: Concepts, contexts, and challenges.* Hillsdale, NJ: Lawrence Erlbaum Associates.

James, W. (1956a). *The will to believe and other essays in popular psychology.* New York, NY: Dover.

James, W. (1956b). *The varieties of religious experience.* New York, NY: New American Library.

Jorgensen, J., & Nafstad, H. E. (2004). Positive psychology: historical, philosophical, and epistemological perspectives. In P. A. Linley & S. Joseph (Eds.), *Positive psychology in practice.* Hoboken, NJ: John Wiley & Sons.

Kabat-Zinn, J. (1990). *Full catastrophe living: using the wisdom of your body and mind to face stress, pain, and illness.* New York, NY: Dell Pub.

Kahneman, D. (1999). Objective happiness. In D. Kahneman, E. Diener, & N. Schwarz (Eds.), *Well-being: The foundations of hedonic psychology* (pp. 3–25). New York, NY: Russell Sage Foundation.

Kahneman, D., Knetsch, J., & Thaler, R. (1990). Experimental tests of the endowment effect and the Coase theorem. *Journal of Political Economy, 98*(6), 1325–1348.

Kasser, T., & Ryan, R. M. (1996a). A dark side of the American dream: Correlates of financial success as a central life aspiration. *Journal of Personality and Social Psychology, 65*, 410–422.

Kasser, T., & Ryan, R. M. (1996b). Further examining the American dream: differential correlates of intrinsic and extrinsic goals. *Personality and Social Psychology Bulletin, 22*, 280–287.

Langer, E., Janis, I., & Wolfer, J. A. (1975). Reduction of psychological stress in surgical patients. *Journal of Experimental Social Psychology, 11*, 155–165.

Langer, E. J. (1994). The illusion of calculated decisions. In R. Schank & E. Langer (Eds.), *Beliefs, reasoning and decision making.* Hillsdale, NJ: Erlbaum.

138   *Sayyed Mohsen Fatemi*

Langer, E. J., Beck, P., Janoff-Bulman, R., & Timko, C. (1984). The relationship between cognitive deprivation and longevity in senile and non-senile elderly populations. *Academic Psychology Bulletin, 6,* 211–226.

Langer, E. J., Blank, A., & Chanowitz, B. (1978). The mindlessness of ostensibly thoughtful action: The role of "placebic" information in interpersonal interactions. *Journal of Personality and Social Psychology, 36,* 635–642.

Langer, E. J., Hatem, M., Joss, J., & Howell, M. (1989). Conditional teaching and mindful learning: The role of uncertainty in education. *Creativity Research Journal, 2,* 139–159.

Langer, E. J., & Piper, A. (1987). The prevention of mindlessness. *Journal of Personality and Social Psychology, 53,* 280–287.

Langer, E. J., & Bodner, T. (1995). *Mindfulness and attention.* Unpublished manuscript, Harvard University, Cambridge, MA.

Langer, E. J., Carson, S., & Shih, M. (in press). Sit still and pay attention? *Journal of Adult Development.*

Langer, E. J., Heffernan, D., & Kiester, M. (1988). *Reducing burnout in an institutional setting: An experimental investigation.* Unpublished manuscript, Harvard University, Cambridge, MA.

Lazar, S. W., Kerr, C., Wasseman, R., Gray, J. R., McGarvey, M., Quinn, B. T., ... Fischl, B. (2005). *Meditation experience is associated with increased cortical thickness.*

Lazarus, R. S., & Folkman, S. (1984). *Stress, appraisal, and coping.* New York, NY: Springer.

Maslow, A. H. (1971). *Farther reaches of human nature.* New York, NY: Penguin Arkana.

Nafstad, H. E. (2003). The neo-liberal ideology and the self-interest paradigm as resistance to change. *Radical Psychology, 3,* 3–21.

Ong, A. D., Bergeman, C. S., Bisconti, T. L., & Wallace, K. A. (2006). Psychological resilience, positive emotions, and successful adaptation to stress in later life. *Journal of Personality and Social Psychology, 91,* 730–749.

Petterson, C., & Seligman, M. E. P. (2003). *Values in Action (VIA). Classification of strengths* (draft dated January, 4, 2003).

Petty, R. E., & Cacioppo, J. T. (1981). *Attitudes and persuasion: Classic and contemporary approaches.* Dubuque, IA: William C. Brown.

Sternberg, R. (2002). Images of mindfulness. *Journal of Social Issues, 56,* 11–26.

7

Art of Mindfulness

Integrating Eastern and Western Approaches

Maja Djikic

Mindfulness, historically associated with meditation techniques that originated principally from Buddhist practices (Hanh, 1976), has permeated Western psychology in the recent decades. There are two distinct approaches to it in the current psychological literature—one based on the practices congruent with the Eastern meditation (Alexander, Langer, Newman, Chandler, & Davies, 1989; Bishop et al., 2004; Kabat-Zinn, 1990), and a uniquely Western approach that does not involve meditation but draws novel distinctions about the objects of one's awareness (Langer, 1989; Langer & Abelson, 1972; Langer, Blank, & Chanowitz, 1978). In this chapter, I shall describe how these two approaches differ in what they considered to be a problem (to which mindfulness is an answer), what they argue to be the underlying causes of the problem, and, finally, what practices they propose would lead to positive outcomes. The differences between the approaches will then be integrated within a unifying framework that focuses on personality development.

The differences between Eastern and Western approaches to psychology—concerning the nature of mind, self, mental illness, well-being, and the best means of examining them all—are so extensive that it would be foolish to attempt to pursue them in this short chapter. It should be kept in mind that the very dichotomy of Eastern and Western, in all of its black-and-white implications, may be called into question. Here, I use it as a shorthand, aware of the impossibility of separating fully the two perspectives. What might be of greater use is to focus specifically on the two traditions of mindfulness that are currently both active within the Western psychology. The most current operational definition of mindfulness from the more traditional, meditative perspective is that it is a form of self-regulation of attention that is present-oriented and is characterized by curiosity, openness, and acceptance (Bishop et al., 2004). This is aligned with Kabat-Zinn's (1990) definition of mindfulness as purposive, present-moment, nonjudgmental awareness. In the alternative, nonmeditative approach that is uniquely Western in its predisposition, Langer (1989, 1997, 2005, 2009)

The Wiley Blackwell Handbook of Mindfulness, First Edition.
Edited by Amanda Ie, Christelle T. Ngnoumen, and Ellen J. Langer.
© 2014 John Wiley & Sons, Ltd. Published 2014 by John Wiley & Sons, Ltd.

operationalizes mindfulness as drawing novel distinctions, which results in being situated in the present, sensitive to context and perspective, and guided (but not governed) by rules and routines. The two sets of operational definitions appear startlingly different, yet, as we shall see upon closer examination, the singularities of each approach can be placed within an underlying framework, wherein each contributes to the elucidation of the other. To do that, however, we need to start with the differences, starting with the formulation of the problem.

The Problem

From the Eastern, Buddhist, perspective, the root problem is suffering (*dukkha*), which includes not only the inevitabilities of sickness, old-age, and death, but also the pain of frequently not getting what we want, and then suffering about that, too (Mosig, 1989). An example here would be something as ubiquitous as the pain of chronic illness or the loss of a loved one. The focus is on the pain that is inevitable in the process of life, and learning ways of being that would obviate suffering that usually stems from it.

From the Western perspective, the problem is mindlessness (Langer et al., 1978; Langer, 1989)—in which we make bad decisions and sometimes no decisions at all by exhibiting routinized, stereotyped, primed, or authority-compliant behaviors. When mindless, we are victimized by the persistence of categories that existed only in the past or that exist only in our minds, struggling and failing in a futile labor against reality. This includes, for example, treating all members of a racial or gender group in the same way, or giving up the struggle for life just because 70–80% of other people who have your diagnosis tend to die from it.

Even within the definition of the problem, there appears to exist a deep philosophical divide between the two approaches. From the Eastern perspective, the problem being remedied begins and ends internally– it is one's way of being or attitude that needs a remedy; to the Western mind, the way of being needs to be accompanied by the right kind of action that will benefit the doer's well-being, in ways both practical and emotional. This being–doing divide, if you will, is reflected in the perspective on the nature of human potential. The Western person tends to think of fulfilling their potential as reflected by and pursued through action, which is propelled forward by a sense of purpose (Jung, 1939/1953; Rogers, 1951), while the predominance of meditative techniques in the East points to the path to self-development through stillness and silence (Walsh & Shapiro, 2006). Finally, this cultural doing versus being divide is reflected even in the definitions of mindfulness—Langer's (1989, 2005) definition of drawing novel distinctions emphasizes activity within awareness, while Kabat-Zinn's (1990) definition emphasizes present-moment, nonjudgmental awareness—a state or quality of awareness.

The Cause

Given that the problems cited above are significantly different, it is no surprise that their causes are likely to diverge further. From the Eastern Buddhist perspective, the cause of the problem of suffering is craving, that is, either attachment or aversion to experiences, emotions, or persons we consider positive or negative (Sheng-yen, 2000). To the Western mind, which generally attempts to solve the problems of content of life, the idea of the solution dealing with the varieties of a megacognitive process, rather than cognitive content, might at first seem rather foreign. To a Western person, for example, the problem of a dying parent is the problem of the loss, rather than the problem of aversion to the loss.

From the Western standpoint, the problem of mindlessness is caused by a lack of choice that stems from being dominated by old categories (and thus leads to the repetition of experience), and by being controlled by the environment. The problem of choice begins with failing to perceive and create choices in one's environment (Langer & Rodin, 1976; Rodin & Langer, 1977), and it is compounded by the problem of the discomfort due to the uncertainty implied in multiplicity of alternatives (McGregor, Zanna, Holmes, & Spencer, 2001). From the evolutionary perspective, it seems reasonable that many of our cognitive and behavioral tendencies would remain relatively stable after being reinforced, since some basic aspects of our environment have tended to remain stable over the millennia (Buss, 1995). Humans as species may have stable preferences and aversions regarding food consumption, or mating. However, when this persistence is mindlessly applied to cognitive categories, it causes a serious and dangerous mismatch between the well-entrenched categories and the emerging (and rapidly changing) world.

This problem of heavy evolutionary emphasis on previous experience as a guide to the future behavior is compounded by the existential uncertainty and anxiety we feel in the face of life choices (McGregor et al., 2001; Peterson, 1999). This fact makes the presence of alternatives anxiety-inducing, given that a multiplicity of alternatives may imply greater probability of error. A person, therefore, may limit the perception of alternatives not only to the point in time after the decision is made, but prior to it as well. As a consequence, the multiplicity of choices we experience at each decision point keeps being veiled by a miasma of anxiety. The price of repetition of past experience in a rapidly evolving world (no matter how comforting or "certain" the behavior may feel) is high—it necessitates that the solutions to the problems we encounter remain out of reach.

From the Western perspective, not only are people controlled and prevented from making better choices by their own routinized past experiences, but also they are controlled by their environment. Frequently, people act because they are primed by cues in their environment, unaware that their behavior is influenced at all (Bargh & Chartrand, 1999). Furthermore, when in the presence of authority figures, instructions are heard as directions, leading to the surrender of responsibility for choices we make (Fromm, 1941; Milgram, 1963). Fromm (1941), who bemoaned the conformity of German populace to Nazi ideology, would not have been surprised that now we are equally mindlessly conformist to the apparent certainties of expert advice, for example, recommendations given by physicians and other health specialists (Langer, 2009).

Finally, even our means of learning promote mindlessness, given the epistemology implicit within our educational system, according to which to know something is to have certainty about a fact. Langer (1997; Langer & Piper, 1987) argued that the very notion of what it means to "pay attention" in the Western world—to pay attention to the fixed aspects of the stimuli, rather than the variable ones—cultivates mindlessness throughout the educational system and beyond.

The causes for the problem (of suffering and mindlessness, respectively), diverge, with the Eastern perspective seeing craving (through either attachment or aversion) as the main cause, while the Western view gravitates toward a multiplicity of causes that take away choices. Given the diversion of the causes, the solutions diverge even further, as we shall see in the next section.

Solutions

The difference between the two approaches regarding the solution to the problem of suffering and mindlessness can be posed as a difference between radical acceptance and radical challenge. From the Eastern, Buddhist perspective, the problem of suffering is to be solved by dissolving craving, which includes the Eightfold Path, the central fold of which is Right Mindfulness (the other seven including Right Thinking, Right Understanding, Right Speech, Right Action, Right Livelihood, Right Effort, and Right Concentration; Kabat-Zinn, 2003; Sheng-yen, 2000). Therefore, craving is dissolved by cultivating a state of mindfulness, in which one approaches experience with accepting, nonjudgmental, and compassionate awareness (Gilbert, 2005; Hayes, Strosahl, & Wilson, 1999; Kabat-Zinn, 1990). Underlying this awareness is a fundamental acceptance of self, environment, and experience, which is achieved mostly through different meditative practices (Walsh & Shapiro, 2006). One aspect of meditation that Western individuals often have trouble with is the very thing that may be therapeutic about it—cultivating stillness.

From the Western perspective, mindfulness is to be achieved not by radical acceptance, but by radical challenge. This means challenging any single perspective, any judgment about the self or the world, any particular outcome, as being absolutely right or wrong, good or bad (Djikic & Langer, 2007). This stance is likely to promote not only tolerance of others but also one's own authenticity. Continually making novel distinctions brings forth a multiplicity of alternatives, the sense of certainty giving way to cultivated tolerance of ambiguity. Langer (2009) argued that educational focus on mindful distinction-making (being attentive to variability), where facts will be taught as necessarily affected by perspective and context, would preempt mindless habits that persist to and through adulthood (Langer, 1993). An awareness of context by drawing novel distinctions leads to being in the present. The fact that the same behavior can be described from multiple perspectives (e.g., as simultaneously both positive and negative) leads to less absolute judgment of any particular behavior. It is this continual active challenge (to a single perspective, single answer, single fact, single authority) that defines the uniquely Western approach to mindfulness. This does not mean that novel distinction-making is more effortful than meditation—both can be effortful at the beginning and can become effortless with time and practice (Tang & Posner, 2009). It only means that from the Western perspective, mindfulness can be approached through activity, and not just the stillness of meditative techniques.

Integration

Given that the two approaches appear so different, how are we to integrate them into a single framework that will accommodate both while elucidating each in a new light? We shall start by outlining the underlying similarity of the approaches, the most conspicuous of which is the similarity of their outcomes.

Novel distinction-making improves attention (Carson, Shih, & Langer, 2001; Levy, Jennings, & Langer, 2001), memory (Langer, 1997), and creativity (Langer & Piper, 1987). In terms of health benefits, it reduces mortality among nursing-home elderly (Alexander et al., 1989; Langer, Beck, Janoff-Bulman, & Timko, 1984) and decreases arthritic pain and alcoholism (Langer, 1997). Finally, in work settings, novel distinction-making decreases burnout and increases productivity (Langer, Heffernan, & Kiester, 1988; Park 1990). Meditative techniques have similar far-reaching effects, particularly with physical and psychological ailments that appear to be stress related (Walsh & Shapiro, 2003). Among their many effects, meditative techniques improve processing speed, concentration, and memory (Murphy & Donovan, 1997). They also reduce cardiovascular and hormonal disorders (Schneider et al., 2005; Murphy & Donovan, 1997), decrease stress and increase immune functioning (Davidson et al., 2003), reduce pain in chronic disorders (Kabat-Zinn, 2003), and reduce mortality among the elderly (Alexander et al., 1989). The overwhelming overlap of effects seems to point to a common factor at the root of the Eastern and Western perspectives on mindfulness.

In terms of the difference in the conception of what constitutes the main problem from Eastern and Western perspectives, that is, positioning the problem of suffering against the problem of mindlessness, it is important to note that both deal with the prevalent unwillingness of individuals to accept reality as it is. With regards to suffering, there is reluctance to face failure, pain, sickness, old-age, or death, as inevitable aspects of existence. Similarly, an individual hides from the reality of alternative interpretations, perspectives, contexts, or behavioral routes by mindlessly acting out primed, routinized, authority-compliant behaviors. It underscores hesitation to acknowledge reality of having a choice, and the necessity of taking the responsibility for it. Suffering, then, is intrinsically linked to the mindless separation from reality.

Even the causes described above, craving (in the form of attachment or aversion) versus the lack of choice, no matter how apparently divergent, are held together by an underlying link, illusory desire. It is unusually difficult to know what we want. For example, if a romantic partner breaks up with me, I might go home and want to eat a whole tub of ice cream. Do I really want the ice cream, do I want a hug from a friend, or perhaps do I want my romantic partner to beg my forgiveness and promptly return to me? It is difficult to know, because, from the Western perspective, the environment and our past experiences control many of the wants we experience as presently ours, though we and the world have changed. We may not want a particular article of clothing or furniture until we have seen a commercial in which these articles are conveniently linked to our other wants—for success or acceptance. I might insist on eating apple pie because I used to love it as an adolescent, though it no longer agrees with my stomach. In the impulse to act, there is no pause in which to consider one's alternatives or choices. Therefore, our wants are to be subjected to the same mindful distinction-making as other objects of our attention, so that a choice can be made, and responsibility can follow. From the Eastern perspective, all desires are illusory when they manifest through either attachment or aversion. Therefore, the displaced desire for ice cream and actual desire for a hug or comfort or to have the partner back are both tinged with the same illusory quality. This aligns with the Western perspective, because when one looks at the thing that we "really" think we want (return of the partner), mindful distinction-making would make us think again. After all, why would we want to be in a relationship with a person who doesn't reciprocate our feelings? Under the light of the mindful distinction-making, the intensity of all attachments and aversions becomes suspect.

The means of pursuing mindfulness that we discussed at first glance seems dia-metrically opposite—radical acceptance versus radical challenge. Yet they are brought together when we consider what is being accepted and what is being challenged. Meditative techniques promote acceptance of reality through present-moment, non-judgmental awareness, while the Western technique of novel distinction-making pro-motes radical challenge to an illusion of a single perspective, a single authority, which make alternatives and choices invisible. While meditative techniques loosen the grip of categories by treating them as potentially equally illusory, novel distinction-making, through evoking a multiplicity of categories, prevents attachment to any single one.

Toward a New Framework

One can conciliate Eastern and Western approaches to mindfulness, but what new framework might illuminate both of these approaches? The clue can be found in a simple question. Given the multiplicity of positive effects of mindfulness, what force compels individuals to keep mindlessly suffering? Instead of looking for causes within the mindfulness framework (either Eastern or Western), I shall attempt to answer this question from a framework that deals with personality development instead.

Personality, though by definition a stable pattern of thoughts, feeling, and disposi-tions (McCrae & Costa, 2008), changes and develops across the life span (Roberts & DelVecchio, 2000). Change in personality, like in any other stable system, is pre-ceded by a dysregulation or fluctuation that needs to reach a critical level before it reorganizes into a new stable configuration (Bak & Chen, 1991; Schiepek Eckert, & Weihrauch, 2003). Often, when this dysregulation (emotional in nature) is involuntary or externally caused (such as in case of trauma or overwhelming life experience), per-sonality change happens quickly and frequently has destructive effects on well-being (Foa, Keane, Friedman, & Cohen, 2009; van der Kolk, 1987). Positive, developmen-tal changes in personality are likely to occur only if the person voluntarily chooses or exposes herself to the emotional dysregulation that can sufficiently disrupt the person-ality system to create a lasting change (Djikic, 2011; Peterson, 1999).

In the West, we have few means for such positive, voluntary dysregulation that promotes personality development. One is psychotherapy—or rather the type of psychotherapy in which the therapists do not dysregulate their clients, but clients dysregulate themselves (Rogers, 1951). Research has shown such discontinuities or fluctuations to occur prior to "breakthrough" growth in psychotherapeutic settings (Hayes, Laurenceau, Feldman, Strauss, & Cardaciotto, 2007). Another potential source of personality development is art. Exposure to art causes subtle fluctuations in personality structure (mediated by emotional fluctuations), across different forms of art (music, literature, visual arts; Djikic, 2011; Djikic, Oatley, & Peterson, 2012; Djikic, Oatley, Zoeterman, & Peterson, 2009). I would argue that mindfulness (from both Eastern and Western perspectives) provides another, unique path to voluntary self-dysregulation, which can lead to salutary changes in one's personality system.

Now, we can come back to the question of why people keep being mindless, despite an enormous amount of evidence showing extraordinary positive physical and psychological effects of being mindful. I would argue that both meditative techniques and novel distinction-making produce subtle fluctuations in one's emotional and personality systems. This is precisely the reason why many people prefer to forfeit the benefits of mindfulness rather than expose themselves to the unsettling tumult of self-dysregulation.

The aspect of meditative techniques that can quickly unsettle novice practitioners is stillness. Stillness produces an existential gap that most people try to avoid by continually talking, thinking, watching TV, checking their berries and tablets, or listening to music. It is the very same gap that allows for the disidentification of awareness from the content of awareness (Walsh & Shapiro, 2006). For novices, the terror and discomfort of stillness are dysregulating, providing a motivation either to stay mindless or to open the space for a new stage of personality development. For those who take the opportunity, the outcomes translate into trait changes, even with regard to the traits that are considered most stable and unchangeable, such as the Big Five (Travis, Arenander, & DuBois, 2004).

From the Western perspective, the process of making novel distinctions is as unsettling as meditation, but for a different reason. Making novel distinctions highlights both the multiplicity of the perspectives, through which one can observe any object in one's awareness, and the continually emerging, changing, nature of reality. Individuals may cling to a single perspective because they may want to experience the existential comfort of "doing or thinking the right thing." Multiple perspectives and the fact that there is no "right thing" are likely to dysregulate individuals who are attempting to be mindful. Furthermore, when the object of awareness is self, the distinctions that are novel usually concern aspects of self that have been occluded, usually because they are, for whatever reason, inappropriate to self. Being mindful thus brings forth the existential anxiety not just about the changing world but about the imperfect self—a state that many individuals may not seek out.

Perhaps we can conclude that mindless people find mindfulness dysregulating (at the start), but that very dysregulation avails them of opportunities for growth. Mindfulness, either from an Eastern or from a Western perspective, has unique qualities that differ from both therapy and exposure to art. Therapy implies the presence of another, and art an indirect presence of another (the artist). It is only with mindfulness that we do not need another to try to develop ourselves. Furthermore, the voluntary nature of practicing mindfulness is undeniable. After all, it is rare that one is pressured into meditation (as is the case with therapy) or accidentally exposed to novel distinction-making (as is the case with art). It allows for personality development for those who prefer to work on themselves by themselves.

Conclusion

For the mindless novices, the process of attempting to be mindful, through meditation or novel distinction-making, will be a struggle no matter how their attempt ends. If it succeeds, they will face dysregulation that is necessary to make the change; if it fails, their mindless actions will keep clashing against the unforgiving demands of reality. They will struggle either way, but only for the former will the struggle lessen over time, as they learn to mindfully accept reality of the self and the world as it is, ever-emerging and unknown.

References

Alexander, C., Langer, E. J., Newman, R., Chandler, H., & Davies, J. (1989). Aging, mindfulness and meditation. *Journal of Personality and Social Psychology, 57*, 950–964.

Bak, P., & Chen, K. (1991). Self-organized criticality. *Scientific American, 264*, 46–53.

Bargh, J. A., & Chartrand, T. L. (1999). The unbearable automaticity of being. *American Psychologist, 54*(7), 462–479.

Bishop, S. R ., Lau, M., Shapiro, S., Carlson, L., Anderson, N. D., Carmody, J., ... Devins, G. (2004). Mindfulness: A proposed operational definition. *Clinical Psychology: Science and Practice, 11*(3), 230–241.

Buss, D. M. (1995). Evolutionary psychology: A new paradigm for psychological science. *Psychological Inquiry, 6*, 1–30.

Carson, S., Shih, M., & Langer, E. J. (2001). Sit still and pay attention? *Journal of Adult Development, 8*(3), 183–188.

Davidson, R. J., Kabat-Zinn, J., Schumacher, J., Rosenkranz, M., Muller, D., Santorelli, S. F., ... Sheridan, J. F. (2003). Alterations in brain and immune function produced by mindfulness meditation. *Psychosomatic Medicine, 65*, 564–570.

Djikic, M. (2011). The effect of music and lyrics on personality. *Psychology of Aesthetics, Creativity, and the Arts, 5*(30), 237–240.

Djikic, M., & Langer, J. (2007). Toward mindful social comparison: When subjective and objective selves are mutually exclusive. *New Ideas in Psychology, 25*, 221–232.

Djikic, M., Oatley, K., & Peterson, J. B. (2012). Serene arts: The effect of personal unsettledness sand painting's narrative structure on personality. *Empirical Studies of the Arts, 30*(20), 183–193.

Djikic, M., Oatley, K., Zoeterman, S., & Peterson, J. B. (2009). On "being moved" by art: How reading fiction transforms the self. *Creativity Research Journal, 21*(1), 24–29.

Foa, E. B., Keane, T., Friedman, M. J., & Cohen, J. A. (2009). Introduction. In E. B. Foa, T. M. Keane, M. J. Friedman, & J. A. Cohen (Eds.), *Effective treatments for PTSD*. New York, NY: The Guilford Press.

Fromm, E. (1941). *Escape from freedom*. New York, NY: Avon.

Gilbert, P. (2005). *Compassion*. New York, NY: Routledge.

Hanh, T. N. (1976). *The miracle of mindfulness: A manual for meditation*. Boston, MA: Beacon.

Hayes, A. M., Laurenceau, J. Feldman, G., Strauss, J., & Cardaciotto, L. (2007). Change is not always linear: The study of nonlinear and discontinuous patterns of change in psychother-apy. *Clinical Psychology Review, 27*, 715–723.

Hayes, S. C., Strosahl, K., & Wilson, K. G. (1999). *Acceptance and commitment therapy*. New York, NY: Guilford Press.

Jung, C. G. (1953). The integration of personality. In H. Read, M. Fordham, & G. Adler (Eds.), *Collected works* (Vol. 8). Princeton, NJ: Princeton University Press. (Original work published 1939)

Kabat-Zinn, J. (1990). *Full catastrophe living: Using the wisdom of your mind to face stress, pain and illness*. New York, NY: Dell.

Kabat-Zinn, J. (2003). Mindfulness-based interventions in context: Past, present, and future. *Clinical Psychology: Science and Practice, 10*, 144–156.

Langer, E. J. (1989). *Mindfulness*. Reading, MA: Addison-Wesley.

Langer, E. J. (1993). Mindful education. *Educational Psychologist, 28*(10), 43–50.

Langer, E. J. (1997). *The power of mindful learning*. Reading, MA: Addison-Wesley.

Langer, E. J. (2005). *On becoming an artist*. New York, NY: Ballantine Books.

Langer, E. J. (2009). *Counter clockwise: Mindful health and the power of possibility*. New York, NY: Ballantine Books.

Langer, E. J., & Abelson, R. P. (1972). The semantics of asking a favor: How to succeed in getting help without really dying. *Journal of Personality and Social Psychology, 24*(1), 26–32.

Langer, E. J., Beck, P., Janoff-Bulman, R., & Timko, C. (1984). The relationship between cognitive deprivation and longevity in senile and non-senile elderly populations. *Academic Psychology Bulletin, 6*, 211–226.

Langer, E. J., Blank, A., & Chanowitz, B. (1978). The mindlessness of ostensibly thoughtful action: The role of "placebic" information in interpersonal interactions. *Journal of Personality and Social Psychology, 36*, 635–642.

Langer, E. J., Heffernan, D., & Kiester, M. (1988). *Reducing burnout in an institutional setting: An experimental investigation*. Unpublished manuscript, Harvard University, Cambridge, MA.

Langer, E. J., & Piper, A. (1987). The prevention of mindlessness. *Journal of Personality and Social Psychology, 11*, 155–165.

Langer, E. J., & Rodin, J. (1976). The effects of choice and enhanced personal responsibility for the aged: A field experiment in an institutional setting. *Journal of Personality and Social Psychology, 34*, 191–198.

Levy, B. R., Jennings, P., & Langer, E. J. (2001). Improving attention in old age. *Journal of Adult Development, 8*(3), 189–192.

McCrae, R. R., & Costa, P. T. (2008). The five-factor theory of personality. In O. P. John, R. W. Robins, & L. A. Pervin (Eds.), *Handbook of personality: Theory and research* (3rd ed., pp. 159–182). New York, NY: Guilford Press.

McGregor, I., Zanna, M. P., Holmes, J. G., & Spencer, J. (2001). Compensatory conviction in the face of personal uncertainty: Going to extremes and being oneself. *Journal of Personality and Social Psychology, 80*(3), 472–488.

Milgram, S. (1963). Behavioral study of obedience. *The Journal of Abnormal and Social Psychology, 67*(4), 371–378.

Mosig, Y. D. (1989). Wisdom and compassion: What the Buddha taught. *Theoretical and Philosophical Psychology, 9*(2), 27–36.

Murphy, M., & Donovan, S. (1997). *The physical and psychological effects of meditation* (2nd ed.). Petaluma, CA: Institute of Noetic Sciences.

Park, K. (1990). *An experimental study of theory-based team building intervention: A case of Korean work groups.* Unpublished doctoral dissertation, Harvard University, Cambridge, MA.

Peterson, J. B. (1999). *Maps of meaning: The architecture of belief.* New York, NY: Routledge.

Roberts, B. W., & DelVecchio, W. F. (2000). The rand-order consistency of personality traits from childhood to old age: A quantitative review of longitudinal studies. *Psychological Bulletin, 126*(1), 3–25.

Rodin, J., & Langer, E. J. (1977). Long-term effects of a control-relevant intervention with the institutionalized aged. *Journal of Personality and Social Psychology, 35*, 897–902.

Rogers, C. R. (1951). *Client-centered therapy: Its current practice, implications, and theory.* Boston, MA: Houghton Mifflin.

Schiepek, Eckert, & Weihrauch (2003). Critical fluctuations and clinical change: Data-based assessment in dynamic systems. *Constructivism in the Human Sciences, 8*(1), 57–84.

Schneider, R., H., Alexander, C. N., Staggers, F., Orme-Johnson, W., Rainforth, M., Salerno, J. W.,... Nidich, S. I. (2005). A randomized controlled trial of stress reduction in African Americans treated for hypertension for over one year. *American Journal of Hypertension, 18*, 88–98.

Sheng-yen, M. (2000). *Setting in motion the Dharma wheel: Talks on the Four Noble Truths of Buddhism.* Elmhurst, NY: Dharma Drum

Tang, Y., & Posner, M. I. (2009). Attention training and attention state training. *Trends in Cognitive Sciences, 13*(5), 222–227.

Travis, F., Arenander, A., & DuBois, D. (2004). Psychological and physiological characteristics of a proposed object-referral/self-referral continuum of self-awareness. *Consciousness and Cognition, 13*, 401–420.

Van der Kolk, B. A. (1987). The psychological consequences of overwhelming life experiences. In B. A. van der Kolk (Ed.), *Psychological trauma* (pp. 1–30). Washington, DC: American Psychiatric Press.

Walsh, R., & Shapiro, S. L. (2003). An analysis of recent meditation research and suggestions for future directions. *The Humanistic Psychologist, 31*(2–3), 86–114.

Walsh, R., & Shapiro, S. L. (2006). The meeting of meditative disciplines and Western psychology. *American Psychologist, 61*(3), 227–239.

Part II

Consciousness, Cognition, and Emotion

Langer and Abelson (1974) were the first to note the overwhelming power of labels in dictating consequent decisions, behavior, and health. Labels, particularly those that describe illness, rapidly constrain individuals' experiences by priming expectations of ill-health and by dictating their attention toward illness cues (Langer, 2000). Many mindfulness-based practices build off this knowledge of how language influences cognition, and have increasingly demonstrated significant, positive effects on various cognitive functions including attention, memory, and executive functions. Mindfulness training has also proved effective in regulating behavior and reorienting general attitudes. This section of the handbook addresses the relationship between mindfulness and cognition, and how this connection moderates behavior.

Mrazek et al.'s chapter provides additional evidence for Langer's assertion that mindlessness is pervasive in our culture. Mrazek et al. discuss the intrinsic relations between the constructs of mindfulness and mind-wandering. Their chapter reviews recent research that places mindfulness and mind-wandering on opposite ends of the same continuum. They also introduce research that suggests the use of mindfulness (defined as a state of sustained nondistraction) as a remedy for mind-wandering (defined as a mindless state of distraction marked by task-unrelated thoughts) and for mind-wandering's associated cognitive impairments and reduced task performance. Relatedly, Kang, Gruber, and Gray present the deautomatizing function of mindfulness, and its facilitation of cognitive and emotional regulation.

Demick reviews the most widely researched cognitive style, field dependence–independence (FDI), to highlight similarities between mindfulness and FDI. He argues that mindfulness and FDI share numerous underlying assumptions (e.g., holism; contextualism; multidimensionality; change; mobility; integration). Mindfulness—similar to the more extensively researched FDI construct—is a comprehensive psychological theory that has the potential of explaining the complex character of everyday life.

The Wiley Blackwell Handbook of Mindfulness, First Edition.
Edited by Amanda Ie, Christelle T. Ngnoumen, and Ellen J. Langer.
© 2014 John Wiley & Sons, Ltd. Published 2014 by John Wiley & Sons, Ltd.

Balcetis, Cole, and Sherali explore the implications of motivated perception and mindfulness in the context of self-regulation. Their chapter discusses how the susceptibility of visual experiences to certain underlying mental states can be exploited to facilitate goal pursuit. They suggest that more research be dedicated to fully uncovering the relationship between mindfulness and motivated perception, and how it interacts with a broader range of self-regulative functions.

Relatedly, Rigby, Ryan, and Schultz examine how mindfulness influences self-regulation and well-being based on the framework of Self-Determination Theory (SDT). They discuss the relationship between mindful awareness and interest-taking, and propose that both facilitate more autonomous self-regulation, greater satisfaction of basic psychological needs, and more investment in intrinsic versus extrinsic life goals and aspirations.

Gantman, Gollwitzer, and Oettingen introduce the idea of mindful mindlessness in goal pursuit. Goal pursuit pertains to the process of selecting goals and planning their implementation. Their chapter clarifies the link between mindfulness–mindlessness and nonconscious goal pursuit through a discussion of both the similarities and differences between conscious and nonconscious goal pursuit.

Luttrell, Briñol, and Petty discuss the relations among mindfulness, attitudes, and persuasion. They address previous debates in the literature concerning persuasion's link to either open- or closed-mindedness states, and demonstrate how persuasion can operate on people's attitudes under both mindful and mindless conditions. The authors also discuss mindfulness's contribution to enhanced body awareness and, in turn, how sensitivity to bodily cues and responses can further influence attitudes.

Herbert begins his chapter with an explanation of how heuristic scripts facilitate decision-making. Automatic cognitive rules of thumb allow us to conserve mental energy while making decisions that would otherwise be complex and cognitively taxing. Herbert provides examples of significant behavioral changes that occur in response to situations that introduce a mindful outlook and that challenge the use of scripted responses.

Automatic reliance on culturally imbued preconceptions contributes to mindlessness. Martin et al. explore what happens when people are caught off guard and must operate outside of heuristics—such as when experiencing a close brush with death. They suggest that the removal of the various cultural lenses that guide human behavior will yield more mindful and authentic selves.

Vannette and Krosnick discuss the implications of optimizing and satisficing on survey and questionnaire tasks. The differences between the cognitive processes of optimizing and satisficing parallel Langer's mindfulness–mindlessness distinctions. The authors assert that comparing the two pairs of cognitive styles can benefit survey methodology and questionnaire construction.

Mindfulness-based interventions and training strengthen cognitive functioning and creativity. Carson reviews theoretical and empirical associations between mindfulness and creativity. She demonstrates how creativity is endemic to Western conceptualizations and practices of mindfulness; according to these Western sociocognitive traditions, "to live creatively is indeed to live mindfully [and to be mindful]." Among Eastern traditions, however, cognitive flexibility and divergent thinking represent two of many beneficial by-products of living mindfully.

Niedderer examines the role of [product] design as an agent for behavior change in social contexts, with a particular focus on the role of emotion in designing artifacts for mindful social interaction. Objects direct our actions both consciously and unconsciously, and can influence the interactions individuals have both with them and with each other. In other words, people largely relate to each other through the mediating influence of products. Furthermore, products influence whether the nature of such social interactions is pleasant or unpleasant as well as mindful or mindless.

Albert argues that there are "mindful" and "mindless" approaches to thinking about time. Through demonstrating how easy it is for people to omit temporal considerations when applying statistical reasoning to predict human behavior, he also sheds light on why people are error-prone when dealing with uncertainty and probability. Albert's chapter finishes with an in-depth analysis of common errors associated with various forms of visually displaying time, and he suggests that the way in which we envision time needs to change in order to reframe and improve our sense of timing, our emotions, as well as our ability to control events more mindfully.

Falk examines the neural correlates of mindfulness practice. While some research has already uncovered the structural and functional correlates of Eastern forms of mindfulness in the brain, Falk argues that more work needs to be done toward understanding the subtleties within camps. In order to more fully understand the similarities and differences among varying approaches to mindfulness, research would need to be dedicated to unveiling the neural underpinnings of Langer's conception of mindfulness, for example, as well as to understand how Langer's model differs from Eastern or Eastern-derived approaches.

References

Langer, E. J. (2000). Mindful learning. *Current Directions in Psychological Science, 9*(6), 220–223.

Langer, E. J., & Abelson, R. P. (1974). A patient by any other name … : Clinician group difference in labeling bias. *Journal of Consulting and Clinical Psychology, 42*, 4–9.

8

Mindfulness
An Antidote for Wandering Minds

Michael D. Mrazek, James M. Broadway,
Dawa T. Phillips, Michael S. Franklin,
Benjamin W. Mooneyham, and
Jonathan W. Schooler

What's in a Name?

Despite the vast flexibility that language offers us for self-expression, we occasionally encounter the limitations of words as imperfect symbols. The word *red* may trigger something relatively universal, but *burgundy* will likely take on a different meaning for a seamstress and a wine aficionado. Words become particularly clumsy when there is not much agreement as to where they point. Most of us use *love* with some trust that others will understand our meaning, yet the word holds a somewhat different significance for each of us. *Mindfulness* has arrived at a similar fate—received with a sense of growing familiarity, but ultimately varied in its meaning. Fortunately, this fate need not stall the pursuit of the benefits that *mindfulness* offers any more than our lumbering use of *love* prevents us from experiencing intimate connection. After all, there are always love letters and operational definitions to help us convey our meanings more clearly.

Mindfulness as Nondistraction

Mindfulness is interpreted in a variety of ways, with ongoing disagreement as to the most privileged and useful definition of this construct (Grossman & Van Dam, 2011). Some meditative traditions have defined mindfulness as sustained nondistraction (Brown & Ryan, 2003; Dreyfus, 2011; Wallace & Shapiro, 2006), whereas multifactor conceptualizations of mindfulness emphasize additional qualities as well, such as an orientation toward one's experiences characterized by curiosity, openness, and acceptance (Baer, Smith, Hopkins, Krietemeyer, & Toney, 2006; Bishop et al., 2004). Another prominent use of *mindfulness* in psychology pioneered by Ellen Langer uses the word to refer to actively drawing novel distinctions, and thereby having greater

The Wiley Blackwell Handbook of Mindfulness, First Edition.
Edited by Amanda Ie, Christelle T. Ngnoumen, and Ellen J. Langer.
© 2014 John Wiley & Sons, Ltd. Published 2014 by John Wiley & Sons, Ltd.

sensitivity to context and perspective (Langer, 1989; Langer & Moldoveanu, 2002). These definitions are by no means exhaustive, and there are many traditions of mindfulness practice that have evolved over millennia and offer further delineation.

Amid this disagreement, there is nevertheless consensus from meditative traditions that sustained attentiveness represents a fundamental element of mindfulness. Although sustained attentiveness is less central to the social psychological view of mindfulness as making novel distinctions, even this form of mindfulness enhances present-moment awareness given that "actively drawing these distinctions keeps us situated in the present" (Langer & Moldoveanu, 2002). Accordingly, we have largely focused our investigations of mindfulness using nondistraction as an operational definition.[1] Our intention has not been to devalue other qualities espoused to be essential to mindfulness, but rather to avoid confusion when using a single term to refer to a variety of different constructs. For instance, multicomponent definitions of mindfulness must indicate whether the various elements are either necessary or sufficient to represent an instance of mindfulness. If one maintains unwavering attention on the breath for hours with a persisting judgment that breathing is wonderful, does the evaluative nature of that experience disqualify the careful focus as mindfulness? While continued discussion on the most privileged definition of mindfulness will almost certainly continue, it may be that different usages of mindfulness are so entrenched that the most practical solution is to accept the term as a catch-all that can provide a useful but unspecific contextualization, within which everyone must explicitly define what they have measured or trained.

Mind-Wandering as Task-Unrelated Thought

In direct contrast to mindfulness, which entails a capacity to avoid distraction, mind-wandering is characteristically described as the interruption of task-focus by task-unrelated thought (TUT; Smallwood & Schooler, 2006). Unlike the struggle to identify a validated and widely accepted measure of mindfulness, there has been somewhat greater consensus with respect to operational definitions of mind-wandering. The most widely used measure is straightforward: periodically interrupting individuals during a task and asking them to report the extent to which their attention was on the task or on task-unrelated concerns, a procedure known as "thought sampling," which measures "probe-caught" mind-wandering. There is a broad literature validating the self-report measures of mind-wandering obtained through thought sampling by using behavioral (Smallwood et al., 2004), event-related potential (ERP; Smallwood, Beach, Schooler, & Handy, 2008), and fMRI methodologies (Christoff, Gordon, Smallwood, Smith, & Schooler, 2009). Such studies suggest that individuals are able to accurately report whether they have been mind-wandering—and even whether they have been aware of it—as revealed by distinct patterns of task performance and neural activation in association with self-reported mind-wandering. Additionally, studies using retrospective reports of mind-wandering after a task has been finished typically find results that are similar to those obtained with thought sampling during the task (Mrazek et al., 2011). This not only provides convergent validity for thought sampling, but also suggests that in at least some task contexts, asking participants to intermittently report their mind-wandering does not substantially alter their behavior or performance (Barron, Riby, Greer, & Smallwood, 2011; Mrazek, Smallwood, Franklin et al., 2012).

Another common measure of mind-wandering involves asking participants to indicate every time they notice that they have been mind-wandering. This measures "self-caught" mind-wandering, providing a straightforward assessment of mind-wandering episodes that have reached meta-awareness (as an explicit re-representation of the contents of one's own consciousness; Schooler, 2002). By contrast, thought sampling queries participants at unpredictable intervals and does not require participants to attend to their thoughts independently of an external prompt. However, because thought-sampling probes occur at varying and unpredictable times during a primary task, this method can be used in conjunction with the self-catching measure to catch people mind-wandering before they notice it themselves (Schooler & Schreiber, 2004).

Several indirect markers of mind-wandering are also available, including those derived from performance markers of inattention in the Sustained Attention to Response Task (SART; Cheyne, Solman, Carriere, & Smilek, 2009; McVay & Kane, 2009; Smallwood et al., 2004; Smallwood, McSpadden, Luus, & Schooler, 2008; Smallwood, Fishman, & Schooler, 2007). The SART is a GO/NOGO task in which participants are asked to respond with a key press as quickly as possible to frequent non-targets and to refrain from responding to rare targets. Different performance markers in this task, such as response times (RTs) or different kinds of errors, have been associated with varying degrees of task disengagement (Cheyne et al., 2009). For example, failures to respond to rare targets (errors of omission) generally indicate a more pronounced state of disengagement than a large coefficient of variability (CV) for RTs (the CV is the standard deviation of RTs divided by the mean). RT CV has been associated with a state of mind-wandering that emerges from a minimally disruptive disengagement of attention characterized by a periodic speeding and slowing of RTs as attention fluctuates slightly (Cheyne et al., 2009; Smallwood, McSpadden, Luus et al., 2008).

Mindfulness and Mind-Wandering as Opposing Constructs

Many behavioral markers of mind-wandering have a distinctly mindless quality, such as rapid and automatic responding during SART (Smallwood et al., 2004), absent-minded forgetting (Smallwood, Baracaia, Lowe, & Obonsawin, 2003), and eye movements during reading that are less sensitive to lexical or linguistic properties of what is being read (Reichle, Reineberg, & Schooler, 2010). Furthermore, ERP studies have demonstrated that instances of mind-wandering are characterized by a reduced awareness and/or sensory processing of task stimuli and other objects in the external environment (Barron et al., 2011; Kam et al., 2011; Smallwood, Beach et al., 2008). The ability to remain mindfully focused on a task therefore appears to be in direct opposition to the tendency for attention to wander to TUTs. Starting from this observation, we began our ongoing series of investigations into the relationship between mindfulness and mind-wandering by first examining whether we could find empirical support for this intuitive notion that mind-wandering and mindfulness are opposing constructs.

Existing work that links mindfulness and mind-wandering has relied heavily on the Mindful Awareness Attention Scale (MAAS; Brown & Ryan, 2003), the most widely used dispositional measure of mindfulness. This scale addresses the extent to which an individual attends to present experience without distraction (e.g., I find myself listening to someone with one ear, doing something else at the same time). Low self-reported mindfulness as measured by the MAAS is associated with fast and error-prone responding in the SART (Cheyne, Carriere, & Smilek, 2006). An adapted version of the MAAS called the MAAS-LO (lapses only) has also been associated with several performance markers of mind-wandering in the SART (Cheyne et al., 2009). These results show that measurement of trait-mindfulness by scales such as MAAS can predict behavioral concomitants of real-time mind-wandering observed during the performance of a task in the lab.

We recently conducted a more comprehensive investigation into the relationship between the MAAS and several convergent measures of mind-wandering (Mrazek, Smallwood, & Schooler, 2012). All participants completed the MAAS, a 10-min mindful breathing task with thought-sampling probes, a 10-min mindful breathing task requiring self-catching of mind-wandering, a 10-min SART, and a self-report measure of trait daydreaming that has been widely used to study mind-wandering (Mason et al., 2007). We found that individuals who reported high levels of mindfulness during daily life also reported less daydreaming. Furthermore, high levels of trait-mindfulness were also associated with less mind-wandering as measured by self-reported TUT during mindful breathing, fewer errors of commission during the SART, and lower RT variability. These results provide converging evidence suggesting that—at least based on their most common operational definitions—mindfulness and mind-wandering are indeed opposing constructs.

Mindfulness as a Tool for Reducing Mind-Wandering

If mindfulness and mind-wandering are inversely related, this suggests that mind-wandering and its disruptive effects on task performance (e.g., Reichle et al., 2010; Smallwood et al., 2003, 2004, 2007) should be reduced by interventions that increase mindfulness. While mindfulness training has been demonstrated to improve executive attention, perceptual sensitivity, and sustained attention (MacLean et al., 2010; Tang et al., 2007), the direct impact of mindfulness training on mind-wandering has until recently been less carefully examined. In fact, to date, there has been little progress in developing empirically proven strategies for reducing mind-wandering.

We recently examined whether a brief mindfulness exercise can reduce mind-wandering, thereby potentially introducing both an effective antidote to mind-wandering and establishing a causal relationship between the presence of mindfulness and the absence of mind-wandering. This expectation is consistent with the many well-documented benefits of mindfulness training (for a review, see Brown, Ryan, & Creswell, 2007). However, many prior studies have utilized intensive meditation training lasting months or years, limiting the applicability of observed improvements for most societal and educational contexts (Brefczynski-Lewis, Lutz, Schaefer, Levinson, & Davidson, 2007; MacLean et al., 2010). Furthermore, from a methodological perspective, mindfulness intervention studies typically include so many different aspects in their intervention that it is difficult to discern which specific element is responsible for any observed changes. What is needed in order to discern the causal role of mindfulness in mitigating mind-wandering is a simple manipulation that directly and specifically targets individuals' ability to remain mindful. Accordingly, we used an 8-min mindful breathing intervention that provides a simple and widely accessible intervention that also affords a high degree of experimental control.[2]

In this investigation, participants were randomly assigned to conditions in which they completed 8 min of mindful breathing, or else in two control conditions, passive relaxation, or reading. Expectation effects and demand characteristics were minimized by informing all participants that they were participating in a study designed to examine effects of relaxation on attention. In the mindful breathing condition, participants were instructed to sit in an upright position while focusing their attention on the sensations of their breath without trying to control the rate of respiration. Participants were asked to return their attention to the breath anytime they became distracted. Participants in the reading condition were asked to browse a popular local newspaper, while those in the passive rest condition were asked to relax without falling asleep. Subsequently, all participants completed a 10-min version of the SART. Relative to the two control conditions, those who first completed 8 min exhibited enhanced performance as measured by behavioral markers of inattention commonly associated with mind-wandering (fewer errors of commission and lower RT variability). The effectiveness of this intervention establishes a causal relationship between the cultivation of mindfulness and subsequent reduction in mind-wandering.[3]

Mind-Wandering and Mental Aptitude

Given the robust relationship between mind-wandering and impaired task performance, the benefits of strategies for reducing mind-wandering clearly have great practical significance. Indeed, mind-wandering is a ubiquitous phenomenon associated with reduced awareness of task stimuli and the external environment (Barron et al., 2011; Kam et al., 2011; Smallwood, McSpadden, & Schooler, 2008), impaired vigilance (Cheyne et al., 2009; McVay & Kane, 2009; Smallwood et al., 2004), absent-minded forgetting (Smallwood et al., 2003), deficits in random-number generation (Teasdale et al., 1995), and poor reading comprehension (Reichle et al., 2010; Schooler et al., 2004; Smallwood, 2011; Smallwood, McSpadden, & Schooler, 2008).

We recently examined whether mind-wandering also impairs performance on measures of mental aptitude—such as working-memory capacity (WMC) and fluid intelligence (gF)—that are predictive of performance in real-world contexts such as academic achievement and job performance (Deary, Strand, Smith, & Fernandes, 2007; Kane, Hambrick, & Conway, 2005; Rohde & Thompson, 2007; te Nijenhuis, van Vianen, & van der Flier, 2007). We conducted four studies employing complementary methodological designs embedding thought sampling into popular measures of these constructs and determined that mind-wandering was consistently associated with worse performance (Mrazek, Franklin, Phillips, Baird, & Schooler, 2013). Indeed, nearly 50% of the shared variance among WMC, fluid intelligence, and performance on the Scholastic Aptitude Test (SAT) was explained by the mind-wandering that occurred during cognitive assessment. These results strongly implicate the capacity to avoid mind-wandering during demanding tasks as an important source of success on measures of general aptitude. Furthermore, mind-wandering during testing may help explain the reliable correlations between measures of mental aptitude as well as their broad predictive utility. In fact, a substantial proportion of what makes tests of general aptitude sufficiently general could be that they create a demanding task context in which mind-wandering is highly disruptive.

Mindfulness Training and Mental Aptitude

Given that the ability to attend to a task without distraction underlies performance in a wide variety of contexts, training this ability should in principle result in a similarly broad enhancement of performance. In a recent randomized controlled investigation, we examined whether a two-week mindfulness training course would be more effective than a comparably demanding nutrition program in decreasing mind-wandering and improving cognitive performance (Mrazek et al., 2013). We found that mindfulness training improved performance on measures of WMC as well as reading comprehension, as measured on the Graduate Record Examination (GRE), while also reducing mind-wandering during these tasks. Notably, improvements in WMC and GRE performance following mindfulness training were mediated by reduced mind-wandering specifically for those who were most prone to distraction at pretesting. This suggests that mindfulness-based interventions benefit individuals who are already proficient at attentional control, and that training to enhance attentional focus may be a key to unlocking latent cognitive skills that were until recently viewed as immutable.

Mindfulness, Mind-Wandering, and Meta-Awareness

Another process that is important to consider in understanding the relationship between mindfulness and mind-wandering is meta-awareness. Meta-awareness is the process of reflecting on the current contents of consciousness (Schooler, 2002). This can serve an important corrective function by reinstating task focus whenever attention becomes diverted to a TUT. As such, meta-awareness is often seen as a tool for minimizing the detrimental effects of mind-wandering (Schooler et al., 2011). This raises the intriguing question of whether strategies exist that might improve attention by enhancing people's awareness of their mind-wandering. One promising direction for exploring this question entails the cultivation of mindfulness through meditative practices.

When mindfulness is defined as nondistraction, it can be clearly distinguished from meta-awareness. It is possible to be fully aware of the sensations of breathing without metaconscious reflection about these sensations. One could even argue that in any given moment, mindfulness and meta-awareness are mutually exclusive: being fully attentive to a given sensation may preclude the possibility of simultaneously reflecting on it. Yet while nondistraction is distinct from conscious reflection about that nondistraction, meta-awareness may nonetheless be a crucial element in the cultivation of mindfulness. For instance, meditative practices designed to cultivate nondistraction in beginners typically require focused attention to a single aspect of sensory experience (e.g., the sensations of breathing) despite the frequent interruption of focus by unrelated distractions or personal concerns. Meta-awareness of each distraction thus promotes meditative focus by providing an opportunity to redirect attention to the object of meditation after a lapse of concentration. How and why this awareness of mind-wandering arises, and the determinants of its frequency of occurrence, remain items in need of investigation.

Recently, Hasenkamp, Wilson-Mendenhall, Duncan, and Barsalou (2012) outlined a model of the temporal sequence of mental events that occur during the practice of meditation: *sustained attention* is periodically interrupted by *mind-wandering* until *awareness of mind-wandering* initiates the *shifting of attention* back to the perceptual target of meditation. In an fMRI investigation of mind-wandering during meditation among experienced meditators, Hasenkamp and colleagues (2012) found that sustained attention and shifting of attention were associated with regions well-established as elements of an attentional control network in the brain, including dorsolateral prefrontal cortex (PFC) and posterior parietal cortex. In contrast, they found that mind-wandering was associated with activation in medial PFC and posterior cingulate cortex, as well as posterior parietal and temporal regions including the hippocampal formation, regions widely associated with a "default network" that is active during rest (Buckner, Andrews-Hanna, & Schachter, 2008) as well as during mind-wandering (Christoff et al., 2009).

Notably, Hasenkamp and colleagues found that *awareness of mind-wandering* was associated with greater activation of bilateral anterior insula (AI) and dorsal anterior cingulate cortex (ACC). These results were interpreted as reflecting the operation of a *salience network* for detecting relevant or salient events—in this case the occurrence of mind-wandering. Although the poor temporal resolution of fMRI makes it difficult to discern the brain regions involved in mental events that occur quickly in succession, these results tentatively suggest that bilateral AI and dorsal ACC may contribute to meta-awareness of mind-wandering in a manner that allows attention to be redirected back to a given task.

In a subsequent article, Hasenkamp and Barsalou (2012) compared individuals with differing amounts of meditation experience in terms of the functional connectivity displayed at rest between brain regions associated with the four phases identified previously during mindfulness meditation. Comparing individuals with high levels of experience to those with low levels, the authors found increased functional connectivity among regions associated with the attentional control network, as well as between these areas and medial PFC, associated with the default network. This suggests that in contrast with the currently dominant view in which the attentional control and default networks are antagonistically related, mindfulness meditation practice may indeed enhance the extent of cooperative functioning between these brain systems (see, e.g., Smallwood, Brown, Baird & Schooler, 2011), perhaps in service of increased meta-awareness of mind-wandering.

The suggestion of a possible relationship between mindfulness and meta-awareness raises the intriguing possibility that cultivating mindfulness might enhance meta-awareness (or vice versa). Existing research regarding the impact of mindfulness training on meta-awareness is mixed. On the one hand, individuals with extensive meditation experience show a stronger association between subjective emotional experience and physiological markers of emotion (i.e., heart period; Sze, Gyurak, Yuan, & Levenson, 2010). The fact that experienced meditators have enhanced meta-awareness of emotions is certainly consistent with the notion that mindfulness training might also improve meta-awareness of mind-wandering. However, Khalsa and colleagues (2008) have shown that advanced meditators do not have any greater interoceptive awareness of heartbeat detection, even though they believe their interoceptive awareness is superior.

In the context of meta-awareness of mind-wandering, it is useful to consider what degree of meta-awareness would be most useful in cultivating mindfulness. While meta-awareness is pivotal to the cultivation of nondistraction, conscious reflection on one's focus is not always necessary or desirable. Before attention has lapsed, meta-awareness is not needed—and in some cases could itself serve as a distraction. It follows that in the course of cultivating mindfulness, the frequency of meta-awareness may resemble an inverted u-shaped function: initially increasing to allow for redirection from distractions, but eventually diminishing when attentional stability makes frequent meta-awareness unnecessary.

Although this would suggest that brief mindfulness training programs should result in increased meta-awareness, demonstrating this change may not be straightforward. For example, as described earlier, we recently found that two weeks of mindfulness training led to reduced mind-wandering during a GRE test (Mrazek et al., 2013). However, we observed that mindfulness training reduced both probe-caught *and* self-caught mind-wandering. This result points to a challenge in establishing whether mindfulness training increases meta-awareness: If mindfulness training reduces mind-wandering, it likewise reduces opportunities to observe meta-awareness of mind-wandering. Thus, in the training experiment just described, it is possible that mindfulness training indeed led to enhanced meta-awareness (of mind-wandering), but that this change was rendered invisible to measurement by overall decreases in mind-wandering. A related challenge is that extensive practice in detecting mind-wandering in the context of meditation might lower an individual's threshold for what subjectively constitutes an instance of mind-wandering. These difficulties indicate that a promising direction for future research would include measuring changes in meta-awareness of mental processes that are themselves unaffected by mindfulness training.

The Ironic Nature of Nondistraction

When telling someone that you research mind-wandering, one of the most common responses is "I would be your perfect participant." It seems that many of us have an intuitive appreciation for how frequently our minds are adrift—as much as half of our waking lives (Killingsworth & Gilbert, 2010). Yet at the same time, many of us are familiar with other contexts in which our minds do not wander at all. We are sometimes completely focused—perhaps on an engrossing film or conversation—in a way that belies our usually wandering minds. Similarly, a child with attention deficit hyperactivity disorder can sometimes attend to a video game for hours despite an inability to remain attentive for even a few minutes in a classroom. Our understanding of what allows mind-wandering to turn off so dramatically in these situations is only just emerging, and the occasional presence of this apparently effortless nondistraction raises an important question regarding the cultivation of mindfulness.

One might think that the key to cultivating nondistraction would be to provide individuals with frequent opportunities to practice nondistraction in those contexts in which it is most natural. After all, 16-year-olds learn how to drive in quiet neighbor-hoods and empty parking lots, not on crowded highways. Yet mindfulness is com-monly trained in contexts where it is particularly difficult: sustaining attention on something of little inherent interest like the sensations of breathing. We suggest this is no accident. There are several possible reasons why tasks characterized by frequent dis-traction are well suited for mindfulness training. For instance, practicing mindfulness in these contexts may reduce the actual occurrence of TUTs. Attending to a simple stimulus, such as the breath, provides fertile ground for distracting thoughts to arise, but such thoughts may lose their disruptive salience when they are continually ignored. A second possibility is that tasks that are not intrinsically engaging require—and there-fore train—greater cognitive control. Yet a third possibility is that continuously mon-itoring one's wandering attention leads to enhanced metacognitive regulation, per-haps increasing awareness of mind-wandering and thereby allowing attention to be redirected from off-task thoughts more quickly. These differing explanations—which are not mutually exclusive—provide an exciting direction for future research.

Mind-Wandering in Relation to Broader Conceptualizations of Mindfulness

We have focused our investigations on mindfulness as nondistraction, which we believe represents the element most central to the concept of mindfulness in meditative tradi-tions and also most directly linked to mind-wandering (Brown & Ryan, 2003; Wallace & Shapiro, 2006). However, more encompassing definitions of mindfulness empha-size additional features of the experience that may also be related to mind-wandering. For example, Bishop and colleagues (2004) have formalized a two-factor theory of mindfulness that emphasizes not only nondistraction but also an attitude of curiosity, openness, and acceptance toward one's experience.[4]

One possibility is that mind-wandering has a similar inverse relationship with both nondistraction and a nonjudgmental orientation. Indeed, being fully attentive to a given sensation may reduce the possibility of being simultaneously evaluative of it. Yet it is also possible that it is the *content* rather than the *occurrence* of mind-wandering that is most strongly associated with the nonjudgmental orientation toward one's experience. Future research should investigate how the actual content of mind-wandering episodes relates to the various subprocesses of multifaceted conceptualiza-tions of mindfulness.

Mind-Wandering in Relation to Western Social Psychological Views of Mindfulness

There is yet another prominent conceptualization of mindfulness also worth considering in relation to mind-wandering: an active state of mind characterized by drawing novel distinctions that results in being (1) situated in the present, (2) sensitive to context and perspective, and (3) guided (but not governed) by rules and routines (Langer, 1975, 1989; Langer & Abelson, 1972; Langer, Blank, & Chanowitz, 1978). This characterization describes a state of active attention to and engagement with one's environment that in some ways stands in contrast to our notion of mind-wandering. For instance, actively drawing novel distinctions can anchor awareness in the here and now. This enhanced awareness of present experience is the opposite of what typically occurs during mind-wandering. As described above, ERP studies have demonstrated that instances of mind-wandering are characterized by a reduced awareness and/or sensory processing of task stimuli and other objects in the external environment (Barron et al., 2011; Kam et al., 2011; Smallwood, Beach et al., 2008). In fact, mindfulness interventions grounded in drawing novel distinctions have been shown to improve attention (Langer, 2000). Several demonstrations have shown that asking participants to notice new things about a stimulus results in better performance than simply asking them to pay attention to the stimulus (Bodner & Langer, 1995; Carson, Shih, & Langer, 2001; Levy, Jennings & Langer, 2001). Although growing evidence suggests that training participants to pay attention to a stimulus can be effective (Mrazek et al., 2013), it may be that a particularly effective way for enhancing sustained attentiveness is combining both attention training and novel distinction drawing.

Another way that mind-wandering can be contrasted with the Western social psychological view of mindfulness is with regards to automatic and habitual responding. Langer contrasts mindfulness with the opposing construct of mindlessness. Mindlessness is a state of mind "characterized by an overreliance on categories and distinctions drawn in the past," "context-dependent and ... oblivious to novel (or simply alternative) aspects of the situation," and in which "rigid invariant behavior" occurs with little awareness (Langer, 1992). As discussed above, many behavioral markers of mind-wandering have a distinctly mindless quality, such as rapid and automatic responding during SART (Smallwood et al., 2004), absent-minded forgetting (Smallwood et al., 2003), and eye movements during reading that are less sensitive to lexical or linguistic properties of what is being read (Reichle et al., 2010). From this perspective, mind-wandering can be construed as a form of mindlessness.

The foregoing discussion suggests that Langer's conceptualization of mindfulness places the construct in opposition to mind-wandering, but this Western social psychological view of mindfulness is not intrinsically distinct from mind-wandering. For instance, TUTs can actively draw novel distinctions while simultaneously distracting attention from a primary task. For this reason, mind-wandering is more clearly distinct from mindfulness when it is defined as nondistraction than when defined as drawing novel distinctions. However, little empirical research has addressed the relationship between mind-wandering and Langer's conceptualization of mindfulness. Future work should explore whether the Mindfulness/Mindlessness Scale (Bodner & Langer,

2001) is associated with validated behavioral and thought-sampling markers of mind-wandering, and whether the positive outcomes associated with mindfulness as measured by this scale are mediated by reduced mind-wandering.

Future Directions: Mindfulness and the Potential Benefits of Mind-Wandering

Given the opposing conceptual relationship between mindfulness and mind-wandering, our understanding of mindfulness will evolve as we discover more about how attention lapses. Yet future research must also keep potential benefits of mind-wandering in view. After all, the human capacity to plan the future and reflect on past experiences has clear adaptive value (Baars, 2010; Smallwood, 2010). There are circumstances in which diverting attention away from the "here and now" is beneficial. Indeed, recent findings suggest that under some circumstances mind-wandering can promote future planning (Baird, Smallwood, & Schooler, 2011) and enhance creative incubation (Baird et al., 2012). Yet the accumulating evidence for the positive outcomes of mindfulness might be interpreted to suggest that mind-wandering is of no benefit, especially within a framework that places these constructs in direct opposition. In contrast, the potential benefits of mind-wandering could be interpreted to suggest a downside to mindfulness. For instance, a practice of mindfulness that eliminated mind-wandering might lead to neglect of distal goals like retirement planning. It may therefore be that mindfulness is most helpful when it affords a degree of control over mind-wandering that allows for its benefits while minimizing its costs.

Acknowledgments

MDM, JMB, MSF, DTP, and JWS are supported through United States Department of Education grant R305A110277 awarded to JWS. The content of this article does not necessarily reflect the position or policy of the U.S. Government, and no official endorsement should be inferred.

Notes

1. Although perhaps obvious, it is worth noting that when we refer to mindfulness as nondistraction, this nondistraction is in the context of a particular activity. For example, if your goal is to engage in a task, but instead you become deeply focused on off-task concerns, this would not be an example of mindfulness, even though your off-task focus may be undistracted.
2. Mindful breathing is a technique that is widely taught in mindfulness training programs around the world, including both modern ones and those based on more traditional approaches. The authors have themselves participated in courses and retreats where these traditional methods were taught to them by qualified teachers holding formal qualification and authorization. This is mentioned here to illustrate the fact that similarity exists between the concise methodologies employed by ongoing research programs and the instructions of longstanding traditions of mindfulness practice.

3. Two unpublished studies have found evidence that meditation training courses are associated with reduced markers of inattention during the SART (Jha, Stanley, Kiyonaga, Wong, & Gelfand, 2009; Wong et al., 2008).
4. Within our framework of defining mindfulness more narrowly as nondistraction, these additional qualities might be understood as precursors, concomitants, or consequences of mindfulness, rather than aspects of mindfulness per se. For example, many meditative traditions teach that the capacity for mindfulness is supported by lessened attachment to experiences, accompanied by a sense of "letting go" of the habitual pursuit of pleasurable experiences and avoidance of painful or boring ones. It is taught that in turn, as mindfulness becomes itself more habitual, attachment to experiences becomes even more diminished, and one is concerned less and less with "getting one's way" all the time. Thus, nondistraction and the attitude of openness and acceptance toward one's experience may arise together in a mutually supportive manner.

References

Baars, B. J. (2010). Spontaneous repetitive thoughts can be adaptive: Postscript on "mind wandering." *Psychological Bulletin, 136*(2), 208.

Baer, R. A., Smith, G. T., Hopkins, J., Krietemeyer, J., & Toney, L. (2006). Using self-report assessment methods to explore facets of mindfulness. *Assessment, 13*(1), 27–45.

Baird, B., Smallwood, J., Mrazek, M. D., Kam, J. W., Franklin, M. S., & Schooler, J. W. (2012). Inspired by distraction: Mind wandering facilitates creative incubation. *Psychological Science, 23*(10), 1117–1122.

Baird, B., Smallwood, J., & Schooler, J. W. (2011). Back to the future: Autobiographical planning and the functionality of mind-wandering. *Consciousness and cognition, 20*(4), 1604–1611.

Barron, E., Riby, L. M., Greer, J., & Smallwood, J. (2011). Absorbed in thought: The effect of mind-wandering on the processing of relevant and irrelevant events. *Psychological Science, 22*(5), 596–601.

Bishop, S. R., Lau, M., Shapiro, S., Carlson, L., Anderson, N. D., Carmody, J., … Devins, G. (2004). Mindfulness: A proposed operational definition. *Clinical Psychology: Science and Practice, 11*(3), 230–241.

Bodner, T., & Langer, E. (1995). *Mindfulness and attention.* Cambridge, MA: Harvard University Press.

Bodner, T., & Langer, E. (2001). *Individual differences in mindfulness: The Langer Mindfulness Scale.* Poster session presented at the annual meeting of the American Psychological Society, Toronto, Ont., Canada.

Brefczynski-Lewis, J. A., Lutz, A., Schaefer, H. S., Levinson, D. B., & Davidson, R. J. (2007). Neural correlates of attentional expertise in long-term meditation practitioners. *Proceedings of the National Academy of Sciences, 104*(27), 11483–11488.

Brown, K. W., & Ryan, R. M. (2003). The benefits of being present: Mindfulness and its role in psychological well-being. *Journal of Personality and Social Psychology, 84*(4), 822–848.

Brown, K. W., Ryan, R. M., & Creswell, J. D. (2007). Mindfulness: Theoretical foundations and evidence for its salutary effects. *Psychological Inquiry, 18*(4), 211–237.

Buckner, R. L., Andrews-Hanna, J. R., & Schachter, D. L. (2008). The brain's default network: Anatomy, function, and relevance to disease. *Annals of the New York Academy of Sciences, 1124,* 1–38.

Carson, S., Shih, M., & Langer, E. (2001). Sit still and pay attention? *Journal of Adult Development, 8*(3), 183–188.

Cheyne, J. A., Carriere, J. S. A., & Smilek, D. (2006). Absent-mindedness: Lapses of conscious awareness and everyday cognitive failures. *Consciousness and Cognition, 15*(3), 578–592.

Cheyne, J., Solman, G. J. F., Carriere, J. S. A., & Smilek, D. (2009). Anatomy of an error: A bidirectional state model of task engagement/disengagement and attention-related errors. *Cognition, 111*(1), 98–113.

Christoff, K., Gordon, A. M., Smallwood, J., Smith, R., & Schooler, J. W. (2009). Experience sampling during fMRI reveals default network and executive system contributions to mind wandering. *Proceedings of the National Academy of Sciences, 106*(21), 8719–8724.

Deary, I. J., Strand, S., Smith, P., & Fernandes, C. (2007). Intelligence and educational achievement. *Intelligence, 35*(1), 13–21.

Dreyfus, G. (2011). Is mindfulness present-centred and non-judgmental? A discussion of the cognitive dimensions of mindfulness. *Contemporary Buddhism, 12*(1), 41–54.

Grossman, P., & Van Dam, N. T. (2011). Mindfulness, by any other name … : trials and tribulations of sati in western psychology and science. *Contemporary Buddhism, 12*(1), 219–239.

Hasenkamp, W., & Barsalou, L. W. (2012). Effects of meditation experience on functional connectivity of distributed brain networks. *Frontiers in Human Neuroscience, 6*(38), 1–14.

Hasenkamp, W., Wilson-Mendenhall, C. D., Duncan, E., & Barsalou, L. W. (2012). Mind wandering and attention during focused meditation: A fine-grained temporal analysis of fluctuating cognitive states. *NeuroImage, 59*(1), 750–760.

Jha, A. P., Stanley, E. A., Kiyonaga, A., Wong, L. M., & Gelfand, L. (2009, October). *Mindfulness training counteracts heightened distractibility in a military cohort.* Poster session presented at the meeting of the Society for Neuroscience, Chicago, IL.

Kam, J. W. Y., Dao, E., Farley, J., Fitzpatrick, K., Smallwood, J., Schooler, J. W., & Handy, T. C. (2011). Slow fluctuations in attentional control of sensory cortex. *Journal of Cognitive Neuroscience, 23*(2), 460–470.

Kane, M. J., Hambrick, D. Z., & Conway, A. R. (2005). Working memory capacity and fluid intelligence are strongly related constructs: Comment on Ackerman, Beier, and Boyle (2005). *Psychological Bulletin, 131*, 66–71.

Langer, E. J. (1975). The illusion of control. *Journal of Personality and Social Psychology, 32*(2), 311.

Langer, E. J. (1989). *Mindfulness.* Reading, MA: Addison-Wesley.

Langer, E. J. (1992). Matters of mind: Mindfulness/mindlessness in perspective. *Consciousness and Cognition, 1*(3), 289–305.

Langer, E. J. (2000). Mindful learning. *Current Directions in Psychological Science, 9*(6), 220–223.

Langer, E. J., & Abelson, R. P. (1972). The semantics of asking a favor: How to succeed in getting help without really dying. *Journal of Personality and Social Psychology, 24*(1), 26–32.

Langer, E. J., Blank, A., & Chanowitz, B. (1978). The mindlessness of ostensibly thoughtful action: The role of "placebic" information in interpersonal interaction. *Journal of Personality and Social Psychology, 36*(6), 635–642.

Langer, E. J., & Moldoveanu, M. (2002). The construct of mindfulness. *Journal of Social Issues, 56*(1), 1–9.

Levy, B. R., Jennings, P., & Langer, E. J. (2001). Improving attention in old age. *Journal of Adult Development, 8*(3), 189–192.

Khalsa, S. S., Rudrauf, D., Damasio, A. R., Davidson, R. J., Lutz, A., & Tranel, D. (2008). Interoceptive awareness in experienced meditators. *Psychophysiology, 45*(4), 671–677.

Killingsworth, M. A., & Gilbert, D. T. (2010). A wandering mind is an unhappy mind. *Science, 330*(6006), 932.

MacLean, K. A., Ferrer, E., Aichele, S. R., Bridwell, D. A., Zanesco, A. P., Jacobs, T. L., … Saron, C. D. (2010). Intensive meditation training improves perceptual discrimination and sustained attention. *Psychological Science, 21*(6), 829–839.

Mason, M. F., Norton, M. I., Van Horn, J. D., Wegner, D. M., Grafton, S. T., & Macrae, C. N. (2007). Wandering minds: The default network and stimulus-independent thought. *Science, 315*(5810), 393–5.

McVay, J. C., & Kane, M. J. (2009). Conducting the train of thought: Working memory capacity, goal neglect, and mind wandering in an executive-control task. *Journal of Experimental Psychology. Learning, Memory, and Cognition, 35*(1), 196–204.

Mrazek, M. D., Chin, J. M., Schmader, T., Hartson, K. A., Smallwood, J., & Schooler, J. W. (2011). Threatened to distraction: Mind-wandering as a consequence of stereotype threat. *Journal of Experimental Social Psychology, 47*(6), 1243–1248.

Mrazek, M. D., Franklin, M. S., Phillips, D. T., Baird, B., & Schooler, J. W. (2013). Mindfulness training improves working memory capacity and GRE performance while reducing mind wandering. *Psychological Science, 24*(5), 776–781.

Mrazek, M. D., Smallwood, J., Franklin, M. S., Baird, B., Chin, J. M., & Schooler, J. W. (2012). The role of mind-wandering in measurements of general aptitude. *Journal of Experimental Psychology: General, 141*(4), 788–798.

Mrazek, M. D., Smallwood, J., & Schooler, J. W. (2012). Mindfulness and mind-wandering: Finding convergence through opposing constructs. *Emotion, 12*(3), 442.

Reichle, E. D., Reineberg, A. E., & Schooler, J. W. (2010). Eye movements during mindless reading. *Psychological Science, 21*(9), 1300–1310.

Rohde, T. E., & Thompson, L. A. (2007). Predicting academic achievement with cognitive ability. *Intelligence, 35*(1), 83–92.

Schooler, J. W. (2002). Re-representing consciousness: Dissociations between experience and meta-consciousness. *Trends in Cognitive Sciences, 6*(8), 339–344.

Schooler, J. W., Reichle, E. D., & Halpern, D. V. (2004). Zoning out while reading: Evidence for dissociations between experience and metaconsciousness. In D. T. Levin (Ed.), *Thinking and seeing: Visual metacognition in adults and children* (pp. 203–226). Cambridge, MA: MIT Press.

Schooler, J., & Schreiber, C. A. (2004). Experience, meta-consciousness, and the paradox of introspection. *Journal of Consciousness Studies, 11*(7–8), 17–39.

Schooler, J. W., Smallwood, J., Christoff, K., Handy, T. C., Reichle, E. D., & Sayette, M. A. (2011). Meta-awareness, perceptual decoupling and the wandering mind. *Trends in Cognitive Sciences, 15*(7), 319–326.

Smallwood, J. (2010). Why the global availability of mind wandering necessitates resource competition: Reply to McVay and Kane (2010). *Psychological Bulletin, 136*, 202–207.

Smallwood, J. (2011). Mind-wandering while reading: Attentional decoupling, mindless reading and the cascade model of inattention. *Language and Linguistics Compass, 5*(2), 63–77.

Smallwood, J. M., Baracaia, S. F., Lowe, M., & Obonsawin, M. (2003). Task unrelated thought whilst encoding information. *Consciousness and Cognition, 12*(3), 452–484.

Smallwood, J., Beach, E., Schooler, J. W., & Handy, T. C. (2008). Going AWOL in the brain: Mind wandering reduces cortical analysis of external events. *Journal of Cognitive Neuroscience, 20*(3), 458–469.

Smallwood, J. M., Brown, K., Baird, B., & Schooler, J. S. (2011). Cooperation between the default mode network and the fronto-parietal network in the production of an internal train of thought. *Brain Research, 1428*(5), 60–70.

Smallwood, J., Davies, J. B., Heim, D., Finnigan, F., Sudberry, M., O'Connor, R., & Obonsawin, M. (2004). Subjective experience and the attentional lapse: Task engagement and disengagement during sustained attention. *Consciousness and Cognition, 13*(4), 657–690.

Smallwood, J., Fishman, D. J., & Schooler, J. W. (2007). Counting the cost of an absent mind: mind wandering as an underrecognized influence on educational performance. *Psychonomic Bulletin & Review, 14*(2), 230–236.

Smallwood, J., McSpadden, M., Luus, B., & Schooler, J. (2008). Segmenting the stream of consciousness: The psychological correlates of temporal structures in the time series data of a continuous performance task. *Brain and Cognition, 66*(1), 50–56.

Smallwood, J., McSpadden, M., & Schooler, J. W. (2008). When attention matters: The curious incident of the wandering mind. *Memory & Cognition, 36*(6), 1144–1150.

Smallwood, J., & Schooler, J. W. (2006). The restless mind. *Psychological Bulletin, 132*(6), 946–958.

Sze, J. A., Gyurak, A., Yuan, J. W., & Levenson, R. W. (2010). Coherence between emotional experience and physiology: Does body awareness training have an impact? *Emotion, 10*(6), 803–814.

Tang, Y. Y., Ma, Y., Wang, J., Fan, Y., Feng, S., Lu, Q., ... Posner, M. I. (2007). Short-term meditation training improves attention and self-regulation. *Proceedings of the National Academy of Sciences, 104*(43), 17152.

te Nijenhuis, J., van Vianen, A. E. M., & van der Flier, H. (2007). Score gains on g-loaded tests: No g. *Intelligence, 35*(3), 283–300.

Teasdale, J. D., Dritschel, B. H., Taylor, M. J., Proctor, L., Lloyd, C. A., Nimmo-Smith, I., & Baddeley, A. D. (1995). Stimulus-independent thought depends on central executive resources. *Memory & Cognition, 23*(5), 551–559.

Wallace, B. A., & Shapiro, S. L. (2006). Mental balance and well-being: Building bridges between Buddhism and Western psychology. *American Psychologist, 61*(7), 690–701.

Wong, L. M., Vugt, M. K., Smallwood, J. S., Carpenter-Cohn, J., Baime, M., & Jha, A. P. (2008, April). *Mindfulness training reduces mind wandering during a sustained attention task.* Poster session presented at the meeting of the Cognitive Neuroscience Society, San Francisco, CA.

9

Mindfulness

Deautomatization of Cognitive and Emotional Life

Yoona Kang, June Gruber, and Jeremy R. Gray

Mindfulness, or a state of nonjudgmental awareness of the present moment, is generally associated with a wide range of psychophysical benefits, such as alleviating various clinical disorders and enhancing well-being (e.g., Chambers, Gullone, & Allen, 2009). However, the number of studies on its underlying mechanisms is more limited. The goal of this review is to consolidate existing empirical findings and theoretical propositions in order to create a model that describes how mindfulness works. Rather than being a single skill, mindfulness includes complex sets of cognitive and affective building blocks operating on multilevel mechanistic processing (e.g., Hölzel et al., 2011). We suggest that though distinct, all these mechanisms of mindfulness have a universal effect of deautomatization, a process in which one's previously established tendency to effortlessly and unconsciously engage in maladaptive behaviors becomes conscious and controlled.

We propose a framework that describes the mechanisms underlying mindfulness that lead to the discontinuation of maladaptive and automatic cognitive and emotional responses. We first elaborate on the concepts of mindfulness as it is conceptualized in two different traditions and discuss automaticity as we use these terms. We then discuss how four components of mindfulness (awareness, attention, present focus, acceptance) can each bring forth the necessary environment for deautomatization to occur. Specifically, mindfulness can instigate four broad subsequent mental processes, including reduction of automatic inference processing, enhancement of cognitive control, facilitation of metacognitive insight, and prevention of thought suppression and distortion. This deautomatizing function of mindfulness, in turn, can promote adaptive self-regulatory strategies and desirable health outcomes.

The Wiley Blackwell Handbook of Mindfulness, First Edition.
Edited by Amanda Ie, Christelle T. Ngnoumen, and Ellen J. Langer.
© 2014 John Wiley & Sons, Ltd. Published 2014 by John Wiley & Sons, Ltd.

Meditation-Oriented and Mindset-Oriented Mindfulness

Mindfulness has at least two distinct meanings in psychology, which we refer to here as "mindset oriented" and "meditation oriented." The conceptual framework on mindset-oriented mindfulness was developed within the Western scientific perspective, and it refers to openness to novel information in the present moment, while having awareness of multiple perspectives, by creating new categories (Langer, 1989, 1997). This understanding in turn enables less judgmental evaluation of others' behavior (Langer, 1975; Langer & Abelson, 1972). Research on mindset-oriented mindfulness stemmed from the opposite concept of mindfulness, namely, mindlessness. Mindless behaviors tend to be automatic, resistant to change, and focused on a single perspective (Langer, 1989). Much of human behavior is based on mindless and unconscious processing, even in ostensively "thoughtful" actions (Langer, Blank, & Chanowitz, 1978). As such, subtle changes in environmental cues can elicit different reactions in similar situations when people are not thoughtfully aware of their behaviors. Mindful individuals, on the other hand, are more likely to engage in conscious thinking and thoughtful actions, and therefore have a higher awareness of multiple perspectives that are context dependent (Langer et al., 1978).

Meditation-oriented mindfulness is derived from Eastern Buddhist meditation traditions and refers to a quality of mind that is practiced or cultivated during meditation (e.g., Kabat-Zinn, 1982). It involves placing one's attention and awareness in the present moment with an attitude of nonjudgmental acceptance (Kabat-Zinn, Lipworth, & Burney, 1985). Though meditation-oriented mindfulness has long been practiced in the Eastern contemplative tradition, only in recent years has it been introduced to and integrated with Western scientific methodologies. Meditation-based mindfulness was shown to be effective first in the treatment of chronic pain (Kabat-Zinn, 1982), and subsequently in various other clinical disorders, including major depression (Teasdale et al., 2000), anxiety (Kabat-Zinn et al., 1992), and substance abuse (e.g., Bowen et al., 2006; Brewer et al., 2009), to list only a few.

Though these two conceptualizations of mindfulness do share various similar components, there are a few important distinctions that differentiate one from the other. For example, mindset-oriented mindfulness focuses on creating new categories, thereby examining old concepts in a new light (Langer, 1989). On the other hand, meditation-oriented mindfulness aims at blurring preestablished categories, especially those of self versus others (e.g., Gyatso, 1986). Furthermore, tasks designed to induce mindset-oriented mindfulness involve goal-oriented cognitive problem solving that requires consideration of information or situations from multiple perspectives to increase creativity and openness (e.g., Langer & Moldoveanu, 2000). In contrast, meditation instructions often include a nongoal-directed and nonjudgmental observation of internal and external stimuli (e.g., Kabat-Zinn, 1990).

Despite differences, both approaches to mindfulness share several common ingredients. First, both involve paying attention and being open to new incoming information with a flexible attitude of curiosity. Second, the acceptance component is important in both traditions. In mindset-oriented mindfulness, one welcomes new information without dismissing, and gives respect to different points of view. Similarly in meditation-oriented mindfulness, one accepts the present moment without criticizing or judging. Third, and most importantly for the purpose of the present review, both approaches of mindfulness affect automaticity, the tendency to effortlessly and unconsciously engage in behaviors. Through both modes of mindfulness, one can allow the awareness of automatic behavioral patterns and then eventually learn to disengage from them (Kabat-Zinn, 1990; Langer, 1989). In other words, both conceptualizations of mindfulness enable the process of deautomatization. Indeed, investigators from both traditions of mindfulness suggest that deautomatization may be one of the central mechanisms of mindfulness (e.g., Deikman, 1966; Langer, 1989; Moore & Malinowski, 2009). Therefore, here we operationalize mindfulness as a general construct that encompasses both conceptualizations of mindfulness, especially given our focus on their common ingredient, deautomatization. We further note that our primarily focus is on mechanisms underlying meditation-oriented mindfulness. We chose to do this because our systemization of deautomatization involves all components pertaining to meditation-oriented mindfulness, but does not include all the components of mindset-oriented mindfulness.

Four Elements of Mindfulness

Mindfulness meditation practice is a form of cognitive training aimed at learning how and where to guide one's attention. This involves maintaining awareness of attention from one moment to the next. Whenever the mind wanders, it is gently but firmly escorted back to the initial target object. This practice trains the mind to be stable, letting it disengage from usual and automatized thought processes. Most discussions of mindfulness include the following four elements: (1) awareness, (2) sustained attention, (3) focus on present moment, and (4) nonjudgmental acceptance (e.g., Kabat-Zinn et al., 1985; Teasdale, Segal, & Williams, 1995). Here, we briefly define and discuss each of the four elements in turn.

Awareness

Awareness is having conscious knowledge of one's internal and external experiences, including bodily sensations, thoughts and emotions, and external events such as sights and sounds (e.g., Brown & Ryan, 2003). Awareness is contrasted with automatic mental reactions that often occur without conscious awareness. Intergroup biases, for example, represent overlearned cultural associations that are automatically and unconsciously activated in response to actual or symbolic categories (Kawakami, Dovidio, Moll, Hermsen, & Russin, 2000). A mindful individual with close awareness of her cognitive processes may be more likely to notice when intergroup biases occur, having accurate awareness of the nature of the bias.

Sustained attention

Sustained attention involves placing one's attention on the ongoing stream of internal and external stimuli. In the state of mindfulness, individuals bring their attention to the target of observation. Whenever mind wanders, attention is gently but firmly brought back to the original target of focus. This component of sustained attention has been associated with positive mental health outcomes, including reduction in ruminative processes (Chambers, Lo, & Allen, 2008) and anxiety (Wells, 2002).

Focus on the present moment

Focusing on the present moment involves directing one's attention, with or without effort, to the internal and external phenomena occurring at each moment of awareness (e.g., Baer, 2003). It is contrasted with states in which the mind is preoccupied with thoughts about the past or the future, such as memories, plans, or fantasies. Rumination, which is associated with increased depressive symptom severity, is an example where perceivers lack focus on the present moment, preoccupied with automatically recurring thoughts from the past such as the causes and consequences of their feelings (e.g., Nolen-Hoeksema, 1991).

Nonjudgmental acceptance

Nonjudgmental acceptance involves experiencing thoughts, sensations, and events as they are at the moment they enter one's consciousness, without judging them as being good or bad, desirable or undesirable, important or trivial (Germer, Siegel, & Fulton, 2005). Acceptance is to allow all experiences—pleasurable, neutral, and painful—to arise without trying to change, control, or avoid them. Acceptance applies to all experiences, concrete (e.g., sensory pain) and abstract (e.g., feelings of rejection). Acceptance allows individuals to appreciate the experience, even in the presence of condemnatory self-evaluations (e.g., "I am a bad person"). When these evaluations do occur, acceptance allows individuals to embrace them as they are, without suppression or distortion (e.g., "Right now I am feeling as though I am a bad person").

Missing one or more components of mindfulness can result in "mindless behavior" (Langer & Piper, 1987). A mindless person has little awareness of the present experiences and is more likely to blindly follow daily routines and impulses. Unconscious processes are more likely to affect the mind when it is not in active control. For example, when mindless, our perceptions and judgments about a person are more likely to be influenced by superficial labels associated with that person (e.g., job title, political orientation). By contrast, a mindful person relies on conscious and deliberate thought processing by having an open and flexible attitude, which can lead to nonjudgmental acceptance of multiple context-dependent perspectives. Acceptance further allows individuals to distinguish events from the thoughts or emotions evoked by them. Therefore, a mindful individual can further notice that some events are uncontrollable, whereas the responses can be controlled with practice. This increased sense of awareness can in turn help change the contexts in which events are experienced. Mindfulness does not necessarily confer greater mental control, but rather, enables an individual to better notice the presence of their own mental control by providing awareness of what is controllable and what is not.

Automaticity and Deautomatization

Much of our mental and emotional life is supported by automatic processes that are unconscious, spontaneous, and seemingly instantaneous (Bargh & Chartrand, 1999). People are often on "autopilot" in their behavior and decision-making, following habits or heuristic routines while their minds are occupied with other thoughts (e.g., Langer & Abelson, 1974). We define automaticity as the ability to effortlessly engage in behaviors without paying conscious attention to their operational details (e.g., LaBerge & Samuels, 1974). Automaticity is usually a desired result of learning that reflects a degree of habit or mastery. It is often adaptive, conserves limited attentional resources, and lessens the self-regulatory burden by freeing up one's limited conscious attention from tasks in which they are no longer needed (e.g., Bargh & Chartrand, 1999). However, automatized mental reactions can also lead to a wide range of detrimental consequences. When an external event is followed by unconscious and automatic reactions, it may become difficult to separate the event itself from thoughts or emotions that it arouses. The automatic and quick reactions may reduce perceived control and lead to helplessness, which is commonly associated with a host of mental problems, such as anxiety disorders (Chorpita & Barlow, 1998), depression (Abramson, Seligman, & Teasdale, 1978), and addiction (Forsyth, Parker, & Finlay, 2003).

Whether automaticity is innate or acquired through learning, the field's consensus has been that automatic reactions are difficult or even impossible to control (e.g., Devine, 1989). However, some recent findings suggest that deautomatization is possible. A highly automatic and unconscious activation and application of intergroup biases were deautomatized when counterstereotyping egalitarian goals were preemptively activated (Moskowitz & Li, 2011), or in positive rather than negative, stereotypic contexts (Wittenbrink, Judd, & Park, 2001). Hypnosis can also be used to initiate deautomatization. In a series of experiments, participants who were given hypnotic suggestion for alexia, the inability to read, showed a reduction or elimination of Stroop interference (Raz, Moreno-Iniguez, Martin, & Zhu, 2007). However, deautomatization that may occur through these paradigms is limited by a number of factors, including short-lived effects and potential difficulty of application in real life. We suggest that another way to instigate deautomatization while allowing perceivers' introspection and control is through mindfulness. A mindful mental set can deautomatize previously established associative categories and other routine modes of behavior, a view that is supported by a growing body of empirical findings.

Mindfulness and Deautomatization

In this section, we discuss how the four integral elements of mindfulness—awareness, attention, focus on the present moment, and acceptance—can enable deautomatization by creating different layers of changes in human behavior, as schematized in Figure 9.1. In doing so, we emphasize that these components of mindfulness often operate in mutually dependent and reciprocal relationships to produce related outcomes,

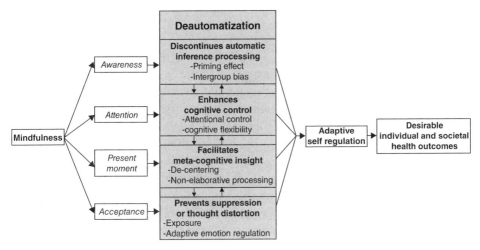

Figure 9.1 A model describing the mechanism of deautomatization facilitated by mindfulness.

and the outcomes often partially overlap. In the current paper, however, we intentionally separate the outcomes of each component for the sake of distinctness. Also, the framework we propose is by no means a comprehensive review on the mechanisms of mindfulness. Mindfulness is a complex phenomenon and probably involves multiple levels of mechanisms that work in independent or interrelated manners (Hölzel et al., 2011; Vago & Silbersweig, 2012), some of which will not be elaborated here for the sake of brevity.

Awareness and deautomatization

Automaticity is often adaptive in that it conserves our limited cognitive resources by utilizing information-processing strategies that are not taxing (Bargh, 1992). However, when our mind relies on automaticity, increased susceptibility to priming effects or reliance on simplifying tactics such as intergroup biases may result. Mindfulness, on the other hand, promotes awareness of the automatic ebb and flow of mental events (Wells, 2006). This awareness can be an important step to discontinue automatic inference processing, such as that which supports priming effect and intergroup bias.

Priming   The priming effect occurs when a preceding stimulus, or prime, influences the perception of or response to a later stimulus (e.g., Salancik & Pfeffer, 1977). Priming effects occur when participants are not aware either of the prime itself or that the prime can affect their subsequent behaviors. For example, brief exposure to words related to elderly stereotypes led people to walk more slowly down the hallway when leaving the experiment than did control participants (Bargh, Chen, & Burrows, 1996). In this study, the words were presented for an extremely brief duration so that they were inaccessible to participants' awareness. In another study, incidental contact with a hot (vs. iced) cup of coffee affected impression formation, influencing people to perceive more (vs. less) interpersonal warmth in a stranger (Williams & Bargh, 2008).

Participants in this study were exposed to a temperature prime for a longer period of time but were not aware of the way it could affect their subsequent social perception.

Awareness of the presence of a prime and its potential effects on one's behavior can eliminate the priming effect. For example, the magnitude of the priming effect is inversely related to the length of exposure to the prime (Fazio, Sanbonmatsu, Powell, & Kardes, 1986), suggesting that priming information is most potent when presented so briefly that it is inaccessible to the perceiver's conscious awareness. In particular, Murphy and Zajonc (1993) showed that awareness eliminates the priming effect by presenting priming stimuli in the form of smiling or scowling faces either for an extremely brief duration or for a longer duration followed by novel Chinese ideographs. Participants preferred the Chinese ideographs that were presented imme- diately after smiling faces only when the smiling faces were presented for a very brief time and thus inaccessible to their conscious awareness. A very short exposure to prim- ing information did not allow individuals' awareness to recognize that the affective information (faces) was unrelated to the later stimuli (Chinese ideographs). On the other hand, when the faces were presented for a longer duration, increased awareness allowed individuals to be capable of separating the affective information from their preference for Chinese ideographs.

A mindful person, who attends to the changing fields of sensations, thoughts, and feelings from moment to moment, may be less influenced by the priming effect, given an increased alertness to the here-and-now and heightened vigilance and clarity of awareness regarding internal and external processing of information. With increased awareness, mindful individuals may be more likely to notice the priming trigger or its psychological effect, bypassing automatic priming reactions. In support of this view, Radel and colleagues (2009) showed that individuals with higher levels of disposi- tional mindfulness as measured by the Mindful Attention Awareness Scale (Brown & Ryan, 2003) were less susceptible to a priming manipulation designed to activate goal motivations, compared to those with low mindfulness. Participants who were exposed to subliminal words related to autonomy (e.g., willing) performed better in a sub- sequent exam than those presented with non goal-related words. Importantly, this effect occurred only among those with low self-reported dispositional mindfulness. The authors conclude that mindful awareness can increase immunity against auto- matic guidance.

Intergroup bias Intergroup biases are often activated and applied by cognitive responses that are based upon automatic categorization, formed by a perceiver's knowledge, beliefs, and expectations about human groups (e.g., Hamilton & Trolier, 1986). The cognitive processes that initiate intergroup bias most often occur auto- matically and unconsciously (Devine, 1989; Pratto & Bargh, 1991), and thus inter- group biases are considered to be an inescapable and necessary by-product of the categorization process (Bargh, 1989). However, current models suggest that inter- group bias reduction is possible when people have awareness of their own bias. Simply being aware of one's mental states or processes—a key ingredient of mindfulness— can reduce these automatized categorizations of feature-related interpretations, such as "I am perceiving this female student to be math-incompetent because there exists a bias that women are incompetent at math" (e.g., Bargh, 1999). This suggests that mindfulness can facilitate deautomatization by fostering awareness of one's presents thoughts and feelings. For example, mindfulness training based on acceptance and commitment decreased racial bias in a naturalistic classroom setting across two sessions and at one-week follow-up (Lillis & Hayes, 2007).

Langer and Moldoveanu (2000) further argue that active awareness permits appreciation of new perspectives and promotes context sensitivity, revealing that behaviors can be understood in multiple ways. For example, mindset-oriented mindful individuals are more likely to appreciate views other than their own, recognizing that there are as many different perspectives as there are different observers (Langer, 1989). This can lead to less judgmental attitudes and reduce bias. For example, experimentally inducing mindfulness in children reduced discrimination against physically handicapped individuals (Langer, Bashner, & Chanowitz, 1985). In another study, greater mindfulness induced by examining multiple (vs. single) aspects of a person reduced biased behaviors, such as slow walking speed activated by age-related bias (Djikic, Langer, & Stapleton, 2008). Whether increased multiple perspective taking or context sensitivity mediated the demonstrated efficacy of mindfulness on bias reduction, however, was not directly tested in these studies.

Collectively, the theoretical rationale and empirical results support the notion that awareness can deter automatic inference processing shown in priming and intergroup bias. We further suggest that awareness in the state of mindfulness is made possible by active control of attention. Mindfulness can promote deautomatization and help control automaticity by training one's attention regulation capacity, which is further illustrated in the following section.

Attention and deautomatization

We now discuss the way mindfulness training can facilitate deautomatization by enhancing attention regulation and cognitive flexibility. Mindfulness practice that involves focusing on a goal object while reducing distraction can enhance the ability to sustain attention on a target object (e.g., Chambers et al., 2009; Shapiro & Schwartz, 2000). In addition, mindfulness practice can offset deleterious effects of cognitive depletion in conditions of low resources (Friese, Messner, & Schaffner, 2012). Practitioners can cultivate the ability to direct their attention to a target of their choice with increased cognitive control, the ability to sustain attention without intentionally choosing the focus of awareness. This can eventually allow the specific focus to change from moment to moment, while maintaining an alert state. We review the effect of mindfulness on facets of cognitive control, including attention regulation and cognitive flexibility.

Attention regulation   Attention is an information-processing capacity that enables selective focus on a particular feature of the environment while inhibiting other competing information. In a state of mindfulness, attention is placed on one specific aspect of goal-relevant information while inhibiting the array of other competing stimuli. Therefore, one critical change during mindfulness training is the enhancement of attentional capacities, indexed by improved performance on tasks that require attention regulation. Mindfulness practice can improve the attention regulation capacity needed to sustain and inhibit attention and allocate attentional resource as intended. In particular, Chambers and colleagues (2008) found that mindfulness cultivates an ability to sustain and control the attentional focus. In this study, participants who underwent a 10-day intensive mindfulness retreat showed increased ability to maintain and shift their focus of attention. Another brief five-day integrative daily meditation program that used mindfulness-based approaches also improved inhibitory attentional control (Tang et al., 2007). Furthermore, a three-month intensive mindfulness retreat improved an ability to allocate attentional resource to task-relevant stimuli (Slagter et al., 2007).

Evidence strongly suggests that mindfulness may be one effective way to train the ability to guide and sustain one's attention in the face of previously established automatic reactions. There are some important similarities between mindfulness training and other attention interventions. For example, both meditation-oriented mindfulness and other attention-training programs emphasize the importance of repetition (e.g., Sohlberg & Raskin, 1996). Attention training and mindfulness both can involve difficulties associated with attempts to control one's internal experience against the mind's strong tendency to habitually wander, often unaware of its own lack of awareness (Langer, 1989). The emphasis of mindfulness on repetition is thus necessary in order to overcome mindlessness and achieve fluency at a task that was initially challenging (e.g., Sohlberg & Mateer, 1987). Similarly, as in attention training, practiced regularly over a longer period of time, the initially transient mindful states can convert into a more stable trait-like condition. Mindfulness training has elements that are also characteristics of an effective attention intervention, such as sufficiently gratifying reinforcement (Sohlberg & Raskin, 1996), as the reward of successful mindfulness training can be extensive with wide-ranging improvements of well-being (for a review, see Germer et al., 2005). In addition, successful attention training should use target stimuli that are common to both the training environment and the real world (Sohlberg & Raskin, 1996). Target stimuli commonly used in mindfulness training are one's breathing and related bodily sensations, and this readily available nature of target stimuli makes it easy to generalize what was learned during practice in a real environment.

Cognitive flexibility   Cognitive flexibility is the ability to adapt information processing strategies and respond to novel and unpredicted information, allowing individuals to switch behavioral responses according to the changing context of the information (Cañas, Quesada, Antolí, & Fajardo, 2003). Mindfulness can increase cognitive flexibility by allowing flexible allocation of attention on the ever-changing landscape of moment-to-moment information (Langer, 1989). The ability to recognize multiple aspects of a target object and choose a task-relevant attentional set is often measured using the Stroop task, where attention has to be withdrawn from processing the over-learned and automatic information (word reading) and placed onto processing novel and relatively less practiced information (naming the ink color), a process of deautomatization. Some evidence indicates that mindfulness reduces Stroop interference. Self-reported dispositional mindfulness predicted enhanced Stroop performance (Galla,

Hale, Shrestha, Loo, & Smalley, 2012). Moore and Malinowski (2009) also report that cognitive flexibility is associated with meditation practice and self-reported levels of mindfulness. In this study, mindfulness meditators who completed at least six weeks of meditation sessions showed a better performance on the Stroop task than those who had no previous mindfulness experience. When a highly automatic reaction has become task-irrelevant, mindfulness meditators could flexibly redirect their attention to the new task-relevant information. Furthermore, Alexander, Langer, Newman, Chandler, and Davies (1989) found that performing 20 min of daily mindfulness practice twice a day over three months was associated with decreased Stroop interference among residents in nursing homes.

We reviewed literature suggesting that mindfulness meditation can improve attention regulation and cognitive flexibility, thereby enabling discontinuation of automatic cognitive processing. We suggested that the repeated training of directing attention in mindfulness meditation can enhance cognitive control, indexed by increased attention control and cognitive flexibility, which then can provide a basis for the deautomatization to occur.

Focus on the present moment and deautomatization

Mindful practice of repeatedly bringing attention back to the present moment can lead to realization that thoughts are simply patterns of the mind rather than accurate reflections of truth or reality. This process is called "metacognitive insight" (Teasdale, 1999), a transition toward regarding thoughts as transient mental events, rather than direct representations of reality. Mindful focus on the present moment can thus enable metacognitive insight, which becomes the basis for de-centering and nonelaborative processing.

De-centering De-centering involves stepping back from mental experiences and observing that thoughts are transient mental events and do not necessarily represent facts based in reality (Segal, Williams, & Teasdale, 2002). De-centering can allow individuals to have some mental distance from their problematic thoughts and emotions, allowing an opportunity to observe their habitual tendency to react automatically. This observation can further offer a sense of choice to respond consciously to an increased number of options instead of reacting unconsciously.

The process and outcomes of de-centering have strong implications in clinical disorders that are characterized by problematic automatized thought patterns. For example, Teasdale (1999) highlights that ruminative and negative self-focused thought patterns can perpetuate depressive episodes. A de-centered view can help reduce rumination by helping individuals to notice recurrent depressogenic thought patterns and respond within a different processing configuration. Specifically, negative thoughts are simply regarded as waves of mental patterns rather than reflections of reality. In support of Teasdale's view, mindfulness-based interventions have shown efficacy in treating major depression (Ma & Teasdale, 2004; Teasdale et al., 2000) and bipolar disorder (Williams et al., 2008). De-centering is a process of changing an individual's relationship to thoughts and feelings, rather than focusing on their details in an attempt to modify them. This reconfigured relationship can free the mind from secondary elaborative processing (Bishop et al., 2004), which will be discussed next.

Nonelaborative processing   A de-centered perspective, by enabling a suspension of conceptual meaning-based processing, can lead to nonelaborative thought processing (Wells, 2006). Nonelaborative processing of information related to physical and psychological pain is of particular importance in mindfulness. The expectation or experience of pain can lead to secondary elaborations on worries and aversion responses that are often unconscious and automatic, making it difficult to separate pain from suffering in the overall experience. With respect to pain, the Buddhist tradition observes that pain is not the same as suffering, as suffering occurs when negative thoughts and fear are projected onto pain sensations (Germer et al., 2005). Similarly, pain can be largely subjective and context dependent. For example, patients who taught themselves to reinterpret the hospital experience in nonthreatening ways took fewer pain relievers and sedatives, and tended to leave the hospital sooner than the untrained patients (Langer, Janis, & Wolfer, 1987). Studies on pain perception further suggest that the expectation of pain can influence the subsequent amplitude of an actual pain experience. For example, expectation of a painful stimulus, a secondary information processing that is purely based on psychological factors, amplified the actual experience of unpleasantness in response to an innocuous stimulus indexed by increased brain responses within areas associated with pain processing (Sawamoto et al., 2000). Siegel and colleagues (2001) also illustrate the way physical pain can be exacerbated by secondary elaborations that often arise automatically upon encountering the pain experience, such as worrying about longer-term consequences of pain. Affected individuals may in turn avoid physical activities altogether for the fear of worsening the symptoms, which can exacerbate psychological stress and muscle deterioration. Mindfulness may provide the initial impetus to discontinue the automatized chronic pain cycle by allowing recognition that a certain portion of the pain experience is self-generated and identify the source of pain that can be changed.

Rumination is another example of elaborative thought processing that involves a highly automatized and repetitive cycle of negative thought patterns and self-focused attention, where negative thoughts about a present problem further compound the condition (Nolen-Hoeksema, 1991). Metacognitive insight, brought about by mindful observation of ever-changing patterns of thoughts, allows relocation of attention from habitual passive thought fixation back to the intended primary focus of attention (Teasdale, 1999). Furthermore, paying attention to one's thought patterns can provide a sense of control over possible courses of actions. Instead of unconsciously following preestablished automatic reactions, a mindful person can consciously monitor emotional experiences, thereby preventing further cycles of rumination (Teasdale et al., 1995). Mindfulness practice was shown to reduce self-reported rumination, as measured by a trait rumination scale (Ramel, Goldin, Carmona, & McQuaid, 2004).

In the next section, we further discuss the concept of mindful acceptance, and how it prevents suppression or thought distortion, thereby facilitating benefits of exposure. Attitude of acceptance may also facilitate adaptive modes of emotion regulation, attenuating automatic reactivity to emotional stimuli.

Acceptance and deautomatization

In the state of mindfulness, the mind is attending to the ongoing stream of ever-changing present experiences with clear awareness. Resulting from these processes may be an enhanced level of acceptance (Chambers et al., 2008). Understanding the futility of trying to achieve permanence in the present moment, which is in a perpetual state of change, can lead to the fundamental insight of acceptance. In the state of nonjudgmental acceptance, all phenomena that enter awareness are observed carefully but not evaluated as good or bad. Instead, all events are experienced with an attitude of acceptance sans threat or defense. Mindfulness involves observing one's own reactive desire to avoid the fear-inducing stimuli without regarding them as harmful or undesirable. This detached stance helps individuals to actually experience fear, which in turn may make the object of fear less threatening. This process is very similar to that of interoceptive exposure.

Exposure   Exposure used in therapy involves introduction to feared object or context in the absence of danger (Joseph & Gray, 2008). Mindfulness encourages a gradual orientation of attention toward fear as it arises, while exploring it with nonjudgmental acceptance. Mindfulness thus involves exposure to fearful stimuli without avoidance, which is a key ingredient for changing undesirable reactivity to fearful stimuli (Samoilov & Goldfried, 2000). Exposure reduces reactivity that would otherwise engender maladaptive automatic cognitive defenses (Baer, 2003). The nonjudgmental acceptance toward internal experience can introduce exposure and reduce anxiety severity by encouraging the experience of anxiety symptoms without attempts to control them (Kabat-Zinn et al., 1992). Kabat-Zinn (1982) also explains that undistorted exposure to the sensations of chronic pain in the absence of catastrophic consequences can lead to desensitization and eventual extinction of the maladaptive reactivity elicited by the pain sensations.

Emotion regulation   Mindfulness cultivates an attitude of nonjudgmental acceptance toward all phenomena, allowing individuals to notice and appreciate all emotional experiences without clinging, whether they are positive or negative. This mode of emotion regulation reduces potentially detrimental emotional reactivity shown in other maladaptive emotion regulation strategies such as suppression or rumination. Arch and Craske (2006) showed that even a very brief 15-min mindfulness practice can help adaptively regulate emotions. Participants who underwent brief mindfulness exercise, compared to controls, were better at decreasing the intensity and negativity of emotional reactivity in response to the highly negatively valenced pictures. Self-reported dispositional mindfulness also is associated with lower arousal within the area of amygdala, an area implicated as a cortical and limbic marker of emotional reactivity, at the baseline (Way, Creswell, Eisenberger, & Lieberman, 2010) as well as during emotional threat (Creswell, Way, Eisenberger, & Lieberman 2007).

Nonjudgmental acceptance is distinct from other emotion-regulation processes, such as suppression, in which an individual attempts to inhibit thoughts that are unacceptable or aversive (Wegner, Schneider, Carter, & White, 1987), or reappraisal, in which individuals reconstrue a situation in a different way than how it was originally experienced (Gross, 1998). Mindfulness does not involve systematic evaluations and cognitive alterations of irrational thoughts. Instead, individuals learn to observe the impermanence of their thoughts and notice that thoughts are not factual threats that call for escape or avoidance responses. This in turn may allow a more accepting and less judgmental stance towards all thoughts, including ruminative thoughts.

Acceptance enables individuals to observe their automatic reactivity to mental events without judging, which can discontinue undesirable automatized behaviors. No longer subjected to former reactive thought patterns, one gains an opportunity to better regulate thoughts and emotions, which can result in improved health outcomes. Indeed, Alexander and colleagues (1989) showed that mindfulness practice can promote psychological health and even predict longevity. Residents in nursing homes who engaged in 20-min mindfulness meditation twice a day for three months exhibited improved mental-health outcomes, measured by a question probing general improvement of mental health (rated by nurses blind to experimental condition) compared to a control group. Furthermore, mindfulness practitioners were more likely to be alive than controls three years after treatment ended. We suggest that acceptance can help regulate thoughts and feelings, contributing to the potentially powerful effect of mindfulness on health outcomes.

Conclusions and Future Directions

Many authors have discussed the deautomatizing function of mindfulness. We provide further elaboration on this model and propose that four core elements of mindfulness—awareness, attention, focus on the present moment, and acceptance—discontinue automaticity. Mindful deautomatization can further promote adaptive self-regulation strategies, which can enhance psychophysical well-being.

Our mental and emotional life is often a succession of automatic and habituated reactions to a constant flow of external and internal stimuli. Automaticity helps to process information process more efficiently than our limited attentional capacity can handle, but there are trade-offs. We reviewed the potential effect of mindfulness in reducing maladaptive automatic cognitive and emotional reactions. The proposed mechanistic approach can be helpful in deconstructing mindfulness and its deautomatizing function into algorithmic steps. Understanding essential components of mindfulness can provide a functional model to test the multifaceted construct of mindfulness, while preventing potentially misguided applications of mindfulness that result in limited or undesired outcomes. We further suggest directions for future research that we hope will flow from this deautomatization model of mindfulness. First, researchers can test whether mindfulness can deautomatize other highly automatic responses. Second, other mechanisms of deautomatization can be tested, such as changes in emotions. Mindfulness has been shown to increase daily experiences of positive emotions such as joy and gratitude (Tang et al., 2007) and decrease negative affect (Chambers et al., 2008). Increased experience of positive emotion facilitated by mindfulness may in turn enhance deautomatization. According to Fredrickson's (1998) "broaden-and-build" model, positive emotions broaden the possible thought–action repertoire by unlatching the rigid processing of automatic operations. Unlike negative emotions that require preparation for a narrow range of specific actions, positive emotions sans threat do not call for quick reactions. Positive emotions thus may open up a mental space, a state where individuals can savor the moment-to-moment experience without mindlessly reacting to incoming stimuli.

Mindfulness practice in clinical or daily life settings can be a new cost-effective and noninvasive treatment or health-enhancement strategy. Both mindset-oriented and meditation-oriented perspectives on the efficacy of mindfulness have been investigated in recent studies, yet their specific underlying properties still remain underexplored. Assessing deautomatization as a potential mechanism of mindfulness can help shed light on better understanding and application of a more advanced contemporary utilization of the 2,500 year-old ancient practice of meditation.

Acknowledgments

The authors thank Judson Brewer for helpful comments. This chapter was originally published as: Kang, Y., Gruber, J., & Gray, J. R. (2013). Mindfulness and de-automatization. *Emotion Review*, 5(2), 192–201. We have updated many of the sections. Reproduced with the permission of Sage.

References

Abramson, L. Y., Seligman, M. E. P., & Teasdale, J. D. (1978). Learned helplessness in humans: Critique and reformulation. *Journal of Abnormal Psychology*, 87(1), 49–74.

Alexander, C. N., Langer, E. J., Newman, R. I., Chandler, H. M., & Davies, J. L. (1989). Transcendental meditation, mindfulness, and longevity: An experimental study with the elderly. *Journal of Personality and Social Psychology*, 57(6), 950–964.

Arch, J. J., & Craske, M. G. (2006). Mechanisms of mindfulness: Emotion regulation following a focused breathing induction. *Behaviour Research and Therapy*, 44(12), 1849–1858.

Baer, R. A. (2003). Mindfulness training as a clinical intervention: A conceptual and empirical review. *Clinical Psychology: Science and Practice*, 10, 125–143.

Bargh, J. A. (1989). Conditional automaticity: Varieties of automatic influence in social perception and cognition. In J. S. Uleman & J. A. Bargh (Eds.), *Unintended thought* (pp. 3–51). New York, NY: Guilford Press.

Bargh, J. A. (1992). The ecology of automaticity: Toward establishing the conditions needed to produce automatic processing effects. *The American Journal of Psychology*, 105(2), 181–199.

Bargh, J. A. (1999). *The cognitive monster: The case against controllability of automatic stereotype effects*. In S. Chaiken & Y. Trope (Eds.), *Dual process theories in social psychology*. New York, NY: Guilford.

Bargh, J. A., & Chartrand, T. L. (1999). The unbearable automaticity of being. *American Psychologist*, 54(7), 462–479.

Bargh, J. A., Chen, M., & Burrows, L. (1996). Automaticity of social behavior: Direct effects of trait construct and stereotype activation on action. *Journal of Personality and Social Psychology*, 71(2), 230–244.

Bishop, S. R., Lau, M., Shapiro, S., Carlson, L., Anderson, N. D., Carmody, J., . . . Devins, G. (2004). Mindfulness: A proposed operational definition. *Clinical Psychology: Science and Practice, 11*, 230–241.

Bowen, S., Witkiewitz, K., Dillworth, T. M., Blume, A. W., Chawla, N., Simpson, T. L., . . . Larimer, M. E. (2006). Mindfulness meditation and substance use in an incarcerated population. *Psychology of Addictive Behaviors, 20*(3), 343–347.

Brewer, J. A., Sinha, R., Chen, J. A., Michalsen, R. N., Babuscio, T. A., Nich, C., . . . Rounsaville, B. J. (2009). Mindfulness training and stress reactivity in substance abuse: Results from a randomized, controlled stage I pilot study. *Substance Abuse, 30*(4), 306–317.

Brown, K. W., & Ryan, R. M. (2003). The benefits of being present: Mindfulness and its role in psychological well-being. *Journal of Personality and Social Psychology, 84*(4), 822–848.

Cañas, J. J., Quesada, J. F., Antolí, A., & Fajardo, I. (2003). Cognitive flexibility and adaptability to environmental changes in dynamic complex problem-solving tasks. *Ergonomics, 46*(5), 482–501.

Chambers, R., Gullone, E., & Allen, N. B. (2009). Mindful emotion regulation: An integrative review. *Clinical Psychology Review, 29*(6), 560–572.

Chambers, R., Lo, B. C. Y., & Allen, N. B. (2008). The impact of intensive mindfulness training on attentional control, cognitive style, and affect. *Cognitive Therapy and Research, 32*, 303–322.

Chorpita, B. F., & Barlow, D. H. (1998). The development of anxiety: The role of control in the early environment. *Psychological Bulletin, 124*(1), 3–21.

Creswell, J. D., Way, B. M., Eisenberger, N. I., & Lieberman, M. D. (2007). Neural correlates of dispositional mindfulness during affect labeling. *Psychosomatic Medicine, 69*, 560–565.

Deikman, A. J. (1966). Implications of experimentally induced contemplative meditation. *The Journal of Nervous and Mental Disease, 142*(2), 101–116.

Devine, P. G. (1989). Stereotypes and prejudice: Their automatic and controlled components. *Journal of Personality and Social Psychology, 56*(1), 5–18.

Djikic, M., Langer, E. J., & Stapleton, S. F. (2008). Reducing stereotyping through mindfulness: Effects on automatic stereotype-activated behaviors. *Journal of Adult Development, 15*, 106–111.

Fazio, R. H., Sanbonmatsu, D. M., Powell, M. C., & Kardes, F. R. (1986). On the automatic activation of attitudes. *Journal of Personality and Social Psychology, 50*(2), 229–238.

Forsyth, J. P., Parker, J. D., & Finlay, C. G. (2003). Anxiety sensitivity, controllability, and experiential avoidance and their relation to drug of choice and addiction severity in a residential sample of substance-abusing veterans. *Addictive Behaviors, 28*(5), 851–870.

Fredrickson, B. L. (1998). What good are positive emotions? *Review of General Psychology, 2*, 300–319.

Friese, M., Messner, C., & Schaffner, Y. (2012). Mindfulness meditation counteracts self-control depletion. *Consciousness and Cognition, 21*(2). 1016–1022.

Galla, B. M., Hale, T. S., Shrestha, A., Loo, S. K, & Smalley, S. L. (2012). The disciplined mind: Associations between the Kentucky Inventory of Mindfulness Skills and attention control. *Mindfulness, 3*(2), 95–103.

Germer, C. K., Siegel, R. D., & Fulton, P. R. (2005). *Mindfulness and psychotherapy.* New York, NY: Guilford Publications.

Gross, J. J. (1998). The emerging field of emotion regulation: An integrative review. *Review of General Psychology, 2*(3), 271–299.

Gyatso, T. K. (1986). *Progressive stages of meditation on emptiness.* Oxford, UK: Longchen.

Hamilton, D. L., & Trolier, T. K. (1986). Stereotypes and stereotyping: An overview of the cognitive approach. In J. Dovidio & S. Gaertner (Eds.), *Prejudice, discrimination, and racism* (pp. 127–163). San Diego, CA: Academic Press.

Hölzel, B. K., Lazar, S. W., Gard, T., Schuman-Olivier, Z., Vago, D. R., & Ott, U. *et al.* (2011). How does mindfulness meditation work? Proposing mechanisms of action from a conceptual and neural perspective. *Perspectives on Psychological Science, 6,* 537–559. doi:10.1177/1745691611419671

Joseph, J. S., & Gray, M. J. (2008). Exposure therapy for posttraumatic stress disorder. *Journal of Behavior Analysis of Offender and Victim: Treatment and Prevention, 1*(4), 69–80.

Kabat-Zinn, J. (1982). An outpatient program in behavioral medicine for chronic pain patients based on the practice of mindfulness meditation: Theoretical considerations and preliminary results. *General Hospital Psychiatry, 4*(1), 33–47.

Kabat-Zinn, J. (1990). *Full catastrophe living.* New York, NY: Delacorte.

Kabat-Zinn, J., Lipworth, L., & Burney, R. (1985). The clinical use of mindfulness meditation for the self-regulation of chronic pain. *Journal of Behavioral Medicine, 8*(2), 163–90.

Kabat-Zinn, J., Massion, A. O., Kristeller, J., Peterson, L. G., Fletcher, K. E., Pbert, L., . . . Santorelli, S. F. (1992). Effectiveness of a meditation-based stress reduction program in the treatment of anxiety disorders. *American Journal of Psychiatry, 149*(7), 936–943.

Kawakami, K., Dovidio, J. F., Moll, J., Hermsen, S., & Russin, A. (2000). Just say no (to stereotyping): Effects of training in the negation of stereotypic associations on stereotype activation. *Journal of Personality and Social Psychology, 78*(5), 871–888.

LaBerge, D., & Samuels, J. S. (1974). Toward a theory of automatic information processing in reading. *Cognitive Psychology, 6,* 293–323.

Langer, E. J. (1975). The illusion of control. *Journal of Personality and Social Psychology, 32*(2), 311–328.

Langer, E. J. (1989). *Mindfulness.* Reading, MA: Addison-Wesley.

Langer, E. J. (1997). *The power of mindful learning.* Reading, MA: Addison-Wesley.

Langer, E. J., & Abelson, R. P. (1972). The semantics of asking a favor: How to succeed in getting help without really dying. *Journal of Personality and Social Psychology, 24*(1), 26–32.

Langer, E. J., & Abelson, R. P. (1974). A patient by any other name . . .: Clinician group difference in labeling bias. *Journal of Consulting and Clinical Psychology, 42*(1), 4–9.

Langer, E. J., Blank, A., & Chanowitz, B. (1978). The mindlessness of ostensibly thoughtful action: The role of "placebic" information in interpersonal interaction. *Journal of Personality and Social Psychology, 36*(6), 635–642.

Langer, E. J., Janis, I., & Wolfer, J. (1987). Reduction of psychological stress in surgical patients. *Journal of Experimental Social Psychology, 11,* 155–165.

Langer, E. J., & Moldoveanu, M. M. (2000). The construct of mindfulness. *Journal of Social Issues, 56*(1), 1–9.

Langer, E. J., & Piper, A. I. (1987). The prevention of mindlessness. *Journal of Personality and Social Psychology, 53*(2), 280–287.

Langer, E. J., Bashner, R. S., & Chanowitz, B. (1985). Decreasing prejudice by increasing discrimination. *Journal of Personality and Social Psychology, 49*(1), 113–120.

Lillis, J., & Hayes, S. C. (2007). Applying acceptance, mindfulness, and values to the reduction of prejudice: A pilot study. *Behavior Modification, 31,* 389–411.

Ma, H. S., & Teasdale, J. D. (2004). Mindfulness-based cognitive therapy for depression: Replication and exploration of differential relapse prevention effects. *Journal of Consulting and Clinical Psychology, 72*(1), 31–40.

Moore, A., & Malinowski, P. (2009). Meditation, mindfulness and cognitive flexibility. *Consciousness and Cognition, 18*(1), 176–86.

Moskowitz, G. B., & Li, P. (2011). Egalitarian goals trigger stereotype inhibition: A proactive form of stereotype control. *Journal of Experimental Social Psychology, 47,* 103–116.

Murphy, S. T., & Zajonc, R. B. (1993). Affect, cognition, and awareness: Affective priming with optimal and suboptimal stimulus exposures. *Journal of Personality and Social Psychology*, *64*(5), 723–739.

Nolen-Hoeksema, S. (1991). Responses to depression and their effects on the duration of depressive episodes. *Journal of Abnormal Psychology*, *100*(4), 569–82.

Pratto, F., & Bargh, J. A. (1991). Stereotyping based on apparently individuating information: Trait and global components of sex stereotypes under attention overload. *Journal of Experimental Social Psychology*, *27*, 26–47.

Radel, R., Sarrazin, P., Legrain, P., & Bobance, L. (2009). Subliminal priming of motivational orientation in educational settings: Effect on academic performance moderated by mindfulness. *Journal of Research in Personality*, *43*, 695–698.

Ramel, W., Goldin, P. R., Carmona, P. E., & McQuaid, J. R. (2004). The effects of mindfulness meditation on cognitive processes and affect in patients with past depression. *Cognitive Therapy and Research*, *28*(4), 433–455.

Raz, A., Moreno-Iniguez, M., Martin, L., & Zhu, H. (2007). Suggestion overrides the stroop effect in highly hypnotizable individuals. *Consciousness and Cognition*, *16*, 331–338.

Salancik, G. R., & Pfeffer, J. (1977). An examination of need-satisfaction models of job attitudes. *Administrative Science Quarterly*, *22*(3), 427–456.

Samoilov, A., & Goldfried, M. R. (2000). Role of emotion in cognitive-behavior therapy. *Clinical Psychology: Science and Practice*, *7*, 373–385.

Sawamoto, N., Honda, M., Okada, T., Hanakawa, T., Kanda, M., Fukuyama, H., . . . Shibasaki, H. (2000). Expectation of pain enhances responses to nonpainful somatosensory stimulation in the anterior cingulate cortex and parietal operculum/posterior insula: An event-related functional magnetic resonance imaging study. *The Journal of Neuroscience*, *20*(19), 7438–7445.

Shapiro, S. L., & Schwartz, G. E. (2000). Intentional systemic mindfulness: An integrative model for self-regulation and health. *Advances in Mind–Body Medicine*, *16*(2), 128–134.

Segal, Z. V., Williams, J., & Teasdale, J. D. (2002). *Mindfulness-based cognitive therapy for depression*. New York, NY: The Guilford Press.

Siegel, R. D., Urdang, M., & Johnson, D. (2001). *Back sense: A revolutionary approach to halting the cycle of back pain*. New York, NY: Broadway Books.

Slagter, H. A., Lutz, A., Greischar, L. L., Francis, A. D., Nieuwenhuis, S., Davis, J. M., & Davidson, R. J. (2007). Mental training affects distribution of limited brain resources. *PLOS Biology*, *5*(6), e138.

Sohlberg, M. M., & Mateer, C. A. (1987). Effectiveness of an attention-training program. *Journal of Clinical & Experimental Neuropsychology*, *9*, 117–130.

Sohlberg, M. M., & Raskin, S. A. (1996). Principles of generalization applied to attention and memory interventions. *The Journal of Head Trauma Rehabilitation*, *11*(2), 65–78.

Tang, Y. Y., Ma, Y., Wang, J., Fan, Y., Feng, S., Lu, Q., . . . Posner, M. I. (2007). Short-term meditation training improves attention and self-regulation. *Journal of Personality and Social Psychology*, *104*(43), 17152–17156.

Teasdale, J. D. (1999). Metacognition, mindfulness and the modification of mood disorders. *Clinical Psychology and Psychotherapy*, *6*, 146–155.

Teasdale, J. D., Segal, Z., & Williams, J. M. (1995). How does cognitive therapy prevent depressive relapse and why should attentional control (mindfulness) training help? *Behavioral Research and Therapy*, *33*(1), 25–39.

Teasdale, J. D., Segal, Z. V., Williams, J. M., Ridgeway, V. A., Soulsby, J. M., & Lau, M. A. (2000) Prevention of relapse/recurrence in major depression by mindfulness-based cognitive therapy, *Journal of Consulting and Clinical Psychology*, *68*, 615–623.

Vago, D. R., & Silbersweig, D. A. (2012). Self-awareness, self-regulation, and self-transcendence (S-ART): A framework for understanding the neurobiological mechanisms of mindfulness. *Frontiers in Human Neuroscience, 6,* 296. doi:10.3389/fnhum.2012 .00296

Way, B. M., Creswell, J. D., Eisenberger, N. I., & Lieberman, M. D. (2010). Dispositional mindfulness and depressive symptomatology: Correlations with limbic and self-referential neural activity during rest. *Emotion, 10,* 12–24.

Wegner, D. M., Schneider, D. J., Carter, S. R., & White, T. L. (1987). Paradoxical effects of thought suppression. *Journal of Personality and Social Psychology, 53*(1), 5–13.

Wells, A. (2002). GAD, metacognition, and mindfulness: An information-processing analysis. *Clinical Psychology, 9*(1), 95–100.

Wells, A. (2006). Detached mindfulness in cognitive therapy: A metacognitive analysis and ten techniques. *Journal of Rational-Emotive & Cognitive-Behavior Therapy, 23*(4), 337–355.

Williams, J. M., Alatiq, Y., Crane, C., Barnhofer, T., Fennell, M. J., Duggan, D. S., . . . Goodwin, G. M. (2008). Mindfulness-based cognitive therapy (MBCT) in bipolar disorder: Preliminary evaluation of immediate effects on between-episode functioning. *Journal of Affective Disorders, 107*(1–3), 275–9.

Williams, L. E., & Bargh, J. A. (2008). Experiencing physical warmth promotes interpersonal warmth. *Science, 322,* 606–607.

Wittenbrink, B., Judd, C. M., & Park, B. (2001). Spontaneous prejudice in context: variability in automatically activated attitudes. *Journal of Personality and Social Psychology, 81*(5), 815–827.

10

Toward a Mindful–Unmindful Cognitive Style

Lessons from the Study of Field Dependence–Independence

Jack Demick

In *Taking Sides: Clashing Views on Controversial Issues in Cognitive Science*, Mason (2004) has posed the question: "Is Mindfulness a Cognitive Style?" In support of the affirmative, she has presented Sternberg's (2000) article on images of mindfulness while in support of the opposing view, she has employed Langer and Moldoveanu's (2000) article on the construct of mindfulness. After comparing mindfulness to related constructs in psychology, namely, abilities, personality traits, and cognitive styles, Sternberg has concluded that "mindfulness has characteristics of all three but seems closest to being a cognitive style" (p. 11). In contrast, Langer and Moldoveanu (2000) have argued that

> ... the concept of mindfulness has some unique characteristics. We are not in complete agreement ... that mindfulness is most like a cognitive style because, in our view, a style is not expected to change over time and through different circumstances, whereas the essence of mindfulness is change. (p. 4)

As a student of the most wildly researched cognitive style to date (cf. Wapner & Demick, 1991), namely, field dependence–independence (FDI), I take the following position. The concept of mindfulness has the potential to be construed as a cognitive (or other) style were both Sternberg and Langer to consider the issues, and the lessons learned, from early and ongoing work on the FDI construct. As stated in their articles in 2000, both Sternberg and Langer and Moldoveanu have employed style conceptualizations that are to some degree inconsistent with contemporary work, some of which has been conducted within my own laboratory.

For example, Sternberg's position that the concept of mindfulness would be enhanced by its association with the more general problem area of cognitive style seems, at first glance, promising for mindfulness researchers. However, his position is tempered by his subsequent statement that the cognitive style movement hit a

The Wiley Blackwell Handbook of Mindfulness, First Edition.
Edited by Amanda Ie, Christelle T. Ngnoumen, and Ellen J. Langer.
© 2014 John Wiley & Sons, Ltd. Published 2014 by John Wiley & Sons, Ltd.

dead end in the 1970s for both theoretical and methodological reasons. Theoretically, cognitive styles, which have often been used to bridge the study of cognition and personality, have not been derived from nor led to any general theories of cognition and/or of personality, leading work on cognitive styles to become isolated from the rest of the psychological literature. Further, research has raised the issue of the generalizability of cognitive styles, namely, whether they are generalized characteristics of individuals or more contextually based. Cognitive styles have also often appeared similar to abilities with some investigators arguing that the poles of many styles may be construed as either more or less adaptive. For example, Sternberg exemplified this notion by citing the FDI cognitive style construct, which he argued has provided data showing that a field-independent (FI) cognitive style is better than a field-dependent (FD) one. Methodologically, he argued that measures of cognitive styles have not corresponded well to their conceptualization and, further, that component measures of a given style have not always corresponded well to each other. In defense of their position, Langer and Moldoveanu (2000) have argued that Sternberg's association of mindfulness with cognitive style categories is inadequate and much too restrictive for the current concept of mindfulness, which involves all senses and does not adhere to the notion of nonchangeability.

I now turn to a basic exposition of the FDI cognitive style construct, in both its original and contemporary forms, as means to consider how work on this particular cognitive style may inform those who wish to develop the concept of mindfulness as an empirically rigorous cognitive (or other) style free from previous criticisms. In doing so, certain of Sternberg's and Langer's assumptions about the nature of styles will be questioned toward arguing that Langer's work has the potential to fit nicely within the general (cognitive) style literature if the latter is accurately construed.

Lessons from FDI Cognitive Style Research

Initial conceptualization

Witkin (1967) introduced the notion of *cognitive style* as a "characteristic, self-consistent mode of functioning found pervasively throughout an individual's cognitive, that is, perceptual and intellectual activities" (p. 234). The particular cognitive style of interest to him was *FDI*. He saw this as a psychological dimension describing individual differences in whether, in space perception, people use cues from the visual field or from their own bodies (postural-kinesthetic cues). Specifically, FDI describes differences in ways of perceiving and structuring a field. FD performance is characterized by *global perception* where items are not well differentiated from the background when the field is structured and where there is a lack of the imposition of organization on the field when it is unstructured. In contrast, FI performance is characterized by *articulated perception* where items are readily disembedded from the surrounding field and where structure is imposed on an unstructured field.

Witkin and colleagues (Witkin, Dyk, Faterson, Goodenough, & Karp, 1962; Witkin & Goodenough, 1981; Witkin, Lewis, Hertzman, Machover, Meissner & Wapner, 1954) have described individuals who are predominantly influenced by field cues (e.g., visual cues) and who cannot easily disembed an object from its surrounding field as FD and individuals who rely primarily on bodily cues and who can easily differentiate objects from the field as FI. They have also found constellations of personality characteristics correlated with these perceptual styles. For example, FD individuals typically exhibit a *global body concept*, a *limited sense of separate identity*, and an *unusual sensitivity to the social surround*. In contrast, FI individuals characteristically show an *articulated body concept*, a *sense of separate identity*, and a *greater ability in analytic tasks*. It has also been documented by these and other researchers that: (1) there are stable individual differences in FDI over long periods of time; (2) over ontogenesis, there are changes from FD to FI and then a reversion to FD in older adulthood; (3) women are more FD than men; (4) FI individuals typically use structured, specialized controls such as intellectualization as a defense mechanism, whereas FD individuals typically employ repression and denial as defenses; also, both appear pathological in the extreme (lability/histrionics in FD, autistic tendencies/withdrawal in FI); (5) FD people are more socially oriented (e.g., more attentive to social cues, prefer being physically close to others, more open emotionally in interpersonal communication), while FI persons are not very interested in others and exhibit greater physical/emotional distancing from them; (6) hunting and gathering people are more FI than sedentary farming people; and (7) whether a particular cognitive style is good or bad depends on its adaptive value in a particular situation; that is, a cognitive style's value is relative to context.

In their early experiments, Witkin and colleagues (Witkin et al., 1954) assessed FDI by the use of three perceptual tasks: (1) the Rod-and-Frame Test or RFT (in a dark room, a subject adjusts to vertical a luminous rod embedded in a tilted square frame); (2) the Body Adjustment Test or BAT (a subject, seated in a chair that is projected into a tilted room, adjusts himself or herself in the chair to upright in the context of the tilted room); and (3) the Embedded Figures Test or EFT (on a paper-and-pencil task, a subject attempts to disembed simple figures from complex designs). Over time, some of the tasks were modified because of their cumbersome nature. That is, the BAT was eliminated, and a portable version of the RFT or Portable Road-and-Frame Test (PRFT) (Oltman, 1968) was developed for those who were unable or did not wish to use a large unlit laboratory. Further, although there was initially a variety of versions of the EFT employed related to subject characteristics and test conditions (e.g., the Preschool Embedded Figures Test or PEFT, the individually administered EFT, the group administered Group Embedded Figures Test or GEFT), the most easily administered GEFT became the norm partly related to the difficulty of obtaining the PEFT and EFT. Thus, in contemporary research, the RFT or more likely the PRFT is used to assess *perception of the upright* (visual vs. postural conflict), while the GEFT is employed to measure *cognitive restructuring ability* (see Demick, in press).

The first iteration of Witkin's research on FDI raised a number of theoretical and methodological issues that became paramount in subsequent work. Theoretical issues included: (1) initial confusion of this work with research assuming the person independent of the environment (e.g., biologically based trait theories); (2) the suspect relationship between FDI cognitive style and ability constructs (e.g., intelligence); (3) the nonvalue-free nature of the FDI construct; and (4) the lack of placing FDI research within a larger theoretical framework. Methodological issues included: (1) whether the FDI construct represented one construct or two (perception of the upright, cognitive restructuring ability); and (2) whether methodological limitations (e.g., women being tested in dark rooms by men) were responsible for some of the classic findings (e.g., with women being more FD than men). These issues re-echo some of Sternberg's previous concerns, and all are relevant for advancing Langer's construct. Thus, each is discussed briefly in turn.

Theoretically, cognitive and other style theories, contrary to the beliefs of some researchers, are *not* similar to trait theories, which assume that the person is independent of the environment. Rather, cognitive styles exemplify interactional theories, which characterize behavior as occurring within a field of interfacing organismic and environmental forces. Theories of cognitive style are, thus, primarily concerned with classifying individuals in terms of the ways in which they construe the environment; a corresponding categorization of types of contexts is not made. Individuals are seen as behaving consistently across contexts as a result of their use of similar modes of construal or recognition of the environment. Little attention is given to explaining variability in an individual's behavior across contexts. Rather, the main focus is on accounting for consistency in behavior across contexts and variability between individuals in the same context. However, Witkin et al. (1962) argued that, unlike traits, the development of FDI was related to both biological-genetic factors and environmental-social factors (e.g., FD is related to socialization patterns emphasizing conformity and dependence on authority, while FI is associated with socialization patterns emphasizing autonomy and independence). Nonetheless, interactive (e.g., cognitive) style theories are characterized by the same strengths and weaknesses as biological style (e.g., temperament) theories, namely, efficiency in generating behavioral predictions, parsimony, issues in dealing with individual differences within a style category or accounting for individual variation in behavior across contexts, and difficulty obtaining empirical support for overly general predictions based on style.

Further, a positive relationship between FDI and intelligence has been argued to be of extreme theoretical importance, for it has led some critics (e.g., McKenna, 1984) to argue strongly that measures of FDI should be viewed more appropriately as measures of cognitive ability rather than of cognitive style. However, the empirical evidence supporting this generalization has been equivocal. Although the direction of the correlation is usually such that those who perform better on the standard FDI tasks, although often limited to the EFT, also perform better on intelligence tests, the correlations have never approached unity, suggesting that FDI tasks assess something more than intelligence tests measure. Although the EFT has correlated with the overall Wechsler scales, the correlations tend to be higher with the performance subtests than with the verbal ones. Although Witkin and Goodenough (1981) highlighted numerous correlations between FDI measures and academic achievement, specific correlations between the EFT and mathematics/science grades, though significant, were reduced to nonsignificance when a general ability measure was taken into account. When statistically controlling for general intellectual ability, some studies reported no relationship between FDI and intelligence, while others provided significant findings, although of varying magnitudes. These different strands of data for me convincingly demonstrate that FDI and intelligence are not the same construct.

The style-ability issue is also linked to the question of whether a value bias enters into the FDI construct. From Witkin's viewpoint, the FDI dimension is value-neutral in so far as each pole—interpersonal skills versus restructuring skills—has qualities that are adaptive depending on particular circumstances. The value-neutral character of the construct is also supported by correlations with educational choices and preference (e.g., FD is associated with careers in helping professions such as social worker and clergy, teaching areas such as social sciences and elementary education, and business occupations such as personnel, advertising, and sales, while FI is related to careers in mathematics, certain science professions such as physics and engineering, several healthcare professions such as medicine and dentistry, and distinct practical occupations such as carpentry and farming). In contrast, however, some researchers (e.g., Silverman, 1991) have found that, under certain conditions (e.g., states of uncertainty), FD individuals show more nonoptimal physiological responses (e.g., veins prone to spasm) than FI individuals. The issue has become further complicated because: (1) at the time of the initial research, analytic skills were valued more highly in society than interpersonal ones; and (2) the term "field dependent," which most often characterized women, was seen then as biased and pejorative, and more recently as sexist. However, in light of society's recent consideration of alternative forms of intelligence such as emotional intelligence (e.g., Salovey & Grewal, 2005), it is unclear as to whether researchers would still take such a strong stand against the dichotomy between cognitive and social-emotional skills. Further, the use of more value-free terminology to describe the two FDI styles (e.g., reversing FD and FI as field sensitivity vs. field insensitivity or, perhaps in an even more value-free manner, referring to FI and FD as self- vs. outer- directedness or articulated vs. global perception) might be developed. Finally, further exploration of alternative measures of social functioning than only those examined by Witkin and colleagues may lead to the possibility that the two groups exhibit interpersonal competencies although in different ways. For example, various aspects of interpersonal communication such as characteristic rate of speech and/or language stereotypy, the quality of interpersonal relationships, and transactions in close relationships are worthy of future empirical research.

Methodologically, if there is only one process involved in both test situations, then the correlations between measures from each should approach unity. If, as in fact, the correlations are of a magnitude that accounts for only a small proportion of the variance—even 36% (r values of magnitude of .60)—there are at least two possible explanations: (1) the correlations might approach unity, but moderator variables (e.g., sex, age, personality characteristics of experimenters and subjects) are not taken into account; or (2) unity of correlations, suggesting one process, does not in fact exist, although the two tasks may have some features in common. This has led some (e.g., Demick, 1991) to advocate strongly that FDI studies need routinely to combine measures from both the RFT and the GEFT into one larger index rather than relying solely on an overall measure from the more easily administered GEFT. Further, in light of the criticism that Witkin's earlier work involved men testing women in dark rooms (RFT), which may have compromised women's performance (cf. Matlin, 1989), Demick, Raymond, and Wapner (1990) uncovered no difference in the performance of undergraduate females related to whether they were tested by male or female experimenters. This finding was extended by Demick and Harkins (1999) to male and female adults across the life span.

Theory development

In response to critics (e.g., Zigler, 1963) who highlighted the atheoretical nature of Witkin's initial conceptualization, Witkin, Goodenough, and Oltman (1979) subsequently discussed FDI cognitive style in terms of Werner's (1957) concept of *psychological differentiation* (using his comparative and developmental theory in which the orthogenetic principle—describing changes over time from dedifferentiated, to differentiated, to differentiated and integrated—plays a prominent role). Specifically, as part of the conceptualization that individual development toward differentiation encompasses biological as well as psychological processes, Witkin et al. (1979) elaborated the differentiation construct by construing differentiation as the most general construct at the apex of a pyramidal structure with its qualities defined by second- and third-order structures. At one level below differentiation, there were three constructs: (1) *self-nonself segregation* (FDI), which was manifest at a third lower order in restructuring skills and interpersonal competencies; (2) *segregation of psychological functions*, which was manifest at a third lower order in structured controls and specialized defenses; and (3) *segregation of neurophysiological functions*, which was manifest at a third lower order in hemispheric specialization.

However, this conceptualization—although based on the orthogenetic principle—was subsequently taken to task for omitting an essential feature of organization, namely, hierarchic integration. In essence, Witkin et al. (1979) seemed to take integration for granted and mentioned its role largely in terms of adaptation. This led other researchers (e.g., Missler, 1986) to suggest that, because of its placement in a differentiation framework, FDI theory became confusing to many.

Contemporary theory and research

When I began work on the FDI cognitive style construct at Clark University initially with Seymour Wapner, one of Witkin's earliest collaborators, I was perplexed by two issues that have occupied much of my attention to the present day, namely, how to portray FDI cognitive style in a more value-free manner and how best to demonstrate hierarchic integration within FDI performance, each of which will be discussed in turn.

The first issue involved the value-free nature of the two opposing styles, which researchers often did not believe. In response, I reasoned that additional research on more complex phenomena might demonstrate and thus heighten the construct's value-free nature. This is indeed what we found in two separate studies. That is, Demick and Harkins (1999) assessed cognitive style and driving skills in adulthood. Two hundred thirty-one individuals in four age groups (20–39, 40–59, 60–74, 75+ years) participated in two sessions (counterbalanced): one in the laboratory (assessing, e.g., driving history, FDI cognitive style, reaction time, selective attention, computerized driving skill) and one on the road (e.g., standard driving road evaluation by licensed instructors). The findings were striking. FDI is a better predictor of driving ability than age, and the two aspects of FDI differentially predict driving ability among the groups (e.g., perception of the upright predicts driving behavior in middle-aged adults, whereas cognitive restructuring ability predicts driving behavior in older adults). Even more striking, however, was the finding that both FD and FI individuals exhibit driving problems although in different ways: FD drivers tend to follow the car in front of them (dependence on context), whereas FI drivers tend to scan the entire visual field and weave in and out of traffic (dependence on body/self) with both styles leading to the possibility of accidents. Not only did this study support the notion that perception of the upright and cognitive restructuring ability represent different constructs but also it identified an important, ecologically valid context (automobile driving) in which both styles may pose problems for drivers regardless of their age.

Finally, Ngnoumen and I (Ngnoumen & Demick, 2013) collaborated more recently on a study assessing the relationships among cognitive style, cognitive flexibility, and world hypotheses or general beliefs about the nature of the world and how reality is constructed (Pepper, 1961). Although not the main thrust of the study, an unexpected finding was that, on the World Hypothesis Scale (Harris, Fontana, & Dowds, 1977), FI individuals endorse world views focused on the person independent of context (formism, mechanism, organicism) while FD persons endorse world views that take context into account (contextualism, dialecticism, transactionalism). From the point of view of contemporary developmental psychology, that those individuals with an FD cognitive style exhibit more developmentally advanced, ecologically valid world views, this is a finding that suggests that the adoption of world views clearly works in favor of FD individuals.

With respect to the second issue, Witkin and Goodenough (1981) noted that despite the inverse relationship between interpersonal competencies and restructuring skills (with the former high and the latter low in FD and vice versa in FI), its magnitude "is sufficiently low to allow for the possibility that these patterns are not the only ones to be found, and that once present, they may be changeable" (p. 62). Though there is generally individual consistency, that is, individuals who are *fixed* (either FD or FI) in their cognitive style, they assumed that there were still others who had access to both characteristics. They designated these last individuals as *mobile*. Thus, I reasoned that, if individuals have the mobility to shift from FD to FI and/or from FI to FD, this state of organization implies hierarchic integration with one style subordinated to the other depending on the individual's goals and task demands. Empirical demonstration of this possibility combine Witkin's previously evoked construct of differentiation with that of hierarchic integration, now making FDI theory completely consistent with Werner's general developmental theory (specifically his orthogenetic principle) and by doing so perhaps reducing confusion on the part of others.

However, identification of the mobility-fixity issue created additional controversy in so far as some argued that, with FDI as a cognitive trait involving a single dimension (biological perspective), people at one end should be consistent, and people at the other end should likewise be consistent. However, others insisted that the trait argument fails to recognize that a large proportion of the variance is unaccounted for in correlations, even of the magnitude of .80 so that there may be systematic variation dependent on the context as well as on the person (interactional perspective). For example, an artist may show great flexibility when moving from the abstract while conceiving of the goal of a painting to responding physiognomically and concretely while executing the painting. Further, by varying the context, one might increase the precision of one's prediction by taking moderator variables into account.

This debate led to consideration of the question as to how to define mobility-flexibility operationally. Assuming that there will be variation in FDI depending on physical, interpersonal, and sociocultural features and demands of the environment in which the assessment occurs, one suggestion was to test subjects in two or more contexts followed by characterizing them as occupying a *range* on the FDI dimension rather than by a measure of average performance. Thus, fixed individuals should be characterized by a narrower range and mobile individuals by a broader range of performance over varied environmental contexts. The problem next became how to select the contexts to be used in such complex testing situations. For example, Reinking (1977) demonstrated that specialized instructions (e.g., alternating those emphasizing an internal or external search for problem-solving cues and vice versa) significantly affect RFT scores. Further, situations changing the interpersonal context of the assessment (e.g., use of experimenters of different sexes, personalities, and/or cognitive styles) might also be employed. More ecologically valid situations introducing different conditions requiring subjects to shift, for example, from the teacher onto the intellectual aspects of an academic task or vice versa or conditions varying the ease and difficulty in cognitive restructuring were also suggested. However, in all these cases, the measure advocated was a range measure based on performance over diverse conditions.

More recently, I (Demick, 2013) became interested in the mobility-fixity problem in the more general context of the study of resilience, a widely popular contemporary construct in developmental psychology over which there is also much controversy. For example, some researchers make a distinction between resiliency (traits of individuals leading to more general "steeling" or "inoculating" functions in future adverse situations) and resilience (dynamic processes leading to favorable outcomes for individuals following adversity), the latter of which seems akin to Rutter's (1979) conceptualization of protective factors. In contrast, my theoretical approach, namely, holistic/systems developmental theory or HSDT (an elaboration and extension of Werner's, 1957, organismic-developmental theory) led me to view resilience as a combination of the psychological trait of strength (cf. hardiness) and flexibility (mobility of cognitive style), the latter of which depends on situational demands and thus takes contextual factors into account.

Toward gaining support for this conceptualization, the following experiment was conducted. Undergraduates were brought into the laboratory and administered: the PRFT, the GEFT, the Stroop (1935) Color–Word Test (as quickly and as accurately as possible, the subject is asked: on Card A, to name 100 color words, e.g., "red" printed in black ink; on Card B, to name the color of 100 color patches; and on Card C, to name the color of the ink in which incongruous color words are printed, e.g., blue printed in "red" ink); the Big Five Personality Inventory (McCrae & Costa, 2012), and Connor and Davidson's (2003) Resiliency Scale (CDRISC). On the basis of the first two tasks, subjects were divided into FD and FI groups. Following this, those FD and FI subjects scoring above the median on the Stroop interference factor (total time on C – total time on B, assumed to be a measure of cognitive flexibility) were considered FDI-mobile, while those below the median retained their original grouping as FD-fixed or FI-fixed.

Further, the Big Five personality traits were employed as proxy measures of psychological strength. That is, only those subjects who scored above the median on

each of the Big Five personality traits, namely, openness to new experience, consci-
entiousness, extraversion, agreeableness, and emotional stability (reverse scoring of
neuroticism scale), taken one at a time, were employed in subsequent analyses. Each
of the five analyses of variance indicated no main effects for cognitive style groupings (FD, FI, FDI) or personality factor groupings (high vs. low) on the CDRISC.
However, analyses did reveal significant interactions of cognitive style by personality
strength for three of five personality traits, namely, emotional stability, extraversion,
and openness to new experience. In these three cases, follow-up analyses indicated
that FDI-mobile individuals scoring high on a given trait exhibited higher resilience
scores on the CDRISC than the FD- and FI-fixed groups. Thus, preliminary findings
for our conceptualization of resilience were provided by our use of an FDI-mobile
group in addition to the two fixed (FD, FI) groups.

Comparisons Between the FDI and Mindfulness Constructs

With close scrutiny and perhaps with some surprise, there are a large number of similarities between the constructs of FDI and mindfulness. These include the following
and, since FDI has been described extensively above, relevant references to Langer's
work will be cited where appropriate. First, the constructs of FDI and mindfulness
may be termed *holistic* in so far as they both address and cut across aspects of the
biological, psychological, and sociocultural levels of functioning and their interrelations. Second, both constructs emphasize the importance of *context*, which is part and
parcel of every analysis. Third, both constructs are *multidimensional* with FDI consisting of perception of the upright and cognitive restructuring ability and mindfulness
comprising openness to novelty, alertness to distinction, sensitivity to different constructs, implicit if not explicit awareness of multiple perspectives, and orientation in
the present. Fourth, the approaches represented by the constructs may both be termed
interactional in that they treat individuals' ways of relating to the environment. Fifth,
both constructs employ a *dichotomy*—FD versus FI, mindfulness versus mindlessness—
to understand individual differences in human functioning. Sixth, the approaches have
both been used more specifically to study *organismic* variables inherent in basic psychological processes such as sex differences (e.g., Kawakami, White, & Langer, 2000),
intelligence (e.g., Brown & Langer, 1990), language (e.g., Langer, 1992), decision-
making (e.g., Langer, 1994), stereotypes (e.g., Levy & Langer, 1994), personality
(e.g., Carson & Langer, 2006), psychopathology (e.g., Langer & Imber, 1980),
placebo effects (e.g., Crum & Langer, 2007), and development especially during old
adulthood (e.g., Langer, 2009a). Seventh, the approaches have both been concerned
with the study of their constructs in terms of human adaptation in *ecologically valid
contexts* such as education (e.g., Langer, 1997), intimate relationships (e.g., Burpee &
Langer, 2005), and automobile-driving behavior (e.g., Demick & Langer, 2013).
Eighth, both approaches espouse *mobility* in functioning as an area worthy of further
investigation (cf. Langer, 2006, on mindfully negotiating the world of academics vs.
art). Ninth, both have considered the *value-free nature*, or lack thereof, in their basic
conceptualization with respect to terminology and content. Tenth, they have both
considered the *best way to operationalize* their essence (e.g., Langer, 2004). Eleventh,

both approaches have demonstrated that *variation in instruction* provided to subjects has the potential to impact the phenomenon under investigation and often in powerfully positive ways (e.g., Langer & Piper, 1987). Finally, they both have implications for the *construction of more grand theories of human functioning with a focus on adaptation and well-being* (e.g., Langer, 2009b) as elaborated below.

Recommendations Toward Conceptualizing Mindfulness as a Cognitive (or Other) Style

Based on the previous review of the history and advancement of the FDI cognitive style, the following recommendations are offered to promote the construct of mindfulness similarly as a (cognitive) style. Theoretically, future research might assess whether mindfulness is stable over time and/or context dependent. It might also address such important issues as ontogenetic and cross-cultural factors inherent early on in development including the origins and course of mindfulness in different societal contexts. Further, consideration of additional individual differences in mindfulness (e.g., among those of differing socioeconomic statuses or SES) might shed light on important social problems, such as productivity in the workplace (e.g., do those of higher SES view work as mindful activity that should be enjoyed in and of itself, whereas those of lower SES construe their job less mindfully as a means to an end, i.e., as a way to earn a paycheck to be able to enjoy one's time off from work?). Future work might also attempt to explore ways to increase the value-free nature of the construct. For example, changes in terminology for its dichotomies—for example, mindfulness versus mindlessness might be renamed mindful versus unmindful (cognitive) styles or perhaps with even less value-laden labels—might be adopted. In line with this, relationships between mindfulness and unmindfulness as cognitive styles might be assessed through comparisons with other cognitive style constructs. For example, given the classic finding in the FDI literature that those with FD cognitive styles show an unusual sensitivity to the social surrounds, does this indicate that FD individuals are at times more mindful? Or might the highly mindful person be able to switch from FD to FI or vice versa, depending on task optimization (FDI mobility)?

Further, assessment of whether an unmindful style is at times more adaptive than a mindful style might contribute to a value-free conceptualization of the construct. For instance, Santostefano (1964) demonstrated that children who were facing surgery exhibited less anxiety and more optimal adaptation if their cognitive style was characterized by leveling (e.g., a preference for simplistic perspectives often leading to repression as a defense mechanism) versus sharpening (e.g., favoring complex perspectives difficult to be assimilated into one's present experience). Thus, a relevant question for mindfulness researchers might become whether an unmindful style may ever serve adaptive functions. Although Langer (1989, 1997, 2009a) appears to argue, based on 40 years of laboratory and field studies, that an unmindful style is never as adaptive as a mindful one since the latter is stress-free, consideration of more complex phenomenon, as occurred in the case of ongoing FDI research on its value-free nature, may counterintuitively uncover that an unmindful style or at least a combination of mindful and unmindful styles may serve some sort of positive function(s). For example, my daughter, a professional dancer, has suggested that the ability to engage automatically (unmindfully) in a dance piece frees the dancer to focus (mindfully) on other performance variables (e.g., freedom of expression, communication of enjoyment, delivery of emotionality), the latter of which are perhaps more important in the context of dance performance. However, this more general construal may be antithetical, perhaps unacceptable, to Langer's perspective, which may then become the biggest stumbling block in viewing her approach as representative of a cognitive style in its most classic sense.

Methodologically, the review of the collective work on FDI suggests for mindfulness researchers that it is often necessary to employ, refine, and/or eliminate different tasks with diverse measures to capture the essence of a construct, particularly a multidimensional one. Thus, the ongoing attempts of Langer and colleagues to develop a paper-and-pencil assessment of mindfulness, although both admirable and already productive, might be furthered by complementing this approach with more standard laboratory techniques that address all levels of organization (biological/physiological, psychological, sociocultural) and their interrelationships.

Conclusions

Although Sternberg (2000) argued that Langer's concept of mindfulness has characteristics of related psychological constructs such as abilities, personality traits, and cognitive styles, he concluded that mindfulness was most akin to cognitive style. However, he then went on to point out the seemingly insurmountable difficulties inherent in contemporary cognitive style theory and research, leading Langer to counter that, given its unique characteristics that involve all senses, the construct of mindfulness is much broader in scope than that of cognitive style. In reaction to common misunderstandings regarding the general nature of cognitive styles, work on the most widely researched cognitive style to date, namely FDI, has been presented to highlight the powerful similarities between mindfulness and FDI given their shared underlying theoretical assumptions (e.g., including holism, contextualism, multidimensionality, change and mobility, integration, ecological validity). Regardless of whether one prefers to view the construct of mindfulness as constituting a classic cognitive style or a more general style, researchers are strongly encouraged to incorporate the powerful heuristic potential of mindfulness within whichever theoretical orientation they employ and however they wish (e.g., alternatively as an ability, a personality trait, or an altogether different construct). As I see it, mindfulness theory—similar to cognitive style theory—represents a viewpoint and an alternative mode of analysis that are extremely helpful in understanding *any* psychological phenomenon. Similar to cognitive style theory, mindfulness theory, as Langer has demonstrated, is relevant not only to social psychology but also to all other subfields of psychology (e.g., cognitive, developmental, educational, clinical, personality, organizational). With further theoretical systematization and development, mindfulness theory—perhaps including a conceptualization of a mindful versus unmindful (cognitive) style—has the potential to become one of our most important psychological theories (cf. Demick, 2000). Mindfulness theory will help us all to conceptualize problems that are more in line with the complex character of everyday life functioning. It will also help psychology both to see itself and to be seen by others as a unified science, one concerned not only with examining isolated aspects of human behavior and experience but also with the study of problems that cut across various aspects of individuals and their environments as well as across various subfields of our discipline (e.g., not only social but also clinical, developmental, cognitive, and organizational). This is crucial for psychology to maintain its status as a holistic entity rather than to be subject to the increasing forces of fragmentation and specialization that currently threaten to eliminate its very existence (Demick & Wapner, 2013).

References

Brown, J. B., & Langer, E. (1990). Mindfulness and intelligence: A comparison. *Educational Psychologist, 25*(3–4), 305–335.

Burpee, L. C., & Langer, E. J. (2005). Mindfulness and marital satisfaction. *Journal of Adult Development, 12*(1), 43–51.

Carson, S. H., & Langer, E. J. (2006). Mindlessness and self-acceptance. *Journal of Rational-Emotive & Cognitive-Behavior Therapy, 24*(1), 29–43.

Connor, K. M., & Davidson, J. R. T. (2003). Development of a new resilience scale: The Connor–Davidson Resilience Scale (CD-RISC). *Depression and Anxiety, 18*(2), 76–82.

Crum, A. J., & Langer, E. J. (2007). Mind-set matters: Exercise and the placebo effect. *Psychological Science, 18*(2), 165–171.

Demick, J. (1991). Organismic factors in field dependence–independence: Gender, personality, psychopathology. In S. Wapner & J. Demick (Eds.), *Field dependence–independence: Cognitive style across the life span* (pp. 209–243). Hillsdale, NJ: Erlbaum.

Demick, J. (2000). Toward a mindful psychological science: Theory and application. *Journal of Social Issues, 56*(1), 141–159.

Demick, J. (2013). *An experimental conceptualization of the nature of resilience: Toward an integrative person-in-environment model.* Manuscript in preparation.

Demick, J. (in press). *A revised manual for the Embedded Figures Test (including computerized GEFT).* Menlo Park, CA: Mind Garden.

Demick, J., & Harkins, D. (1999). Cognitive style and driving skills in adulthood: Implications for licensing of older adults. *International Association of Traffic Science and Safety (IATSS) Research, 23*(1), 1–16.

Demick, J., & Langer, E. J. (2013). *Toward mindful driving in older adults.* Manuscript in preparation.

Demick, J., Raymond, N., & Wapner, S. (1990, March). *Gender of subject, gender of experimenter, field dependence–independence, and moral reasoning.* Paper presented at Eastern Psychological Association annual meeting, Philadelphia, PA.

Demick, J., & Wapner, S. (2013). *Toward integrating psychology: Strategies from holistic/systems developmental theory (HSDT).* Manuscript in preparation.

Harris, M., Fontana, A. F., & Dowds, B. N. (1977). The World Hypothesis Scale: Rationale, reliability and validity. *Journal of Personality Assessment, 41*(5), 537–547.

Kawakami, C., White, J. B., & Langer, E. J. (2000). Mindful and masculine: Freeing women leaders from the constraints of gender roles. *Journal of Social Issues, 56*(1), 49–63.

Langer, E. J. (1989). *Mindfulness.* Reading, MA: Addison-Wesley.

Langer, E. J. (1992). Interpersonal mindlessness and language. *Communication Monographs, 59*, 324–327.

Langer, E. J. (1994). The illusion of calculated decisions. In R. P. Abelson, R. C. Shank, & E. J. Langer (Eds.), *Beliefs, reasoning, and decision making: Psychologic in honor of Bob Abelson* (pp. 33–54). Hillsdale, NJ: Erlbaum.

Langer, E. J. (1997). *The power of mindful learning*. Reading, MA: Addison-Wesley.

Langer, E. J. (2004). *Langer Mindfulness Scale user guide and technical manual*. Worthington: IDS Publishing Cooperation.

Langer, E. J. (2006). *On becoming an artist: Reinventing yourself through mindful creativity*. New York, NY: Ballantine Books.

Langer, E. J. (2009a). *Counterclockwise: Mindful health and the power of possibility*. New York, NY: Random House.

Langer, E. J. (2009b). Well-being: Mindfulness versus positive evaluation. In Lopez, S. J., & Snyder, C. R. (Eds.), *The Oxford handbook of positive psychology* (2nd ed., pp. 279–294). New York, NY: Oxford University Press.

Langer, E. J., & Imber, L. (1980). Role of mindlessness in the perception of deviance. *Journal of Personality and Social Psychology, 39*(3), 360–367.

Langer, E. J., & Moldoveanu, M. (2000). The construct of mindfulness. *Journal of Social Issues, 56*(1), 1–9.

Langer, E. J., & Piper, A. I. (1987). The prevention of mindlessness. *Journal of Personality and Social Psychology, 53*(2), 280–287.

Levy, B., & Langer, E. J. (1994). Aging free from negative stereotypes: Successful memory in China and among the American deaf. *Journal of Personality and Social Psychology, 66*(6), 989–997.

Mason, M. (2004). *Taking sides: Clashing views on controversial issues in cognitive science*. New York, NY: McGraw-Hill/Dushkin.

Matlin, M. W. (1989). *Cognition* (2nd ed.). Fort Worth, TX: Holt, Reinhart and Winston.

McCrae, R. R., & Costa, P. T. (2012). *Personality in adulthood: A five-factor theory perspective* (2nd ed.). New York, NY: Guilford Press.

McKenna, F. P. (1984). Measures of field dependence: Cognitive style or cognitive ability? *Journal of Personality and Social Psychology, 47*(3), 593–603.

Missler, R. A. (1986). Analytic and synthetic cognitive functioning: A critical review of evidence bearing on field dependence. *Journal of Research on Personality, 20*, 1–33.

Ngnoumen, C. T., & Demick, J. (2013). *Relations among cognitive style, cognitive flexibility, and world hypotheses: Old wine in new bottles or new wine in old bottles?* Manuscript in preparation.

Oltman, P. K. (1968). A portable rod-and-frame apparatus. *Perceptual and Motor Skills, 26*, 503–506.

Pepper, S. C. (1961). *World hypotheses: A study in evidence*. Berkeley, CA: University of California Press.

Reinking, R. H. (1977). Cognitive set influences on Witkin's rod-and-frame test. *Perceptual and Motor Skills, 66*, 999–1012.

Rutter, M. (1979). Protective factors in children's responses to stress and disadvantage. *Annals, Academy of Medicine, Singapore, 8*(3), 324–338.

Salovey, P., & Grewal, D. (2005). The science of emotional intelligence. *Current Directions in Psychological Science, 14*(6), 281–285.

Santostefano, S. G. (1964). A developmental study of the cognitive control of "leveling sharpening." *Merrill Palmer Quarterly of Behavior and Development, 10*(4), 343–360.

Silverman, A. J. (1991). Psychophysiological and brain lateralization studies in field dependence–independence. In S. Wapner & J. Demick (Eds.), *Field dependence–independence: Cognitive style across the life span* (pp. 61–77). Hillsdale, NJ: Erlbaum.

Sternberg, R. J. (2000). Images of mindfulness. *Journal of Social Issues, 56*(1), 11–26.

Stroop, J. R. (1935). Studies of interference in serial verbal reactions. *Journal of Experimental Psychology, 18,* 643–661.

Wapner, S., & Demick, J. (Eds.). (1991). *Field dependence–independence: Cognitive style across the life span.* Hillsdale, NJ: Erlbaum.

Werner, H. (1957). *A comparative psychology of mental development.* New York, NY: International Universities Press.

Witkin, H. (1967). A cognitive-style approach to cross-cultural research. *International Journal of Psychology, 2,* 233–250.

Witkin, H. A., Dyk, R. B., Faterson, H. F., Goodenough, D. R., & Karp, S. A. (1962). *Psychological differentiation: Studies of development.* New York, NY: Wiley.

Witkin, H. A., & Goodenough, D. R. (1981). *Cognitive style: Essences and origins.* New York, NY: International Universities Press.

Witkin, H. A., Goodenough, D. R., & Oltman, P. K. (1979). Psychological differentiation: Current status. *Journal of Personality and Social Psychology, 37,* 1127–1145.

Witkin, H. A., Lewis, H. B., Hertzman, M., Machover, K., Meissner, P. B., & Wapner, S. (1954). *Personality through perception: An experimental and clinical study.* New York, NY: Harper.

Zigler, E. (1963). A measure in search of a theory? *Contemporary Psychology, 8,* 133–135.

11

The Motivated and Mindful Perceiver

Relationships Among Motivated Perception, Mindfulness, and Self-Regulation

Emily Balcetis, Shana Cole, and Sana Sherali

In 2011, the American Psychological Association surveyed Americans about their life goals. The majority reported that they wanted to improve in several domains. Fifty-two percent of respondents steadfastly resolved to save more money. Likewise, 77% of adults set goals to eat a healthier diet, 75% intended to exercise more, and 58% intended to sleep more. In the same survey, however, 73% acknowledged that they did not have the willpower to actually meet the goals they set. They are likely right. Although many people recognize that balancing the number of calories consumed against daily activity levels is one of the most important aspects of fitness, only 15% of Americans say they count calories (Consumer Reports, 2011). Of those overweight individuals who need it the most, only 20% exercise the amount they should each day to be fit (Mendes, 2009). And over the past 30 years, the percent of Americans acknowledging that they get insufficient amounts of sleep each night continued to rise (Centers for Disease Control and Prevention, 2011). Even after people set important life goals, are committed to pursuing them, and are aware of steps to take to meet them, people still come up against challenges that thwart their efforts to pursue and achieve these goals.

When faced with problems that threaten goal progress, people call upon strategies to help manage their goals. Often, these strategies are deliberate, calculated, conscious, and cognitive ones. For instance, 55% of people say they find ways to remind themselves of their long-term goal, 50% actively force themselves to resist temptations, and 40% talk to themselves in encouraging ways (American Psychological Association, 2012). Unfortunately, these deliberate tactics are not always helpful. Because they require effort, intention, and ability, these strategies may be difficult to enact when people are tired, depleted, or cognitively taxed. As a result, conscious strategies sometimes fail to produce meaningful changes in behavior. Despite the deficiencies of some cognitive strategies, people do succeed at some goals sometimes. In this chapter, we discuss a strategy that may complement explicit cognitive approaches to goal pursuit.

The Wiley Blackwell Handbook of Mindfulness, First Edition.
Edited by Amanda Ie, Christelle T. Ngnoumen, and Ellen J. Langer.
© 2014 John Wiley & Sons, Ltd. Published 2014 by John Wiley & Sons, Ltd.

Namely, we describe how a nonconscious phenomenon, known as *motivated visual perception,* may assist in some aspects of self-regulation.

Motivated perception is a phenomenon in which one's desires, goals, and needs produce biased visual experiences (Balcetis & Dunning, 2006; Dunning & Balcetis, 2013). Motivated perceivers can and often do see their surroundings in ways that support their goals. In this chapter, we discuss properties that suggest motivated perception can be a functional tool used to assist in the effective management of goals. We draw parallels between qualities of motivated perception and qualities of another phenomenon known to assist in goal pursuit—mindfulness. We discuss three qualities common to both motivated perception and mindfulness: *active construction, heightened awareness,* and *flexibility.* We propose that these qualities may be particularly useful tools in the pursuit and attainment of goals. Moreover, we suggest possible sequential and simultaneous effects of motivated perception and mindfulness. Mindfulness may lead to motivated perception, and mindfulness may interact with motivated perception in the service of successful goal pursuit.

The first quality of motivated perception, common to mindfulness as well, is *active construction.* Perception is not a passive process. Instead, people actively and creatively form visual representations of their world that support their goals. Motivations, in particular, lead to the construction of rose-colored perceptual experiences. The specific form of active construction that motivated perception takes allows people to view some contents of the world as they would like them to appear (see Balcetis & Lassiter, 2010). Likewise, states of mindfulness create an openness for new information (Langer, 1997; see Langer, Blank, & Chanowitz, 1978, for work on mindlessness and a lack of information gathering), which fosters an ability to create novel categories and to new conclusions from the information provided (Langer & Moldoveanu, 2000). Both motivations and mindfulness lead people to make sense of information in novel ways. Motivated perception and mindfulness are related to an active construction of the world, and motivated perception in particular shapes those constructions to align with desires.

The second quality descriptive of motivated perception and mindfulness is *heightened awareness.* Motivations direct attention (Dijksterhuis & Aarts, 2010). People preferentially attend to visual information that can help goal pursuit. Motivations also create a perceptual sensitivity for information related to desired end states. People are quicker to detect visual information that is relevant to active goals. In a similar fashion, states of mindfulness lead people to be aware of more of their environment and direct attention to various parts of it (Langer, 1989). Both motivated perception and mindfulness are related to increased attention to and greater resources for the processing of goal-relevant visual information.

The third quality descriptive of motivated perception and mindfulness is *flexibility.* Motivations produce perceptual experiences that shift adaptively in accordance with changing goals or changes in one's ability to pursue those goals (Dijksterhuis & Aarts, 2010). Indeed, perception is responsive to changing goals. Likewise, mindful states lead people to engage in the present and respond to contextual demands (Langer, 2000). Both motivated perception and mindfulness are related to the flexible adaptation of representations; both change in accordance with current contextual demands. In sum, like states of mindfulness, motivated perception is an active, constructive process that directs attention to opportunities for goal pursuit, as goals shift and change. Active construction, heightened awareness, and flexibility are three qualities that ultimately assist in the pursuit of goals.

This review holds the following objectives. We will first describe the phenomenon of motivated perception. We focus on research that attests to three of its qualities: active construction specifically of rose-colored glasses, heightened awareness, and flexible adaptation. We use these three qualities to suggest parallels between motivated perception and mindfulness. Finally, we conjecture on the relationship between motivated perception and mindfulness, and discuss whether they may work in collaboration to affect self-regulation.

Defining Motivated Perception

Perception is not a product; it is an active process. Perception combines bottom-up features of the outside world with top-down influences specific to perceivers. Sensory information, including light, edges, curves, and textures, stimulates receptor cells in the eyes and brain. Quickly, but not quite immediately, related thoughts, feelings, and previous experiences come to mind, often outside of awareness or conscious monitoring. These accessible psychological states are combined with physical sensations to create a perceptual experience. As noted by psychologists (Bruner, 1957), philosophers (Wittgenstein, 1968), and those who defy singular categorization (James, 1890), sensation is a passive process of gathering visual stimulation from the environment, but perception is more; perception is the process of actively combining sensations and concurrently activated cognitions. Perception is created with input from both current sensory experiences as well as psychological experiences specific to the perceiver.

Multiple psychological states may inform perceptual experience. For example, beliefs stemming from political affiliations influenced perceptions of Obama's skin tone prior to the 2008 election; American voters who agreed with Obama perceived his skin tone to be lighter than those who disagreed with him (Caruso, Mead, & Balcetis, 2009). In another study, the underlying inclination to maintain self-esteem led people to see their own faces as more attractive than they actually were (Epley & Whitchurch, 2008). However, psychological processes involved in social comparison led people to see their own faces as less attractive after looking at photographs of beautiful models (Zell & Balcetis, 2012). Psychological states impact people's perceptual experiences.

While several types of psychological experiences may influence perceptual processing, this chapter discusses one specific factor that has the ability to powerfully shape perception. Specifically, the goals that perceivers pursue and motivational states that accompany those goals influence visual experience (Balcetis & Dunning, 2006; Dunning & Balcetis, 2013). For instance, people literally see a glass of water as larger when they have goals to satisfy their thirst compared to when they do not (Veltkamp, Aarts, & Custers, 2008). People's desires, needs, interests, and aspirations help to clarify vague or muddled visual information, direct attention, and prioritize processing to influence visual experience. This phenomenon is termed motivated visual perception.

At the very early stages of information processing, as people first look at the world around them, perception may be systematically altered in accordance with active goals. These perceptual biases occur quickly and often outside of awareness, without requiring conscious effort. In the sections that follow, we will discuss empirical evidence suggesting that motivated perception can be defined by three qualities—active construction, heightened awareness, and flexibility. In concert, these qualities suggest motivations influence perception in ways that assist in meeting active goals.

Motivated Perception as Active Construction of Rose-Colored Glasses

Seeing the object of one's desire can satisfy a goal. In a metaphoric sense, people who wear rose-colored glasses, and see the contents of the world in ways that align with their wants and wishes, may find their goals satisfied. Longing to spot a celebrity while visiting New York, the weary tourist sitting down for pancakes at a diner might find her goal satisfied when she spots a fellow diner who appears to be, or is a convincing enough doppelganger for, Donnie Wahlberg, the singer-turned-B-list-actor 15 years past his prime. Likewise, the anxious graduate student preparing for his first departmental presentation might have a strong goal to impress his difficult-to-please advisor. He might find his goal satisfied when he scans the audience during his talk and interprets the slight upward curl of his advisor's lips as a smile. People's motivations, wants, and desires shape the ways in which they identify people, objects, or other information that might be seen in multiple ways.

In order to facilitate goal pursuit, the visual system actively constructs perceptual experiences that appear to advance people's wants, desires, and needs. We have provided empirical evidence for these claims. In one study, we experimentally manipulated people's goals and thereby created desires to see an image in a particular way (Balcetis & Dunning, 2006, Study 2). Specifically, participants knew that they might taste delicious, gourmet Jelly Belly candies. They also knew that they might instead taste disgusting, partially liquefied canned beans mashed together in a Ziploc bag. We told participants that neither they nor the experimenter would choose which food they would eat. Instead, a computer program would randomly choose one picture of an animal. The type of animal presented would determine which of the two foods participants would consume. Some participants were told that if the computer randomly presented an image of a farm animal, they would eat the candies, but if it presented an image of a sea animal, they would eat the canned beans. These outcome pairings were reversed for other participants. Thus, in this paradigm, we experimentally created the goal for participants to eat the candy instead of the beans, and with the particular outcome structure we assigned, we manipulated the desire for participants to see one type of animal rather than the other.

After inducing these goals, we presented participants with an image of an animal. Although it appeared like a random selection, the computer always presented participants with the same bistable, ambiguous image for 100 ms. The image could be interpreted as either the head of a horse or the body of a seal. When participants had the desire to see farm animals, 67% saw the image as a horse, and when participants had the desire to see sea animals, 71% saw the image as a seal. The goal to eat delicious jellybeans instead of disgusting canned beans and the desire to see a specific animal that could satisfy the goal influenced perceptual categorization of the ambiguous image. People saw what they wanted to see. The goals and desires people held influenced their perceptual construction of an image that could be interpreted in multiple ways.

Of course, it is possible that participants simply lied or misrepresented what they actually saw. For example, one might wonder whether observers had actually seen both interpretations of the image and then simply chose to report only the one that best served their goals. We tested this alternative possibility. Again, we presented participants with the ambiguous image that could be interpreted as either a horse or a seal (Balcetis & Dunning; Study 5). Participants learned that they would sample freshly squeezed orange juice if the computer presented them with a farm animal or would sample a repulsive, pickle-scented gelatinous veggie smoothie if the computer presented them with a sea animal. For other participants, the outcomes were reversed. Again, participants saw the ambiguous image for 100 ms. However, before perceivers reported what they saw, we staged a computer error. The computer seemed to crash and the experimenter feigned surprise. The experimenter quickly conjectured that the error was because the outcome pairings actually should have been switched. Although the experimenter had originally told participants that farm animals were paired with orange juice, the mistake was that sea animals were supposed to be paired with orange juice. What the experimenter effectively did at that point was switch participants' goals and desires, but, importantly, only after the ambiguous image disappeared from view. After making this switch, the experimenter asked participants whether the computer presented anything before the crash.

We predicted that the goals and desires we originally created for participants at the beginning of the session would influence their perceptual categorization of the ambiguous drawing. That is, we predicted that at the time they saw the object, people's goals would influence their perceptions. However, an alternative possibility is that participants might have seen that the image could be interpreted in multiple ways and, when given the chance, might instead choose to report the interpretation that represented the new outcome structure. In this paradigm, participants were capable of and given free rein to report the interpretation that served their current goals rather than the original goals if they had actually seen multiple interpretations. However, the data suggested participants did not do so. Instead, participants overwhelmingly reported seeing an animal that reflected their original desires. In fact, 100% of participants who originally held the goal to detect farm animals reported seeing a horse, even though this meant that they all would sample the less desirable veggie smoothie as a result. That is, their goals and desires at the time the ambiguous figure appeared on the screen influenced how participants perceptually constructed the images. Even when they had the opportunity to switch their reports, they could not do so because they had seen only one interpretation. Goals, desires, and motivations actively shaped production of conscious visual experiences.

Motivated perception is the result of an active process of perceptual construction that incorporates the goals of the perceiver with sensory input from the environment.

While visual information related to unwanted outcomes could have been seen or the bistable nature of the figure could have been recognized, they were not. Instead, motivations led people literally see what they want to see. Motivations lead people to understand multifaceted, inexplicit, and ambiguous visual information in ways that assist in meeting active goals.

Motivated Perception Heightens Awareness of Goal-Relevant Opportunities

Successful goal pursuit requires identifying and attending to information, locations, and objects that might help people accomplish goals. For instance, when looking for a relationship partner, one needs to notice attractive and viable companions. The lonely divorcee hoping for a new chance at love may find an opportunity to pursue her goals when noticing that the striking gent across the bar has winked in her direction. Motivations increase awareness of people, objects, and information related to goals.

Motivated perception heightens awareness of opportunities for goal pursuit by increasing the ease with which people attend to and detect information that can assist in effectively reaching goals. Specifically, multiple visceral and social goals direct and hold visual attention to objects related to these active motivational states. Moreover, the process by which attention is directed to goal-relevant objects is automatic and does not require conscious intent (Vogt, De Houwer, Moors, 2011; Vogt, De Houwer, Moors, van Damme, & Crombez, 2010). Motivations direct attention quickly and efficiently without requiring effort or awareness.

Visceral motivations direct attention. For example, in our lab, we found that activating the goal to satisfy one's thirst directed participants' visual attention to beverages (Balcetis, Cole, & Sherali, 2012). Some participants consumed a serving of dry, salty pretzels constituting 40% of their daily intake of sodium, while others were invited to drink water until they felt their thirst was quenched. We then presented participants with an image of an array of objects, which for some participants included a bottle of water, on a computer screen. Using hidden eye-tracking technology that covertly monitored eye gaze outside of participants' awareness, we found that thirsty people spent more time looking at the bottle of water than a similarly sized control object. Quenched participants, on the other hand, showed little attentional preference for the water. The goal to reduce thirst directed visual attention to the goal-relevant object.

In addition to basic physiological motivations, social goals can also direct attention to objects that can assist in goal pursuit. For instance, interpersonal goals to connect with others direct visual attention. People who frequently engaged in casual sex and visualized sexual fantasies experienced an active goal to find an intimate partner; these people then found their attention drawn to and fixated on physically attractive members of the opposite sex (Maner, Gailliot, Rouby, & Miller, 2007; Study 1). Likewise, when people are lonely, the active goal to restore social connectedness directs visual attention. Participants who received feedback that they were likely to experience a future of loneliness and exclusion spent a greater percentage of time subsequently looking at photographs of smiling faces compared to faces depicting other expressions (DeWall, Maner, & Rouby, 2009). This attentional bias for smiling faces occurred more for the group of people who felt alone compared to people who learned their future would bring about unfortunate injuries or those who learned their future would be filled with rewarding relationships. Although participants in these two control conditions experienced equally strong affective responses, it was only people in the exclusion condition, who held a goal to restore feelings of connectedness, who directed their attention to the smiling faces that in some way could reestablish those feelings.

The goal to protect one's own relationship from outside threat can also direct attention. Participants in romantic relationships who felt jealous of their partner's other friendships experienced a goal to protect their long-term relationship against threats. These jealous partners found their attention fixated on physically attractive members of their own sex who might act as potential rivals (Maner et al., 2007; Study 3). Those people who felt less jealous or threatened did not fixate on the attractive others.

Goals to regulate emotions also direct attention. In the lab, participants were told to suppress the feelings that might come from seeing appealing and disturbing pictures (Xing & Isaacowitz, 2006). Using eye-tracking technology, the researchers found that participants who had the goal to control their emotions devoted far less attention to negative than positive images. They literally looked away from the images they found disturbing and toward the images they found pleasant. Motivations can direct attention to aspects of the environment that can help achieve goal states.

Even when direction of eye gaze is fixed and attentional orienting constrained, motivations facilitate the detection of goal-relevant information. That is, motivations may increase perceptual sensitivity for goal-relevant information. Motivations may reduce the strength of the input or stimulation required for the formation of a perceptual conclusion. For example, a lost hiker looking down the unfamiliar path and desperately searching for a clue as to the way out of a dark forest might notice the faint reassuring glow of a tiny candle flickering up ahead. On the other hand, a confident hiker looking down the well-known path might only notice the light if it is beaming from a strong flashlight. Even when one's eyes are fixed on a location, motivations may increase perceptual sensitivity for goal-relevant objects or visual information.

We empirically tested whether motivations increase perceptual sensitivity by exposing participants to a perceptual experience known as binocular rivalry (Balcetis, Dunning, & Granot, 2012). Binocular rivalry is an artificial phenomenon that occurs in the lab when researchers present two incompatible images to participants simultaneously, one to each eye. For instance, we presented a letter to participants' left eyes and a number to their right eyes, or vice versa. To do this, we had participants wear goggles containing different colored lenses covering each eye that filtered one particular color. For instance, some participants wore a red lens over their left eye, and when they had the experience of looking with only their left eye, they could not perceive any red-colored stimulus. All participants wore one red lens and one green lens, and we presented a number and a letter, in either red or green font. The number and the letter were fairly transparent and layered on top of one another. When the images were presented for a short duration, instead of seeing a muddled composite image, perceivers actually consciously experienced seeing only one of the two images—either the letter or the number—and had no awareness that another image could have appeared.

We demonstrated that goals and desires predicted which image reached conscious awareness under conditions of binocular rivalry. In one experiment, we experimentally induced goals by associating letters with possible financial gain and numbers with financial loss for some participants (Balcetis et al., 2012). Other participants received the reverse reward structure. Participants knew that if they saw more letters than numbers, they would earn tickets for a raffle that included substantial cash prizes; if they saw more numbers than letters, they would not earn the chance to participate in the raffle. Thus, participants had an active goal to win money and thus a desire to see letters rather than numbers. While viewing the images, participants wore the colored goggles that filtered out different elements of the stimulus for each eye. As a result, one eye was presented with a letter, and the other eye was presented with a number.

To test whether participants consciously perceived the rewarding or costly visual information, we presented the rivaling images for 300 ms. This presentation duration was long enough for participants to experience perceiving either the letter or number but was not long enough for them to consciously perceive the other stimulus. The desire to see the image associated with reward influenced their perceptual experience. Participants were more likely to consciously see the image associated with financial gain rather than loss. These data suggest that desires created a perceptual sensitivity that prioritized the recognition of rewarding, goal-promoting rather than costly, goal-hindering visual information.

Motivated perception increases awareness of goal-relevant objects and information in the environment. To be successful at goal pursuit, people must gather information and recognize when they are involved in situations that afford the pursuit of goals (Webb & Sheeran, 2004). By directing attention to and increasing perceptual sensitivity for objects that are capable of satisfying goals, motivated perception allows people to identify, detect, and eventually act on opportunities for goal pursuit more quickly. Thus, motivated perception may assist in successful self-regulation by increasing awareness of available opportunities for goal pursuit.

Motivated Perception as a Flexible Strategy

For perception to assist effectively with goal pursuit, perceptual experiences must shift quickly as goals change. Holding steadfast to one plan or set of behavioral intentions will do little good if opportunities change, the situation requires adaptation, or one's goals shift. The quarterback who in the huddle called a specific play, but after getting to the line of scrimmage sees a defensive lineup he was not expecting, is better able to meet his team's goals by calling an audible and changing the play. When situational demands change, plans, behaviors, and intentions must shift quickly and easily. Successful self-regulation requires flexibility.

To assist in goal pursuit, perceptual experiences should change quickly in accordance with shifting motivations. To test this, we tweaked the binocular rivalry paradigm described above. In one study (Balcetis et al., 2012, Study 3), participants knew that whether numbers or letters appeared would have consequences for the money they would win or lose. But in this study, they also learned that this reward structure would affect them in only half of the blocks. In the other blocks, the financial gains and losses would affect someone sitting next door—a person whom participants were compelled to dislike. Prior to the binocular rivalry experience, we gave participants false information about this supposed next-door neighbor. We implied that the neighbor was overwhelmingly confident in their abilities, eager to win, and unwilling to cooperate to help the participant's financial outcome. Participants earnestly reported their subsequent dislike for this person. Thus, every minute or two, the recipient of the rewards or costs would alternate between the participants themselves and a disliked other. Participants' motivations would shift; we tested whether their perceptions would also shift.

Participants' desires to increase their own financial gain and their disinterest in helping the neighbor influenced the perceptual experiences they had during binocular rivalry. Specifically, when the rewards benefited themselves, participants for whom numbers were associated with financial gain saw 19% more numbers than letters in the rivaling stimuli. However, when the same reward structure would instead benefit the disliked neighbor, that perceptual bias disappeared completely. These data suggest that perceptual experiences changed as goals shifted every few minutes.

Motivated perception is flexible and responsive to quickly changing goals that the situation specifies. As goals shift, so too do people's perceptual experiences. People maintain multiple goals simultaneously and, as a result of limited resources, must prioritize and flexibly shift the pursuit of one goal over another (Johnson, Chang, & Lord, 2006). Visual perception is sensitive to such shifting priorities. Indeed, attention is allocated to those goals that are the most valued or hold the highest expectancy of success—qualities that shift depending on perceivers' needs and the resources available for pursuit of particular goals (Vogt, De Houwer, & Crombez, 2011). Such flexibility is an important component of successful self-regulation. Furthermore, given research that suggests perceptual experiences flexibly shift with changing goals, motivated perception may be an apt tool for self-regulation.

Is Motivated Perception a State of Mindfulness?

We have defined and described motivated perception through three qualities and suggested how these qualities may assist in self-regulation. First, motivated perception is an active process of construction in which people organize visual information in novel ways that allow them to see what they desire to see, which can assist in accomplishing goals. Second, motivated perception is marked by an increased awareness for opportunities and objects that will assist goal pursuit. Third, perceptual experiences transform quickly as goals shift, and situational demands require change.

These three qualities that describe motivated perception also describe states of mindfulness. Mindful approaches to information processing are also marked by active construction and incorporation of psychological experiences, heightened awareness of the environment, and flexibility as opportunities and means change. We conjecture that motivated perception may be likened, in some sense, to a state of mindfulness.

Effects of Mindfulness on Motivated Perception

While no research has explicitly, directly, and strictly tested the overlap between motivated perception and mindfulness, some circumstantial evidence speaks to the relationship between the two. One line of research studied people considered experts in mindfulness, who gained their expertise through the practice of Buddhist meditation. Researchers tested whether Buddhist meditation would affect perceptual experience (Hodgins & Adair, 2010). They found that people who regularly engaged in Buddhist-based meditation experienced less bias in their perceptual conclusions. For example, meditators more quickly detected alternative interpretations of ambiguous figures. They recognized that a bistable image could be categorized as both a saxophone player and a woman's profile, suggesting they constructed perceptual experiences that were less constrained by active thoughts. Meditators also directed attention to more aspects of the visual scene than people who did not meditate. When focusing their attention on the number of times players passed basketballs, meditators were more likely than nonmeditators to also notice that a person dressed in a gorilla suit walked through the game. Meditators' attention was less directed and less selective. From these data, the researchers concluded that mindfulness eliminated perceptual bias and as a result reduced motivated perception. Further, they inferred that motivated perception is a result not of mindfulness but of mind*less*ness.

We caution against these two conclusions for multiple reasons. Hodgins and Adair (2010) tested whether Buddhist meditation attenuated perceptual bias, and their data suggested it did. However, the conclusion that the specific phenomenon of motivated perception itself was reduced through meditation-induced mindfulness is circumspect if not erroneous. To be sure, meditators compared to nonmeditators formed a fuller, richer, and more complete representation of the visual information in question. General perceptual bias was reduced. However, left untested in this line of research was the interaction between meditation and motivation. The experimenters did not manipulate goal states or activate motivations. If anything, both meditators and nonmeditators held the same single goal—to report accurately what they saw. From the fact that meditators actually performed better than nonmeditators, as measured by accurately reporting more of the visual information, we assert that the data may actually suggest that meditation *exacerbates* motivated perception. In other words, the only goal active for all participants was the goal to report what appeared, and meditators seemed to do this better.

That said, one cannot conclude that states of mindfulness that accompany meditation attenuate or accentuate motivated perception, as motivations were not manipulated. That meditators saw the world more completely could itself be evidence of motivated perception if they had the goal to do so, or it could be evidence of some third variable not tested in the study. Thus, the data Hodgins and Adair (2010) collected do suggest that perceptual bias is reduced, but from those data, one cannot make causal statements as to whether meditation or mindfulness affects motivated perception.

Perceptual Accuracy From Mindfulness or Motivated Perception

Another line of research also tested the relationship between mindfulness and perception. Ellen Langer and colleagues (Langer, Djikic, Pirson, Madenci, & Donohue, 2010) tested whether mindfulness increased perceptual accuracy. In their paradigm, some participants adopted the mindset of a mindful airline pilot. Results suggested that these mindful perceivers were better able to accurately identify smaller letters on an eye chart compared to energized people who were simply excited and worked up after exercising.

While it is possible that mindfulness causes increased perceptual accuracy, we propose that another possibility exists; mindful information processing may simultaneously activate the phenomenon of motivated perception. We posit that the mindful pilot manipulation may have also increased the motivation to accurately perceive the full contents of their environment, given the importance of doing so for pilots. Participants in the control condition, who were energized after just exercising, did not have a strong active goal to perceive accurately. Certainly, the mindful state improved perceptual accuracy. It is also possible that motivations improved perceptual accuracy, and in so doing served the relevant self-regulatory challenges faced by the perceiver. Did mindfulness, motivated perception, or their interaction lead to perceptual accuracy, and did these factors serve the self-regulatory needs of the perceiver at that moment? By simultaneously testing the effects of both states, future research might suggest more strongly whether mindfulness and motivation work in concert to manage goals.

Circumstantial Evidence Relating Motivated Perception, Mindfulness, and Self-Regulation

In our lab, we have taken preliminary steps to outline the relationship between mindfulness and the self-regulatory functions served by motivated perception. Before we describe how we have tested the relationship between these two constructs, we must first explain a specific perceptual domain that is affected by motivations. Specifically, motivations influence the perception of distances in the environment (Balcetis & Dunning, 2010; Cole, Balcetis, & Zhang, 2013). Why would motivations influence distance perception? Emerging theories build upon classic goal gradient work to suggest that biased perceptions of the environment encourage action. Actual proximity to a goal-relevant object mobilizes goal-directed behaviors (Hull, 1932). As physical distance to goal-promoting objects decreases, goal-directed approach behavior increases (Dollard & Miller, 1950). For instance, rats' rate of running speed increased as they physically approached a food reward (Crespi, 1942). Similarly, rats exerted more effort against a restraining harness when they were in close physical proximity to food or water (Brown, 1948). Actual distance to goal-relevant objects plays an important role in regulating action in the service of goal pursuit.

We suggest that just as actual proximity relates to goal-relevant action, so too may the mere misperception of proximity. If a goal-relevant object simply appears close, people may be more likely to act in ways that will assist goal pursuit. In other words, hungry people might move faster to grab a sandwich if the food looks close. People might run harder in the last few meters of a race if the finish line appears like it is just ahead. If an object that can help people reach an active goal appears close, people may work harder and faster to reach that object. The appearance of proximity may increase people's attempts to reach, acquire, or grab hold of goal-relevant objects.

If this is true, then when a goal is active, an object that is capable of satisfying the goal should be misperceived as closer than that same object when the goal is not active. Evidence suggests that this is in fact the case. We asked participants to consume many pretzels or to drink as much water as they could (Balcetis & Dunning, 2010; Study 1). Then, we asked them to estimate the distance to a bottle of water. The same bottle of water appeared 10% closer to the thirsty people than to people who quenched their thirst. This evidence suggests that objects appear closer when they will help achieve an active goal. Further, we have conjectured that this is because proximity increases action tendencies.

If proximity encourages action, then the reverse may also be true; elongating actual distances, or simply increasing the perception of distance, should discourage action. The discouragement of action is especially important when there are temptations that may threaten goal progress in the environment. Increasing the distance between the self and temptations may help discourage people from giving in to those temptations. Indeed, lay knowledge and general intuitions seem to concur with this conjecture. People routinely push their plates away to avoid overeating. They also walk across the street from the bakery to avoid purchasing tempting sugary snacks. Nutritionists and weight-management programs routinely advise dieting clients to literally increase the distance between themselves and tempting objects to avoid giving in to them (Beck, 2012). In addition, some empirical research suggests that people are fundamentally predisposed to increasing the distance between themselves and temptations; people were faster to respond to temptation-related words by making a pushing motion away from the words (Fishbach & Shah, 2006). As the researchers noted, "people secure attainment of goals by keeping a distance from tempting objects ..." (p. 821). When tempting objects are located further away, people should be less likely to act on them.

If it is true that goals are best pursued if temptations are actually located far away, then a successful self-regulatory strategy would be to misperceive temptations as further away. If motivated perception serves self-regulatory functions, then the distance between oneself and tempting objects that thwart goal pursuit should appear great for people who have strong goals. Furthermore, if mindfulness assists in self-regulation in the same way as motivated perception, then mindfulness should also relate to distance perception in similar ways. More mindful people should misperceive tempting objects that hamper goal pursuit as further away.

In ongoing research in our lab, we tested whether motivations and mindfulness led to perceptions of tempting food objects as further away. We exposed dieters and nondieters to a table full of salty and sugary snacks (Cole & Balcetis, 2012). Consistent with the claim that motivated perception assists self-regulation, perceivers who had strong dieting goals perceived the table to be further away than did perceivers who were not dieting. In addition, we tested whether mindfulness predicted exaggerated perceptions of distance to temptations. Participants completed Langer's Mindfulness Scale (Langer, 2004). Our results are consistent with the claim that mindfulness and motivated perception together assist self-regulation. We found a significant positive correlation between scores on the mindfulness scale and perceptions of distance to the unhealthy snacks. More mindful dieters estimated that the distance between themselves and the temptations that would thwart their healthy eating goals was greater than less mindful dieters.

This work serves as the first simultaneous test of the motivated perception (specifically distance perception), mindfulness, and self-regulatory functions. If actual proximity encourages action, then objects that can help achieve goals should appear closer than those same objects when goals are not active. Likewise, if actual remoteness discourages action, then objects that have the potential to thwart active goals should appear further away. In fact, it seems that temptations that could undermine goal pursuit do appear further away, especially among more mindful people.

A Call for Future Research

Although existing research provides circumstantial evidence suggesting the relationship between mindfulness and motivated perception, we caution against the conclusion that mindfulness heightens, reduces, or causes motivated perception. We believe that conclusions of these sorts are premature simply because the proper experimental design has not yet been used in the literature to warrant these inferences. To be sure, mindfulness is often assessed through self-reports of personal tendencies to meditate or measures of chronic individual differences in mindful approaches to information processing. Indeed, our own research has only tested mindfulness as a chronic individual difference measure. The problem is that individual differences in the propensity to be mindful may correlate with other factors that experimenters do not measure. Thus, experimental manipulations of mindfulness are needed to make causal inference. However, strong experimental manipulations of mindful states are difficult to produce in the lab. Indeed, theorists conjecture that successful mindfulness may require extensive practice. Only when experimental manipulations of both mindful states of being and goal states are empirically and rigorously tested can alternative explanations be ruled out, causal effects be measured, and the interaction of both psychological effects be tested. Researchers must independently manipulate mindful states and goal states to determine whether mindfulness and motivated perception work independently, assist one another, or impair one another in the service of self-regulation.

Because of the absence of experimental paradigms, the similarities between motivated perception and mindfulness are still conjectured ones at this point. Very little empirical research has examined the relationships between the two, and the research that has may be open to alternative interpretations. Additional rigorous work is needed to fully explore the relationships between the two. If empirical research does support these relationships, strategies and interventions could target inducing both mindful and motivated states in order to change how people represent the world around them in ways that aid successful self-regulation.

Conclusion

While on a camping trip, former Senator Barry Goldwater of Arizona reportedly saw it as shaving cream. Inventor George Washington Carver saw it as axel grease for a truck. But most hungry American children grow up identifying that thick, gummy brown substance as peanut butter. Similarly, WD-40 began its life as a top secret formula to be applied as an antirust coating on intercontinental ballistic missiles, before people like company founder Norm Larsen saw the sprayable oil as a steadfast remedy for for keeping squirrels out of birdhouses. Some people look at everyday concoctions and see them in very different ways than do others. They construct novel labels, categories, uses for, and ideas about how the items may serve their current goals. Maybe these unorthodox reconstruals occur through a mindful approach to life and business, or perhaps they are the result of motivated perceptual biases.

It is possible to liken motivated perception to a mindful state of being. Both phenomena appear to serve self-regulation, and may do so through three similar processes. Indeed, both are states of *active construction* where people situate themselves in the present and find their experiences are the result of active, fleeting psychological states. Both are states of *heightened awareness*. People scour the environment and find themselves sensitive to information related to their current psychological states. Finally, both mindfulness and motivated perception are marked by flexible responses to changing situational demands and variant needs. While just a sticky mess to the mindless, motivated and mindful perceivers may take a jar of Jiffy, slather it on their faces, and see a new world of possibilities.

References

Bruner, J. S. (1957). On perceptual readiness. *Psychological Review, 64*(2), 123–152.

American Psychological Association. (2012). *What Americans think of willpower: A survey of perception of willpower & its role in achieving lifestyle and behavior-change goals.* Retrieved from http://www.apa.org/helpcenter/stress-willpower.pdf

Balcetis, E., Cole, S., & Sherali, S. (2012). [Goal-relevant objects attract attention]. Unpublished raw data.

Balcetis, E., & Dunning, D. (2006). See what you want to see: Motivational influences on visual perception. *Journal of Personality and Social Psychology, 91*, 612–625.

Balcetis, E., & Dunning, D. (2010). Wishful seeing: Desired objects are seen as closer. *Psychological Science, 21*, 147–152.

Balcetis, E., Dunning, D., & Granot, Y. (2012). Subjective value determines initial dominance in binocular rivalry. *Journal of Experimental Social Psychology, 48*, 122–129.

Balcetis, E., & Lassiter, G. D. (2010). *The social psychology of visual perception.* New York, NY: Psychology Press.

Beck, J. (2012). Daily diet solutions. *Beck Diet Solution.* Retrieved from http://www. beckdietsolution.com/daily-diet-solutions/

Brown, D. (1948). Primary sensory neuropathy with muscular changes associated with carcinoma. *Journal of Neurology, Neurosurgery, & Psychiatry, 11,* 73–87.

Caruso, E., Mead, N., & Balcetis, E. (2009). Political partisanship influences perception of biracial candidates' skin tone. *Proceedings of the National Academy of Sciences, 106,* 20168–20173.

Centers for Disease Control and Prevention. (2011). Unhealthy sleep-related behaviors—12 States, 2009. *Morbidity and Mortality Weekly Report, 60,* 1–277.

Cole, S., & Balcetis, E. (2012). [Distance perception to tempting and healthy food items]. Unpublished raw data.

Cole, S., Balcetis, E., & Zhang, S. (2013). Visual perception and regulatory conflict: Motivation and physiology influence distance perception. *Journal of Experimental Psychology: General, 142*(1): 18–22.

Consumer Reports. (2011, January). Are we fooling ourselves: 90 percent of Americans say their diet is healthy, CR poll finds. *Consumer Report.* Retrieved from http://www. consumerreports.org/health/healthy-living/diet-nutrition/diets-dieting/healthy-diet/ overview/index.htm

Crespi, L. P. (1942). Quantitative variation of incentive and performance in the white rat. *American Journal of Psychology, 55,* 467–517.

DeWall, C. N., Maner, J. K., & Rouby, D. A. (2009). Social exclusion and early-state interpersonal perception: Selective attention to signs of acceptance. *Journal of Personality and Social Psychology, 96,* 729–41.

Dijksterhuis, A., & Aarts, H. (2010). Goals, attention, and (un)consciousness. *Annual Review of Psychology, 16,* 467–490.

Dollard, J., & Miller, N. (1950). *Personality and psychotherapy: An analysis in terms of learning, thinking, and culture* (New York, NY: McGraw-Hill).

Dunning, D., & Balcetis, E. (2013). Wishful seeing: How preferences shape visual perception. *Current Directions in Psychological Science, 22,* 33–37.

Epley, N., & Whitchurch, E. (2008). Mirror, mirror on the wall: Enhancement in self-recognition. *Personality and Social Psychology Bulletin, 34,* 1159–1170.

Fishbach, A., & Shah, J. Y. (2006). Self control in action: Implicit dispositions toward goals and away from temptations. *Journal of Personality and Social Psychology, 90*(5), 820–832.

Hodgins, H. S., & Adair, K. C. (2010). Attentional processes and meditation. *Consciousness and Cognition: An International Journal, 19,* 872–878.

Hull, L. C. (1932). The goal gradient hypothesis and maze learning. *Psychological Review, 39,* 25–43.

James, W. (1890). *Principles of psychology—Vol. 1.* New York, NY: Cosimo.

Johnson, R. E., Chang, C.-H., & Lord, R. G. (2006). Moving from cognition to behavior: What the research says. *Psychological Bulletin, 132,* 381–415.

Langer, E. (1989). Minding matters: The consequences of mindlessness–mindfulness. In L. Berkowitz (Ed.), *Advances in Experimental Social Psychology* (pp. 137–173). San Diego, CA: Academic Press.

Langer, E. (1997). *The power of mindful learning.* Reading, MA: Addison-Wesley.

Langer, E., Blank, A., & Chanowitz, B. (1978). The mindlessness of ostensibly thoughtful action: The role of "placebic" information in interpersonal interaction. *Journal of Personality and Social Psychology, 36,* 635–642.

Langer, E. J. (2000). Mindful learning. *Current Directions in Psychological Science*, 9, 220–223.

Langer, E., Djikic, M., Pirson, M., Madenci, A., & Donohue, R. (2010). Believing is seeing: Using mindlessness (mindfully) to improve visual acuity. *Psychological Science*, 21, 661–666.

Langer, E. J. (2004). *Langer mindfulness scale user guide and technical manual*. Worthington, OH: IDS Publishing Corporation.

Langer, E. J., & Moldoveanu, M. (2000). The construct of mindfulness. *Journal of Social Issues*, 56, 1–9.

Maner, J. K., Gailliot, M. T., Rouby, D. A., & Miller, S. L. (2007). Can't take my eyes off you: Attentional adhesion to mates and rivals. *Journal of Personality and Social Psychology*, 93, 389–401.

Mendes, E. (2009). In U.S. nearly half exercise less than three days a week. *Gallup-Healthways Well-Being Index*. Retrieved from http://www.gallup.com/poll/118570/nearly-half-exercise-less-three-days-week.aspx

Veltkamp, M., Aarts, H., & Custers, R. (2008). Perception in the service of goal pursuit: Motivation to attain goals enhances the perceived size of goal-instrument objects. *Social Cognition*, 26, 720–736.

Vogt, J., De Houwer, J., & Crombez, G. (2011). Multiple goal management starts with attention: Goal prioritizing affects the allocation of spatial attention to goal-relevant events. *Experimental Psychology*, 58, 55–61.

Vogt, J., De Houwer, J., & Moors, A. (2011). Unintended allocation of spatial attention to goal-relevant but not to goal-related events. *Social Psychology*, 42, 48–55.

Vogt, J., De Houwer, J., Moors, A., van Damme, S., & Crombez, G. (2010). The automatic orienting of attention to goal-relevant stimuli. *Acta Psychologica*, 134, 61–69.

Webb, T. L., & Sheeran, P. (2004). Identifying good opportunities to act: Implementation intentions and cue discrimination. *European Journal of Social Psychology*, 34, 407–419.

Wittgenstein, L. (1968). Notes for lectures on "private experience" and "sense data." *Philosophical Review*, 77, 275–320.

Xing, C., Isaacowitz, D. M. (2006). Aiming at happiness: how motivation affects attention to and memory for emotional images. *Motivation & Emotion*, 30, 243–250.

Zell, E., & Balcetis, E. (2012). The influence of social comparison on visual representation of one's face. *PLoS ONE*, 7(5), e36742.

Further Reading

Bartlett, F. C. (1932). *Remembering*. London, UK: Cambridge University Press.

Brown, D., Dysart, M., & Forte, M. (1984). Differences in visual sensitivity among mindfulness meditators and non-meditators. *Perceptual and Motor Skills*, 58, 727–733.

Bruner, J. S., & Goodman, C. C. (1947). Value and need as organizing factors in perception. *Journal of Abnormal and Social Psychology*, 42, 33–44.

Kawakami, K., Phills, C. E., Greenwald, A. G., Simard, D., Pontiero, J., Brnjas, A., ... Dovidio, J. F. (2012). In perfect harmony: Synchronizing the self to activated social categories. *Journal of Personality and Social Psychology*, 102, 562–575.

Langer, E. J., & Bodner, T. (1995). *Mindfulness and attention*. Unpublished manuscript, Harvard University, Cambridge, MA.

Vogt, J., Lozo, L., Koster, E.H., & De Houwer, J. (2011). On the role of goal relevance in emotional attention: Disgust evokes early attention to cleanliness. *Cognition & Emotion*, 25, 466–477.

12

Mindfulness, Interest-Taking, and Self-Regulation

A Self-Determination Theory Perspective on the Role of Awareness in Optimal Functioning

C. Scott Rigby, Patricia P. Schultz, and Richard M. Ryan

For the past quarter century, there has been a steady escalation of interest in mindfulness, along with the circumstances that facilitate it, and its psychological, behavioral, and health-related outcomes. Across this work, the construct of mindfulness has been variously defined (e.g., see Baer, Smith, & Allen, 2004; Brown & Ryan, 2003; Langer, 1978), contingent on scholars' line of research or theoretical perspective. Although differing in other respects, definitions of mindfulness across these schools of thought commonly recognize that the basic elements of mindfulness include attention to present-moment experience along with an attitude of receptivity and openness. Furthermore, in all instances, mindfulness is seen as a state of high-quality awareness that can enhance self-functioning, explaining the burgeoning popularity of mindfulness concepts, practices, and interventions.

In this chapter, we delve into the connections between high-quality awareness and self-regulation as researched and studied within our work on *self-determination theory* (SDT; Deci & Ryan, 2000; Ryan & Deci, 2000), an established empirically based theory of human motivation and optimal self-functioning. In considering this issue, we discuss two forms of awareness considered within SDT to exemplify open, receptive, and nondefensive processing, and which have been shown to facilitate integrative self-regulation.

The first of these is *mindful awareness* viewed as an open and receptive awareness of what is presently occurring (Brown & Ryan, 2003; Ryan & Rigby, in press; Schultz & Ryan, in press). In mindfulness, what is occurring in the present is observed without being grasped, manipulated, or actively processed. Instead, one allows experiences, thoughts, and perceptions to pass before one without attachment or judgment. Mindfulness so defined has been linked in numerous studies to enhanced self-regulation and wellness (Brown, Ryan & Creswell, 2007).

The Wiley Blackwell Handbook of Mindfulness, First Edition.
Edited by Amanda Ie, Christelle T. Ngnoumen, and Ellen J. Langer.
© 2014 John Wiley & Sons, Ltd. Published 2014 by John Wiley & Sons, Ltd.

A second form of open and receptive awareness is a more focused form of mindful attention we label *interest-taking* (Ryan & Deci, 2008a; Weinstein, Przybylski & Ryan, 2012). Whereas mindful awareness as defined in Brown & Ryan (2003) emphasizes an open and receptive mode that is heavily influenced by Buddhist conceptions of mindfulness, interest-taking is drawn from early studies within SDT of self-regulation and growth that described "relaxed interest" and reflectivity (e.g., see Deci & Ryan, 1985). In interest taking, one actively reflects in a curious and non-defensive way upon a selected phenomenon. Because the mind is actively engaging and exploring an "object" of focus, interest-taking is distinct from many definitions of mindfulness outlined within Buddhist traditions. However, both mindfulness and interest-taking share a receptive, open attitude—one that is free from ego involvement and other forms of judgmental thinking. The concept of interest-taking also shares interesting parallels with Langer's (1989, 1997) conception of mindfulness as creative cognitive engagement with an object of interest, in which one is open to information and multiple perspectives, as portrayed in multiple chapters within this volume.

What connects mindful awareness and interest-taking within SDT is that both entail high-quality awareness, which, because of its nondefensive nature, allows for more informed and congruent self-regulation. In fact, trait measures of mindfulness and propensities toward interest-taking are highly correlated (e.g., $r = .57$, Weinstein et al., 2012), suggesting their shared characteristics. SDT further proposes that, albeit in somewhat distinct ways, both mindful awareness and interest-taking: (1) facilitate more autonomous self-regulation; (2) potentiate greater satisfaction of basic psychological needs by enhancing people's experiences of autonomy, competence, and relatedness; and (3) conduce to more investment in intrinsic (e.g., growth, intimacy) versus extrinsic (financial success, fame) life goals and aspirations. Herein we discuss research supporting each of these three propositions, as well as the processes through which these potentiating relations occur, thus illustrating some of the major psychological pathways through which mindful awareness and interest-taking are connected to enhanced self-functioning, high-quality relationships, and the positive life outcomes associated with them. First, however, we provide an overview of how high-quality awareness came to be studied within SDT, and how it interlaces with the concept of self-regulation.

Awareness and SDT: Overview of Their Connections

Although mindful awareness as a foundation for self-determined functioning was discussed early on in SDT (e.g., Deci & Ryan, 1980), more refined theory and research coordinating concepts of awareness and motivation within SDT began in earnest with the work of Brown and Ryan (2003). Hypothesizing that quality of awareness relates to the quality of self-regulation, Brown and Ryan sought to provide an operational definition of mindfulness that could be used in furthering research on this relation, and in exploring the many other salutary effects of mindfulness. In developing their Mindful Awareness and Attention Scale (MAAS) Brown and Ryan drew heavily on Buddhist thought in both the Zen and Tibetan traditions. These Eastern traditions have commonly described mindfulness as a core, "natural" state of mind character-ized by open and receptive awareness that conduces towards greater self-regulation and well-being. Thus, Brown and Ryan conceptualized (and operationalized) mind-fulness as an attribute that could be assessed in all individuals, regardless of whether they engaged in specific mindfulness-cultivating practices (Brown, Ryan, Loverich, Biegel, & West, 2011). They also operationalized mindfulness both as a dispositional, or individual difference, variable (capturing propensities to be more or less mindful) and as a state variable that fluctuates from situation to situation (showing the vulner-ability of mindfulness to contexts). That is, mindfulness is understood as an attribute that varies both between persons and within person (see Brown & Ryan, 2007).

In line with their thesis that mindfulness supports autonomous regulation, Brown and Ryan (2003) used an experiencing sampling methodology to show that at both dispositional and state levels of analysis, mindfulness was indeed associated with more autonomous functioning. Specifically, in both adult and college samples, participants were asked at varied points within their day to rate their current mindfulness, mood, and other state-related variables, as well as to complete a measure assessing their rela-tive autonomy in the moment. Results revealed that the more mindful the person was, both in general and in any given moment, the more they experienced their actions as autonomously undertaken and volitional (see also Levesque & Brown, 2007). These findings thus lent support to the overall thesis that mindful awareness supports autonomous functioning. However, this is a complex relation, about which we shall need to elaborate further.

In their conceptualization of mindfulness, Brown and Ryan (2003) specifically delineated between *awareness* and *attention*, both of which can be more or less mind-ful. Awareness refers to the subjective experience of internal and external phenomena; it represents the pure perception of the field of events that encompass our reality at any given moment. At its fundamental level, awareness can be understood as a cogni-tive process whereby phenomena are simply perceived. Such perceptions are occurring constantly in our minds: We sit on a park bench reading a book as our peripheral vision senses the branches of a nearby tree swaying in the breeze and simultaneously feel the air brushing across our cheek. After some time, our ears pick up the distant rumble of an approaching storm. All of these perceptual inputs constitute the field of awareness that our senses bring to us moment to moment.

Attention, by contrast, is an aspect of consciousness whereby we select from this rich field of perceived phenomena an object of focus (Brown & Ryan, 2004). Attention is thus a conscious engagement with selected phenomena that enter awareness, marked by focusing that awareness on a certain phenomenon that emerges in the field of awareness. Simply put, what we perceive in our minds—our awareness—presents an opportunity space of phenomena from which we can then select for focused attention.

One form of mindful attention has recently been described within SDT through the concept of *interest-taking* (see Deci, Ryan, Schultz, & Niemiec, in press; Ryan & Deci, 2008a; Weinstein et al., 2012). Like mindful awareness, interest-taking is con-ceptualized as a relaxed attention that is open and receptive. But whereas, in mindful-ness, one is actively aware of phenomena as they occur without actively choosing and exploring from said phenomena, in interest-taking awareness is directed (i.e., actively focused) on specific phenomena that may be salient in the individual's experience.

Interest-taking is thus a focused receptivity or detached curiosity and wonder about something that arises. Through mindful awareness, people receive what is occurring and observe what unfolds in experience without being strongly focused or selective; through interest-taking, people bring relaxed interest and a receptive attention actively to bear on selected inner or outer events of significance (see Deci et al., in press; Ryan & Deci, 2008a).

For instance, Weinstein (2009) performed an experiment in which participants wrote an essay about their qualities as a friend, and then were rejected by another (confederate) participant, leading to negative feelings. In her experiment, Weinstein had participants write about a distracting topic, write about their feelings and reactions, or write about feelings and reactions while "taking an interest" in what occurred for them. The latter "interest-taking" condition was assumed to conduce toward a more reflective, nonjudgmental perspective on inner and outer events. Participants in all conditions were then given the friendship profiles of both the person who rejected them and a neutral participant uninvolved in previous tasks. Although participants in all conditions rated the rejecter negatively, only those in the "interest-taking" group showed no transfer of this negatively to the "innocent" participant, suggesting more integrated self-regulation in this emotional context. They also showed less distress as an aftereffect of rejection.

Both of these types of high-quality awareness can be occupied with outer sensory activations, such as sights and sounds in our environments. But of course this is not the only source of experience: Internal processes also generate phenomena that, like the stimuli in the external world, we are aware of only to varying degrees. As we sit with our book on the park bench, a nostalgic daydream might arise sparked by the words we read. In this case, there is a sixth source of perception, which is the mind itself—or, more specifically, the fount of thoughts and emotions that arise endogenously in the mind and felt somatically (e.g., heart pounding from joy). Proust (2003) referred to such risings of thought and emotion as "involuntary memory" via a phenomenon called the "Madeleine effect," in which he described the example of a rich stream of memories being sparked spontaneously simply by the act of dipping a cookie (a madeleine) into his drink. Thus, awareness and attention are not limited only to perceptions arising through the five senses; we can also more or less mindfully observe thoughts and feelings as they rise within us. Even strong emotions that many times we see as inexorably part of the self can be observed as they wax and wane. Because such thoughts and emotions need no proximal external stimulus, they cannot be reduced to merely the reaction to something occurring through the primary senses. Put differently, even without any immediate sensory input, thoughts and emotions spontaneously arise.

Yet what arises can be illuminated with more or less high-quality awareness or attention, a point particularly relevant to the discussion of mindfulness (Epstein, 1995). For example, consider that we can experience an emotion without being attentive, or sometimes even aware, of that emotion. We may, for example, feel angry without conscious attention that "I am angry." In fact, anger may not even be recognized, especially if that might represent a threat to one's self-image (Ryan, Deci, Grolnick, & La Guardia, 2006). Alternatively, rather than being swept away by anger, or balling up one's fists in denial, a person can allow awareness of anger to become clear and/or bring active attention to the emotional experience itself. Being aware of the emotion, however, it is different than judging it as bad or good or having positive or negative reactions to this affective state; it is simply a neutral, receptive openness. If done with the observant mode associated with mindfulness, the person may, in fact, gain enhanced emotion awareness.

Brown and Ryan (2003) illustrated this facilitating effect of mindfulness on emotion awareness. They assessed participants' current emotional states using both an explicit (self-report) scale and an implicit measure based on the Implicit Association Test (IAT; Greenwald & Farnham, 2000). They found that whereas people low in mindfulness showed no correlation between self-reported and implicitly measured emotion states, those high in mindfulness showed robust positive correlations between these indicators. This suggests that mindful persons have greater awareness of their background emotional states.

Similarly, with regard to interest-taking, Roth (2013) recently reported on two experiments in which people were exposed to a highly emotional film sequence. Roth then had them suppress their emotions, reappraise their emotions, or "take-interest" in what they experienced. He then had them return to the laboratory days later to reexperience the film. Of the three groups, the interest-taking group showed lower arousal, both subjectively and physiologically assessed, even while demonstrating better memory for the film. Put differently, taking interest in one's emotions seems to have inoculated against being "tossed about" by those emotions, while also allowing for a clearer mental processing of the film itself.

Indeed, important in both SDT research and work on awareness is the notion that shows that people can be unaware, or only dimly aware, of their inner preferences and motives, which leads them to more controlled forms of regulation. For example, Weinstein, Ryan, et al. (2012) showed that people vary in their awareness of sexual preferences, such that some persons did not consciously report preferences for which they showed an affective proneness. Those persons tended to come from homes where parents were controlling or authoritarian. Similarly, Niemiec et al. (2010) showed that persons low in mindfulness were more likely to act defensively when faced with existential threats. In contrast, people higher in mindfulness more fully processed existential threats and thus were less subsequently affected by them when making judgments about others. These data suggest that a low quality of awareness can lead to compromised, controlled, and defensive functioning, whereas mindfulness can supply a protective or ameliorative factor.

Awareness: The Qualitative Concept of "Openness"

Kabat-Zinn (1990) and many others have described mindfulness as having an *attitudinal* or qualitative component. This qualitative component of mindfulness is often referred to as a state of "open" awareness or "receptive" attention. Yet what is meant by open or receptive in this context is not always clear. As noted by Brown, Ryan, and Creswell (2007), openness describes a state of consciousness most associated with *observing* rather than *controlling*. It is a bare display of what is taking place at any given moment. Self-control, by contrast, involves a state of consciousness during which we are not observing, but directing, our energies towards a desired goal. When observing, we are conscious of the *self as a process* (Brown & Ryan, 2004; Ryan & Rigby, in press) and are primarily focused on allowing perceptions to unfold without constraining or shaping them towards a specific goal or outcome. Openness, therefore, refers to a quality of consciousness that is not evaluative or actively shaped by preexisting ideas or intentions, but is fully receptive to allowing the experience to simply occur "as it is." It is for this reason that the concept of observing (rather than shaping) is used to define the experience of *open* awareness.

Taking on the role of the "observer self" also implies a conscious state in which we are not only openly observant of experiences as they are perceived through our five senses, but similarly positioned as an observer of our own thoughts and emotions as they arise—either in response to specific external precipitants or as they spontaneously arise by themselves. Situated as an observer that is "openly aware," we are mindful and fully cognizant of thoughts and emotions as they occur, but are not controlled or "caught up" within them. For example, a nostalgic memory does not carry us away into a reverie (pleasant or otherwise) that shifts our focus away from the present moment, nor does a strong emotion gain such a tight grip on us that we are no longer an observer but are driven by the emotion in how we interpret an experience, or in the actions we take, potentially crowding out the flexibility and openness to the experience as it exists without such emotional clouding.

This is easier said than done! Moreover, it presupposes a number of psychological capacities associated with emotion regulation (Ryan et al., 2006). Specifically, within mature emotion regulation, emotional phenomena are allowed as *informational* inputs—they provide important information. In less mature emotion regulation, emotions are *controlling* inputs—one's behavior is driven or controlled by feelings or reactions (Vansteenkiste & Ryan, 2013). One can see from this description how mindful awareness and attention to what is occurring allow emotions to be treated as more informational input. One can be aware of what one feels without "attaching to it" or feeling compelled to identify the feeling with oneself, a huge aid in self-regulation. The distinction between consciousness (context) and mental content, also referred to as *decentering* and *desensitization* (Martin, 1997), enhances autonomous self-regulation because behavior is guided by authentic awareness rather than distorted self-cognitions. This is one reason why mindfulness training has become an important element in treatment of impulsive disorders, such as borderline personality (Ryan, 2005).

Self-Determination Theory and Mindfulness: The Three Propositions

The continuum of motivation and mindfulness

As we have noted, SDT sees the quality of awareness as foundational to autonomous functioning, and thus as integrally associated with quality of self-regulation. Within SDT, motivational quality is understood in terms of a continuum of relative autonomy (Ryan & Connell, 1989) with more autonomous forms of self-regulation associated with greater well-being and positive performance outcomes (e.g., Blais, Sabourin, Boucher, & Vallerand, 1990; Gagné & Deci, 2005; Reeve & Jang, 2006; Ryan, Patrick, Deci & Williams, 2008). We now consider some of the forms of self-regulation along that continuum and how they are more or less infused with mindfulness.

Intrinsic motivation   Intrinsic motivation is defined by having deep interest and enjoyment in activities themselves. There is a here-and-now component to most intrinsically motivated activities that is also conducive to mindfulness. For example, the present centered attention to what is occurring that one might experience in playing tennis can be conducive to both performance and a mindful and positive experience. The focus on immediacy can even feel transcendent, especially if it is absent of judgment and instead is open and perceptual, as articulated famously in Gallwey's depictions of the "inner game" (Gallwey, 1974), and Csikszentmihalyi's depictions of "flow" (Csikszentmihalyi, 1990). It is this quality of experience that leads people to pursue such activities; it is simply for the enjoyment they bring without the need for any additional incentive or outcome. This, too, conduces to mindfulness, in so far as, when being mindful, agendas and instrumental investments must be suspended. Thus, it is important to both mindful states and intrinsic motivation that one's engagement is not shaped by extrinsic agendas, whether they be tangible rewards or some attainment of nirvana.

At the same time, intrinsic motivation and mindfulness are distinct constructs. For instance, one can be intrinsically motivated and not particularly in a mindful state. This happens when one is "lost" or absorbed in experience without the observant capacity to oversee the flow of events. In immersion, one can be mindless with respect to what is occurring in and around one. In such absorption, we find that individuals can make poor choices, such as playing video games for too long (Przybylski, Rigby, & Ryan, 2010; Rigby & Ryan, 2011). That is, absorption, and sometimes flow states, can be marked by an immersion that can pull one out of mindful awareness. Thus, while a person can be both intrinsically motivated and mindful (and these are generally positively correlated), these are not identical.

Beyond intrinsic motivation, many things we pursue are not done purely for their own sake. They are instrumental in achieving some other outcome, and can thus be said to be extrinsically motivated. Simply put, we are "doing X to achieve Y." Here, the notion of motivational quality becomes quite relevant, as the instrumental reasons for pursuing activities can vary greatly with respect to their motivational quality. Self-determination theory outlines four distinct types of extrinsic motivation (or regulation) that fall along a continuum of motivational quality, and each of which is differentially related to mindful awareness.

External regulation   External regulation refers to a person's behavior being regulated by purely external contingencies, such as pursuing a reward, or acting to avoid an explicit punishment, and it represents the least autonomous form of behavioral regulation. Here, one has no personal investment or valuing of the activity, and because action is merely a means to an end, motivational quality for the activity is typically quite low. The person often invests the minimal energy required for outcome attainment, and behaviors are not easily maintained or transferred to environments unless contingencies remain operative (Ryan & Deci, 2000). As understood within SDT, in external regulation there has been little or no internalization, upon which maintenance and transfer depend.

Because external regulation is characterized by controlling contingencies, the focus of attention is instrumental and at the same time draining of energy because it involves self-control. In fact, considerable evidence shows depletion and loss of vitality as consequences of external regulation (e.g., Ryan, Bernstein, & Brown, 2010; Ryan & Deci, 2008b). In short, external regulation is not conducive to mindful awareness, in part because it both directs and constraints awareness and attention, and in addition entails active internal control over competing propensities.

Introjected regulation   Introjected regulation occurs when one has internalized some of the reasons for pursuing the activity but has not yet identified with the activity as being valuable or interesting. Instead, in introjection, the individual is motivated to sustain feelings of worth and esteem. Thus, they are driven to attain self- and other-approval, and to avoid feelings of guilt, shame, or anxiety associated with failure at introjected goals or standards. Thus, while there is no explicit contingency controlling the person, intrapsychic pressures control behavior. There is some internalization, but it is also accompanied by inner conflict, pressure, and ego depletion.

A particularly important way in which introjection has been studied within SDT is through the concepts of *ego involvement* (Ryan, 1982) and contingent self-esteem (Roth, Assor, Niemiec, Ryan, & Deci, 2009). Ego involvement entails a motivated form of perception in which the individual is focused on maintaining or enhancing feelings of self-worth. Ego involvement is thus a form of engagement and attention shaped by our ego needs, rather than representing a position of being fully open to experience (Niemiec, Ryan, & Brown, 2008). The dynamics of ego involvement are largely incompatible with having a relaxed interest in, or open, receptive, and detached focus on the relevant experiences because one is instead defensively focused on self-esteem maintenance. In fact, when mindful, self-esteem is not an issue (Ryan & Brown, 2003), and when one becomes mindful of potential ego involvement, ego involvement itself tends to dissipate.

Identified regulation   Identified regulation occurs when one personally values the goals they are trying to attain through acting, even if the activity itself is not inherently interesting. Here, motivational quality is significantly higher than in introjected or external forms of regulation, as there is a more personally relevant and valued reason for pursuing the behavior in question, leading to better performance and persistence (Burton, Lydon, D'Alessandro, & Koestner, 2006). Yet identifications can be more or less *compartmentalized* (Ryan & Deci, 2008aa), and thus the relationship of identified regulation to mindfulness is complex. Persons higher in mindfulness are likely less prone to compartmentalization, in so far as greater mindfulness would allow one to observe one's actual valuing processes, and identify activities and domains of value and that are more truly self-congruent and internally consistent. Nonetheless, identifications, even when volitional, can be absorbing, and like intrinsic motivation their moment-to-moment pursuit can be more or less mindful.

Integrated regulation   Integrated regulation is considered to be the highest quality form of regulation within SDT's continuum of regulatory styles. Integrated regulation is in evidence when one not only values an activity, but also finds that activity congruent with one's other values and propensities. Here, both mindful awareness and interest-taking can play a central role, allowing one to better detect discrepancies and conflicts inherent in one's actions and thoughts. In other words, this open awareness provides a self-compatibility check to avoid incongruent behaviors or to blend congruent behaviors with values that are already part of the self. One may, for example, not only see exercise as personally valuable to overall health, but also recognize how it increases one's vitality and energy for spending time on other valued pursuits such as caring for work and family. Integration of an activity with other aspects important to the self is conducive to a more balanced and fulfilled life because all these different values and behaviors may help to harmonize need satisfaction (Milyavskaya et al., 2009). In contrast, when a specific regulation is strongly identified with, but not integrated, one can let it predominate over other valued activities (e.g., exercise taking over family time), leading to distress.

Processes of internalization   Within SDT, the process of moving from more external or introjected forms of regulation towards identified and integrated forms of regulation is called *internalization,* and it is assumed that under supportive conditions, people are prone to increasingly internalize and integrate social norms and regulations. The one proviso is when these social norms or regulations are inherently in conflict with basic need satisfactions and the sentiments related to them (Deci & Ryan, 2012). Further, as we have mentioned, greater internalization is positively related to mindfulness (e.g., Brown & Ryan, 2003; Weinstein, Pryzbylski, & Ryan, 2013), as well as other indicators of positive functioning.

Higher quality regulatory styles—such as identified and integrated functioning— are largely a function of finding the personal value in experiences and activities, and "leaning forward" into these behaviors because one truly takes an interest in the benefit they have to one's self. Mindful engagement with life experiences naturally conduce towards this process of internalization and more autonomous functioning by removing the ego involvements that cloud one's ability to be open and receptive to the potential value of experiences. In addition, the open awareness that is the hallmark of mindfulness would be expected to aid in deeper integration of experiences into the self by enhancing one's ability to see new points of connection and relevance between what is happening in the moment with other held experiences and values. In sum, mindfulness is expected to promote higher quality motivation and greater autonomous functioning by facilitating the process of internalization and decreasing the experience of control that arises by higher levels of ego involvement and introjection.

Thus, both theories of mindfulness and self-determination theory contain qualitative dimensions. In mindfulness theory, we have discussed the importance of the qualitative dimension of receptive openness. In SDT, we can see the importance of autonomy as a qualitative distinction in the continuum of self-regulation. We also see that openness and nondefensiveness, as entailed in mindful awareness and autonomy, are positively correlated (Hodgins & Knee, 2002; Schultz & Ryan, in press), and as one moves up SDT's continuum of autonomy, mindfulness is increasingly implicated.

We shall now turn to the relations between mindful awareness, interest-taking and two other core aspects of self-determination theory, namely basic need satisfaction (Deci & Ryan, 2000; Deci et al., in press) and the emphasis people put on intrinsic versus extrinsic goal pursuits (Kasser & Ryan, 1996).

Awareness as potentiating basic need satisfaction

A core tenet of self-determination theory posits that just as humans are governed by basic physiological needs—such as those for food and water—they also have some basic psychological needs that are universal and cross-developmental in nature. When persons pursue activities and relationships that are satisfying these needs, they are more persistent and experience greater integrity and wellness. Conversely, when social contexts or inner conflicts thwart or frustrate satisfaction of basic psychological needs, negative consequences including lower motivation (Deci & Ryan, 2000) and vitality (Ryan & Deci, 2008b) accrue.

Specifically, SDT specifies three basic psychological needs (although the list remains open) that fulfill the criteria of essential nutriments for the maintenance of growth, integrity, and wellness. The satisfaction of these needs invariably yields greater well-being and positive psychological, social, and physical outcomes. We next discuss each of these needs, namely the needs for competence relatedness and autonomy, and how mindful awareness and interest-taking can play a key role in potentiating their satisfaction.

Competence   Competence refers to our basic need to feel effective and successful in what we undertake (Deci & Ryan, 1985; Harter, 2012; White, 1959). Going further, competence is satisfied by the process of growth and elaboration of our skills and abilities. We have the desire not simply to succeed, but to grow by undertaking new challenges that stretch our abilities without overwhelming us. This is often achieved through pursuing optimal challenges that enable us to grow and increase our capacities and skills (Deci & Ryan, 1985).

A key contributor to experiencing greater competence satisfaction occurs when one perceives they are receiving strong *informational feedback* on performance (Deci & Ryan, 1985). Feedback is seen as informational when it is perceived to be directly useful to the individual in improving their performance and assisting in personal growth. By contrast, *controlling feedback* is experienced when feedback is perceived as judgmental or evaluative rather than supporting future growth or success, and is thus less useful in helping individuals improve their mastery.

Here, mindfulness plays an important potentiating role: by attenuating the tendency to engage in ego-protection and freeing up one's mental energy to focus and assimilate all possible information, mindfulness greatly facilitates the capacity to absorb information in an open fashion. This receptive state allows for feedback to enhance mastery (competence) and increase success and growth. Put differently, it is expected that mindfulness will lead to a greater propensity to perceive feedback on performance as being informational (rather than controlling), because (1) one is less predisposed to feel ego-involved in the feedback itself and (2) one is more receptive to all sources of information that are occurring in the moment, and can be potentially used for growth and improvement. By contrast, when less mindful and more ego-involved, information that could be helpful for growth is curtailed as the individual selectively attends or filters information in order to protect self-esteem. Thus, we can see direct relations between mindfulness and competence need satisfaction.

Autonomy   A second basic psychological need postulated by SDT is the need for autonomy. Autonomy literally means "regulation by the self." The need for autonomy is thus best understood as the need that supports propensities to self-regulation; the need to feel volitional, integrated, and congruent in acting. When autonomous, the individual endorses the actions she or he is taking, and the path being traveled. By contrast, autonomy is thwarted when the person feels controlled, or experiences pressure, manipulation, or undesired constraints compelling their actions. Controlled actions thus feel alien (or "heteron") as covered in the word heteronomous.

It is important within SDT to distinguish autonomy from the concept of independence (Ryan & Lynch, 1989; Van Petegem, Vansteenkiste & Beyers, 2013). Independence concerns nonreliance on others. There are many circumstances in which one can be autonomously dependent on others—that is, to willingly rely on them— a fact that is true across cultures (Ryan, La Guardia, Solky-Butzel, Chirkov, & Kim, 2005). It is also the case that one can be compelled to rely on others or to be nonautonomously dependent. Similarly, one can be autonomously or heteronomously independent, depending on why one is acting without social help or support.

In any case, many factors have been shown to facilitate autonomy satisfactions, including factors that are both developmental and situational. In terms of situations, feelings of autonomy can be enhanced or thwarted by factors such as how requests, goals, or rules are presented, how messages are framed and "incentivized," and how meaningful are the options and opportunities for choice. With more controlling messages, salient surveillance or evaluation, and contingent use of rewards or sanctions, decreased experiences of autonomy and lower levels of motivation and vitality can be expected. By contrast, when more autonomy supportive communications and practices are used, opposite effects are had, as evidenced in multiple domains such as education (e.g., Black & Deci, 2000; Reeve, Ryan, Deci, & Jang, 2007), sports coaching (e.g., Bartholomew, Ntoumanis, Ryan, Bosch, & Thogersen-Ntoumani, 2011), and work environments (e.g., Baard, Deci & Ryan, 2004). Results consistently show that when individuals perceive greater support for their autonomy (and less controlling environments), they manifest a wide range of positive outcomes, including greater well-being, and vitality, a result shown across diverse cultures (e.g., Jang, Reeve, Ryan, & Kim, 2009).

As previously noted, situational mindfulness covaries with situational autonomy (Brown & Ryan, 2003, 2007). In addition to these situational factors, research has shown that feeling more autonomous in life is also a trait-level variable (e.g., Deci & Ryan, 1985; Weinstein et al., 2012). Simply put, individuals appear to have different baseline levels of autonomous functioning, with those exhibiting greater autonomy showing the positive benefits outlines above. Most importantly, for this discussion, researchers have found a consistently strong relationship between dispositional autonomy and dispositional mindfulness (Brown & Ryan, 2003; Weinstein et al., 2012).

As with our discussion of competence, there are several potential mechanisms through which mindfulness may significantly bolster greater autonomy satisfactions. First and foremost is through the pathway of decreased ego involvement discussed previously: When one is not able to bring an openness to the perception of events, and is constrained by feelings of defensiveness, rigidity in thinking, or other preconceptions in order to protect or enhance the "me-self," there is a higher likelihood of feeling more controlled forms of regulation, including external regulation and, in particular, introjected regulation marked by feelings of internal guilt, pressure, or compulsion (Mageau, Carpentier & Vallerand, 2011; Vansteenkiste & Ryan, 2013). These are states of mind that are in contrast to feeling autonomy satisfaction and integrated, harmonious regulation.

In many circumstances, controlling pressures and the potential for thwarted autonomy (e.g., from teachers, managers, parents, etc.) can be quite high. This is particularly true where people feel threats to security (Grolnick, 2003) or pressures from above (e.g., Assor, Kaplan, Kanat-Maymon, & Roth, 2005; Pelletier & Sharp, 2009). However, if mindfulness is active, such ego involvements will not dominate the interactions between manager/teacher and subordinate, nor overwhelm the person's functioning. For example, Schultz, Niemiec, Legate, Williams, and Ryan (2013) recently assessed dispositional mindfulness in a heterogeneous sample of working adults, surveyed online about the conditions of their work, adjustment, and well-being. Results showed that although controlling work climates were associated with need thwarting in employees and more negative mental and physical wellness, mindfulness moderated that relation. Specifically, when conditions were autonomy supportive, those high and low in mindfulness benefited similarly. But under the adverse conditions of controlling supervision or management, mindful people displayed less psychological need thwarting, and in turn less distress. This is in keeping with experimental studies showing that mindfulness buffers people in stressful situations, through both less threatening appraisals of and more active coping with difficult circumstances (see Weinstein, Brown, & Ryan, 2009).

Relatedness   Relatedness is the final basic psychological need postulated by SDT, referring to people's fundamental need for interpersonal connections that are experienced as supportive and meaningful (Ryan, 1995; see also Baumeister & Leary, 1995). While today it is increasingly easy to use social networking technologies to connect and share the details of our lives with a multitude of individuals, relatedness satisfaction requires something more substantial: relatedness satisfaction is not just a function of the *quantity* of interpersonal connections, but the *quality* of these connections. That is, we want to feel that "I matter" to others, and in turn that others matter to us. It is characterized by relationships in which we feel understood, supported, and cared about.

A key aspect to creating this kind of qualitatively meaningful connection is the capacity to be emotionally available and present for others (Deci, La Guardia, Moller,

Scheiner, & Ryan, 2006; La Guardia & Patrick, 2008). Given that mindfulness is largely defined by the state of "open awareness" we have outlined above, it follows that the capacity for meaningful connection to others—connections in which we are fully present and available to support and communicate—will occur when we are able to be fully in the moment, unburdened by "rigid" beliefs, defensive ego-protections, or other preconceptions that we bring to our interactions. By remaining flexible and open to what we are hearing from those around us, we are in the optimal position to respond in ways that are relevant and reflect empathy and a fuller understanding of the circumstances at hand. In this way, mindfulness contributes directly to potentiating greater opportunities for relatedness satisfaction.

Consider, for example, the important role of autonomy support in the experience of relatedness. Research has shown that relatedness is enhanced when an individual feels that another is supportive of their autonomy, a dynamic that spans from infancy (e.g., Whipple, Bernier, & Mageau, 2011) through adulthood (e.g., Baard et al., 2004) to old age (e.g., Kasser & Ryan, 1999). Barnes, Brown, Krusemark, Campbell, and Rogge (2007) found that mindfulness, assessed by the MAAS, predicted greater relationship satisfaction and investment. In this research, partners discussed a salient conflict. After the discussion, partners higher in mindfulness showed less negativity, anger, hostility, anxiety, and withdrawal. In addition, mindfulness positively predicted higher reports of love, commitment, and support for the partner following the discussion. Other studies have demonstrated that mindfulness is related to higher empathy and compassion for others (Beitel, Ferrer, & Cecero, 2005; Brown et al., 2007; Shapiro, Schwartz, & Bonner, 1998). It thus seems that this open receptiveness to internal and external cues, which defines mindfulness, may allow persons to be more present and responsive in interpersonal settings, enhancing relatedness satisfaction and connectedness.

Although we have focused on mindful awareness as potentiating relatedness need fulfillment, evidence points to the facilitating impact of interest-taking as well. For example, Weinstein et al. (2012) measured interest taking, along with other aspects of autonomy, and showed that it was associated with greater need fulfillment both between and within levels of analysis. Moreover, interactions with more interest-taking partners were characterized by greater closeness, empathy, and satisfaction.

Mindfulness as potentiating intrinsic versus extrinsic goal pursuits

In an attempt to understand how differing life goals and aspirations may influence behavior and well-being, a minitheory was developed within SDT called Goal Content Theory (GCT; Ryan & Deci, 2002). This is based on the empirically derived distinction between intrinsic and extrinsic goal contents (e.g., Kasser & Ryan, 1996), and the hypothesis that these different types of goals would influence well-being in different directions as a function of their relations to basic psychological need satisfactions (e.g., Ryan, Sheldon, Kasser, & Deci, 1996).

Several decades of research have confirmed that, indeed, not all goals in life are created equally: Intrinsic goals such as pursuing personal growth, community, or intimacy with others are inherently more likely to satisfy basic psychological needs, especially for autonomy and relatedness, and thus foster wellness; whereas extrinsic goals such as strivings for wealth, fame, or image (Sheldon, Ryan, Deci, & Kasser, 2004) can actually interfere with basic needs fulfillment. This was shown in a longitudinal study of postcollege young adults. These adults tended to get what they wished for—those with strong extrinsic goals attained such goals, and those with intrinsic goals also attained theirs. Yet, whereas intrinsic attainments enhanced wellness, extrinsic attainments did not. In addition, extrinsic attainments were associated with increased symptoms of ill-being, while intrinsic goal attainment was associated with lower ill-being. Therefore, the pursuit of intrinsic goals yields benefits to happiness and well-being, whereas extrinsic goals, even when attained, can result in fewer wellness benefits and increased risk for ill-being.

Just as mindfulness is seen as intensifying basic need satisfactions regarding competence, autonomy, and relatedness, we likewise see mindfulness as playing a facilitating role in emphasizing intrinsic goals and aspirations over extrinsic ones. If one is holding more open awareness of an experience, and is more in touch with one's feelings, thoughts, basic needs, and reactions, it follows that the greater satisfactions that are derived from intrinsic goals and aspirations will be recognized and create a stronger value for these activities (and, subsequently, greater motivation and sustained engagement).

Indeed, initial research has shown positive relations between intrinsic goals and both mindful awareness and interest-taking. For example, Brown and Kasser (2005) showed that people assessed as high in mindfulness behaved in ways that were more ecologically responsible, reflecting the intrinsic aspiration of community contribution. Brown, Kasser, Ryan, Linley, and Orzech (2009) found that people higher in mindfulness were less susceptible to consumerist messages, less dissatisfied with their current economic circumstances, and less stressed by aspirations for more. Mindfulness is also associated with placing more emphasis on close relationships, another intrinsic goal (Brown & Kasser, 2005). Similar to these findings with mindfulness, Weinstein and colleagues (2012) found a positive relationship between interest-taking and more intrinsic values. It thus appears that people who are more mindful tend toward the principles of living reflective of Buddhist ideals, which derive from recognition of how all things are interdependent, and implicate our responsibilities for compassionate living (Hanh, 1998).

Conclusion

Various approaches to well-being and performance have concluded that mindfulness is a positive state, and agree that mindfulness contributes to self-regulation and well-being of the individual, and of those around him or her (e.g., Brown et al., 2007). In this chapter, we have been focusing on the integration of mindfulness with one well-established theory of human motivation and personality development, namely self-determination theory (Ryan & Deci, 2000). SDT concerns the conditions under which we experience greater well-being, vitality, and personal growth. As discussed, achieving such positive outcomes is largely related to functioning in autonomous rather than controlled ways, obtaining the satisfaction of basic psychological needs for competence, autonomy, and relatedness, and pursuing goals that are consistent with the optimal satisfaction of these needs. We argued herein that mindfulness has been shown to have positive relations with all three of these processes (Ryan, Huta, & Deci, 2008). That is, mindfulness is a psychological state that facilitates autonomous self-regulation, and potentiates the satisfaction of basic psychological needs as well as the personal importance of intrinsic versus extrinsic goals and values. Moreover, SDT also points to an additional, more actively focused yet open and receptive mode of awareness, namely interest-taking, as also facilitating better behavioral and emotional regulation.

Underlying these potentiation effects of mindful awareness and interest-taking is the fact that these high-quality states of awareness are characterized by open awareness and a lack of ego involvement and biases, allowing one to have greater clarity about what is happening in the moment. This further enables the informational use of feedback and perceptions for growth and success (competence satisfaction), identification of meaningful and interesting paths of response that are truly of value to the self (autonomy satisfaction), and the ability to be more fully "present" in interactions with others (enabling greater relatedness satisfaction). When more mindful, persons also cope better with stressors and adverse conditions (Schultz et al., 2013; Weinstein et al., 2009). Finally, when mindful, one has a greater awareness of the value of intrinsic goal pursuits, which in turn yields increased basic need satisfaction and well-being, and a lessened emphasis on extrinsic goals, which are also related to higher levels of ego involvement and contingent self-esteem. This linkage between mindfulness and more intrinsic, and less materialistic goal contents is important in a world where needs and wants can be readily confused, and where the globe's scarce resources can be better used for human wellness.

Much interesting work lies ahead in understanding the relations between mindfulness and interest-taking in greater detail, potentially leading to process models that bring greater clarity to their relations. It is possible that the openness and receptivity present in mindfulness facilitate interest taking by allowing for salient events to come into awareness more easily and with greater clarity. Interest-taking may subsequently supplement this with a more active, integrative engagement with what arises. Although both constructs have shown similar positive relations to basic need satisfaction and well-being, such hypothesized relations between the two concepts await further experimental and qualitative study.

References

Assor, A., Kaplan, H., Kanat-Maymon, Y., & Roth, G. (2005). Directly controlling teachers' behaviors as predictors of poor motivation and engagement in girls and boys: The role of anger and anxiety. *Learning and Instruction, 15*, 397–413.

Baard, P. P., Deci, E. L., & Ryan, R. M. (2004). Intrinsic need satisfaction: A motivational basis of performance and well-being in two work settings. *Journal of Applied Social Psychology, 34*, 2045–2068.

Baer, R. A., Smith, G. T., & Allen, K. B. (2004). Assessment of mindfulness by self-report: The Kentucky Inventory of Mindfulness Skills. *Assessment, 11*(3), 191–206. doi:10.1177/1073191104268029

Barnes, S., Brown, K. W., Krusemark, E., Campbell, W. K., & Rogge, R. D. (2007). The role of mindfulness in romantic relationship satisfaction and responses to relationship stress. *Journal of Marital and Family Therapy, 33*, 482–500.

Bartholomew, K. J., Ntoumanis, N., Ryan, R. M., Bosch, J., & Thogersen-Ntoumani, C. (2011). Self-determination theory and diminished functioning: The role of interpersonal control and psychological need thwarting. *Personality and Social Psychology Bulletin, 37*, 1459–1473. doi:10.1177/0146167211413125

Baumeister, R. F., & Leary, M. R. (1995). The need to belong: Desire for interpersonal attachments as a fundamental human motivation. *Psychological Bulletin, 117*, 497–529.

Beitel, M., Ferrer, E., & Cecero, J. J. (2005). Psychological mindedness and awareness of self and others. *Journal of Clinical Psychology, 61*, 739–750.

Black, A. E., & Deci, E. L. (2000). The effects of instructors' autonomy support and students' autonomous motivation on learning organic chemistry: A self-determination theory perspective. *Science Education, 84*, 740–756.

Blais, M. R., Sabourin, S., Boucher, C., & Vallerand, R. J. (1990). Toward a motivational model of couple happiness. *Journal of Personality and Social Psychology, 59*, 1021–1031.

Brown, K. W., & Kasser, T. (2005). Are psychological and ecological well-being compatible? The role of values, mindfulness, and lifestyle. *Social Indicators Research, 74*, 349–368.

Brown, K. W., Kasser, T., Ryan, R. M., Linley, P. A., & Orzech, K. (2009). When what one has is enough: Mindfulness, financial desire discrepancy, and subjective well-being. *Journal of Research in Personality, 43*, 727–736.

Brown, K. W., & Ryan, R. M. (2003). The benefits of being present: Mindfulness and its role in psychological well-being. *Journal of Personality and Social Psychology, 84*, 822–848.

Brown, K. W., & Ryan, R. M. (2004). Fostering healthy self-regulation from within and without: A self-determination theory perspective. In A. Linley & S. Joseph (Eds.), *Positive psychology in practice* (pp. 105–124). Hoboken, NJ: Wiley.

Brown, K. W., & Ryan, R. M. (2007). Multilevel modeling of motivation: A self-determination theory analysis of basic psychological needs. In A. D. Ong & M. van Dulmen (Eds.), *Handbook of methods in positive psychology* (pp. 530–541). New York, NY: Oxford University Press.

Brown, K. W., Ryan, R. M., & Creswell, J. D. (2007). Mindfulness: Theoretical foundations and evidence for its salutary effects. *Psychological Inquiry, 18*, 211–237.

Brown, K. W., Ryan, R. M., Loverich, T. M., Biegel, G. M., & West, H. A. M. (2011). Out of the armchair and into the streets: Measuring mindfulness advances knowledge and improves interventions: Reply to Grossman. *Psychological Assessment, 23*, 1041–6.

Burton, K. D., Lydon, J. E., D'Alessandro, D. U., & Koestner, R. (2006). The differential effects of intrinsic and identified motivation on well-being and performance: Prospective, experimental and implicit approaches to self-determination theory. *Journal of Personality and Social Psychology, 91*, 750–762.

Csikszentmihalyi, Mihaly (1990). *Flow: The psychology of optimal experience*. New York, NY: Harper & Row.

Deci, E. L., La Guardia, J. G., Moller, A. C., Scheiner, M., & Ryan, R. M. (2006). On the benefits of giving as well as receiving autonomy support: Mutuality in close friendships. *Personality and Social Psychology Bulletin, 32*, 313–327.

Deci, E. L., & Ryan, R. M. (1980). Self-determination theory: When mind mediates behavior. *Journal of Mind and Behavior, 1*, 33–44.

Deci, E. L., & Ryan, R. M. (1985). The general causality orientations scale: Self-determination in personality. *Journal of Research in Personality, 19*, 109–134.

Deci, E. L., & Ryan, R. M. (2000). The "what" and the "why" of goal pursuits: Human needs and the self-determination of behavior. *Psychological Inquiry, 11*, 227–268.

Deci, E. L., & Ryan, R. M. (2012). Motivation, personality, and development within embedded social contexts: An overview of self-determination theory. In R. M. Ryan (Ed.), *Oxford handbook of human motivation* (pp. 85–107). Oxford, UK: Oxford University Press.

Deci, E. L., Ryan, R. M., Schultz, P. P., Niemiec, C. P. (in press). Being aware and functioning fully: Mindfulness and interest-taking within self-determination theory. In K. W. Brown, R. M. Ryan, & J. D. Creswell (Eds.), *Handbook of mindfulness*. New York, NY: Guilford.

Epstein, M. (1995). *Thoughts without a thinker*. New York, NY: Basic Books.

Gagné, M., & Deci, E. L. (2005). Self-determination theory and work motivation. *Journal of Organizational Behavior, 26*, 331–362.

Gallwey, W. Timothy (1974). *The inner game of tennis* (1st ed.). New York, NY: Random House.

Greenwald, A. G., & Farnham, S. D. (2000). Using the Implicit Association Test to measure self-esteem and self-concept. *Journal of Personality and Social Psychology, 79*, 1022–1038.

Grolnick, W. S. (2003). *The psychology of parental control: How well-meant parenting backfires*. Mahwah, NJ: Erlbaum.

Hanh, T. N. (1998). *Interbeing: Fourteen guidelines for engaged Buddhism*. Berkeley, CA: Parallax Press.

Harter, S. (2012). Emerging self-processes during childhood and adolescence. In M. R. Leary & J. P. Tangney (Eds.), *Handbook of self and identity* (2nd ed., pp. 680–715). New York, NY: Guilford Press; US.

Hodgins, H. S., & Knee, C. R. (2002). The integrating self and conscious experience. In E. L. Deci & R. M. Ryan (Eds.), *Handbook of self-determination research* (pp. 87–100). Rochester, NY: University Of Rochester Press.

Jang, H., Reeve, J., Ryan, R. M., & Kim, A. (2009). Can self-determination theory explain what underlies the productive, satisfying learning experiences of collectivistically-oriented Korean students? *Journal of Educational Psychology, 101*, 644–661.

Kabat-Zinn, J. (1990). *Full catastrophe living: Using the wisdom of your mind to face stress, pain and illness*. New York, NY: Dell.

Kasser, T., & Ryan, R. M. (1996). Further examining the American dream: Differential correlates of intrinsic and extrinsic goals. *Personality and Social Psychology Bulletin, 22*, 280–287.

Kasser, V. M., & Ryan, R. M. (1999). The relation of psychological needs for autonomy and relatedness to health, vitality, well-being and mortality in a nursing home. *Journal of Applied Social Psychology, 29*, 935–954.

La Guardia, J. G., & Patrick, H. (2008). Self-determination theory as a fundamental theory of close relationships. *Canadian Psychology, 49*, 201–209.

Langer, E. J. (1978). Rethinking the role of thought in social interaction. In J. H. Harvey, W. J. Ickes, & R. F. Kidd (Eds.), *New directions in attribution research* (Vol. 2, pp. 36–58). Hillsdale, NJ: Lawrence Erlbaum Associates.

Langer, E. J. (1989). *Mindfulness*. Reading, MA: Addison-Wesley.

Langer, E. J. (1997). *The art of mindful learning*. Reading, MA: Addison-Wesley.

Levesque, C., & Brown, K. W. (2007). Mindfulness as a moderator of the effect of implicit motivational self-concept on day-to-day behavioral motivation. *Motivation and Emotion, 31*, 284–299.

Mageau, G. A., Carpentier, J., & Vallerand, R. J. (2011). The role of self-esteem contingencies in the distinction between obsessive and harmonious passion. *European Journal of Social Psychology, 41*, 720–729.

Martin, J. R. (1997). Mindfulness: A proposed common factor. *Journal of Psychotherapy Integration, 7*, 291–312.

Milyavskaya, M., Gingras, I., Mageau, G. A., Koestner, R., Gagnon, H., Fang, J., & Boiche, J. (2009). Balance across contexts: Importance of balanced need satisfaction across various life domains. *Personality and Social Psychology, 38*, 1031–1045.

Niemiec, C. P., Brown, K. W., Kashdan, T. B., Cozzolino, P. J., Breen, W. E., Levesque-Bristol, C., & Ryan, R. M. (2010). Being present in the face of existential threat: The role of trait mindfulness in reducing defensive responses to mortality salience. *Journal of Personality and Social Psychology, 99*, 344–365.

Niemiec, C. P., Ryan, R. M., & Brown, K. W. (2008). The role of awareness and autonomy in quieting the ego: A self-determination theory perspective. In H. A. Wayment & J. J. Bauer (Eds.), *Transcending self-interest: Psychological explorations of the quiet ego* (pp. 107–116). Washington, DC: American Psychological Association.

Pelletier, L. G., & Sharp, E. C. (2009). Administrative pressures and teachers' interpersonal behavior in the classroom. *Theory and Research in Education, 7*, 174–183.

Proust, M. (2003). *In search of lost time* (C. K. Scott-Moncrieff, T. Kilmartin, & D. J. Enright, Trans.). New York, NY: Modern Library.

Przybylski, A. K., Rigby, C. S., & Ryan, R. M. (2010). A motivational model of videogame engagement. *Review of General Psychology, 14*, 154–166.

Reeve, J., Ryan, R. M., Deci, E. L., & Jang, H. (2007). Understanding and promoting autonomous self-regulation: A self-determination theory perspective. In D. Schunk & B. Zimmerman (Eds.), *Motivation and self-regulated learning: Theory, research, and application* (pp. 223–244). Mahwah, NJ: Lawrence Erlbaum.

Reeve, J. M., & Jang, H. (2006). What teachers say and do to support students' autonomy during a learning activity. *Journal of Educational Psychology, 98*, 209–218.

Rigby, S., & Ryan, R. M. (2011). *Glued to games: How video games draw us in and hold us spellbound*. Santa Barbara, CA: Praeger.

Roth, G. (2013). *The benefits of emotional integration and the costs of emotional avoidance*. Paper presented at the 5th International Conference on Self-Determination Theory, Rochester, NY.

Roth, G., Assor, A., Niemiec, C. P., Ryan, R. M., & Deci, E. L. (2009). The emotional and academic consequences of parental conditional regard: Comparing conditional positive regard, conditional negative regard, and autonomy support as parenting practices. *Developmental Psychology, 45*, 1119–1142.

Ryan, R. M. (1982). Control and information in the intrapersonal sphere: An extension of cognitive evaluation theory. *Journal of Personality and Social Psychology, 43*, 450–461.

Ryan, R. M. (1995). Psychological needs and the facilitation of integrative processes. *Journal of Personality, 63*, 397–427.

Ryan, R. M. (2005). The developmental line of autonomy in the etiology, dynamics, and treatment of borderline personality disorders. *Development and Psychopathology, 17*, 987–1006.

Ryan, R. M., Bernstein, J. H., & Brown, K. W. (2010). Weekends, work, and wellbeing: Psychological need satisfactions and day of the week effects on mood, vitality, and physical symptoms. *Journal of Social and Clinical Psychology, 29*, 95–122.

Ryan, R. M., & Brown, K. W. (2003). Why we don't need self-esteem: Basic needs, mindfulness, and the authentic self. *Psychological Inquiry, 14*, 71–76

Ryan, R. M., & Connell, J. P. (1989). Perceived locus of causality and internalization: Examining reasons for acting in two domains. *Journal of Personality and Social Psychology, 57*, 749–761.

Ryan, R. M., & Deci, E. L. (2000). Self-determination theory and the facilitation of intrinsic motivation, social development and well-being. *American Psychologist, 55,* 68–78.

Ryan, R. M., & Deci, E. L. (2002). Overview of self-determination theory: An organismic dialectical perspective. In E.L Deci & R. M. Ryan (Eds.), *Handbook of self-determination research* (pp. 3–33). Rochester, NY: University of Rochester Press.

Ryan, R. M., & Deci, E. L. (2008a). A self-determination theory approach to psychotherapy: The motivational basis for effective change. *Canadian Psychology, 49,* 186–193.

Ryan, R. M., & Deci, E. L. (2008b). From ego depletion to vitality: Theory and findings concerning the facilitation of energy available to the self. *Social and Personality Psychology Compass, 2,* 702–717.

Ryan, R. M., Deci, E. L., Grolnick, W. S., & La Guardia, J. G. (2006). The significance of autonomy and autonomy support in psychological development and psychopathology. In D. Cicchetti & D. Cohen (Eds.), *Developmental psychopathology: Volume 1, Theory and methods* (2nd ed., pp. 295–849). New York, NY: John Wiley & Sons.

Ryan, R. M., Huta, V., & Deci, E. L. (2008). Living well: A self-determination theory perspective on eudaimonia. *Journal of Happiness Studies, 9,* 139–170.

Ryan, R. M., La Guardia, J. G., Solky-Butzel, J., Chirkov, V., & Kim, Y. (2005). On the interpersonal regulation of emotions: Emotional reliance across gender, relationships and cultures. *Personal Relationships, 12,* 145–163.

Ryan, R. M., & Lynch, J. (1989). Emotional autonomy versus detachment: Revisiting the vicissitudes of adolescence and young adulthood. *Child Development, 60,* 340–356.

Ryan, R. M., Patrick, H., Deci, E. L., & Williams, G. C. (2008). Facilitating health behaviour change and its maintenance: Interventions based on self-determination theory. *European Health Psychologist, 10,* 1–4.

Ryan, R. M., & Rigby, C. S. (in press). Did the Buddha have a self? No-self, self and mindfulness in Buddhist thought and western psychologies. In. K. W. Brown, R. M. Ryan, & J. D. Creswell (Eds.), *Handbook of mindfulness.* New York, NY: The Guilford Press.

Ryan, R. M., Sheldon, K. M., Kasser, T., & Deci, E. L. (1996). All goals are not created equal: An organismic perspective on the nature of goals and their regulation. In P. M. Gollwitzer & J. A. Bargh (Eds.), *The psychology of action: linking cognition and motivation to behavior* (pp. 7–26). New York, NY: Guilford.

Schultz, P. P., & Ryan, R. M. (in press). The "why," "what," and "how" of healthy self-regulation: Mindfulness and well-being from a self-determination theory perspective. In B. Ostafin (Ed.), *Handbook of mindfulness and self-regulation.* New York, NY: Springer.

Schultz, P. P., Niemiec, C. P., Legate, N., Williams, G. C., & Ryan, R. M. (2013). Zen and the art of wellness at work: mindfulness, work climate, and psychological need satisfaction in employee well-being. Unpublished manuscript, University of Rochester.

Shapiro, S.L., Schwartz, G, & Bonner, G. (1998). Effects of mindfulness-based stress reduction on medical and premedical students. *Journal of Behavioral Medicine, 21,* 581–599.

Sheldon, K. M., Ryan, R. M., Deci, E. L., & Kasser, T. (2004). The independent effects of goal contents and motives on well-being: It's both what you pursue and why you pursue it. *Personality and Social Psychology Bulletin, 30,* 475–486.

Van Petegem, S., Vansteenkiste, M., & Beyers, W. (2013). The jingle-jangle fallacy in adolescent autonomy in the family: In search of an underlying structure. *Journal of Youth and Adolescence, 42*(7), 994–1014.

Vansteenkiste, M., & Ryan, R. M. (2013). On psychological growth and vulnerability: Basic psychological need satisfaction and need frustration as a unifying principle. *Journal of Psychotherapy Integration.*

Weinstein, N. (2009). *Interest-taking and carry-over effects of incidental rejection emotions.* Unpublished dissertation, University of Rochester, Rochester, NY.

Weinstein, N., Brown, K. W., & Ryan, R. M. (2009). A multi-method examination of the effects of mindfulness on stress attribution, coping, and emotional well-being. *Journal of Research in Personality, 43*, 374–385.

Weinstein, N., Przybylski, A. K., Ryan, R. M. (2012). The index of autonomous functioning: Development of a scale of human autonomy. *Journal of Research in Personality, 46*, 397–413.

Weinstein, N., Pryzbylski, A., & Ryan, R. M. (2013). The integrative process: New research and future directions. *New Directions in Psychology, 22*, 69–74.

Weinstein, N., Ryan, W. S., DeHaan, C. R., Przybylski, A. K., Legate, N., & Ryan, R. M. (2012). Parental autonomy support and discrepancies between implicit and explicit sexual identities: Dynamics of self-acceptance and defense. *Journal of Personality and Social Psychology, 102*, 815–832.

Whipple, N., Bernier, A., & Mageau, G. A. (2011). A dimensional approach to maternal attachment state of mind: Relations to maternal sensitivity and maternal autonomy-support. *Developmental Psychology, 47*, 396–403.

White, R. W. (1959). Motivation reconsidered: The concept of competence. *Psychological Review, 66*, 297–333.

Further Reading

Kasser, T., & Ryan, R. M. (2001). Be careful what you wish for: Optimal functioning and the relative attainment of intrinsic and extrinsic goals. In P. Schmuck & K. M. Sheldon (Eds.), *Life goals and well-being: Towards a positive psychology of human striving* (pp. 115–129). Goettingen: Hogrefe & Huber.

Niemiec, C. P., Ryan, R. M., & Deci, E. L. (2009). The path taken: Consequences of attaining intrinsic and extrinsic aspirations in post-college life. *Journal of Research in Personality, 43*, 291–306.

Ryan, R. M., Curren, R. R., & Deci, E. L. (2013). What humans need: Flourishing in Aristotelian philosophy and self-determination theory. In A. S. Waterman (Ed.), *The best within us: Positive psychology perspectives on eudaimonic functioning* (pp. 57–75). Washington, DC: American Psychological Association Books.

Weinstein, N., Hodgins, H. S., & Ryan, R. M. (2010). Autonomy and control in dyads: Effects on interaction quality and joint creative performance. *Personality and Social Psychology Bulletin, 36*, 1603–1617.

13

Mindful Mindlessness
in Goal Pursuit

Ana P. Gantman, Peter M. Gollwitzer, and Gabriele Oettingen

> The great thing, then, in all education is to *make our nervous system our ally instead of our enemy.*
>
> (James 1890/1950, p. 122)

Mindfulness is the process of drawing novel distinctions (e.g., Langer 1992). Processing information mindfully requires that attention be administered as devoid of preexisting appraisals and categories as possible. In doing so, the mindful individual is able to make direct contact with the external world rather than experiencing stimuli through the lens of a preexisting filter. Mindlessness, on the other hand, is the process of using preexisting rules and routines without considering aspects of the current situation that may be different from those prescribed by the preexisting schema.

To practice mindfulness, one must create new categories, be open to new information, and maintain awareness of more than one perspective (Langer, 1989). By the creation of new categories, problems are solved effectively and creatively. For example, a mindful approach to the question of who to hire as a computer programmer in a noisy work environment may bring to light that a deaf applicant may be better qualified than a hearing applicant of equal programming ability (Langer, 1989). Mindfulness can also manifest as freeing oneself from functional fixedness such that one is able to see multiple, creative uses for an object that is typically used only for one: a bicycle bell is a doorknob, a key can function like a knife. When one is mindful of the environment, it's not that one has a hammer and everything is a nail, so to speak, but rather, with mindfulness, everything is a Swiss army knife.

When one is open to new information, categories do not have to be considered exclusive definitions. For example, in teaching students the definition of a concept or a word, it is better to replace the common definition structure of "X is Y" with "X can be Y" to allow students to draw novel analogies and conjure up clever examples of the phenomenon instead of only those most common or prototypical (Langer,

The Wiley Blackwell Handbook of Mindfulness, First Edition.
Edited by Amanda Ie, Christelle T. Ngnoumen, and Ellen J. Langer.
© 2014 John Wiley & Sons, Ltd. Published 2014 by John Wiley & Sons, Ltd.

1989). For example, if a student understands studying to be memorization, that student may fail to recognize when academic pursuits call for conceptual understanding or novel idea generation and thus fail to try to study when different methods are required.

When one maintains awareness of multiple perspectives, interpretations of a given situation proliferate. A lily can be a subject of study to a botanist, something to avoid for someone allergic, a collection of cells and proteins to a molecular biologist, a present to a romantic, and a symbol of the Virgin Mary to an art historian. A pointed question in a scientific talk can sound like constructive criticism to some and acerbic attack to others. Once these multiple perspectives are considered, individuals can better solve misunderstandings and resolve conflicts. Remembering these disparate perspectives may also help reduce the correspondence bias, and allow for the consideration of others' negative behavior as well intentioned or merely unintentional.

In defining mindfulness, it is important to note that it is not just self-awareness (e.g., Duval & Wicklund, 1972); when objects in the environment such as a mirror, tape-recorder, or the sound of one's own voice, are present in the environment, they are reminders of the self-as-object and so draw the focus of attention of the individual as "Me." The highly objectively self-aware individual regards the self as an entity in the environment that can be evaluated as any other. Mindfulness is a state of conscious awareness in which the individual as "I" actively constructs categories and distinctions. In contrast, mindlessness is a state of mind characterized by an overreliance on categories and distinctions drawn in the past—it is not simply taking the "I" out of experience. The individual is context-dependent and as such oblivious to novel (or simply alternative) aspects of the situation. Mindlessness is seen as similar to more familiar concepts such as habit, functional fixedness, overlearned and automatic (vs. controlled) processing where controlled processing is the conscious processing of information within a given context. Mindlessness is insensitive to novel aspects of a familiar situation (Langer, 1992); and as opposed to habit, it is not dependent on repetition—exposure to a rigid definition can lead to mindless information processing upon the very next exposure, causing uncritically accepted information to lead to premature cognitive commitments (Chanowitz & Langer, 1981).

While the mindfulness/mindlessness distinction seems similar to the distinction between conscious and nonconscious action, it does not map perfectly onto it. The distinction between conscious and nonconscious action has been with psychology since William James, under many different names. In *The Principles of Psychology* (1890/1950), James discusses habit and the will in two separate chapters. On habit (by which he means to pick out those actions that are initiated without a conscious act of the will), James discusses skill acquisition and the way in which experts, such as marksmen and pianists, are able to perform complex sets of smaller actions that comprise the greater action of hitting the target or playing a score. According to James, we can see evidence for automatic action when the first in the set of actions triggers the next, and so on, until the full act is complete, and the initiation of each of the composite actions does not require an act of conscious awareness to initiate. For the purposes of this chapter, we will adopt a similar definition, with the caveat that nonconscious goal pursuit is to be differentiated from the modern definition of habit, in which situational context cues a particular action independent of goals (Neal, Wood, Labrecque, & Lally, 2012).

With regard to the will, James describes acts of the will as those actions that were predicted by the conscious intentions of the actor, and these actions are meant to serve as a contrast to what James believed were the primary actions of man, the automated ones. While the majority of contemporary research on motivation and goal pursuit has focused on these actions (and so not treated them as secondary), we have learned much about the antecedents, determinants, and potential strategies for maximizing conscious goal pursuit. More recently, however, there has been a surge in research on automatic behavior and, in particular, automated goal-directed behavior, or nonconscious goal pursuit.

Mindfulness and modern automaticity research share a fundamental theoretical thread: the environment plays a powerful role in the generation of human behavior, and social psychology tends to overestimate the role of the individual's mental states or intentions. Bargh and Chartrand (1999) made this connection explicit at the beginning of their paper "the unbearable automaticity of being" in which they both summarize and spark research on priming and automaticity. In particular, the authors cite Langer's (1978) chapter "Rethinking the role of thought in social interaction," in which Langer argues that many of the theories of attribution popular in the 1970s assumed mindful individuals carefully observing the scenes they were in and actively considering the minds of those around them. In accordance with this observation, Bargh and Chartrand (1999) argued that our behaviors, judgments, and goals can also be activated outside of awareness, and that historically this fact either has been regarded as a negative aspect of human nature or, more commonly, has been downplayed by psychologists. While much research published after this article has focused on automaticity in goal pursuit, in many ways both folk and empirical psychology of the will or conscious goal pursuit has remained focused on the causal efficacy of a conscious agent.

In order to further clarify the link between mindfulness/mindlessness and nonconscious goal pursuit, we will discuss the current state of research of both similarities and differences between conscious and nonconscious goal pursuit, also raising the question of what happens when consciousness is brought back to bear on actions that have already been automated. However, before we address these issues, we will discuss two prevalent problems of conscious goal pursuit. In goal selection, there is the challenge to commit to and strive for goals that are not only attractive but also feasible. To meet this challenge, research has proposed to engage in mental contrasting (summary by Oettingen, 2012), which means mentally juxtaposing a desired future with obstacles of present reality. In goal implementation, there is the challenge of weakness of the will, which occurs when one has set an appropriate goal but fails to effectively strive for it. To meet this challenge, research has proposed forming if–then plans called implementation intentions, linking a given critical cue with a goal-directed response (Gollwitzer, 1993, 1999). We will argue that both of these self-regulation strategies capitalize on mindful as well as mindless processes, and thus allow for mindful mindlessness in goal pursuit (i.e., selecting goals and planning their implementation). Finally, we will discuss the importance of turning a mindful eye to the common distinction psychology makes between conscious and nonconscious goal pursuit.

Conscious Goal Pursuit

Conscious goal pursuit may be subdivided into two primary component parts: goal selection and goal implementation. Goal selection involves deciding on and committing to an intention, and research in this domain has mostly focused on the determinants of goal selection (Bargh, Gollwitzer, & Oettingen, 2010). If individuals act mindlessly, these determinants may or may not predict goal selection. As of yet, there is only one theory that provides a self-regulation strategy that allows mindful goal selection. According to Fantasy Realization Theory (Oettingen, 2012), mental contrasting allows for the mindful selection of goals by contrasting the desired future with the obstacles in present reality. Goal implementation, on the other hand, comprises the deployment of behaviors aimed at bringing about the desired outcome specified by the goal. Research has focused on determinants of goal implementation and their varied effects on goal attainment. As with goal selection, there is research on one extant self-regulation strategy (i.e., furnishing goal intentions with implementation intentions) that allows for the mindful planning out in advance of how a chosen goal is to be implemented.

Determinants of goal selection: Desirability and feasibility

Research on goals has focused on the factors both at the individual and at the contextual level that predict goal selection. To approach goal selection mindlessly is to fail to consider carefully which goals are both desirable and feasible. Undesirable goals are worth only little time and effort to complete, and unfeasible goals lure individuals to spend time and energy on a future that may not be possible. Moreover, mindless goal selection may be driven by individual and contextual determinants (e.g., habits, peer pressure) without any consideration of new perspectives or possibilities. In other words, in mindless goal selection, suboptimal determinants for success may take the reins.

One central determinant of goal selection is an individual's perceived desirability of a goal. According to Ajzen and Fishbein (1980; Fishbein & Ajzen, 1975), high perceived desirability is the sum total of the perceived possible positive and negative consequences associated with the attainment of the goal. Each valenced assessment is weighted by its perceived likelihood of coming to fruition. While it is commonly assumed that individuals select desirable goals (Bargh et al., 2010), as suggested by Bandura (1977, 1997), feasibility concerns play an important role in forming goal commitments as well. Individuals recognize the importance of the likelihood of goal attainment in goal selection, meaning they consider whether they feel that they can perform the behaviors relevant to the desired goal. Thus, self-efficacy beliefs (or, according to Ajzen, 1991, "control beliefs") contribute much to perceived feasibility. To harbor high self-efficacy beliefs, people benefit from successes in the past, but they do not need to have previously made successful responses; rather, beliefs can also be based on observing similar others making similar responses (Bandura, 1977).

Practically, however, individuals may not let themselves be guided by the relative perceived desirability and feasibility of potential goals, but rather act independently of these beliefs. Unfortunately, this means that mindlessness may lead people to put too much effort towards nearly impossible outcomes and thus prevent people from pursuing goals that are both worthwhile and within their grasp. Acting according to perceived desirability or feasibility, however, can be promoted by engaging in mindful reasoning (Oettingen, 2012).

Mindful goal selection

As of yet, there is one theory that spells out what type of mindful reasoning makes people respect expectancies or feasibility criteria, thereby strategically guiding their own goal selection and subsequent goal striving (i.e., goal pursuit). According to Fantasy Realization Theory (Oettingen, 2012), there are four primary strategies for thinking about a desired future. First, there is mental contrasting in which the desired future is contrasted with obstacles in the way of realizing that future. This strategy allows for commitment to attractive goals that are also feasible, and to disengage from those that are unattainable. In contrast, dwelling, thinking only about the present reality, and indulging, thinking only about the positive future, lead to moderate commitments no matter whether the goal is perceived as highly feasible or unreachable. Finally, reverse contrasting, in which the present reality is acknowledged first and the desired future second, also does not allow for feasibility-dependent goal pursuit.

Mental contrasting pulls commitment and performance to match expectations (i.e., feasibility). By using mental contrasting, the individual is able to identify a discrepancy between the desired future and the present reality. This in turn activates expectations (i.e., the question of "Can I reach the desired outcome?" is raised). If expectations for success are high, people will experience high goal commitment and the affective, cognitive and behavioral consequences that come with it. If expectations are low, individuals will experience low goal commitment, having recognized that the discrepancy between fantasy and reality is not worth the effort it would take to close it or that it cannot be closed; these individuals will disengage from turning desired outcomes into goals and thus protect their resources. Indulging and dwelling protect a person's resources less than mental contrasting because they do not allow for the allocation of resources in an expectation-dependent manner; the former strategies lead to an unchanged, medium level of engagement even when no engagement (in the case of low expectations of success) or full engagement (in the case of high expectations of success) would be the resource-efficient way to act.

Various studies have tested the effects of mental contrasting as compared to indulging and dwelling on goal commitment and goal striving (Oettingen, 2000; Oettingen, Hönig, & Gollwitzer, 2000; Oettingen, Mayer, Thorpe, Janetzke, & Lorenz, 2005; Oettingen, Pak & Schnetter, 2001; summary by Oettingen, 2012). For example, in one study, freshmen enrolled in a vocational school for computer programming (Oettingen et al., 2001; Study 4) first indicated their expectations of excelling in mathematics. Then, they named positive aspects they desired that would come from excelling in mathematics (participants named aspects such as feelings of pride and increasing job prospects) and aspects of present reality that might hinder their success (participants named aspects such as getting distracted and feeling lazy).

Students were then randomly assigned to one of three conditions: In the mental contrasting condition, participants had to elaborate on two aspects of the desired future and two aspects of present reality, in alternating order, starting with an aspect of the desired future. Participants in the indulging only condition elaborated on four aspects of the desired future; in the dwelling condition, they elaborated only on four aspects of present reality. Afterwards, participants indicated how energized (e.g., active, energetic) they felt. Two weeks after the experiment, participants' teachers reported how much effort each student had exhibited over the last two weeks and provided each student with a grade for that time period. Participants in the mental contrasting group with high expectations of success felt the most energized, invested the most effort, and received the highest grades. Conversely, participants in the mental contrasting group with low expectations of success felt the least energized, invested the least effort, and received the lowest course grades. Participants in the indulging and dwelling conditions felt moderately energized, exerted moderate effort, and received moderate grades independent of their expectations of success.

Spanning various life domains, a multitude of studies replicated these results. For example, experiments reveal the benefits of mental contrasting when studying abroad (Oettingen et al., 2001; Study 2), learning a second language (Oettingen et al., 2000; Study 1), getting to know an attractive stranger (Oettingen, 2000; Study 1), finding a balance between work and family life (Oettingen, 2000; Study 2), cigarette-smoking cessation (Oettingen, Mayer & Thorpe, 2010), and pursuing important individual interpersonal wishes (e.g., establishing a good relationship with one's mother; Oettingen et al., 2001; Studies 1 and 3). Strength of goal commitment has been assessed by cognitive (e.g., making plans), affective (e.g., feeling responsible for the desired ending), motivational (e.g., feelings of energization), and behavioral indicators (e.g., invested effort and markers of success). Indicators were measured via self-report, other-reported observations, or physiological measures directly after the experiment, weeks later, or both. Across studies, the results reveal the same pattern: participants in the mental contrasting group with high expectations showed the strongest goal commitment and goal striving. For those in the mental contrasting group with low expectations, people showed the least goal commitment and goal striving. Participants who indulged in a desired future or dwelled on present reality showed unchanged, medium-level commitment independent of their expectations of success, and this was also true for reverse mental contrasting. By mentally contrasting a desired future with the obstacles of present reality, individuals effectively become open to new information regarding whether to pursue the desired future, mindfully opening themselves up to the possibility of goal disengagement or creating a new categorization for an old wish: a goal that is high on desirability but also on feasibility.

A mindless mechanism

Though engaging in mental contrasting requires drawing mindful contrasts, the processes by which mental contrasting facilitates smart goal selection rely on changes in implicit cognitions. Mental contrasting facilitates the anchoring of the desired future onto the present reality and the formation of a link between them; from this mental exercise, individuals are able to see what it is in their current situation that stands in the way of their wishes—they form a relational link "X stands in the way of Y." When reverse contrasting, the desired future has nothing to hang onto, and so no "standing in the way" relationship is formed between the obstacle (X) and the future (Y). In other words, by relinquishing old associations with a desired future and replacing a relational "standing in the way" link between the future and reality, expectations become activated and guide behavior accordingly.

Recent work has directly investigated the mechanisms behind the effects of mental contrasting. In one set of studies, Kappes, Singmann, and Oettingen (2012; Study 1), used a primed lexical decision task to measure the strength of associations between obstacles and instrumental behavior following mental contrasting as compared to reverse contrasting (thinking about the present reality prior to the desired future) and an irrelevant content control exercise. In Study 1, participants listed both an interpersonal concern and a health concern, and used mental contrasting or reverse contrasting on the interpersonal concern only. Individuals' idiosyncratic desired futures and obstacles were put into a primed lexical decision task. Only those participants in the mental contrasting condition with high expectations showed a facilitation effect in classifying their instrumental behavior target as a word when it was preceded (primed) by their obstacle. This effect did not hold for health goals, which none of the participants elaborated on, or for participants in the mental contrasting condition with low expectations, reverse contrasting, and irrelevant contrast conditions.

In the second study, Kappes et al. (2012; Study 2) tested whether the strength of the association between perceived obstacle and instrumental behavior would mediate the expectancy-dependent change in that behavior. In this study, participants are told that a common obstacle to maintaining health in college is taking the elevator instead of the stairs. This set up the desired future as feeling healthy, the obstacle as using the elevator, and their instrumental behavior as taking the stairs. As in the previous study, there were three conditions: mental contrasting, reverse contrasting, and an irrelevant contrasting condition. In the same primed lexical decision task, only those individuals in the mental contrasting condition with high expectations showed a faster classification time in identifying the target word "exercise" as a word (as opposed to a nonword) after seeing the word "elevator." After the strength of this associative link was measured, participants were told that the second part of the study would take place on another floor; whether participants took the stairs to and from the other part of the study served as the behavioral measure. As predicted, the stronger the association between the obstacle in present reality and the behavior to overcome it, the more likely that participants were to take the stairs, suggesting that newly created associative links drive the positive effects of mental contrasting for goal commitment and subsequent goal enactment (Kappes et al., 2012). Further research has shown that this is also true for associative links that mental contrasting creates between the desired future and the obstacle of present reality (Kappes & Oettingen, 2012).

Using mental contrasting to select goals allows for the formation of new insights about one's desired future. Mental contrasting creates implicit associative links between the desired future and relevant obstacle of reality, as well as between obstacles and instrumental behaviors to overcome them. Note that the associative links have been formed on the basis of mindful reasoning; that is, they were formed on the basis of extensive elaborations of both a nonexisting desired future and an existing negative reality, and thus the resulting associations should be relatively trustworthy. Once individuals have used mental contrasting to select an attractive and feasible goal, they can be confident that mindless behavior toward that goal, that is, behavior that is initiated from implicit cognition (i.e., strong associative links), will be aimed at this goal.

Determinants of goal implementation

As with goal selection, if individuals do not mindfully plan goal implementation, they may leave the outcome of goal pursuit to the influence of individual and contextual determinants. In other words, there are many factors that determine how a given goal will be pursued, and many of these factors are outside of the individual's awareness or control. Research on goals has focused on the factors both at the individual and at the contextual level that predict successful goal implementation. To approach goal implementation mindlessly is to act in ways usually associated with these factors. Often, these factors are common features of the person and the situational context—for a health-conscious individual, an apple in a store becomes an opportunity to meet the goal to eat more fruit. Without considering familiar aspects of the context in a new way, goal implementation will likely proceed according to its individual- and context-level determinants.

But situational contexts can promote or hamper goal attainment. Over time, individuals may come to associate a particular cue in their context with a particular action simply because the two have been coactivated repeatedly, and these actions can be antagonistic to the actions required to meet one's goals. According to Wood and colleagues (Wood & Neal, 2007; Neal, Wood, and Quinn, 2006), habitual behaviors are cued directly by context and do not depend on goals. These actions are perfectly mindless—they are behaviors that are associated with context and so are deployed without consideration. For example, in one study, people were given a bag of either fresh or stale popcorn before entering a movie theater. Among individuals who do not usually eat popcorn during movies, those with fresh popcorn ate more than those with stale popcorn. Among individuals who regularly eat popcorn while they watched movies, popcorn was consumed regardless of quality (Neal, Wood, Wu, & Kurlander, 2011). While this phenomenon is specifically not goal-related, it clearly demonstrates the potential for powerful associations between context and action to affect a person's behavior when encountering a particular context. Without planning in advance or mindfully reconsidering familiar contexts, old habits reign, and unfortunately these habits often run counter to individuals' explicit goals. Mindless goal strivers will thus likely fall prey to these individual- and contextual-level predictors, which in turn determine whether people successfully implement their goals.

As of yet, there is one strategy for reinterpreting cues from one's context to make them actionable, and which can capitalize on the mind's ability to associate an action with a feature in context. Forming implementation intentions (Gollwitzer, 1993, 1999) requires that individuals understand aspects of their context from a new, more goal-relevant perspective, and in doing so they can form new associative links between contextual cues and goal-directed behaviors to maximize goal attainment.

Mindful planning

If an individual takes a mindless approach to goal implementation, letting former, unconsidered associations between contextual cues and behaviors take the reins, goal attainment may prove impossible. Research on goal pursuit has identified many types of challenges that people may encounter during goal implementation that can result in failure to achieve the selected goal. These include: failing to get started, getting derailed, not calling a halt to ineffective behavior, ceasing goal striving too soon, and overextending oneself (Gollwitzer & Sheeran, 2006). Succumbing to any of these challenges is typically referred to as weakness of the will (Holton, 2009). One way to maximize goal striving in the face of these problems is to make mindful plans that construe familiar contextual cues as opportunities for goal striving and to link these cues with goal-directed behavior (i.e., form implementation intentions).

Furnishing mere goal intentions with implementation intentions optimizes goal striving. For example, if one has the goal intention to read more books, forming plans that delineate the when, where, and how of the goal-directed behaviors will help goal attainment. It is particularly effective to form such plans as an "if–then" statement, such as "If I encounter situation X, then I will perform goal-directed behavior Y!" or, more specifically, "If I am getting into bed for the night, then I will open my book!" Numerous studies suggest that furnishing goal intentions with implementation intentions leads to higher goal-attainment rates than goal intentions alone.

People can break longstanding habits by forming strong implementation intentions (e.g., if–then plans that spell out a response contrary to the habitual response to the critical situation; Holland, Aarts, & Langendam, 2006). Cohen, Bayer, Jaudas, and Gollwitzer (2008; Study 2) used implementation intentions to counter dominant responses in a Simon task. In this task paradigm, participants are asked to respond to a nonspatial aspect of a stimulus (i.e., whether a presented tone is high or low) by pressing a left or right key, and to ignore the fact that the stimulus appears on the left or right side of the screen, and so a key on either the same or opposite side of the stimulus is needed. The difficulty of correct responding is high when the location of the tone (e.g., right) and the required key press (e.g., left) are incongruent, as the dominant response is to press the key that corresponds with the side that the stimulus appeared on.

Similarly, other automatic responses, such as stereotyping, can be blocked by implementation intentions designed to run counter to them. For example, Mendoza, Gollwitzer, and Amodio (2010) have added to findings that implementation intentions can also be used to suppress the behavioral expression of implicit stereotypes (see also Stewart & Payne, 2008). In their study, individuals completed the Shooter Task paradigm in which individuals choose whether or not to simulate shooting at Black or White targets holding guns or nongun objects. In a correct response, individuals shoot at threatening, gun-wielding targets, and not innocent targets who merely have their hands full. In Study 1, individuals were given no task instructions or a goal intention to ignore irrelevant information, or formed an implementation intention aimed at ignoring irrelevant information. Individuals with implementation intentions made fewer errors than either those with goal intentions alone or no further instructions. In Study 2, the target of the implementation intention was facilitation, and so they formed the strategy "If I see a target holding a gun, then I will shoot at it!" These participants also outperformed participants with a goal intention containing the same strategic information and participants with no further instructions (Mendoza, Gollwitzer, & Amodio 2010).

Implementation intentions not only override dominant or habitual responses, but generally facilitate goal implementation. In a recent meta-analysis (Gollwitzer & Sheeran, 2006), the overall impact of furnishing goals with implementation intentions on goal attainment was $d = .65$, based on 8,461 participants in 94 tests. These tests were on a wide variety of samples, including children with ADHD, adults with schizophrenia, the elderly, and heroin addicts, and tested a wide variety of goals, including taking vitamins, performance on a Stroop task, negotiation outcomes, academic performance, and exercise (Gollwitzer & Sheeran, 2006).

A(nother) mindless mechanism

Implementation intentions capitalize on the associative structure of the mind. The if–then plan forms a strong associative link between a contextual cue and the goal-directed response. Research investigating the mechanisms of the success of implementation intentions identified changes in how individuals regard the context and the linked behavior. Due to the formation of implementation intentions, the relevant contextual cue becomes mentally activated and so more highly accessible (Gollwitzer, 1999). For instance, Webb and Sheeran (2004; Studies 2 and 3) observed that implementation intentions improve cue detection (fewer misses and more hits), without engendering false alarms. Moreover, using a dichotic listening task paradigm in which participants had to listen to two strings of verbal information, one in each ear, Achtziger, Bayer, and Gollwitzer (2012) asked participants to focus attention on one or the other stream. Achtziger and colleagues found that words describing the critical situation specified in the "if" part of the implementation intentions were highly disruptive to focused attention in implementation-intention participants compared to mere goal-intention participants, demonstrating the heightened accessibility of the contextual cue.

The success of implementation intentions in maximizing goal striving derives from heightened accessibility not only to contextual cues but also to the formation of a strong associative link between the contextual cue and the specified goal-directed behavior (Webb & Sheeran, 2007, 2008). These associative links seem to be stable over time (Papies, Aarts, & de Vries, 2009) and allow for the activation of the representation of the goal-directed response even by subliminal presentation of the specified contextual cue (Webb & Sheeran, 2007). In other words, the associative link between the representation of the specified if-component and then-component exhibits features of automaticity, including immediacy, efficiency, and redundancy of conscious intent (Gollwitzer, 1999). If–then planners act more quickly (e.g., Gollwitzer & Brandstätter, 1997; Experiment 3), deal more effectively with cognitive load (Brandstätter, Lengfelder, & Gollwitzer, 2001), and do not depend on conscious intentions to act in the specified situation (Bayer, Achtziger, Gollwitzer, & Moskowitz, 2009).

Using implementation intentions to implement goals allows individuals to open up their understanding of their context to a new, more goal-relevant perspective. Aspects of the context that might have previously gone entirely unnoticed gain heightened accessibility. Moreover, implementation intentions capitalize on the associative quality of the mind. Once people form implementation intentions, they have created a strong associative link between the contextual cue and the goal-directed behavior, such that the context triggers the behavior automatically. As with mental contrasting, the mindless mechanism behind this strategy does not carry the same dangers of other (not mindfully planned) behaviors.

It is important to note, however, that the authors are not advocating for completely mindless goal pursuit that may cause individuals to miss novel opportunities in the environment or evidence that goal disengagement is the best course of action. Instead, we recommend the combination of mental contrasting and implementation intentions, which allows for mindful goal selection and mindful goal implementation via mindless mechanisms—even the automaticity associated with these mindless mechanisms allows for flexibility in action to some degree, such as the ability to respond to feedback (Rosenbaum, Vaughan, Meulenbroek, Jax, & Cohen, 2009) and learn implicit rules (Eitam, Hassin, & Schul, 2008), which will be discussed in more detail later in this chapter. In other words, mental contrasting with implementation intentions allows for mindful mindlessness in goal pursuit via mindful goal selection and the mindful planning of automatic goal implementation.

Mindful mindlessness in goal pursuit

The authors recommend combining the two strategies for effective goal pursuit, mental contrasting for mindful goal selection with subsequent effortful striving, and implementation intentions for mindful planning of goal implementation. When combined, mental contrasting with implementation intentions (MCII) provides a strategy for maximizing goal pursuit that capitalizes on the notion of strategic automaticity. Moreover, because mental contrasting allows for the recategorization of the desired future and the reality in a manner that respects expectations, and implementation intentions allow for reinterpreting aspects of the context as opportunities to act, both strategies utilize aspects of mindfulness. At the same time, however, both strategies for goal pursuit rely on automaticity and the notion that mindfully formed links are then followed strictly based on their association (i.e., mindlessly). The two strategies together can be described as a mindfully mindless self-regulation strategy.

More specifically, MCII leads to greater rates of goal attainment than either mental contrasting or implementations alone (Adriaanse et al., 2010; Christiansen, Oettingen, Dahme, & Klinger, 2010; Stadler, Oettingen, & Gollwitzer, 2009, 2010; review by Oettingen, 2012). The two strategies complement each other, as mental contrasting facilitates the pursuit of goals with high expectations for success and fosters high goal commitment and effortful goal striving, while implementation intentions work best on goals to which individuals are highly committed (Sheeran et al., 2005; Study 1). Moreover, mental contrasting allows for the identification of idiosyncratic obstacles, which can then be specified in the if-component of implementation intentions as a critical contextual cue, thus creating a maximally tailored self-regulation strategy.

In two studies demonstrating the power of MCII, Adriaanse and colleagues (2010) found that mental contrasting with implementation intentions led to greater reduction in unhealthy snacking compared to controls who only listed healthy snack options (Study 1) and mental contrasting alone or implementation intentions alone (Study 2). Together, the two strategies target both goal selection and goal implementation to optimize goal attainment; mental contrasting relies on the formation of a new insight into the contrast between one's desired future and the present reality, changes the meaning of the present reality towards being an obstacle, and implicitly links the obstacle to instrumental means. Forming implementation intentions provides a new, goal-relevant perspective on one's context and explicitly links goal-relevant opportunities (e.g., obstacles) to instrumental means. This creates strategic automaticity, the delegation of control of goal-directed behavior to contextual cues.

Not only does MCII allow for personally tailored strategies, but the general mental procedure can be taught, making MCII a metacognitive strategy applicable to multiple domains. For example, Stadler, Oettingen, and Gollwitzer (2009) taught participants the MCII technique. This intervention allowed participants to apply MCII independently to any desire of their choosing. When participants applied MCII to their individual health concerns, they exercised more often than individuals who were only provided with health-related information. Participants in the MCII group exercised nearly twice as much as before the intervention, and positive effects began to appear directly after the intervention and remained throughout the 16-week study. Finally, MCII has been tested beyond the health domain and was found to successfully promote adolescents preparing for standardized tests (Duckworth, Grant, Loew, Oettingen, & Gollwitzer, 2011; review by Oettingen, 2012). In summary, MCII works with both aspects of the mind—the so-called conscious controller uses mental contrasting to select and strive for expectancy-respecting goals and forms implementation intentions in advance of encountering the critical context, while the automatic "unconscious self" takes over after these mindful steps have been completed.

Nonconscious Goal Pursuit

As previously mentioned, many models of human motivation assume an agentic conscious controller, but much research over the past two decades has focused on the automated will, the activation of goals outside of the awareness of the agent. Much like the birth of mindlessness research, this surge in research derives from the observation that the current state of a given body of research (attribution for mindlessness, motivation for nonconscious goals) overemphasizes mental content and underemphasizes the direct causal power of context on an individual's actions.

According to Langer (1989), much of the research on attribution assumed that individuals were constantly assessing what was going on in the minds of those around them, but in reality, it is likely that those individuals were not giving any thought to their surroundings at all. The fundamental attribution error, then, was not a failure to consider the situation with regard to the causal factors contributing to the actions of others, but rather a failure to consider any cause at all. As a result of this observation, Langer and colleagues conducted a now classic experiment in social psychology in which a confederate asked someone waiting in line at a fax machine if they could skip them in line either because they were "in a rush" or because they needed to "make a copy." She argued that if participants were paying attention to the content of the request instead of the format, they would not allow the person who explained that they needed to make a copy cut in line. If people were only paying attention to the form or using a preexisting schema, they would allow the person with a nonexistent reason for cutting the line to pass (Langer, 1978).

First generation of research: Similarities regardless of awareness

According to the Auto-Motive Theory, goals may be activated indirectly (i.e., outside of awareness) through the repeated pairing of a given situation and its related goal; the contextual cues eventually activate the goal through the established associative link (Bargh, 1990; Bargh & Gollwitzer, 1994). This model predicts that both conscious and nonconscious activation of goals should lead to similar goal-attainment rates and qualities of goal striving (Bargh, Gollwitzer, Lee-Chai, et al., 2001). Accordingly, nonconsciously activated goals exhibit hallmarks of goal pursuit. In particular, nonconscious goals lead to goal-directed action, stay active until completed, produce persistence in the face of setbacks, and promote resumption after interruption (Bargh et al., 2001). We are able to see evidence for such hallmarks by the use of priming, in which goal-related words are either embedded in a seemingly unrelated task, as in a supraliminal ("above the threshold of consciousness") priming procedure such as a word search puzzle, or flashed on the screen below the level of awareness as in subliminal priming (Bargh & Chartrand, 2000).

In line with Auto-Motive Theory, the first generation of research on nonconscious goal pursuit has focused on the similarities between conscious and nonconscious goal pursuit (Bargh et al., 2001; review by Gollwitzer, Parks-Stamm, & Oettingen, 2009). For example, participants with both conscious and nonconscious goals experience the phenomenon of goal projection (Kawada, Oettingen, Gollwitzer, & Bargh, 2004) in which an active goal in the agent leads to the perception of others having that same goal. Moreover, both conscious and nonconscious goals have similar effects on affect following success and failure. In particular, participants primed with an achievement goal, who succeeded on a task, experienced greater positive affect than those who completed the task without having been primed, and those primed with achievement who failed at the task experienced greater negative affect than those who were not primed (Leander, Moore, & Chartrand, 2009).

More recently, research has focused on whether nonconscious goals exhibit equivalent flexibility in goal striving as conscious goals. Much evidence has supported the flexibility of nonconscious goal striving as compared to no goal controls. For instance, participants with a nonconscious goal to achieve perform better than participants with no goal on implicit and unintentional learning tasks, in which success requires adapting to a dynamic environment, as well as the Wisconsin Card Sorting Task and the Iowa Gambling Task (Eitam, Hassin, & Schul, 2008; Hassin, Bargh, & Zimmerman, 2009). Such evidence is in line with cognitive work on perceptual motor acts, in particular, Feedback Control Theory, in which feedback from the environment determines whether a motion has departed from the current goal or not (summary by Rosenbaum et al., 2009).

In a more recent study (Gantman, Gollwitzer, & Oettingen, 2012), we asked the question of whether nonconscious goals are as flexible as conscious goals. We found that participants with conscious and nonconscious goals alike exhibit optional flexibility: they spontaneously discover simpler means more frequently than participants with no goal. In addition, both conscious and nonconscious goal striving allowed for the fast discovery of a new solution when such flexibility was mandatory for task completion (i.e., mandatory flexibility). Taken together, these studies highlight a similarity between conscious and nonconscious goal striving—both allow for flexibility, either by incorporating feedback from the environment or by recognizing novel opportunities for success.

Second generation of research: Awareness-based differences

Follow-up research has also addressed differences in conscious versus nonconscious goal striving. For instance, Govorun and Payne (2006) found differences in capacity, such that conscious goal striving is more subject to ego-depletion effects than nonconscious goal striving. Given recent research suggesting that knowledge of ego-depletion may be related to the emergence of the phenomenon (Job, Dweck, & Walton, 2010), it is possible that this difference in goal striving may be dependent on awareness of the goal in conjunction with the belief that self-regulatory resources are limited. After all, it does not make sense to bring the notion of limited self-regulatory resources in goal striving to bear on a situation in which one does not think there is goal striving in the first place.

Other work (Oettingen, Grant, Smith Skinner, & Gollwitzer, 2006) more directly investigated the difference in awareness of the goal in conscious and nonconscious goal pursuit. While this difference seems obvious, no preceding work has focused on potential affective consequences of this difference or what happens when nonconscious goal strivers are made aware of their (nonconsciously activated) goal-directed behavior. In order to study this question, Oettingen and colleagues (2006) provided participants with a task that required cooperation and induced either a conscious or a nonconscious goal of competitiveness (associated with expected, norm-conforming behavior and unexpected, norm-violating behavior, respectively). The participants given the nonconscious goal of competitiveness showed heightened negative affect as a result of their conflicting, norm-incongruent behavior (namely, acting competitively in a cooperation-based task) compared to those with a conscious goal to act competitively. Apparently, participants in the nonconscious condition could not explain their behavior. The authors call the phenomenon of people faced with their own unexpected behavior the "explanatory vacuum."

A later study by Parks-Stamm, Oettingen, and Gollwitzer (2010) hypothesized that the increased negative affect in the nonconscious goal condition arose specifically from the lack of explanation for the behavior. The authors found that the heightened negative affect in the nonconscious goal condition could be reduced when a plausible explanation for primed competitive behavior (in this case, acting too quickly was equivalent to acting competitively) was made available. More precisely, the authors replicated the previous study with the addition of a prior, seemingly unrelated study that asked half of the participants to perform quickly and half to perform accurately. Of the participants in the explanatory vacuum, those who engaged in the prior speed task showed less negative affect than those in the accuracy task, suggesting that when primed goal-directed behaviors can be explained (i.e., by having just done a task as quickly as possible) the negative affect associated with the explanatory vacuum does not arise. While this is preliminary evidence suggesting that people when primed with nonconscious goals may at times feel the need to explain their nonconscious goal pursuit, much research has investigated the effects of explicit awareness of goal-directed behavior, specifically when it has detrimental effects on performance.

Explicit awareness of goal-directed behavior

Explicit awareness of the goal to perform well is associated with the pressure to excel (Bargh et al., 2010), which can lead to the phenomenon called "choking under pressure." According to the *explicit monitoring theory,* performance pressure leads people to attempt to exert conscious control over the execution of physical behaviors (Baumeister, 1984; Lewis and Linder, 1997). In particular, Beilock and Carr (2001) proposed that "choking" in a behavioral task occurs when performance pressure leads people to attempt to exert conscious control over the execution of physical behaviors that have become automated.

When behaviors have automated, consciously monitoring the enactment of learned physical skills results in suboptimal performance as the behavior no longer requires conscious direction. Empirical demonstrations of the detrimental result of adding conscious control have included golf putting (Lewis & Linder, 1997), squash (Masters, Polman, & Hammond, 1993), and basketball played before a home audience (Baumeister & Steinhilber, 1984). Masters and colleagues (1993) called this tendency to exert conscious control over automated behaviors "conscious reinvestment." They created a Reinvestment Scale that measures this tendency to exert conscious control under pressure and found that individuals who scored highly on this scale performed worse at a golf-putting task under pressure than those who were low in reinvestment and under pressure, despite evincing equal skill level in the no-pressure condition (Masters et al., 1993). This work suggests that awareness of the goal to perform well (operationalized as pressure) may recruit thoughts that are detrimental to successful performance.

Other recent research by Bijleveld, Custers, and Aarts (2011) has focused on the nonconscious presentation of rewards. The Attentional Blink is a task in which focused attention devoted to the details of the task hurts performance (Arend, Johnston, & Shapiro, 2006; Dale & Arnell, 2010). These authors presented high-value versus low-value monetary rewards for performance on the Attentional Blink paradigm either consciously or nonconsciously. Bjileveld and colleagues found that nonconscious high-value rewards were associated with improved performance on Attentional Blink trials, while the effect of a high-value incentive disappeared when it was presented consciously.

For test anxious college students, forming implementation intentions was found to ward off the tendency to consciously reinvest in the task at hand, thus facilitating performance on a math exam. In particular, implementation intentions aimed at ignoring distracting thoughts improved performance over and above those designed to facilitate task performance, suggesting that test anxiety hinders math test performance because it is distracting. Apparently, implementation intentions allow for the strategic automation of control over distracting thoughts so that conscious reinvestment is no longer a problem (Parks-Stamm, Gollwitzer, & Oettingen, 2010). Given that conscious awareness of performance goals may lead to detriments in performance, and that people may experience negative affect at the recognition of behavior elicited by counternormative nonconscious goals (i.e., experience an explanatory vacuum), it seems that the boundary between conscious and nonconscious goal pursuit is permeable and would benefit from further consideration.

A Mindful Perspective on the Conscious/Nonconscious Dichotomy in Goal Research

Finally, the notions of conscious and nonconscious goals in psychological research may benefit from the look of a mindful eye, particularly on the ways in which we use strong words with minimal thought. With regard to nonconscious goal pursuit, especially when conducting studies involving the use of supra- or subliminal priming techniques, it is easy to refer casually to the participants in the study who will receive the nonneutral form of the manipulation as the "unconscious group" (vis-à-vis the "conscious" or the "control group"). While this shorthand is in most cases harmless, in the context of goal pursuit it obscures something important about those participants in the "unconscious" group; they are not, in fact, unconscious. When we fail to think about what else might be going on in the minds of our primed participants, we not only fail to understand something important about priming but fail to fully grasp the meaning of priming in the real world.

Not only are those participants in the "unconscious" (sometimes referred to as "nonconscious") priming conditions aware, in the sense of phenomenal consciousness,[1] but also they are able to think about the behaviors that they have been presumably primed into performing. Moreover, can we induce thinking about these behaviors, and are these behaviors regarded differently from those that have not been directly primed in a laboratory setting? Future research would benefit from considering these issues.

There are two basic possible responses to this question. The first is simply that we act based on primed behavior much more often than we realize, and so whatever the regular, lay conception of action is, that is how we regard primed behaviors. On the other hand, particularly with regard to the priming of goals outside of awareness (Bargh et al., 2001), it may be the case that, as individuals are capable of forming explicit goals and subsequently (at least sometimes) carrying out the actions that follow from those goals as the result of a deliberate plan (Gollwitzer & Oettingen, 2011), people may find the possibility of acting on a goal that has been activated outside of awareness unsettling.

The explanatory vacuum phenomenon suggests that there might be resistance to this idea not only by scientists (as suggested by Bargh and Chartrand, 1999) but also at least by college undergraduates. Parks-Stamm, Oettingen, and Gollwitzer (2010; Study 2), conducted a follow-up explanatory vacuum study to determine whether finding an explanation for one's unexpected (and, in this case, primed) behavior happens reflexively, or whether individuals acting in an explanatory vacuum need to be prompted to notice that they lack an explanation for their behavior. They found that when participants were given extra time to reflect about their goals in the study, this had no effect on negative affect; only those participants with a prior goal to explain their behavior showed reduced negative affect as compared to those whose prior goal could not. In other words, it is possible that participants reflexively search for explanations for norm-violating behavior, suggesting that, even unprompted, students seek to understand the origins of unexpected primed behaviors in their minds and are likely unsatisfied by answers more in line with the concept of nonconscious goal pursuit.

The strong dichotomy between conscious and nonconscious goal pursuit in the field and its matching folk psychology seems to be embedded in the way that people think about themselves and their own behavior; if individuals spontaneously think about the origins of their actions when they could not have been predicted by the individuals' conscious intentions, it may be to repair or bolster beliefs in the conscious controller or to undermine concerns about the lack of controllability of one's own actions. We can see, however, from the self-regulation literature and the benefits of using mental contrasting with implementation intentions to maximize goal attainment that conscious and nonconscious goal pursuit can be strategically combined. If we dissolve the distinction, especially given that the unconscious seems quite increasingly capable of doing what consciousness can (Hassin, in press), we can begin to better understand the way in which we are agents and how to maximize our agentic efficacy. Once we expand our ideas of these two categories, we, both as psychologists and as lay theorists, can expand the concept of the agentic self to include our nonconscious actions.

Summary and Conclusion

In this chapter, we have introduced the idea of mindful mindlessness in goal pursuit or strategic automaticity. We have argued that individuals select and implement their goals based on the influence of individual and contextual determinants that may include mindless associations. There exist two strategies for moderating the influence of these determinants on goal pursuit. For goal selection and effortful goal striving, individuals who mentally contrast the desired future with present reality gain insight into and respect their expectations for success. For those with high expectations of success, future and negative reality (obstacle) become linked, and the reality (obstacle) becomes linked to instrumental behavior, resulting in new implicit, associative links that may be acted on mindlessly. For goal implementation, individuals who furnish mere goal intentions with implementation intentions select opportunities in their context and specify how to act on them. The if–then structure (best combined with high goal commitment and fitting obstacles) forms a strong link between the eliciting situation and the relevant goal-directed behavior. This, too, results in an implicit link between opportunity and relevant action that can be mindlessly followed to successful goal pursuit. Such faith in these associative links is, of course, only warranted by the mindful manner in which they were set.

In this chapter, we have also reviewed literature on both similarities and differences between conscious and nonconscious goals. Of note is the fact that individuals acting with nonconscious goals are unaware of the purpose of their purposeful behavior, and if that behavior is norm-violating, negative affect arises. This behavior is lower on the spectrum of awareness of automated behavior than the phenomenon of "choking under pressure" or the tendency to consciously reinvest attention in the task at hand when it can be successfully performed automatically. In these cases, it seems that explicit awareness of the goal leads to a decrease in goal-attainment rates compared to individuals without this tendency. By taking a mindful approach to these findings in the literature, we can shine new light on the distinction between conscious and nonconscious goal striving, suggesting that to retain an understanding of this dichotomy in a strong sense may keep further research from fully understanding goal pursuit more broadly.

Note

1. Not to be confused with the fact that priming can be considered a case where there is access but not phenomenal consciousness *of the particular stimuli* (Block, 2002).

References

Achtziger, A., Bayer, U. C., & Gollwitzer, P. M. (2012). Committing to implementation intentions: Attention and memory effects for selected situational cues. *Motivation & Emotion*, *36*, 287–300.

Adriaanse, M. A., Oettingen, G., Gollwitzer, P. M., Hennes, E. P., de Ridder, D. T. D., & de Witt, J. B. F. (2010). When planning is not enough: Fighting unhealthy snacking habits by mental contrasting with implementation intentions (MCII). *European Journal of Social Psychology*, *40*, 1277–1293.

Ajzen, I. (1991). The theory of planned behavior. *Organizational Behavior and Human Decision Processes*, *50*, 179–211.

Ajzen, I., & Fishbein, M. (1980). *Understanding attitudes and predicting social behavior*. Englewood Cliffs, NJ: Prentice-Hall.

Arend, I., Johnston, S., & Shapiro, K. (2006). Task-irrelevant visual motion and flicker attenuate the attentional blink. *Psychonomic Bulletin and Review*, *13*, 600–607.

Bandura, A. (1977). Self-efficacy: Toward a unifying theory of behavioral change. *Psychological Review*, *84*, 191–215.

Bandura, A. (1997). *Self-efficacy: The exercise of control*. New York, NY: Freeman.

Bargh, J. A., & Chartrand, T. L. (1999). The unbearable automaticity of being. *American Psychologist*, *54*, 462–479.

Bargh, J. A., & Chartrand, T. L. (2000). The mind in the middle: A practical guide to priming and automaticity research. In H. T. Reis & C. M. Judd (Eds.), *Handbook of research methods in social and personality psychology* (pp. 253–285). New York, NY: Cambridge University Press.

Bargh, J. A., Gollwitzer, P. M., Lee-Chai, A., Barndollar, K., & Troetschel, R. (2001). The automated will: Nonconscious activation and pursuit of behavioral goals. *Journal of Personality and Social Psychology, 81,* 1014–1027.

Bargh, J. A. (1990). Auto-motives: Preconscious determinants of social interactions. In E. T. Higgins & R. M. Sorrentino (Eds.), *Handbook of motivation and cognition* (Vol. 2, pp. 93–130). New York, NY: Guilford Press.

Bargh, J. A., & Gollwitzer, P. M. (1994). Environmental control of goal-directed action: Automatic and strategic contingencies between situations and behavior. In W. D. Spaulding (Ed.), *Integrative views of motivation, cognition, and emotion* (pp. 71–124). Lincoln, NE: University of Nebraska Press.

Bargh, J. A., Gollwitzer, P. M., & Oettingen, G. (2010). *Motivation.* In S. Fiske, D. Gilbert, & G. Lindzey (Eds.), *Handbook of social psychology* (5th ed., pp. 268–316). New York, NY: Wiley.

Baumeister, R. F. (1984). Choking under pressure: Self-consciousness and paradoxical effects of incentives on skillful performance. *Journal of Personality and Social Psychology, 46,* 610–620.

Baumeister, R. F., & Steinhilber, A. (1984). Paradoxical effects of supportive audiences on performance under pressure: The home field disadvantage in sports championships. *Journal of Personality and Social Psychology, 47,* 85–93.

Bayer, U. C., Achtziger, A., Gollwitzer, P. M., & Moskowitz, G. (2009). Responding to subliminal cues: Do if–then plans facilitate action preparation and initiation without conscious intent? *Social Cognition, 27,* 183–201.

Beilock, S. L., & Carr, T. H. (2001). On the fragility of skilled performance: What governs choking under pressure? *Journal of Experimental Psychology: General, 130,* 701–725.

Bijleveld, E., Custers, R., & Aarts, H. (2011). Once the money is in sight: Distinctive effects of conscious and nonconscious rewards on task performance. *Journal of Experimental Social Psychology, 47,* 865–869.

Block, N. (2002). Concepts of consciousness. In D. Chalmers (Ed.), *Philosophy of mind: Classical and contemporary readings* (pp. 206–218). New York, NY: Oxford University Press.

Brandstätter, V., Lengfelder, A., & Gollwitzer, P. M. (2001). Implementation intentions and efficient action initiation. *Journal of Personality and Social Psychology, 81,* 946–960.

Cohen, A. L., Bayer, U. C., Jaudas, A., & Gollwitzer, P. M. (2008). Self-regulatory strategy and executive control: Implementation intentions modulate task switching and Simon task performance. *Psychological Research, 72,* 12–26.

Chanowitz, B., & Langer, E. J. (1981). Premature cognitive commitment. *Journal of Personality and Social Psychology, 6,* 1051–1063.

Christiansen, S., Oettingen, G., Dahme, B., & Klinger, R. (2010). A short goal-pursuit intervention to improve physical capacity: A randomized clinical trial in chronic back pain patients. *Pain, 149,* 444–452.

Cohen, A. L., Bayer, U. C., Jaudas, A., & Gollwitzer, P. M. (2008). Self-regulatory strategy and executive control: Implementation intentions modulate task switching and Simon task performance. *Psychological Research, 72,* 12–26.

Dale, G., & Arnell, K. M. (2010). Individual differences in dispositional focus of attention predict attentional blink magnitude. *Attention, Perception, & Psychophysics, 72,* 602–606.

Duckworth, A. L., Grant, H., Loew, B., Oettingen, G., & Gollwitzer, P. M. (2011). Self-regulation strategies improve self-discipline in adolescents: Benefits of mental contrasting and implementation intentions. *Educational Psychology, 31,* 17–26.

Duval, S., & Wicklund, R. A. (1972). *A theory of objective self-awareness.* San Diego, CA: Academic Press.

Eitam, B., Hassin, R. R., & Schul, Y. (2008). Non-conscious goal pursuit in novel environments: The case of implicit learning. *Psychological Science, 19,* 261–267.

Fishbein, M., & Ajzen, I. (1975). *Belief, attitude, intention, and behavior: An introduction to theory and research.* Reading, MA: Addison-Wesley.

Gantman, A. P., Gollwitzer, P. M., & Oettingen, G. (2012). Flexibility in conscious and non-conscious goal striving: Exhibiting optional and mandatory flexibility. Manuscript in preparation.

Govorun, O., & Payne, B. K. (2006). Ego depletion and prejudice: Separating automatic and controlled components. *Social Cognition, 24,* 111–136.

Gollwitzer, P. M. (1993). Goal achievement: The role of intentions. *European Review of Social Psychology, 4,* 141–185.

Gollwitzer, P. M. (1999). Implementation intentions: Strong effects of simple plans. *American Psychologist, 54,* 493–503.

Gollwitzer, P. M., & Brandstätter, V. (1997). Implementation intentions and effective goal pursuit. *Journal of Personality and Social Psychology, 73,* 186–199.

Gollwitzer, P. M., & Oettingen, G. (2011). Planning promotes goal striving. In K. D. Vohs & R. F. Baumeister (Eds.), *Handbook of self-regulation: Research, theory, and applications* (2nd ed.). New York, NY: Guilford.

Gollwitzer, P. M., Parks-Stamm, E. J., & Oettingen, G. (2009). Living on the edge: Shifting between nonconscious and conscious goal pursuit. In E. Morsella, J. A. Bargh, & P. M. Gollwitzer (Eds.), *Oxford handbook of human action* (pp. 603–624). New York, NY: Oxford University Press.

Gollwitzer, P. M., & Sheeran, P. (2006). Implementation intentions and goal achievement: A meta-analysis of effects and processes. *Advances in Experimental Social Psychology, 38,* 69–119.

Hassin, R. R. (in press). Yes it can: On the functional abilities of the human unconscious. *Social Cognition.*

Hassin, R. R., Bargh, J. A., & Zimmerman, S. (2009). Automatic and flexible: The case of nonconscious goal pursuit. *Social Cognition, 27,* 20–36.

Holland, R. W., Aarts, H., & Langendam, D. (2006). Breaking and creating habits on the working floor: A field-experiment on the power of implementation intentions. *Journal of Experimental Social Psychology, 42,* 776–783.

Holton, R (2009). *Willing, wanting, waiting.* New York, NY: Oxford University Press.

James, W. (1950). *The principles of psychology.* Oxford, UK: Holt. (Original work published 1890)

Job, V., Dweck, C. S., & Walton, G. M. (2010). Ego depletion—is it all in your head? Implicit theories about willpower affect self-regulation. *Psychological Science, 21,* 1686–1693.

Kappes, A., & Oettingen, G. (2012). The emergence of goal commitment: Mental contrasting connects future and reality. *Journal of Personality and Social Psychology.* Manuscript in preparation.

Kappes, A., Singmann, H., & Oettingen, G. (2012). Mental contrasting instigates behavior by linking reality with instrumental behavior. *Journal of Experimental Social Psychology, 48,* 811–818.

Kawada, C., Oettingen, G., Gollwitzer, P. M., & Bargh, J. A. (2004). The projection of implicit and explicit goals. *Journal of Personality and Social Psychology, 86,* 545–559.

Langer, E. (1992). Matters of mind: Mindfullness/mindlessness in perspective. *Consciousness and Cognition, 1,* 289–305.

Langer, E. J. (1978). Rethinking the role of thought in social interaction. In J. H. Harvey, W. Ickes, & R. F. Kidd (Eds.), *New directions in attribution research* (Vol. 2, pp. 35–58). Hillsdale, NJ: Erlbaum.

Langer, E. J. (1989). *Mindfulness.* Reading, MA: Addison-Wesley.

Leander, N. P., Moore, S. M., & Chartrand, T. L. (2009). Mystery moods: Their origins and consequences. In G. Moskowitz & H. Grant (Eds.), *The psychology of goals* (pp. 480–504). New York, NY: Guilford Press.

Lewis, B. P., & Linder, D. E. (1997). Thinking about choking? Attentional processes and paradoxical performance. *Personality and Social Psychology Bulletin, 23,* 937–944.

Masters, R. S., Polman, R. C., & Hammond, N. V. (1993). "Reinvestment": A dimension of personality implicated in skill breakdown under pressure. *Personality and Individual Differences, 14,* 655–666.

Mendoza, S. A., Gollwitzer, P. M., & Amodio, D. M. (2010). Reducing the expression of implicit stereotypes: Reflexive control through implementation intentions. *Personality and Social Psychology Bulletin, 36,* 512–523.

Neal, D. T., Wood, W., Labrecque, J., & Lally, P. (2012). How do habits guide behavior? Perceived and actual triggers of habits in daily life. *Journal of Experimental Social Psychology, 48,* 492–498.

Neal, D. T., Wood, W., & Quinn, J. M. (2006). Habits: A repeat performance. *Current Directions in Psychological Science, 15,* 198–202.

Neal, D. T., Wood, W., Wu, M., & Kurlander, D. (2011). The pull of the past: When do habits persist despite conflict with motives? *Personality and Social Psychology Bulletin, 37,* 1428–1437.

Oettingen, G. (2000). Expectancy effects on behavior depend on self-regulatory thought. *Social Cognition, 18,* 101–129.

Oettingen, G. (2012). Future thought and behaviour change. *European Review of Social Psychology, 23,* 1–63.

Oettingen, G., Grant, H., Smith, P. K., Skinner, M., & Gollwitzer, P. M. (2006). Nonconscious goal pursuit: Acting in an explanatory vacuum. *Journal of Experimental Social Psychology, 42,* 668–675.

Oettingen, G., Hönig, G., & Gollwitzer, P. M. (2000). Effective self-regulation of goal attainment. *International Journal of Educational Research, 33,* 705–732.

Oettingen, G., Mayer, D., & Thorpe, J. S. (2010). Self-regulation of commitment to reduce cigarette consumption: Mental contrasting of future with reality. *Psychology and Health, 25,* 961–977.

Oettingen, O., Mayer, D., Thorpe, J. S., Janetzke, H., & Lorenz, S. (2005). Turning fantasies about positive and negative futures into self-improvement goals. *Motivation and Emotion, 29,* 237–267.

Oettingen, G., Pak, H., & Schnetter, K. (2001). Self-regulation of goal-setting: Turning free fantasies about the future into binding goals. *Journal of Personality and Social Psychology, 80,* 736–753.

Papies, E. K., Aarts, H., & de Vries, N. K. (2009). Planning is for doing: Implementation intentions go beyond the mere creation of goal-directed associations. *Journal of Experimental Social Psychology, 45,* 1148–1151.

Parks-Stamm, E. J., Oettingen, G., & Gollwitzer, P. M. (2010). Making sense of one's actions in an explanatory vacuum: The interpretation of nonconscious goal-striving. *Journal of Experimental and Social Psychology, 46,* 531–542.

Parks-Stamm, E. J., Gollwitzer, P. M., & Oettingen, G. (2010). Implementation intentions and test anxiety: Shielding academic performance from distraction. *Learning and Individual Differences, 20,* 30–33.

Rosenbaum, D. A., Vaughan, J., Meulenbroek, R. G. J., Jax, S., & Cohen, R. G. (2009). Smart moves: The psychology of everyday perceptual motor acts. In E. Morsella, J. A. Bargh, & P. M. Gollwitzer (Eds.), *Oxford handbook of human action* (pp. 603–624). New York, NY: Oxford University Press.

Stadler, G., Oettingen, G., & Gollwitzer, P. M. (2009). Physical activity in women: Effects of a self-regulation intervention. *American Journal of Preventive Medicine, 36*, 29–34.

Stadler, G., Oettingen, G., & Gollwitzer, P. M. (2010). Intervention effects of information and self-regulation on eating fruits and vegetables over two years. *Health Psychology, 29*, 274–283.

Stewart, B. D., & Payne, B. K. (2008). Bringing automatic stereotyping under control: Implementation intentions as efficient means of thought control. *Personality and Social Psychology Bulletin, 34*, 1332–1345.

Sheeran, P., Aarts, H., Custers, R., Rivis, A., Webb, T. L., & Cooke, R. (2005). The goal-dependent automaticity of drinking habits. *British Journal of Social Psychology, 44*, 47–64.

Webb, T. L., & Sheeran, P. (2004). Identifying good opportunities to act: Implementation intentions and cue discrimination. *European Journal of Social Psychology, 34*, 407–419.

Webb, T. L., & Sheeran, P. (2007). How do implementation intentions promote goal attainment? A test of component processes. *Journal of Experimental Social Psychology, 43*, 295–302.

Webb, T. L., & Sheeran, P. (2008). Mechanisms of implementation intention effects: The role of goal intentions, self-efficacy, and accessibility of plan components. *British Journal of Social Psychology, 47*, 373–395.

Wood, W., & Neal, D. T. (2007). A new look at habits and the interface between habits and goals. *Psychological Review, 114*, 843–863.

14

Mindful Versus Mindless Thinking and Persuasion

Andrew Luttrell, Pablo Briñol, and Richard E. Petty

Although the construct of mindfulness has seen diverging definitions in the field of psychology (Gethin, 2011), general themes among these definitions are relevant to attitudes and persuasion. One of these accounts of mindfulness, representing a more Western approach, is that provided by Langer (1989; Langer & Moldoveanu, 2000). In this account, mindfulness is seen as bringing one's full resources to a cognitive task by using multiple perspectives and attending to context, which creates novel ways to consider the relevant information. As we describe in this review, this active process of elaboration can be linked to the concept of the *central route* to persuasion. In contrast to mindfulness, the persuasion literature views mindlessness as a way of approaching the same cognitive tasks with reduced attention and a reliance on previously developed means of interpreting information. This second approach, based on reliance on mental shortcuts, associative inferences, and heuristics, can be linked to the concept of the *peripheral route* to persuasion. Briefly stated, mindful engagement in a task is characterized by openness and elaborative thinking, whereas mindless engagement is characterized by rigidity and less elaborative rule-governed behavior.

Other definitions of mindfulness stem more from the Buddhist practice of mindful meditation. Like Langer's formulation, this view of mindfulness involves openness centered in the present moment, but there are additional processes inherent in these conceptualizations of mindfulness that are not components of Langer's approach. These more Eastern formulations emphasize various mental processes that characterize the state of mindfulness (Bishop et al., 2004; Brown & Ryan, 2003; Kabat-Zinn, 2003). Of most relevance to the persuasion processes that will be reviewed later are openness to current experiences, shifting perspectives of self, and the nonjudgment of thoughts. Simply put, people experiencing a state of mindfulness are those who demonstrate an openness to the present and have experiences unburdened by personal concerns, previous events, or future possibilities (e.g., Bishop et al., 2004; Brown & Ryan, 2003; Hölzel et al., 2011; Martin, 1997). Shifting perspectives of self refers to

The Wiley Blackwell Handbook of Mindfulness, First Edition.
Edited by Amanda Ie, Christelle T. Ngnoumen, and Ellen J. Langer.
© 2014 John Wiley & Sons, Ltd. Published 2014 by John Wiley & Sons, Ltd.

a tendency to see oneself as changing, following from Buddhist beliefs regarding the impermanence of the self (Hölzel et al., 2011). The nonjudgment of thoughts refers to the act of noticing one's thoughts and letting them pass without personalizing or evaluating them (Bishop et al., 2004; Dreyfus, 2011; Kabat-Zinn, 2003; Shapiro, Carlson, Astin, & Freedman, 2005). As we describe shortly, the characteristics of mindfulness from these theoretical perspectives are applicable to the domain of attitudes and persuasion.

The study of attitudes and persuasion is one of the key elements of social psychology and beyond (e.g., marketing, political science, etc.). Attitudes refer to people's evaluations of a target, which can be an object, a place, an issue, oneself, or another person. Attitudes are important because a person's attitude can often predict their relevant behavior. Persuasion refers to the processes by which a person's attitude can change. After encountering persuasive messages of any type, one's attitude toward the topic of the message can shift. There are a number of variables that can either facilitate or inhibit persuasion. The extent of mindfulness is one such variable.

Mindfulness and Attitude Change

Persuasion can occur at all levels of mindfulness. That is, some processes of persuasion can occur when people are in a relatively mindless state, and others can occur when people are in a more mindful state, and everywhere in between. First, many social influence variables operate under conditions of mindlessness. For instance, in their classic study, Langer, Blank, and Chanowitz (1978) examined people's compliance with a simple request that followed the familiar structure of acceptable persuasive requests (i.e., including a reason) and varied whether or not the content of the request was compelling. Specifically, an experimenter approached people who were about to use a photocopier and asked to use the machine first. This request came with a reason that conveyed no real information and was vacuous (i.e., "because I have to make copies"), a reason that did convey information (i.e., "because I'm in a rush"), or included no reason at all for the request. Their results revealed that people were more compliant with the request when it was accompanied by some reason than when the request was made in isolation, even if the reason was vacuous. Importantly, the persuasive advantage of providing a vacuous reason was present under relatively mindless conditions. Under conditions characterized by increased thought, Langer et al. (1978) found that including a vacuous reason was no more persuasive than merely making the request alone. Thus, under conditions of mindlessness, simple heuristics such as provision of a reason can enhance a communication's persuasive impact.

In a similar vein, research using a traditional persuasion paradigm showed that increasing the number of arguments for a position—whether strong or weak—can increase persuasion when thinking was low. However, when thinking was high, only increasing the number of strong arguments increases persuasion. Increasing the number of weak arguments reduced persuasion when people were being thoughtful (Petty & Cacioppo, 1984).

Other influence techniques also have been explicitly identified as persuasion variables that operate primarily under mindless conditions. For example, the

"That's-Not-All" technique in which persuasion increases when initial offers are followed either by a reduced price or by the inclusion of an upgrade on the offer has been shown to be more effective under conditions of mindlessness (Pollock, Smith, Knowles, & Bruce, 1998). Additionally, some researchers have argued that other compliance strategies are successful because they *induce* a state of mindlessness (Dolinski & Nawrat, 1998; Fennis & Janssen, 2010), including the Foot-In-The-Door technique (Burger, 1999), the Door-In-The-Face technique (Cialdini et al., 1975), and the Fear-Then-Relief technique. That is, some have argued that these techniques work because they reduce the ability and/or motivation for people to think mindfully about requests. In these cases, mindful consideration of a request could *undermine* the persuasiveness of the request as people might generate reasons to deny the request; however, if an influence technique prevents people from reaching a state of mindful consideration, a request might be agreed to without much thought.

The persuasion literature is replete with examples of people succumbing to simple strategies when they are not thinking much. For example, people might go along with an authority without much thinking because experts are presumed to be correct (e.g., Chaiken, 1980; Petty, Cacioppo, & Goldman, 1981), or they might become more attracted to a restaurant if the parking lot is full rather than empty, taking the apparent popularity of the place as social proof that it must be good (Cialdini, 2001), or because that restaurant is going to be open only for a limited, restricted period of time (Lynn, 1991). Indeed, people often do not have the time or mental resources to think about every request and persuasive appeal that passes by them each day or every decision they must make. As a result, everybody can fall prey to simple decision rules or triggers that can operate in a fairly automatic manner. However, persuasion does not *always* operate in a mindless way.

There are many other processes that guide persuasion when people operate mindfully. In fact, the very same variables that can lead to mindless change can also produce mindful change under different circumstances. Petty and Briñol (2012) argued that variables such as those mentioned above (scarcity, authority, and social consensus) can operate in different ways, depending on the situation. For example, consider the general social influence principle of liking. The dominant understanding of why people tend to be persuaded by people they like is that it operates as a fairly automatic heuristic (e.g., I like this person; therefore, I should go along with their proposal). However, in accord with contemporary multiprocess theories of influence such as the elaboration likelihood model (Petty & Cacioppo, 1986) and the heuristic-systematic model (HSM; Chaiken, Liberman, & Eagly, 1989), it is now clear that variables such as source attractiveness and processes such as liking affect judgments in different ways depending on how motivated and able people are to think about the appeal or request. That is, depending on the message recipient's motivation and ability to think, factors such as liking or attractiveness can influence persuasion in multiple ways, including not only serving as a simple cue, but also by some other more mindful processes. We describe these next.

Mindful Change

As noted, attitudes can change through automatic, mindless processes as well as through more deliberative, mindful mechanisms. Although both mindless and mindful processes are possible, the consequences of those processes are different. According to the ELM, attitudes formed or changed through low thinking processes typically associated with mindless approaches are less persistent, resistant to change, and predictive of behavior than attitudes changed via high thinking processes linked to mindfulness. This is because elaboration typically involves accessing relevant information from both external and internal sources, scrutinizing, making inferences, generating new arguments, and drawing new conclusions about the merits of the attitude object (Petty & Cacioppo, 1986). These mental activities involve people adding something of their own to the information available and are likely to lead to the integration of all relevant information into the underlying structure for the attitude object, therefore making the adopted evaluation not only stable, but also coherent and resistant. Thus, deliberative attitudes based on high amounts of thinking are *stronger* than attitudes based on little thought (see Petty, Haugtvedt, & Smith, 1995, for a review). The mental operations associated with elaborative thinking share a number of similarities with what has been proposed for mindful thinking. The components of mindful thinking of most relevance to the concept of elaboration include the tendency to think about alternatives, being open to new information, perceiving change, and the nonjudgment of one's thoughts.

First, mindfulness has been described as a tendency to think flexibly (Langer & Moldoveanu, 2000). In social psychology, similar tendencies have been examined in work on creativity and divergent thinking and in the proposed function of positive emotions (e.g., Fredrickson, 1998, 2001). Within the field of persuasion research, this tendency can relate to the thoughts that people have in response to a persuasive message and to the evaluative information used when reflecting on an attitude. Regarding message-evoked thoughts, *cognitive response theory* (Greenwald, 1968; Petty, Ostrom, & Brock, 1981) proposed that persuasion is driven by a person's own thoughts evoked by a persuasive message. This approach stood in contrast to the prior focus on the extent to which these messages were simply learned (see McGuire, 1985). According to the research derived from cognitive response theory, a person can have both thoughts relevant to and thoughts irrelevant to a persuasive communication. The relevant thoughts can also vary in the extent to which they are positive, negative, or neutral toward the message. Some research has even demonstrated that when people are directly asked to generate thoughts of a particular valence in a persuasion context, they can spontaneously generate *unrequested* thoughts of the opposite valence, which also inform resulting attitudes (Tormala, Falces, Briñol, & Petty, 2007). This phenomenon may be even more likely under conditions of mindfulness that facilitate flexible thinking. Clearly, there are many ways a person can think about a persuasive message, all of which have their own influence on the resulting attitudes.

Although this research has shed light on the extent to which a person can think in alternative directions to that intended in the persuasive appeal, when encountering a persuasive message, people may also think in alternative valence when considering the target of evaluation itself, in the absence of any attempts at persuasion. For example, when a person has both positive and negative reactions to an object, person, or idea, that individual is said to have an *ambivalent attitude* (for a review, see Conner & Armitage, 2008). Thus, ambivalence reflects endorsement of both positive and negative aspects of a particular topic, agreeing with both the benefits and detriments simultaneously. Ambivalence can also exist at a different level; a person's automatic evaluation of an object, obtained via an implicit measure, can conflict with the evaluation obtained on a more deliberative, explicit self-report measure. When this occurs, the person's attitude is characterized by *implicit ambivalence* (Petty & Briñol, 2009; Petty, Briñol, & Johnson, 2012; Petty, Tormala, Briñol, & Jarvis, 2006). Research on attitude strength has shown that highly ambivalent attitudes—whether explicit or implicit—are not as functional in guiding thoughts and behavior as relatively less ambivalent attitudes. Existing research has also shown that people find attitudinal ambivalence to be aversive and are thus motivated to reduce the evaluative conflict implied by competing positivity and negativity (Jonas, Diehl, & Brömer, 1997; Newby-Clark, McGregor, & Zanna, 2002; van Harreveld, van der Pligt, & de Liver, 2009).

Of most relevance here, a mindfulness approach can lead to a different conceptualization and response to ambivalent attitudes. On the one hand, with its promotion of more diverse thinking, mindfulness could provoke more frequent attitudinal ambivalence. Some research has shown that attitudes can be more mixed among people and cultures characterized by greater tendencies to think dialectically. Dialectical thinking refers to greater acceptance of contradiction in reasoning (for a review, see Spencer-Rodgers, Williams, & Peng, 2010). For example, Peng and Nisbett (1999) note that in dialectical thinking, "good and bad . . . coexist in everything" (p. 743). Such a tendency to think in this way has been related to the characteristics of mindful thought. Previous work has shown that those who tend to think more dialectically demonstrate greater ambivalence in their self-evaluations by generating and endorsing both positive and negative evaluations of themselves (Boucher, Peng, Shi, & Wang, 2009; Spencer-Rodgers, Peng, Wang, & Hou, 2004). They are also more likely to experience mixed emotions than those who tend to think less dialectically (Bagozzi, Wong, & Yi, 1999; Goetz, Spencer-Rodgers, & Peng, 2008; Shiota, Campos, Gonzaga, Keltner, & Peng, 2010; Spencer-Rodgers, Peng, & Wang, 2010).

In accord with this view, Langer (1994) notes that uncertainty, which often accompanies ambivalence (e.g., Jonas et al., 1997), promotes mindfulness and consideration of new information (see also Tiedens & Linton, 2001). Thus, when considering both positive and negative information about some topic mindfully, it may itself contribute to ambivalence in the objective sense (i.e., coexistence of both positive and negative reactions to a single object). Intriguingly, however, whereas mindfulness might increase the frequency of objectively ambivalent attitudes, it may also contribute to a reduction of the aversive subjective feeling that typically accompanies ambivalence. Because the notion that there is a single correct evaluation can be classified as a relatively mindless belief, perhaps it is primarily for people who hold this belief that the coexistence of positive and negative reactions to something will signal an actual conflict that must be resolved. For more mindful individuals, however, such evaluative uncertainty may provoke a search for more information, but perhaps more in the spirit of curiosity. Future research should explore the complex relationship between mindfulness and the presence of objective and subjective ambivalence, as well as the consequences for subsequent information processing.

Second, mindfulness has been characterized by openness to new information and by new ways of considering some object or issue. In fact, mindfulness scales have been found to correlate with the Openness to Experience Scale of the Big Five (Giluk, 2009). For instance, an important element of Bishop et al.'s (2004) two-component model of mindfulness is that of greater acceptance of each moment of experience. That is, someone who is being mindful is not trying to reach a particular conclusion or end-state and will thus entertain any new information or experiences as relevant. Such openness is also prominent in many other theoretical formulations of mindfulness (e.g., Brown & Ryan, 2003; Hölzel et al., 2011; Martin, 1997). Similarly, Chanowitz and Langer (1981) introduced the notion of "premature cognitive commitment," which is a tendency to adhere strictly to previously encountered information. They further suggested that such a tendency is particularly mindless because of the failure to reconsider beliefs and perceptions after they are initially formed. Under mindful states, however, preexisting cognitions may be more open to scrutiny and change (Langer, 1989; Langer & Moldoveanu, 2000). By its nature, the persuasive effects of a communication can depend on how open a person is to information that contradicts a currently held attitude. Several variables have been examined for their ability to affect a person's openness to, or willingness to process, counterattitudinal communication. These include an attitude's strength, personal motivations, self-affirmation, general individual differences in open- versus closed mindsets, and attitudes toward change, to name just few of the most relevant ones.

When a person's preexisting attitude is relatively weak, that attitude is more susceptible to change in response to persuasive appeals (Krosnick & Petty, 1995). For example, when people are relatively doubtful about an attitude or possess an attitude that is relatively ambivalent, they are more likely to process new information; thus, when a persuasive message contains arguments that are adequately strong, those with more doubtful or ambivalent attitudes are more persuaded by the message (Edwards, 2003; Jonas et al., 1997; Petty et al., 2006; Tiedens & Linton, 2001; Weary & Jacobson, 1997). Also, work on motivated reasoning has been applied to persuasion contexts, with people showing more openness to persuasive messages containing attitude-congruent arguments and less openness to persuasive messages containing attitude-incongruent arguments (Kunda, 1990).

A different body of literature has proposed that a persuasive message can represent a threat to a person's self-concept (Jacks & O'Brien, 2004). As such, giving people an opportunity to self-affirm (i.e., focusing them on personally important values) generally makes them more open to a counterattitudinal persuasive message (Cohen, Aronson, & Steele, 2000; see also Briñol, Petty, Gallardo & DeMarree, 2007; Jacks & O'Brien, 2004).

Finally, persuasion has been related to open- versus closed-mindedness motivations. In particular, the construct *need for cognitive closure*, occasionally related explicitly to open- versus closed-mindedness (e.g., Kruglanski, 2004), has been shown to affect openness to persuasion. The need for cognitive closure refers to a general motivation for firm conclusions rather than ambiguity (for reviews, see Kruglanski, 2004; Kruglanski & Fishman, 2009; Kruglanski & Webster, 1996). In particular, in some research, when people had a preexisting basis for an opinion, those operating under a high need for cognitive closure (either having scored high on a measure of dispositional need for closure or having been in a condition in which quick closure was valued) were less persuaded by a message than those operating under a low need for cognitive closure. In other words, the more closed-minded (high need for closure) people clung to the initial basis for an opinion (similar to "premature cognitive commitment") and resisted new information, whereas the more open-minded (low need for closure) people were more open to new information and did not cling as strongly to their initial opinions. Thus, just as research on mindfulness has highlighted the importance of "openness" in understanding how people engage with their experiences, so too does attitudes and persuasion research highlight the role that a state of openness plays in approaching persuasive messages.

Third, mindfulness has been described in relation to perceptions of impermanence. That is, having drawn from Buddhist notions that a permanent, static self is the source of psychological distress (e.g., Olendzki, 2010), some have suggested that a state of mindfulness can facilitate a shift in how the self is perceived toward flexibility (Hölzel et al., 2011). Some social psychology research has examined a related distinction between perceptions of the self as changeable versus more permanent, separating people with "entity" theories, which suggest current attributes will remain relatively permanent over time, from people who hold "incremental" theories, which suggest that current attributes are open to change and improvement (Dweck, Chiu, & Hong, 1995). Work more closely relevant to attitudes and persuasion has also considered these perceptions of changeability. For instance, people can vary in how much stability they perceive in their attitudes, with some perceiving an attitude as being relatively more stable over time than others (Petrocelli, Clarkson, Tormala, & Hendrix, 2010). Other work has shown that people also differ in the extent to which they perceive themselves as generally resisting (vs. being persuaded by) persuasive communications, implying variability in how permanent they perceive their attitudes to be (Briñol, Rucker, Tormala, & Petty, 2004). In fact, people can apply different beliefs to persuasion resistance, believing in some cases that resistance (and thus strong attitude consistency over time) is good and in other cases that resistance is bad, relating perhaps to more general implicit theories regarding the changeability of one's attitudes (Rydell, Hugenberg, & McConnell, 2006). It is important to note, however, that *perceptions* of change are often independent of actual change. Indeed, it is clear that people often make errors in assessing whether they have changed or not (Bem & McConnell, 1970; Goethals & Cooper, 1975; see Briñol & Petty, 2012, for a review). In a programmatic line of studies, Schryer and Ross (2012) have shown that people can fail to recognize change in either their attitudes or themselves, even when there actually has been change. In fact, they also show that people can see some change when there actually has been none.

Finally, mindfulness is often described as encompassing the nonjudgment of thoughts. Not only is it a key component in one of the most often cited definitions of mindfulness ("paying attention in a particular way: on purpose, in the present moment, and non-judgmentally"; Kabat-Zinn, 1994, p. 4), but it also plays a role in many other accounts of mindfulness (Bishop et al., 2004; Gethin, 2011; Shapiro et al., 2005; cf. Dreyfus, 2011). In psychology, this can be related to therapy approaches that emphasize metacognitive techniques, such as the metacognitive therapy proposed by Adrian Wells (2012). In persuasion research, the importance of *metacognition* has also been shown. As previously noted, persuasive messages can evoke a variety of thoughts, and importantly, these thoughts can themselves be evaluated. This highlights the distinction between *primary cognitions* and *secondary cognitions*, or between cognition and metacognition (Briñol & DeMarree, 2012; Petty, Briñol, Tormala, & Wegener, 2007).

Primary cognitions refer to the initial thoughts themselves, whereas secondary cognitions involve judgments and evaluations of the primary cognitions. These secondary cognitions can take many forms that influence the persuasion process. In particular, thoughts (or "primary cognitions") can be judged on their perceived valence, on how many there seem to be, on their perceived target (i.e., what the thoughts are about), on where they seemed to come from, on how confidently they can be held, and on how desirable they are, each exerting effects on the persuasion process (Petty et al., 2007; Wagner, Briñol, & Petty, 2012). Although there are a number of judgments that people can make about their thoughts, most persuasion research has focused on one particular metacognitive factor—the confidence people have in their thoughts. Confidence in thoughts is important because as thoughts are held with greater confidence, people are more likely to use those thoughts in forming their attitudes and other judgments (Petty, Briñol, & Tormala, 2002). In contrast, when people doubt the validity of their thoughts, their thoughts are less likely to have an impact on judgments.

Although this research has uncovered the many ways in which people feel and think about their own thoughts, mindfulness is characterized by the *nonjudgment* of thoughts. Linking the distinction between primary and secondary cognitions to mindfulness, Bishop et al. (2004) write that a state of mindfulness is said to "*inhibit secondary elaborative processing* of the thoughts, feelings, and sensations that arise in the stream of consciousness" (p. 233). Relatedly, some proponents of mindfulness-based therapies have suggested that thoughts can be treated as material objects (Brown, Ryan, & Creswell, 2007). This allows clients to separate themselves from their thoughts by treating those thoughts more objectively. In a recent series of studies testing the application of this approach to attitudes, Briñol, Gascó, Petty, and Horcajo (2013) asked people to write down either positive or negative thoughts about Mediterranean diets. Upon doing so, they were randomly assigned to one of three conditions. In one, they were asked to take the page on which they wrote their thoughts and place it in a trash can, "throwing away" their thoughts. In the other condition, they were asked to take the page on which they wrote their thoughts, fold it up, and keep it in a safe place such as their pocket, wallet, or purse. In the third, control condition, participants were asked to merely fold the corners of the page where the thoughts were written and leave it on the table. After performing one of these actions, all participants were then asked to rate their attitudes regarding the Mediterranean diet. As expected, results indicate that when people in the control condition were asked to generate positive (vs. negative) thoughts about the topic, they later reported more positive (vs. negative) attitudes. How thoughts were treated (as if they were material objects), however, had a significant impact on how those thoughts influenced attitudes. For people who kept their written thoughts close to them, those thoughts had a more pronounced effect on attitudes than in the control condition. In contrast, for people who placed their written thoughts in the trash, the effect of the thoughts on attitudes was attenuated compared to the control group.

Consistent with the idea that mindfulness treatments promote a more objective and distant relationship with people's own thoughts (e.g., Brown et al., 2007), this research showed that detaching and separating (in this case, literally) from one's negative thoughts can produce more positive evaluations. Importantly, the very same treatment (thought disposal) produced the opposite effect when thoughts were positive. This finding suggests that techniques involved in some mindfulness treatments can backfire at least for some people and for some situations, particularly those in which positive thoughts are present. The research by Briñol and colleagues (2013) also suggests a new, simple strategy for magnifying thought impact by having people develop a closer relationship with their positive thoughts (e.g., carrying them).

It seems obvious from these results that it is important to know which specific processes are responsible for the reported effectiveness of clinically relevant mindfulness treatments. It is also important to consider that mindfulness researchers have proposed that merely distancing oneself from thoughts may not always be mindful. Rather, there can be a difference between distancing the self from one's thoughts and disconnecting oneself from one's thoughts (Shapiro et al., 2005). Further research is needed to address this distinction in the treatment of one's thoughts and the effects it can have on resulting attitudes.

Elaboration Likelihood Model of Persuasion (ELM)

As noted earlier, the available literature has suggested that attitudes are sometimes changed by relatively low thought mechanisms, but at other times they are changed with a great deal of thinking. Sometimes the thinking is relatively mindless, and sometimes it is more mindful. Notably, the accumulated research on persuasion shows that sometimes variables such as using an attractive source or putting people in a good mood have a positive effect on persuasion, but sometimes the effect is negative. In order to understand these complexities, contemporary multiprocess theories of persuasion were developed. As anticipated earlier, we use one of these theories—the ELM—to organize the literature.

The ELM (Petty & Cacioppo, 1986) was developed in an attempt to integrate the literature on persuasion by proposing that there are a finite set of processes by which variables can affect attitudes and that these processes require different amounts of thought. Thoughtful persuasion was referred to as following the *central route*, whereas low-thought persuasion was said to follow the *peripheral route*. A common finding in research guided by the ELM is that when people are motivated and able to think about a message, their attitudes are influenced by their assessment of the merits of the appeal, but when they are relatively unmotivated to think, attitudes are influenced by simple cues in the persuasion setting (see Petty & Wegener, 1999; Petty & Briñol, 2012, for reviews).

The ELM is an early example of what became an explosion of dual process and dual system theories that distinguished thoughtful from nonthoughtful persuasion (see Chaiken & Trope, 1999; Sherman, Gawronski, & Trope, in press).[1] According to the ELM, the extent of thinking is important not only because it determines the route to persuasion and the process by which a variable affects attitudes, but also because more thoughtful persuasion tends to be more consequential. Specifically, attitudes changed with high thought tend to be more persistent over time, resistant to change, and predictive of behavior than attitudes changed by low thought processes (Petty, Haugtvedt, & Smith, 1995).

In the remainder of this section, we outline the ways in which the ELM specifies that a variable relevant to mindfulness (our own body) can affect the extent of persuasion. We will review some of the main roles our body can serve in the persuasion process, including (1) serving as simple cues to the merits of a proposal, (2) affecting the direction of the thinking, (3) affecting the amount of thinking that takes place, and (4) affecting evaluations of the thoughts generated.

Body Awareness and Persuasion

One effect of mindfulness that has not yet been discussed is the association between mindfulness and body awareness. Hölzel et al. (2011) proposed that mindfulness can increase one's body awareness (i.e., the ability to notice one's own bodily sensations), noting, for example, that several items in the Five Facet Mindfulness Questionnaire (Baer, Smith, Hopkins, Krietemeyer, & Toney, 2006) are directly related to the experience of body awareness. Not only do people who practice mindfulness meditation report a change in their awareness of bodily sensations (Hölzel, Ott, Hempel, & Stark, 2006, as cited in Hölzel et al., 2011), but some recent neuroscience evidence implies a relationship between mindfulness and neural regions previously associated with interoception (insula) and other bodily sensations (secondary somatosensory cortex; Farb et al., 2010; Gard et al., 2011; Grant, Courtemanche, Duerden, Duncan, & Rainville, 2010). Although this evidence is only suggestive, it supports the proposed mindfulness–body awareness link, making bodily awareness an interesting component of mindfulness that warrants attention and one that can extend to other areas of research as well.

Within the realm of attitudes and persuasion, a substantial amount of research has considered the role that the bodily responses of the recipient of persuasion play in forming and modifying attitudes. Specifically, the posture, movement, and actions of one's body can influence both the way in which the person processes persuasive communications and the resulting attitudes. These processes have been referred to as *embodied persuasion* (Briñol & Petty, 2008). An early example of this work revealed that when individuals were asked to move their heads up and down (supposedly in order to test the quality of headphones) while listening to a persuasive message, they became more favorable toward the topic of the message than individuals who were asked to move their heads from side to side (simulating the movements associated with shaking "no") while listening to the same message (Wells & Petty, 1980). Just as we like things better when nodding (vs. shaking) our heads, when we smile or approach something, we tend to have more positive attitudes than when we frown or perform an avoidant behavior. Thus, making smiling expressions or moving things toward us can produce more favorable attitudes (e.g., Cacioppo, Priester, & Berntson, 1993). Similar findings have been found for a large number of behaviors, postures, and body movements.

These effects of embodied persuasion can be understood both through a more traditional mindfulness framework and through the ELM. Consideration of each approach should stimulate theory when it comes to understanding how one's body can impact attitudes. The mindfulness framework might predict that the impact of body manipulations such as the direction of one's head movements would depend on a person's body awareness, which increases with mindfulness experience. It is important to know that mindfulness theory has suggested that a radical mind–body dualism is a relatively mindless notion and that a more mindful approach is to consider the two concepts as more closely integrated with a reciprocal influence between processes traditionally defined as "body" (i.e., embodied) and "mind" (i.e., cognition; see Langer, 1992). Consistent with an integrated mind–body approach, some research on emotion has demonstrated that embodiment effects are moderated by individual differences in body awareness (for an extensive review on individual differences in persuasion, see Briñol & Petty, 2005).

In relevant work, Laird and Bresler (1992) have reported that people differ consistently and stably in how large an impact a bodily state will have on a variety of cognitive processes (including metacognitive processes) relevant to attitude change. These differences were first identified in research on emotion. In a series of studies, they found that when people were induced to engage in emotional behaviors, some reported feeling the corresponding emotions, whereas other people were unaffected by their behaviors. These differences in the extent to which the body affected the experience of emotion have been found in people's response to manipulations of their facial expressions, postures, tone of voice, patterns of gaze, and level of autonomic arousal. Furthermore, these individual differences have been related to a number of psychological constructs, such as field independence and private self-consciousness, and to other factors, such as body weight (e.g., Duclos & Laird, 2001; Schnall & Laird, 2003). For example, inducing an internal state of disgust (vs. control) led people to make more severe moral judgments, but this effect held only for those who reported to be relatively more sensitive to their own bodily responses (Schnall, Haidt, Clore, & Jordan, 2008). Future research should further clarify whether participants with greater awareness of their bodily responses felt more disgust or if they experienced the same level of the emotion but used it to a greater extent to inform their moral judgments.

Taken together, these studies suggest that body awareness can increase the effects of body responses on judgment. However, it is important to note that body awareness could also lead to decreased effects of bodily postures and movements on some occasions. For example, when thinking carefully, people can be influenced by their own bodily information such as smiling when rating how good they look that day. In those cases, greater sensitivity to one's body can increase its subsequent impact on judgment. However, if people believe that their judgments are somehow being biased or influenced by their bodily feelings, and they do not want this to occur, they may adjust their judgments in a direction opposite to the expected bias (*correction processes*; Wegener & Petty, 1997). In these cases, greater sensitivity to the body might reduce its impact on judgment. Similar to research on priming showing that sensitivity to external inductions can increase or decrease its impact on judgment (Lombardi, Higgins, & Bargh, 1987; Petty, DeMarree, Briñol, Horcajo, & Strathman, 2008), future research should examine the conditions in which body awareness increases or decreases embodied persuasion.

The effects of embodiment on attitudes can also be understood through the ELM, identifying how one's body can influence persuasion at various levels of elaboration. According to the ELM, when people are at a low level of elaboration (i.e., under low thinking conditions), signals from one's body can serve as simple cues that can be associated with an object of evaluation. For instance, when people viewed a neutral image (i.e., a Chinese ideograph), whether they were pulling up on a table versus pushing down on a table affected attitudes toward the image such that those who were pulling their arms toward themselves had more positive attitudes than those who were pushing away (Cacioppo et al., 1993). In another illustration, Strack, Martin, and Stepper (1988) had individuals hold a pen either between their teeth or between their lips, activating or inhibiting facial muscles usually associated with smiling. Their results demonstrated that those who activated smiling muscles judged cartoons as more humorous than those who inhibited smiling muscles. These results often have been interpreted as the result of classical conditioning. Aside from using mere associations with arm flexion, smiling, or head nodding, people can also rely on simple heuristics about their bodily states when forming or changing attitudes (e.g., if my heart is beating fast, I must like this object; Valins, 1966). Thus, the body can serve as a simple cue to persuasion when motivation and ability to think are low.

When elaboration is not constrained, bodily sensations can affect how much a person thinks about a persuasive message. One such bodily state relates to posture. In an early study, for instance, people showed greater processing of an audio message when they were lying down (powerless posture) versus standing up (powerful posture; Petty, Wells, Heesacker, Brock, & Cacioppo, 1983). Other research also found that posture affects thinking such that people in an upright posture (vs. slumped over) spend more time pursuing cognitive tasks (Riskind & Gotay, 1982). Consistent with the idea that posture can affect thinking, another recent study showed that participants holding a heavy clipboard (a body sensation metaphorically associated with effort) were differentially persuaded by the strength of the message arguments (i.e., suggesting that they paid careful attention to the message), whereas those holding a lighter clipboard were not (Jostmann, Lakens, & Schubert, 2009).

Under conditions of high elaboration, body responses can bias the valence of a person's thoughts in response to a message. For instance, when people are asked to categorize words as good or bad, they are quicker to categorize positive words as good while enacting an "approach" motion (e.g., flexing one's arm or pulling a lever towards oneself) and quicker to categorize negative words as bad while enacting an "avoidance" motion (e.g., extending one's arm or pushing a lever away from oneself; Chen & Bargh, 1999; Neumann & Strack, 2000). Thus, this research suggests that when a person is engaged in thinking, their bodily movements can facilitate the generation of thoughts in a particular direction, a phenomenon likely to be of great consequence in persuasion domains wherein thoughts of a particular valence are strongly linked with resulting attitudes (Petty et al., 1981).

Finally, a person's body can affect attitudes not only by biasing the content of primary cognitions but also by affecting the evaluations of those thoughts. That is, bodily responses can influence secondary cognitions as well as primary cognitions. In particular, body movements and posture can affect reliance on thoughts through a self-validation process. In the first series of studies on embodied validation, Briñol and

Petty (2003) found that head movements could affect the confidence people had in their thoughts and thereby have an impact on attitudes. Specifically, when people listened through headphones to strong arguments advocating that students be required to carry personal identification cards on campus, vertical head movements led to more favorable attitudes than horizontal movements, as would be expected if vertical movements increased confidence in one's favorable thoughts. However, when people listened to weak arguments in favor of the identification cards, vertical movements led to less favorable attitudes than horizontal movements, as would be expected if vertical movements increased confidence in one's negative thoughts.

Similar validation effects have been shown for other embodiment variables like body posture such that sitting in a more confident posture (sitting up straight) as opposed to sitting in a more doubtful posture (sitting slouched forward) led to greater thought confidence and subsequently more thought-consistent attitudes (Briñol, Petty, & Wagner, 2009). As noted, body movement and postures can operate through multiple processes, including affecting thinking. Therefore, it is important to specify the conditions under which the body is likely to operate through these primary cognitive processes or though more metacognitive processes such as self-validation. One of the moderating conditions identified so far is the timing of the bodily induction. That is, the confidence that emerges from the body should be salient *following* (or at least during) thought generation rather than prior to thought generation.

In research illustrating this aspect (Paredes, Stavraki, Briñol, & Petty, 2013), participants were first exposed to a story that elicited mostly positive thoughts (about an employee's good day at work) or negative thoughts (about an employee's bad day at work). After writing their thoughts, participants were asked to hold a pen with their teeth (smile) or with their lips (control). Finally, all participants reported the extent to which they liked the story. In line with previous work showing that happiness can validate thoughts (Briñol, Petty, & Barden, 2007), it was predicted and found that the thoughts participants generated affected evaluations of the story only among those in the smiling condition. It is important to emphasize that the induction of smiling in this study followed (rather than preceded) the processing of the story, making it unlikely that the thoughts generated in response to the stories were affected by something that did not take place until later. Indeed, bodily responses are more likely to operate through a self-validation process when induced after (vs. before) thinking (see Briñol, Petty, & Wagner, 2012, for a review on embodied validation).

In sum, at each level of elaboration, a person's bodily movements, sensations, and responses can play a unique role in the attitude-change process. Given the relationships between mindfulness and body awareness that have been proposed, the means by which the body can affect evaluations should be of interest to mindfulness researchers, especially because of evidence that suggests the effects of embodiment are strongest among people most attentive to their own bodies. Presumably, if mindfulness does indeed foster greater body awareness, with increased mindfulness, there may also be an increased influence of one's body on attitudes and persuasion processes. Further research, however, is necessary to establish whether or not this is the case.

In conclusion, we have seen how the body can influence attitudes by serving as a simple cue, by affecting either the amount or direction of thinking, and by affecting what people think about their own thoughts (i.e., metacognition). Consistent with the ELM, these psychological processes relevant to embodied attitude change operate at different points along an elaboration continuum. Under low thinking conditions, bodily responses, like other variables (e.g., source attractiveness), can influence attitudes via a variety of low-effort processes. When the likelihood of thinking is relatively high, these same bodily responses can impact persuasion by affecting the direction of the thoughts that come to mind or the validation of those thoughts. Furthermore, body postures and actions can influence attitudes by affecting the amount of thinking when elaboration is not constrained to be very low or high. As should be clear by now, understanding these processes is essential in order to predict *whether*, *when*, and *how* attitudes will change, as well as to predict whether, when, and how attitudes will result in further behavioral changes.

Note

1. See the *unimodel* by Kruglanski and Thompson (1999), for a "single-process" approach to understanding high versus low thought persuasion; and see Petty, Wheeler, and Bizer (1999) and Petty & Briñol (2006), for discussions.

References

Baer, R. A., Smith, G. T., Hopkins, J., Krietemeyer, J., & Toney, L. (2006). Using self-report assessment methods to explore facets of mindfulness. *Assessment*, *13*(1), 27–45. doi:10.1177/1073191105283504

Bagozzi, R. P., Wong, N., & Yi, Y. (1999). The role of culture and gender in the relationship between positive and negative affect. *Cognition & Emotion*, *13*(6), 641–672. doi:10.1080/026999399379023

Bem, D. J., & McConnell, H. K. (1970). Testing the self-perception explanation of dissonance phenomena: on the salience of premanipulation attitudes. *Journal of Personality and Social Psychology*, *14*(1), 23.

Bishop, S. R., Lau, M., Shapiro, S., Carlson, L., Anderson, N. D., Carmody, J., . . . Devins, G. (2004). Mindfulness: A proposed operational definition. *Clinical Psychology: Science and Practice*, *11*(3), 230–241. doi:10.1093/clipsy.bph077

Boucher, H. C., Peng, K., Shi, J., & Wang, L. (2009). Culture and implicit self-esteem: Chinese are "good" and "bad" at the same time. *Journal of Cross-Cultural Psychology*, *40*(1), 24–45. doi:10.1177/0022022108326195.

Briñol, P., & DeMarree, K. G. (2012). Social metacognition: Thinking about thinking in social psychology. In P. Briñol & K. G. DeMarree (Eds.), *Social metacognition* (pp. 141–158). New York, NY: Psychology Press.

Briñol, P., Gascó, M., Petty, R. E., & Horcajo, J. (2013). Treating thoughts as material objects can increase or decrease their impact on evaluation. *Psychological Science*, *24*(1), 41–47. doi:10.1177/0956797612449176

Briñol, P., & Petty, R. E. (2003). Overt head movements and persuasion: A self-validation analysis. *Journal of Personality and Social Psychology*, *84*(6), 1123–1139. doi:10.1037/0022-3514.84.6.1123

Briñol, P., & Petty, R. E. (2005). Individual differences in attitude change. In D. Albarracín, B. T. Johnson, & M. P. Zanna (Eds.), *The handbook of attitudes and attitude change* (pp. 575–615). Mahwah, NJ: Erlbaum.

Briñol, P., & Petty, R. E. (2008). Embodied persuasion: Fundamental processes by which bodily responses can impact attitudes. In G. R. Semin & E. R. Smith (Eds.), *Embodied grounding: Social, cognitive, affective, and neuroscientific approaches* (pp. 184–207). Cambridge, UK: Cambridge University Press.

Briñol, P., & Petty, R. E. (2012). Knowing our attitudes and how to change them. In S. Vazire & T. D. Wilson (Eds.), *Handbook of self-knowledge* (pp. 157–180). New York, NY: Psychology Press.

Briñol, P., Petty, R. E., & Barden, J. (2007). Happiness versus sadness as a determinant of thought confidence in persuasion: A self-validation analysis. *Journal of Personality and Social Psychology, 93,* 711–727.

Briñol, P., Petty, R. E., & Wagner, B. (2009). Body posture effects on self-evaluation: A self-validation approach. *European Journal of Social Psychology, 39*(6), 1053–1064. doi:10.1002/ejsp.607

Briñol, P., Petty, R. E., & Wagner, B. (2012). Embodied validation: Our body can change and also validate our thoughts. In P. Briñol & K. G. DeMarree (Eds.), *Social metacognition* (pp. 141–158). New York, NY: Psychology Press.

Briñol, P., Petty, R. E., Gallardo, I., & DeMarree, K. G. (2007). The effect of self-affirmation in non-threatening persuasion domains: Timing affects the process. *Personality and Social Psychology Bulletin, 33,* 1533–1546.

Briñol, P., Rucker, D. D., Tormala, Z. L., & Petty, R. E. (2004). Individual differences in resistance to persuasion: The role of beliefs and meta-beliefs. In E. S. Knowles & J. A. Linn (Eds.), *Resistance and persuasion* (pp. 83–104). Mahwah, NJ: Lawrence Erlbaum Associates.

Brown, K. W., & Ryan, R. M. (2003). The benefits of being present: Mindfulness and its role in psychological well-being. *Journal of Personality and Social Psychology, 84*(4), 822–848. doi:10.1037/0022-3514.84.4.822

Brown, K. W., Ryan, R. M., & Creswell, J. D. (2007). Mindfulness: Theoretical foundations and evidence for its salutary effects. *Psychological Inquiry, 18*(4), 211–237. doi:10.1080/10478400701598298

Burger, J. M. (1999). The Foot-in-the-Door compliance procedure: A multiple-process analysis and review. *Personality and Social Psychology Review, 3*(4), 303–325. doi:10.1207/s15327957pspr0304_2

Cacioppo, J. T., Priester, J. R., & Berntson, G. G. (1993). Rudimentary determinants of attitudes: II. Arm flexion and extension have differential effects on attitudes. *Journal of Personality and Social Psychology, 65*(1), 5–17. doi:10.1037/0022-3514.65.1.5

Chaiken, S. (1980). Heuristic versus systematic information processing and the use of source versus message cues in persuasion. *Journal of Personality and Social Psychology, 39*(5), 752–766. doi:10.1037/0022-3514.39.5.752

Chaiken, S., Liberman, A., & Eagly, A. H. (1989). Heuristic and systematic processing within and beyond the persuasion context. In J. S. Uleman & J. A. Bargh (Eds.), *Unintended thought* (pp. 212–252). New York, NY: Guilford Press.

Chaiken, S., & Trope, Y. (Eds.). (1999). *Dual process theories in social psychology.* New York, NY: Guilford Press.

Chanowitz, B., & Langer, E. J. (1981). Premature cognitive commitment. *Journal of Personality and Social Psychology, 41*(6), 1051–1063. doi:10.1037/0022-3514.41.6.1051

Chen, M., & Bargh, J. A. (1999). Consequences of automatic evaluation: Immediate behavioral predispositions to approach or avoid the stimulus. *Personality and Social Psychology Bulletin, 25*(2), 215–224. doi:10.1177/0146167299025002007

Cialdini, R. B. (2001). *Influence: Science and practice* (4th ed.). Boston, MA: Allyn & Bacon.

Cialdini, R. B., Vincent, J. E., Lewis, S. K., Catalan, J., Wheeler, D., & Darby, B. L. (1975). Reciprocal concessions procedure for inducing compliance: The door-in-the-face technique. *Journal of Personality and Social Psychology, 31*(2), 206–215. doi:10.1037/h0076284

Cohen, G. L., Aronson, J., & Steele, C. M. (2000). When beliefs yield to evidence: Reducing biased evaluation by affirming the self. *Personality and Social Psychology Bulletin, 26*(9), 1151–1164. doi:10.1177/01461672002611011

Conner, M., & Armitage, C. J. (2008). Attitudinal ambivalence. In W. D. Crano & R. Prislin (Eds.), *Attitudes and attitude change* (pp. 261–286). New York, NY: Psychology Press.

Dolinski, D., & Nawrat, R. (1998). "Fear-then-relief" procedure for producing compliance: Beware when the danger is over. *Journal of Experimental Social Psychology, 34*(1), 27–50. doi:10.1006/jesp.1997.1341

Dreyfus, G. (2011). Is mindfulness present-centred and non-judgmental? A discussion of the cognitive dimensions of mindfulness. *Contemporary Buddhism, 12*(1), 41–54. doi:10.1080/14639947.2011.564815

Duclos, S. E., & Laird, J. D. (2001). The deliberate control of emotional experience through control of expressions. *Cognition & Emotion, 15*(1), 27–56. doi:10.1080/02699930126057

Dweck, C. S., Chiu, C.-y., & Hong, Y.-y. (1995). Implicit theories and their role in judgments and reactions: A world from two perspectives. *Psychological Inquiry, 6*(4), 267–285. doi:10.1207/s15327965pli0604_1

Edwards, J. A. (2003). The interactive effects of processing preference and motivation on information processing: Causal uncertainty and the MBTI in a persuasion context. *Journal of Research in Personality, 37*(2), 89–99. doi:10.1016/s0092-6566(02)00537-8

Farb, N. A. S., Anderson, A. K., Mayberg, H., Bean, J., McKeon, D., & Segal, Z. V. (2010). Minding one's emotions: Mindfulness training alters the neural expression of sadness. *Emotion, 10*(1), 25–33. doi:10.1037/a0017151

Fennis, B., & Janssen, L. (2010). Mindlessness revisited: Sequential request techniques foster compliance by draining self-control resources. *Current Psychology, 29*(3), 235–246. doi:10.1007/s12144-010-9082-x

Fredrickson, B. L. (1998). What good are positive emotions? *Review of General Psychology, 2*(3), 300–319. doi:10.1037/1089-2680.2.3.300

Fredrickson, B. L. (2001). The role of positive emotions in positive psychology: The broaden-and-build theory of positive emotions. *American Psychologist, 56*(3), 218–226. doi:10.1037/0003-066x.56.3.218

Gard, T., Hölzel, B. K., Sack, A. T., Hempel, H., Lazar, S. W., Vaitl, D., & Ott, U. (2011). Pain attenuation through mindfulness is associated with decreased cognitive control and increased sensory processing in the brain. *Cerebral Cortex, 22*(11), 2692–2702. doi:10.1093/cercor/bhr352

Gethin, R. (2011). On some definitions of mindfulness. *Contemporary Buddhism, 12*(1), 263–279. doi:10.1080/14639947.2011.564843

Giluk, T. L. (2009). Mindfulness, Big Five personality, and affect: A meta-analysis. *Personality and Individual Differences, 47*(8), 805–811. doi:http://dx.doi.org/10.1016/j.paid.2009.06.026

Goethals, G. R., & Cooper, J. (1975). When dissonance is reduced: The timing of self-justificatory attitude change. *Journal of Personality and Social Psychology, 32*(2), 361–367. doi:10.1037/0022-3514.32.2.361

Goetz, J., Spencer-Rodgers, J., & Peng, K. (2008). Dialectical emotions: How cultural epistemologies influence the experience and regulation of emotional complexity. In R. M.

Sorrentino & S. Yamaguchi (Eds.), *Handbook of motivation and cognition across cultures* (pp. 517–538). New York, NY: Elsevier.

Grant, J. A., Courtemanche, J., Duerden, E. G., Duncan, G. H., & Rainville, P. (2010). Cortical thickness and pain sensitivity in Zen meditators. *Emotion, 10*(1), 43–53. doi:10.1037/a0018334

Greenwald, A. G. (1968). Cognitive learning, cognitive response to persuasion, and attitude change. In A. G. Greenwald, T. C. Brock, & T. M. Ostrom (Eds.), *Psychological foundations of attitudes* (pp. 147–170). New York, NY: Academic Press.

Hölzel, B. K., Lazar, S. W., Gard, T., Schuman-Olivier, Z., Vago, D. R., & Ott, U. (2011). How does mindfulness meditation work? Proposing mechanisms of action from a conceptual and neural perspective. *Perspectives on Psychological Science, 6*(6), 537–559. doi:10.1177/1745691611419671

Hölzel, B. K., Ott, U., Hempel, H., & Stark, R. (2006). *Wie wirkt Achtsamkeit? Eine Interviewstudie mit erfahrenen Meditierenden (How does mindfulness work? An interview study with experienced meditators).* Paper presented at the 24th Symposium of the Section for Clinical Psychology and Psychotherapy of the German Society for Psychology, Würzburg, Germany.

Jacks, J. Z., & O'Brien, M. E. (2004). Decreasing resistance by affirming the self. In E. D. Knowles & J. A. Linn (Eds.), *Resistance and persuasion* (pp. 235–257). Mahwah, NJ: Lawrence Erlbaum.

Jonas, K., Diehl, M., & Brömer, P. (1997). Effects of attitudinal ambivalence on information processing and attitude-intention consistency. *Journal of Experimental Social Psychology, 33*(2), 190–210. doi:10.1006/jesp.1996.1317

Jostmann, N. B., Lakens, D., & Schubert, T. W. (2009). Weight as an embodiment of importance. *Psychological Science, 20*(9), 1169–1174. doi:10.1111/j.1467-9280.2009.02426.x

Kabat-Zinn, J. (1994). *Wherever you go, there you are: Mindfulness meditation in everyday life.* New York, NY: Hyperion.

Kabat-Zinn, J. (2003). Mindfulness-based interventions in context: Past, present, and future. *Clinical Psychology: Science and Practice, 10*(2), 144–156. doi:10.1093/clipsy.bpg016

Krosnick, J. A., & Petty, R. E. (1995). Attitude strength: An overview. In R. E. Petty & J. A. Krosnick (Eds.), *Attitude strength: Antecedents and consequences* (pp. 1–24). Hillsdale, NJ: Lawrence Erlbaum Associates.

Kruglanski, A. W. (2004). *The psychology of closed mindedness.* New York, NY: Psychology Press.

Kruglanski, A. W., & Fishman, S. (2009). The need for cognitive closure. In M. R. Leary & R. H. Hoyle (Eds.), *Handbook of individual differences in social behavior* (pp. 343–353). New York, NY: Guilford Press.

Kruglanski, A. W., & Thompson, E. P. (1999). Persuasion by a single route: A view from the unimodel. *Psychological Inquiry, 10,* 83–109.

Kruglanski, A. W., & Webster, D. M. (1996). Motivated closing of the mind: "Seizing" and "freezing." *Psychological Review, 103*(2), 263–283. doi:10.1037/0033-295x.103.2.263

Kunda, Z. (1990). The case for motivated reasoning. *Psychological Bulletin, 108*(3), 480–498. doi:10.1037/0033-2909.108.3.480

Laird, J. D., & Bresler, C. (1992). The process of emotional experience: A self-perception theory. In M. S. Clark (Ed.), *Emotion* (pp. 213–234). Thousand Oaks, CA: Sage Publications.

Langer, E. J. (1989). Minding matters: The consequences of mindlessness–mindfulness. In L. Berkowitz (Ed.), *Advances in experimental social psychology* (Vol. 22, pp. 137–173). San Diego, CA: Academic Press.

Langer, E. J. (1992). Matters of mind: Mindfulness/mindlessness in perspective. *Consciousness and Cognition, 1*(3), 289–305. doi:http://dx.doi.org/10.1016/1053-8100(92)90066-J

Langer, E. J. (1994). The illusion of calculated decisions. In R. C. Schank & E. J. Langer (Eds.), *Beliefs, reasoning, and decision making: Psycho-logic in honor of Bob Abelson* (pp. 33–53). Hillsdale, NJ: Lawrence Erlbaum Associates.

Langer, E. J., Blank, A., & Chanowitz, B. (1978). The mindlessness of ostensibly thoughtful action: The role of "placebic" information in interpersonal interaction. *Journal of Personality and Social Psychology, 36*(6), 635–642. doi:10.1037/0022-3514.36.6.635

Langer, E. J., & Moldoveanu, M. (2000). The construct of mindfulness. *Journal of Social Issues, 56*(1), 1–9. doi:10.1111/0022-4537.00148

Lombardi, W. J., Higgins, E. T., & Bargh, J. A. (1987). The role of consciousness in priming effects on categorization: Assimilation versus contrast as a function of awareness of the priming task. *Personality and Social Psychology Bulletin, 13*(3), 411–429. doi:10.1177/0146167287133009

Lynn, M. (1991). Scarcity effects on desirability: A quantitative review of the commodity theory literature. *Psychology and Marketing, 8,* 43–57.

Martin, J. R. (1997). Mindfulness: A proposed common factor. *Journal of Psychotherapy Integration, 7*(4), 291–312. doi:10.1023/B:JOPI.0000010885.18025.bc

McGuire, W. J. (1985). Attitudes and attitude change. *Handbook of Social Psychology, 2*(3), 233–346.

Neumann, R., & Strack, F. (2000). Approach and avoidance: The influence of proprioceptive and exteroceptive cues on encoding of affective information. *Journal of Personality and Social Psychology, 79*(1), 39–48. doi:10.1037/0022-3514.79.1.39

Newby-Clark, I. R., McGregor, I., & Zanna, M. P. (2002). Thinking and caring about cognitive inconsistency: When and for whom does attitudinal ambivalence feel uncomfortable? *Journal of Personality and Social Psychology, 82*(2), 157–166. doi:10.1037/0022-3514.82.2.157

Olendzki, A. (2010). *Unlimiting mind: The radically experiential psychology of Buddhism.* Boston, MA: Wisdom Publications.

Paredes, B., Stavraki, M., Briñol, P., & Petty, R. E. (2013). Smiling after thinking increases reliance on thoughts. *Social Psychology, 44*(5), 349–353. doi:10.1027/1864-9335/a000131

Peng, K., & Nisbett, R. E. (1999). Culture, dialectics, and reasoning about contradiction. *American Psychologist, 54*(9), 741–754. doi:10.1037/0003-066x.54.9.741

Petrocelli, J. V., Clarkson, J. J., Tormala, Z. L., & Hendrix, K. S. (2010). Perceiving stability as a means to attitude certainty: The role of implicit theories of attitudes. *Journal of Experimental Social Psychology, 46*(6), 874–883. doi:10.1016/j.jesp.2010.07.012

Petty, R. E., & Briñol, P. (2006). Understanding social judgment: Multiple systems and processes. *Psychological Inquiry, 17,* 217–223.

Petty, R. E., & Briñol, P. (2009). Implicit ambivalence: A meta-cognitive approach. In R. E. Petty, R. H. Fazio, & P. Briñol (Eds.), *Attitudes: Insights from the new implicit measures* (pp. 119–161). New York, NY: Psychology Press.

Petty, R. E., & Briñol, P. (2012). A multiprocess approach to social influence. In D. T. Kenrick, N. Goldstein & S. L. Braver (Eds.), *Six degrees of social influence: Science, application, and the psychology of Robert Cialdini* (pp. 49–58). New York, NY: Oxford University Press.

Petty, R. E., Briñol, P., & Johnson, I. (2012). Implicit ambivalence. In B. Gawronski & F. Strack (Eds.), *Cognitive consistency: A fundamental principle in social cognition* (pp. 178–201). New York, NY: Guilford Press.

Petty, R. E., Briñol, P., & Tormala, Z. L. (2002). Thought confidence as a determinant of persuasion: The self-validation hypothesis. *Journal of Personality and Social Psychology, 82*(5), 722–741. doi:10.1037/0022-3514.82.5.722

Petty, R. E., Briñol, P., Tormala, Z. L., & Wegener, D. T. (2007). The role of meta-cognition in social judgment. In A. W. Kruglanski & E. T. Higgins (Eds.), *Social psychology: Handbook of basic principles* (2nd ed., pp. 254–284). New York, NY: Guilford Press.

Petty, R. E., & Cacioppo, J. T. (1984). The effects of involvement on responses to argument quantity and quality: Central and peripheral routes to persuasion. *Journal of Personality and Social Psychology, 46*(1), 69–81. doi:10.1037/0022-3514.46.1.69

Petty, R. E., & Cacioppo, J. T. (1986). The elaboration likelihood model of persuasion. In L. Berkowitz (Ed.), *Advances in experimental social psychology* (Vol. 19, pp. 123–205). New York, NY: Academic Press.

Petty, R. E., Cacioppo, J. T., & Goldman, R. (1981). Personal involvement as a determinant of argument-based persuasion. *Journal of Personality and Social Psychology, 41*(5), 847–855. doi:10.1037/0022-3514.41.5.847

Petty, R. E., DeMarree, K. G., Briñol, P., Horcajo, J., & Strathman, A. J. (2008). Need for cognition can magnify or attenuate priming effects in social judgment. *Personality and Social Psychology Bulletin, 34*(7), 900–912.

Petty, R. E., Haugtvedt, C. P., & Smith, S. M. (1995). Elaboration as a determinant of attitude strength: Creating attitudes that are persistent, resistant, and predictive of behavior. In R. E. Petty & J. A. Krosnick (Eds.), *Attitude strength: Antecedents and consequences* (pp. 93–130). Hillsdale, NJ: Lawrence Erlbaum Associates.

Petty, R. E., Ostrom, T. M., & Brock, T. C. (1981). *Cognitive responses in persuasion*. Hillsdale, NJ: Lawrence Erlbaum Associates.

Petty, R. E., Tormala, Z. L., Briñol, P., & Jarvis, W. B. G. (2006). Implicit ambivalence from attitude change: An exploration of the PAST model. *Journal of Personality and Social Psychology, 90*(1), 21–41. doi:10.1037/0022-3514.90.1.21

Petty, R. E., & Wegener, D. T. (1999). The Elaboration Likelihood Model: Current status and controversies. In S. Chaiken & Y. Trope (Eds.), *Dual process theories in social psychology* (pp. 41–72). New York, NY: Guilford Press.

Petty, R. E., Wells, G. L., Heesacker, M., Brock, T. C., & Cacioppo, J. T. (1983). The effects of recipient posture on persuasion: A cognitive response analysis. *Personality and Social Psychology Bulletin, 9*(2), 209–222. doi:10.1177/0146167283092004

Petty, R. E., Wheeler, S. C., & Bizer, G. Y. (1999). Is there one persuasion process or more? Lumping versus splitting in attitude change theories. *Psychological Inquiry, 10*, 156–163.

Pollock, C. L., Smith, S. D., Knowles, E. S., & Bruce, H. J. (1998). Mindfulness limits compliance with the That's-Not-All Technique. *Personality and Social Psychology Bulletin, 24*(11), 1153–1157. doi:10.1177/01461672982411002

Riskind, J. H., & Gotay, C. C. (1982). Physical posture: Could it have regulatory or feedback effects on motivation and emotion? *Motivation and Emotion, 6*(3), 273–298. doi:10.1007/bf00992249

Rydell, R. J., Hugenberg, K., & McConnell, A. R. (2006). Resistance can be good or bad: How theories of resistance and dissonance affect attitude certainty. *Personality and Social Psychology Bulletin, 32*(6), 740–750. doi:10.1177/0146167205286110

Schnall, S., Haidt, J., Clore, G. L., & Jordan, A. H. (2008). Disgust as embodied moral judgment. *Personality and Social Psychology Bulletin, 34*(8), 1096–1109. doi:10.1177/0146167208317771

Schnall, S., & Laird, J. (2003). Keep smiling: Enduring effects of facial expressions and postures on emotional experience and memory. *Cognition & Emotion, 17*(5), 787–797. doi:10.1080/02699930302286

Schryer, E., & Ross, M. (2012). People's thoughts about their personal past and futures. In P. Briñol & K. G. DeMarree (Eds.), *Social metacognition* (pp. 141–158). New York, NY: Psychology Press.

Shapiro, S. L., Carlson, L. E., Astin, J. A., & Freedman, B. (2005). Mechanisms of mindfulness. *Journal of Clinical Psychology*, *62*(3), 373–386.

Sherman, J., Gawronski, B., & Trope, Y. (Eds.) (in press). *Dual-process theories of the social mind*. New York, NY: Guildford Press.

Shiota, M. N., Campos, B., Gonzaga, G. C., Keltner, D., & Peng, K. (2010). I love you but…: Cultural differences in complexity of emotional experience during interaction with a romantic partner. *Cognition and Emotion*, *24*(5), 786–799. doi:10.1080/02699930902990480

Spencer-Rodgers, J., Peng, K., & Wang, L. (2010). Dialecticism and the co-occurrence of positive and negative emotions across cultures. *Journal of Cross-Cultural Psychology*, *41*(1), 109–115. doi:10.1177/0022022109349508

Spencer-Rodgers, J., Peng, K., Wang, L., & Hou, Y. (2004). Dialectical self-esteem and East–West differences in psychological well-being. *Personality and Social Psychology Bulletin*, *30*(11), 1416–1432. doi:10.1177/0146167204264243

Spencer-Rodgers, J., Williams, M. J., & Peng, K. (2010). Cultural differences in expectations of change and tolerance for contradiction: A decade of empirical research. *Personality and Social Psychology Review*, *14*(3), 296–312. doi:10.1177/1088868310362982

Strack, F., Martin, L. L., & Stepper, S. (1988). Inhibiting and facilitating conditions of the human smile: A nonobtrusive test of the facial feedback hypothesis. *Journal of Personality and Social Psychology*, *54*(5), 768–777. doi:10.1037/0022-3514.54.5.768

Tiedens, L.Z., & Linton, S. (2001). Judgment under emotional certainty and uncertainty: The effects of specific emotions on information processing. *Journal of Personality and Social Psychology*, *81*(6), 973–988. doi:10.1037/0022-3514.81.6.973

Tormala, Z. L., Falces, C., Briñol, P., & Petty, R. E. (2007). Ease of retrieval effects in social judgment: The role of unrequested cognitions. *Journal of Personality and Social Psychology*, *93*(2), 143–157. doi:10.1037/0022-3514.93.2.143

Valins, S. (1966). Cognitive effects of false heart-rate feedback. *Journal of Personality and Social Psychology*, *4*(4), 400–408. doi:10.1037/h0023791

van Harreveld, F., van der Pligt, J., & de Liver, Y. N. (2009). The agony of ambivalence and ways to resolve it: Introducing the MAID model. *Personality and Social Psychology Review*, *13*(1), 45–61. doi:10.1177/1088868308324518

Wagner, B., Briñol, P., & Petty, R. (2012). Dimensions of metacognitive judgment: Implications for attitude change. In P. Briñol & K. G. DeMarree (Eds.), *Social metacognition* (pp. 43–61). New York, NY: Psychology Press.

Weary, G., & Jacobson, J. A. (1997). Causal uncertainty beliefs and diagnostic information seeking. *Journal of Personality and Social Psychology*, *73*(4), 839–848. doi:10.1037/0022-3514.73.4.839

Wegener, D. T., & Petty, R. E. (1997). The flexible correction model: The role of naive theories of bias in bias correction. In M. P. Zanna (Ed.), *Advances in experimental social psychology* (Vol. 29, pp. 141–208). San Diego, CA: Academic Press.

Wells, A. (2012). Metacognition and psychological therapy. In P. Briñol & K. G. DeMarree (Eds.), *Social metacognition* (pp. 141–158). New York, NY: Psychology Press.

Wells, G. L., & Petty, R. E. (1980). The effects of overt head movements on persuasion: Compatibility and incompatibility of responses. *Basic and Applied Social Psychology*, *1*(3), 219–230. doi:10.1207/s15324834basp0103_2

278 *Andrew Luttrell et al.*

Further Reading

Briñol, P., & Petty, R. E. (2009). Persuasion: Insights from the self-validation hypothesis. In M. P. Zanna (Ed.), *Advances in experimental social psychology* (Vol. 41, pp. 69–118). New York, NY: Academic Press.

Petty, R. E., & Wegener, D. T. (1998). Attitude change: Multiple roles for persuasion variables. In D. T. Gilbert, S. T. Fiske, & G. Lindzey (Eds.), *The handbook of social psychology* (4th ed., Vol. 1, pp. 323–390). Boston, MA: McGraw-Hill.

15

Mindfulness and Heuristics

Wray Herbert

A while back, some friends and I attended a jazz concert at a venue in Virginia's Piedmont region, about an hour from Washington, DC. This is rolling farm and horse country, and the campus entry was a narrow curving road. I was enjoying the late afternoon sunshine on the lawns and trees, when an unlikely road sign snapped me to attention. It was an otherwise inconspicuous sign, except for the speed limit it posted: 14 mph.

We slowed down, suddenly mindful of the speedometer, which of course was the intention. Later on, when I was back at my desk, I decided to do just a little bit of Internet research. It turns out that such peculiar speed limits are not vanishingly rare. A Grifton, North Carolina, RV park sets its limit at 7 mph. A Bend, Oregon, resort sets it at 19 mph. A Pike Road, Alabama, residential development, imposes an 18 mph limit, and another in Erie, Pennsylvania, 13 mph.

I have no way of knowing if these are part of a larger trend, or if the planners in these communities have any formal training in psychological science, but they clearly have an intuitive grasp of the human mind—and specifically the way we process information and make choices. Had the sign in Virginia set the speed limit at 5 mph, 10 mph, or 20 mph, none of us would have noticed, much less slowed down. We would have continued along on auto-pilot, and there's a good chance we would have exceeded the speed limit. As it was, we not only noted and honored the odd restriction but discussed it and remembered it.

We go through much of our lives on auto-pilot. It's not always as literal as in this example, though piloting planes and cars is not a bad metaphor. All of life's piloting is in essence a series of judgments and decisions, and most of them we make rapidly and mindlessly. This is for the most part a good thing—essential to daily functioning, in fact. Think of your daily commute—or any other drive you make regularly. How much of it do you actually process consciously? Chances are, very little. You leave home and arrive at your destination. The decision-making in between—shifting gears, signaling and making turns, following a route, braking—takes place outside of awareness, automatically.

The pioneering work of Harvard University psychological scientist, Ellen Langer, revealed that mindlessness is not limited to rote behavior, like typewriting. Indeed, what she called "pseudothinking" encompasses fairly complex evaluations of others' motivations (Langer, Blank, & Chanowitz, 1978). In her landmark study of favors—requests and responses—she demonstrated that even decisions to help others are automatic, under certain circumstances. Langer had confederates approach people who were waiting in line to use a photocopying machine, asking if they could cut ahead. Sometimes these line cutters gave an explanation—"I'm in a rush"—while other times they gave an uninteresting and meaningless explanation—"I need to make copies." When the request was not a big imposition—five copies, say—almost all of the people said okay, even when offered the nonexplanation. They could well have said, "Well, I obviously need to make copies, too, or I wouldn't be standing in line," but they didn't; they stepped aside (Langer et al., 1978).

These results suggest that we all use a simple script for such simple requests: We say yes, no matter what the reason. If the workers had mindfully examined the request—weighing its merits, their own work demands, and so forth—they probably would have refused those with a lame reason for cutting in line.

If we didn't make decisions this way, we would be paralyzed. Imagine that every time you went to the grocery store, you had to weigh every decision: the nutritional value of this cereal compared to that one, or that other one; the cost of this yogurt compared to that one, or compared to something else entirely? We don't want to make these informed but labored choices over and over, so we rely on cognitive rules of thumb, or heuristics.

But there are other times in life when we want and need to slow down our thinking, and scientists are homing in on methods for doing this. Consider those speed limits again. What the planners in those RV parks and condominium communities and hospital zones knew intuitively was something called the Pique Technique, first described by social psychologist, Michael Santos, nearly two decades ago (Santos, Leve, & Pratkanis, 1994). It's called that because strange requests—or commands in the case of the speed limits—are believed to literally pique our attention, snapping us out of the automatic scripts we use to get us through so much of life. A 14-mph speed sign arrests our attention, just as a child darting across the road would, more dramatically, forcing us to slow down our thinking and become more deliberate.

The original research on the pique technique focused on panhandlers. The scientists recruited confederates to pose as panhandlers on the wharf in Santa Cruz, California. The wharf is a very popular spot in this beach community, for both locals and tourists, and there are a lot of down-and-out panhandlers trying to beg spare change. Most people use an unconscious, automatic schema—a kind of heuristic—to deal with begging, which is to avoid eye contact, keep walking and talking, and otherwise ignore the beggars' requests. This is known as a refusal script—"I say no to panhandlers"—but it allows us to say no without really engaging the panhandlers in any real way. This refusal script is evident on Santa Cruz's wharf, because panhandlers are so prevalent that it would be difficult to acknowledge even a fraction of them.

But Santos and colleagues found a way to stop the scripted version. Instead of asking for spare change or "a quarter"—the usual requests—the experimental panhandlers made either of two requests: "Can you spare 17 cents?" or "Can you spare 37 cents?" Santos compared the outcomes of these strange panhandlers' requests to the "traditional" requests for "any change" or "a quarter." Note that one surprising request was for more than a quarter, one for less—controlling for the value of the money requested.

The results were dramatic. When asked for spare change, the compliance rate was 44%. That rate increased to 64% when faux panhandlers asked for a "a quarter," and when they asked for 17 cents or 37 cents, the compliance rate reached 75%. That is, three out of every four people gave money in a situation where they are scripted to refuse automatically.

This heuristic script is not part of human nature, as far as we know. We almost certainly learn, based on many experiences, not to invest time and effort weighing every panhandler's request, just as we avoid investing time and effort in grocery shopping. Princeton social psychologist, Susan Fiske, once described humans as "cognitive misers"—meaning we're very stingy with our brain power (Fiske & Taylor, 1991). It's a limited resource, and it's cognitively much more efficient to divert our attention or mumble something incomprehensible, instead of listening to a personal story and weighing the merits of the request. Stopping to listen is effortful, and we're much less generous with our effort than we are with loose change.

It's not exactly clear what's going on in our heads when we stop our scripted actions and begin to question our heuristic responses. Are we really stopping to ask more questions? Engaging with another human's story in a meaningful way? Santa Clara University psychologist Jerry Burger and colleagues raised these questions and more in a recent paper on the pique technique and mindfulness (Burger, Hornisher, Martin, Newman, & Pringle, 2007). Santos, in his Santa Cruz panhandler studies, concluded that the technique worked because it aroused curiosity and refocused attention, but the Santa Clara researchers weren't so sure of this. They wanted to look more closely, and did in a couple experiments.

Santos had also found that passers-by asked more questions when confronted with a peculiar request from a panhandler. They wanted to know why these people needed money, suggesting some kind of mindful engagement with their lives. But listening—really listening and weighing pros and cons of a request—takes cognitive effort. Burger and colleagues wondered if the passers-by were really making this effort, so they did a modified version of the panhandler study. When passers-by asked about the unusual request, the panhandlers either gave a reasonable answer—"I need to buy a stamp"—or gave a meaningless one—"I need to buy some things." If the pique technique really leads to mindful deliberation and thus to compliance, one would expect compliance following a meaningful explanation only.

That's not exactly what they found. The pique technique did work as predicted, and as previously shown, but the panhandlers' explanations did not make any difference. Those who bothered to ask about the request went on to give money, regardless of the meaningfulness of the panhandlers' responses. In other words, they weren't really looking for a convincing argument from the panhandlers, and they didn't mindfully weigh the responses. The very act of asking was a sign that they had already made up their minds to give.

So, what affected their decisions? What were they thinking, if not about the worthiness of the panhandler's need and request? Burger suggests a couple of possibilities. One possibility is that, rather than slowing down and considering the panhandler's request in a mindful way, the subjects simply switched to a different script—one that's been called an "acquaintance script." The acquaintance script says basically, "I help people I know" and leads to knee-jerk compliance. Compellingly, even strangers can qualify as "people I know" after just a few moments of dialogue, and indeed these researchers found a boost in generosity only among those who asked for an explanation.

It's also possible that those who gave money had already decided to give before asking for more information. That is, perhaps the kind of person who engages in conversation with a panhandler is the kind of person who responds to an unusual request for money. It's not clear, but it does seem that people who respond to the pique technique do so effortlessly—they are just as miserly with their cognitive resources as the rest of us.

The early work of Ellen Langer and Robert Abelson demonstrated just how common such scripts are in everyday life—and how arbitrary they can be. These scientists demonstrated in a 1972 study that the decision to help an accident victim—or not—can be determined by something as simple as the word order of the victim's request, even when the meaning of the request remains unchanged. They had confederates feign a knee injury in a department store and ask for help from passing strangers. Bystanders were much more likely to help in response to legitimate requests in which the syntax put emphasis on the victim's need and distress over the call for assistance (Langer & Abelson, 1972).

These scripts are a form of what some behavioral scientists label System 1 thinking. System 1 thinking is fast, automatic, impressionistic, emotional, and usually unconscious—and for better or worse, it's our primary mode of cognition. It's "on" most of the time, unless we make the conscious decision to slow down, deliberate, or calculate rationally. System 1 thinking relies not only on cultural scripts that we learn, but also on more deep-seated heuristics and biases—some of which may have been evolutionary adaptations. Much of the work on heuristics and biases derives from the pioneering early work of Daniel Kahneman and the late Amos Tversky, but others have identified dozens of these deep-rooted habits of mind—cognitive shortcuts—that shape much of our day-to-day thought and behavior (Kahneman, 2011; Kahneman & Tversky, 1979).

This is the sense in which I use the word mindful in this article. These automatic cognitive biases can be very helpful—in the sense that they conserve mental energy—but they are mindless, and can be perilous, leading to bad decisions. To live mindfully is to be aware of these heuristics and biases, and cultural scripts, and to de-bias them when more deliberate judgments and decisions serve us better.

Take another example: Scientists and clinicians are interested in the dynamic interaction of perception and aggression. Looking for trouble, and seeing it, may be a deep cognitive bias—a negativity bias—that distorts normal emotional processing. Indeed, some experts wonder: Does seeing anger and hostility in others actually elicit angry feelings and aggression, creating a vicious, self-fulfilling, cycle? In other words, do some people act mean simply because they see the world as a mean place?

A team of psychological scientists in the UK decided to find out. Led by Marcus Munafo of the University of Bristol, the investigators ran a series of experiments to verify if such a negativity bias does in fact lead to aggressive behavior and, further, to see if such distorted emotional processing might be corrected (Penton-Voak et al., 2013). They did this by having a group of healthy adults look at, and react to, pictures of morphed faces. Think of your own facial expressions. Some are clearly happy, others unambiguously angry. But these are extremes, and most are somewhere in between—with some being very difficult to read at all. The volunteers looked at a lot of these ambiguous, difficult-to-interpret faces and were forced to label them happy or angry.

This determined each volunteer's baseline level of negativity bias—how likely they were to see anger in ambiguous faces. Then, the scientists trained some, but only some, of the volunteers—using feedback to nudge them away from this negativity bias. When they labeled a neutral face as angry, the feedback indicated that this was not correct—that it was in fact a happy face. Over many trials with many different faces, these volunteers learned to see happiness in some of the ambiguous faces that they previously identified as angry.

Or at least that's the theory behind the intervention. To check, the scientists retested all the volunteers, using similar morphed faces. The results were intriguing. Those who underwent training showed a clear shift, compared to controls, in perception of anger. They were more likely to label ambiguous faces as happy rather than angry. What's more, these de-biased volunteers were themselves less angry and aggressive, as measured by an emotional inventory. In other words, it appears that the intervention did modify the volunteers' negativity bias, which could lead to beneficial changes in behavior.

The volunteers in this first study were healthy adults, like you and me, with no history of aggression or violence. How would such an intervention work with people known for their anger and belligerence? Munafo and colleagues decided to test the training on a group of teenagers who were already at high risk for adult criminality. The volunteers had all been referred to a youth program for delinquent teens, either by the courts or by schools, and many already had records of aggression and criminal offenses.

The training was basically the same as before, except that it lasted longer—four sessions over a week's time. The teenagers also kept a diary over this time, noting every incident of anger and aggression, from verbal abuse to physical assault. Staff members at the youth program also rated each of the volunteer's behaviors, to corroborate the teenagers' self-reports. These diary entries and staff observations continued through the final reevaluation two weeks later.

The results were very encouraging, and theoretically interesting. Those who received the bias-modification training shifted their perceptions, seeing less anger in ambiguous faces. In addition, these teenagers were much less aggressive—based on both self-reports and staff assessments—when they were assessed two weeks later. Two weeks is not a long time, but these findings do raise the hope that these training effects will persist, even with adolescents at high risk for conduct disorder and lives of crime.

Both of these experiments relied on explicit feedback to change the way volunteers judge others' emotions. The scientists wonder if it might be possible to get the same result with another approach, specifically by making volunteers adapt visually to angry faces. It's known that prolonged viewing of any image alters the perception of related images afterward, so the scientists forced some volunteers—healthy adults again—to focus on angry faces only, while controls looked at a mix of emotional faces.

The results were essentially the same. Those who were forced to adapt to angry faces subsequently shifted their emotional perception, seeing more happiness in ambiguous faces. And once again, they themselves were less angry and aggressive.

So, did the training break the vicious cycle of perceived anger and aggression? Did it create a "virtuous cycle," boosting perceived happiness and diminishing aggression? It's not certain, but that's how the scientists would like to interpret the results, and they see an intriguing parallel in the working of antidepressant drugs. It's been proposed that medication leads to rapid changes in emotion processing biases, which in turn allows cognitive changes that improve mood. That is, improvement in mood results from changes in emotion perception, not the other way around. These new findings suggest a similar mechanism at work with aggression. If so, these results might point to a simple, fast, and cost-effective way to keep the troubled from looking for trouble.

The negativity bias is well known and well documented. But let's turn to another, less obvious heuristic, with large implications for the way we live our lives. Baby boomers are right now starting to reach retirement age, and huge numbers will cross this threshold in the decade ahead. But retirement is an odd notion when you think of it, and a modern one in the scheme of human history. For our ancestors, the idea that you had earned enough money for one lifetime, that it was OK to stop working and enjoy the fruits of your labor, would have been incomprehensible. Indeed, until quite recently the deal was: You worked, you ate and otherwise consumed what you had earned, and then you worked some more. Then, you died.

This is still true for way too many of the world's people, who continue to live hand to mouth. But there are also many more people—and a growing number every year—who don't really have to work anymore, but do, who forgo the leisure of their golden years to earn yet more money. The per capita GDP worldwide has increased 200 times in the past two centuries and continues to grow, meaning that there are many people who have more wealth than they will ever live to enjoy.

So, why not just stop working and earning? Why do people keep toiling long beyond when they have to? Of course, the lucky ones do it because they love their work, and others want to bequeath something to their kids or hedge against misfortune. But what about those who lack these motivations but earn too much money anyway?

Psychological scientist, Christopher Hsee, of the University of Chicago's Booth School of Business, is interested in these workers. Working with colleagues at the University of Miami and Shanghai Jiao Tong University, he wanted to explore the possibility that working people are driven by some powerful, deep-rooted need to keep working and amassing wealth (Hsee, Zhang, Cai, & Zhang, 2013). Is it possible, they asked, that unthinking accumulation of money is the mind's default position?

To study this question, Hsee developed a stripped-down laboratory simulation of the big question facing baby boomers all over the country: if and when to retire. Let's call it the Retirement Game. Many are familiar with the Ultimatum Game, which is a similar simulation for studying people's selfish and unselfish motives. It does not pretend to capture real life in all its complexity but instead isolates human choice in its most basic form. That's what the Retirement Game does, as well. It's a microcosm of a lifetime, in which people must make decisions about how much to work, for what rewards, and when to quit.

Here is how the Retirement Game simulation works. One by one, volunteers come into the lab and don a pair of headphones. During the first 5 min of the experiment—the earning phase of life—they can choose to relax and listen to pleasant piano music or to disrupt the music and listen to grating noise. The music is meant to simulate leisure, the noise work. Whenever volunteers are listening to noise, they earn "income" in the form of chocolates. Then, in the second 5-min phase, they get to enjoy the rewards of their hard work, eating as much of their amassed chocolate as they like. Hsee ran several versions of this simulation to explore different aspects of decision-making about work and retirement.

In the first and simplest, some volunteers were much better earners than others. They banked a chocolate for every 20 episodes of noise, while their low-earning counterparts had to endure 120 episodes of noise for the same chocolate. The idea was to see if earning rate had any effect on retirement decisions, and it clearly did. Those who were well paid were much more likely to keep working—and to sock away more than they needed. In fact, they earned so much that they ended up leaving much more on the table than they ate. This is the equivalent of working until the day you die, amassing a lot of wealth but enjoying little of it. It's what Hsee labels mindless accumulation.

The low earners also earned more than they needed or wanted for enjoyment, though not as much as the high earners. This suggests that everyone has some bias toward mindless accumulation, regardless of their earning power. Hsee wanted to see if this automatic bias might be modified, so in a second study, some of the volunteers were asked beforehand to predict the optimal rewards they would want, while others were just left to their own devices. Hsee suspected that merely thinking about how much accumulated wealth they would want and need might temper mindless earning.

The findings were clear. Those who stopped to think about the future and how much wealth they would really need earned less over their "lifetime" than those who did not deliberate. In fact, they stopped earning almost exactly at the optimal level, while those who did not think about the future continued to accumulate excessively. In other words, they did not automatically forecast what they would really need. Finally, and most importantly, those who slowed down and thought about these issues—work, wealth, need—were happier than the others. The more people earned, the less happy they were. Apparently, it's not true that having financial bragging rights—who has the most toys—is in itself a source of joy.

Hsee ran a couple more versions of the Retirement Game. The most important additional finding was that if people are required to stop earning (if there is an earnings cap that kicks in when people have earned enough to satisfy their needs for a lifetime), they will realize that more work is pointless, and they stop. It seems that people, or volunteers in the Retirement Game, at least, did not enjoy working simply for the sake of working. What's more, the people who had a cap on their wealth accumulation were happier, both while they were earners and later in retirement.

This never-stop-working heuristic is probably rooted in our evolutionary past. Our ancestors lived in a world of scarcity, and their pervasive neediness lingers and shapes much modern thought and behavior. Here's another example. Everyone knows by now that the U.S. is in the midst of an obesity epidemic, but for all the hand wringing, nobody really knows why. Experts have offered many theories about why Americans eat too much, especially too much fattening food, but these remain theories. It's because Americans are ill-informed about diet and nutrition, and simply do not understand that double cheeseburgers are loaded with fat and calories. Or it's because we're constantly bombarded with stimulating ads for tempting but unhealthful snacks. Or it's because we simply lack the self-discipline of earlier generations. Or all of the above.

Or perhaps something else entirely. Two University of Miami marketing experts, Juliano Laran and Anthony Salerno, are now offering a new and provocative idea about why Americans make poor food choices, along with some preliminary evidence to back it up (Laran & Salerno, 2013). They contend that the news we're exposed to every day, specifically information about the economic crisis, adversity, and struggle in a harsh world, is triggering a live-for-today mindset that makes us short-sighted about diet. For reasons rooted deep in our evolutionary past, living in a harsh world makes us focus on immediate reproductive success, which makes us fiercely competitive for scarce resources. This sense of immediacy makes us dismiss the future and focus on the here and now, including a filling diet rich in calories. Once adaptive, this life strategy leads, in modern-day America, to too many French fries and helpings of chocolate mocha ice cream.

At least that's the theory, which the psychological scientists tested in a few experiments. In the first one, they invited passers-by to join in a taste test for a new kind of M&M. Half the volunteers were given a bowl full of this new candy and were told that the secret ingredient in the new M&Ms was a new, high-calorie chocolate. The others, the controls, also got a bowl of M&Ms, but they were told that the new chocolate was low-calorie. All the volunteers were told that they could sample the product until the next part of the study.

This was a ruse. The scientists were actually measuring their consumption. But during this waiting period, some read a text that emphasized harshness and deprivation, with words like "survival," "persistence," "shortfall," and "adversity." The controls read a text with neutral words. The idea was that those who were subconsciously primed to think about scarcity and struggle would eat more if they were offered high-calorie food, more than if they were offered a low-calorie option. And they did. They also ate more of the high-calorie candy than did controls, and less of the low-calorie candy. In other words, they were responding to their (perceived) world of deprivation by packing away the calories.

Excessive consumption of chocolate can lead to obesity. But isn't it possible that chocolate eaters are simply seeking pleasure, indulging themselves rather than coping with a scarcity of food? The scientists wanted to make sure that the high-calorie eating was related to perceived deprivation rather than mere indulgence, a possibility they addressed in a second study. They again primed some volunteers to think about a harsh world of scarce resources, while others were primed to think about comfort, enjoyment, pleasure, and indulgence. Then, half the volunteers in each group were given a small amount of money, which was intended to satisfy their psychological need for resources and thus diminish their calorie seeking.

The scientists tested this by offering all the volunteers a choice between a garden salad and cupcakes. As predicted, those primed for a harsh world were less likely to choose cake if they were given monetary resources than if they were not, suggesting that they didn't need the calories to cope with deprivation. Those primed for pleasure seeking were, like the controls, just as likely to take the cake if they had been paid or not. In short, the deep psychic need for scarce resources is altogether different from mere indulgence in taste. Even a tiny amount of money appears to decrease calorie seeking.

So, is there a way to put these findings to good use, to deliberately decrease calorie seeking? Perhaps so. In a final experiment, Laran and Salerno tried to reverse the short-sighted scarcity bias that leads to high-calorie eating. They again primed only some volunteers to think about scarcity. Then, they used a second kind of priming to make some of these scarcity-minded volunteers, and some controls, focus on the slow passage of time; others were primed to think about the rapid passage of time. The idea was that taking the long view of time would undo the sense of urgency leading to unhealthful eating. And that's what they found. When offered a choice of salad or a cheese-and-turkey sandwich, the scarcity-minded volunteers opted for the high-calorie sandwich only when mindful of fleeting time. If they were primed to think of time as slow and plentiful, they were much less likely to opt for the immediate calories, and more apt to eat salad. Looked at another way, reorienting people's distorted sense of time and urgency is a strategy that appears to help them make healthful food choices.

The world can seem like a competitive and unforgiving place these days, with so many people out of work and the economy struggling. All Americans have to do is turn on the TV to get daily reminders of the world's cruelty and suffering. While it's not clear just how these findings might translate into strategies to undo this unrelenting daily priming, these findings suggest that it may not be enough simply to inform people about the calories and nutrition in this or that food and expect them to make disciplined food choices.

This is also true of another serious personal and public health problem—alcoholism—which appears to be driven in part by mindless, automatic decision-making. Imagine this scenario: You're at an informal social gathering, and you wander into the kitchen in search of a cold Coke. You open the refrigerator, but there are no soft drinks to be found. Instead, you face a fridge packed with cases of beer and icy quarts of vodka.

How do you react? Well, if you're like most people, you think, "Damn. No Coke," and look elsewhere or forget it. But if you're an alcoholic, your reaction—your rapid, visceral reaction—would likely be quite different. You'd be drawn in. Your memory would instantly call up past associations with liquor, and you might even feel a craving—even if you haven't had a drink in a long time. Then, either you would contemplate reaching for a bottle, or you would push yourself away from this cache of booze—pronto.

Alcoholics have an abnormal, automatic attraction to temptation, and most relapses result from poor impulse control. Yet most clinical treatments for problem drinking focus on reflection—the higher order reasons for maintaining sobriety—health, family life. Might it be possible to counter this unconscious bias for booze on a more basic level, defusing the powerful cognitive bias that magnetically draws alcoholics to a drink?

That's the theory that a team of European psychological scientists have been exploring. The University of Amsterdam's Reinout Wiers and colleagues wondered if it might be possible to use physical and mental training to manipulate alcoholics' "approach bias" for booze (Wiers, Eberl, Rinck, Becker, & Lindenmeyer, 2011). They developed a therapeutic technique called "cognitive bias modification," or CBM, which uses a joystick to change alcoholics' approach bias to an avoidance bias for temptation.

They tested the theory and technique in an actual rehab facility, the Salus Clinic in Germany. They recruited more than 200 alcoholic patients who were at least three weeks out of detox, and assessed their craving level and their unconscious attraction to alcohol. Then, half the patients participated in four 15-min CBM sessions on four consecutive days. This consisted of deliberately pushing the joystick in reaction to pictures of beer, whiskey, and so forth (literally and figuratively pushing the temptation away), and pulling the joystick in response to pictures of soft drinks. The control subjects had no training or sham training sessions.

When the scientists retested and compared the patients, the findings were hopeful. The patients trained on the joystick—and only those patients—reversed their cognitive bias; that is, their alcoholic approach tendency became a strong alcoholic avoidance tendency. Craving for alcohol also decreased in these patients, while craving for soft drinks increased.

That's all good, but what about the only result that really matters to the alcoholics: Did they stay sober? Following this brief training, all the patients went through the usual alcoholic treatment program, averaging about three months; then they went home. The scientists followed up a year later, and the results were mixed. Specifically, 46% of those with CBM training had relapsed a year later, compared to 59% of the controls.

The majority of alcoholics fail when they try to quit. So, these results, while inconclusive, are not discouraging. At the least, they may provide an additional tool for the recovering alcoholic to wield in the ongoing struggle to slam the door on temptation.

These are just a few examples of the untoward consequences of mindlessness in everyday judgment and decision-making. There are many more, affecting everything from personal finance to environmental policy to charity and even romance. The stakes are high, and one of the clearest messages from the research so far is that these habits are powerful and highly resistant to change. Yet this sampling of studies offers some preliminary but encouraging evidence that they are not impervious to change.

References

Burger, J. M., Hornisher, J., Martin, V. E., Newman, G., & Pringle, S. (2007). The pique technique: Overcoming mindlessness or shifting heuristics? *Journal of Applied Social Psychology*, *37*, 2086–2096.

Fiske, S. T., & Taylor, S. E. (1991). *Social cognition* (2nd ed.). New York, NY: McGraw-Hill.

Hsee, C. K., Zhang, J., Cai, C. F., & Zhang, S. (2013). Overearning. *Psychological Science*, *24*(6), 852–859.

Kahneman, D. (2011). *Thinking fast and slow*. New York, NY: Macmillan.

Kahneman, D., & Tversky, A. (1979). Prospect theory: An analysis of decision under risk. *Econometrica, 47*(2), 263–291.

Langer, E., Blank, A., & Chanowitz, B. (1978). The mindlessness of ostensibly thoughtful action: The role of "placebic" information in interpersonal interaction. *Journal of Personality and Social Psychology, 36*(6), 635–642.

Langer, E. J., & Abelson, R. P. (1972). The semantics of asking a favor: How to succeed in getting help without really dying. *Journal of Personality and Social Psychology, 24*(1), 26–32.

Laran, J., & Salerno, A. (2013). Life-history strategy, food choice, and caloric consumption. *Psychological Science, 24*(2), 157–173.

Penton-Voak, I. S., Thomas, J., Gage, S. H., McMurran, M., McDonald, S., & Munafo, M. R. (2013). Increasing recognition of happiness in ambiguous facial expressions reduces anger and aggressive behavior. *Psychological Science, 24*(5), 688–697.

Santos, M. D., Leve, C., & Pratkanis, A.R. (1994). Hey buddy, can you spare seventeen cents? Mindful persuasion and the pique technique. *Journal of Applied Social Psychology, 24*, 755–764.

Wiers, R. W., Eberl, C., Rinck, M., Becker, E. S., & Lindenmeyer, J. (2011). Retraining automatic action tendencies changes alcoholic patients' approach bias for alcohol and improves treatment outcomes. *Psychological Science, 22*(4), 490–497.

Further Reading

Herbert, W. (2010). *On second thought: Outsmarting your mind's hard-wired habits*. New York, NY: Crown.

16

I-D Compensation

Exploring the Relations Among Mindfulness, a Close Brush With Death, and Our Hunter-Gatherer Heritage

Leonard L. Martin, Matthew A. Sanders, Amey Kulkarni, Wyatt C. Anderson, and Whitney L. Heppner

What would the world look like if mindfulness were the rule rather than the exception? In some ways, we already know the answer to that question. Research has shown that when people behave mindfully, they are more creative (Langer & Eisenkraft, 2009), healthier (Langer, 2009), and more liked by their interaction partners (Langer, Cohen, & Djikic, 2012). They learn better (Langer, Hatem, & Howell, 1989), exhibit less stereotyping (Djikic, Langer, & Stapleton, 2008), display greater self-acceptance (Carson & Langer, 2006), and even live longer (Alexander, Langer, Newman, Chandler, & Davies, 1989).

But what if more people were more mindful more of the time? What if mindfulness were the default state rather than a state that needed to be induced with special manipulations? The outcome, we believe, would be surprisingly ordinary—but in a good way. It might parallel the effects some people display after a close brush with death. There would be no great "transport to bliss," just a "paradoxical combination of total familiarity with surprised satisfaction" (Wren-Lewis, 1994, p. 110).

In this chapter, we suggest that the connections between mindfulness and a close brush with death are more than skin deep. The two phenomena produce similar effects because they initiate the same general process. They induce people to decrease their automatic reliance on preconceptions, especially those introjected from their culture.

In making this point, we describe some features of mindfulness as well as some aftereffects of a close brush with death. We suggest that in both cases, people shed cultural introjects and guide their behavior using a more authentic self. Next, we raise the possibility that this self is the one that evolved when our ancestors were living in immediate-return hunter-gatherer societies. To make this case, we discuss aspects of immediate-return hunter-gatherer societies and contrast them with aspects

The Wiley Blackwell Handbook of Mindfulness, First Edition.
Edited by Amanda Ie, Christelle T. Ngnoumen, and Ellen J. Langer.
© 2014 John Wiley & Sons, Ltd. Published 2014 by John Wiley & Sons, Ltd.

of modern, complex delayed-return societies. We conclude that compared to the immediate-return ones, modern societies foster mindlessness. They do so, in part, by encouraging people to interpret the world through a fixed set of justifying stories (e.g., just-world beliefs). When people drop these stories, they stop living in their head and guide their behavior more authentically. In short, they become mindful. We end the chapter by tying these ideas together using I-D compensation theory (Martin, 1999). Finally, we describe what the world would look like if mindfulness were the rule rather than the exception.

As a prelude, we can say that if mindfulness were the rule, the world would look more like an immediate-return hunter-gatherer world. That does not mean that people would be living in the forest and foraging for food. It means they would live in the present, adjust their knowledge in response to subtle changes in their environment, and behave more authentically. Moreover, the effects would be synergistic. Increasing mindfulness would foster an immediate-return lifestyle, which, in turn, would foster greater mindfulness, and so on. Before we make these points, though, we need to say what we mean by mindfulness.

Defining Mindfulness and Mindlessness

Mindfulness can be defined as the process of actively making new distinctions about objects in one's awareness (Langer & Moldoveanu, 2000). It can be contrasted with mindlessness in which people adhere to entrenched categorizations from the past. When people are mindful, they adjust their cognitive processing strategies to match their current conditions, they stay attuned to the present, and they are more open to new information. They are also more sensitive to subtle variations in their environment, they display more cognitive flexibility, and they are more able to apply new categories as needed (Brown & Langer, 1990).

When people are mindless, on the other hand, they adhere rigidly to a single perspective and are less responsive to subtle changes in their environment. Moreover, the single perspective they use may be a preexisting one they accepted more or less unquestioningly from their culture and that they apply more or less unthinkingly. As a result, people may perform well-practiced behaviors in a very competent way yet make a mistake because they performed the behavior in the wrong place at the wrong time (Langer, Blank, & Chanowitz, 1978; Reason, 1984).

The distinction between mindfulness and mindlessness can be seen quite clearly in the real-life example of a man who lived in England most of his life but who had occasion to drive a car in the United States. He had no problem driving on the right-hand side of the road once he was behind the wheel and driving. His problem was getting in the car. He repeatedly found himself trying to enter from the passenger side, which, of course, is the driver's side in an English car. Why was he better at driving than entering?

While he was driving, he was paying attention. He was guiding his behavior on the basis of the ongoing changes in his environment. In a word, he was mindful. As he was getting in the car, however, he was preoccupied with where he was going, whether he had everything he needed, what he was going to say to his coworker when he got to his office, and so on. So, he enacted automatically the same routine he always enacted when getting ready to drive his car. He opened the door in his usual way, which turned out to be the wrong thing for him to do in his current situation. In a word, he was mindless.

Of course, living mindfully does more than confer simple performance benefits. It facilitates the expression of broad psychological variables such as authenticity (Carson & Langer, 2006). When people live mindfully, they engage more fully with the environment, pay attention to what they are doing, and respond in real time to subtle, changing aspects in the environment. In addition, because they focus on what they are doing, they do not become especially concerned with the impression they are making on others. They do not worry about winning the approval of others or enhancing their self-esteem. Instead, they guide their behavior on the basis of their personal values in relation to their current context.

When people live mindlessly, on the other hand, they guide their behavior using preexisting scripts and categories, and discount their genuine feelings and values. This may lead them to approach situations from a single perspective and miss other ways in which they could have responded to the situation. To make matters worse, it is likely that they adopted their single perspective without checking to see if it was valid for them as individuals or for the situation in which they currently found themselves (Chanowitz & Langer, 1981). As a result, they may base their behavior on information that seems universally valid but that was not valid for them as individuals or for their current situation.

Consider how the mismatch between received cultural knowledge and authentic knowledge can create a problem in the domain of happiness. When people are asked, "How happy are you?" they can answer using either of two general strategies. They can assess their actual feelings, or they can consult what appear to be relevant cultural theories. Such theories specify the conditions people need to satisfy in order to be happy. People are happy, for example, if they drive the right car, marry the right spouse, or get the right job. In this way, people can judge their happiness simply by seeing if their current situation matches the specified situation. No introspection is needed.

To see if people based their happiness judgments on their feelings or the cultural theories, Csikszentmihalyi and LeFevre (1989) contacted people at various times in various contexts and asked them how happy they were. One generally recognized cultural theory suggests that people are happier when they engage in leisure activity rather than work. Although this theory may be true for some people some of the time, it is not true for all people all of the time. So, if people based their happiness judgments on this theory, they may say they are happier at leisure, even if they experience more positive feelings at work.

Consistent with this observation, Csikszentmihalyi and LeFevre (1989) found that some participants reported experiencing more engagement and flow at work than at leisure. When asked if they would rather be doing something else, however, these same people answered "Yes" more often at work than at leisure. What did they want to be doing instead of working? They wanted to be engaged in leisure activities. They based their happiness judgments on the cultural theory rather than their actual feelings. This is a form of mindlessness. The participants had internalized a cultural theory and applied it in a nonthinking way to a situation in which the theory did not apply.

In sum, there are many advantages to being mindful. It can help people stay attuned to the present, update their knowledge, and adjust their cognitive strategies to reflect changes in the demands of their environment. It can also help them avoid acting on the basis of entrenched categorizations or inaccurate cultural givens. It might even help them be happy. Despite these benefits, people are often mindless. Why? Do people have some inherent weakness that leads them to mindlessness? Is there some factor in our society that fosters mindlessness? Before we can say what the world would be like if mindfulness were the rule, we need to know what it would take to make mindfulness the rule.

In general, we can say that mindfulness manipulations produce their positive effects by inducing people to consider multiple perspectives. They reduce people's automatic application of fixed conceptions. So, if we could get people to stop applying their preconceptions in an automatic way, we could make them more mindful. If we could get them to do this permanently, we could induce them to be mindful in a permanent way. That's when mindfulness would be the rule rather than the exception.

Is there a way to induce people permanently to stop the automatic application of their preconceptions? We believe there is. We could give them a close brush with death.

Death and Mindfulness

For some people, almost dying is the best thing that ever happened to them (Hablitzel, 2006). What makes it so good? It leads people to trivialize the trivial and stop taking life for granted. In short, it makes people mindful. A woman dying of cancer explained it this way:

> When you're dying, you're stripped of everything that's important to society—money, image—so all you have left is that honesty. It takes so much energy to pretend when you can use that energy for other things. … all that crap just flies off of you; it just sort of comes off you like layers of skin. All of a sudden, you're starting from scratch, like when you were born. … I believe in myself now. I never had that before. And I am not afraid of being who I am. (Kuhl, 2002, p. 230)

Thus, a close brush with death, like mindfulness, can lead people to shed aspects of their culture, adopt multiple perspectives, and behave in a more authentic way. It can also lead people to:

1 display an enhanced sense of living in the present;
2 drop values introjected from their culture;
3 feel free to refuse doing things they do not want to do;
4 experience high levels of self-forgiveness;
5 care more about other people but care less what other people think of them;
6 display less interest in material things, fame, and money;
7 display a greater appreciation for nature and the ordinary things in life (e.g., a sunset, hugging a child);
8 express low levels of self-aggrandizement;
9 keep daily frustrations and trivialities from bogging them down; and
10 stop taking life for granted.

Although these features are not exactly those associated with mindfulness, there is considerable overlap. Both phenomena lead people to shed aspects of their culture, focus more on the present, pay less attention to what other people think of them, adjust their cognitive strategies in response to subtle changes in their situation, and live more authentically (for a review, see Flynn, 1984; Grey, 1985; Greyson, 1983; Kinnier, Tribbensee, Rose, & Vaugh, 2001; Martin, Campbell, & Henry, 2005; Noyes, 1982–1983; Ring, 1984). Further evidence of a commonality between mindfulness and a close brush with death can be seen in the process through which the two produce their effects.

To understand this process, we have to consider that not all close brushes with death lead to psychological growth. Two conditions are needed. Both can be seen in the story of a woman (known to one of the authors) who survived a head-on car crash. She was driving on the highway when another car travelling in the opposite direction suddenly swerved over the median and headed straight for her car. Everything happened so fast that there was little the woman could do. There was no time to hit the brakes. No time to steer away. In fact, the woman had time for only two thoughts: "This is it" and "It's OK."

As counterintuitive as this reaction may be, it is not unusual. It has been observed in many people who faced their imminent death—but then survived (Greyson & Stevenson, 1980; Noyes, 1980; Roberts & Owen, 1988). The first feature that seems critical to producing the positive aftereffects is having an absolutely vivid and convincing encounter with death. People have to believe they really are dying. Right here, right now, like this. It is not enough for them simply to contemplate their mortality or to realize they could have been on a flight that went down. They need to believe with absolute certainty they are about to die.

The second critical ingredient seems to arise naturally out of the first. It is acceptance (Noyes, 1980). When people have a vivid, immediate confrontation with death, they let go. They stop trying to force their preconceptions onto reality—probably because they can't. Death is too big of a reality. People know they are going to die no matter what they think. So, they invest less in their thoughts, goals, and plans. They shed their preconceptions, and this seems to be the ingredient that is most directly responsible for the positive aftereffects of a close brush with death (Cole & Pargament, 1999; Noyes, 1980).

We can get further insight into this letting-go process from a passage in Chesterton's (2009) novel *The Ball and the Cross*. The protagonist in the novel has a close brush with death and then expresses the following insight:

At the highest crisis of some incurable anguish there will suddenly fall upon the man the stillness of an insane contentment. It is not hope, for hope is broken and romantic and concerned with the future; this is complete and of the present. It is not faith for faith by its very nature is fierce; and as it were at once doubtful and defiant; but this is simply a satisfaction. It is not knowledge, for intellect seems to have no particular part in it. Nor is it (as the modern idiots would certainly say it is) a mere numbness or negative paralysis of the power of grief. It is not negative in the least: it is as positive as good news. (Chesterton, 2009, p. 10)

What is it about a close brush with death that can make it as positive as good news and that produces features similar to mindfulness? According to Wren-Lewis (1994), a close brush with death turns off our hyperactive survival mechanism. He suggested, more precisely, that each of us possesses a set of operations, a hypothetical survival mechanism, that works to maintain our personal well-being. This mechanism motivates us to watch our weight, get our papers published, ask for a raise, and so on. In this way, the mechanism can be useful. It helps us survive and thrive.

According to Wren-Lewis, however, the mechanism has become overactive. It has led each of us to become myopically focused on our own agenda and to perceive the world as hostile and competitive rather than as benign and cooperative. It makes us miss the peace and beauty available in each moment. A close brush with death can break that spell because it turns the survival mechanism off. In the words of Wren-Lewis (2004), "when the brain approaches the point of complete shutdown, the conditioned patterns of thought, feeling, and perception lose their grip on consciousness" (p. 91).

The catch, of course, is that when the brush with death is merely a close one, the person is not dead. But it's too late. The survival mechanism has been turned off. So, when people return from the brink, the goals, standards, and expectations they introjected mindlessly from their culture are no longer there to color their perceptions. This allows people to adapt to reality as it is and stop trying to fit reality into their preconceptions. This is how a close brush with death sets the stage for mindfulness.

But why a close brush with death? Couldn't other traumas produce similar effects? Although it is true that other traumas can produce psychological growth (Tedeschi & Calhoun, 2004), they seem to do so through a rebuilding process rather than a letting-go process. As Wren-Lewis (2004) noted, most traumas shatter benign or optimistic world assumptions (Janoff-Bulman, 1992). For example, people generally assume that the world is safe, that they will not become a victim of crime, or that they will not succumb to a debilitating disease, at least not while they are young. Traumatic life events, however, challenge these assumptions. When this happens, people need to rebuild their assumptions. If they do so in a way that reflects their changed situation, they may experience psychological growth (Tedeschi & Calhoun, 2004).

A close brush with death, however, is different. It does not challenge positive assumptions. It challenges negative ones. People may spend a lot of time worrying about life, including lots of little things that may seem important to them at the time but really aren't. Have I lost enough weight? Will I get that next paper published? Why wasn't I invited to that party? A close brush with death invalidates those concerns. They don't matter when you are dead.

What happens, though, if you come close to death but don't die? Wouldn't the concerns become important again? It seems not. It seems a close brush with death can lead people to see their concerns for what they are, and always have been in the grand scheme of things: barren pursuits (Martin & Kleiber, 2005). And once people see things this way, there is no going back. When people return from the brink, they drop their preconceptions and open up to "an essentially benign inner reality underlying a world which had hitherto been superficially perceived as hostile, competitive and 'red in tooth and claw'" (Wren-Lewis, 2004, pp. 91–92).

A woman dying from cancer described it this way:

> There's less fear in my life because I'm not in the loop of stress that most of us get into
> from working and worrying about money and the kids, rather than just being with what
> is. It's about acceptance rather than still struggling to make it your way. All the ego stuff,
> all the future fear—'God, did I gain weight? Am I turning gray?' Most of those things
> aren't important any more. It's like really downsizing to the essence. It wasn't things
> that I wanted. It was a way of life. And so I systematically set out to live it. A lot of
> the programming from my youth was still there before the illness, like 'You need to be
> successful.' You're in this prison. I've switched to what's important." (Branfman, 1996)

Thus, a close brush with death, like mindfulness, can lead people to drop the fixed
set of goals, standards, and expectations they may have introjected from their culture
and that were contributing negatively to their well-being (Flynn, 1984; Ring, 1984;
Sutherland, 1992). By dropping these preconceptions, people can open up to greater
acceptance of themselves and see more options in the world around them. As Kuhl
(2002) put it, when people cannot escape death, "they embrace life, their own life. The
'prescription' of how to live given by family, culture, profession, religion, or friends
loses its grasp" (p. 227).

Thus, a close brush with death can lead people to let go of harmful and inaccurate preconceptions and guide their behavior on the basis of their current experience.
This, in turn, allows them to focus on the present, show less concern with making an
impression on others, and live more authentically. These are features associated with
mindfulness. Moreover, people may display these features for years after a close brush
with death (Furn, 1987).

In sum, mindfulness manipulations and a close brush with death may produce their
effects in a similar way. They reduce the likelihood that people automatically apply their
preconceptions. Although this observation helps explain why mindfulness and a close
brush with death produce similar effects, it leaves other questions unanswered. For
example, why does the shedding of cultural preconceptions lead people to experience
greater openness and authenticity? Why doesn't it leave them confused or motivate
them to defend or restore their preconceptions? How do people guide their behavior once they have dropped their cultural preconceptions? Are there alternate goals,
standards, and values they adopt? If so, what are they and where do they come from?
Fortunately, we are not the first to ask questions like these. So, there are places we can
look for answers.

The Drift Back to the Self

Personality researchers have known for years that stable individual differences do not
always reveal themselves in behavior. Sometimes, extraverts act like introverts, and
introverts act like extraverts. So, researchers have tried to outline the variables that
lead people to guide their behavior on the basis of their stable dispositions (Kenrick &
Funder, 1988).

Caspi and Moffitt (1993) proposed that people rely on their stable individual differences when (1) they are in a situation in which the old guides do not apply, (2) the new

guides are not yet known, and (3) they experience a press to behave. In short, people turn to idiosyncratic guides when they feel a need to respond but have no external guides for their behavior.

Turner (1969) developed a similar, though broader, model based on his investigations of rituals in small-scale societies. He suggested that these rituals could be divided into three stages. In the first, or preritual, stage, the initiates guide their behavior on the basis of the cultural knowledge they picked up over the course of their life. The second stage comprises the actual ritual, which is designed intentionally to render the initiates' preritual conceptions inapplicable. The initiates may be threatened, for example, yet not be allowed to turn to their parents for support. In the third stage, the postritual stage, the initiates are provided with the knowledge they need to become fully integrated members of their society.

The stage most relevant to mindfulness is the middle stage, the stage in which the initiates drop their old knowledge but have not yet acquired the new knowledge. According to Turner, in this stage the initiates are stripped of their cultural roles and identities, and have only their basic human predispositions to guide their behavior. So, they behave in a way that is common to all humans and which exists apart from culture.

Is it possible that mindfulness manipulations, including a close brush with death, work in an analogous way? They invalidate people's preexisting guides but leave intact the press to act. With the preexisting guides gone and no readily available external substitute, people act in accord with some basic aspect of their nature. If this hypothesis is correct, we would see some overlap between the features associated with mindfulness or a close brush with death and the features of basic human nature. Of course, no one can say for sure what basic human nature is, but we can take some educated guesses. We propose that basic human nature encompasses features humans evolved as they lived in immediate-return hunter-gatherer societies (Martin, 1999). Thus, mindfulness and a close brush with death wakes people up to their authentic self, the self that reflects their hunter-gatherer heritage.

Our Immediate-Return Heritage

For at least 95% of its existence, our species lived as hunter-gatherers. More precisely, they lived as immediate-return hunter-gatherers. Hunters-gatherers are people who obtain less than 5% of their subsistence from farming and/or herding (Murdock, 1981). Immediate-return hunter-gatherers are those for whom this percent goes down to zero or close to it. According to Marlowe (2002), "Even if foragers [immediate-return hunter-gatherers] are not living fossils, surely they are the best living models of what life was like prior to agriculture" (p. 249). By studying these societies, we may learn something about the world for which our biology was adapted (Martin & Shirk, 2008). This may be the world to which we return when we shed the preconceptions we've adopted from our modern, complex delayed-return society. This is the world we might see if mindfulness were the rule. So, what are the features of immediate-return societies?

Changing company and changing places

One of the more distinctive features of immediate-return societies is their fluidity. These societies are made up of small family groups (with the modal size being 24 members) that exist as part of a larger population spread out over the landscape. There is much movement of individuals in and out of the local groups. In fact, the membership of these groups may change on a daily basis. In addition, the whole group may move every few weeks (Woodburn, 1979), and when it does, the decision is based on a series of ad hoc individual decisions, not on the decision of a leader or on consensus reached in discussion (Turnbull, 1962).

Bird-David (1992) analogized immediate-return societies to drops of oil floating on water. When the drops come together, they coalesce into a larger drop. This larger drop can split easily into smaller ones, however, which may coalesce to form other larger drops. Likewise, members of immediate-return societies "perpetually coalesce with, and depart from, each other" (Bird-David, 1992, p. 597). The formal term is fission and fusion. To state it colloquially, members of immediate-return societies vote with their feet. They can choose which relationships to pursue and which to abandon. They do so through visits, meal sharing, cooperative work, and even through the positioning of the openings of their huts. Thus, they have greater latitude to direct their lives authentically rather than in accordance with formal cultural orthodox.

These features led Ingold (1980) to define immediate-return hunter-gatherer societies as

> a loose and unbounded association of individuals or families, each related to one or more others through immediate kinship, occupying a particular locale and its environs. It is the outcome of a series of choices about where to go, and with whom to affiliate, in order to make the best of environmental resources which are never quite the same, in abundance or distribution, from one season or year to the next. (p. 403; see also Winterhalder & Smith, 1992)

Unlike the delayed-return societies in which most people now live, in immediate-return societies there are no sanctioned authorities, no binding contracts, and a weaker top-down influence of formal cultural conventions. Such societies may foster authenticity.

Relational autonomy

Although members of immediate-return societies move frequently, they do not see this movement as a burden. They see it as a gift. It allows them to maintain their autonomy. It is important to note, though, that their autonomy is not the isolated individualism often seen in modern Western cultures. It is much more relational. It grows out of a history of continuing involvement with others in contexts of joint, practical activity. Each member of the society acts with the other members in mind and can assume that the others will do the same (Bird-David, 1992; Ingold, 1980). Each actively avoids infringing on the autonomy of the others and can be confident the other members will actively avoid infringing on their autonomy.

One way immediate-return societies foster autonomy is through the intentional avoidance of long-term commitments. Such commitments entail dominance and inequality. The first party holds power over the second party until the latter delivers on their end of the deal. By avoiding such commitments, members of immediate-return societies experience considerable freedom to guide their lives on the basis of their personal values and interests.

Heaps of randomly associated elements

In a society that values autonomy as highly as immediate-return societies do, there can be no single, correct version of events. After all, if the interpretation of one person is considered correct, a different interpretation held by another person must be incorrect. Members of immediate-return societies actively avoid this inequality. Thus, people are free to explore their own interpretation of events.

At the individual level, the absence of formalized rights and wrongs fosters autonomy and exploration. At the cultural level, it fosters instability (Brunton, 1989). Immediate-return societies have few verbalized rules of behavior, their rituals are highly variable (and may even be dispensed with altogether), and there is no single, clear idea of a moral order. Their knowledge is generally idiosyncratic and gained by personal experience rather than handed down by others. As one immediate-return hunter-gatherer put it, "None of us are quite sure of anything except of who and where we are at that particular moment" (Brunton, 1989, p. 677). In these societies, there are fewer top-down pressures to constrain people's interpretations of events.

Although there is less pressure to conform to generally agreed-upon conventions in immediate-return societies, the behavior of people in these societies is not random. As Turnbull (1962) noted:

> In the forest life appears to be free and easy, happy-go-lucky, with a certain amount of perpetual disorder as a result. But in fact, behind all the disorder there *is* order and reason; reaching everywhere is the firm, controlling hand of the forest itself. … The forest, the great provider, is the one standard by which all deeds and thoughts are judged; it is the chief, the lawgiver, the leader, and the final arbitrator. (p. 126)

In this way, behavior in immediate-return societies displays yet another feature of mindfulness. It is guided by rules but not determined by them (Carson & Langer, 2006).

Living in the present

In immediate-return societies, people receive relatively immediate feedback with regard to their efforts (Barnard & Woodburn, 1988; Meillassoux, 1973). This does not mean they obtain immediate gratification. It means they know within a relatively a short time whether their efforts have paid off. They will know within a few hours, for example, if their hunt has been successful. If it has, they can return to the camp to eat. If it has not, they have time to search for an alternative food source.

This immediacy allows members of immediate-return societies to maintain an extreme focus on the present. They

> are bound to the momentary present, scarcely ever striking out new lines for themselves, never forecasting the distant future, and seldom making provisions for the near future. Capable of anticipating its future needs only for a very brief span. Accumulation is difficult, long-term planning is impossible. (Forde & Douglas, 1956, p. 332)

Members of immediate-return societies seem to live by the motto "If it is not here and now what does it matter where (or when) it is?" (Turnbull, 1983, p. 122). This immediacy fosters flexibility and adaptation to subtle changes in the environment, which are also features of mindfulness.

In sum, life in an immediate-return society involves frequent changes in group membership and location, less pressure to conform, no sanctioned authorities, no binding commitments, and little in the way of stable, agreed upon cultural orthodox. As a result, members of these societies experience high levels of autonomy, learning that is idiosyncratic, and a strong tendency to live in the present. We believe these features foster mindfulness, and we believe they are harder to come by in delayed-return societies. We propose, therefore, that our ancestral societies fostered mindfulness, whereas our modern, complex, delayed-return societies do not. That is why the shedding of delayed-return cultural values, which can result from a close brush with death, can foster mindfulness.

The Problem With Delayed-Return Societies

Humans made the transition from hunter-gatherer life to a more sedentary life in densely populated communities over the course of thousands of years. For simplicity's sake, though, anthropologists point to 10,000 years ago as the time when things changed. It is around this time that humans were forced into domesticating plants and animals in a widespread and irreversible way.

It was also around this time that humans began domesticating themselves (Harris, 1989). By settling down, humans changed their societies in ways that had significant effects on their psychology—not all of them good. Diamond (1987) calls the transition to agriculture the worst mistake in the history of the human race. It is "a catastrophe from which we have never fully recovered" (p. 64). The problem, in short, is that the transition resulted in the development of delayed-return societies, and these societies often demand from their members behavior that is discordant with their immediate-return nature (Martin, 1999).

For example, in modern, complex societies, people are often required to exert immediate effort for delayed, uncertain payoffs (Martin, 1999; Woodburn, 1979). They may plant crops, work for a paycheck, or save for retirement. In each case, people work toward an outcome they will not receive for days, weeks, months, or even years—if then. This input–outcome disjunction may lead people to experience a great deal of insecurity, possibly over long stretches of time. As a result, people may look for assurance that their efforts are going to pay off. The evidence suggests that people do this in two general ways (both of which have implications for mindfulness).

The first way is structural or societal. People developed formal cultural mechanisms that demand the long-term cooperation of specific members of society (Martin, 1999; Woodburn, 1979). These mechanisms include laws and binding contracts as well as agents designed to enforce those laws and contracts such as courts and police. When members of delayed-return societies enter into formal binding relationships, each member is expected to uphold their end of the deal. If they fail to do so, not only is there no payoff, but also there are negative social consequences.

When people take a job, for example, they may sign a contract indicating that they will be paid at the end of each month. This contract gives them assurance that their efforts throughout the month will eventually produce their desired outcome, namely the paycheck. If the paycheck does not arrive, the workers can take the employer to court for breach of contract and hope to obtain their compensation that way. In short, the members of delayed-return societies intentionally subject themselves to binding social arrangements in an effort to assure themselves that their efforts will pay off. These arrangements may give people the reassurance they seek, but they do so at a cost. They heighten conformity and obedience, and reduce autonomy as well as self-exploration. In other words, they reduce the opportunity for flexible, mindful, authentic behavior.

Barry, Child, and Bacon (1959) and Zern (1983) provided some evidence for this connection in their comparisons of hunting and fishing societies (i.e., immediate return) with herding and farming societies (i.e., delayed return). They noted that in hunting and fishing societies, each day's food comes from that day's catch, and there is a relatively short delay between a person's efforts and feedback regarding the effectiveness of those efforts. Moreover, if a person's initial efforts meet with failure, he or she could switch to Plan B to acquire their desired resources. This flexibility means that deviations from the established routine are not necessarily feared. So, the child-rearing practices in immediate-return societies emphasize personal initiative, exploration, and individual skill. They can try different things. This is a feature associated with mindfulness.

In farming and herding societies, on the other hand, there are established rules that prescribed the best-known way to acquire resources. With farming, for example, people must plow the fields, plant the seeds, water the fields, monitor them for weeds and pests, harvest the grain, and store it safely—and each of these steps must be done in the right way at the right time. If all goes well, the chances are good the farmers will reap the benefits of their effort. If all does not go well, however, there is no time to start over, and the consequences for the entire society may be severe, widespread, and long-term (e.g., hunger or starvation). It is not surprising, therefore, that in delayed-return societies, the child-rearing practices emphasize obedience, conformity, the acceptance of culturally given values, and the fixed application of preexisting rules. These are features associated with mindlessness.

The second strategy people in delayed-return societies use to assure themselves that their efforts will pay off is intrapersonal. They adopt justifying stories such as the Protestant work ethic and just-world beliefs. When people work toward a college degree, for example, they exert effort for years before they can even begin to consider obtaining their sought-after outcome—and even then the outcome may not be obtained. If it is not, then they wasted years of their life. To assure themselves that they are not wasting their time, people may try to convince themselves that the world is just and that their efforts will pay off. So, when there is a conflict between their reassuring stories and reality, people often maintain the stories at the expense of reality (e.g., they blame an innocent victim). This is a form of mindlessness.

Hafer (2000) showed that a delayed-return orientation can heighten this kind of reality distortion. She had participants describe either their long-term plans or the university courses they were currently taking. Then, she had them watch an interview in which a student described how she had contracted a sexually transmitted disease. Some participants heard that the student contracted the disease by accident (innocent victim), whereas others heard that she contracted the disease through her own negligence (blameworthy victim).

Hafer found that participants who believed in a just world and who had focused on their long-terms goals were more likely than those who focused on their courses to blame the innocent victim. It would be pointless for these participants to pursue their long-term goals if the world was not just. Yet, the existence of an innocent victim suggests that the world is not just. So, they distorted that reality. They construed the innocent victim as blameworthy. In short, the delayed-return orientation (i.e., focus on long-term goals) led the participants to maintain a fixed interpretation of events even when that interpretation did not map on to reality. This is a form of mindlessness.

In sum, members of delayed-return societies have established social and cognitive mechanisms designed to assure them that their efforts will payoff. Although these mechanisms may perform their function, they also foster a high level of conformity and encourage the application of preexisting knowledge structures. In other words, they foster mindlessness. It is not surprising, therefore, that manipulations that induce people to drop aspects of these societies lead people to be mindful. They shift people away from the misplaced pressures of a delayed-return society toward the immediacy and authenticity of their immediate-return self.

I-D compensation theory

So far, we've distinguished between mindfulness and mindlessness and noted that a close brush with death can produce features similar to those of mindfulness. We also noted that some of these features are seen more often in immediate-return societies than in delayed-return societies. We raised the possibility that these features may be especially compatible with our basic human nature and noted that situational ambiguity can induce people to turn toward that nature as a guide for their behavior. Therefore, when people drop aspects of their delayed-return society, as with a mindfulness manipulation, they guide their behavior using their basic human nature, which reveals itself in a focus on the present, flexible updating of knowledge structures, and a reduced reliance on received orthodox. These are the features of a mindful society.

Now, we can integrate these general observations into a coherent story using I-D compensation theory (Martin, 1999). It is useful to start by unpacking the name of the theory. The *I* stands for the immediate-return nature of human beings, the *D* stands for the delayed-return nature of the societies in which most people live now, and *compensation* stands for the steps people take to reconcile their immediate-return nature with the constraints placed on them by their delayed-return societies. The general idea is that when people experience discordance between their immediate-return biology and their delayed culture, they take steps to reconcile the two.

More specifically, the theory starts with the assumption that humans possess a set of sensitivities and predispositions that helped their distant ancestors survive and reproduce in the context of immediate-return societies. This is one reason people function optimally when they live in small temporal windows, receive frequent feedback that they are progressing toward their goals, and behave in accord with their personal goals and values. These are the features toward which our biology is attuned.

People may experience psychological difficulties, however, when they live in delayed-return societies. These societies can lead people to behave in ways that are not compatible with their immediate-return biology. There are incompatibilities, for example, in our diet (Cordain et al., 2005), economies (Gowdy, 1999), and population pressure (Cohen, 1985). The main incompatibility on which I-D compensation theory focuses is that between people's efforts and the feedback they receive with regard to those efforts.

Humans function optimally when they receive frequent reliable feedback that they are progressing toward their goals (Carver & Scheier, 1990; Csikszentmihalyi, 1990). This feedback may have characterized the immediate-return societies of our ancestral past, but the feedback can be harder to come by in modern delayed-return societies. In modern societies, people often have to engage in immediate effort for delayed, uncertain outcomes. This effort–outcome disjunction can lead people to experience long periods of insecurity. To cope with this insecurity, people developed complex cultural mechanisms such as contracts and agents to enforce them (Cohen, 1985) and justifying stories such as just-world beliefs (Martin, 1999). In the context of I-D compensation theory, these coping mechanisms reflect people's attempts to create conditions compatible with their immediate-return biology. They are compensations by an immediate-return organism trying to thrive in a delayed-return world.

Not only are people's compensations associated with justifying stories and reassuring social mechanisms, but also they may be associated with rumination, negative affect, and heightened self-focus (Martin & Tesser, 2006). Interestingly, these are the basic ingredients of many phenomena that have been identified by social psychologists (e.g., dissonance, prejudice, defensive self-esteem). So, according to I-D compensation theory, when people adopt an immediate-return orientation, they may be less susceptible to these phenomena.

Empirical evidence

One general hypothesis that can be derived from I-D compensation theory is that people experience a greater need to justify their efforts when they are living in a delayed-return society (i.e., engaging in immediate effort for delayed, uncertain payoff).

We tested this hypothesis by looking at meaning in life. Although there is generally a positive correlation between meaning in life and life satisfaction (Steger & Kashdan, 2007), this correlation is not always observed. It tends to occur mostly among people who are actively searching for meaning (Steger, Oishi, & Kesebir, 2011). If people do not need to justify their behavior, they don't need a justifying story. Who needs to develop and defend a justifying story? People in delayed-return society. They need a way to justify their immediate efforts for delayed, uncertain payoff. Thus, the correlation between meaning in life and life satisfaction is likely to be higher among people in a delayed-return society.

We tested this hypothesis priming aspects of immediate-return and delayed-return cultures and then having participants rate their meaning in life as well as their life satisfaction. More precisely, we presented participants with 14 sentences and asked them to sort the sentences into seven pairs. For some participants, the sentences reflected the features of immediate-return, forager societies (e.g., "Long-term, binding contracts inhibit people's freedom"). For others, the sentences reflected the features of modern, complex, delayed–return society (e.g., "Long-term, binding contracts assure us of that our efforts will pay off"). This made participants think about the features of immediate-return and delayed-return societies, respectively. After participants completed this priming task, they rated the extent to which they had found meaning in their life and the extent to which they were searching for meaning in their life. Then, they rated their satisfaction with life.

The results supported our justification hypothesis. There was a stronger correlation between having found meaning and life satisfaction among participants who had been primed with aspects of delayed-return societies. The results suggest more generally that exposure to the values of modern, complex, delayed-return societies heightened participants' need to have a story to make sense of their life.

Of course, having a story does not by itself lead to mindlessness. Mindlessness occurs, in essence, when people guide their behavior using a preexisting story rather than the features of the actual situation. In a second study, we explored the way in which a delayed-return orientation might lead people to do this.

We began by assessing participants' belief in a just word (e.g., I feel that people get what they are entitled to have). Then, we primed aspects of immediate-return and delayed-return societies. After that, we had participants read about an interview in which a student explained how she had contracted a sexually transmitted disease. Some participants read that the student had contracted the disease by accident (innocent victim), whereas others read that she had contracted the disease through her own negligence (blameworthy victim). Then, we assessed the extent to which participants blamed the student for contracting the disease.

We hypothesized that participants who were primed with aspects of a delayed-return world would have more of a need to defend their view that the world is just. After all, it would be pointless for them to engage in immediate effort for delayed payoff unless they were assured of the payoff. A just world (like meaning in life) can assure them that their efforts will pay off. The existence of an innocent victim, however, suggests that the world is not just. So, if people are motivated to see the world as just, they may simply distort that reality. They may construe the innocent victim as blameworthy. This is what we found.

Participants who believed in a just world and who were primed with the aspects of a delayed-return society were more likely to rate the innocent victim as blameworthy. In other words, they were more likely to force the story in their head onto the world whether or not the story fit. This is a form of mindlessness.

In sum, these studies suggest that people have a greater need for a coherent story and a greater tendency to apply that story at the expense of reality when they are in a delayed-return orientation. This is how living in a delayed-return society can foster mindlessness.

When mindfulness rules

Now, we have enough background to address the main question: What would the world be like if mindfulness was the rule rather than the exception? The answer, in short, is that people would display features associated with mindfulness, a close brush with death, and living in an immediate-return way. We discuss each in turn.

As we noted in our introduction, if mindfulness were the rule, people would be more creative, healthier, and more liked by their interaction partners. They would learn better, exhibit less stereotyping, display greater self-acceptance, and even live longer. They would also reduce their automatic acceptance and application of introjected cultural values, be more sensitive to subtle variations in their environment, and be better able to apply new categories as needed.

According to I-D compensation theory, if mindfulness were the rule, people would also be less susceptible to a wide array of traditional social psychology phenomena. This is because when people behave mindfully they experience less uncertainty, negative affect, and self-concern. As a result, they would be less likely to display phenomena that have these features as their underlying components. So, if mindfulness were the rule, people might experience less dissonance, less defensive self-esteem, less blaming of innocent victims, less outgroup derogation, and fewer breakdowns in self-control.

If mindfulness were the rule, people would also display better coping. They would do this for two reasons. First, mindfulness can facilitate acceptance. Life situations become problems, in part, because they block important goals (Martin & Tesser, 2006). A spinal cord injury, for example, could challenge people's ability to have children, take care of their self, or support their family. One component of successful coping is knowing when to let go of blocked goals (Wrosch, Scheier, Carver, & Schulz, 2003). Smith, Jankovic, Loewenstein, and Ubel (2009), for example, found that people who accepted their colostomies as irreversible were better adjusted one year after their surgery than people who maintained hope they might improve back to their presurgery selves. More generally, in a mindful world, people would shed their fixed conceptions of how life should be and adjust instead to the way it really is.

For more clues regarding what the world would look like if mindlessness were the rule, we can turn to our second source of information: people who have had a close brush with death. As we noted previously, a close brush with death can help people shed introjected cultural values, focus on the present, and experience greater acceptance of the self. Although these changes can be profound, they typically manifest themselves in ordinary ways. As Wren-Lewis (1994) put it:

> The change is a subtle one, in keeping with that sense of absolute ordinariness: I haven't for example become anything like my earlier stereotypes of the mystic or "enlightened being." I haven't lost my taste for meat or wine or humor or detective fiction, or good company; I still feel sexual pleasure, I still enjoy being appreciated by others, and my scientific curiosity is as great as ever. In fact all these things seem "very good" as never before—but I am no longer bothered to *pursue* any of them, nor much worried when such desires aren't met, since in the new consciousness, satisfaction is the basic essence of existence itself, not the result of desire-gratification. So while I still make choices and pursue goals, this has become for me a kind of secondary game, not the focus of living. (p. 111)

So, what would the world look like if people were more mindful? It would look profoundly ordinary. The overall effect of a close brush with death is to wake people up to the present. It makes them more mindful. A woman dying of cancer was clear about this when she attributed her psychological growth to "Mindfulness. Being aware of how I spend each moment of the day. ... [Ordinarily] We don't see our options" (Branfman, 1996). If mindfulness were the rule, people would see more options in the ways they could interact with the world. They would not be locked into a single perspective.

Wren-Lewis (1994) noted how his close brush with death allowed him to develop alternate interpretations of many of the unpleasant aspects of life including pain and death:

> I now experience such a pain in the way nature must surely mean it to be experienced, mainly as a signal of something to be avoided if possible, or other organs not functioning properly. I found that the painful stimulus remains unpleasant precisely so long as I ignore the signal.

Regarding death, he wrote

> Although I still intend to avoid it as long as possible in life's secondary game and still mourn the loss of friends, it has in itself a very special kind of beauty, like the dying leaves of autumn, whose splendor we are allowed to see in ordinary consciousness because our minds don't associate it with the ultimate taboo. (Wren-Lewis, p. 114)

Observations like these lead us to believe that if mindfulness were the rule, people would be less likely to struggle against the world. They would adjust their knowledge to the subtle changes in the world rather than trying to force the world to conform to their preconceptions. As a result, they might come, like Wren-Lewis (1988), to "know exactly why the Bible says that God looked upon the creation and saw that it was good" (p. 115).

Our third source of information for how the world would look if mindfulness were the rule is immediate-return societies. According to numerous reports, members of these societies are happy. As Turnbull (1962) noted of the M'buti, an immediate-return society in Africa

> They are a people who had found in the forest something that made their life more than just worth living, something that made it, with all its hardships and problems and tragedies, a wonderful thing full of joy and happiness and free of care. (pp. 25–26)

Everett (2008) provided a very similar description of the Pirahãs [pee da HAN], a group in Brazil. He wrote, "the Pirahãs or an unusually happy and contented people" (p. 279). They

> showed no evidence of depression, chronic fatigue, extreme anxiety, panic attacks, or other psychological ailments common in many industrialized societies. ... They regularly face dangerous reptiles, mammals, bugs, and other creatures. They live with threats of violence from outsiders who frequently invaded their land. When I am there, with a much easier life than the Pirahãs themselves, I still find there's plenty for me to get worked up about. The thing is, I do get worked up, but they do not. I have never heard a Pirahã say that they are worried. In fact, so far as I can tell, the Pirahãs have no word for *worry* in their language. (p. 278)

One way in which an immediate-return orientation fosters happiness is by inducing people to focus on the present. This immediate temporal focus may help people avoid phenomena that can undermine psychological well-being, such as rumination (Martin & Tesser, 2006). As Everett (2008) observed:

> The Pirahãs share some of our concerns, of course, since many of our concerns derive from our biology, independent of our culture ... But they live most of their lives outside these concerns because they have independently discovered the usefulness of living one day at a time. The Pirahãs simply make the immediate their focus of concentration, and thereby, at a single stroke, they eliminate huge sources of worry, fear, and despair that plague so many of us in Western societies. (p. 273)

It seems likely that if mindfulness were the rule, people would focus more on the present and display less worry, fear, and despair.

Of course, focusing on the present may work well for people in immediate-return societies, but it may seem more difficult to accomplish in a delayed-return society and may even seem counterproductive. This is not necessarily the case, however. People can attain long-term goals by focusing on the subcomponents, by focusing on what they are doing at the moment. They can live in the present without living for the present. In fact, doing so seems to enhance long-term persistence and the ability to delay gratification (Stock & Cervone, 1990). This is because each small success operates as feedback that people are making progress toward their long-term goals (Frey & Preston, 1980). In this way, people can turn a delayed-return situation into an immediate-return one (Martin, 1999).

In fact, from an I-D compensation perspective, this would be the main advantage of living in a world in which mindfulness was the rule. That world would be more compatible with our immediate-return biology. If mindfulness were the rule, people would thrive even when they faced pressures that otherwise would be considered delayed return (e.g., pursuing long-term goals).

Where to from here?

Does the picture we have painted seem too good to be true? Could widespread mindfulness really give rise to a world in which people were more creative, coped better, and experienced greater happiness? We believe it could.

Keep in mind that there is evidence for most of our conclusions, and when we did speculate, we did not deviate far from that evidence. Remember also that the immediate-return lifestyle is one that served our species well for the first 95% of its existence. It may very well be the lifestyle with which our biology is most compatible. In fact, we consider it to be our birthright. It comes naturally to us once the constraints of our delayed-return societies are removed. If this conjecture is true, the real marvel is not that mindfulness can lead people to experience the world in the ways we have described. "The real marvel seems to be that the world isn't experienced like this by everyone all the time, since this is, quite simply, the way things are" (Wren-Lewis, 1994, p. 110).

So, what would the world look like if people were more mindful? In many ways, it would look like the world of 100,000 years ago. That does not mean we would be living in the forest and foraging for food. It means we would be paying attention, seeing more options in the ways we could interpret the world, adjusting our behavior in response to subtle changes in the environment, and behaving authentically rather than through fixed cultural knowledge we may have introjected mindlessly.

And the good news is that we don't have to undergo anything as dramatic as a close brush with death to develop an immediate-return orientation. It can come naturally to us if we let it. Wren-Lewis (1994) captured this sentiment well, when he said:

> What I suspect we need is not any kind of path or discipline, but a collection of tricks or devices for catching the Dark at the corner of the eye, as it were, and learning how to spot its just-waiting-to-be-seen presence, combined with strategies for stopping the hyperactive survival-programs from immediately explaining the perception away. (p. 114)

Perhaps with the help of a few mindfulness exercises (Langer & Piper, 1987), we could all learn to let go and look at the world and say, "It is good."

References

Alexander, C., Langer, E. J., Newman, R., Chandler, H., & Davies, J. (1989). Aging, mindfulness and meditation. *Journal of Personality and Social Psychology, 57,* 950–964.

Barnard, A., & Woodburn, J. (1988). Property, power and ideology in hunter-gathering societies: An introduction. In T. Ingold, D. Riches, & Woodburn (Eds.), *Hunters and gatherers* (Vol. 2, pp. 4–31). Oxford, UK: Berg.

Barry, H., Child, I. L., & Bacon, M. K. (1959). Child relation of child training to subsistence economy. *American Anthropologist, 61,* 51–63.

Bird-David, N. (1992). Beyond "The Original Affluent society": A culturalist reformulation. *Current Anthropology, 33,* 115–137.

Branfman, F. (1996). How a terminal diagnosis saved Jackie McEntee's life. Retrieved from trulyalive.org, http://www.trulyalive.org/individuals/jackie_mcentee.htm

Brown, J., & Langer, E. (1990). Mindfulness and intelligence: A comparison. *Educational Psychologist, 25*[Special issue: Intelligence and Intelligence Testing], 305–335.

Brunton, R. (1989). The cultural instability of egalitarian societies. *Man, 24*, 673–681.

Carson, S. H., & Langer, E. J. (2006). Mindfulness and self-acceptance. *Journal of Rational-Emotive & Cognitive Behavior Therapy, 24*, 29–43.

Carver, C. S., & Scheier, M. F. (1990). Origins and functions of positive and negative affect: A control-process view. *Psychological Review, 97*, 19–35.

Caspi, A., & Moffitt, T. E. (1993). When do individual differences matter? A paradoxical theory of personality coherence. *Psychological Inquiry, 4*, 247–271.

Chanowitz, B., & Langer, E. J. (1981). Premature cognitive commitment. *Journal of Personality and Social Psychology, 41*, 1051–1063.

Chesterton, G. K. (2009). *The ball and the cross.* Lawrence, KS: Digireads.com.

Cohen, M. N. (1985). Prehistoric hunter-gatherers: The meaning of social complexity. In T. D. Price & J. A. Brown (Eds.), *Prehistoric hunter-gatherers* (pp. 99–117). Orlando, FL: Academic Press.

Cole, B. S., & Pargament, K. I. (1999). Spiritual surrender: A paradoxical path to control. In W. R. Miller (Ed.), *Integrating spirituality into treatment: Resources for practitioners* (pp. 179–198). Washington, DC: American Psychological Association.

Cordain, L., Boyd Eaton, S., Sebastian, A., Mann, N., Lindeberg, S., Watkins, B. A., ... & Brand-Miller, J. (2005). Origins and evolution of the Western diet: health implications for the 21st century. *American Journal of Clinical Nutrition, 81*, 341–354.

Csikszentmihalyi, M. (1990). *Flow: The psychology of optimal experience.* New York, NY: Harper-Collins.

Csikszentmihalyi, M., & LeFevre, J. D. (1989). Optimal experience in work and leisure. *Journal of Personality and Social Psychology, 56*, 815–22.

Diamond, J. (1987). The worst mistake in the history of the human race. *Discover Magazine, May*, 64–66.

Djikic, M., Langer, E. J., & Stapleton, S. F. (2008). Reducing stereotyping through mindfulness: Effects on automatic stereotype-activated behaviors. *Journal of Adult Development, 15*, 106–111.

Everett, D. L. (2008). *Don't sleep, there are snakes.* New York, NY: Pantheon Books.

Frey, P. S., & Preston, J. (1980). Children's delay of gratification as a function of task contingency and the reward-related contents of task. *Journal of Social Psychology, 111*, 281–291.

Flynn, C. P. (1984). Meanings and implications of near-death experiencer transformations. In B. Greyson & C. P. Flynn (Eds.), *The near-death experience: Problems, prospects, perspectives* (pp. 278–289). Springfield, IL: Charles C. Thomas.

Forde, D., & Douglas, M. (1956). Primitive economics. In H. L. Shapiro (Ed.), *Man, culture, and society* (pp. 330–344). New York, NY: Oxford University Press.

Furn, B. G. (1987) Adjustment and the near-death experience: A conceptual and therapeutic model. *Journal of Near-Death Studies, 6*, 4–19.

Gowdy, J. (1999). Hunter-gatherers and the mythology of the market. (pp. 391–398). In R. B. Lee & R. Daly (Eds.), *The Cambridge encyclopedia of hunters and gatherers.* Cambridge, UK: The Cambridge University Press.

Grey, M. (1985). *Return from death: An exploration of the near-death experience.* London, UK: Arkana.

Greyson, B. (1983). Near-death experiences and personal values. *American Journal of Psychiatry, 140*, 618–620.

Greyson, B., & Stevenson, I. (1980). The phenomenology of near-death experiences. *American Journal of Psychiatry, 137*, 1193–1196.

Hablitzel, W. E. (2006). *Dying was the best thing that ever happened to me*. Austin, TX: Greenleaf Books.

Hafer, C. L. (2000). Investment in long-term goals and commitment to just means drive the need to believe in a just world. *Personality and Social Psychology Bulletin, 26*, 1059–1073.

Harris, M. (1989). *Our kind: Who we are, where we came from, where we are going*. New York, NY: HarperCollins.

Ingold, T. (1980). *The appropriation of nature: Essays on human ecology and social relations*. Iowa City, IA: University of Iowa Press.

Janoff-Bulman, R. (1992). *Shattered assumptions: Towards a new psychology of trauma*. New York, NY: Free Press.

Kenrick, D. T., & Funder, D. C. (1988). Profiting from controversy: Lessons from the person-situation debate. *American Psychologist, 43*, 23–34.

Kinnier, R. R., Tribbensee, N. E., Rose, C. A., & Vaugh, S. M. (2001). In the final analysis: More wisdom from people who have faced death. *Journal of Counseling and Development, 79*, 171–177.

Kuhl, D. (2002). *What dying people want: Practical wisdom for the end of life*. New York, NY: Public Affairs.

Langer, E., & Eisenkraft, N. T. (2009). Orchestral performance and the footprint of mindfulness. *Psychology of Music, 37*, 125–136.

Langer, E. J. (2009). *Counterclockwise: Mindful health and the power of possibility*. New York, NY: Ballantine Books.

Langer, E. J., Blank, A., & Chanowitz, B. (1978). The mindlessness of ostensibly thoughtful action: The role of 'placebic' information in interpersonal interaction. *Journal of Personality and Social Psychology, 36*, 635–642.

Langer, E. J., Cohen, M., & Djikic, M. (2012). Mindfulness as a psychological attractor: The effect on children. *Journal of Applied Social Psychology, 42*, 1114–1122.

Langer, E., Hatem, M. J., & Howell, M. J. (1989). Conditional teaching and mindful learning: The role of uncertainty in education. *Creativity Research Journal, 2*, 139–150.

Langer, E. J., & Moldoveanu, M. (2000). The construct of mindfulness. *Journal of Social Issues, 56*, 1–9.

Langer, E. J., & Piper, A. I. (1987). The prevention of mindlessness. *Journal of Personality and Social Psychology, 53*, 280–287.

Marlowe, F. (2002). Why the Hadza are still hunter-gatherers. In S. Kent (Ed.), *Ethnicity, hunter-gatherers, and the "other": Association or assimilation in Africa* (pp. 247–275). Washington, DC: Smithsonian Institution Press.

Martin, L. L. (1999). I-D compensation theory: Some implications of trying to satisfy immediate-return needs in a delayed-return culture. *Psychological Inquiry, 10*, 195–208.

Martin, L. L., Campbell, W. K., & Henry, C. D. (2005). The roar of awakening: Mortality acknowledgment as a call to authentic living. In J. Greenberg, S. L. Koole, & T. Pyszczynski (Eds.), *Handbook of experimental existential psychology* (pp. 431–448). New York, NY: Guilford Press, 2004.

Martin, L. L., & Kleiber, D. A. (2005). Letting go of the negative: Psychological growth from a close brush with death. *Traumatology, 11*, 221–232.

Martin, L. L., & Shirk, S. (2008). Immediate return societies: What can they tell us about the self and social relationships in our society? In J. V. Wood & A. Tesser (Eds.), *The self and social relationships* (pp. 161–182). New York, NY: Psychology Press.

Martin, L. L., & Tesser, A. (2006). Extending the goal progress theory of rumination: Goal re-evaluation and growth. In L. J. Sanna & E. C. Chang (Eds.), *Judgments over time: The interplay of thoughts, feelings, and behaviors* (pp. 145–162). New York, NY: Oxford University Press.

Meillassoux, C. (1973). On the mode of production of the hunting band. In P. Alexandre (Ed.), *French perspectives in African studies* (pp. 187–203). Oxford, UK: Oxford University Press for the International African Institute.

Murdock, G. P. (1981). *Atlas of world cultures*. Pittsburgh, PA: University of Pittsburgh Press.

Noyes, R. (1980). Attitude change following near-death experiences. *Psychiatry, 43*, 234–242.

Noyes, R., Jr. (1982–1983). The human experience of death, or what can we learn from near-death experiences? *Omega, 13*, 251–259.

Reason, J. (1984). The psychopathology of everyday slips. *The Sciences, Sep/Oct*, 45–48.

Ring, K. (1984). *Heading toward omega: In search of the meaning of near death experience*. New York, NY: William Morrow and Company.

Roberts, G. A., & Owen, J. H. (1988). The near-death experience. *British Journal of Psychiatry, 153*, 607–617.

Smith, D. M., Jankovic, A., Loewenstein, G., & Ubel, P. A. (2009). Happily hopeless: Adaptation to a permanent, but not to a temporary, disability. *Health Psychology, 28*, 787–791.

Steger, M. F., & Kashdan, T. B. (2007). Stability and specificity of meaning in life and life satisfaction over one year. *Journal of Happiness Studies, 8*, 161–179.

Steger, M. F., Oishi, S., & Kesebir, S. (2011). Is a life without meaning satisfying? The moderating role of the search for meaning in satisfaction with life judgments. *The Journal of Positive Psychology, 6*, 173–180.

Stock, J., & Cervone, D. (1990). Proximal goal-setting and self-regulatory processes. *Cognitive Therapy and Research, 14*, 483–498.

Sutherland, C. (1992). *Transformed by the light*. Sydney, Australia: Random House Australia.

Tedeschi, R. G., & Calhoun, L. G. (2004). Posttraumatic growth: Conceptual foundations and empirical evidence. *Psychological Inquiry, 15*, 1–18.

Turnbull, C. M. (1962). *The forest people*. New York, NY: Simon & Schuster.

Turnbull, C. M. (1983). *The Mbuti Pygmies: change and adaptation*. New York, NY: Holt, Rinehart Winston.

Turner, V. (1969). *The ritual process: Structure and anti-structure*. New York, NY: Aldine deGruyter.

Winterhalder, B., & Smith, E. A. (1992). Evolutionary ecology and the social sciences. In E. A. Smith & B. Winterhalder (Eds.), *Evolutionary ecology and human behavior* (pp. 3–23). New York, NY: Aldine de Gruyter.

Woodburn, J. C. (1979). Minimal politics: The political organization of the Hadza of North Tanzania. In W. A. Shack & P. S. Cohen (Eds.), *Politics in leadership: A comparative perspective* (pp. 224–246). Oxford, UK: Clarendon Press.

Wren-Lewis, J. (1988). The darkness of God: A personal report on consciousness transformation through an encounter with death. *Journal of Humanistic Psychology, 28*, 105–122.

Wren-Lewis, J. (1994). Aftereffects of near-death experiences: A survival mechanism hypothesis. *Journal of Transpersonal Psychology, 26*, 107–115.

Wren-Lewis, J. (2004). The implications of near-death experiences (NDEs) for understanding posttraumatic growth. *Psychological Inquiry, 15*, 90–92.

Wrosch, C., Scheier, M. F., Carver, C. S., & Schulz, R. (2003). The importance of goal disengagement in adaptive self-regulation: When giving up is beneficial. *Self and Identity, 2*, 1–20.

Zern, D. S. (1983). The relationship of certain group-oriented and individualistically oriented child-rearing dimensions to cultural complexity in a cross-cultural sample. *Genetic Psychology Monographs, 108*, 3–20.

17

Answering Questions
A Comparison of Survey Satisficing and Mindlessness
David L. Vannette and Jon A. Krosnick

Introduction

While the large literature on mindlessness has evolved in psychology, a remarkably related literature has evolved quite separately in the literature on survey methodology. In that context, researchers have been interested in understanding why different question wordings sometimes yield systematically different answers from survey respondents. Inspired by Simon's (1957) notion of satisficing, Krosnick (1999) proposed that respondents might sometimes devote considerable cognitive effort to answering survey questions accurately and might at other times devote little or no effort and instead seek to generate answers quickly on the basis of little thinking. This distinction parallels the notions of mindfulness and mindlessness, so building a bridge between the two literatures seems potentially promising to yield new and valuable insights and may generate interesting hypotheses that could advance research in both mindfulness and survey satisficing. In this chapter, we seek to bridge these literatures.

We begin by describing the survey questionnaire response process, with particular emphasis on the cognitive features of responding to questions. Beginning with a description of what researchers believe is the optimal response process; we then introduce the theory of survey satisficing and contrast it with the optimal process. Next, we describe specific response strategies that the theory proposes respondents may employ in order to shortcut the response process. Noting the operation of these strategies, we offer a set of general implications and recommendations for optimal questionnaire design.

Having established the notion of survey satisficing, the final section of the chapter contrasts it with mindfulness and mindlessness, and proposes a set of potential benefits of understanding satisficing theory for mindfulness researchers. Lastly, we outline some proposals for ways that understanding mindfulness and mindlessness might benefit survey researchers in areas such as momentary assessment, cognitive interviewing,

The Wiley Blackwell Handbook of Mindfulness, First Edition.
Edited by Amanda Ie, Christelle T. Ngnoumen, and Ellen J. Langer.
© 2014 John Wiley & Sons, Ltd. Published 2014 by John Wiley & Sons, Ltd.

and respondent recruitment. To do this, we draw on findings in the literature in mind-fulness and mindlessness that may be relevant to survey research and suggest some novel applications of these concepts in the domain of survey research.

In the course of telling this story, we offer advice for researchers regarding how best to design survey questions to measure constructs accurately and overcome the distorting impact of satisficing. Because mindfulness researchers routinely measure the extent to which people are mindful or mindless by administering questionnaires, our advice may be useful to these researchers by helping them to design more effective measures.

Optimal Responses

Cognitive features of the response process

When a respondent is answering a question in a questionnaire, the accuracy of the obtained data is dependent partly on how well people perform the required cognitive tasks. Specifically, a person must execute a set of mental processes in order to offer a valid response. These processes have been outlined by a number of researchers, several of whom have proposed four stages (Cannell, Miller, & Oksenberg, 1981; Sudman, Bradburn, & Schwarz, 1996; Tourangeau, Rips, & Rasinski, 2000): (1) comprehen-sion, where respondents interpret the intended meaning of the question; (2) retrieval, which involves the respondent searching memory for all relevant information; (3) judgment, which involves integrating retrieved information into summary judgments; and (4) responding in a way that conveys the judgment. Proceeding carefully through each of these stages constitutes what has come to be called *optimizing*.

Many motives may lead a person to optimize the response process when answering a question, including desires for self-expression, interpersonal response, intellectual challenge, self-understanding, feelings of altruism, or emotional catharsis (see, e.g., Warwick & Lininger, 1975). Questionnaires often require a great amount of effort to complete optimally, and the expenditure of this effort in answering questionnaires can also be motivated by desires of the respondent to help researchers or for gratification from successful performance, to help employers improve working conditions, to help manufacturers produce better quality products that suit consumers' needs better, or to help governments make better informed policy decisions. To the extent that these sorts of motives inspire a person to optimize the response process, responses seem more likely to reflect the "true" values of the constructs being assessed.

Satisficing, a Breakdown in Optimal Responding

Satisficing

As much as researchers hope that respondents optimize the response process for each question in a questionnaire, the reality of responding may often be less than ideal. In fact, some people may agree to complete a questionnaire simply through a relatively automatic compliance process (e.g., Cialdini, 1988) or because they are required to do so in order to fulfill a course requirement or to earn financial remuneration for questionnaire completion. Thus, they may have no intrinsic motivation to provide high-quality answers to the questions.

Simon posited that, when faced with the demanding information-processing tasks of everyday life, people often expend only the amount of effort necessary to make an acceptable or satisfactory decision, a strategy Simon called *satisficing* (Simon, 1957). Presented as a simple metaphor about how people behave, this notion was a useful starting point for developing a theory of the questionnaire response process in particular. Krosnick (1991) theorized that respondents may sometimes not be sufficiently motivated to provide high-quality data and therefore may engage in satisficing during the survey response process.

Satisficing is thought to occur because optimizing is sometimes more cognitively demanding than a respondent is willing or able to execute in answering a question. Questionnaires routinely require respondents to answer multiple questions, sometimes for hours at a time during the longest face-to-face interviews. Even in shorter questionnaires, respondents are often asked to answer extensive batteries of questions, and these questions can be cognitively demanding. Taken together, these features of questionnaires may increase the chances of respondent satisficing (Krosnick, 1999; Krosnick, Narayan, & Smith, 1996; McClendon, 1986, 1991; Narayan & Krosnick, 1996).

In the face of the significant cognitive demands of the response process, respondents may not optimize when answering every single question and may instead shortcut or completely skip some stages of optimizing (Krosnick, 1999). Some respondents are motivated to expend the considerable cognitive effort necessary to optimize their responses. However, the sources and duration of this motivation may vary across respondents and across questions within a single questionnaire. Respondents may expend their resource of available effort early in the questionnaire-completion process, before all questions have been answered. As motivation fades, such respondents may lose interest and become increasingly fatigued, impatient, or distracted. Yet questions remain to be answered, even after a respondent is no longer fully engaged with the reporting process or motivated to optimize their responses. This presents respondents with a dilemma: they have agreed to complete a questionnaire and may have even been promised an incentive as a reward for completion, but they now lack the motivation to provide optimal responses to what must often feel to the respondent like an unending stream of questions.

In this situation, some respondents will break off, stopping the process of answering questions before all have been answered. But perhaps more often, respondents may continue answering but change their response strategy. Instead of continuing the cognitively demanding process of optimizing, some respondents may choose to expend less mental effort in any or all stages of the response process. This behavior is called "survey satisficing" (Krosnick, 1991). As they satisfice, respondents may interpret a question's meaning and then search memory incompletely or in a biased manner, integrate retrieved information superficially, and then report their response. In this formulation, respondents complete all four steps of the response process but shortcut stages 2 and or 3, an approach called *weak satisficing*.

As questionnaire completion continues, respondent motivation may decrease, and fatigue may increase, leading to further degradation in the response process. When this occurs, the respondent may fail to implement the retrieval and judgment stages altogether and may instead exert only minimal effort to interpret the question and provide a response that appears plausible. Yet this answer is selected without referring to any internal psychological cues specifically relevant to the attitude, belief, or event of interest. Instead, the respondent may look to the wording of the question for a cue, pointing to a response that can be easily selected and easily defended if necessary. If no such cue is present, the respondent may select an answer completely arbitrarily. In this case, the respondent provides what may appear to be a sensible answer to each question but without having actually delivered any meaningful information. This is termed *strong satisficing*.

Optimizing and strong satisficing can be thought of as being at the poles of a continuum of cognitive effort, with weak satisficing occurring to varying degrees between the poles. When optimizing, respondents thoroughly retrieve and carefully integrate relevant information. When strong satisficing occurs, respondents do not retrieve or integrate any relevant information from memory before providing a response. Weak satisficing, then, is a label encapsulating a range of potential levels of incompleteness in the response process; retrieval may be thorough, while integration is incomplete, or vice versa.

Satisficing Response Strategies

According to the theory of satisficing, respondents may satisfice in a series of specific ways depending on the format and features of the question that has been asked and the response options that have been provided. This section outlines the primary satisficing response strategies that have been documented in the literature.

Don't know?

One response strategy thought to be a manifestation of strong satisficing is selecting an offered "don't known" option. When a respondent is asked about a subjective phenomenon, researchers routinely presume that the responses provided reflect opinions or information that the respondent had in their memories. Even if the specific requested judgment does not already exist in long-term memory, a respondent might draw on available information to construct a judgment (e.g., Zaller & Feldman, 1992). Under this set of assumptions, responses to a question, whether previously extant or newly formed, then reflect the respondent's true opinion on the matter under investigation.

However, questions sometimes focus on a matter about which the respondent knows nothing and cannot form a judgment. In this case, researchers would prefer the respondent indicate this lack of relevant information by stating that he/she has "no opinion" (NO) or by offering a "don't know" (DK) response. If the question is worded in such a way that respondents feel that they ought to have an opinion, then they may provide an arbitrary, seemingly substantive response in order to avoid appearing to be embarrassingly uninformed. Thus, some respondents may provide a nonattitude in the guise of a meaningful answer (Converse, 1964).

Consistent with this argument, the reliability of questionnaire responses over time is often moderate to low (Achen, 1975; Converse & Markus, 1979; Feldman, 1989; Jennings & Niemi, 1978). This low response reliability has been taken by some to indicate that many respondents don't have true opinions about issues and are indeed responding at random. More disconcerting are findings that respondents sometimes offer apparently meaningful opinions on extremely obscure or fictitious issues about which they are extremely unlikely to know anything (Bishop, 2005; Bishop, Tuchfarber, & Oldendick, 1986; Hawkins & Coney, 1981; Paulhus, Harms, Bruce, & Lysy, 2003; Schwarz, 1996), again suggesting that they are likely reporting nonattitudes.

To reduce the chance of arbitrary responses being given to questions, some experts have suggested that NO or DK response options should always be offered to respondents (e.g., Vaillancourt, 1973). However, other researchers caution against offering DK or NO response options, because they may induce respondents who do have meaningful opinions to fail to report those opinions (Krosnick, 1991; Krosnick et al., 2002). Along these lines, Oppenheim (1992) speculated that some people give a "don't know" response in order to avoid thinking. Further supporting this recommendation to avoid DK options is evidence that voting behavior is better predicted by estimates of respondents' political candidate preferences when researchers discourage DK responses (Krosnick et al., 2002; Visser, Krosnick, Marquette, & Curtin, 2000). Additionally, respondents who are encouraged to guess after providing a DK response tend to provide the correct answer to factual questions about political knowledge at better than chance rates (Mondak & Davis, 2001). This indicates that discouraging DK responses leads to more valid data than encouraging such responses.

Satisficing theory focuses on people who have relevant considerations available in memory but must construct overall evaluations by integrating those considerations, rather than simply retrieving existing judgments already in memory. If a person is low in ability to optimally conduct a memory search and information integration or low in motivation to do so, or task difficulty is high, and a "don't know" option is explicitly offered, he or she may choose to satisfice by selecting it (Krosnick, 1991). If the NO option were to be omitted from the question instead, these respondents might be less likely to satisfice and might therefore optimize instead. Consequently, offering a NO option may forego collection of useful data by discouraging some respondents from providing thoughtful answers.

Even if a NO option is omitted from a question, some respondents may volunteer that they have no opinion. Interviewers or interactive software can respond by saying, "we'll make a note of that, but it would be very helpful if you'd be willing to answer the question, even if you're not completely sure of your answer." The people who volunteer a NO answer a second time in response to this probe can be viewed as genuinely having no information to offer. This approach collects meaningful response from the largest group of respondents. This recommendation is in line with common practice among most major survey organizations, who train their interviewers to probe respondents when they say that they don't know the answer to a question and encourage respondents to provide a substantive response instead, even using wording such as "what is your best guess?" to elicit responses.

Acquiescence

A response strategy thought to result from weak satisficing is agreeing with assertions made in questions. This is relevant to one of the most commonly used question-and-response formats, which utilizes what is called a "Likert scale," after the work of Rensis Likert (1932). Respondents read a statement and indicate the degree to which they agree or disagree with the statement. This format offers the opportunity for efficiency: many different constructs can be measured with a series of questions without changing the response options from question to question.

A great deal of research shows that some respondents are biased toward agreeing with just about any statement when presented with such an agree/disagree scale or when asked a question with true/false response options or implicit yes/no response options (e.g., "Do you like tomatoes?"). This agreement tendency is known as *acquiescence bias* and is thought to occur for a number of reasons. Some respondents are inclined to agree because they wish to conform to social norms that dictate agreeableness and politeness (Bass, 1956; Brown & Levinson, 1987; Campbell, Converse, Miller, & Stokes, 1960). Another cause is the tendency that some respondents are inclined to defer to people who seem to be of higher social status and better informed, including an interviewer or researcher (Carr, 1971; Lenski & Leggett, 1960).

Satisficing is also thought to be a cause of acquiescence bias. Respondents who fail to exert the mental effort required to fully evaluate the plausibility of a statement or respondents who have limited cognitive skills to do so may be inclined to manifest acquiescence bias. People implementing weak satisficing evaluate the plausibility of a statement by thinking of reasons why the statement might be valid and quickly grow fatigued and terminate the evaluation process before thoroughly considering reasons why the statement might be invalid. Thus, satisficing individuals tend toward agreeing with a statement rather than disagreeing with it (Krosnick, 1991).

Evidence of acquiescence bias comes from studies showing that some respondents agree with a statement *and* with its opposite and from evidence that more people agree with a statement than disagree with its opposite. About 15–20% of respondents appear to manifest acquiescence on average across studies (for reviews of this literature, see Krosnick & Presser, 2010; Saris, Revilla, & Krosnick, 2010). Consistent with satisficing theory, acquiescence is most common when respondent ability to optimize is low, when motivation to do so is low, and when a question requires substantial cognitive work in order to be answered optimally. Thus, acquiescence bias can present a major challenge to researchers, so a number of different approaches have been developed to attempt to address this problem.

To overcome this problem, some researchers have pursued approaches aimed at mitigating acquiescence bias rather than abandoning the agree/disagree, true/false, and yes/no response formats. One common approach is balancing batteries of questions, where half of the statements are arranged such that affirmative answers indicate high levels of the construct of interest, and the other half of the statements are such that affirmative answers indicate low levels of the construct. This approach assumes that acquiescence will be equivalent across items for each respondent, so a tendency to agree with all statements will cancel out and place such respondents in the middle of the possible range of final scores. However, there is no theoretically justified reason why these respondents should be placed at the scale midpoint. Thus, simply balancing a set of questions may not improve the validity of measurement.

The more effective solution is to offer questions with construct-specific response choices. That is, if a question is meant to assess the personal importance of an issue to a respondent, it is preferable to ask the respondent, "How important is this issue to you? Extremely important, very important, moderately important, slightly important, or not important at all?" rather than asking them to agree or disagree with a statement such as, "This issue is important to me." The former approach eliminated any pressure in the question toward an affirmative answer.

Response-order effects

Another manifestation of weak satisficing is impact of the order in which response options are presented to respondents (Schuman & Presser, 1996). Respondents are often asked to choose among a set of offered nominal or ordinal response choices. Respondents inclined to satisfice may devote confirmatory-biased thinking to initially considered options and terminate the evaluation process before thoroughly evaluating those choices or others that are offered by the question. In short, satisficing respondents may be inclined to settle for the first plausible response option they identify. This yields what are called response-order effects (Krosnick, 1999; Krosnick & Alwin, 1987).

When questions are presented visually, typically on paper or a computer screen, people tend to choose the first nominal response options presented. This is known as a *primacy effect,* and considerable evidence indicates that such primacy effects are especially likely to occur under the conditions thought to foster satisficing (Chang & Krosnick, 2010; Krosnick & Alwin, 1987; Malhotra, 2009; Narayan & Krosnick, 1996). Recency effects occur when nominal sets of response options are presented orally. Respondents have the most time to implement confirmatory-biased thinking after hearing the final response option, and options heard most recently are most likely to be remembered after hearing a question. All this biases respondents toward selecting the last option they hear (Holbrook, Krosnick, Moore, & Tourangeau, 2007; Krosnick & Alwin, 1987). Primacy effects also occur with visually and orally presented ordinal rating scales because of a tendency for respondents to select the first response option they consider that falls within their "latitude of acceptance" of plausible responses. These effects tend to occur most among respondents with a low ability to optimize, when motivation to optimize is low, and when answering a question requires considerable cognitive work (Holbrook et al., 2007).

Response-order effects can be managed by randomly assigning different respondents to read or hear the response choices in one of various different orders. Because the researcher directs this assignment, it is possible to control statistically for the systematic variance thus created in the data. It is best to do so with interactions between the order manipulation and attributes of respondents indicating their cognitive ability (e.g., years of education) and motivation (e.g., their need for cognition).

Nondifferentiation in using rating scales

Many survey practitioners believe that answering a series of questions with the same response alternatives is easier and more enjoyable for respondents and more efficient for interviewers than constantly changing response alternatives from question to question (e.g., Lavrakas, 1987, pp. 145–146). This belief frequently leads survey designers to group questions together that offer the same response alternatives. For example, respondents might be asked to consider a series of brands of candy bars and to indicate for each one whether they like it a great deal, like it somewhat, like it only a little, or don't like it at all.

In recent years, researchers have come to recognize that there is an inherent danger in asking respondents to rate a series of objects on a common scale. In most cases, researchers hope that respondents will differentiate among the objects in their ratings. In the candy bar example, researchers might want to use the rating data to make inferences about which brands are preferred. Unfortunately, this is sometimes difficult to do, because some respondents fail to differentiate between the objects in their ratings, instead giving all or almost all of the objects the same rating (see, e.g., Krosnick & Alwin, 1988). Doing so may sometimes be the result of a careful consideration of the merits of the objects, but this response strategy could also be the result of strong satisficing. Satisficing respondents could, for example, simply select a point on the response scale that appears to be reasonable for the first object, and then rate all of the remaining objects at that point. Therefore, this response pattern might appear more often under the conditions that foster satisficing.

A number of studies have found evidence consistent with this prediction. Nondifferentiation is more common among respondents with less education (Krosnick & Alwin, 1988; Rogers & Herzog, 1984). Nondifferentiation is more common toward the end of a questionnaire than toward the beginning (Coker & Knowles, 1987; Herzog & Bachman, 1981; Knowles, 1988; Knowles, Cook, & Neville, 1989a, 1989b; Knowles, Lundeen, & Irwin, 1988; Kraut, Wolfson, & Rothenberg, 1975; Krosnick & Alwin, 1988; Neville & Knowles, n.d.; Rogers & Herzog, 1984), particularly among respondents low in verbal ability (Knowles et al., 1989a, 1989b). Furthermore, placing rating questions later in a questionnaire makes correlations between ratings on the same scale more positive or less negative (Andrews, 1984; Herzog & Bachman, 1981; Krosnick & Alwin, 1988; Rogers & Herzog, 1984), which are the expected results of nondifferentiation (see Krosnick & Alwin, 1988).

Reducing the Likelihood of Satisficing

Researchers cannot control the ability level that a respondent brings to a questionnaire, but researchers can influence an individual's motivation to optimize and can influence the cognitive posed by a questionnaire. In order to minimize the likelihood of satisficing, questionnaire designers should take steps to maximize respondent motivation and to minimize task difficulty. Motivation can be enhanced by creating a sense of accountability among respondents, by providing instructions asking respondents to commit to thinking carefully and generating accurate answers, and by telling respondents why the research project's findings will be valuable and have constructive impact. Task difficulty can be minimized by taking steps to make it easy for people to interpret questions, to retrieve information from memory, to integrate the information into a judgment, and to report that judgment.

For example, interpretation is presumably more difficult for questions written with rarely used words or words with various different meanings. Similarly, retrieval may be made more difficult by questions that ask about multiple objects rather than just one. It is useful to think of the difficulty of the judgment phase as a function of the *decomposability* of the decision to be made; the more constituent decisions that must be made and integrated into a single summary judgment, the more difficult this phase will be (see Armstrong, Denniston, & Gordon, 1975). A question can be difficult to answer at the point of response selection if the answer choices use familiar words with obvious meanings.

Mindful Versus Mindless Responding to Questionnaires

Mindfulness and mindlessness

Thus far, we have talked about the cognitive and contextual conditions that are associated with satisficing behavior by people answering questionnaires. Now, we turn to the literature on *mindfulness* and *mindlessness* to apply these concepts to the question-answering context of questionnaires.

Mindfulness has been described in a number of different ways, such as "bringing one's complete attention to the present experience on a moment-to-moment basis" (Marlatt & Kristeller, 1999) or as "paying attention in a particular way: on purpose, in the present moment, and nonjudgmentally" (Kabat-Zinn, 1994). Most definitions of mindfulness contain three key components. First, mindfulness is a state of consciousness, not a trait of individuals (Lau et al., 2006). Second, this state of consciousness focuses attention on the present moment, the "here and now" (Herndon, 2008). Third, this present-moment attention is marked by consciousness of both internal and external phenomenon, or "both the content and context of information" (Langer, 1992).

In contrast, according to Langer (1992), "mindlessness concerns rigid invariant behavior that occurs with little or no conscious awareness" (Langer, 1992). Mindlessness is a state of reduced attention to the present moment that is typified by implementing cognitively scripted behavior without conscious awareness (Langer, 1975).

The contrast of mindfulness and mindless maps onto the contrast of optimizing and satisficing only partially and awkwardly. On the one hand, a mindful state seems necessary in order for optimizing to occur. That is, a respondent must focus their complete attention on the process of answering questions, with considerable cognitive awareness. However, satisficing could also occur in that way. That is, a satisficing respondent may be quite aware that they are choosing to shortcut the thinking process while answering questions and may execute satisficing mindfully, with attention and conscious awareness focused on that activity.

Furthermore, satisficing seems not to parallel mindlessness. To the extent that mindlessness involves the state of acting without thinking, it is similar to satisficing in that there is little conscious thought involved. But satisficing involves selecting among offered responses in ways that minimize cognitive effort, whereas mindless behavior involves relying on scripts and habits when taking actions. Thus, there is not necessarily a close parallel between these two distinctions.

It is intriguing to think about what would happen during the process of questionnaire completion if the respondent were in a state of mindlessness, behaving according to habits and scripts with very little conscious attention or thought. One circumstance in which this might occur is if a respondent is completing an online questionnaire simply to earn a financial reward and with no intention to even read or think about the questions at all (see, e.g., Yeager et al., 2011). And perhaps some college students completing a questionnaire in order to meet a course requirement might do this as well. It might be interesting to explore the behavioral habits or scripts that people execute under such circumstances in order to answer questions, in order perhaps to detect this behavior by observing patterns of responses.

Another possibility worth noting is that mindlessness may be a state into which respondents creep as they progress through a questionnaire. For example, a person completing a questionnaire may begin in a state of conscious awareness, executing cognitive processes thoughtfully and diligently. But as the questionnaire progresses, respondents might become fatigued and increasingly unwilling to think carefully. As a result, people may become increasingly mindless as time passes, and more questions are answered.

It is also interesting to think about the possibility of transforming respondents from being in a mindless state to being mindful. Specifically, the mindfulness literature suggests exploring the possibility that respondents could be told explicitly about the four stages of optimal question answering: interpretation, retrieval, integration, and judgment. Perhaps encouraging respondents explicitly to perform these cognitive tasks might lead people to be more effortful and responsible—in short, more mindful in a good way. But perhaps encouraging people to introspect and attempt to control the working of their minds would interfere with ordinarily effective processing and would yield reductions in report accuracy. Future studies could explore this possibility.

Indeed, one instantiation of this general concept is a core component of what is known as *cognitive interviewing*, an increasingly popular pretesting method used to identify problems with wordings or formats employed in questionnaires (Beatty & Willis, 2007). During this pretesting procedure, respondents are first asked to restate each question in their own words and then think out loud to verbalize all their thoughts when generating an answer to the question. The purpose of this procedure is to gain insights into how people interpret questions, to identify instances in which misinterpretations occur, so questions must be rewritten. It seems obvious that the procedure itself will induce a state of mindfulness, so the answers that pretest respondents provide are likely to reflect that mindful state. If the same state would be desirable during all questionnaire completion, it might be interesting to see what methods could be used to induce it without considerably lengthening the interview process the way that cognitive interviewing does.

Are there benefits of satisficing for assessing mindlessness?

One might imagine that if a questionnaire's purpose were to predict or understand behavior performed mindlessly, then optimizing during questionnaire responding would not be desirable. Instead, we might want people to answer a questionnaire in just the way they will ultimately act in the situation of interest: thinking only superficially. Thus, it might seem that satisficing would be desirable to accomplish such research goals.

There are two principal reasons that we do not share this perspective. First, we view the goal of questionnaire measurement of subjective phenomena to be the accurate assessment of the contents of an individual's memory. Thus, if the contents of memory are incompletely measured and/or the measures are biased, then we are handicapped in any effort to describe how the information in a person's memory will later impact their thinking or action. The process of mindless behavior involves superficial or biased retrieval from memory, so the challenge of explaining such behavior is to document the superficiality and bias in the process. To assess the contents in an incomplete or biased fashion is to incorrectly assign that incompleteness and bias to the contents, not to the process by which they are retrieved and applied.

The second reason why satisficing is undesirable, even for understanding behavioral phenomena that may involve mindlessness, is that its particular manifestation for any given measure is presumably a function of the question form employed. If a "don't know" alternative is offered, satisficing might manifest itself as a selection of it. If a question is closed-ended, a response-order effect may be manifested in the form of selecting the first reasonable response. If a question is in an agree/disagree format, satisficing may drive respondents toward affirmative answers. Yet these biases are not substantively informative about the contents of respondents' memories. They reflect primarily the question format that the researcher happens to have chosen to measure the construct of interest. How could such biases possibly help a researcher to understand the sources of mindless behavior performed without a question stimulating it? We think they cannot, and so we believe satisficing is best avoided, even when assessing mindless behaviors.

Benefits of bridging the mindfulness and satisficing literatures

Satisficing theory may offer some thoughts of value to mindfulness research. First, awareness of satisficing when completing questionnaires is useful for mindfulness researchers to consider any time that mindfulness is measured using questionnaires, which seems to be quite often (Baer, 2004; Cardaciotto, Herbert, Forman, Moitra, & Farrow, 2008; Herndon, 2008; Lau et al., 2006; Van Dam, Earleywine, & Borders, 2010). Satisficing can have dramatic impacts on data reliability and validity, so it is important that researchers in any domain making use of questionnaires apply concerted and concrete efforts to reduce satisficing by task difficulty and increasing respondent motivation. We hope that this chapter raises awareness of the causes of satisficing and the risks that it poses to questionnaire-based research on mindfulness in such a way that helps measurement to improve and science to advance more rapidly.

Second, satisficing theory might stimulate new hypotheses and directions in the area of mindfulness research. For example, as with satisficing, perhaps when people are being mindless, they are more prone to acquiescence bias or deciding that they "don't know" something that they might actually hold in memory (e.g., Chiesa, Calati, & Serretti, 2011). To our knowledge, exploration of this possibility has not been conducted in either the mindfulness or survey research domains. The predictions made by satisficing theory could be tested in the contexts of mindlessness and mindfulness to identify whether the predicted patterns arise in each. Perhaps participants trained to be mindful are more motivated during the question-response process and will demonstrate more optimizing behavior rather than satisficing. Similarly, perhaps participants that are mindlessly engaging in the question-response process will be less motivated and more likely to exhibit satisficing behaviors.

In addition, mindfulness researchers may benefit from the sizable and accumulating literature on the causes of satisficing (Krosnick, 1991). Under the headings of ability, motivation, and task difficulty, many concrete attributes of individuals, situations, and questions have been identified as catalyzers of satisficing. These same factors might combine in the same additive and interactive ways in inducing mindless behavior, a possibility worth exploring in future research.

There may also be benefits for survey researchers from understanding the concepts of mindfulness and mindlessness, and the literature on them. Particular subfields and techniques of survey research may be uniquely suited to take advantage of the concepts and methods of mindfulness training, while others may benefit from understanding mindless behavior. For example, cognitive interviewing seems well positioned to benefit from incorporating the concepts and training techniques thought to induce mindfulness. Similarly, techniques for stimulating mindfulness may be useful for researchers employing Ecological Momentary Assessment, which is a survey practice where respondents are called at intervals throughout a day and asked to report their behavioral and cognitive processes and states in the natural settings (Stone & Shiffman, 1994). Lastly, there may be a place for exploring the extent to which mindless responding to requests (Langer, Blank, & Chanowitz, 1978) might be useful to exploit in the context of increasing survey participation rates. In other words, there may be a parallel between "May I use the copy machine? I need to make some copies." and "Would you please complete this survey? We need your responses." If potential respondents might mindlessly comply with the request to participate in a survey, given the appropriate request framework and length, then there may be implications for how survey interviewers should make the initial request for participation in order to increase response rates.

These observations and potential links between mindfulness and mindlessness research and survey methodology are largely speculative, but we believe that they may act as a starting point for exciting new research directions that could provide benefits for research in both fields. These and other questions could provide meaningful new incentives to bridge the fields of mindfulness and satisficing research. We hope that this chapter acts as a starting point to stimulate new ideas and applications of existing theories, concepts, and techniques in important psychological and methodological research.

Conclusion

In this chapter, we have outlined the cognitive features of responding to questionnaires and described satisficing theory, a framework for understanding the conditions that predict when people are likely to engage in suboptimal questionnaire responding. We then described a series of concrete steps that researchers should take to reduce opportunities for satisficing when designing questionnaires. We hope that this evidence-based advice will prove useful to mindfulness researchers whenever they use questionnaires.

Next, we turned to examining the potential conceptual parallels and connections that may exist between optimizing and mindfulness, and satisficing and mindlessness. While these concepts are in many ways complementary, they do not completely overlap, and neither can fully explain the other in the context of the questionnaire-response process. Despite this lack of perfect correspondence between the concepts, there may be significant benefits that mindfulness researchers could gain from an understanding of satisficing. By applying the optimal questionnaire design principles suggested by satisficing theory, researchers can reduce opportunities for satisficing among their participants, which should have the effect of improving data reliability and validity. Furthermore, satisficing theory presents opportunities to ask new and interesting questions about the effects of mindfulness and mindlessness in light of satisficing theory. There are also opportunities for survey methodology research to benefit from understanding the integrating concepts and techniques from mindfulness and mindlessness research in hopes of improving both data quality and survey participation. We hope that this chapter provides important insights and guidance that will help move both mindfulness research and survey methodology forward by improving data collection and offering new areas for research.

References

Achen, C. H. (1975). Mass political attitudes and the survey response. *The American Political Science Review, 69*(4), 1218–1231.

Andrews, F. M. (1984). Construct validity and error components of survey measures: A structural modeling approach. *Public Opinion Quarterly, 48*(2), 409–442.

Armstrong, J. S., Denniston, W. B., Jr., & Gordon, M. M. (1975). The use of the decomposition principle in making judgments. *Organizational Behavior and Human Performance, 14*(2), 257–263.

Baer, R. A. (2004). Assessment of mindfulness by self-report: The Kentucky Inventory of Mindfulness Skills. *Assessment, 11*(3), 191–206.

Bass, B. M. (1956). Development and evaluation of a scale for measuring social acquiescence. *Journal of Abnormal Psychology, 53*, 296–299.

Beatty, P. C., & Willis, G. B. (2007). The practice of cognitive interviewing. *Public Opinion Quarterly, 71*(2), 287–311.

Bishop, G. F. (2005). *The illusion of public opinion: Fact and artifact in American public opinion polls.* Oxford, UK: Rowan & Littlefield.

Bishop, G. F., Tuchfarber, A. J., & Oldendick, R. W. (1986). Opinions on fictitious issues: The pressure to answer survey questions. *Public Opinion Quarterly, 50*(2), 240–250.

Brown, P., & Levinson, S. C. (1987). *Politeness: Some universals in language use*. New York, NY: Cambridge University Press.

Campbell, A., Converse, P. E., Miller, W. E., & Stokes, D. E. (1960). *The American voter.* New York, NY: John Wiley & Sons.

Cannell, C. F., Miller, P. V., & Oksenberg, L. (1981). Research on interviewing techniques. *Sociological Methodology, 12*, 389–437.

Cardaciotto, L., Herbert, J. D., Forman, E. M., Moitra, E., & Farrow, V. (2008). The assessment of present-moment awareness and acceptance: The Philadelphia Mindfulness Scale. *Assessment, 15*(2), 204–223.

Carr, L. G. (1971). The Srole items and acquiescence. *American Sociological Review.*

Chang, L., & Krosnick, J. A. (2010). Comparing oral interviewing with self-administered computerized questionnaires: An experiment. *Public Opinion Quarterly, 74*(1), 154–167.

Chiesa, A., Calati, R., & Serretti, A. (2011). Does mindfulness training improve cognitive abilities? A systematic review of neuropsychological findings. *Clinical Psychology Review, 31*(3), 449–464.

Cialdini, R. B. (1988). *Influence: Science and practice*. Glenview, IL: Scott, Foresman.

Coker, M. C., & Knowles, E. S. (1987). *Testing alters the test scores: Test–retest improvements in anxiety also occur within a test*. Paper presented at the Annual Meeting of the Midwestern Psychological Association, Chicago.

Converse, P. E. (1964). The nature of belief systems in mass publics. In D. Apter (Ed.), *Ideology and discontent*. New York, NY: Free Press.

Converse, P. E., & Markus, G. B. (1979). Plus ca change … : The New CPS Election Study Panel. *The American Political Science Review, 73*(1), 32–49.

Feldman, S. (1989). Measuring issue preferences: The problem of response instability. *Political Analysis, 1*, 25–60.

Hawkins, D. I., & Coney, K. A. (1981). Uninformed response error in survey research. *Journal of Marketing Research, 18*(3), 370–374.

Herndon, F. (2008). Testing mindfulness with perceptual and cognitive factors: External vs. internal encoding, and the cognitive failures questionnaire. *Personality and Individual Differences, 44*(1), 32–41.

Herzog, A. R., & Bachman, J. G. (1981). Effects of questionnaire length on response quality. *Public Opinion Quarterly, 45*(4), 549–559.

Holbrook, A. L., Krosnick, J. A., Moore, D., & Tourangeau, R. (2007). Response order effects in dichotomous categorical questions presented orally the impact of question and respondent attributes. *Public Opinion Quarterly, 71*(3), 325–348.

Jennings, M. K., & Niemi, R. G. (1978). The persistence of political orientations: An over-time analysis of two generations. *British Journal of Political Science, 8*(3), 333–363.

Kabat-Zinn, J. (1994). *Wherever you go, there you are*. New York, NY: Hyperion.

Knowles, E. S. (1988). Item context effects on personality scales: measuring changes the measure. *Journal of Personality and Social Psychology, 55*(2), 312–320.

Knowles, E. S., Cook, D. A., & Neville, J. W. (1989a). *Assessing adjustment improves subsequent adjustment scores*. Paper presented at the Annual Meeting of the American Psychological Association, New Orleans, LA.

Knowles, E. S., Cook, D. A., & Neville, J. W. (1989b). *Modifiers of context effect on personality tests: Verbal ability and need for cognition*. Paper presented at the Annual Meeting of the American Psychological Society.

Knowles, E. S., Lundeen, E. J., & Irwin, M. E. (1988). *Experience with the personality test changes factor loadings on externality but not self-monitoring*. Paper presented at the 60th Annual Convention of the Midwestern Psychological Association, Chicago, IL.

Kraut, A. I., Wolfson, A. D., & Rothenberg, A. (1975). Some effects of position on opinion survey items. *Journal of Applied Psychology, 60*(6), 774.

Krosnick, J. A. (1991). Response strategies for coping with the cognitive demands of attitude measures in surveys. *Applied Cognitive Psychology, 5*(3), 213–236.

Krosnick, J. A. (1999). Survey research. *Annual Review of Psychology, 50*(1), 537–567.

Krosnick, J. A., & Alwin, D. F. (1987). An evaluation of a cognitive theory of response-order effects in survey measurement. *Public Opinion Quarterly, 51*(2), 201–219.

Krosnick, J. A., & Alwin, D. F. (1988). A test of the form-resistant correlation hypothesis: Ratings, rankings, and the measurement of values. *Public Opinion Quarterly, 52*(4), 526–538.

Krosnick, J. A., Holbrook, A. L., Berent, M. K., Carson, R. T., Hanemann, W. M., Kopp, R. J., … Conaway, M. (2002). The impact of "no opinion" response options on data quality: Non-attitude reduction or an invitation to satisfice? *Public Opinion Quarterly, 66*(3), 371–403.

Krosnick, J. A., Narayan, S. S., & Smith, W. R. (1996). Satisficing in surveys: Initial evidence. *New Directions for Evaluation, 70,* 29–44.

Krosnick, J. A., & Presser, S. (2010). Question and questionnaire design. In P. V. Marsden (Ed.), *Handbook of survey research.* Bingley, UK: Emerald Group Publishing.

Langer, E. J. (1975). The illusion of control. *Journal of Personality and Social Psychology, 32*(2), 311–328.

Langer, E. J. (1992). Matters of mind: Mindfulness/mindlessness in perspective. *Consciousness and Cognition, 1*(3), 289–305.

Langer, E. J., Blank, A., & Chanowitz, B. (1978). The mindlessness of ostensibly thoughtful action: The role of "placebic" information in interpersonal interaction. *Journal of Personality and Social Psychology, 36,* 635–642.

Lau, M. A., Bishop, S. R., Segal, Z. V., Buis, T., Anderson, N. D., Carlson, L., … Devins, G. (2006). The Toronto mindfulness scale: Development and validation. *Journal of Clinical Psychology, 62*(12), 1445–1467.

Lavrakas, P. J. (1987). *Telephone survey methods: Sampling, selection, and supervision.* Beverly Hills, CA: Sage Publications.

Lenski, G. E., & Leggett, J. C. (1960). Caste, class, and deference in the research interview. *American Journal of Sociology, 65*(5), 463–467.

Likert, R. (1932). A technique for the measurement of attitudes. *Archives of Psychology, 140,* 5–55.

Malhotra, N. (2009). Completion time and response order effects in web surveys. *Public Opinion Quarterly, 72*(5), 914–934.

Marlatt, G. A., & Kristeller, J. L. (1999). Mindfulness and meditation. In W. R. Miller (Ed.), *Integrating spirituality in treatment* (pp. 67–84). Washington, DC: American Psychological Association.

McClendon, M. J. (1986). Unanticipated effects of no opinion filters on attitudes and attitude strength. *Sociological Perspectives, 29*(3), 379–395.

McClendon, M. J. (1991). Acquiescence and recency response-order effects in interview surveys. *Sociological Methods & Research.*

Mondak, J. J., & Davis, B. C. (2001). Asked and answered: Knowledge levels when we will not take "don't know" for an answer. *Political Behavior, 23*(3), 199–224.

Narayan, S. S., & Krosnick, J. A. (1996). Education moderates some response effects in attitude measurement. *Public Opinion Quarterly, 60*(1), 58–88.

Neville, J. W., & Knowles, E. S. (n.d.). *Serial position effects on extracted MMPI scales.* Unpublished manuscript.

Oppenheim, A. N. (1992). *Questionnaire design, interviewing, and attitude measurement.* London, UK: Pinter.

Paulhus, D. L., Harms, P. D., Bruce, M. N., & Lysy, D. C. (2003). The over-claiming technique: Measuring self-enhancement independent of ability. *Journal of Personality and Social Psychology, 84*(4), 890–904.

Rogers, W. L., & Herzog, A. R. (1984). *Response style characteristics and their relationship to age and item covariances.* Unpublished manuscript.

Saris, W. E., Revilla, M., & Krosnick, J. A. (2010). Comparing questions with agree/disagree response options to questions with item-specific response options. *Survey Research Methods, 4,* 61–79.

Schuman, H., & Presser, S. (1996). *Questions and answers in attitude surveys: Experiments on question form, wording, and context.* London, UK: Sage Publications.

Schwarz, N. (1996). *Cognition and communication: Judgmental biases, research methods, and the logic of conversation.* Malwah, NJ: Erlbaum.

Simon, H. A. (1957). *Models of man.* New York, NY: Wiley.

Stone, A. A., & Shiffman, S. (1994). Ecological momentary assessment (EMA) in behavorial medicine. *Annals of Behavioral Medicine, 16,* 199–202.

Sudman, S., Bradburn, N. M., & Schwarz, N. (1996). *Thinking about answers: The application of cognitive processes to survey methodology.* San Francisco, CA: Jossey-Bass.

Tourangeau, R., Rips, L. J., & Rasinski, K. A. (2000). *The psychology of survey response.* Cambridge, UK: Cambridge University Press.

Vaillancourt, P. M. (1973). Stability of children's survey responses. *Public Opinion Quarterly, 37*(3), 373–387.

Van Dam, N. T., Earleywine, M., & Borders, A. (2010). Measuring mindfulness? An item response theory analysis of the Mindful Attention Awareness Scale. *Personality and Individual Differences, 49*(7), 805–810.

Visser, P. S., Krosnick, J. A., Marquette, J., & Curtin, M. (2000). Improving election forecasting: Allocation of undecided respondents, identification of likely voters, and response order effects. In *Election polls, the news media, and democracy.* New York, NY: Chatham House.

Warwick, D. P., & Lininger, C. A. (1975). *The sample survey: Theory and practice.* New York, NY: McGraw-Hill.

Yeager, D. S., Krosnick, J. A., Chang, L., Javitz, H. S., Levendusky, M. S., Simpser, A., & Wang, R. (2011). Comparing the accuracy of RDD telephone surveys and internet surveys conducted with probability and non-probability samples. *Public Opinion Quarterly, 75*(4), 709–747.

Zaller, J., & Feldman, S. (1992). A simple theory of the survey response: Answering questions versus revealing preferences. *American Journal of Political Science, 36*(3), 579–616.

18

The Impact of Mindfulness on Creativity Research and Creativity Enhancement

Shelley Carson

The qualities of mindfulness are important components of creative ideation. The *mindful* state, in which an individual actively and nonjudgmentally notices novel aspects of objects and situations, forms an internal cognitive environment in which associations that lead to new products, discoveries, inventions, and processes can occur. In contrast, the *mindless* state—in which an individual adheres to preconceived conceptualizations of objects and events in the environment (without noting differences in context)—discourages the production of creative ideas, discoveries, and products.

Consider, for example, the classic case of Scottish biologist, Alexander Fleming: Before leaving on holiday with his family, Fleming left several culture plates containing variants of the staphylococcus bacterium uncovered on a bench in his laboratory. Some of the culture plates became contaminated with an air-borne microorganism. When Fleming returned, he noticed that in some of the contaminated plates, a white fluffy mold was growing. He further noticed that the bacteria near the mold were dying, or "undergoing lysis," as Fleming recounted in his original report. Fleming then examined the mold more closely and began to culture it (Fleming, 1929).

Although much more work would still need to be done to convert that serendipitous contaminant into penicillin, the discovery of a medical miracle occurred in a Scottish laboratory in 1928, because a biologist *mindfully* observed an anomaly on a culture plate—rather than *mindlessly* categorizing it as "contaminated" and discarding it.

There are many first-hand accounts of the discovery or invention of scientific and artistic products that highlight the importance of a mindful state. There is also a growing body of cognitive and neuroscience research that associates the state of mindfulness either directly or indirectly with the creative process. In this chapter, I will first define creativity and two separate but complementary traditions of mindfulness research. I will also underscore the need for creativity in the 21st century. I will then examine how mindfulness is related to a variety of characteristics that define the creative individual,

The Wiley Blackwell Handbook of Mindfulness, First Edition.
Edited by Amanda Ie, Christelle T. Ngnoumen, and Ellen J. Langer.
© 2014 John Wiley & Sons, Ltd. Published 2014 by John Wiley & Sons, Ltd.

and I will describe how mindfulness informs the creative insight process. Finally, I will demonstrate how an attitude of mindfulness may enhance our natural creative abilities.

Definitions of Mindfulness and Creativity

Creativity has been associated both theoretically and empirically with two different traditions of mindfulness research. While both traditions emphasize being present in the moment and viewing the self and the environment in a nonjudgmental way, there are definite distinctions in the theory, research, and practice of both traditions.

The Western tradition of mindfulness

The first tradition, which I will refer to as the Western tradition, views mindfulness as a flexible state of mind that results from drawing novel distinctions about the situation and the environment. This tradition is derived from the work of Harvard social psychologist Ellen Langer and her associates, based on their empirical work in the field of choice and decision-making processes (Langer, 1989, 1997). The *mindful* person is actively engaged in the present and sensitive to both context and perspective. In the mindful state, a person is noticing new aspects of experience on many levels simultaneously and is typically *guided* by rules and routines but not *governed* by them. In contrast, *mindlessness* is a rigid state in which a person adheres to a single perspective and interacts with the environment with preconceived automatic responses, oblivious to context or perspective. The mindless person tends to pigeon-hole experiences and objects into rigid categories. Thought processes and behavior in the mindless state are *governed*, rather than guided by, rules and routines that have been established (usually by others) in the past. In the Western tradition, mindfulness is encouraged by teaching individuals to view information from multiple perspectives and to categorize information and experience in provisional rather than absolute ways (Langer, 2000).

The Eastern tradition of mindfulness

The second construct of mindfulness, which I will refer to as the Eastern tradition, has its roots in Zen Buddhist philosophy, and has been popularized in the West by the work of Buddhist monk, Thich Nhat Hanh (1975), and University of Massachusetts scientist, Jon Kabat-Zinn (1990). In this tradition, the mindful state is associated with a specific type of meditation in which attention and conscious awareness are focused on present-state thoughts, emotions, and perceptions of one's surroundings.

The goal of mindfulness meditation in the Eastern tradition is to achieve a nonjudgmental state of quiet mind that promotes *acceptance* of the self and the environment. In contrast, the goal of mindfulness in the Western tradition is to view phenomena nonjudgmentally from multiple perspectives and then *choose* the perspective that makes the most sense in the given context. The difference might be described as quiet acceptance versus active choice.

Definition of creativity

While the definition of creativity has long been debated, most researchers in the field have agreed that two elements need to be present for an idea or product to be considered creative: first, it must be *novel* or *original,* and second, it has to be *useful* or *adaptive.* In other words, it has to serve a purpose for at least some portion of the population (Barron, 1969). For example, the scribblings of a toddler who has just learned to hold a crayon are *novel* and *original,* but they are not typically considered *creative* under our definition because they are not *useful* or *adaptive* for some portion of the population. Of course, the *mindful* person could dispute this example and point out that judging the toddler's scribblings as nonuseful would be to prematurely categorize them and ignore the adaptive aspects of learning to use a drawing implement or of having one's fledgling attempts at art hung on the refrigerator door by a doting mother. Thus, we immediately run into a dilemma posed by the intersection of science and mindfulness. In order to study a construct scientifically, we must be able to define and measure it; however, the very act of defining and measuring a thing involves limiting (perhaps mindlessly) its description and functions to those that can be concretely defined and measured.

In my research, I define creativity as follows: it is the ability to combine or recombine bits of information in novel or original ways to arrive at an idea or product that is useful or serves a purpose (Carson, 2010). "Bits of information" can be stored in the individual's unique brain repository of knowledge, memories, and skills, or they can arrive from the external environment through the sensory organs. This definition combines the elements of *novel/original* and *useful/adaptive* with the well-accepted theory that creative thinking involves the forming of associative elements into new combinations (Mednick, 1962).

Many people confuse the concept of creativity with that of *talent.* For example, I often have people tell me that they are not creative because they cannot even draw a stick figure. The ability to draw realistically is a matter of talent, however, rather than creativity. Talent is technical ability in a particular domain of endeavor (such as perfect pitch in music or mathematical calculation skills). Creative capacity (which is innate in all of us) surpasses the boundaries of domains and is transferrable to many areas of one's life.

The Importance of Creativity in the 21st Century

We are all aware of the comfort and richness that human creativity has brought to our lives. From advances in modern medicine to the invention of hand-held communication devices to music, poetry, and art that calm or motivate us, we have all benefitted from the creativity of those who have gone before us. We also benefit from our own major or minor acts of creativity, which may include anything from patenting inventions to pursuits such as painting, journaling, playing music, gardening, or cooking. Recent studies indicate that engaging in creative activity can reduce stress, regulate mood, and increase longevity (Cohen et al., 2006).

The purpose of human creativity, however, is not only personal enrichment; it has historically served as a survival mechanism for our species. Our human predecessors were not strong enough to fight off large predators nor fast enough to outrun them; we were able to survive as a species due primarily to our human ingenuity that allowed our predecessors to build tools, weapons, and shelters. In other words, we humans were able to conceive of that which did not already exist and actually bring it into existence to meet our survival needs. Creativity is our survival mechanism today, as well; it is a vital resource for meeting the challenges and dangers, as well as the opportunities, of the accelerated-change climate of the 21st century.

The recent explosion in information and technology, which has facilitated cyber-communication and globalization, has also transformed the way we learn, the way we do business, and the way we relate to each other. As the rulebooks for virtually *every* aspect of human endeavor and interaction are changing before our eyes, the need for creative solutions to never-before-imagined problems has intensified. Creativity is no longer limited to the work of artists, writers, musicians, and scientists; it is also a valued commodity in professions from athletes (Eisenberg, 2005) to military officers (Matthew, 2009). Further, according to a recent worldwide study of CEOs, creativity is now considered the most important leadership quality for business executives (IBM Corporation, 2010).

Businesses that do not innovate risk falling behind their competitors. It is no longer possible to rest on previously successful products or to conduct business in the same old way that has worked in the past. One example is the spectacular collapse of U.S. automaker General Motors, which required a large infusion of taxpayer capital to keep its doors open. Analysts attributed the collapse to a corporate culture that sacrificed innovation, creativity, and long-term vision in favor of short-term returns on investment (Maynard, 2008).

Creative solutions are needed for problems such as a faltering world economy, an increase in global terrorism, and deadly physical and mental disorders such as heart disease and depression. In recognition of this realization, former UK Prime Minister, Gordon Brown, has suggested that creativity and innovation are the most critical factors in the future of the UK economy (Brown, 2009). Creative solutions are also needed for problems at the personal level, including everything from how to comfort a child who hasn't made the soccer team to how to prepare for a productive and engaging retirement.

Clearly, the need for creativity at both the individual and the societal level is now being recognized and acknowledged. Our human ingenuity and creativity are the greatest assets we possess for successfully negotiating this rapidly changing modern world (Carson, 2010). If an attitude of mindfulness (in either the Western or Eastern tradition) can enhance these assets, then the broad implementation of mindfulness strategies becomes an important component in 21st century growth and survival.

Mindfulness and the Characteristics of Highly Creative People

Creative accomplishments are the result of a confluence of factors existing within the individual, including (but not limited to) personality traits, such as openness and self-confidence (Feist, 1999); creative thinking skills; and intrinsic motivation

(Amabile, 1996). Aspects of mindfulness in both the Western and Eastern traditions are crucial to each of these factors.

Personality traits

The personality trait most robustly associated with creativity across multiple studies is openness to experience (Feist, 1999). Openness to experience represents the tendency to view ideas, events, and experiences in a nonjudgmental and interested manner. It is characterized by active imagination, intellectual curiosity, and a preference for variety (Costa & McCrae, 1992). Langer (1989), in her classic book on mindfulness in the Western tradition, relates that "Openness, not only to new information, but to different points of view is also an important feature of mindfulness" (p. 68).

Likewise, Bishop et al. (2004), in proposing an operational definition of mindfulness in the Eastern tradition, describes one of the two main components of mindfulness as "an orientation that is characterized by curiosity, openness, and acceptance" (p. 232). Baer and colleagues found that measures of Eastern mindfulness were significantly and highly correlated with the openness to experience trait (Baer, Smith, Hopkins, Krietemeyer, & Toney, 2006). In a comparison of personality traits among experienced Dutch mindfulness meditators and nonmeditators, van den Hurk and colleagues found that the mindfulness meditators had significantly higher openness to experience scores than did the nonmeditators (van den Hurk et al., 2011). These investigators also found that openness to experience was positively correlated with the amount of mindfulness meditation experience within the meditator group. It is unclear from these findings, however, whether increased mindfulness meditation enhances openness or whether individuals who are high in openness may be more likely to engage in mindfulness meditation.

Clearly, mindfulness is associated with openness to experience, which is, in turn, an important component of creativity. Although personality traits such as openness are by nature fairly stable across the lifespan, studies have shown that it *is* possible to increase openness through training and practice (Jackson, Hill, Payne, Roberts, & Stine-Morrow, 2012). Mindfulness exercises may be one method of increasing this creativity-related personality trait.

A second personality trait, self-confidence, is also crucial to creativity (Feist, 1999). Self-confidence is the belief in one's own powers and abilities. Because creative ideas are by definition novel and original, they may represent a change from previously accepted ways of doing things and thus may be met with substantial criticism and even hostility. Without self-confidence, the creative individual will have difficulty pursuing a creative idea to fruition in the face of that criticism and the desire of others to maintain the status quo. Consider, for example, the case of Vincent van Gogh. His art was either highly criticized or ignored during his lifetime; yet he is now considered to be one of the prominent artists of the 19th century. If he had lacked confidence in his own artistic mission, he would never have made a substantial mark on the art field, and the world would not have benefitted from his starry nights and colorful sunflowers.

Mindfulness in the Western tradition suggests that self-confidence is a mind*ful* decision and that low self-image is often a mind*less* response to social comparisons (Langer,

1989, 2005). Social comparison research has found that upward comparisons (comparing ourselves to someone who is perceived as more competent or successful than we are) can lead to decreased self-regard, while downward comparisons (comparing ourselves to someone who is perceived as less competent or successful) can only temporarily boost self-regard. Ultimately, however, the tendency to continually compare ourselves with others—whether through upward or downward comparisons—has a negative effect on self-esteem and self-confidence (White, Langer, Yariv, & Welch, 2006). In a study of whether mindfulness training can reduce the negative effects of social comparison on self-confidence, researchers from Harvard asked participants to draw pictures that would be subject to either upward or downward social comparison. Some of the participants received brief mindfulness training before the experiment in which they practiced viewing potentially negative events from multiple perspectives. As predicted, mindfulness training made the participants less vulnerable to the effects of social comparisons (Langer, Pirson, & Delizonna, 2010). Researchers note, however, that social comparisons can actually be beneficial to self-confidence and self-esteem when they are viewed *mindfully*, with an eye toward noting specific areas in which an individual might seek personal growth and improvement (Carson & Langer, 2006).

In another study, researchers asked tourists in Rome to draw pictures of things in their environment (Grant, Langer, Falk, & Capodilupo, 2004). The authors hypothesized that those who were drawing in an art environment (the Pantheon) would have less confidence in their work due to unfavorable social comparison (they were surrounded by paintings done by European masters), while those in a nonart environment (the Coliseum) would have somewhat more self-confidence in their work. This hypothesis was confirmed, suggesting that upward social comparison in the art environment condition had a detrimental effect on the tourists' self-confidence in their ability to draw. In a second study, the authors hypothesized that those subjects who were given a mindfulness manipulation would feel more confident in their drawing than those who did not receive the mindfulness manipulation. This hypothesis was likewise confirmed, suggesting that increasing mindfulness may also increase self-confidence in one's work.

Several studies have found that mindfulness meditation in the Eastern tradition has a positive effect on self-confidence and self-esteem. Many of these studies are associated with the positive benefits for self-confidence that arise from Mindfulness-Based Stress Reduction (MSBR) in the treatment of psychopathology, such as depression or anxiety disorders (e.g., Goldin & Gross, 2010). Other studies have examined the effect of mindfulness-based programs on self-confidence in the context of performance. In one study, researchers put amateur archers and golfers through a four-week mindfulness program (Kaufman, Glass, & Arnkoff, 2009). Both groups improved in terms of confidence and reduced performance-related anxiety. The practice of mindfulness meditation emphasizes awareness of self without judgment of self. One of the mindfulness meditative strategies for improving self-confidence involves noticing the self-doubt that may invade our ongoing internal dialog without judging that dialog or giving the self-doubt power over our self-concept.

There is also evidence that Eastern mindfulness as a *trait* (that is, the tendency to be nonjudgmentally present in the current moment) is associated with high self-confidence and self-esteem. When researchers gave standard measures of both

Convergent thinking

Directing all of one's
knowledge toward a problem that
has a singular and specific solution

Divergent thinking

Using the contents of memory to
generate multiple solutions to a
problem in an open-ended manner

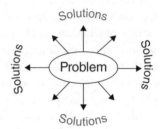

Figure 18.1 Divergent and convergent thinking. Carson, 2010. Reproduced with permission from John Wiley & Sons, Ltd.

mindfulness and self-esteem to several large samples of U.S. college students and adults from the general population, they found that the measures were highly and significantly correlated (Brown & Ryan, 2003). People who are highly mindful appear to be self-confident as well.

Self-confidence is important to creative endeavor. The creative individual must have confidence in their work in order to overcome potential criticism and to sustain the effort associated with the creative process. Mindfulness skills (whether practiced through informal Western mindfulness techniques or more formal Eastern mindfulness programs) may augment self-confidence and reduce concern about negative evaluations and social comparisons.

Creative thinking skills

The thinking skill that is most often associated with creativity is the tendency to use a *divergent* thinking style. Divergent thinking, first described by Guilford (1956), is one of the hallmarks of the creative mind. In fact, many researchers who study creativity use tests of divergent thinking as a measure of *trait* creativity or *potential* creativity (Eysenck, 1995). The essence of divergent thinking is the ability to generate multiple novel or unique solutions to a problem. In contrast, *convergent* thinking is the ability to focus on finding the one correct solution to a problem (see Figure 18.1). As an example, determining how many states in the United States have a capital city that begins with the letter "T" would be solved using convergent thinking, while generating unusual uses for a common household object would employ a divergent thinking style. When used as a measure of creativity, divergent thinking is assessed in terms of the fluency (number of solutions), originality (statistical infrequency of solutions), and flexibility (number of different categories of solutions) of responses to a specific prompt (such as listing as many uses for a brick as possible; Torrance, 1968). While both convergent and divergent thinking styles are necessary to the creative process, creative ideas tend to be generated using divergent thinking, and the ability to think divergently is predictive of real-life creative achievement (Carson, Peterson, and Higgins, 2005).

Divergent thinking has been associated with a neurological state of broadened attentional focus (Martindale, 1999). A body of research indicates that positive affect also broadens attentional focus and increases divergent thinking (Ashby, Isen, & Turken, 1999; Fredrickson & Branigan, 2005). By promoting awareness of the present environment and actively noticing new things, Western mindfulness encourages broadened attentional focus. Further, mindfulness manipulations have been shown to actively increase positive affect and promote creative engagement with the environment (Grant et al., 2004). In a study of seniors, mindfulness and active engagement with the environment were associated with higher levels of divergent thinking (Parisi, Stine-Morrow, Noh, & Morrow, 2009). This same group of researchers found that divergent thinking scores of seniors who had been given a mindfulness manipulation to actively engage with the environment increased significantly over those of a control group (Stine-Morrow, Parisi, Morrow, & Park, 2008).

Direct evidence for a connection between Eastern mindfulness and divergent thinking has also been reported. Colzato, Ozturk, and Hommel (2012) looked at the effects of two different types of meditation on convergent and divergent thinking in a group of Dutch subjects. Each subject participated in three sessions (one session of focused-attention meditation, one of open-monitoring meditation, and one visualization session that was used as a control condition), after which they were given divergent thinking tasks. The researchers found that the open-monitoring meditation (a type of mindfulness) led to significantly higher divergent thinking scores than either the focused-attention meditation or the control exercise.

These findings suggest that mindfulness—in both Eastern and Western traditions—is associated with divergent thinking. Further, it appears that practicing simple mindfulness exercises can actually improve divergent thinking skills.

Another related creative thinking skill is cognitive flexibility (Dietrich, 2004). Cognitive flexibility is defined as the ability of a person to change their conceptual system or point of reference in response to appropriate environmental stimuli (Scott, 1962). Being able to shift one's focus in response to context allows a person to look at events, objects, and concepts in a new light. For example, Alexander Fleming, in our earlier example, was able to shift his focus from viewing the mold in his specimen plates as an unwanted invader to an object of potential scientific interest. Consider also the example of Swiss engineer, George de Mestral. After returning from an Alpine hunting trip with his dog in 1941, de Mestral found that both his jacket and the dog's fur were covered with small burrs. De Mestral could have mindlessly viewed this situation as an annoyance; however, he was able to adopt a mindful attitude of noticing new things. He became fascinated with how the burrs hooked themselves onto material or fur and examined one of them under the microscope. This mindful examination of the lowly burr led to the invention of Velcro (Freeman & Golden, 1997).

Langer's (1989) Western conception of mindfulness emphasizes several aspects of cognitive flexibility, including the act of noticing new distinctions in familiar objects and the act of creating new categories depending on context rather than holding mindlessly onto predetermined rigid categories. Langer calls this tendency to pigeonhole or put objects or people into rigid categories "premature cognitive commitment"

Figure 18.2   Carson, 2010. Reproduced with permission from John Wiley & Sons, Ltd.

(Langer, 1989, p. 22). Research has shown that being able to categorize items in broader and more fluid categories that change depending on context is a key component of creative thinking (Runco & Chand, 1995). For instance, consider how one might categorize the object shown in Figure 18.2.

To rigidly categorize it as a chair would be a premature cognitive commitment to see it as a piece of furniture on which one sits. This categorization makes it less likely that one could view it differently depending upon the situation. It could be, for example, a weapon, a table, a source of firewood, a stepping stool, or a barricade to keep a pet in the back hall. By maintaining flexible and fluid categories (e.g., thinking of it as an object that *could be* used as chair), it is more likely that one could see creative possibilities for this or other objects or situations.

In an elegant laboratory experiment, Langer and Piper (1987) illustrated the creative value of maintaining flexible categories. They introduced several items to subjects in either a mindless/rigid ("Object A is a dog's rubber chew toy") or a mindful/flexible ("Object A *could be* a dog's rubber chew toy") manner. Later in the experiment, subjects were called upon to erase some pencil marks made earlier; those in the mindful/flexible condition were significantly more likely than those in the mindless/rigid condition to make the connection that the dog's rubber chew toy could be used as an eraser.

Cognitive flexibility has also been studied relative to the Eastern tradition of mindfulness. In a study of experienced mindfulness meditators versus nonmeditators, British researchers found that the mindfulness meditators had better scores than nonmeditators on two neuropsychological measures of cognitive flexibility. They also found that there was a significant correlation between scores on a mindfulness measure and the cognitive flexibility measures (Moore & Malinowski, 2009). In another recent study, researchers found that mindfulness meditators who had undergone an eight-session mindfulness program had significantly lower scores than meditation-naïve controls on a measure of cognitive rigidity (the opposite of cognitive flexibility; Greenberg, Reiner, & Meiran, 2012). Yet another study of mindfulness meditation practice and cognitive flexibility indicated that experienced meditators performed better on a perspective-switching task. Experienced meditators were able to identify more alternative perspectives for ambiguous images and could identify the first perspective more quickly than did nonmeditators (Hodgins & Adair, 2010).

Intrinsic motivation

While there are debates about what types of *extrinsic* motivation (including rewards, fame, shame, and competition) tend to increase creativity (Eisenberg & Cameron, 1996), there is no doubt that *intrinsic* motivation is a major factor in creative achievement (Hennessey, 2010). Intrinsic motivation is defined as "the inherent tendency to seek out novelty and challenges, to extend and exercise one's capacities, to explore, and to learn" in the absence of specific external rewards (Ryan & Deci, 2000, p. 70).

High levels of internal motivation and the human capacity to lose oneself in a project appear to be integral to the creative process. Isaac Newton, for example, would become immersed in his work and not leave his rooms at Cambridge University for weeks at a time, according to reports from his assistant, Whiston. Whiston claimed to have been rebuffed if he so much as interrupted Newton to leave him a plate of food (Westfall, 1994). This kind of intrinsic motivation is associated with a state of flow, in which a person experiences a sense of timelessness and is totally absorbed and completely confident in their ability to engage the task at hand (Csikszentmihalyi, 1996).

The state of flow and strong intrinsic motivation are highly rewarding. However, many—perhaps most—people do not feel intensely intrinsically motivated by their work and may pass their days feeling unfulfilled or unchallenged by their activities. According to Western mindfulness theory, these people may be approaching their work mindlessly. By purposefully noticing new aspects of their work and becoming engaged in the present, they should be able to mindfully increase their engagement and intrinsic motivation (Langer, 1989). To test this theory, Langer, Russell, and Eisenkraft (2009) asked members of a large symphony orchestra to play well-known compositions twice: once with the instruction to recreate the best performance of the piece that they could remember playing (the control condition) and once with the instruction to incorporate subtle new nuances into the performance (the mindful condition). Orchestra members completed questionnaires on how engaged they were and how much they enjoyed playing the pieces after each performance. The performances were recorded and played for an audience at a later time. Across two separate studies, musicians rated playing the musical pieces as much more enjoyable in the mindful condition than in the control condition, suggesting higher intrinsic motivation. Further, the audiences preferred the recordings of the pieces played in the mindful condition over those played in the control condition, suggesting that the increase in intrinsic motivation for the musicians was associated with better and more creative performance.

In the drawing study mentioned earlier, Grant and colleagues (2004) had subjects draw pictures in a stressful environment (a dentist's office). Some subjects were given a simple mindfulness manipulation before the experiment "Draw distinctions between the things that you see and observe how they change." The subjects who were given this simple mindfulness suggestion reported enjoying the drawing task more and feeling more competent in their abilities, even though their stress level remained as high as that in the control group.

Intrinsic motivation, the internally rewarded push to explore and work toward a goal, is a driving force behind creative achievement. The state of mindfulness, defined by open awareness and interested attention in the current environment, has been associated with autonomous or intrinsic motivation (Deci & Ryan, 2008). As we have seen, mindful manipulations appear to enhance intrinsic motivation in creative activities such as drawing and performing music. Intrinsic motivation appears to be yet another pathway through which creativity and mindfulness intersect.

Mindfulness, Brain States, and Creative Insight

Graham Wallas (1926), in his classic book *The Art of Thought*, was among the first to identify a set of stages in the creative process, which he based on descriptions provided by creative luminaries in letters, diaries, and interviews. In my work with over 1,000 creative individuals, I have found that the stages set forth by Wallas are confirmed by descriptions of the creative process from modern luminaries who have never heard of Wallas's work; thus, the following stages appear to be more or less universal. They include stages of *preparation* (gathering knowledge, honing domain-specific skills, creative problem-finding), *incubation* (allowing a creative problem to develop below the level of conscious awareness), *illumination* or *insight* (the aha! experience when a creative idea bursts forth into consciousness), and *verification* (testing the idea for soundness and then fleshing it out to create the finished idea or product.

While most of this creative process is fairly transparent, the stages of incubation and insight have traditionally been treated as somewhat mystical. The ancient Greeks believed that creative ideas were imparted to men through the breath of the gods. (Our word *inspiration* actually means to "breathe in.") William Blake credited some of his creative insights to small spirits who surrounded him and often jostled him to get his attention (Shaw, 2000). Other luminaries have credited angels or deceased relatives with providing their insights (Carson, 2010).

There is a spontaneous nature to creative insight. Mozart has described how a symphony appeared suddenly within his mind with all the orchestral parts discernible (Ghiselin, 1952); likewise, the mathematician, Poincaré, has described how equations "rose in crowds" in his head, without his bidding, and then interlocked. He had but to write them down (Ghiselin,1952, p. 25).

Reports such as these, as well as the many impressive works that appear to have been spawned by spontaneous moments of insight or inspiration, may suggest that some people are born with a creative "gift," while others are just simply not creative. Modern neuroscience investigations suggest otherwise. Brain-imaging research and psychophysiological studies using EEG technology indicate that highly creative individuals employ specific brain-activation patterns when engaging in creative problem solving (e.g., Howard-Jones, Blakemore, Samuel, Summers, & Claxton, 2005; Martindale, 1999). These patterns may represent a tendency to access spontaneous creative material (Dietrich, 2004). Brain structures, however, appear to be no different in highly creative individuals than in those who do not exhibit much creative aptitude. The difference, then, between high and low creative individuals appears to be in their ability to access brain activation states that allow information being processed below the level of conscious awareness to make its way into the conscious theater of the mind (Carson, 2011).

If we can learn to access the brain activation states demonstrated by highly creative individuals, we may be able to enhance our own level of creativity. Recent findings, based on neuro-feedback studies (Gruzelier, 2009) cognitive-behavioral interventions (e.g., Straube, Glauer, Dilger, Mentzel, & Miltner, 2006), and cognitive rehabilitation programs (e.g., Chiaravalloti, Leavitt, Wylie, & DeLuca, 2012), suggest that we *can* manipulate our brain activation states. In other words, we can *teach ourselves* to be more creative. Simple mindfulness exercises and meditation instructions may be one technique for teaching creativity, as we shall see in following section.

Neuroscientists have been investigating the brain states associated with mindfulness meditation for more than a decade, beginning with the famous "lama in the lab" studies (Goleman, 2003), which were inspired by meetings in the year 2000 between the Dalai Lama and leading U.S. scientists. Clearly, experienced meditators are able to achieve an altered state of consciousness as indicated by their brain-activation patterns; what is interesting is that characteristics of these brain patterns are also noted in highly creative people when they are generating solutions to creative problems (Gruzelier, 2009).

Defocused attention and mildly disinhibited cognitive states during the incubation and insight stages of the creative process may allow increased sensory stimuli, unusual associations, and mental images into conscious awareness that can then be combined and recombined to form creative ideas (Carson, 2011). Access to information that is typically filtered out of consciousness has been shown to predict both divergent thinking and creative achievement in high-functioning individuals (Carson, Peterson, & Higgins, 2003). This disinhibited state corresponds to a type of "receptive" attention that is cultivated in mindfulness meditation (Jha, Krompinger, & Baime, 2007). Receptive attention aims to remain open to the whole field of awareness, including to stimuli that would be considered extraneous or irrelevant. Thus, mindfulness meditators who practice receptive attention may more readily access creative material that has been incubating in associational areas of the brain.

From a brain-activation-pattern perspective, both the defocused and disinhibited brain states associated with creative insight and the receptive attention state of mindfulness meditators are characterized by greater levels of cortical alpha and theta-bandwidth activity, especially in the prefrontal cortex (Lagopoulos et al., 2009; Martindale, 1999; Takahashi et al., 2005). Alpha waves (between 8 and 13 Hz) are typically associated with a relaxed mental state and a broadened attentional focus that is inwardly directed. While there is debate over the interpretation of theta waves (between 4 and 7 Hz) in association with meditation, theta seems to evoke heightened awareness and efficient cognitive processing.

Researchers at Northwestern University have detected increased alpha activity followed by a short burst of gamma wave activity in the right temporal lobe just before subjects report experiencing an aha! moment when solving insight problems (Jung-Beeman et al., 2004). The authors speculate that the gamma burst is related to unconscious material being ushered into conscious awareness where it is perceived as a moment of insight. At least one study (Faber et al., 2004) found that open or mindful meditation was accompanied by increased gamma activity in the temporal lobe as well. Ostafin and Kassman (2012) reported that subjects with higher trait mindfulness were, indeed, better than those with low trait mindfulness at solving problems that required a moment of insight. Further, these authors found that subjects who had received a short mindfulness induction were better at solving the insight problems than those who did not receive the mindfulness induction, suggesting that mindfulness techniques can be used to enhance the experience of sudden moments of insight.

The similarity between brain activation states of highly creative people and those of mindfulness meditators suggests that creativity and mindfulness may have physiological as well as theoretical similarities. Roy Horan (2009), in a review of the neuropsychological connection between creativity and mindfulness meditation, suggests that mindfulness meditation creates "a relaxed, yet alert, witness state ... [that] could then conceivably activate weak or nonexistent associations leading to creative inspiration" (p. 205).

The research on creative insight highlights the similarities between a state of mindfulness and the brain state that appears to facilitate creative idea generation. Along with the findings on personality traits, creative thinking skills, and intrinsic motivation, this research presents a growing body of work on the interface between mindfulness and creativity. Because mindfulness techniques are easy to implement, they may provide us with a method of universally enhancing our creative capacity.

Mindful Conclusions

In this chapter, I have reviewed how constructs of mindfulness, from both the Western socio/cognitive tradition and the Eastern meditative tradition, are associated with creativity through the pathways of personality traits, cognitive processes, and motivational factors. I have emphasized the importance of creativity if we are to address present-day challenges at both the societal and individual levels. I have demonstrated that mindfulness is related to the creative-insight process. Mindfulness—in the form of actively noticing new things in our environment and making choices based on current context, as well as in the formal and informal practice of mindful meditation—may allow us to enhance creativity through a variety of neural, cognitive, emotional, and social mechanisms. The effect of specific mindfulness techniques and suggestions on creative idea generation, production, and performance is an area ripe for future research.

Creativity is not limited to the arts and sciences. Creativity is important in all aspects of life—from how we arrange the items in our living space to how we live our lives. Each of us is a work in progress, and daily we experience the stages of the creative process in our work, in our personal activities, and in our personal growth. To live creatively is indeed to live mindfully.

References

Amabile, T. M. (1996). *Creativity in context*. Boulder, CO: Westview Press.

Ashby, F. G., Isen, A. M., & Turken, A. U. (1999). A neuropsychological theory of positive affect and its influence on cognition. *Psychological Review, 106*, 529–550.

Baer, R. A., Smith, G. T., Hopkins, J., Krietemeyer, J., & Toney, L. (2006). Using self-report assessment methods to explore facets of mindfulness. *Assessment, 13*(1), 27–45.

Barron, F. (1969). *Creative person and creative process*. New York, NY: Holt, Rinehart, and Winston.

Bishop, S. R., Lau, M., Shapiro, S., Carlson, L., Anderson, N. D., Carmody, J.,…Devins, G. (2004). Mindfulness: A proposed operational definition. *Clinical Psychology: Science and Practice, 11*(3), 230–241.

Brown, G. (2009). Talk given at the Innovation Edge conference in London, U.K., on March 10, 2009, sponsored by the National Endowment for Science Technology and the Arts (NESTA). Retrieved from http://www.nesta.org.uk/assets/external_video/public_services_innovation_summit__gordon_brown

Brown, K. W., & Ryan, R. M. (2003). The benefits of being present: Mindfulness and its role in psychological well-being. *Journal of Personality and Social Psychology, 84*, 822–848.

Carson, S. (2010). *Your creative brain: Seven steps to maximize imagination, productivity, and innovation in your life*. San Francisco, CA: Jossey-Bass.

Carson, S. H. (2011). Creativity and psychopathology: A genetic shared-vulnerability model. *Canadian Journal of Psychiatry, 56*(3), 144–153.

Carson, S., & Langer, E. J. (2006). Mindfulness and self-acceptance. *Journal of Rational Emotive Behavioral Therapy, 24*(1), 29–43.

Carson, S., Peterson, J. B., & Higgins, D. (2005). Reliability, validity and factor structure of the Creative Achievement Questionnaire. *Creativity Research Journal, 17*(1), 37–50.

Carson, S.H., Peterson, J. B., & Higgins, D. M. (2003). Decreased latent inhibition is associated with increased creative achievement in high-functioning individuals. *Journal of Personality and Social Psychology, 85*(3), 499–506.

Chiaravalloti, N. D., Leavitt, V., Wylie, G., DeLuca, J. (2012). Increased cerebral activation after behavioral treatment for memory deficts in MS. *Journal of Neurology, 259*(7), 1337–1346.

Cohen, G. D., Perlstein, S., Chapline, J., Kelly, J., Firth, K. M., & Simmens, S. (2006). The impact of professionally conducted cultural programs on the physical health, mental health, and social functioning of older adults. *The Gerontologist, 46*(6), 726–734.

Colzato, L. S., Ozturk, A., & Hommel, B. (2012). Meditate to create: The impact of focused-attention and open-monitoring training on convergent and divergent thinking. *Frontiers in Psychology, 3*, doi:10.3389/fpsyg.2012.00116.

Costa, P. T., & McCrae, R. R. (1992). *Revised NEO Personality Inventory and NEO Five-Factor Inventory professional manual*. Odessa, FL: Psychological Assessment Resources.

Csikszentmihalyi, M. (1996). *Creativity: Flow and the psychology of discovery and invention*. New York, NY: Harper Collins.

Deci, E. L., & Ryan, R. M. (2008). Self-determination theory: A macrotheory of human motivation, development, and health. *Canadian Psychology, 49*(3), 182–185.

Dietrich, A. (2004). The cognitive neuroscience of creativity. *Psychonomic Bulletin and Review*, *11*(6), 1011–1026.

Eisenberg, J. (2005). *Creativity in sport: The triumph of imagination*. Toronto, ON: Chestnut.

Eisenberg, R., & Cameron, J. (1996). Detrimental effects of reward: Reality or myth? *American Psychologist*, *51*(11), 1153–1166.

Eysenck, H. J. (1995). *Genius: The natural history of creativity*. Cambridge, UK: Cambridge University Press.

Faber, P. L., Lehmann, D., Gianotti, L. R. R., Kaelin, M., & Pascual-Marqui, R. D. (2004). *Scalp and intacerebral (LORETA) theta and gamma EEG coherence in meditation*. Paper presented at the Meeting of the International Society for Neuronal Regulation, April 2004, Winterthur, Switzerland.

Feist, G. F. (1999). The influence of personality on artistic and scientific creativity. In R. J. Sternberg (Ed.), *Handbook of creativity* (pp. 273–296). Cambridge, UK: Cambridge University Press.

Fleming, A. (1929). On the antibacterial action of cultures of a penicillium with special reference to their use in the isolation of *B. influenzae*. *British Journal of Experimental Pathology*, *10*, 226–236.

Fredrickson, B. L., & Branigan, C. A. (2005). Positive emotions broaden the scope of attention and thought–action repertoires. *Cognition and Emotion*, *19*, 313–332.

Freeman, A., & Golden, B. (1997). *Why didn't I think of that: Bizarre origins of ingenious inventions we couldn't live without*. New York, NY: Wiley.

Ghiselin, B. (1952). *The creative process*. Berkeley, CA: University of California Press.

Goldin, P. R., & Gross, J. J. (2010). Effects of Mindfulness-Based Stress Reduction (MBSR) on emotion regulation in social anxiety disorder. *Emotion*, *10*(1), 83–91.

Goleman, D. (2003). *Destructive emotions: A scientific dialog with the Dalai Lama*. New York, NY: Bantam.

Grant, A. M., Langer, E. J., Falk, E., & Capodilupo, C. (2004). Mindful creativity: Drawing to draw distinctions. *Creativity Research Journal*, *16*, 261–265.

Greenberg, J, Reiner, K., & Meiran, N. (2012). "Mind the trap": Mindfulness practice reduces cognitive rigidity. *PLoS ONE*, *7*(5): e36206.

Gruzelier, J. (2009). A theory of alpha/theta neurofeedback, creative performance enhancement, long distance functional connectivity and psychological integration. *Cognitive Processing*, *10* (Supplement 1), S101–S109.

Guilford, J. P. (1956). The structure of intellect. *Psychological Bulletin 53*, 267–293.

Hanh, T. N. (1975) *The miracle of mindfulness*. Boston, MA: Beacon Press.

Hennessey, B. A. (2010). The creativity–motivation connection. In J. C. Kaufman & R. J. Sternbeerg (Eds.), *The Cambridge handbook of creativity* (pp. 342–365). New York, NY: Cambridge University Press.

Hodgins, H. S., & Adair, K. C. (2010). Attentional processes and meditation. *Consciousness and Cognition*, *19*(4), 872–878.

Horan, R. (2009). The neuropsychological connection between creativity and meditation. *Creativity Research Journal*, *21*, 199–222.

Howard-Jones, P. A., Blakemore, S. J., Samuel, E. A., Summers, I. R., & Claxton, G. (2005). Semantic divergence and creative story generation: An fMRI investigation. *Cognitive Brain Research*, *25*, 240–250.

IBM Corporation. (2010). *IBM 2010 Global CEO Study*. New York, NY: IBM Global Business Services.

Jackson, J. J., Hill, P. L., Payne, B. R., Roberts, B. W., & Stine-Morrow, E. A. (2012). Can an old dog learn (and want to experience) new tricks? Cognitive training increases openness to experience in older adults. *Psychology and Aging*, *27*(2), 286–292.

Jha, A. P., Krompinger, J., & Baime, M. J. (2007). Mindfulness training modifies subsystems of attention. *Cognitive, Affective, & Behavioral Neuroscience, 7*(2), 109–119.

Jung-Beeman, M., Bowden, E. M., Haberman, J., Frymiare, J. L., Arambel-Liu, S., & Greenblatt, R., ... Kounios, J. (2004). Neural activity when people solve verbal problems with insight. *PLoS Biology, 2*, 500–510.

Kabat-Zinn, J. (1990). *Full catastrophe living: Using the wisdom of your body and mind to face stress, pain, and illness.* New York, NY: Dell.

Kaufman, K. A., Glass, C. R., & Arnkoff, D. B. (2009). Evaluation of Mindful Sport Performance Enhancement (MSPE): A new approach to promote flow in athletes. *Journal of Clinical Sport Psychology, 4*, 334–356.

Lagopoulos, J., Xu, J., Rasmussen, I., Vik, A., Malhi, G. S., Eliassen, C. F. ... , & Ellingsen, Ø. (2009). Increased theta and alpha EEG activity during nondirective meditation. *Journal of Alternative and Complementary Medicine, 15*(11), 1187–1192.

Langer, E. (2005). *On becoming an artist: Reinventing yourself through mindful creativity.* New York, NY: Ballantine Books.

Langer, E. J (1989). *Mindfulness.* Reading, MA: Addison-Wesley.

Langer, E. J (1997). *The power of mindful learning.* Reading, MA: Addison-Wesley.

Langer, E. J. (2000). The construct of mindfulness. *Journal of Social Issues, 56*(1), 1–9.

Langer, E. J., & Piper, A. I. (1987). The prevention of mindlessness. *Journal of Personality and Social Psychology, 53*(2), 280–287.

Langer, E. J., Pirson, M., & Delizonna, L. (2010). The mindlessness of social comparisons. *Psychology of Aesthetics, Creativity, and the Arts, 4*(2), 68–74.

Langer, E. J., Russell, T., & Eisenkraft, N. (2009). Orchestral performance and the footprint of mindfulness. *Psychology of Music, 37*(2), 125–136.

Martindale, C. (1999). Biological basis of creativity. In R. J. Sternberg (Ed.), *Handbook of creativity.* Cambridge, UK: Cambridge University Press.

Matthew, C. T. (2009). Leader creativity as a predictor of leading change in organizations. *Journal of Applied Social Psychology, 39*(1), 1–41.

Maynard, M. (2008). With eye on profits, G. M. began missing on innovation. *New York Times* (December 5, 2008), p. B1. Retrieved from http://www.nytimes.com/2008/12/06/business/06motors.html?pagewanted=all

Mednick, S. (1962). The associative basis of the creative process. *Psychological Review, 69*, 220–232.

Moore, A., & Malinowski, P. (2009). Meditation, mindfulness and cognitive flexibility. *Consciousness and Cognition, 18*, 176–186.

Ostafin, B. D., & Kassman, K. T. (2012). Stepping out of history: Mindfulness improves insight problem solving. *Consciousness and Cognition, 21*, 1031–1036.

Parisi, J. M., Stine-Morrow, E. A. L., Noh, S. R., & Morrow, D. G. (2009). Predispositional engagement, activity engagement, and cognition among older adults. *Aging, Neuropsychology, and Cognition, 16*, 485–504.

Runco, M. A., & Chand, I. (1995) Creativity and cognition. *Educational Psychology Review, 7*(3), 243–267.

Ryan, R. M., & Deci, E. L. (2000). Self-determination theory and the facilitation of intrinsic motivation, social development, and well-being. *American Psychologist, 55*, 68–78.

Scott, W. A. (1962). Cognitive complexity and cognitive flexibility. *Sociometry, 25*(4), 405–414.

Shaw, K. (2000). *The mammoth book of oddballs and eccentrics.* New York, NY: Carroll & Graf.

Stine-Morrow, E. A. L., Parisi, J. M., Morrow, D. G., & Park, D. C. (2008). The effects of an engaged lifestyle on cognitive vitality: A field experiment. *Psychology and Aging, 23*(4), 778–786.

Straube, T., Glauer, M., Dilger, S., Mentzel, H. J., & Miltner, W. H. (2006). Effects of cognitive-behavioral therapy on brain activation in specific phobia. *NeuroImage, 29*(1), 125–35.

Takahashi, T., Murata, T., Hamada, T., Omori, M., Kosaka, H., Kikuchi, M., …Wada, Y. (2005). Changes in EEG and autonomic nervous activity during meditation and their association with personality traits. *International Journal of Psychophysiology, 55*, 199–207.

Torrance, E. P. (1968). Examples and rationales of test tasks for assessing creative abilities. *Journal of Creative Behavior, 2*(3), 165–178.

van den Hurk, P. A. M., Wingens, T., Giommi, F., Barendregt, H. P., Speckens, A. E. M., & van Schie, H. T. (2011). On the relationship between the practice of mindfulness meditation and personality—An exploratory analysis of the mediating role of mindfulness skills. *Mindfulness, 2*, 194–200.

Wallas, G. (1926). *The art of thought*. New York, NY: Harcourt-Brace.

Westfall, R. (1994). *The life of Isaac Newton*. Cambridge, UK: Cambridge University Press.

White, J. B., Langer, E. J., Yariv, L., & Welch IV, J. C. (2006). Frequent social comparisons and destructive emotions and behaviors: The dark side of social comparisons. *Journal of Adult Development, 13*(1), 36–44.

19

Mediating Mindful Social Interactions Through Design

Kristina Niedderer

Introduction: Mindfulness in Design

This chapter focuses on design as an agent for behavior change in social contexts. In particular, it discusses the role of emotion in designing artifacts for mindful social interaction. Behavior change is increasingly important for building a sustainable future, whether social, ecological, or economic. For example, research into behavior change is one of the current objectives of the Economic and Social Research Council, UK (ESRC, 2012, p. 6). At the same time, the role of design in implementing behavior change is becoming more widely recognized (e.g., Brown, 2008; Brown & Wyatt, 2010; Lockton, 2012; Lockton, Harrison, & Stanton, 2009; Tromp, Hekkert, & Verbeek, 2011). Design plays an important role within behavior change, because "every act of design involves choices that are deeply interested, in the sense that they necessarily serve someone's needs before (or to the exclusion of) those of other parties" (Greenfield, 2011). Furthermore, objects direct our actions both consciously and unconsciously, and can influence the interaction we have with them and with other people (Norman, 2002, pp. 1, 34; Pearce, 1995, p. 166). This shifts the traditional focus on human–object interaction to one that is concerned with "how human beings relate to other human beings through the mediating influence of products" (Buchanan, 2001, p. 11). Examples are found in many contexts, such as the built environment and a plethora of analog and digital consumer products including cell phones, furniture, and tableware. The use of artifacts can also affect social interaction in desired and undesired ways (Dunne & Raby, 2001; Ilstedt Hjelm, 2004; Norman, 2002), and for it to be *mindless* or *mindful* (Langer, 1989; Niedderer, 2007).

Mindlessness reinforces entrenched behaviors and beliefs without paying attention to the specific situation and its context, and can therefore lead to errors and inappropriate personal or social judgments and behaviors (Langer, 1989, pp. 25, 43). For example, cell phones are designed to connect people, which is their desirable characteristic.

The Wiley Blackwell Handbook of Mindfulness, First Edition.
Edited by Amanda Ie, Christelle T. Ngnoumen, and Ellen J. Langer.
© 2014 John Wiley & Sons, Ltd. Published 2014 by John Wiley & Sons, Ltd.

However, they can also disrupt the interaction between people. For instance, where a person takes a call while in conversation with another person, the first interaction is disrupted in favor of the second: people who take such calls seem often oblivious, that is, mindless, of this consequence of their action. Similarly, in public spaces, on trains or buses, people often shout into their phones, unaware of their disrupting impact on other people's conversations or activities (Srivastava, 2005, p. 123). *Mindfulness*, in contrast, refers to a mindset of openness and alertness, which regards any information as novel, pays attention to the specific context, and considers the information from different perspectives, in order to enable the creation of new categories (Langer, 1997, p. 111). Mindfulness can aid behavior change, because it encourages reconsidering our actions and their causes, helping to adjust them to new situations and challenges (Langer & Moldoveanu, 2000b). For example, a mindful person might decide not to answer the call from their cell phone when in conversation, but to call back afterwards or, if taking a call in a public space, might lower their voice to an appropriate level so as not to disturb others.

The state of mindfulness, however, is elusive as demonstrated by the example of the cell phone and many others (e.g., Langer, 1989, pp. 2, 9ff; Langer & Moldoveanu, 2000a, p. 3). In order to achieve mindfulness, it is necessary to break through established patterns of experience and preconceptions (Langer, 1989, pp. 19–42; Udall, 1996, p. 107). This breakthrough to mindfulness is usually facilitated through an external agent (Langer, 1989, pp. 81–114; Udall, 1996, p. 107), which must be capable of disrupting consciousness in order to cause this breakthrough. This external agent is often provided by educational or legal contexts through a person (e.g., trainer, therapist) or the law (e.g., embodied in law-reinforcing street signs; Niedderer, 2004, pp. 47, 120, 142; Niedderer, 2007, p. 12). Alternatively, an artifact can be designed in such a way that it stimulates mindfulness where a mindful context is not available (Niedderer, 2004, 2007, 2013). Such design is termed *mindful design* (Niedderer, 2013). The concept of mindfulness refers here to the attentiveness of the user towards the social, environmental, etc. consequences of their actions performed with an object (Niedderer, 2007, p. 4; Niedderer, 2013). An object that specifically induces mindfulness of the social consequences of the user's actions is termed a performative object (Niedderer, 2007, p. 3). In order to induce mindfulness, performative objects need to cause both awareness and attentiveness. Awareness pertains to consciousness of an experience per se, while attentiveness refers to the caring attention towards the content of that experience (Langer, 1989, p. 61ff; Metzinger, 1995, pp. 8–21; Niedderer, 2007, p. 8; Udall, 1996, p. 11). Performative objects can induce mindfulness by means of their function: this is understood as "the plan of action that the object represents" (Pearce, 1995, p. 166), and which comprises a twofold process: First, the *disruption* of function, which raises awareness because it requires some additional or alternative action to continue the intended use of the object; second, the *thematization*, which directs attentiveness through the way in which it leads the user's awareness towards the content of physical actions—and their symbolic meanings—and causes reflection (Niedderer, 2007, p. 10).

The concept of the performative object has been used implicitly widely in the design of games or in concept designs, or otherwise as part of safety devices such as warning notices on computers (e.g., when saving a document) which briefly disrupt

Figure 19.1 Come a little bit closer bench for Droog by Nina Farkache, 2001. Photographer: Robaard/Theuwkens (Styling by Marjo Kranenborg, CMK).

our consciousness and require an additional action to complete the command (e.g., "save/don't save/cancel"). One example identified as a performative object is the bench "Come a little bit closer," designed in 2001 by Nina Farkache of Droog Design (Droog, 2012; Lovegrove, 2002, pp. 62–63; Ramakers, 2002, p. 57; Figure 19.1). The upper surface of the bench is covered with glass marbles, which act as ball bearings on which the seating shells float. Because the seating shells are not fixed (disruption), the design allows users physically to move closer without changing seats (thematization). The ability to move closer physically suggests symbolically moving closer on a social level. In this way, the design questions people's behavior in public places—which is to avoid strangers and to sit down at opposite ends of a public bench—by offering alternative actions. Similarly, with the example of a person shouting into their cell phone in public, in applying the concept of performative object one could imagine the phone "shouting back" to make the person mindful of their own voice level (disruption). By adjusting the level of their own voice, they could readjust the level of the phone voice to their need (thematization).

Various examples of performative objects suggest that mindless responses in social encounters are significantly influenced by emotions (Niedderer, 2004, p. 150). On the one hand, emotions can be seen as beneficial because they offer swift responses to problems of physical and social survival (Keltner & Ekman, 2000, p. 163). On the other hand, emotions can be perceived as causing mindless behavior because they are based on "premature cognitive commitments," that is, beliefs we take for granted, unaware that they are our construct and that there are many other perspectives. This is because of the dependency of emotions on context in relation to which they tend to be "learned in a single-minded way" (Langer, 1989, p. 175).

This chapter presents a theoretical analysis of the role of emotion in designing for mindful social interaction with the purpose of providing a framework for the design and application of performative objects in real world situations. The work is situated in the context of design for behavior change (Lockton, 2012). It complements behavioral, user-centered and emotional design approaches by offering an alternative to the ubiquituous design approach of efficient functionality (Niedderer, 2007, p. 9). It therefore focuses on the early design concept stage, rather than the later design process. The chapter first examines the understanding of mindfulness with regard to aspects of content, choice, and complexity. Second, the nature and role of emotions in causing mindfulness are discussed. Third, a mindful-emotional framework is proposed as an interpretive tool that provides robust guidance (1) for the analysis of social situations or environments and (2) for designing performative objects in these situations. The discussion takes a functional approach (Burgoon, Berger, & Waldron, 2000, p. 108; Keltner & Gross, 1999), to provide a unifying basis for the analysis of mindfulness, emotions, and design, and which links actions as observable consequences to the underlying goals or intentions and vice versa (Lockton, 2012, p. 7; Roseman, Wiest, & Swartz, 1994, p. 207). Two examples serve to ground the discussion in everyday life experience and which are used to build the argument throughout the chapter. The first example is people's use of public benches, in relation to which the Droog Design bench has been identified as a matching performative object. The second example is the use of cell phones in public spaces. The final discussion draws together the different aspects of emotion and mindfulness in these examples to demonstrate how the framework can be applied first to the analysis of objects, and second to the analysis of a situation to provide the starting point for a new design approach.

Mindfulness: Content, Choice, and Complexity

If performative objects cause awareness of a social experience or action and attentiveness to the content of that experience or action, we must ask what is the nature of this content, how does it emerge from experience/action, and how may it be embodied in the design to guide the user towards it? An example of mindless behavior relates to people using benches in public places who commonly sit at opposite ends of a bench (Figure 19.2a and Figure 19.2b). This behavior may have a number of reasons, such as the protection of one's personal space, the creation of a physically or socially safe and comfortable distance from others, or the courtesy of not infringing someone else's personal space (Burgess, 1982; Evans & Wener, 2007, pp. 90, 92; Fried & DeFazio, 1974; Goffman, 1966). In addition, people often put their bags next to them to prevent anyone sitting close to them, erecting a physical and social barrier where none has been designed (Figure 19.3). In the traditional design of public benches (Figure 19.4), social interaction—whether this is people deliberately sharing a bench or whether this is strangers avoiding each other—does not typically feature as a consideration. In the first case, sitting side by side does not aid communication,

(a)

(b)

Figure 19.2 (a) Two people on a public bench in a train station in Cambridgeshire, UK. Photograph: Kristina Niedderer. (b) Two people on a public bench in a city center in the West Midlands, UK. Photograph: Kristina Niedderer.

Figure 19.3 A person on a public bench with their bag next to them, Cambridgeshire, UK. Photograph: Kristina Niedderer.

Figure 19.4 A common public bench, Cambridgeshire, UK. Photograph: Kristina Niedderer.

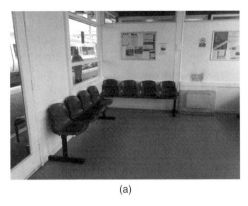 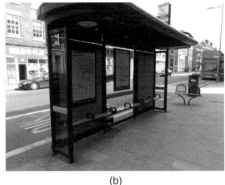

(a)   (b)

Figure 19.5 (a) Public seating at a train station, Cambridgeshire, UK. Photograph: Kristina Niedderer. (b) Public seating at a bus stop, West Midlands, UK. Photograph: Kristina Niedderer.

because it makes visual contact difficult. In the second case, although some designs of public benches hint at the avoidance behavior of people by designing benches with individual seating spaces instead of a uniform shared seating surface (Figure 19.5a and Figure 19.5b), these measures do not appear to provide a sufficient barrier, and hence cause people to create the necessary barriers for themselves.

The cultural or social preconceptions, also termed premature cognitive commitments (Langer, 1989, p. 19ff), which cause such behaviors, are both learned and context dependent. For example, we may have learned as children that strangers are potentially dangerous and therefore to be avoided (p. 175). Whether consciously or unconsciously, such beliefs can create barriers in the form of negative emotions, such as fear or disgust, which in turn lead to emotional actions of avoidance (Keltner & and Gross, 1999; Langer, 1989, p. 175; Roseman et al., 1994), such as those observed in the context of public benches. A change of context can further change how we judge people and how we behave towards them (Langer, 1989, pp. 35, 175). For example: we might judge a stranger sitting down next to us in the dentist's waiting room to be a fellow sufferer for whom we are prepared to make space; at the doctor's, although we might still judge them to be a fellow sufferer, we might fear them to have a potentially contagious disease and sit as far apart as possible; a stranger approaching us at a party is likely to be defined as a potential friend who offers the opportunity of an interesting new acquaintance, while we might avoid the same person if we met them in the street at night; and we may be comfortable engaging in discussion with a well-dressed person sitting down on a park bench next to us, while a person who looks scruffy may make us vacate our space. These examples demonstrate that there is a rich amount of cues, that our interpretation of them is socially and culturally conditioned, and that this interpretation might in due course be affecting our judgment and behavior appropriately or inappropriately.

The question is how design can break down such preconceptions. With regard to the use of benches in public places, the Droog Design bench can be seen to provide an opportunity for social interaction between strangers that always existed, but that is not usually taken up (or permissible), due to cultural or social beliefs (premature cognitive commitment). The cue here is in the movability of the seating shells, which challenges preconceptions of what a bench commonly is like, and which therefore is likely to attract the user's attention. Beyond causing attention, it is the possibility of increasing or decreasing the distance between the shells, and hence that between the users of the bench, which points to the aspect of individual space and social distance, and which constitutes the theme and mindful content of the design. With regard to this theme, the bench appears to offer an obvious set of choices: to stay where one has settled on the bench, to move closer, or to move further away from another person on the bench. The aspect of choice is important because choice makes us mindful. It requires conscious reflection on the different options available (Langer, 1989, p. 123), which in turn can lead to (1) a greater sensitivity to one's environment, (2) more openness to new information, (3) the creation of new categories for structuring perception, and (4) enhanced awareness of multiple perspectives in problem solving (Langer & Moldoveanu, 2000a, p. 2). This suggests that mindful design needs to offer the user choices. Adding more choices can be expected to increase reflection and thus mindfulness, while too many options might make a design potentially confusing to use (Norman, 2002, p. xii). Apart from this functional aspect of choice, the bench can also offer different options for interpretation, some of which may be culturally dependent and therefore vary. For example, the ability to move quickly to and fro on the bench reminds one of the children's game of "catch me," where a child touches another child or adult and runs away quickly not to be touched in return. The aspect of play suggests fun, offering a desirable alternative to avoidance. This shows that there can be a second level of interpretation, and potentially several more, based on the link between physical and symbolic actions and their interpretation, adding complexity, which can further enhance mindfulness (Burgoon et al., 2000, p. 112).

Both choice and complexity have to refer to the theme(s) addressed, which in the first instance is the emotional action that can be observed (e.g., avoidance behavior), and which is a result of the emotions and the underlying premature cognitive commitments. The example of the cell phone can offer some further insights with regard to the causes of mindless behavior. One of the differences between the two examples is that benches—in their most rudimentary form, perhaps as a shared rock or tree trunk—are as old as humankind. In contrast, modern cell phones have been around for about three decades, and have only come into wider public use since the 1990s (theguardian, 2010). Because of this short time span, customs or rules of how to behave with cell phones are as yet not well established (Srivastava, 2005, p. 123). For example, when our cell phone rings in a meeting, we have a dilemma of how to behave: carry on with the conversation in the meeting, or answer the call? The lack of social rules leads to such mindless behavior as taking the phone when in meetings, shouting into the phone in public spaces, or more dangerously answering the phone while driving or walking across a road (Bianchi & Phillips, 2005; Hatfield & Murphy, 2005; Palen, Salzman, & Youngs, 2000; Walsh & White, 2007). While traditional face-to-face social interaction is ruled by well-established rituals that guide us how to enter an existing conversation (Goffman, 1982, pp. 5–10; Rothenbuhler, 1998, p. 4), the use of the cell phone constitutes a new territory, which appears to override or ignore many of the rules established to manage face-to-face interaction.

Only gradually, social rules or customs of how to behave with cell phones are emerging, often guided through reminders such as signs or announcements for example, in quiet coaches of trains, or in the music hall or theatre before a performance. Looking more closely, the impetus underlying this dilemma of whether or when to answer or talk on your phone appears to be a conflict of emotions. For example, motivations for answering your phone might be curiosity or the fear of missing out, a perceived duty, love, or perhaps boredom. Simultaneously, the action of answering a call might signal a lack of priority or disrespect for other person(s) in the same space while the decision not to take the phone might communicate priority and respect (Srivastava, 2005, p. 124ff).

The example of the cell phone reveals several layers that can be addressed by design to stimulate mindfulness. In using a cell phone, we can have three levels of interaction: human–object interaction (first level), for example, when we dial a number; intentional human–human interaction with the person (second level) for which the phone is designed; and unintentional human–human interaction (third level) with those with whom we are in the same space and which is generally ignored. Also, people's interaction can have primary goals, that is, the intended goal of their conversation, as well as secondary goals, which have the aim to support and enable the first goal (Burgoon et al., 2000, p. 112). Secondary goals may include, for example maintaining the seamless flow of the conversation, managing one's emotional states, maintaining one's personal image or face, or recognizing and interpreting environmental and social cues (Burgoon et al., 2000, p. 108). Third, because it can travel, the cell phone is part of a more diverse set of situations. Each of these three aspects can be used to address the identified mindful intent or theme. In addition, each of these different themes offers several choices and levels of interpretation that can be used to induce mindfulness. Because of this complexity, if we were to design a cell phone as a performative object, it would be possible to embed solutions to several issues such as a specific situation or certain emotional actions. For example, when phoning while walking on the sidewalk, the phone might be programmed to alert us to stop talking when we enter the zone of a pedestrian crossing or by deterring us from jaywalking. When in a meeting, the phone could question our emotional motivation for answering the call or, when raising our voice, the cell phone could "shout back" to alert us to the level of our voice. In order to do so, the design would need to address second and or third-level interaction (thematization), while influencing first-level interaction with the main function(s) of the phone (disruption), for example, a change in voice transfer or level may raise awareness of the user's own voice and its impact on others. Interestingly, approaches in this direction are already under way (e.g., Siewiorek et al., 2003) but have mostly remained at a conceptual stage.

To summarize, the mindful intent or theme addressed by any performative object can relate to either one or several of the three levels of interaction identified—within a specific situation or context—and where this is otherwise mindless. In order to address an identified mindful intent, the object's function and people's common use of it have to relate. Choice and complexity in embedding the theme in the object play an important role in causing mindfulness. Further, mindless social behavior and use of objects appear to be motivated by (a conflict of) emotions based on social and cultural preconceptions.

The Dual Role of Emotions in Designing Mindfulness

The following discussion examines the nature and role of emotions in social context. The aim is to better observe and recognize causes of mindless behavior to aid the understanding of how to design performative objects. The discussion adopts a social functional approach to emotion (Keltner & Gross, 1999; Keltner & Haidt, 1999; Roseman et al., 1994). The functional approach defines emotions broadly as "brief, rapid responses involving physiological, experiential, and behavioral activity that helps humans respond to survival-related problems and opportunities" (Keltner & Ekman, 2000, p. 163). It treats emotions as a complex system linking actions, causes, and consequences (Keltner & Gross, 1999, pp. 472–473), which offers "solutions to problems and opportunities related to physical and social survival" (Keltner & Gross, 1999, p. 467). The social functional approach is based on the belief that people—by their nature—are social and that emotions serve the purpose of "coordinating social interactions and relationships" (Keltner & Haidt, 1999, p. 508). Because the social functional approach elicits and relates the social nature of emotions, emotional actions, and their consequences, it can serve as a means to analyze complex social situations as a key to designing performative objects. With regard to investigating emotions as a cause for mindless action, this understanding of emotions provides three cues. First, it emphasizes the immediate nature of emotions; second, it refers to the regulating role of emotions in social interaction; and third, it defines emotions in terms of the actions they effect.

Emotions have evolved to be immediate and swift to enable survival-related actions, which require little or no time for reflection, and can be partially or fully subconscious (Gelder, 2006). Being able to operate certain tasks subconsciously is beneficial in that it enables us to operate efficiently in everyday life. For example, the skills and seamless operation required by the superfast typist break down when consciousness is directed towards them (Langer, 1989, pp. 19–22). While, on the one hand, this immediacy is beneficial, on the other hand it can make us unreflective and mindless (Burgoon et al., 2000, p. 112). In the context of emotions, this can cause problems when the emotions' specific situation or context changes. It then requires a change of emotional response, which, due to its immediacy, may not be realized (Langer, 1989, p. 175). In other words, while emotions enable a rapid response—which is good for "survival" in familiar situations—they may prevent mindful awareness of the different options available for "survival" in any new or changing (social) situation. They thus lead us to judge any situation from a single perspective. This will be the perspective or belief most familiar to us, which we have learned previously, and which we experience "without an awareness that they could be otherwise" (Langer, 1989, p. 175). Referring back to the use of public seating, in the context of public transport, as a matter of protecting their personal space, people's most common single perspective is that strangers are to be avoided (Evans & Wener, 2007, p. 92). In terms of the cell phone, this single-mindedness is encouraged by the design through the exclusive focus on the person at the other end of the connection, at the expense of any interaction outside this connection. Designing choice and complexity into the phone may be able to address this single-mindedness and lead to mindful new perspectives.

Emotions also have an important role in regulating personal relations and interactions (Keltner & Haidt, 1999, p. 508), such as "forming attachments, maintaining cooperative relations, or avoiding physical threats" (Keltner & Gross, 1999, p. 472). Emotions can pertain to personal (individual, intrapersonal), social, and/or societal levels (p. 475). The social level can be divided into dyadic relationships between two people and group interactions between several individuals, while the cultural level pertains to the "beliefs, norms, and cultural models" shared by an extended group of people (Keltner & Haidt, 1999, p. 506). The different social levels of emotions have different functions. At a cultural level, they provide a broad context that offers moral guidance (Keltner & Haidt, 1999, p. 513; Keltner, Horberg, & Oveis, 2006, pp. 161–175). For example, in certain cultures, kissing in public is deemed inappropriate because of cultural or religious beliefs, and breaking them may incur punishment; or on public transport, in some cultures, vacating a seat for a frail person or pregnant woman is a moral obligation. An individual's benefit and their "survival," however, are the foremost goal of emotions (Keltner & Haidt, 1999, p. 508). This priority creates a tenuous relationship between personal and social survival. There are many examples in life that require making this choice, such as: a politician deciding whether to stand back in favor of the unity of their party; a spouse choosing between her career or the well-being of their family; a soldier putting himself in harm's way. This dichotomy between personal interest and social benefit is borne out also in the examples of the public bench and the cell phone, albeit in a less dramatic way. For example, protecting one's personal space on a public bench by putting one's bag down diminishes the space of others and might deter them from sitting down. The cell phone in a meeting or public space may disrupt one conversation in favor of another and disturb the comfort of the many in favor of the satisfaction of a single person (Srivastava, 2005, p. 123). While functional accounts of emotions tend to focus on the beneficial consequences of emotions (Keltner & Gross, 1999, p. 473) and their ability to provide moral guidance and stability within a given system (Keltner, Horberg, & Oveis, 2006, pp. 161–175), the understanding of emotions from the perspective of mindfulness is often critical (Langer, 1989, p. 175). The mindful perspective questions established cultural-emotional systems concerning their continued validity and relevance to any specific situation, regarding them as single-minded and unreflective, and proposing that "mindful awareness of different options [and perspectives] gives us more control, which in turn encourages us to be more mindful" (Langer, 1989, p. 202). These two views of emotions may be negotiated if we accept that, in principle, emotions offer beneficial solutions by "regulat[ing] the individual's relation to the external environment" (Keltner & Gross, 1999, p. 468) through a balancing action. For example, the function of anger is assumed to restore equitable relations (p. 474). This in general may be seen as beneficial. However, how this is achieved may differ and may be achieved either in a desirable way (e.g., mutual negotiation) or in an undesirable way (e.g., hitting somebody in retaliation; Keltner & Gross, 1999, p. 474; Roseman et al., 1994, p. 207). This means, where (negative) emotions cause a mindless approach to social interaction, performative objects need to be designed to manage this imbalance to afford responsible action. This requires creating awareness of the different perspectives available including the individual/dyadic/group levels of emotional responses, the underlying cultural and social values that drive them, and the tensions between them.

Emotional actions are an essential part of the capacity of emotions to regulate emotional and interrelational imbalances, because emotions are linked to specific patterns of behavior that relate emotional goals, action tendencies, and actions (Roseman et al., 1994, p. 215). Specific emotions, such as anger or fear, have specific regulating patterns, such as seeking redress or avoidance. For example, anger seeking redress may result in the wish to hurt someone (goal), the conscious or unconscious intention to do so, which may or may not be executed (action tendency), and the action of hitting someone (action; pp. 207, 216). Emotions may further be categorized into three different pairs of emotional action patterns: positive or negative, appetitive or aversive, and "approach and withdrawal orientated" (Keltner & Gross, 1999, p. 475). In designing performative objects, mindful attention is likely to focus on situations where emotional actions occur that are negative or aversive, or seek avoidance, because these are most likely to relate to unsatisfactory or problematic situations—although context dependent, the reverse could be the case. Returning to the example of the public bench, one may work backward from the observable action (to sit down at the opposite end) to get to the underlying causes. Based on the idea of emotional patterns, this behavior can be interpreted as belonging to a particular set of emotions, that of avoidance, of which the most prominent is fear, although others such as contempt or disgust can also be considered. In relation to the context, we can further search for social and cultural motivations (premature cognitive commitments), which may underpin and lead to the observable actions.

Generally emotions and their actions are assumed to have a functional relationship in terms of cause and effect for the purpose of rebalancing any given situation. For instance, appeasement can be interpreted as a result of embarrassment or shame, and seeking redress may be seen as the function of anger (Keltner & Gross, 1999, p. 473). However, not all behavioral responses of emotions follow this pattern. There are accidental or nonfunctional consequences, which are more difficult to relate to the cause of the emotions (p. 473) and therefore are less predictable. "For example, anger might plausibly have several consequences, including [. . .] eating binges, and irrational bouts of house-cleaning, that do not relate to the assumed function of anger, the restoration of just relations" (p. 474).

Trying to understand the purpose of nonfunctional actions, it appears that they offer a way of reducing emotional tension within an individual. Although they do not change the environmental situation that has caused the negative emotions, they generate positive emotions that can partially overlay or cancel out negative emotions (Cohn, Fredrickson, Brown, Mikels, & Conway, 2009, p. 8). For example, irrational bouts of housework when angry might have an ameliorating effect by releasing the physical energy set free by a rush of adrenaline, or by causing positive emotions, such as satisfaction of a task completed, which can overlay and reduce or cancel out the first emotion. In the example of the Droog bench, the emotions of curiosity and/or fun can be seen to overlay those of fear, thus strengthening perceptions of safety, which creates openness to other stimuli, such as social concerns. Similar observations have been made in other functional accounts of emotion pertaining to risk appraisal (Peters, Burraston, & Metz, 2004, p. 1362). The connection between emotional goal/intent and action links emotions to the use of objects, which—by means of their function or "plan for action"—may also cause discrete actions (Niedderer, 2007, p. 9) akin to the functional and nonfunctional actions of emotions (Keltner & Gross, 1999, p. 473). Through this analog mechanism, objects have the potential to impact emotional action and—if designed correctly—can achieve a mindful-mediating effect. For example, water glasses are designed to hold water for drinking and are usually used for that purpose. However, a glass might be used for other, related purposes such as holding pens, or as a vase. This alternative use still adheres to the function of the glass as a container. In yet another situation, such as a pub brawl, the glass might be used very differently as a weapon (Winder & Wesson, 2006, p. 14). The use (or abuse) of the glass in response to emotions compares with the irrational bouts of housework, releasing emotions rather than solving a problem. Performative objects must therefore seek to harness functional and common nonfunctional emotional actions with objects. Thereby, choice may be used to direct attention mindfully towards desired goals, while nonfunctional behaviors may offer unexpected scenarios that provide useful alternative perspectives and solutions.

The discussion of the three aspects of emotions, their immediate nature, their role in social interaction, and the actions they effect, has revealed a number of ways in which emotions can cause mindlessness and which provide potential themes and approaches for designing performative objects. At the same time, recognizing their beneficial affect (Burgoon et al., 2000, p. 118; Keltner & Haidt, 1999, p. 511), emotions may also have the potential to serve as a subliminal tool in designing for mindfulness by providing an incentive or motivation for users to act with and use objects in desired ways. Thus, emotions might be used beneficially to complement the causal function of performative objects that serves to create awareness of unreflective emotional behavior by means of a disruption. This will be beneficial because we tend to blame ourselves when objects do not work in the way we expect them to (Norman, 2002, p. vii, x, 1ff). To counter such a potentially negative experience, the use of the positive influence of emotions could provide suitable direction and motivation to complete the action with the object. This could have the benefit of increasing both the desire to use the object, an aspect that has been researched widely in emotional design (e.g., Norman, 2004; Spillers, 2003), and the motivation to change undesirable emotional actions, based either on emotional appeal or on opposing emotions canceling each other out.

A Mindful-Emotional Framework for Designing Social Interaction

Following the analysis of mindfulness and emotion, this section draws together the key points of the discussion to establish a mindful-emotional framework. The aim of the framework is to aid the design of performative objects by serving as an interpretive tool for analyzing social situations and the use of design objects within them, with regard to any emotional actions and their mindful or mindless consequences. When originally developed, the concept of the performative object focused mainly on the functional aspects of causing mindfulness, without considering how to identify a context-related thematic starting point (Niedderer, 2004, pp. 147–149). The framework presented here aims to enable designers to identify such a context-related starting point through the analysis of actual social situations and interactions, and the social consequences of the objects they design for them. This is contrary to the starting point of traditional design briefs or scenarios that focus on the desired purpose or function of a new product. In doing so, the framework can help to promote deep thinking and to identify the purpose and responsible affordances of a product at the early conceptual stage of the design process. The framework thus complements other design approaches such as design for behavior change (Lockton, 2010), socially responsible design (Tromp et al., 2011), emotional design (e.g., Desmet & Hekkert, 2002; Weerdesteijn, Desmet, & Gielen, 2005), and user-centered design (e.g., Sanders & Simons, 2009; Sanders & Stappers, 2008) by providing an alternative starting point.

The discussion of mindfulness and emotions has revealed several key points. It has highlighted choice and complexity as key aspects for causing mindfulness, whereby choice pertains to the different possible options for action, and complexity pertains to the different possible perspectives and levels of interpretation. Further, the discussion has shown that emotions are likely to cause mindless action because they are by their nature unreflective and focus the mind on a single perspective. The mindful content or theme of performative objects therefore needs to focus on the different aspects of emotions, including: different kinds of emotions (e.g., anger, joy, frustration, fear); the corresponding functional and nonfunctional actions and goals, and any underlying beliefs that cause these emotions; different social levels of emotions (individual, dyadic, group, cultural) and any tensions between them. Parallels between actions and functions of emotions and objects allow for addressing one through the other, and thus for designing choice and complexity to raise awareness of emotions and their social consequences. Finally, while one set of emotions may cause mindlessness (e.g., negative, avoidance, and aversive emotions), emotions of the opposing set (e.g., positive, appetitive, and approach-oriented emotions) may be used as a mechanism to counter the first and act as an incentive (or deterrent) to change the user's action. In the following, these findings are expressed as a set of guidelines for designing performative objects. The guidelines offer three steps for consideration at the concept development phase of designing, including (1) identification of the design problem, (2) identification of the potential design solution, and (3) identification of different ways of implementation.

Step 1: Identification of the design problem

The design problem can be defined generally as a lack of mindful interaction or intent within a specific social situation. Specifics may be identified by investigating the following potential indicators:

- the mode(s) of interaction: human–object; human–object–human; human–object–human group;
- the level(s) of emotional interaction: individual, social/dyadic, social/group;
- emotional actions, both functional and nonfunctional relating to the above;

- what set of emotions any identified emotions belong to (positive, appetitive, and approach oriented or negative, avoidance, aversive);
- the individual/social/cultural level of emotions and any underlying premature cognitive commitments that could drive the emotional actions;
- any tensions between personal, social, and/or societal levels of emotions.

Step 2: Identification of the potential design solution

In response to the identified problem, the designer needs to identify and embody in the design mindful options for mediating or improving the social situation or interaction. These need to address any undesirable emotional actions, goals, social levels, etc. identified under Step 1, create awareness of them, and offer alternative perspectives and actions. In order to do so, the designer may identify:

- different choices of emotional actions as a means of creating reflection;
- different possible perspectives of the emotion/emotional actions to provide complexity;
- desirable emotions that may be used as an incentive or to cancel out undesirable emotions.

Step 3: Identification of different ways of implementation

In order to implement the selected mindful options, the designer needs to identify how these options can be embodied in the mindful design object. There are three ways in which this may be achieved:

- creating choice by offering different options for responding to the function of the object, which need to:
  - operate on both a pragmatic and symbolic level;
  - relate to the individual emotional functional or nonfunctional action on the pragmatic level;
  - relate to the social or societal emotions and their underlying norms or beliefs on the symbolic level;
- creating awareness of multiple perspectives by embedding different functional/ nonfunctional actions in the object that are related to different social perspectives, which need to:
  - refer to different social emotions and/or to different cultural norms and beliefs;
  - offer multiple level interpretations that are new/different to that of the individual emotional action, and related premature cognitive commitments;
- using positive emotions as a motivation to encourage desired action, which requires identifying:
  - any emotions/emotional actions that complement the emotions/emotional actions that are perceived as problematic (e.g., fear/avoidance—curiosity/ appetitive);

- whether/how they may be perceived as a reward or whether they work on the basis of empathy;
- whether/how they may work as an incentive or deterrent, or to cancel out negative emotions.

In summary, this above emotional-mindful design framework aims to provide a flexible tool for designers for analyzing and addressing emotion-related mindless social interactions using emotion regulation based on a mindful design approach.

Discussion: Applying the Mindful-Emotional Framework

The following discussion revisits the examples of the Droog Design bench and the cell phone in order to demonstrate how the framework might be applied, and to discuss a number of issues concerning design and behavior change relating to the idea of the performative object. Having recognized the Droog bench as a performative object previously, the analysis can be expected to reveal matching observations answering to each point of the framework, thus demonstrating how the analytical framework provides a structure for analyzing design examples. In contrast, the example of the cell phone demonstrates how to apply the framework to a (new) social situation. When analyzing examples of performative objects and social situations, in theory, the guidelines need to be applied to the former in reverse order because the emotional action needs to be induced from the function of the object, while the analysis of social situations begins with observing emotional actions. In practice, however, emotional and object functions are implied and compared simultaneously. Therefore, the analysis follows a logical order, rather than a strictly sequential order.

Example 1: "Come a little bit closer bench" by Nina Farkache, 2001 (Droog, 2012)

With the help of the emotional-mindful framework, one can now construct a full and systematic analysis of the bench. The contextual situation (Step 1), which the object suggests by association with traditional benches, is people's habitual behavior in public places. The mode and level of interaction in this context are generally a human–object interaction combined with a dyadic human–human interaction, although in some cases this might extend to interaction of an individual with a group. The emotional action addressed by the bench is one of people sitting down at opposite ends to avoid strangers (Figure 19.2a and Figure 19.2b; Evans & Wener, 2007). The action of avoidance points to the group of avoidance-orientated emotions, which includes fear, disgust, or contempt (Keltner & Haidt, 1999, p. 369; Keltner, Young, & Buswell, 1997, p. 513; Roseman et al., 1994, p. 207). The cultural beliefs and norms causing such emotions may include the protection of one's personal space and having learned that strangers may pose a potential danger (Langer, 1989, p. 175). These beliefs may cause emotional tension at the dyadic level, for example, between people who take two seats and thus bar others from sitting down, forcing them to ask for space or remain standing. In terms of mindful options, the bench addresses emotions of avoidance by offering the option of decreasing physical/social distance without changing seats through the movable seating shells. Beyond the functional level, the bench offers a second level of playfulness and additional complexity. Both solutions can be seen to invoke positive emotions, such as surprise (about the moving shells), curiosity (should I move closer?), and fun (an aspect of play). Concerning the implementation of these mindful options in the design, choice is created through the movable shells offering a choice of moving closer, staying put, or creating more distance. Although this function pertains to the individual, it affects their social interaction both physically and symbolically, thus questioning the individual's beliefs and behavior towards strangers. Through this analysis, we can see how the framework allows for a systematic study of the mindful and emotional actions and consequences of the design in relation to the social situation.

Example 2: The use of cell phones in public spaces

The example of the cell phone starts from an existing situation that is used to build up towards a speculative design specification. This demonstrates how the framework can be applied where there is no known performative object. For this purpose, the example draws together the various aspects of cell-phone usage in the context of public spaces, and particularly public transport, in order to identify potential mindful actions that could inform the design of cell phones. The example draws on observations by the author and on findings from research on this subject (e.g., Monk, Carroll, Parker, & Blythe, 2004; Srivastava, 2005). The aim is to demonstrate how to develop deep thinking about a product and its consequences before starting the actual design process. The purpose is to enhance our understanding and approach to designing products for users by the explicit addition of responsible use for social interaction.

In the context of cell-phone use, it is possible to identify all three modes and levels of interaction: the individualistic interaction of people with their cell phones; the dyadic interaction between the caller and the person called; and the interaction between the cell-phone user and any group surrounding them, although such group interaction can also be broken down into multiple dyadic interactions. In terms of emotional actions, there is the individual calling, answering a call, or talking loudly on the phone, which may be motivated by a range of positive and negative emotions as discussed above. In relation to the group, emotional action can be lacking or passive (e.g., ignoring interaction with and by other people) or disruptive (e.g., deliberately loud voice), indicating a lack of social concern and responsibility, or lack of respect for others. Whether this lack of concern is based on carelessness, or because the interaction with the phone does not fit established patterns and rituals of interaction, cannot be established without user research. It suggests, however, that, contrary to the bench, mindlessness with the cell phone is based on a lack of predefined cultural norms, creating tensions between the individual and the group.

Mindful solutions for mediating such social tensions will thus need to bring the group perspective to the mind of the individual, such as feeling disturbed by inappropriately talking loud or listening to a one-sided, trivial, or inappropriately intimate conversation. One can imagine a number of choices concerning emotional action in this context, for example, answering or not answering the phone, leaving the joint (group) space or sending an SMS, or talking quietly or louder. Although some of these options are beginning to enter protocols for people's behavior with cell phones, especially talking loudly or loud ringtones remain problematic. The key issue therefore is to integrate an awareness of the different perspectives and choices into the design while raising positive emotions. Indeed, some aspects are already designed into the phone but they are not always used. For example, the phone can be set to silent or to vibrate. Another solution might be to display a message that needs a response before the call can be taken, similar to the warning messages on computers. If such messages offered different choices in a humorous way, they might instill positive emotions and acceptance by the user. When deciding to answer a call, the user might be encouraged to consider lowering the volume of their speech through the phone responding with appropriate and proportional audible feedback.

This discussion is only able to highlight some of the most obvious ideas, because its main purpose has been to demonstrate how the framework enables identifying under-lying emotions and emotional actions, and potential mindful choices and perspectives as a basis for developing design solutions that can create awareness of these issues. The example of the cell phone also indicates how user behavior coemerges with the objects used, and how design can be used to impact not just user behavior but also social interactions and attitudes.

Conclusion: Mindful Design for Behavior Change

This chapter has investigated the role of emotion in designing for mindfulness. The study has used a small number of real-world and hypothetical examples to demonstrate the broader application of performative objects as a contribution to design for behav-ior change. Focusing on performative objects, the investigation has first reviewed the aspects of choice and complexity as means for causing mindfulness. Second, the func-tional analysis of emotions has revealed their dual role in causing mindless and mindful social interaction. On the one hand, emotions can cause mindlessness because of their immediate context-dependent nature; on the other hand, emotions can be used as an incentive (or deterrent) in designing for mindfulness. The analysis of examples has revealed two possibilities for the intervention of design in social situations: (1) situ-ations where social interaction is problematic due to mindlessness; and (2) situations where an opportunity for mindful social interaction is not recognized. In both situa-tions, existing objects may be redesigned to facilitate mindful interaction. Instead of a discrete object, we can also imagine the redesign of a larger entity such as an interior or exterior environment. In this regard, several examples of performative architecture exist (e.g., Sheldon Scenarios, 2002). Other opportunities for the redesign of inte-rior environments arise from research reports that highlight problem areas, such as aggressive drinking behavior in pubs (Winder & Wesson, 2006).

The outcome of this study is a mindful-emotional framework, which can be used both for the analysis of design objects and for the analysis of social situations to elicit underlying emotions, emotional actions, and premature cognitive commitments. It is further offered as robust guidance to inform the design of performative objects. The contribution and benefit of this research are a better understanding of the design and broader application of performative objects, and their potential to contribute to behavior change. It will be appreciated that currently this framework is speculative and demonstrates what may be rather than what is (March, 1984, p. 269). Finally, the analysis has pointed to a number of opportunities for further work, which can be used to test the framework in real-world situations.

Acknowledgments

I would like to acknowledge the support of the University of Wolverhampton, School of Art and Design, in granting me a research sabbatical to undertake the work for this chapter. I also would like to thank a number of colleagues for their encouragement and support, including Professor Dew Harrison, Professor Ken Manktelow, and Dr. Caroline Wesson. In particular, I would like to thank Professors Robert Jerrard and David Durling for their advice in editing.

References

Bianchi, A., & Phillips, J. G. (2005). Psychological predictors of problem mobile phone use. *Cyberpsychology & Behavior, 8*(1), 39–51.

Brown, T. (2008). Design thinking. *Harvard Business Review,* June.

Brown, T., & Wyatt, J. (2010). Design thinking for social innovation. *Stanford Social Innovation Review,* Winter. Retrieved from http://www.ssireview.org/articles/entry/design_thinking_for_social_innovation/

Buchanan, R. (2001). Design research and the new learning. *Design Issues, 17*(4), 3–23.

Burgess. J. W. (1982). Interpersonal spacing behavior between surrounding nearest neighbors reflects both familiarity and environmental density. *Ethology and Sociobiology, 4*(1), 11–17.

Burgoon, J. K., Berger, C. R., & Waldron, V. R. (2000). Mindfulness and interpersonal communication. *Journal of Social Issues, 56*(1), 105–127.

Cohn, M. A., Fredrickson, B. L., Brown, S. L., Mikels, J. A., & Conway, A. M. (2009). Happiness unpacked: Positive emotions increase life satisfaction by building resilience. *Emotion, 9*(3), 361–368. Retrieved from http://www.ncbi.nlm.nih.gov/pmc/articles/PMC3126102/pdf/nihms-222302.pdf

Desmet, P. M. A., & Hekkert, P. (2002). The basis of product emotions. In W. Green & P. Jordan (Eds.), *Pleasure with products, beyond usability* (pp. 60–68). London, UK: Taylor & Francis, .

Droog (2012). *Come a little bit closer bench, by Nina Farkache, 2001.* Retrieved from http://www.droog.com/store/furniture/come-a-little-bit-closer-bench/

Dunne, A., & Raby, F. (2001). *Design noir: The secret life of electronic objects.* Basel, Switzerland: Birkhäuser and London, UK: August.

ESRC. (2012). *Economic and social research council delivery plan 2011–2015. Economic and Social Research Council.* Retrieved from http://www.esrc.ac.uk/_images/ESRC%20Delivery%20Plan%202011–15_tcm8-13455.pdf

Evans, G. W., Wener, R. E. (2007). Crowding and personal space invasion on the train: Please don't make me sit in the middle. *Journal of Environmental Psychology, 27,* 90–94.

Fried, M. L., & DeFazio, V. J. (1974). Territoriality and boundary conflicts in the subway. *Psychiatry: Journal for the Study of Interpersonal Processes, 37*(1), 47–59.

Gelder, B. de (2006). Towards the neurobiology of emotional body language. *Nature Reviews Neuroscience, 7*, 242–249. Retrieved from http://www.beatricedegelder.com/documents/degelderNRN2006.pdf

Goffman, E. (1966). *Behavior in public places: Notes on the social organization of gatherings.* New York, NY: Free Press.

Goffman, E. (1982). *Interaction ritual. Essays on face-to-face behavior.* New York, NY: Pantheon Books (Reprint of 1967 Anchor Ed.).

Greenfield, A. (2011). *Weeks 43–44: International garbageman.* New York, NY: Urbanscale. Retrieved from http://urbanscale.org/news/2011/11/03/weeks-43-44-international-garbageman/

Hatfield, J., & Murphy, S. (2005). The effects of mobile phone use on pedestrian crossing behaviour at signalised and unsignalised intersections. *Accident Analysis & Prevention, 39*(1), 197–205.

Ilstedt Hjelm, S. I. (2004). *Making sense. Design for well-being (Doctoral thesis).* Stockholm, Sweden: KTH.

Keltner, D., & Ekman, P. (2000). Emotion: An overview. In A. Kazdin (Ed.), *Encyclopedia of psychology* (pp. 162–167). London, UK: Oxford University Press.

Keltner, D., & Gross, J. J. (1999). Functional accounts of emotions. *Cognition and Emotion, 13*(5), 467–480.

Keltner, D., & Haidt, J. (1999). Social functions of emotions at four levels of analysis. *Cognition and Emotion, 13*(5), 505–521.

Keltner, D., Horberg, E. J., & Oveis, C. (2006). Emotions as moral institutions. In J. P. Forgas (Ed.), *Affect in social thinking and behaviour, frontiers of social psychology* (Vol. 8, pp. 161–175). New York, NY: Psychology Press.

Keltner, D., Young, R. C., & Buswell, B. N. (1997). Appeasement in human emotion, social practice, and personality. *Aggressive Behavior, 23*, 359–374.

Langer, E. J. (1989). *Mindfulness.* New York, NY: Addison-Wesley.

Langer, E. J. (1997). *The power of mindful learning.* Cambridge, MA: Perseus.

Langer, E. J., & Moldoveanu, M. (2000a). The construct of mindfulness. *Journal of Social Issues, 56*(1), 1–9.

Langer, E. J., & Moldoveanu, M. (2000b). Mindfulness research and the future. *Journal of Social Issues, 56*(1), 129–139.

Lovegrove, R. (Ed.). (2002). *The international design yearbook 2002.* London, UK: Laurence King.

Lockton, D. (2010). *Design for intent.* Retrieved from http://www.danlockton.com/dwi/Main_Page

Lockton, D. (2012). POSIWID and determinism in design for behaviour change. *Working Paper Series, April 2012*, Brunel University. Retrieved from http://bura.brunel.ac.uk/handle/2438/6394

Lockton, D., Harrison, D., & Stanton, N. A. (2009). Choice architecture and design with intent. *Proceedings of NDM9, the Ninth International Conference on Naturalistic Decision Making.* London, UK: The British Computer Society, June 2009. Retrieved from http://bura.brunel.ac.uk/handle/2438/3558

March, L. (1984). The logic of design. In N. Cross (Ed.), *Developments in design methodology* (pp. 265–276). Chichester, UK: John Wiley & Sons.

Metzinger, T. (Ed). (1995). *Conscious experience.* Thorverton, UK: Imprint Academic.

Monk, A., Carroll, J., Parker, S., & Blythe, M. (2004). Why are mobile phones annoying? *Behaviour & Information Technology, 23*(1), 33–41.

Niedderer, K. (2004). *Designing the performative object: A study in designing mindful interaction through artefacts* (Ph.D. thesis). University of Plymouth, Plymouth, UK.

Niedderer, K. (2007). Designing mindful interaction: The category of the performative object. *Design Issues, 23*(1), 3–17.

Niedderer, K. (2013). Mindful design as a driver for social behaviour change. In *Proceedings of the IASDR Conference 2013*. Tokyo, Japan: IASDR.

Norman, D. A. (2002). *The design of everyday things*. New York, NY: Basic Books.

Norman, D. A. (2004). *Emotional design: Why we love (or hate) everyday things*. New York, NY: Basic Books.

Palen, L., Salzman, M., & Youngs, E. (2000). Going wireless: Behavior & practice of new mobile phone users. *ACM 2000 Conference on Computer Supported Cooperative Work*, December 2–6, Philadelphia, PA. Retrieved from http://www.cs.colorado.edu/~palen/Papers/cscwPalen.pdf

Pearce, S. M. (1995). *On collecting: An investigation into collecting in the European tradition*. London, UK: Routledge.

Peters, E. M., Burraston, B., & Metz, C. K. (2004). An emotion-based model of risk perception and stigma susceptibility: Cognitive appraisals of emotion, affective reactivity, worldviews and risk perceptions in the generation of technological stigma. *Risk Analysis, 24*(5), 1349–1367.

Ramakers, R. (2002). *Less + more: Droog design in context*. Rotterdam, Netherlands: 010.

Roseman, I. J., Wiest, C., & Swartz, T. S. (1994). Phenomenology, behaviours and goals differentiate discrete emotions. *Journal of Personality and Social Psychology, 67*(2), 206–221.

Rothenbuhler, E. W. (1998). *Ritual communication*. London, UK: Sage.

Sanders, E. B.-N., & Simons, G. (2009). A social vision for value co-creation in design. *Open source business resource, December 2009: Value co-creation*. Retrieved from http://www.maketools.com/articles-papers/Social_Vision_for_Value_CoCreation_in_Design.pdf

Sanders, E. B.-N., & Stappers, P. J. (2008). Co-creation and the new landscapes of design. Retrieved from http://www.maketools.com/articles-papers/CoCreation_Sanders_Stappers_08_preprint.pdf (preprint of an article submitted for consideration in CoDesign, Taylor & Francis, March 2008. CoDesign is available online at http://journalsonline.tandf.co.uk)

Sheldon Scenarios. (2002). *Sheldon Scenarios: Introduction and context*. Retrieved from http://www.2.gvsu.edu/~wittenbp/scenario/about/about.intro.html

Siewiorek, D., Smailagic, A., Furukawa, J., Moraveji, N., Reiger, K., & Shaffer, J. (2003). SenSay: A context-aware mobile phone. *Proceedings of the 7th International Symposium of Wearable Computers*, ISWC 03 (pp. 248–250). Retrieved from http://www.cs.cmu.edu/afs/cs.cmu.edu/Web/People/aura/docdir/sensay_iswc.pdf

Spillers, F. (2003). Emotion as a cognitive artifact and the design implications for products that are perceived as pleasurable. *Cognition, 7*, 1–14. Retrieved from http://www.experiencedynamics.com

Srivastava, L. (2005). Mobile phones and the evolution of social behaviour. *Behaviour & Information Technology, 24*(2), 111–129.

theguardian. (2010). *From bricks to the iPhone: 25 years of the mobile phones*, February 14, 2010 Retrieved from http://www.theguardian.com/technology/gallery/2010/feb/14/mobile-phones-gadgets-iphone

Tromp, N., Hekkert, P., & Verbeek, P. (2011). Design for socially responsible behaviour: A classification of influence based on intended user experience. *Design Issues, 27*(3), 3–19.

Udall, N. (1996). *An investigation into the heuristics of mindfulness in higher art and design education* (Ph.D. thesis). University of Surrey, Guildford, UK.

Walsh, S. P., & White, K. M. (2007). Me, my mobile, and I: The role of self- and prototypical identity influences in the prediction of mobile phone behavior. *Journal of Applied Social Psychology, 37*(10), 2405–2434. Retrieved from http://www.cs.colorado.edu/~palen/palen_papers/palen-mobilephones.pdf

Weerdesteijn, J. M. W., Desmet, P. M. A., & Gielen, M. A. (2005). Moving design: To design emotion through movement. *The Design Journal, 8*(1), 28–40.

Winder, B., & Wesson, C. J. (2006). *Last orders for alcohol related violence*. Report prepared for the British Glass Institute, Nottingham Trent University, Nottingham, UK.

20

On Being Mindful of Time

Stuart Albert

The most mindless approach to time is simply to ignore time completely. Whenever we attempt to reason logically or invoke statistical or mathematical principles to explain or predict human behavior, it is easy to omit temporal considerations. Here are two examples.

The A-Temporal Logic of Probability

Here's a simple problem (Mlodinow, 2008, pp. 51–52). A woman has two children. We know that one is a girl. What are the odds that the other is also female?

If you said 50–50, a statistician would say that you were wrong. The right answer is 33%. Here's why. We know that the woman has a girl. What are the remaining logical possibilities? They are: girl–girl, girl–boy, and boy–girl. So, the odds are 1 in 3 that the other child will be a girl. The boy–boy pair is ruled out because we know that at least one child is a girl.

Tricky, right? But there is also something fishy going on. Notice that this description of the problem does not tell us the actual sequence of events. Let's bring time back into this story and see what happens.

Let's assume that the first child born was a girl. Before the second child was conceived, the mother might have wondered what the odds were that she would end up with two girls. The answer depends on *when* she asked the question. If she asked the question *before* she had *any* children, the odds of ending up with two girls are one in four. There are four possibilities: boy–boy, girl–girl, girl–boy, and boy–girl. But *after* she *had* one girl, the odds change. *Then* odds that the next child will be a female are simply 50/50. So, how is it that we got the 33% answer above and the 50% answer here?

The Wiley Blackwell Handbook of Mindfulness, First Edition.
Edited by Amanda Ie, Christelle T. Ngnoumen, and Ellen J. Langer.
© 2014 John Wiley & Sons, Ltd. Published 2014 by John Wiley & Sons, Ltd.

The answer has to do with time and timing. The problem as initially presented stated that *one* child was a girl. It didn't say that the *first* child born was a girl, and then the mother wondered about the sex of the next child. What is called a "wrong" answer is actually more realistic. It was based on our understanding that events unfold in sequences, and that questions about odds are often raised in the context of trying to predict the future. Those of you who said 50–50 simply made a series of reasonable assumptions *about the real world*.

Let me give you a second example of a-temporal statistical thinking. It comes from a review of Leonard Mlodinow's book, *The Drunkards Walk* (Johnson, 2008, p. 14).

The O. J. Simpson Trial

Leonard Mlodinow recalls the O. J. Simpson trial, in which the prosecution depicted the defendant as an inveterate wife abuser. One of Simpson's lawyers, Alan Dershowitz, countered with statistics: in the United States, four million women are battered every year by the male partners, yet only one in 2,500 is ultimately murdered by her partner.

> The jury maybe found that persuasive, but it's a spurious argument. Nicole Brown Simpson was already dead. The relevant question was what percentage of all battered women who are murdered are killed by their abusers. The answer, Mlodinow notes, didn't come up in the trial. It was 90 percent.

In the O. J. Simpson story, the key is also one of timing. In one case, we are looking at the problem prospectively. A woman is battered and then murdered (forget about who did it for the moment). What are the odds of that happening? Not great. Relatively few battered women end up murdered by their male partners. (Needless to say, we all want the answer to be zero.) But now reverse the sequence. Assume that a battered woman is already dead. She was one of a relatively small number of battered women who met this fate. The question is, who did it? What are the odds that the person who abused her was the killer? The odds, it turns out, are remarkably high, 90%. So, statistically, the odds that O. J. Simpson killed his wife were 90%, not 1 in 2,500 or 0.04% as Dershowitz claimed.

Why do we make these so-called mistakes? The reviewer of Mlodinow's book, George Johnson, a distinguished scientist and science writer, comments: "The brain, no matter how well schooled, is just plain bad at dealing with randomness and probability" (Johnson, 2008, p. 14). And a few paragraphs later, he adds: "Trust your instincts … and you're bound to go wrong" (Johnson, 2008, p. 14). I think the source of the difficulty has been misdiagnosed. The problem isn't our instincts. It isn't randomness. It isn't that our poor brain "can't be schooled." All of these things may be true in some situations. But I think an important reason why we make "errors" is that we have left time (in this case, temporal sequences) out of the way we formulate mathematical and statistical questions, *without realizing that we have done so*. We think we have a *real* problem before us, and we set out to solve it. In fact, we have an *imaginary* problem posing as a real one. Real problems always have a temporal order associated with them.

These two examples describe life in the Gated Community of logic and mathematics in which time, with the accompanying fear of change and death, is kept out. When we do include time in our thinking, we tend to use standard ways of visually displaying it, the time line, the circular face of a clock, for example. In this chapter, I want to examine and critique these common forms of visually displaying time. I also want to suggest alternatives to what Langer describes as the limiting mindset of linear time (Langer, 1989, pp. 32–33).

Lines and Arrows

One of the most common ways of visually representing time is the time line. It is the *x*-axis of many graphs and diagrams. A time line has direction. Usually, by convention, the past is to the left, and the future is to the right. But a time line has a number of other characteristics in addition to direction. It is usually drawn horizontally, which means that we view it head on, perpendicular to our line of sight. It is also usually drawn as a straight line rather than one that is curved or bumpy, so as to provide a constant reference point against which change can be observed.

The art historian, Herbert Read, claimed that images precede ideas and that new images make it possible to think in new ways (Read, 1965 p. 70). So, if we want to improve our sense of timing, and hence our ability to more mindfully control events, I think we need to change the shapes we use to plot, graph, chart, and display temporal information. The way we usually graph and plot data leaves out important information about time, even when we think we have included it. Let me show you what I mean, by describing two alternatives to the straight and horizontal time line.

V0 and V2 Projections

Figure 20.1 is a standard graph of some hypothetical data using what I call a V0 projection, and another graph using the same data, which I call a V2 projection.

The top graph does not have a vanishing point: there is no depth to it, hence, the name, a V0 (V zero) projection. I now plot the same data using two vanishing points, an idea suggested by Brueghel's 1565 painting, Peasant Wedding.[1] Notice what we have gained by displaying data in this way.

1   One of the most important features of the V2 projection is the sharp vertical edge of the corner—which represents the present. This line reminds us that the future may not be a continuation of the past. Once we turn the corner, we may run into something completely unexpected.
2   Because the V2 projection has depth, it reminds us to look farther back in time, to ask about origins.
3   The right vanishing point reminds us to think long term. We will miss risks and opportunities if we do not.
4   The V2 projection also has an inside, which we cannot see. That reminds us to look for what is not immediately visible or apparent.

V0 Projection

V2 Projection

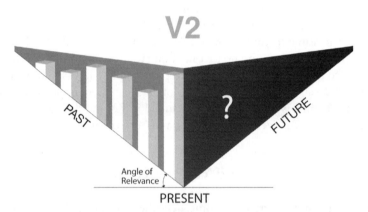

Figure 20.1   Standard graph of some hypothetical data.

5 The V2 projection makes it possible to note the comparative importance of the past relative to the future. We can do this by making one side longer than the other, as might be the case in the Middle East, where the past dominates thinking.
6 Finally, we can show the diminished relevance of the past for present decisions by adjusting "R," the angle or relevance. If we increase "R," the past becomes smaller more quickly, reflecting its reduced importance. When R is 90°, one sees only the present. The past has vanished. When the past is not relevant, one has achieved closure.

Compare the V2 projection with the standard graph (the V0 projection) in which time is treated almost as a constant, as a stable, level floor from which to observe variation. The message is subtle. The future may be up in the air, but we are rooted. Everything will turn out fine. After all, what goes up goes down. We will return to equilibrium. It is almost as if we are seated on firm ground watching the spectacle of change unfold above us like a display of fireworks.

When we plot change in this way, as *change over time*, we think we have captured the essence of change, namely variation. But captured is the key word. We have defanged and corralled the real threat, which is the speed of time's passage and the prospect of radical discontinuity. We feel this sense of motion in the V2 projection in a way that we do not in the V0 projection. We are aware that events may change more quickly and unpredictably than we can cope with. The V0 projection has not exactly killed the experience of time passing (our eye still can travel left to right on the graph), but we have slowed or arrested its motion. Adding a vanishing point reminds us of how much we do not know about the past and the future, which opens the door to another kind of understanding based on new information.

I think that the standard HTL (horizontal time line) graph should be *X-rated*. Warning: viewer discretion advised. The full frontal presentation of the data leaves important aspects of time out of the picture. The V0 projection is one way the Conventional Mind creates a view of the world that is time-impoverished. It is a perspective that is not mindful of the richness of temporal experience and the possibility of new perspectives.

Two additional comments before I leave the V2 projection. Notice that there is no loss in accuracy in plotting data on the V2 graph: the *y*-axis shrinks proportionally. Second, it is somewhat amusing to find in the structure of a 16th-century painting a better way to capture the dynamism of events in the 21st century.

In the V2 projection, I have taken the standard time line and bent it. I now want to explore another modification. Instead of the time line being drawn as a horizontal line, I want to put in on a diagonal.

The T Map

Figure 20.2, which I call a T map, is another way to highlight qualities that the V0 projection leaves out. The essential idea is to rotate the standard time line (T) up from its usual horizontal position so that it is now on a diagonal.

As we move along this diagonal, let's assume that first A happens, then B, then C, etc. At each of these points, if we look to the right, we see the future as it appears at that moment (the future horizon, or FH). If we look to the left, we see the past, or rather what we remember of it (the past horizon, or PH). Each moment provides a unique view of the past and future as seen from that point in time.

Now, let's assume that we have reached point C. At point C, we look to the right and see events D and E coming. The arrow tells us when D is expected. The dotted lines define what I call the angle of risk (AOR), the risk that D could arrive earlier or later than expected.

Now, proceed further up the diagonal. At some point, we look back into the past. We think that C happened before B. But our memory is faulty. B happened before C, as indicated on the diagonal time line. Some events are no longer remembered at all. They are beyond the horizon.

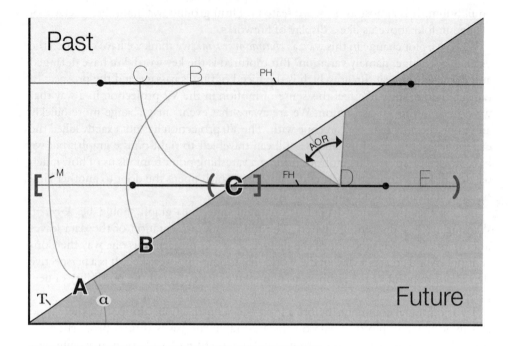

Figure 20.2 T Map, another way to highlight qualities omitted by the V0 projection.

Advantages of the T Map

The T map has a number of advantages:

1 When we think about the past and future in order to decide what to do today, we have at our disposal all the tenses of our natural language. For example, the future perfect: "I'll sell now. That way, *I will have sold* before a downward spiral begins, something I missed last year." If a graphic display does not contain, or suggest, the same rich set of relationships that the tense structure of our natural language provides, then the display is time impoverished.[2] Individuals who rely on it can easily miss some of the facts and relationships that they need to make good decisions about timing. They will not be mindful, open to new possibilities.

2 Our view of the past and future continually changes. We need to think about what the future will look *like at different points in the future, including the fact that we ourselves are changing.*

3 Any given moment, any point like point C on the T map can be grouped with either the past [] and/or with the future (). Which grouping one chooses can affect how urgent a situation is perceived to be, and how quickly one feels one must act. For example, if one has been working on a task for a very long time,

one wants to complete it (the present moment is grouped with the past). "Let's get it done. We have been working on this forever," you can hear someone say. But if the present is seen as the first step of a new and possibly uncertain future, one may decide to be more cautious. After all, first steps set precedents.

4   The T map makes it easy to compare expectation with reality. What occurred earlier or later than expected or predicted, and why?

5   The T map gives us a better understanding of timing risks. A large financial firm is failing. Should the government jump in and try to save it? The concept of moral hazard raises a red flag. If the government saves the firm, so the standard reasoning goes, that will encourage others to take excessive risks in the future. What that line of reasoning omits is what the T-map calls to our attention. First, the present time may be the wrong time (that is, the wrong place on the T map) to invoke the concept of *moral hazard*. If a firm is large and linked to others, its failure could bring down the entire system. Second, the government can learn from its mistakes. If its actions were counterproductive, it won't repeat them. The government—as well as everyone else—will be at a different point on the diagonal time line in the future. Its view of the past and future will be different, and that will influence what it decides to do. The T map brings these considerations to mind in a way that the V0 projection does not.

6   By adjusting alpha, we can change how important the past is relative to the future. When alpha is small, the past has greater significance. When it is large, decisions about timing are more influenced by the future. When it is 90°, we can't see the past at all. When it is zero, we can't even see the future, and hence are unlikely to take it into account.

7   Because the T map places historical or real-time events on a diagonal, the future arrives at an angle. That reminds us, as did the V2 projection, that the future may not be a continuation of the past.

8   The T map helps keep us in the present, the present of time past, and the present of time future.

9   The T map helps us remain open to new information. We will be better prepared for events happening at times different from what we expected. We know that the AOR is likely to vary over time.

10   The T map makes it easy to think about why one time may be better than other to take a particular action based on what the past and future look like at that time. The most powerful timing rules, the ones we rely on to decide *when* to act are *triples*, refer to past, present, and future. I illustrate these triples in the table below reproduced from *When: The Art of Perfect Timing* (Albert, 2013). I've placed a YES in those cells when the window of opportunity is open, and an action can be successful, NO when it is closed, and acting is impossible or inadvisable (Table 20.1).

As the table illustrates, decisions about timing dependon what was (or was thought to be) possible in the past, present, and future. So, if you want to understand the emotions associated with a timing decision, you need to consider all three time periods. For example, compare Row 5 (NO—YES—NO) with Row 7 (YES—YES—NO). The rows are highlighted. In both, the decision is the same: Act now. But there is a difference. In Row 5, this is your first and only chance. The time wasn't right until now,

Table 20.1 Timing triples.

| | When is the time right to act? | | |
Past	Present	Future	Timing rule or implication
NO	NO	NO	Forget about it! No time is right.
YES	YES	YES	Timing doesn't matter. Any time will do.
YES	NO	NO	I'm sorry. It's too late.
NO	NO	YES	Not yet, but the right time will come.
NO	YES	NO	Act now! Opportunities are fleeting.
YES	NO	YES	It looks like you will get a second chance.
YES	YES	NO	Hurry. Act now, before it's too late.
NO	YES	YES	Finally. But don't worry: there's no rush.

Albert 2013. Reproduced with permission from John Wiley & Sons, Ltd.

and the moment is fleeting. Acting later will be impossible. In Row 7, this is your last chance to take advantage of an opportunity that was always present. We feel differently about these two situations, although our decision is the same.

The Plane: Time as a Musical Score

I now want to consider another alternative. I want to represent time not as a line, whether horizontal or placed at an angle, but as a plane, more specifically a plane that has the vertical and horizontal structure of a musical score.[3] The score, in Langer's terms, is a new category of visual display (Langer, 1989, p. 63), a new way to illustrate and depict temporal processes and phenomena. For those of you who don't happen to be musicians, here is what a tiny portion of the score for Beethoven's Fifth Symphony looks like (Figure 20.3).[4]

As you can see, different instruments (arrayed vertically) play different parts. The notes comprising each part are played in sequence, from left to right, on or between sets of horizontal lines. Notes played at the same time create chords or harmonies, or, in some music, dissonance. Notes played one after another create melodies. The relationships among the notes comprising the horizontal and vertical dimensions define and create the overall composition.

If you think for a moment about your own actions and those of others, the analogy to a musical score should become clear. Many things are going on simultaneously both inside and outside of your immediate environment. Every action, event, or process has its own rhythm, pace, and sequence. Different actors (individuals, groups, organizations, etc.) will be playing their own tunes, or at least trying to. The way these different actions (notes and melodies) play out together—whether they are in harmony, create dissonance, result in a long period of silence, or just produce noise—create the temporal patterns that define and create your environment.

At the most fundamental (and simplified) level, musical patterns are composed of seven elements. The first five describe the *horizontal dimension* of the pattern: how

Figure 20.3 Small portion of the score for Beethoven's Fifth Symphony.

the actions and events that comprise it unfold in time, how quickly they develop, in what order, with what gaps, how long each lasts, and so on. The sixth adds the *vertical* dimension. Most patterns are tall; they will have multiple levels or tracks like floors in a multistorey building. The seventh element is measurement. Measurement is really a metaelement: it applies to all of the previous six. Here is a list of the seven elements.

1 *Sequence.* This element describes the order of things, what follows what.
2 *Temporal punctuation.* This element directs our attention to beginnings, middles, pauses, endings, etc. Temporal punctuation functions like linguistic punctuation. It both groups (what falls between punctuation marks) and separates.
3 *Interval/duration.* This element deals with time in terms of duration. How long until X happens? How long will Y last? How long has Z been going on, etc.?
4 *Rate or tempo.* This element refers to how quickly something is happening.

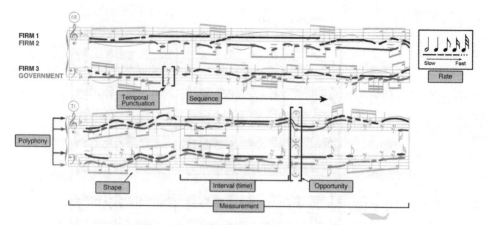

Figure 20.4 Seven elements of temporal architecture.

5 *Shape.* This element describes *rhythms and other patterns of movement,* such as cycles, feedback loops, peaks and valleys, etc.
6 *Polyphony.* Poly—meaning many—adds the vertical dimension. In any pattern, many things may be going on simultaneously, each with its own trajectory. Polyphony raises the question of their interrelationship.
7 *Measurement.* Patterns come in different sizes. A pattern may exist at one timescale but not at another.

So that you can see these elements as part of a simple musical score, one that involves polyphony, I have superimposed labels for these elements in the Bach fugue[5] in Figure 20.4.

Let's assume that Firms A, B, and C take various actions (sequences of notes) over time. The government is also involved. It has its own course of action. The bottom set of four tracks is a continuation of the top set. There is a time (indicated by the thin vertical rectangle), when all four parts pause (the musical symbol for a rest), which may open a window of opportunity for something new.

I call the patterns that the six elements above form with each other at different levels of scale temporal architecture. Here is a more complete definition (Albert, 2013, appendix).

> Temporal architecture is the art and science of finding, creating, analyzing, and using music-like patterns. These patterns, which have the vertical and horizontal structure of musical scores, form when multiple processes are aligned, synchronized, superimposed, or otherwise related to each other in time. The life span of these patterns can vary from seconds to years. Temporal architecture includes the study of the *functions* or *purposes* that these patterns serve, the *qualities* and *meanings* they express, the *emotions* they provoke, the *intentions* they realize or resist, and perhaps most important for the practical actor, the *actions that they permit or prohibit.*

The advantage of a musical score representation of time is that it can help overcome mindless thinking. The musical plane (the vertically and horizontally organized score) is better able to capture the way we experience time than a succession of numbered points on a line or a series of locations on a circular dial of a watch or clock. Let me give you three examples of why this is the case.

Points

When we make decisions or envision choices, we often think of time as a point, that is, as a specific location or place on time line or calendar. When to do X? Answer: 3 o'clock on Friday. I call this way of thinking *Cat-Point thinking*, meaning that we envision a certain category of action occurring at a certain point in time. Thinking about time as a specific location, however, can cause us to miss innovative solutions as well as many of the risks associated with a course of action. Here's an example.

The Healthy Lunch

A company wants to ensure that its executives embrace a healthy life style. What can it do? Let's assume for the purpose of this example that most employees eat in the company dining room. The standard economic solution is to make sure that there are a large number of healthy alternatives available, and that they are priced right: 10 cents for an apple, 10 dollars for apple pie. Provide the right alternatives, add the right incentives, and individuals will make the right choice. This is a Cat-Point formulation. The problem of how to modify human behavior is framed as a problem of choice at a given point in time.

Now, let's look at the problem of how to encourage individuals to eat a healthy lunch in terms of a musical score. Can there be other solutions? Thomas Schelling (1992, p. 173) describes one in which a company's employees were required to order lunch as soon as they arrived in the morning. They then had to eat only what they had ordered. The company reasoned that, since employees would still be full from breakfast, they would make healthier choices about what to eat. I've displayed this solution in the diagram below. Sketching a score diagram (a simplified musical score; see Figure 20.5) allows us to more precisely surface, explore, and understand the risks and benefits associated with this "offbeat" solution.

To read the diagram, look from left to right along each track. The top track (Track 1) shows the sequence of ordering and eating (O and E). In the company's solution, the short time between ordering and eating lunch has been substantially increased and realigned so that the person now orders lunch when he or she arrives at work. The bottom track (Track 2) shows the daily rhythm of hunger and satiation. The employee arrives at the office presumably still full from breakfast, grows hungry, eats lunch, and then gradually becomes hungry again.

I have placed the explicit actions a person takes, ordering and eating, on the treble track, and the actions going on in the background, usually in a lower pitch (the rumblings in one's stomach) on the base track.

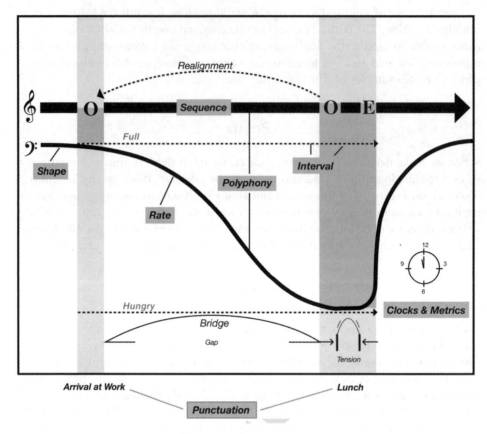

Figure 20.5   Score diagram of the healthy lunch.

All seven elements of temporal architecture are present in this diagram:

- *Sequence.* There are two sequences involved: breakfast followed by lunch, and ordering lunch, followed by eating it.
- *Temporal punctuation.* There are three punctuation marks in the company's solution: breakfast, arriving at the office, and lunch.
- *Interval duration.* The critical intervals are the time between breakfast, arriving at the office, ordering lunch, and then eating it.
- *Rate.* How quickly will the person become hungry after eating breakfast?
- *Shape.* The curve that describes how hungry the person becomes as the day progresses.
- *Polyphony.* There are two tracks indicating two separate processes that are going on at the same time.
- Finally, we need to consider *measurement or clocks and metrics,* the fact this composition is being played out over minutes and hours rather than days and weeks.

To think about a situation musically means, among other things, to look for rhythm. In this diagram, there are two identical rhythms, a short–long pattern that repeats at different timescales. The first is the rhythm of ordering and eating. Ordering is preparatory and takes a relatively short time in comparison with eating, which takes a longer time. In poetry, this rhythm would be called iambic, a short and unstressed syllable followed by longer stressed syllable, that is, one given emphasis. If it took hours to order a meal that was consumed in seconds, the company's solution would be less likely to work, since the odds would increase that during the long process of ordering, the person would become hungry. Notice that the same short–long rhythm repeats over the course of the day. One feels full for a brief time after eating followed by a much longer period during which one gradually becomes hungry again—which leads to the next meal. One then decides what to eat and eats it, and the pattern repeats. As in fractal geometry, the same pattern occurs at different timescales.

The two vertical columns indicate the company's solution. The right column represents the synchronous risk of ordering while hungry, the left column the advantage of ordering while full. Musically, we can think in terms of chords, two or more notes sounding at the same time. Ordering a big meal when one is hungry, or a small meal when one is not, is consonant; the two conditions are in harmony. Ordering a huge steak when one is not hungry, or a small appetizer when one is famished, is dissonant.

The diagram provides us with information about the risk of ordering the wrong foods when one is very hungry. There are, however, other risks. If employees eat a sugary breakfast, or if they skipped breakfast entirely, they might become very hungry at 10:30. So, for the company's plan to work, the gap between arriving at the office and eating lunch must be bridged. No midmorning snacking on donuts. When we modify the interval between ordering and eating, or the time when people eat or don't eat breakfast, everything changes. We might find ourselves doing something that we might later regret, or pleased that we have avoided a temptation. Like the design of a physical structure, a well-understood temporal structure warns us of potential weaknesses so that we can avoid the risks of a "structural" failure (in this case a decision make at the wrong time, or a gap that can't be bridged). When we think mindfully about a situation, we become open to new and potentially valuable information (Langer, 1989, p. 66). We learn about the risks to which our plans and projects are subject, and how they might be avoided.

Sometimes, changing the temporal architecture of a product or service can lead to a new industry. Think about how a credit card works. The mechanism is a simple modification of the sequence-alignment architecture of the healthy lunch example. Before credit cards were in common use, a customer went to a store, selected a product, paid for it, and brought it home. A credit card inverts this sequence and inserts a long interval between stages. A customer buys the item, brings it home, and then some time later pays for it. The result is a new industry. What has also changed is the relationship between when a product is purchased, when the customer earns the money to pay the product, and when—over time—he or she actually pays for it. In the healthy lunch example, the risk was snacking before lunch. In the case of credit cards, the risk is not being able to pay the bill when it arrives. Comedian Art Buchwald describes what happens when a "Fly-Now-Pay Later plan collides with a failure to make a payment on time. A man from the travel agency comes to your house with a curious electric machine. You sit down in it, the current is turned on, and the machine removes all your memories of Europe (Bly, 1990, p. 19)."

The advantage of the plane compared to the point is that there are more distinctions and relationships (Langer, 1989, pp. 153–170) that can be drawn and hence more ways to solve problems. The vertical dimension adds "thickness." That helps us think about all the synchronous risks, requirements, and rewards (opportunities) that occur when actions and events occur at the same time.

Lines

The time line is implicit in our thinking about the relationship between the present and the future. Let me give you an example of *time-line thinking* and how a score representation of that relationship would be useful in overcoming its limitations. It is the story of Thales, the ancient Greek philosopher who invented, and profited from, the concept of options. Here is Tom Copeland and Vladimir Antikarov's version. The original story had to do with olive oil. I've taken poetic license and changed olive oil to wine, for reasons that will become apparent.

The Greek Philosopher Thales

> ... Thales [a sophist philosopher who lived on the island of Milos in the Mediterranean] read the tealeaves and interpreted them as forecasting a bountiful grape harvest that year. In fact, the reading was so favorable that Thales took his life's savings, a modest amount of money, and bargained with the owners of the wine presses to grant him the right to rent their presses for the usual rate during the harvest season in return for his life saving.
>
> Sure enough, the harvest exceeded all expectations, and when the wine growers rushed to the presses ..., Thales was there. He paid the usual rent to the press owners, as required by contract, then turned around and charged the market price—a much higher amount— for use of the presses, which were in high demand. Thales made a fortune ... (Copland & Antikarov, 2001, pp. 6–7).

All this can be discussed in the technical language of options; puts and calls, the exercise price, the time to expiration, the risk-free interest rate over the life of the option (if one could be envisioned), and so on.

Thales thought that he had solved the problem of timing. The principle, he would argue, is simple. Delay important decisions until you can see what is coming: then act. This is an example of call time-line thinking. In time-line thinking we think about time in terms of direction and distance. One moment follows the next like points on a line. The distant future is more remote—further down the line—than the immediate future. The idea is that if you can get close to the future point you are interested in, you will be better able to pierce the darkness that conceals it, and hence be prepared for what is coming. But if we look at the situation Thales described and are *mindful of context,* we can see that Thales's plan has serious risks associated with it.

What Could Go Wrong? A Failure to Consider Context

In this version of the story, imagine that Thales had tried the same tactic three years in a row. Each year he was increasingly successful, so he went to a group of individuals who many years later would call themselves a bank, and borrowed heavily so that he could rent more presses. He was becoming a rich man. But he wanted more, so he pawned everything he owned to expand his operation. After three years, the owners of the presses had enough. They didn't want to make any kind of deal with Thales. In the end, Thales and the owners did reach an agreement, but at a much higher price.

Then a stranger came to town. His name was Beck. Beck claimed that he had invented something called beer. No one paid much attention, but when Beck came down from the mountains where his "laboratory" was located, he was holding a jug of amber liquid. People took a sip. They liked it. They took another sip, and then one after that. Three weeks later, Beck set up a booth at the yearly wine festival promoting his new drink. Soon, wine had competition, particularly since Beck didn't charge very much for his new discovery (as a bench scientist, he didn't yet understand pricing).

Meanwhile, some presses, which had been brought into service, had not been used for a long time. As a result, they developed mechanical problems. Unfortunately, these weren't discovered until the week before they were to be used. The needed parts had to be shipped from Italy. En route, not only did the boat run into a serious storm that delayed the shipment, but when the boat arrived, the captain disclosed that over 90% of the parts were lost, including a sailor who tried to save the shipment but was swept overboard.

All this didn't matter in the end for Thales, however, because just when the grapes were to be harvested, he had a stroke. He had previous symptoms, but ignored them. He lingered for three days and then died. At the funeral, the owners of the wine presses expressed great sorrow, praised his courage and good name, but said nothing to his three sons about the deal their father had struck with them for the rental of the presses. Six months after Thales died, his sons, wanting to carry on his work, took up the study of philosophy. Many years later, all three died in poverty.

This alternative scenario, while fanciful, includes contextual factors that might reasonably be present in any situation like this: competition, supply-chain issues, the health of the main players, the failure of technology, the need for succession planning, and so on. Let's look at this revisionist history in terms of the seven elements that make up a musical score.

Sequence

Let's begin with the wine presses. Every technology has a life cycle. First, it is invented, then put to use. After a while, it will fail and need repairs. Ultimately, it will be discarded, replaced, or superseded as new technology is developed, or its intended use changes. Thales might not know when these different stages will occur, but he can be certain that wine presses, like any technology, will move through them (possibly many times). Since he was betting his life's fortune, he needed to think about the life stage of the presses. Would they be in good working condition when they were needed? There was a second sequence; namely, the warning signs preceding his stroke. I included this sequence as a reminder that any time-rich description includes internal events (what is going on in the life of an individual, inside a firm or organization) and not just external ones. When I sketch a score diagram, I generally put external factors in the treble clef and the internal one in the bass clef, as I did in the healthy-lunch example.

Temporal punctuation

Temporal punctuation refers to beginnings, ending, pauses, etc. that break up the flow of time.[6] The date of the yearly wine festival is an example. The approximate date of the harvest season is another example. Punctuation helps us to anticipate the events that surround each punctuation mark, and therefore anticipate what might occur and when. Borders and boundaries are inherently times of risk and opportunity.

Interval/duration

Thales needed to recognize that unused equipment might develop problems over time, problems that will be discovered only when the equipment is used, which may be too late to get them resolved in time.

Rate and tempo

Thales needed to ask the right questions. How quickly will beer catch on? How will the market for a product develop: all at once, in fits and starts, or at a slow steady pace? Is there a time during the year when customers will be more open to new products or when new products can gain the most exposure? In this example, if Beck missed the yearly wine festival (*punctuation*), the threat raised by his new product would materialize more slowly.

Shape

When we think about shape, we look for patterns of rise and fall, for rhythms of various kinds, or for anything that is different from a simple linear process. In this example, because grapes ripen at more or less at the same time, and because they can't be stored for long periods of time, the demand for the presses will be immediate. It is the long growing season, combined with a short harvest, that brings about the spike in demand. If this shape were reversed, a short growing season followed by a long harvest, the presses would not be overwhelmed, and their owners would not be able to charge high rents for the their use.

Polyphony

Polyphony means many voiced. To listen to polyphonic music, you have to follow each melodic strand separately, making a mental effort to disentangle the way it is interwoven with others.

   In the Thales story, we can see how three independent strands come together. Bad weather develops (one melodic strand) just when the shipment of spare parts is needed (a second melodic strand), which occurs right when the demand for the idle presses will be greatest (a third melodic strand), creating the perfect storm.

Measurement: clocks and metrics

Thales is not a young man. This may be his only chance to make a killing, so he is willing to risk his life's fortune on one bet. Beck, on the other hand, is a young man. He can take his time; think long term. Different actors pay attention to different clocks, which affects what they do and when.

Of course, if Thales knew nothing about technology, if he was only interested in a single deal, if he had no one to whom he wanted to leave his fortune, or if he was independently wealthy, and didn't care whether he lost money, none of the above considerations would matter.

If Thales was thinking about time at all, he was engaged in *time-line thinking*. He was looking horizontally out from the present into future, rather than vertically, trying to find patterns in what was going on at the same time at different timescales. Those patterns, which were the source of synchronous and asynchronous risk, weren't secret. Thales just had to know where to look for them. It is almost as if there were a magician that kept Thales looking in one direction while the real action was going on someplace else. To be mindful requires that we pay attention to the larger context of action.

There were not only a number of risks that Thales did not see, but also a number of missed opportunities.

Missed Opportunities: What a Score Representation + the T Map Might Have Revealed

1 Thales missed the fact that mechanical presses break down. He could have performed an initial inspection and included a clause in the contract to the effect that the presses must be in good working order. When we are mindful, we recognize that fixed elements may not be fixed at all: they can, and will, change.

2 Thales apparently didn't anticipate the need for replacement parts. If he had, it would have raised questions about their availability. That in turn would have revealed that the parts came from Italy. He could have considered the prospect of bad weather and how that would affect shipping schedules. As a result, he could have stockpiled spare parts. He didn't think about the larger temporal and historical *context* of his actions.

3 Thales failed to think about succession planning, namely future context. He could have told his sons what he was doing and included them in the contract.

4 Thales could have placed all the meteorologists in the area under an exclusive contract so he would have a monopoly on weather forecasting. The two-dimensional structure of a musical score directs our attention to the vertical as well as the horizontal, to what should (or should not) be done simultaneously. Our actions can be chords, not just a string of single notes.

5 Thales could have taken better care of himself. He should not have ignored early warning signs of stroke, assuming they were present, and might have taken out life insurance (had such existed). A musical score reminds us that every element, such as a person's health, has a shape. Nothing remains constant forever.

6   Thales missed the need for a multiyear contract. If he made a fortune one year, the cost of renting the presses wouldn't be out of sight the next. He didn't think about the future, *as seen from the future*, a perspective that is make salient by when we display time using the diagonal line of the T map.

7   Thales could have created a secondary market for his contract, and sold it to others when it became clear that the harvest would be a good one *before* it was discovered that the presses needed repair. When we think about a situation mindfully, we discover that there are multiple points where we can intervene.

All of these opportunities were missed because Thales did not have a sufficiently rich time-rich description of the situation before him: He didn't know the score!

Circles

In addition to the time line, the most common visual representation of time is the circle, as can be found on the numbered dial of our watch, or on the face of a clock. We can also find circles in the way we represent important logical concepts, such as a feedback loop (Figure 20.6).

The difficult with visualizing feedback as a circle is that it leaves the state of the entity receiving the feedback unchanged, as if it were not subject to effects of time. Adding a time lag, an interval before feedback is received, while helpful, is not enough to surface all of the relevant time-dependent factors involved in thinking about feedback. So, instead of a circle, let's consider the concept of feedback from the perspective of a two track musical score (Figure 20.7).

In the diagram above, an action is taken. Some time later, it has an impact, which lasts for some period of time. I've labeled this interval ED2 to indicate that the interval is composed of at least three stages. At some point, the consequences of an action exist. Then they are *d*etected. Then they are *d*isclosed or communicated to relevant

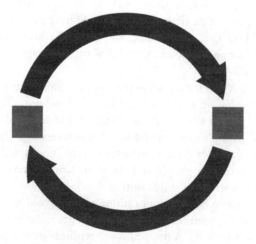

Figure 20.6 Standard feedback loop.

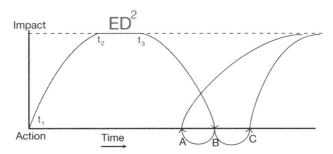

Figure 20.7 Feedback as a score diagram.

parties, including those waiting for feedback. I've included two kinds of loops in the diagram, one that loops backward (B to A), and one that loops forward (B to C). In the backward loop, the actor acts before, or in anticipation, of feedback. In the forward loop, she acts after she has received feedback. This two-level diagram brings the following intervals to our attention.

1 The time from when an action is taken until the first consequences of that action begin to appear (*e*).
2 How long before these consequences are *d*etected.
3 How long before they are communicated (*d*isclosed).
4 Finally, how long before or after receiving feedback new action is initiated.

Each of these intervals defines a specific risk as well as presents a potential opportunity. An action may have little impact—ever. Alternatively, an action may have immediate and dramatic consequences for all involved. But what if the consequences are hidden or kept secret, and as a result, a person makes the wrong decision? Or perhaps feedback is so delayed that the person no longer wants or needs it. She may have left the organization or moved on to another position. Considering the four intervals above introduces a set of distinctions that makes us more mindful about what consequences follow or might follow from our actions, and when we will find out about them.

Conclusion

My suggestion in this chapter is that when we visually display temporal processes, we should use the stratified vertical and horizontal structure of a musical score. We need the two-dimensional plane of a score to capture the richness of temporal experience, which a line, even one that curves back on itself as a circle, cannot provide. Thus, when we think about causality, we should think in terms of chords and chord progressions rather than simply about what comes *before* or *after* something else. The latter treats time as a single dimension, represented by the time line. Chords remind us to consider the vertical, to think about what can or should cooccur. To think about time mindfully, we need to consider simultaneity as well as succession. Without copresence nothing would exist, and there could be no possible experience of succession. As Husserl said, "Simultaneity is nothing without temporal succession and temporal succession is nothing without simultaneity, and thus correlatively, constitution of simultaneity and constitution of temporal succession are inseparable (Husserl, 1991, p. 386).

Another way to say this is that to be mindful of time requires a time-rich description, one that includes all seven elements of temporal architecture, and the patterns that the first six of these elements form with each other at different timescales. Time-rich descriptions are needed if we are to find the novel distinctions that lead to new ideas and new solutions, which is at the center of a mindful approach to time and to temporal processes in general.

Notes

1. See a discussion by Weismann (1974, pp. 210–213).
2. I discuss the issue of time-impoverished description more fully in Albert (2013).
3. This discussion closely follows ideas I developed in Albert (2013).
4. http://www.wmich.edu/mus-gened/mus170/BeethovenSymph5-4.gif
5. Bach (1745).
6. See also Weick (1977).

References

Albert, S. (2013). *When: the art of perfect timing*. San Francisco, CA: Jossey Bass.

Bach, J. S. (1745). *The art of the fugue, no. 7. Die Kunst der Fuge, Vol. 1 BWV 1080* (Frankfurt: CF Peters).

Bly, R. (1990). *American poetry*. New York, NY: Harper & Row.

Copland, T., & Antikarov, V. (2001) *Real options: A practitioner's guide*. New York, NY: TEXERE LLC.

Husserl, E. (1991). *On the phenomenology of the consciousness of internal time* (J. Barnett Brough, Trans.). Dordrecht, Netherlands: Kluwer Academic.

Johnson, G. (2008, June 8). Playing the odds. *New York Times Book Review*, p. 14.

Langer, E. (1989). *Mindfulness*. Cambridge, MA: Lifelong Books, Da Capo Press.

Mlodinow, L. (2008). *The drunkard's walk: How randomness rules our lives*. New York, NY: Random House.

Read, H. (1965). *Icon and idea*. New York, NY: Shocken Books.

Schelling, T. C. (1992). Self-command: A new discipline. In G. Loewenstein & J. Elster (Eds.), *Choice over time*. New York, NY: Russell Sage Foundation.

Weick, K. (1977). Enactment processes in organizations. In A. Staw & G. Salancik (Eds.), *New directions in organizational behavior*. New York, NY: St. Clair.

Weismann, D. (1974). *The visual arts as human experience*. Englewood Cliffs, NJ: Prentice-Hall.

21

Mindfulness and the Neuroscience of Influence

Emily B. Falk

The concept of mindfulness as present-oriented awareness, coupled with flexibility in thinking and creating new categories (Langer, 1989), has been directly applied to problems ranging from conceptualizing and promoting creativity to reducing prejudice to improving health and longevity (Alexander, Langer, Newman, Chandler, & Davies, 1989; Langer, 1989, 2009; Langer, Bashner, & Chanowitz, 1985; Langer & Imber, 1980). From an academic standpoint, the basic tenets of mindlessness versus mindfulness recur throughout social psychology. These ideas form a theoretical basis for models explaining a range of human behaviors, whether directly referred to in these terms or not. Indeed, this conceptualization of mindfulness and Eastern-inspired forms of mindfulness have been highly influential in elucidating the overlap and connection between mind and body, and in promoting health and well-being.

Given the powerful effects of mindfulness on health, a growing body of literature has examined biological correlates of mindfulness practice. For example, neuroscientists have begun to uncover structural and functional correlates of Eastern-inspired forms of mindfulness in the brain. Although relatively little work has specifically examined the neural correlates of Langer's mindfulness (present-oriented awareness, coupled with flexibility in thinking and creating new categories), in the current chapter, I argue that doing so will shed light on important social neuroscience questions. First, extending current research beyond Eastern-inspired forms of mindfulness and related concepts such as mindfulness meditation to also understand the neural bases and effects of Langer's social-cognitive mindfulness can help clarify common and distinct mechanisms associated with each. Second, understanding these neural underpinnings may shed light on common and distinct pathways leading to the cognitive and health benefits of each form of mindfulness. Third, this type of work will facilitate more efficient

The Wiley Blackwell Handbook of Mindfulness, First Edition.
Edited by Amanda Ie, Christelle T. Ngnoumen, and Ellen J. Langer.
© 2014 John Wiley & Sons, Ltd. Published 2014 by John Wiley & Sons, Ltd.

connection to the existing social psychological literature. Finally, Langer's mindfulness as a dispositional trait is also likely a moderator of many commonly studied neurocognitive effects, and so its inclusion in social neuroscience investigations could shed light on a variety of neurocognitive processes. Thus, more work incorporating measures of dispositional mindfulness, as well as examining situations that promote state mindfulness, is likely to expand our understanding of the brain and its associated psychology beyond what has already been addressed by extant social-cognitive neuroscience research on mindfulness.

Given that most neuroscience research on mindfulness has focused on Eastern-inspired forms of mindfulness, in the current chapter I will provide a brief overview of social-cognitive neuroscience investigations of the neural correlates of this form of mindfulness. In addition, I will speculate about ways in which Langer's mindfulness (which is defined in more social-cognitive terms, as compared to Eastern forms of mindfulness and mindfulness meditation) might operate in similar or distinct ways from the forms of mindfulness studied in existing neuroimaging research. I will address the idea that trait mindfulness is likely to moderate many well-documented social-cognitive neuroscience findings. As one example to illustrate how this might be conceptualized, I will focus on Langer's social-cognitive mindfulness as a potential moderator of the neural bases of persuasion and social influence, as well as ways in which mindfulness may help explain certain brain-as-predictor relationships that are presently poorly understood. Questions include: In what ways might mindfulness moderate currently observed neural correlates of social influence? Can a mindfulness lens help explain why neural activity predicts variance in behavior change that is not currently explained by self-report?

Mindfulness and the Brain

A growing body of research explores the neural correlates of mindfulness meditation and other Eastern-inspired forms of mindfulness (Cahn & Polich, 2006; Treadway & Lazar, 2009). This growth parallels increased interest in scientific mechanisms that underlie the effects of Eastern forms of mindfulness intervention on health-relevant outcomes (Baer, 2006; Didonna, 2009). Many of these studies seek to understand the neural processes that take place during mindfulness meditation, as well as longer-term structural and functional consequences of such meditation.

Given that enriched experience fosters brain development across the lifespan, it is logical that mindfulness of a variety of forms should also alter the structure and function of the brain. In particular, it is now widely accepted that the brain is plastic, undergoing changes throughout life, according to experience (Maguire et al., 2000; Rosenzweig, Bennet, & Diamond, 1972). In her discussion of mindful aging, Langer (1989) notes that this capacity for development throughout the lifespan is often ignored; instead, Western society conceptualizes growing older in terms of inevitable decline. Consistent with Langer's view, a number of studies of mindfulness meditation and other Eastern-inspired forms of mindfulness also reinforce the conclusion that the mind, body, and brain are plastic.

Structural changes associated with mindfulness

Studies of mindfulness meditation have examined the neural and behavioral consequences of mindfulness meditation in terms of both brain structure and function. For
example, studies examining brain structure have demonstrated that long-term mindfulness meditation practice results in structural changes in cortical thickness (Lazar
et al., 2005), as well as increased gray-matter concentration implicated in bodily
perception (such as the anterior insula; Hölzel et al., 2008); thus, paralleling other
strength-models (Muraven & Baumeister, 2000), it is possible that long-term mindfulness practice builds brain function as other forms of exercise build muscle. Experimental evidence also suggests that mindfulness practice can alter the structure of brain
systems (effectively toning brain "muscles" to engage in relevant cognitive and affective processing). For example, participants who are randomly assigned to a mindfulness
meditation intervention, compared to waitlist controls, show widespread structural
changes across the brain (including changes in neural regions such as the posterior cingulate cortex, the temporo-parietal junction, and the cerebellum; Hölzel et al., 2011).

Functional changes associated with state mindfulness

Functional magnetic resonance imaging (fMRI) studies have also demonstrated differences in the brain activity observed: between meditators and nonmeditators; between
those higher and lower in trait mindfulness; and between those assigned to mindfulness interventions versus controls. Participants randomly assigned to mindfulness-
based stress reduction also demonstrate widespread increases in functional
connectivity compared to control subjects (Kilpatrick et al., 2011). Finally, participants randomly assigned to a mindfulness meditation intervention evidence positive
changes in immune function (Davidson et al., 2003). Consistent findings across these
studies implicate neural systems involved in bodily perception, attention, and emotion regulation in mindfulness-related practice; however, the direction of effects across
studies has not been consistent.

Studies comparing meditators and nonmeditators have demonstrated differences in
neural regions associated with attentional control (e.g., dorsal anterior cingulate cortex [dACC]) and with perception of bodily states (e.g., anterior insula), though the
direction of results has not been consistent across studies (Brefczynski-Lewis, Lutz,
Schaefer, Levinson, & Davidson, 2007; Hölzel et al., 2007); on the one hand, meditation increases attentional control and hence should be reflected with increased neural
activity in attentional processing regions. However, meditators also have become more
skilled at achieving these results as they practice and hence may not require the same
degree of activity in order to achieve parallel results (Treadway & Lazar, 2009). One
recent study demonstrated increased activity in attention networks during mindfulness meditation compared to mindwandering in novice meditators, suggesting one
pathway through which effects of mindfulness may initially take hold (Dickenson,
Berkman, Arch, & Lieberman, 2013).

Studies comparing short-term mindfulness training to control conditions also suggest that mindfulness practitioners show better ability to regulate anticipatory anxiety
and unpleasant emotions associated with pain (Gard et al., 2011; Zeidan et al., 2011).

Perhaps counterintuitively, this ability is associated with increased activity in neural regions associated with sensory perception, and decreased activity in lateral prefrontal emotion-regulation regions (Gard et al., 2011; Zeidan et al., 2011). It is possible that cultivation of present-minded awareness allows practitioners to dissociate sensation from evaluation. Participants who are assigned to mindfulness training also show functional changes in left-sided activation (previously implicated in positive affect), suggesting that the practice may alter this basic functioning (Davidson et al., 2003).

Complementing the experimental findings described, long-term practice of meditation is also associated with decreased prefrontal cortical activity during exposure to emotional images; whereas nonmeditators employing mindfulness techniques show decreased reactivity in neural regions implicated in affective processing (e.g., the amygdala). Thus, activity in experienced meditators employing mindfulness techniques suggests increased acceptance of current emotional states, and lack of neural changes in the face of affective stimuli (Taylor et al., 2011). This type of equanimity in the face of change is one characteristic that characterizes Eastern forms of mindfulness.

Another possibility that is consistent with Langer's description of mindfulness is that mindfulness intervention expands the practitioner's ability to flexibly interpret their position within context. For example, participants assigned to a mindfulness intervention condition differ from controls in how their brains come to represent the self (Farb et al., 2007): those who have practiced mindfulness-based stress reduction over the course of weeks show more dissociation between neural representations of the self across time (e.g., in terms of stable traits, which the authors refer to as "narrative focus"), and in the present moment (which the authors refer to as "experiential focus"), than novices. To the extent that individuals are able to see themselves from multiple other perspectives, we would expect to observe increased ability to think flexibly about a range of topics (potentially including pain).

Functional differences associated with trait mindfulness

A separate group of studies have examined neural responses to a range of tasks in nonmeditators according to levels of trait mindfulness—in other words, whereas the studies above examine differences associated with specific mindfulness related activities (e.g., meditation), studies of trait mindfulness examine variability according to participants' self-reports of how they tend to approach the world and scenarios encountered. This early group of studies has focused primarily on the relationship between trait mindfulness and emotion regulation. Findings suggest that those higher in some forms of dispositional mindfulness (Brown & Ryan, 2003) may recruit prefrontal resources more easily during emotion regulation of different kinds, including affect labeling (Creswell, Way, Eisenberger, & Lieberman, 2007) and reappraisal (Modinos, Ormel, & Aleman, 2010). Levels of trait mindfulness also moderate responses to highly arousing images very early in the processing stream (Brown, Goodman, & Inzlicht, 2013).

Summary and extensions

In sum, reviews of the neural bases of Eastern-inspired forms of mindfulness suggest that mindfulness practices such as mindfulness meditation produce unique patterns of neural activation that "[appear] to promote long-term structural and functional changes in brain regions important for performing clinically relevant functions" (Treadway & Lazar, 2009), and that mindfulness meditation evokes substantially different patterns of activity from the brain at "rest" (Treadway & Lazar, 2009). In particular, consistent patterns across studies link mindfulness to structural and functional changes in brain regions associated with bodily perception and emotional processing. Results are consistent with the emphasis of mindfulness practitioners and researchers on mind–body connection, and may suggest mechanisms relevant to health effects of mindfulness.

Although not as thoroughly studied within the neuroscience community to this point, Langer's form of mindfulness shares common ideals with more Eastern-inspired forms of mindfulness-related meditation practices; however, they are conceptually distinct in several key ways (Langer, 1989). Both types of mindfulness have been associated with positive health effects and broader indices of well-being (Didonna, 2009; Langer, 1989). More Eastern forms of mindfulness, and mindfulness meditation in particular are conceptualized as being practiced effortfully. By contrast, Langer's mindfulness is conceptualized in terms of finding new ways of categorizing and viewing daily encounters in a way that Langer argues is not more effortful than the alternative (mindlessness). As such, results reviewed above pertaining to trait levels of mindfulness are likely to be most relevant to elucidating the neural correlates of Langer's form of mindfulness, and in understanding how it might moderate other social, cognitive and affective processes. For example, as reviewed, a small number of studies have demonstrated that trait mindfulness moderates brain responses to emotional stimuli during affect labeling and reappraisal tasks. Langer argues that mindfulness allows us to see the world from multiple points of view and, as such, might allow a wider range of labels and interpretations for any given experience, as well as, by definition, greater facility with reappraisal.

Although social neuroscience studies of mindfulness have focused most heavily on changes in attention and emotion regulation related to mindfulness, decades of social psychological research suggest that mindfulness also moderates many other basic social psychological processes. Thus, incorporation of measures of mindfulness into a wider range of social neuroscience investigations is likely to inform our understanding of both the brain and mindfulness. As one example of how this might be accomplished, I devote the remaining portion of this chapter to an exploration of one set of core concepts in social psychology (persuasion and social influence) and ways in which mindfulness might moderate the neural bases of these processes.

Mindfulness as a Moderator of the Neural Bases of Social Influence: An Exploration of Broader Incorporation of Mindfulness in Social Neuroscience

Neural correlates of persuasion and social influence

In contrast to the decades of research that have characterized psychological and physiological mechanisms of persuasion and other forms of social influence (Allport,

1935; Chaiken, Liberman, & Eagly, 1989; Eagly & Chaiken, 2005; Hovland, 1949; Hovland, Janis, & Kelley, 1953; Petty & Brinol, 2012; Petty & Cacioppo, 1986a, 1986b), neuroimaging work examining the brain's representation of these processes is in a relative state of infancy (Falk & Lieberman, 2013; Falk, Way, & Jasinska, 2012; Lieberman, 2010). As such, there is still much to uncover. Researchers interested in understanding persuasion and social influence have looked to the brain in order to answer questions that have been challenging to answer using self-reports and direct behavioral observation alone, and to identify common and distinct mechanisms of a range of persuasion and broader influence processes. Given that mindfulness clearly moderates individuals' responses to potential sources of social influence (Langer, Blank, & Chanowitz, 1978; Santos, Leve, & Pratkanis, 1994), examining the conditions under which mindfulness moderates neural responses to social inputs, and in what ways, is likely to shed light on both mechanisms of influence and on basic neuroscientific questions about the social brain.

Much of the recent neuroimaging work on social influence has focused on the ventral striatum and ventromedial prefrontal cortex (VMPFC; Falk, Way, & Jasinska, 2012), which are key components of the brain's reward system (Haber & Knutson, 2010; Knutson, Adams, Fong, & Hommer, 2001; Knutson & Cooper, 2005; McClure, York, & Montague, 2004). Across several studies, activity within these putative reward structures, during exposure to social information, is associated with participants conforming to the opinion of others. For example, in one early study of the neural bases of influence effects (Klucharev, Hytonen, Rijpkema, Smidts, & Fernandez, 2009), neural activity was recorded using fMRI, while male participants were presented with female faces and asked to rate the faces according to attractiveness. Directly following their own rating of the faces, participants were subsequently presented with the ratings of peers. Following the scanner session, participants rerated the faces. Discrepancy between the participants' initial ratings and the "peer" ratings led to subsequent conformity on average (changing one's opinion in the second rating session to be consistent with the group). In the brain, decreased activity in the ventral striatum was associated with discrepancy between one's own opinion and the opinion of the group. This "discrepancy signal" was specific to social influence—the neural signal was greater when the reference group ratings were said to be provided by other people, as compared to when the reference group ratings were said to be generated by a computer. In addition to tracking social value of stimuli during initial exposure to the opinions of others (Klucharev et al., 2009), activity in the brain's reward system also appears to be positively associated with ratings of others, when they are higher, compared to lower, than participant's initial ratings (Zaki, Schirmer, & Mitchell, 2011).

A parallel study by Campbell-Meiklejohn, Bach, Roepstorff, Dolan, and Frith (2010) examined the converse effect. In this study, participants made ratings of music, which were sometimes concordant and sometimes discordant with information provided about the ratings of "musical experts." Results from this study indicated that participants showed increased activity in the ventral striatum when their own opinions about music were consistent with the opinions of two "expert raters" (Campbell-Meiklejohn et al., 2010). This activity overlapped with activity in response to being given monetary rewards in response to their ratings. This provides evidence first for modulation of the reward system by social, in addition to nonsocial, rewards. Second, this overlapping neural activity between monetary and social rewards may suggest that being consistent with experts produces a reward signal in the brain. The authors speculate that this reward may come from the feeling that concordance with expert ratings suggests that one has good musical taste, or taste that is socially valued.

Follow-up work by Campbell-Meiklejohn and colleagues (2012) pharmacologically manipulated levels of dopamine in the brain by administering the dopamine reuptake inhibitor, methylphenidate (also known as Ritalin), in order to examine its effects on conformity. The researchers found that the Ritalin group showed more exaggerated conformity effects as compared to a placebo control group (Campbell-Meiklejohn et al., 2012). Although neural effects were not assessed in this study, these data are consistent with the hypothesis that dopamine signaling in the striatum sensitizes individuals to the opinions of group members, and associated social rewards of conformity (Falk, Way, et al., 2012).

Finally, just as activity in the brain's reward system is moderated by directly provided social cues (e.g., the preferences or ratings of others), activity within the reward system is also moderated by indirect signals of social value (in effect "social placebos") and can be modulated by the mere presence of others. One clear demonstration of this effect comes from a study in which participants were asked to taste and rate wines that were priced at different levels. Although the actual wine fed to participants was held constant, participants believed that the wines they were tasting were different. They rated the more expensive wines as tasting better and showed increased activity within the brain's reward system (in the VMPFC) while drinking wines that they believed to be more expensive (Plassmann, O'Doherty, Shiv, & Rangel, 2008). Receptivity to peer influence in adolescence also appears to be tied to the brain's reward system (Casey, Getz, & Galvan, 2008; Steinberg, 2008), and the VS in particular (Chein, Albert, O'Brien, Uckert, & Steinberg, 2010). The mere presence of peers increases adolescents' susceptibility to risk taking and is associated with heightened sensitivity within the VS (Chein et al., 2010). In addition, during adolescence, the brain's emotional systems develop more quickly than the brain's cognitive control system, which results in an imbalance of the strength of emotional signals in relation to the brain's capacity to exert cognitive control and regulate such emotions (Casey et al., 2008; Chein et al., 2010; Steinberg, 2008).

One way of viewing this body of research suggests reason for pessimism—the mindless use of an "expensive = good" heuristic (Cialdini, 2009) may trick us, and cost us money, and the presence of peers may lead to risky behavior in adolescence. Levels of activity within the VS are associated with risky behavior in the presence of peers in teens, and VMPFC are associated with participants willingness to pay for items (Plassmann, O'Doherty, & Rangel, 2007), as well as purchase decisions (Knutson, Rick, Wimmer, Prelec, & Loewenstein, 2007). Furthermore, encoding of value signals in these brain regions appears to occur outside of our conscious awareness and in cases where we aren't consciously evaluating (Tusche, Bode, & Haynes, 2010).

These data may also suggest a silver lining, however. As Langer has noted, mindfulness training may increase the ability of the VMPFC to focus selectively on cues that maximize happiness. The brain's reward system, and VMPFC in particular, encodes and integrates many different value signals (e.g., healthiness and taste, in addition to social value, when choosing foods; Hare, Camerer, & Rangel, 2009; Hare,

Malmaud, & Rangel, 2011). The VMPFC gives different weight to attributes according to one's motivational goals (Hare et al., 2009, 2011). Given that the VMPFC responds to many different possible forms of value, the mindful consumer might actively choose to focus on some attributes over others to maximize happiness. As such, the VMPFC may be a fruitful target for studies examining effects of mindfulness interventions on happiness. Likewise, the mindful teen might be in a better position to conceptualize many ways of being "cool."

In sum, in multiple separate studies, activity in the reward system appears to be modulated by social feedback. Neural activity within the reward system appears to increase when one is in line with a valued reference group, and to decrease when one is out of line. Across different paradigms, activity within the brain's reward system covaried with the fit between participants' opinions and the opinions of others. These data are consistent with the idea that the social reward of fitting in promotes conformity (Cialdini & Goldstein, 2004).

Potential moderation by mindfulness

How might these findings be moderated by mindfulness? We might expect that more mindful people, or people in a more mindful state, might evidence different responses to persuasion and other forms of social influence effects than those who are less mindful. First, it is well documented that, although mindfulness can open us to the views of others, it can also reduce mindless susceptibility to social influence. As noted by Langer (1989): "Once we become mindfully aware of views other than our own, we start to realize that there are as many different views as there are different observers" (p. 68). She further suggests that by seeing the multiple possible viewpoints that one might take on, we gain more choice with respect to how we respond.

Thus, instead of mindlessly changing her opinion of music based on the views of an expert, an expert rating might prompt a more mindful consumer to consider the different aspects of a song that the expert would have considered to arrive at the displayed rating. This, in turn, might be associated with greater neural activity in perspective taking and executive control regions of the brain. By contrast, in a situation where others rate a face or a piece of music differently than we have, instead of viewing the discrepancy as a threat, we may be prompted to consider other possible ways of viewing the stimulus, which, in addition to neural systems associated with perspective taking, might also be associated with more extensive processing in sensory regions of the brain (mindfulness is likely to change the way we physically see, hear, etc.), as well as within the reward system (mindfully processing stimuli is likely to be rewarding).

This concept is also consistent with literature in the emotion regulation literature suggesting that emotions can be up- or downregulated in a top-down fashion (Ochsner et al., 2009). In the context of social influence, mindfulness might not systematically change the ratings that individuals make (e.g., in the music study described above, more and less mindful people might each change their opinion following expert ratings), but might do so for very different reasons (heuristically expert → authority → change, versus expert → prompts consideration of different stimulus features → person finds beauty where they hadn't heard it previously).

The differing mechanisms that lead to social influence in mindful and mindless participants could be evident in examining neural activity in a way that is not evident based on observing the outcome of self-reports such as the second ratings described above, or even in the number of reasons generated (NB: elaboration, as captured in the classic Elaboration Likelihood Model of persuasion, and mindfulness are not synonyms, and may be represented quite differently in the brain). For example, arguments may be processed centrally with a relatively high degree of elaboration without being mindful, and mindful processing does not necessarily require more effort than mindless thought (Langer, 1989). High degrees of elaboration can engage more mindful critiques of arguments, however, effortful processing can also call to mind knowledge acquired under other circumstances that need not apply in the current circumstance, and/or overlearned beliefs may serve as starting points for seemingly logical arguments that constrain the way a thinker views the current situation. In other words, it is possible to engage in high degrees of elaboration without mindfulness. Likewise, it is possible to process cues mindfully and peripherally (Langer, 1992). To the extent that arguments are considered within the framework of ideas that were acquired under one context, without full consideration of the current context, these so-called premature cognitive commitments may still limit the degree to which incoming information can be fully leveraged. Within the brain, we might expect that increased mindfulness would be associated with greater connectivity across networks that link sensory input, memory, and generation of novel concepts, or in systems associated with abstract thought.

Thus, in addition to considering central versus peripheral processing in furthering our understanding of the neural bases of persuasion and the neural precursors of behavior change, it will also likely prove useful to consider mindfulness. Research examining trait mindfulness as a moderator of currently documented effects will be of interest in defining the boundary conditions of the effects observed. Furthermore, in considering these results and their potential moderation by mindfulness, it is important to keep in mind that no brain region operates in isolation, just as no psychological process operates outside of a social context. Thus, the involvement of any neural system in the process of making an attitudinal evaluation is actually a product of the interaction of multiple brain systems, which in turn is operating within a social context.

Acknowledging this complexity, Wil Cunningham and colleagues have suggested that incoming stimuli are initially registered in relatively fast-operating, affective processing regions, including the brain's reward system, but are subsequently iteratively reprocessed between such affective processing regions and higher level executive control systems (Cunningham & Zelazo, 2007; Cunningham, Zelazo, Packer, & Van Bavel, 2007). In parallel with the Elaboration Likelihood Model, they suggest that the degree of iterative reprocessing depends on contextual factors, internal motivation, and social cues. The results of this iterative reprocessing are stimulus evaluation and goal-directed action. Mindfulness is likely to affect this process in at least two ways. First, increased mindfulness may increase connection and processing of incoming stimuli between affective processing regions and the executive control system. Second, mindful consideration of different aspects of the incoming stimulus is likely to alter the weight given to different aspects of the stimulus.

As currently conceptualized in investigations of the neural bases of social influence, neural activity in the ventral striatum is thought to index a discrepancy signal wherein agreement with others is more rewarding than not agreeing. Subsequent viewing of stimuli that others value is also conceptualized as more rewarding than viewing stimuli that others don't value. However, participants who are more mindful might spontaneously have more ways of conceptualizing beauty or quality, due to their increased tendency to actively construct distinctions and see novel distinctions in the ordinary (Langer, 1992). They might show more facility in simultaneously maintaining their initial preference rating, while seeing the merits of the peers supposed ratings (Langer, 1989). Hence, more mindful participants might not view initial discrepancy between the participant and peer ratings as prompting a need to conform, but might instead prompt participants to consider what might be beautiful in the face of another and/or what might be viewed as strange or undesirable (in effect making more categories of attractive and unattractive). Participants processing the social cues in a more mindless fashion, by contrast, might have more difficulty simultaneously representing positive evaluations of both their own view and a seemingly contrasting view. Neural evidence for such effects might parallel the results suggesting that mindfulness alters neural representations of the self across time (Farb et al., 2007), such that individuals higher in trait mindfulness, or those exposed to a mindfulness intervention, might show both more discrepancy in representations of the self across time, and less of a discrepancy signal to information contradicting their own view, and might show less discrepancy within the reward system when confronted with potentially contrasting views to their own.

Finally, the idea that one key pathway to social influence is through the brain's reward system also suggests a potential route to leverage influence to actively recreate such rewards in situations when we might not otherwise experience reward. Indeed, a number of forms of meditation, and other religious activities, appear to achieve salutatory effects, perhaps by reducing negative affect or increasing social support. In the first section, I reviewed evidence suggesting that mindfulness meditation reduces unpleasantness and anxiety associated with pain and is also associated with decreased activity in lateral prefrontal brain regions that have been implicated in cognitive control and emotion regulation (Gard et al., 2011; Zeidan et al., 2011). Interestingly, in a separate line of work, Christian participants with strong beliefs in the power of intercessory prayer evidenced decreased activity in medial and lateral prefrontal executive control brain regions when they believed that messages were delivered by individuals with charismatic abilities, compared to the same statements delivered by individuals not labeled as having such powers (Schjoedt, Stodkilde-Jorgensen, Geertz, Lund, & Roepstorff, 2011). As Langer (1989, 2009) argues, placebos are very powerful in part due to the power of the mind–body relationship, and this may also apply to active intervention by prayer and other forms of mind focus. Although many of us require outside influence to spur our bodies into responding (e.g., through the use of placebo medicines or through strong belief in intercessory prayer), it is likely possible to activate parallel brain mechanisms without such stimuli, and hence achieve similar results. Just as placebos can help the mind/body heal itself, attention to certain forms of external cues can also alter our pleasure and corresponding neural activity in response to experiences (Langer, 2009).

Mindfulness and brain–behavior relationships

The neuroscience studies reviewed above manipulate psychological processes as independent variables and treat neural activity as a dependent variable. These "brain-mapping" studies are useful in exploring the neural mechanism that are associated with psychological processes of interest (e.g., mindfulness, social influence), and can help identify psychological phenomena that share common versus distinct underlying neural mechanisms. A growing body of literature, however, has also begun to harness what we have learned from such brain-mapping studies in social and cognitive neuroscience and neuroeconomics to predict outcomes outside of the lab. In particular, we can use our knowledge of the brain in order to choose neural regions a priori that are hypothesized to predict outcomes outside of the neuroimaging lab. In this type of brain-as-predictor model, neural activity during basic laboratory tasks is used to predict real-world outcomes longitudinally outside of the laboratory (Berkman & Falk, 2013).

Employing this type of brain-as-predictor approach can help us test competing theories and can help us link what we have learned about the brain in the controlled laboratory environment to more complex real-world behaviors. However, in many cases, neural activity predicts behavior change above and beyond self-report measures (Falk, 2010). In other words, these studies might suggest that the brain contains information that is implicitly registered but is not accessed by conscious self-report. For example, neural activity in VMPFC, in response to public-health-service announcements, has been used to predict individual health-behavior change over the course of weeks (Falk, Berkman, Mann, Harrison, & Lieberman, 2010) or months (Falk, Berkman, Whalen, & Lieberman, 2011), above and beyond what is explained by participants' reports of their attitudes toward the health behaviors, their intentions with respect to the behaviors, their confidence in their ability to change, and their ability to relate to the ads. Likewise, neural activity in VMPFC has also been used to predict population-level behavior change in response to persuasive messages (Falk, Berkman, & Lieberman, 2012) and other socially relevant stimuli (Berns & Moore, 2012), above and beyond participants' self-reports.

Thus, one logical question is whether the information encoded in the brain is inaccessible to self-report because it cannot be consciously accessed, or whether, instead, the information is not captured by self-reports due to mindlessness. It has long been recognized that many important psychological processes occur outside of conscious awareness, and that conscious introspection can alter or disrupt these processes (Dijksterhuis, 2004; Nisbett & Wilson, 1977). However, Langer (1989) suggested that some of the processes that we conceptualize as subconscious might be made conscious if we attended to our own thoughts more clearly. She argues that just as placebos can alter the relationship between brain and body, so too we might alter these processes without the need for a pill. It stands to reason, then, that if it is possible to exert top-down control over the body by being more in touch with the mind, one might also be better in touch with the mind by attending more to the body; as practitioners of nearly all forms of mindfulness suggest, the dissociation between mind and body creates a false dichotomy that may have negative consequences when it comes to understanding ourselves and the antecedents of well-being. Of course, it is also likely that some of the discrepancy between variance in behavioral outcomes that is predicted by the brain, and not by self-report, will be resolved by measuring other self-report constructs that have not yet been explored, and by examining moderators of influence processes. For example, in addition to using mindfulness as a tool to improve our ability to forecast our actions, mindfulness is likely to moderate the strength of the relationship between neural activity and behaviors that follow.

Summary and Conclusion

In this chapter, I have reviewed evidence for systematic changes in brain structure and function brought on by diverse forms of experience, including the active practice of mindfulness meditation, as well as trait mindfulness. Although the neural correlates of Eastern forms of mindfulness and mindfulness meditation have been more extensively explored than more social-cognitive forms of mindfulness, such as Langer's mindfulness, we now know that lived experience alters the brain throughout life. Hence, mindfulness or mindlessness, too, should affect the brain accordingly. The current literature on mindfulness meditation falls into three categories: studies of long-time meditators compared to novices, studies comparing those who have undergone a relatively brief mindfulness training intervention (on the order of days or weeks) compared to a control group, and studies examining dispositional mindfulness. Across studies, neural systems associated with attention, perception of bodily awareness, and emotion regulation differ between those higher and lower in mindfulness. This is true of short-term functional variation within specific networks as well as differences in structure.

Findings from studies of dispositional mindfulness are likely to provide the best starting point for forming hypotheses about how social-cognitive mindfulness is likely to moderate brain function in contexts beyond those currently studied. Mindfulness is likely to moderate a much wider range of processes than have been currently explored or documented in the social neuroscience literature. The incorporation of trait and state levels of mindfulness within neuroscientific investigations stands to benefit both our understanding of the clinical and social psychological phenomena under study and our understanding of brain function.

As one example of how mindfulness might be more deeply integrated into social neuroscience inquiry, I reviewed selected examples of neuroimaging findings pertaining to the neural bases of social influence and speculated about how mindfulness might moderate underlying neural function within this context. In particular, a growing body of studies suggest that the brain's reward system is sensitive to a wide range of social cues, including whether our opinions conform to the opinions of others. Researchers have suggested that the social rewards of conformity may have had evolutionary benefits in terms of group cohesion and protection of individuals within the group (Cialdini & Goldstein, 2004; Lieberman & Eisenberger, 2009). However, several factors contribute to any given overall evaluation of the value of a stimulus, which are integrated within the VMPFC (Hare et al., 2009, 2011). Increased mindfulness might lead to increased control over the weighting of these different value signals, expansion of the list of attributes that are seen as desirable, and increased happiness through focus on social cues as one of many possible ways of computing value.

Likewise, increased mindfulness may facilitate parallel effects to forms of placebic influence exerted by sugar pills or certain religious rituals or beliefs. Mindfulness meditation increases attention to bodily states and increases present-oriented awareness. Correspondingly, mindfulness is associated with increased activity in neural systems associated with sensory awareness and with decreased activity in cognitive control regions. These findings may suggest that mindfulness practice decreases active engagement of cognitive control, or simply that less effort is required to achieve parallel results. In either case, increased mindfulness may allow individuals to simulate social influence effects within their own minds and bodies to achieve positive results.

Further study that simultaneously examines neural function during experiences of influence, including connectivity between regions, as well as changes in structure in response to changes in mindfulness may be especially helpful in uncovering links between state and trait levels of mindfulness, and the ways that we are mindfully or mindlessly open to cues from those around us. In turn, this form of investigation stands to increase not only our understanding of mindfulness and of influence but also our ability to integrate diverse forms of measurement to predict behavioral outcomes.

References

Alexander, C. N., Langer, E. J., Newman, R. I., Chandler, H. M., & Davies, J. L. (1989). Transcendental meditation, mindfulness, and longevity: an experimental study with the elderly. *Journal of Personality and Social Psychology, 57*(6), 950–964.

Allport, G. W. (1935). Attitudes. In C. M. Murchison (Ed.), *Handbook of social psychology*. Winchester, MA: Clark University Press.

Baer, R. A. (Ed.). (2006). *Mindfulness-based treatment approaches: Clinician's guide to evidence base and applications.* San Diego, CA: Elsevier Academic Press.

Berkman, E. T., & Falk, E. B. (2013). Beyond brain mapping: Using the brain to predict real-world outcomes. *Current Directions in Psychological Science, 22*(1), 45–55.

Berns, G. S., & Moore, S. E. (2012). A neural predictor of cultural popularity. *Journal of Consumer Psychology, 22,* 154–160.

Brefczynski-Lewis, J. A., Lutz, A., Schaefer, H. S., Levinson, D. B., & Davidson, R. J. (2007). Neural correlates of attentional expertise in long-term meditation practitioners. *Proceedings of the National Academy of Sciences of the United States of America, 104*(27), 11483–11488.

Brown, K. W., Goodman, R. J., & Inzlicht, M. (2013). Dispositional mindfulness and the attenuation of neural responses to emotional stimuli. *Social Cognitive and Affective Neuroscience, 8*(1), 93–99.

Brown, K. W., & Ryan, R. M. (2003). The benefits of being present: mindfulness and its role in psychological well-being. *Journal of Personality and Social Psychology, 84,* 822–848.

Cahn, B. R., & Polich, J. (2006). Meditation states and traits: EEG, ERP, and neuroimaging studies. *Psychological Bulletin, 132*(2), 180–211.

Campbell-Meiklejohn, D. K., Bach, D. R., Roepstorff, A., Dolan, R. J., & Frith, C. D. (2010). How the opinion of others affects our valuation of objects. *Current Biology, 20*(13), 1165–1170.

Campbell-Meiklejohn, D. K., Simonsen, A., Jensen, M., Wohlert, V., Gjerløff, T., Scheel-Kruger, J., … Roepstorff, A. (2012). Modulation of social influence by methylphenidate. *Neuropsychopharmacology, 37*(6), 1517–1525.

Casey, B. J., Getz, S., & Galvan, A. (2008). The adolescent brain. *Developmental Review, 28*(1), 62–77.

Chaiken, S., Liberman, A., & Eagly, A. H. (1989). Heuristic and systematic information processing within and beyond the persuasion context. In J. S. Uleman & J. A. Bargh (Eds.), *Unintended thought* (pp. 212–252). New York, NY: Guilford Press.

Chein, J., Albert, D., O'Brien, L., Uckert, K., & Steinberg, L. (2010). Peers increase adolescent risk taking by enhancing activity in the brain's reward circuitry. *Developmental Science, 14*(2), F1–F10.

Cialdini, R. B. (2009). *Influence: science and practice* (5th ed.). Boston, MA: Pearson Education.

Cialdini, R. B., & Goldstein, N. J. (2004). Social influence: compliance and conformity. *Annual Review of Psychology, 55*, 591–621.

Creswell, J. D., Way, B. M., Eisenberger, N. I., & Lieberman, M. D. (2007). Neural correlates of dispositional mindfulness during affect labeling. *Psychosomatic Medicine, 69*(6), 560–565.

Cunningham, W. A., & Zelazo, P. (2007). Attitudes and evaluations: a social cognitive neuroscience perspective. *Trends in Cognitive Sciences, 11*(3), 97–104.

Cunningham, W. A., Zelazo, P., Packer, D. J., & Van Bavel, J. J. (2007). The iterative reprocessing model: A multilevel framework for attitudes and evaluation. *Social Cognition, 25*(5), 736–760.

Davidson, R. J., Kabat-Zinn, J., Schumacher, J., Rosenkranz, M., Muller, D., Santorelli, S. F., … Sheridan, J. F. (2003). Alterations in brain and immune function produced by mindfulness meditation. *Psychosomatic Medicine, 65*(4), 564–570.

Dickenson, J., Berkman, E. T., Arch, J., & Lieberman, M. D. (2013). Neural correlates of focused attention during a brief mindfulness induction. *Social Cognitive and Affective Neuroscience, 8*(1), 40–47.

Didonna, F. (Ed.). (2009). *Clinical handbook of mindfulness.* New York, NY: Springer New York.

Dijksterhuis, A. (2004). Think different: the merits of unconscious thought in preference development and decision making. *Journal of Personality and Social Psychology, 87*(5), 586–598.

Eagly, A. H., & Chaiken, S. (2005). *Attitude research in the 21st century: The current state of knowledge.* Mahwah, NJ: Lawrence Erlbaum Associates.

Falk, E. B. (2010). Communication neuroscience as a tool for health psychologists. *Health Psychology, 29*(4), 355–357.

Falk, E. B., Berkman, E. T., & Lieberman, M. D. (2012). From neural responses to population behavior: Neural focus group predicts population-level media effects. *Psychological Science, 23*(5), 439–445.

Falk, E. B., Berkman, E. T., Mann, T., Harrison, B., & Lieberman, M. D. (2010). Predicting persuasion-induced behavior change from the brain. *Journal of Neuroscience, 30*(25), 8421–8424.

Falk, E. B., Berkman, E. T., Whalen, D., & Lieberman, M. D. (2011). Neural activity during health messaging predicts reductions in smoking above and beyond self-report. *Health Psychology, 30*(2), 177–185.

Falk, E. B., & Lieberman, M. D. (2013). The neural bases of attitudes, evaluation and behavior change. In F. Krueger & J. Grafman (Eds.), *The neural basis of human belief systems* (pp. 71–94). New York, NY: Psychology Press.

Falk, E. B., Way, B. M., & Jasinska, A. J. (2012). An imaging genetics approach to understanding social influence. *Frontiers in Human Neuroscience, 6*(168), 1–13.

Farb, N. A., Segal, Z. V., Mayberg, H., Bean, J., McKeon, D., Fatima, Z., & Anderson, A. K. (2007). Attending to the present: mindfulness meditation reveals distinct neural modes of self-reference. *Social Cognitive and Affective Neuroscience, 2*(4), 313–322.

Gard, T., Hölzel, B. K., Sack, A. T., Hempel, H., Lazar, S. W., Vaitl, D., & Ott, U. (2011). Pain attenuation through mindfulness is associated with decreased cognitive control and increased sensory processing in the brain. *Cerebral Cortex.*

Haber, S. N., & Knutson, B. (2010). The reward circuit: linking primate anatomy and human imaging. *Neuropsychopharmacology, 35*(1), 4–26.

Hare, T. A., Camerer, C. F., & Rangel, A. (2009). Self-control in decision-making involves modulation of the vmPFC valuation system. *Science, 324*(5927), 646–648.

Hare, T. A., Malmaud, J., & Rangel, A. (2011). Focusing attention on the health aspects of foods changes value signals in vmPFC and improves dietary choice. *Journal of Neuroscience, 31*(30), 11077–11087.

Hölzel, B. K., Carmody, J., Vangel, M., Congleton, C., Yerramsetti, S. M., Gard, T., & Lazar, S. W. (2011). Mindfulness practice leads to increases in regional brain gray matter density. *Psychiatry Research, 191*(1), 36–43.

Hölzel, B. K., Ott, U., Gard, T., Hempel, H., Weygandt, M., Morgen, K., & Vaitl, D. (2008). Investigation of mindfulness meditation practitioners with voxel-based morphometry. *Social Cognitive and Affective Neuroscience, 3*(1), 55–61.

Hölzel, B. K., Ott, U., Hempel, H., Hackl, A., Wolf, K., Stark, R., & Vaitl, D. (2007). Differential engagement of anterior cingulate and adjacent medial frontal cortex in adept meditators and non-meditators. *Neuroscience Letters, 421*(1), 16–21.

Hovland, C. I. (1949). Reconciling conflicting results derived from experimental and survey studies of attitude change. *American Psychologist, 14*, 8–17.

Hovland, C. I., Janis, I. L., & Kelley, H. H. (1953). *Communication and persuasion: Psychological studies of opinion change.* New Haven, CT: Yale University Press.

Kilpatrick, L. A., Suyenobu, B. Y., Smith, S. R., Bueller, J. A., Goodman, T., Creswell, J. D., ... Naliboff, B. D. (2011). Impact of mindfulness-based stress reduction training on intrinsic brain connectivity. *Neuroimage, 56*(1), 290–298.

Klucharev, V., Hytonen, K., Rijpkema, M., Smidts, A., & Fernandez, G. (2009). Reinforcement learning signal predicts social conformity. *Neuron, 61*(1), 140–151.

Knutson, B., Adams, C. M., Fong, G. W., & Hommer, D. (2001). Anticipation of increasing monetary reward selectively recruits nucleus accumbens. *Journal of Neuroscience, 21*(RC 159), 105.

Knutson, B., & Cooper, J. C. (2005). Functional magnetic resonance imaging of reward prediction. *Current Opinion in Neurology, 18*(4), 411–417.

Knutson, B., Rick, S., Wimmer, G. E., Prelec, D., & Loewenstein, G. (2007). Neural predictors of purchases. *Neuron, 53*(1), 147–156.

Langer, E. J. (1989). *Mindfulness.* Cambridge, MA: Perseus Books.

Langer, E. J. (1992). Matters of mind: Mindfulness/mindlessness in perspective. *Consciousness and Cognition, 1*(3), 289–305.

Langer, E. J. (2009). *Counter clockwise: Mindful health and the power of possibility.* New York, NY: Random House.

Langer, E. J., Bashner, R. S., & Chanowitz, B. (1985). Decreasing prejudice by increasing discrimination. *Journal of Personality and Social Psychology, 49*(1), 113–120.

Langer, E. J., Blank, A., & Chanowitz, B. (1978). The mindlessness of ostensibly thoughtful action: The role of "placebic" information in interpersonal interaction. *Journal of Personality and Social Psychology, 36*, 635–642.

Langer, E. J., & Imber, L. (1980). Role of mindlessness in the perception of deviance. *Journal of Personality and Social Psychology, 39*(3), 360–367.

Lazar, S. W., Kerr, C. E., Wasserman, R. H., Gray, J. R., Greve, D. N., Treadway, M. T., ... Fischl, B. (2005). Meditation experience is associated with increased cortical thickness. *Neuroreport, 16*(17), 1893–1897.

402 Emily B. Falk

Lieberman, M. D. (2010). Social cognitive neuroscience. In S. Fiske, D. Gilbert, & G. Lindzey (Eds.), *Handbook of social psychology* (5th ed., pp. 143–193). New York, NY: McGraw-Hill.

Lieberman, M. D., & Eisenberger, N. I. (2009). Pains and pleasures of social life. *Science, 323*(5916), 890–891.

Maguire, E. A., Gadian, D. G., Johnsrude, I. S., Good, C. D., Ashburner, J., Frackowiak, R. S., & Frith, C. D. (2000). Navigation-related structural change in the hippocampi of taxi drivers. *Proceedings of the National Academy of Sciences of the United States of America, 97*(8), 4398–4403.

McClure, S. M., York, M. K., & Montague, P. R. (2004). The neural substrates of reward processing in humans: the modern role of FMRI. *Neuroscientist, 10*(3), 260–268.

Modinos, G., Ormel, J., & Aleman, A. (2010). Individual differences in dispositional mindfulness and brain activity involved in reappraisal of emotion. *Social Cognitive and Affective Neuroscience, 5*(4), 369–377.

Muraven, M., & Baumeister, R. F. (2000). Self-regulation and depletion of limited resources: does self-control resemble a muscle? *Psychological Bulletin, 126*(2), 247–259.

Nisbett, R., & Wilson, T. (1977). Telling more than we can know: Verbal reports on mental processes. *Psychological Review, 84*(3), 231–259.

Ochsner, K., Ray, R., Hughes, B., McRae, K., Cooper, J. C., Weber, J., … Gross, J. J. (2009). Bottom-up and top-down processes in emotion generation: Common and distinct neural mechanisms. *Psychological Science, 20*(11), 1322–1331.

Petty, R. E., & Brinol, P. (2012). The Elaboration Likelihood Model. In A. W. Kruglanski, P. A. M. Van Lange, & E. T. Higgens (Eds.), *Handbook of theories of social psychology* (Vol. 1, pp. 224–245). London, UK: Sage Publications.

Petty, R. E., & Cacioppo, J. T. (1986a). *Communication and persuasion: Central and peripheral routes to attitude change.* New York, NY: Springer.

Petty, R. E., & Cacioppo, J. T. (1986b). The elaboration likelihood model of persuasion. *Advances in Experimental Social Psychology, 19*, 123–205.

Plassmann, H., O'Doherty, J., & Rangel, A. (2007). Orbitofrontal cortex encodes willingness to pay in everyday economic transactions. *Journal of Neuroscience, 27*(37), 9984–9988.

Plassmann, H., O'Doherty, J., Shiv, B., & Rangel, A. (2008). Marketing actions can modulate neural representations of experienced pleasantness. *Proceedings of the National Academy of Sciences of the United States of America, 105*(3), 1050–1054.

Rosenzweig, M., Bennet, E. L., & Diamond, M. (1972). Brain changes in response to experience. *Scientific American, 226*(2), 22–29.

Santos, M. D., Leve, C., & Pratkanis, A. R. (1994). Hey buddy, can you spare seventeen cents? Mindful persuasion and the pique technique. *Journal of Applied Social Psychology, 24*, 755–764.

Schjoedt, U., Stodkilde-Jorgensen, H., Geertz, A. W., Lund, T. E., & Roepstorff, A. (2011). The power of charisma—perceived charisma inhibits the frontal executive network of believers in intercessory prayer. *Social Cognitive and Affective Neuroscience, 6*(1), 119–127.

Steinberg, L. (2008). A social neuroscience perspective on adolescent risk-taking. *Developmental Review, 28*(1), 78–106.

Taylor, V. A., Grant, J., Daneault, V., Scavone, G., Breton, E., Roffe-Vidal, S., … Beauregard, M. (2011). Impact of mindfulness on the neural responses to emotional pictures in experienced and beginner meditators. *Neuroimage, 57*(4), 1524–1533.

Treadway, M. T., & Lazar, S. W. (2009). The neurobiology of mindfulness. In F. Didonna (Ed.), *Clinical handbook of mindfulness.* New York, NY: Springer.

Tusche, A., Bode, S., & Haynes, J. D. (2010). Neural responses to unattended products predict later consumer choices. *Journal of Neuroscience, 30*(23), 8024–8031.

Zaki, J., Schirmer, J., & Mitchell, J. P. (2011). Social influence modulates the neural computation of value. *Psychological Science, 22*(7), 894–900.

Zeidan, F., Martucci, K. T., Kraft, R. A., Gordon, N. S., McHaffie, J. G., & Coghill, R. C. (2011). Brain mechanisms supporting the modulation of pain by mindfulness meditation. *Journal of Neuroscience, 31*(14), 5540–5548.

Part III

Leadership and Organizational Behavior

Applications of mindfulness interventions in organizational contexts have been shown to promote more effective leadership and distress tolerance in work-related settings. The incorporation of mindfulness training and meditation into the workplace has also been shown to foster greater collective mindfulness and more mindful organizational cultures. This section of the handbook addresses the broadening of managerial cognition and behavior that is offered when mindfulness is brought into the workplace.

Sutcliffe and Vogus review the literature on collective mindfulness, particularly, the process by which the application of core elements of both Western- and Eastern-based mindfulness practices enables organizations to function more efficiently and manage uncertainty, complexity, and change. Jordan and Johannessen combine the concepts of mindfulness and organizational defenses to shed light on challenges that are specific to collective mindfulness—for example, challenges to maintaining mindful organizational cultures over time—and demonstrate how this opens up new directions for research on mindful organizing. Through the use of case studies, Ritchie-Dunham shows how the application of Langer's conception of mindfulness into organizational practices can help leaders effectively deal with the uncertainties introduced by social change. More specifically, he explores the application of mindfulness solution in the contexts of an electric company, school, and textile company. Pirson addresses mindfulness within the work context. He outlines the beneficial outcomes associated with bringing mindfulness into varying work environments including schools, businesses, and hospitals. He demonstrates how mindful management affects different aspects of the organizational context including culture, learning and innovation, and decision-making. Riskin discusses the current and potential roles of both Western- and Eastern-based mindfulness teachings in the context of law and dispute resolution, while Rogers offers a look at the latest methods developed to help integrate both approaches to mindfulness into the legal profession.

The Wiley Blackwell Handbook of Mindfulness, First Edition.
Edited by Amanda Ie, Christelle T. Ngnoumen, and Ellen J. Langer.
© 2014 John Wiley & Sons, Ltd. Published 2014 by John Wiley & Sons, Ltd.

22

Organizing for Mindfulness

Kathleen M. Sutcliffe and Timothy J. Vogus

*It all started with a one-inch-wide band of fire that crept across
the fireline into fresh grass...*

—Cerro Grande firefighter

On the evening of May 4, 2000, as part of a 10-year plan to reduce hazardous fuels, firefighters preemptively ignited a controlled burn[1] on a steep hillside in the Bandolier National Monument outside of Santa Fe New Mexico.[2] Early in the burn, personnel realistically expected that the burn plan was doable, that resources were sufficient, that the dispatch system was responsive, and that the weather conditions were suitable. But, as the burn became unexpectedly more active and complex, small misjudgments grew and created larger problems that eventually grew into a crisis. Within 48 hr, events overwhelmed firefighting crews and the system. A tiny spot fire that kept flaring up every time firefighters thought they had put it out eventually escaped and grew into the Cerro Grande wildfire, one of the most devastating wildfires in United States history—a fire so hot it melted the soil. By the time the fire was controlled several weeks later, 18,000 people had been evacuated, 48,000 acres had been consumed, and 274 homes and laboratory buildings had been destroyed. Total damages to Los Alamos, New Mexico, the adjacent Los Alamos National Laboratories, and Santa Clara Canyon, site of the historical Pueblo Puye Cliff Dwellings, exceeded $1 billion.

The question of how a small band of fire can produce a billion dollars in damage naturally has many answers. Critics claimed, for example, that leadership was inadequate; that monument and forest service leaders recklessly proceeded with the plan in the face of strong countervailing evidence.[3] But our analysis painted a more complex picture (Weick & Sutcliffe, 2007). Failures at Cerro Grande were tied to what leaders and firefighters expected, their inability to "see" that their expectations were not being fulfilled and to catch early indications that they were not, and their inabilities to make

The Wiley Blackwell Handbook of Mindfulness, First Edition.
Edited by Amanda Ie, Christelle T. Ngnoumen, and Ellen J. Langer.
© 2014 John Wiley & Sons, Ltd. Published 2014 by John Wiley & Sons, Ltd.

small adjustments that could have forestalled the crisis. In our view, failures at Cerro Grande were failures in collective mindfulness (Weick & Sutcliffe, 2007).

In this chapter, we examine collective mindfulness[4] and the mechanisms of mindful organizing as means for managing amidst uncertainty, complexity, and change. Although some organizations and institutions experience crises on the scale of Cerro Grande, most organizations experience crises of a much smaller scale every day. After all, crises are relative to what organizations and their members expect won't go wrong. When Federal Express grounds a faulty aircraft because a worn part cannot be repaired, it may not cost lives for Federal Express, but it is a relative disaster to the millions of customers who were expecting an engine part, proposal, manuscript, or legal brief. It is a disaster to those who counted on Federal Express and expected that it would not fail in delivering what it had promised. Small events gone wrong may not cost billions of dollars in damages, but they can cost reputations, market shares, and careers. When organizations organize for mindfulness, they are less likely to be blindsided by events that they didn't see coming and less likely to be disabled by events that do catch them unawares (Weick & Sutcliffe, 2007).

We begin by describing the conceptual foundation of collective mindfulness, which followed initial work by Langer and colleagues (e.g., Langer & Abelson, 1972; Langer, 1978, 1989a) and was fueled by our research on high-risk organizations. We then describe processes of mindful organizing and move on to examine how this research domain has evolved over the past decade by reviewing some of the more recent empirical research. Then, we discuss how processes of mindful organizing link Western and Eastern conceptions of mindfulness and end with a set of research questions and prospective avenues for future research.

Conceptual Background

The perspective on organizational mindfulness that we articulate in this chapter emerged from research on *high-reliability organizations* (HROs)—organizations such as aircraft carriers, air-traffic control (and commercial aviation more generally), and nuclear power-generation plants (see Rochlin, LaPorte, & Roberts, 1987; Roberts, 1990; Weick, Sutcliffe, & Obstfeld, 1999) that operate complex technologies in complex, dynamic, interdependent, and time-pressured social and political environments.[5] Although diverse, studies have shown that these high-risk organizations share a set of operating commonalities and characteristics that enable nearly error-free performance in settings in which errors should be plentiful (see Roberts, 1993; Vogus, 2011). Specifically, HROs possess highly trained personnel, continuous training, effective reward systems, frequent process audits, and continuous improvement efforts. More distinctively, these organizations are characterized by an organization-wide sense of vulnerability, a widely distributed sense of accountability for reliability, deep concern about misperception, misconception, and misunderstanding that is generalized across a wide set of tasks, and redundancy and a variety of checks and counterchecks as precautions against potential mistakes (Roberts, 1990; Schulman, 2004).

We began our research when the HRO literature was considered to be an "exotic outlier" at the periphery of mainstream organization theory (Weick et al., 1999, p. 81), disconnected from studies of more ordinary, everyday organizations. Scholars such as sociologist, Dick Scott (1994, p. 25), had questioned this state of affairs and had proposed that this growing body of research be more broadly diffused and integrated into research on organizational effectiveness and organizational learning. During this same period, changes were occurring in organizational environments; environmental volatility and complexity appeared to be increasing, as were pressures for higher quality and more highly reliable performance across many industry sectors (Ilinitch, D'Aveni, & Lewin, 1996; Sitkin, Sutcliffe, & Schroeder, 1994). Our preliminary analyses of the HRO literature suggested that HROs warranted closer attention both theoretically and practically because of their capabilities to adapt and to suppress inertia in complex, dynamic environments. Thus, our goal was not only to better explain how HROs achieve highly reliable performance but also to create bridges between HRO research and mainstream organization and management theory.

Our work built on, but differed from, earlier studies of high reliability, which tended to focus on system characteristics, bureaucratic mechanisms such as organizational structure and formal processes (e.g., policies and procedures, extensive training, etc.), technological redundancy, and other activities aimed at anticipating or precluding untoward events (Roberts, 1990, 1993). Organization theorists had proposed for some time that the capacity to repeatedly produce high-quality collective outcomes came from highly standardized routines and reproducible actions or patterns of activity (e.g., Hannan & Freeman, 1984, pp. 153–154). But, in our comprehensive, integrated reanalysis of studies of HROs, we observed different patterns and proposed that organizations concerned with reliable performance under trying conditions enact "aggregate mental processes" (Weick & Roberts, 1993, p. 357; Weick et al., 1999).

The focus on collective mental processes reflected growing currents in psychology (e.g., Langer, 1989a) and organization theory. Sandelands and Stablein (1987), for example, described organizations as mental entities capable of thought, and Hutchins (1990, 1991) followed, suggesting that organizations are distributed information-processing systems. Westrum (1992, 1997) argued that highly reliable organizations are generative, thinking, and protected by a comprehensive envelope of human thought (Westrum, 1997, p. 237). Similarly, Weick and Roberts (1993), drawing together insights from a number of scholars including Asch (1952) and Ryle (1949), argued that reliable operations on naval aircraft carrier flight decks resulted from the "collective mind," embodied in the interrelating of social activities. Two important unanswered questions guided the development of our work on collective mindfulness: How is this capability of mind brought about? And what form does it take?

HROs avoid mistakes or small problems that can cumulate and achieve highly reliable performance not because of organizational invariance, but rather because they are able to continually manage fluctuations (Schulman, 1993; Weick et al., 1999, p. 88). The uncertainty, complexity, and volatility facing HROs make them vulnerable to surprises and conditions that can change without warning, and these changes can have large and negative consequences. To remain reliable, these organizational systems must be able to handle unforeseen situations in ways that forestall negative consequences. This requires capabilities or processes that enable people in these organizations to become aware of variations, vulnerabilities, and discrepancies, focus on them, and act on them. These capabilities don't necessarily come from standard operating routines, in part because unvarying procedures and static hierarchy cannot handle what is not anticipated. HROs manage unanticipated situations and fluctuations in working conditions through well-developed and stable processes of cognition and variations in action patterns. Following Langer (1989a), we labeled this capability to induce a rich awareness of discriminatory detail and a capacity for action, collective mindfulness.

In our original conception, mindfulness was not about single individuals being mindful or engaging in meditative practices. Rather, it was about patterns of organizing that result in a quality of organizational attention that increases the likelihood that people will notice unique details of situations and act upon them (Weick & Sutcliffe, 2006, 2007). Mindfulness goes beyond the awareness of current operations and projecting into the future to include deeper exploration and refinement of expectations and the development of capabilities to deal with present and emerging challenges (Weick & Sutcliffe, 2007). In other words, mindfulness functions by counteracting the tendency to simplify events into familiar categories, strengthening the capability to anomalize events (Weick & Sutcliffe, 2006, p. 518), and improving capabilities to cope more wisely with what is seen (i.e., held in mind).

Processes of Mindful Organizing

Mindful organizing is a function of a collective's (such as a subunit or work group) attention to context and capacities to act. It provides a basis for individuals to interact continuously as they develop, refine, and update shared understanding of the situations they face and their capabilities to act on that understanding. When workgroup members focus sustained attention to operational challenges, they enhance the likelihood that they will develop, deepen, and update a shared understanding of their local context and emerging vulnerabilities. As they better understand what they face, they enhance the collective's ability to marshal the necessary resources and capabilities to act on that understanding in a flexible manner that is tailored to the unexpected contingency. Five interrelated processes constitute mindful organizing: preoccupation with failure, reluctance to simplify interpretations, sensitivity to operations, commitment to resilience, and flexible decision structures. Collectively, these processes and associated practices help people focus attention on perceptual details that are typically lost when they coordinate their actions and share their interpretations (Weick, 2011). This expands capabilities both to anticipate and defend against foreseeable risks or surprises and to bounce back from dangers after they have become manifest (Wildavsky, 1991, p. 77). More simply, processes of mindfulness increase the likelihood that organizational members will be able to detect and correct or cope with errors and unexpected events more swiftly. We describe these processes of mindful organizing in more detail below.

Preoccupation with failure

A preoccupation with failure reflects the organization's ongoing wariness that analytic error is embedded in ongoing activities (Weick et al., 1999, p. 91). This "intelligent wariness" (Reason, 1997) drives proactive and preemptive analyses of possible vulnerabilities and treats small failures, mistakes, and near misses as indicators of potentially larger problems. Worrying about failure is a distinctive quality of mindful organizing. People are encouraged to actively search for the innocuous or seemingly insignificant deviations (e.g., weak signals) that might not warrant attention but might indicate that the system is acting in unexpected ways. This concern with failure is an effort to avoid hubris, the liabilities of success (Miller, 1993), or the arrogance of optimism (Landau & Chisholm, 1995), which sometimes contribute to inertia and mindlessness.

Reluctance to simplify interpretations

Reluctance to simplify interpretations means that a collective does not take the past as an infallible guide to the future. Instead, its members are socialized to make fewer assumptions, to bring more perspectives to bear on problems and decisions, and to actively question received wisdom and ensure that key variables are not overlooked. In practice, this means frequently discussing alternatives as to how to go about their everyday work (Vogus & Sutcliffe, 2007a). In part, this is an issue of requisite variety. The law of requisite variety asserts that the variety of a system such as an organization, team, or individual, must be as great as the variety of the environment that it is trying to regulate (Ashby, 1956). It is often assumed that random variety is "requisite," but, in fact, the type of variety that is brought to bear is critical (see Dimov, Shepherd, & Sutcliffe, 2007). The variety sought by more mindful organizations is that which provides insight into their particular environments and ongoing activities. In other words, through questioning assumptions and offering diverse alternatives, a reluctance to simplify interpretations enlarges the interpretive variety of a work group such that its members are able to see more possibilities. Consequently, reluctance to simplify interpretations is the means by which organizations can create and draw on requisite variety, and more effectively detect and cope with the unexpected.

Sensitivity to current operations

Sensitivity to operations means creating and maintaining an integrated big picture of current situations through ongoing attention to real-time information. Organizations that have real-time information and situational understanding can forestall the compounding of small problems or failures by making a number of small adjustments. Small adjustments are opportunities to stop mistakes and errors from lining up in such a way that they grow into a bigger crisis. Many untoward events originate in latent failures; loopholes in the system's defenses such as defects in supervision, training, briefings, and hazard identification (Reason, 1997). Being in close touch with what is happening here and now means that latent problems can get the attention they need.

Commitment to resilience

A commitment to resilience involves ongoing enlargement of capabilities to recover from the unforeseen and unanticipated. Such capabilities include greater skill at improvisation, learning, multitasking, and adapting (Sutcliffe & Vogus, 2003). Most organizations, like people, try to anticipate possible dangers by creating, improving, and revising plans and procedures to incorporate the lessons from past experience. But it is not possible to totally reduce uncertainty and create procedures to antici-pate all situations and conditions that shape people's work (Wildavsky, 1991). Thus, more mindful organizations have a strong commitment to developing a capacity to cope with unanticipated surprises as they come up. Capabilities for resilience are a consequence of an extensive action repertoire, which is built through training and simulation, varied job experiences, learning from negative feedback, and ad hoc net-works that allow for rapid pooling of expertise to handle unanticipated events (Weick et al., 1999).

Flexible decision structures

Flexible decision structures (also referred to as deference to expertise; Weick et al., 1999; Weick & Sutcliffe, 2007) arise when, in the face of problems or unexpected events, a collective pools the necessary expertise and utilizes it by enabling the person or people with the greatest expertise in handling the problem at hand to make deci-sions, regardless of formal rank. Typically, in hierarchical organizations, important choices are made by important decision makers who can participate in many choices. Mindful organizing expresses a different priority. When unexpected problems arise, the organization loosens the designation of who is the "important" decision maker in order to allow decision-making to migrate along with problems (see Roberts, Stout, & Halpern, 1994, p. 622). The result is that hierarchical rank is subordinated to exper-tise, which increases the likelihood that new capabilities will be matched with new problems assuring that emerging problems will get quick attention before they blow up. In other words, the organization has more skills and expertise to draw on. This flexibility enables the system to deal with inevitable uncertainty and imperfect knowl-edge (Weick et al., 1999).

A preoccupation with failure, reluctance to simplify interpretations, and sensitivity to operations are aimed at anticipating vulnerabilities, contingencies, or discrepancies either to preclude them or to prevent them from accumulating into bigger problems or crises (Weick & Sutcliffe, 2007). Jointly, these three processes enable a rich rep-resentation of the complexity of potential threats. A commitment to resilience and flexible decision structures jointly comprise the pool of expertise and the capacity to use it in a flexible manner that allows for swift recovery from unexpected events. Taken as a whole, these processes constitute mindful organizing.

Research on Organizational Mindfulness

Although theory on organizational mindfulness has grown over the past decade, empirical research has lagged. Below, we selectively review the more general findings— for example, evidence of construct validity and linkages to important outcomes. We start by reviewing a number of studies from healthcare, where research on organizational mindfulness is most prominent. Then, we review some research from outside the healthcare domain.

Organizational mindfulness in healthcare

Medical errors are a pervasive problem in healthcare organizations. Although the actual number of medical errors and their preventability are contested (Classen et al., 2011; Hayward & Hofer, 2001), the facts are that medical errors are frequent and costly in terms of human lives and expense to the healthcare system (Institute of Medicine, 2000). Moreover, one of the more troubling facts about errors is that most of them are not "objective" facts waiting to be picked up for the asking. Errors become errors after the fact, in the dynamic unfolding of the uncertainties and vagaries of medical treatment. They are, as Paget (1990, p. 93) argues, "an indigenous feature of the work process as it unfolds." Mindful organizing, with its emphasis on improving system awareness and alertness as well as the capacity to act, is an important means to managing error and its untoward consequences in the healthcare context.

Vogus and Sutcliffe (2007a) sought to establish construct reliability as well as the convergent, discriminant, and criterion validity of a 9-item measure of mindful organizing in a study of 1685 registered nurses from 125 nursing units in 13 hospitals. The results confirmed that the measure was a precise, unidimensional measure of mindful organizing at the unit level that closely resembled the content domains identified in earlier work (e.g., Weick et al., 1999; Weick & Sutcliffe, 2001). Vogus and Sutcliffe (2007b) also examined the relationship between mindful organizing and the commission of medication errors. The findings showed that fewer medication errors occurred over the subsequent six months on units with higher levels of mindful organizing. Moreover, the negative association between medication errors and mindful organizing was stronger when registered nurses reported high levels of trust in their nurse managers and when units reported extensive use of standardized care protocols. Additionally, Vogus (2004) examined antecedents of mindful organizing and some mechanisms through which these antecedents have their effects. He found that human resource (HR) practices such as selective staffing, extensive training, developmental performance appraisal, and decentralized decision-making were positively associated with mindful organizing and performance reliability. These practices resulted in higher levels of mindful organizing by increasing the levels of trust and respect in communications and interactions. In another study of hospital nursing units, Vogus, Tangirala, Lehman, and Ramanujam (2012) explored the effects of workgroup professional characteristics on mindful organizing. They found that professional experience had a curvilinear relationship with mindful organizing (i.e., a positive relationship with diminishing returns at high levels of experience). They further found that the effects of experience on mindful organizing were diminished when a workgroup had high variability in its experience, but they were strengthened when members of a workgroup collectively had high professional commitment.

Additional research confirms the validity of the mindful organizing construct. In a laboratory study of student teams, Vogus and colleagues (2012) examined the discriminant validity of mindful organizing and demonstrated its distinctiveness from several related work-group constructs including communication frequency, transactive memory, and several teamwork behaviors. In addition, the findings showed that mindful organizing uniquely predicted the likelihood that a team would build a safe bridge that withstood testing. That is, a one-unit increase in mindful organizing (on a 1–7 scale) made a team 2.5 times more likely to build a safe bridge.

Other studies in healthcare affirm the salutary effects of mindful organizing. For example, Madsen, Desai, Roberts and Wong (2006) and Roberts, Madsen, Desai, and Van Stralen (2005) conducted a qualitative longitudinal study of a Pediatric Intensive Care Unit (PICU) and found that the introduction of mindful organizing practices was associated with lower levels of patient deterioration on the unit, an exceptional achievement given the medical fragility of the patients. Caregivers were continually alert to the possibility that they had missed something (preoccupation with failure). Constant in-service training contributed to caregivers' abilities to interpret and question data that appeared relevant to their working hypotheses (reluctance to simplify interpretations). Collaborative rounding by the entire patient care team created an up-to-date picture of potential threats to safety for each patient (sensitivity to operations). Frequent postevent debriefings enlarged the repertoire of possible actions caregivers could take in the future to recover more quickly from unexpected events (commitment to resilience), and patient care decisions migrated to bedside caregivers who had more experience with a specific patient (deference to expertise). In another study, Knox, Simpson, and Garite (1999) studied hospital obstetrical units and found that those with better safety performance and fewer malpractice claims were distinguished by the features of mindful organizing. Vogus and colleagues (2012) similarly found that higher levels of mindful organizing were associated with higher manager ratings of patient safety and care quality.

Organizational mindfulness in nonhigh-risk contexts

Ray, Baker, and Plowman (2011) examined organizational mindfulness in a sample of U.S. business schools with dual goals of empirically validating the organizational mindfulness construct and exploring the usefulness of mindful organizing for the educational context. In addition to validating a measure of mindfulness and its constituent processes, Ray et al. found that individuals in different organizational roles (e.g., Deans, Associate Deans, and Department Chairs) differed in the extent to which they perceive their colleges to be mindful: Individuals at the top have more positive perceptions of mindfulness than those in other roles. In a rigorous longitudinal case study of Novo Nordisk, Rerup (2009) found that stable focused attention to weak signals (i.e., preoccupation with failure, reluctance to simplify interpretations, and sensitivity to operations) led to recovery from crisis and subsequent highly reliable performance. In a study of habitual entrepreneurs, Rerup (2005) found that the processes of mindful organizing contributed to venture success, but that this relationship may be curvilinear (suggesting that mindfulness is helpful only up to a point). Lastly, Vogus and Welbourne (2003) examined innovation in a sample of software firms and found evidence that HR practices unleashed practices of mindful organizing that contributed to reliable innovation over time.

Mindful Organizing as Integrating Western and Eastern Conceptions

As research on organizational mindfulness has grown, the artificial distinctions between Western and Eastern views have blurred. Langer (1989b, p. 79) early on highlighted similarities in Western and Eastern conceptions of the mindful state, and noted that differences lay in processes and techniques through which mindfulness is achieved. For example, Langer noted that the mindful state of deautomatization, in which "old categories break down and the individual is no longer trapped by stereotypes … and rigid distinctions," is similar to the mindful state described in her work (Langer, 1989b, p. 79). Still, the idea that a "chasm" exists between West and East perspectives persists among some scholars, particularly those studying individual mindfulness. But a chasm exists among scholars studying organizational mindfulness as well (see Weick & Sutcliffe, 2006).

In our initial conceptualization of organizational mindfulness, we built on Langer's (1989a, 1997) early thinking that "routines induce mindless action and that performance improves when coded information is differentiated more fully and more creatively" (Weick & Sutcliffe, 2006, p. 516). We argued that differentiation "is a joint product of refining existing categories, adopting new categories, and developing greater awareness of multiple perspectives on context." Through this lens, a variant of an information-processing perspective, organizations consist of embedded routines through which information is stored, processed, and coded in a computational manner (Lant & Shapira, 2001). Mindless information processing induces mindless action (and subsequent poor performance), so there is a need to counteract these tendencies in organizations (Weick & Sutcliffe, 2006; Levinthal & Rerup, 2006). From this perspective, mindfulness is seen as an antidote to mindlessness. In other words, organizing in a way that enables seeing similarities in things thought different and differences in things thought similar (Langer, 2005, p. 16) is privileged (Weick & Sutcliffe, 2006). Through this "Western" lens, perception and conception are in the foreground.

In contrast, Eastern perspectives on mindfulness more explicitly associate it with processes of attention and attending. For example, mindfulness is described as "non-superficial awareness. It sees things deeply, down below the level of concepts and opinions … it manifests itself primarily as a constant and unwavering attention that never flags and never turns away" (Gunaratana, 2002, pp. 147–148). It emphasizes a state of consciousness in which attention is focused on present-moment phenomena occurring both externally and internally (Dane, 2011). As Wallace (2005, p. 226) describes, mindfulness is "the nonforgetfulness of the mind with respect to a familiar object having the function of nondistraction." Mindfulness also entails "enhanced attention to and awareness of current experience or present reality" (Brown & Ryan, 2003, p. 822). Through this lens, mindfulness is seen as a way to discipline attention by making it more stable and vivid. From this "Eastern" perspective, becoming alert and aware, and keeping present details in mind are in the foreground.

A closer consideration of organizational mindfulness shows how it blends and integrates the two perspectives. It accentuates perceptions (i.e., awareness of details) of the Eastern perspective, and also accentuates conceptions (i.e., differentiation of conceptual categories) of the Western perspective. This suggests that the chasm may be more artificial than real at least as it pertains to our understanding of organizational mindfulness.

To better understand these links and how organizational mindfulness works, it is necessary to understand what it means to organize. "[O]rganizing implies generalizing…the subsumption of heterogeneous particulars under generic categories" (Tsoukas, 2005, p. 124). Organizing requires coordinating. But coordinating has important implications for generalizing. As the need for coordination increases, "interdependent people substitute categorically-based knowing for perceptually-based knowing" (Weick, 2011, p. 24). In other words, people impose discrete concepts on continuous perceptions. But the danger in substituting (known as a shareability constraint [Baron & Misovich, 1999, p. 587; Freyd, 1983, p. 192]) is that perceptual details get lost as people shift away from details. Processes of mindful organizing weaken the shareability constraint, and develop both sides of mindfulness: the capability to discriminate details and the capability to continuously notice. Mindful organizing provides a basis for this dual capability.

Processes of mindful organizing enable organizations to differentiate coded information more fully and more creatively, and develop a rich awareness of detail. "Such differentiation is a joint product of refining existing categories, adopting new categories, and developing greater awareness of multiple perspectives on context" (Weick & Sutcliffe, 2006, p. 516). The differentiation that results from conceptual refinement embodies the Western perspective. It is one means to improve attention. But the five mindful organizing processes also influence concentration (e.g., attentional stability) and insight (i.e., attentional vividness; Weick & Putnam, 2006; Weick & Sutcliffe, 2006), which is at the core of the Eastern perspective. Preoccupation with failure, with its focus on emerging failures, induces concentration and potentially vivid insights. Reluctance to simplify interpretations and sensitivity to operations increase the vividness of insight by replacing conceptual categories with awareness of current details, but possibly at the expense of concentration. Commitment to resilience involves vivid attention to whatever is at hand in an effort to ascertain how one might resume whatever was interrupted. Finally, deference to expertise made possible by flexible decision structures involves efforts to stabilize attention by routing decisions to experts who are best able to focus on the present phenomenon without distraction. In sum, although organizational mindfulness derives from a Western perspective on mindfulness, it also operates in a manner consistent with an Eastern perspective.

Future Directions and Conclusion

Although research on organizational mindfulness is growing, there are a number of unresolved questions and promising directions for future research. Among the many issues that need further conceptual development and empirical research, we single out five: linking individual and organizational mindfulness; the effects of organizational mindfulness on organizational members; the interplay between affect and mindfulness; mechanisms through which mindfulness is created; and the outcomes of mindfulness.

We have broadly referred to variety in perspectives on mindfulness, but at no point in this chapter have we focused on individual mindfulness. That omission reflects our perspective that organizational mindfulness is collectively enacted, resulting not from individual mindsets or intrapsychic processes in individual minds, but rather from patterns of action and interaction (Weick & Sutcliffe, 2007). Two important unanswered questions are: Is there a link between individual and organizational mindfulness? And, if so, through what mediating mechanisms might the two be linked? Fiol and O'Connor (2003), for example, propose that individual mindfulness leads to organizational mindfulness, and they are linked through top executive team scanning and interpretation practices. If individual mindfulness is established as an antecedent of organizational mindfulness, one could explore the extent to which routines of mindful practice can be enabled through employee training programs or other methods and, in turn, generate both individual and organizational mindfulness (Sadler-Smith & Shefy, 2007).

Little is known about the subjective experience of working in contexts where mindful organizing predominates. On the one hand, some have proposed that organizational mindfulness is effortful and costly (Levinthal & Rerup, 2006; Vogus & Welbourne, 2003), particularly in terms of the sustained commitment and effort required from front-line employees where mindful organizing processes usually are deployed (Roe & Schulman, 2008). High commitment and intensive effort, on the one hand, could lead to employee exhaustion and turnover. On the other hand, processes of mindful organizing might increase engagement and lower turnover because it provides social support and resources that can improve the work environment, improve performance, and also enhance learning (Weick et al., 1999). These competing hypotheses merit further exploration.

There may also be a reciprocal relationship over time between mindful organizing and individual-level affective and normative processes. Organizational commitment describes an employee's psychological attachment to an organization. Affective commitment reflects the employee's positive emotional attachment, whereas normative commitment reflects the extent to which an individual commits to an organization out of obligation (Meyer, Allen, & Smith, 1993). Affective commitment, might lead an individual or group to engage in the discretionary behaviors that comprise mindful organizing. Mindful organizing also might influence affective commitment to an organization. That is, mindful organizing with its intense focus on delivering highly reliable performance may align with the deeply held organizational values that inspired individuals to join the organization. Concomitantly, mindful organizing could fuel normative commitment. The goal of assuring highly reliable performance might generate normative commitment in the form of a moral duty rather than indebtedness (Meyer & Parfyonova, 2010) and lead employees to fulfill their obligations to their organization (e.g., collaborating with coworkers and staying up to date on new knowledge in their profession and industry). Thus, the effects of mindful organizing on employee commitment might further reinforce and deepen the processes of mindful organizing over time.

As theorized, mindful organizing processes improve overall reliability by enhancing attention to perceptual details, conceptualization of those details, and the ability to act on what is "seen." Although researchers have examined reliable outcomes more generally, such as the reliable administration of medication, more research examining the more proximal outcomes (e.g., alertness, awareness of details, attention, etc.) is needed. This could be supplemented by laboratory experiments or in-depth observational studies. In addition, few studies have investigated interventions to induce organizational mindfulness. And it is not known whether particular practices under some circumstances may inadvertently have perverse effects (e.g., serve to make attention less stable and less vivid; Weick & Sutcliffe, 2006, p. 519). Thus, field experiments that track the implementation and effects of particular mindful practices over time (e.g., a new leadership practice such as safety rounds in hospitals) would be useful empirically and practically, and would help to catalog the theoretical conditions under which organizational mindfulness is most likely to emerge.

Research on organizational mindfulness emerged, in part, to better understand organizing processes that counteract failures of foresight (i.e., failure to discover and correct discrepancies that can grow into crises). For decades, scholars have taken for granted "failure of foresight" as the most prominent explanation for crises and accidents (Reason, 1997). But a recent study by Barton and Sutcliffe (2009) calls into question this received wisdom. In their study of wildland firefighting, they found that awareness of small cues was not sufficient to interrupt ongoing patterns of action that were under way. Psychological and contextual factors created strong "dysfunctional" momentum that prevented firefighters from changing course, which, in most cases, led to negative outcomes. These findings suggest that organizational mindfulness may be critical to present-moment awareness and distinctive understandings, but it may be insufficient to overcome momentum and inertia in current actions. These findings suggest that there is a need for longitudinal studies that examine how mindful organizing influences the capability to change course or adapt and adjust in real time.

For high-risk organizations and some organizations in other industries concerned with safety and reliability (e.g., healthcare), mindfulness is a potentially costly strategy (Levinthal & Rerup, 2006; Rerup, 2005; Vogus & Welbourne, 2003) but worth the cost because the costs of failure are often catastrophic. But what leads more ordinary organizations to embrace mindful organizing in the absence of obvious threats (e.g., business schools; Ray et al., 2011)? One proposition is that mainstream organizations choose to pursue mindful organizing in the absence of obvious threats for reasons of organizational identity and appropriateness (what kind of organization do we want to be, and how do we want to go about our business?), rather than reasons related to consequentiality (Weick et al., 1999, p. 114). Although organizational mindfulness is an expression of organizational identity, the choice to pursue it is likely to be shaped by the organization's top leaders. But issues of consequentiality still matter, as mindfulness may be crucial to ongoing competitiveness and innovation (Barton, 2010). Thus, exploring organizational mindfulness in lower risk organizations might necessitate an expansion of what it means to be highly reliable or to be reliability-seeking (Vogus & Welbourne, 2003).

Finally, we need to better understand the outcomes of mindful organizing. There is growing evidence of the salutary effects of mindful organizing on reliability and safety (e.g., Bigley & Roberts, 2001; Madsen et al., 2006; Rerup, 2009; Vogus & Sutcliffe, 2007a, 2007b; Vogus et al., 2012). But examining a wider array of outcomes may be useful. For example, what is the link between organizational mindfulness and organizational resilience? Resilience requires "improvement in overall capability, i.e., a generalized capacity to investigate, to learn, and to act, without knowing in advance what one will be called to act upon" (Wildavsky, 1991, p. 70). Operating resiliently means "learning through fast negative feedback, which dampens oscillations" (Wildavsky, 1991, p. 120) and highlights the importance of general knowledge, technical facility, and command over resources so that knowledge can be combined in unexpected ways to address emerging threats. It also may be useful to explore the extent to which mindfulness influences opportunity outcomes such as successfully entering new markets or introducing new innovations. Are organizations with higher levels of organizational mindfulness better able to detect and respond to market opportunities and otherwise adapt more quickly? Evidence suggests that organizational mindfulness is associated with innovation (Vogus & Welbourne, 2003), but this relationship and its form require further and more direct examination.

To summarize, we have described the origins of organizational mindfulness, the processes through which it is enacted, discussed extant research efforts in this domain, and closed with gaps in current research and fruitful avenues for scholars to pursue. Capabilities to recognize small disturbances and vulnerabilities as they emerge and to cope wisely before these turn into a tragic flaw would seem both theoretically interesting and organizationally important. Scholars have made some progress, but there is much more work to be done.

Notes

1. Although wildland firefighting is generally reactive as firefighters suppress fires, in recent years it has become much more proactive as a means to manage dead trees and debris on the forest floor (e.g., hazardous fuels in forests) and stimulate germination of desirable vegetation.
2. See Weick and Sutcliffe (2007) for a more extensive description and analysis of the Cerro Grande fire.
3. Critics insisted that everyone knew that that area, at that time of year, was prone to dry humidity and high winds; conditions that exacerbate fire danger. If firefighters proceeded with the burn, they risked disaster if they lost control of it. At the same time, it could be disastrous if they did not proceed with the burn. The slopes of Cerro Grande already were dry. If there were a lightning strike or human carelessness, which are not unusual in the spring, the area could ignite with catastrophic consequences. Thus, if the burn wasn't initiated, the same winds that militated against starting it might drive an uncontrolled wildland fire toward Los Alamos, with terrible consequences.
4. We use the terms *collective mindfulness*, *organizational mindfulness*, and *mindful organizing* interchangeably throughout this chapter.
5. High reliability generally conveys the idea that high risk and high effectiveness can coexist, that some organizations must perform well under very trying conditions, and that it takes intensive effort to do so.

References

Asch, S. E. (1952). *Social psychology.* Englewood Cliffs, NJ: Prentice-Hall.

Ashby, W. R. (1956). *An introduction to cybernetics.* London, UK: Chapman-Hall.

Baron, R. M., & Misovich, S. J. (1999). On the relationship between social and cognitive modes of organization. In S. Chaiken & Y. Trope (Eds.), *Dual-process theories in social psychology* (pp. 586–605). New York, NY: The Guilford Press.

Barton, M. A. (2010). *Shaping entrepreneurial opportunities: Managing uncertainty and equiv-ocality in the entrepreneurial process* (Doctoral dissertation). University of Michigan, Ann Arbor.

Barton, M. A., & Sutcliffe, K. M. (2009). Overcoming dysfunctional momentum: Organiza-tional safety as a social achievement. *Human Relations, 62*(9), 1327–1356.

Bigley, G. A., & Roberts, K. H. (2001). The incident command system: High-reliability orga-nizing for complex and volatile environments. *Academy of Management Journal, 44*(6), 1281–1299.

Brown, K. W., & Ryan, R. M. (2003). The benefits of being present: Mindfulness and its role in psychological well-being. *Journal of Personality and Social Psychology, 84*(4), 822–848.

Classen, D., Resar, R., Griffin, F., Federico, F., Frankel, T., Kimmel, N., … James, B. (2011). "Global trigger tool" shows that adverse events in hospitals may be ten times greater than previously measured. *Health Affairs, 30*(4), 581–589.

Dane, E. (2011). Paying attention to mindfulness and its effects on task performance in the workplace. *Journal of Management, 37*, 997–1018.

Dimov, D. P., Shepherd, D. A., & Sutcliffe, K. M. (2007). Requisite expertise, firm reputation and status in venture capital investment allocation decisions. *Journal of Business Venturing, 22*, 481–502.

Fiol, M., & O'Connor, E. J. (2003). Waking up! Mindfulness in the face of bandwagons. *Academy of Management Review, 28*(1), 54–70.

Freyd, J. J. (1983). Shareability: The social psychology of epistemology. *Cognitive Science, 7*, 191–210.

Gunaratana, B. H. (2002). *Mindfulness in plain English.* Boston, MA: Wisdom Publications.

Hannan, M. T., & Freeman, J. (1984). Structural inertia and organizational change. *American Sociological Review, 49*, 149–164.

Hayward, R. A., & Hofer, T. P. (2001). Estimating hospital deaths due to medical errors: Preventability is in the eye of the reviewer. *Journal of the American Medical Association, 286*(4), 415–420.

Hutchins, E. (1990). The technology of team navigation. In J. Galegher (Ed.), *Intellectual teamwork: Social and technological foundations of cooperative work* (pp. 191–220). Hillsdale, NJ: Lawrence Erlbaum.

Hutchins, E. (1991). The social organization of distributed cogntion. In L. B. Resnick, J. M. Levine & S. D. Teasley (Eds.), *Perspectives on socially shared cognition* (pp. 283–307). Wash-ington DC: American Psychological Association.

Ilinitch, A. Y., D'Aveni, R. A., & Lewin, A. Y. (1996). New organizational forms and strategies for managing hypercompetitive environments. *Organization Science, 2*, 211–220.

Institute of Medicine. (2000). *To err is human: Building a safer health system.* Washington, DC: National Academies Press.

Knox, G. E., Simpson, K. R., & Garite, T. J. (1999). High reliability perinatal units: An approach to the prevention of patient injury and medical malpractice claims. *Journal of Healthcare Risk Management, 19*(2), 24–32.

Langer, E. J. (1978). Rethinking the role of thought in social interaction. In J. H. Harvey, W. J. Ickes, & R. F. Kidd (Eds.), *New directions in attribution research* (Vol. 2, pp. 35–57). Hillsdale, NJ: Erlbaum.

Langer, E. J. (1989a). Minding matters: The consequences of mindlessness–mindfulness. In L. Berkowitz (Ed.), *Advances in experimental social psychology* (Vol. 22, pp. 137–173). San Diego, CA: Academic.

Langer, E. J. (1989b). *Mindfulness.* Cambridge, MA: De Capro Press.

Langer, E. J. (1997). *The power of mindful learning.* Reading, MA: Addison-Wesley.

Langer, E. J. (2005). *On becoming an artist: Reinventing yourself through mindful creativity.* New York, NY: Ballantine.

Langer, E. J., & Abelson, R. P. (1972). The semantics of asking a favor: How to succeed in getting help without really dying, *Journal of Personality and Social Psychology, 24*(1), 26–32.

Landau, M., & Chisholm, D. (1995). The arrogance of optimism: Notes on faiure avoidance management. *Journal of Contingencies and Crisis Management, 3,* 67–80.

Lant, T. K., & Shapira, Z. (2001). *Organizational cognition: Computation and interpretation.* Mahwah, NJ: Lawrence Erlbaum Associates.

Levinthal, D. A., & Rerup, C. (2006). Crossing an apparent chasm: Bridging mindful and less mindful perspectives on organizational learning. *Organization Science, 17*(4), 502–513.

Madsen, P. M., Desai, V. M., Roberts, K. H., & Wong, D. (2006). Mitigating hazards through continuing design: The birth and evolution of a pediatric intensive care unit. *Organization Science, 17*(2), 239–248.

Meyer, J. P., Allen, N. J., & Smith, C. A. (1993). Commitment to organizations and occupations: Extension and test of a three component conceptualization. *Journal of Applied Psychology, 78*(4), 538–551.

Meyer, J. P., & Parfyonova, N. M. (2010). Normative commitment in the workplace: A theoretical analysis and reconceptualization. *Human Resource Management Review, 20,* 283–294.

Miller, D. (1993). The architecture of simplicity. *Academy of Management Review, 18,* 116–138.

Paget, M. A. (1990). Life mirrors work mirrors text mirrors life. *Social Problems, 37*(2), 137–148.

Ray, J. L., Baker, L. T., & Plowman, D. A. (2011). Organizing mindfulness in business schools. *Academy of Management Learning and Education, 10*(2), 188–203.

Reason, J. (1997). *Managing the risk of organizational accidents.* Aldeshot, UK: Ashgate.

Rerup, C. (2005). Learning from past experience: Footnotes on mindfulness and habitual entrepreneurship. *Scandinavian Journal of Management, 21,* 451–472.

Rerup, C. (2009). Attentional triangulation: Learning from unexpected rare crises. *Organization Science, 20*(5), 876–893.

Roberts, K. H. (1990). Some characteristics of one type of high reliability organization. *Organization Science, 1*(2), 160–176.

Roberts, K. H. (Ed). (1993). *New challenges to understanding organizations.* New York, NY: Macmillan.

Roberts, K. H., Madsen, P. M., Desai, V. M., & Van Stralen, D. (2005). A case of the birth and death of a high reliability healthcare organization. *Quality and Safety in Health Care, 14,* 216–220.

Roberts, K. H., Stout, S. K., & Halpern, J. J. (1994). Decision dynamics in two high reliability organizations. *Management Science, 40,* 614–624.

Rochlin, G., LaPorte, T., & Roberts, K. H. (1987). The self-designing high reliability organization: Aircraft carrier flight operation at sea. *Naval War College Review, 40,* 76–90.

Roe, E., & Schulman, P. (2008). *High reliability management.* Stanford, CA: Stanford University Press.

Ryle, G. (1949). *The concept of mind.* Chicago, IL: University of Chicago Press.

Sadler-Smith, E., & Shefy, E. (2007). Developing intuitive awareness in management education. *Academy of Management Learning & Education, 6,* 196–206.

Sandelands, L. E., & Stablein, R. E. (1987). The concept of organization mind. In S. Bacharach & N. DiTomaso (Eds.), *Research in the sociology of organizations* (Vol. 5, pp. 135–161). Greenwich, CT: JAI.

Schulman, P. R. (1993). The negotiated order of organizational reliability. *Administration and Society, 25,* 353–372.

Schulman, P. P. (2004). General attributes of safe organizations. *Quality & Safety in Health Care, 13*(Supplement 2), ii39–ii44.

Scott, W. R. (1994). Open peer commentaries on "Accidents in High-Risk Systems." *Technology Studies, 1,* 23–25.

Sitkin, S. B., Sutcliffe, K. M., & Schroeder, R. G. (1994). Distinguishing control from learning in total quality management: A contingency perspective. *Academy of Management Review, 18*(3), 537–564.

Sutcliffe, K. M., & Vogus, T. J. (2003). Organizing for resilience. In K. S. Cameron, J. E. Dutton, & R. E. Quinn (Eds.), *Positive organizational scholarship: Foundations of a new discipline* (pp. 94–110). San Francisco, CA: Berrett-Koehler.

Tsoukas, H. 2005. *Complex knowledge: Studies in organizational epistemology.* Oxford, UK: Oxford University Press.

Vogus, T. J. (2004). *In search of mechanisms: How do HR practices affect organizational performance?* (Doctoral dissertation). University of Michigan, Ann Arbor.

Vogus, T. J. (2011). Mindful organizing: Establishing and extending the foundations of highly reliable performance. In K. S. Cameron & G. Spreitzer (Eds.), *Handbook of positive organizational scholarship* (pp. 664–676). Oxford, UK: Oxford University Press.

Vogus, T. J., & Sutcliffe, K. M. (2007a). The impact of safety organizing, trusted leadership, and care pathways on reported medication errors in hospital nursing units. *Medical Care, 41*(10), 992–1002.

Vogus, T. J., & Sutcliffe, K. M. (2007b). The Safety Organizing Scale: Development and validation of a behavioral measure of safety culture in hospital nursing units. *Medical Care, 45*(1), 46–54.

Vogus, T. J., Tangirala, S., Lehman, D. W., & Ramanujam, R. (2012). The antecdents and consequences of mindful organizing in workgroups. Working paper.

Vogus, T. J., & Welbourne, T. M. (2003). Structuring for high reliability: HR practices and mindful processes in reliability-seeking organizations. *Journal of Organizational Behavior, 24,* 877–903.

Wallace, B. A. (2005). *Balancing the mind.* Ithaca, NY: Snow Lion.

Weick, K. E. (2011). Organizing for transient reliability: The production of dynamic non-events. *Journal of Contingencies and Crisis Management, 19*(1), 21–27.

Weick, K. E., & Putnam, T. (2006). Organizing for mindfulness: Eastern wisdom and Western knowledge. *Journal of Management Inquiry, 15*(3), 275–287.

Weick, K. E., & Roberts, K. H. (1993). Collective mind in organizations: Heedful interrelating on flight decks. *Administrative Science Quarterly, 38,* 357–381.

Weick, K. E., & Sutcliffe, K. M. (2001). *Managing the unexpected: Assuring high performance in an age of complexity.* San Francisco, CA: Jossey-Bass.

Weick, K. E., & Sutcliffe, K. M. (2006). Mindfulness and the quality of organizational attention. *Organization Science, 17*(4), 514–524.

Weick, K. E., & Sutcliffe, K. M. (2007). *Managing the unexpected: Resilient performance in an age of uncertainty* (2nd ed.). San Francisco, CA: Jossey-Bass.

Weick, K. E., Sutcliffe, K. M., & Obstfeld, D. (1999). Organizing for high reliability: Processes of collective mindfulness. *Research in Organizational Behavior, 21,* 81–123.

Westrum, R. (1992). Cultures with requisite imagination. In J. A. Wise, D. Hopkin, & P. Stager (Eds.), *Verification and validation of complex systems: Human factors issues* (pp. 401–416). Berlin: Springer.

Westrum, R. (1997). Social factors in safety-critical systems. In F. Redmill & J. Rajan (Eds.), *Human factors in safety critical systems* (pp. 233–256). London, UK: Butterworth-Heinemann.

Wildavsky, A. (1991). *Searching for safety* (4th ed.). New Brunswick, NJ: Transcation.

Further Reading

Endsley, M. R. (1995). Toward a theory of situation awareness in dynamic systems. *Human Factors, 37*(1), 32–64.

Weick, K. E. (2009). *Making sense of the organization: The impermanent organization.* Chichester, UK: John Wiley & Sons.

Weick, K. E., Sutcliffe, K. M., & Obstfeld, D. (2005). Organizing and the process of sensemaking. *Organization Science, 16*(4), 409–421.

23

Mindfulness and Organizational Defenses

Exploring Organizational and Institutional Challenges to Mindfulness

Silvia Jordan and Idar Alfred Johannessen

Introduction

What are the particular characteristics and challenges that arise when we consider mindfulness as a social and organizational practice? In this chapter, we propose to consider organizational and institutional sources of defensiveness (Argyris, 1990a; Argyris & Schön, 1978; McGivern & Ferlie, 2007; Power, 2007; Schön, 1983; Vince, 2001, 2002; Vince & Saleem, 2004) that can get in the way of implementing and maintaining organizational mindfulness. Combining the concepts of mindfulness and organizational defenses enables us to shed light on challenges that are specific to collective mindfulness and opens up new directions for research on mindful organizing.

An extensive body of research, particularly studies of high-reliability organizations (HROs), has applied the concept of mindfulness to work teams and processes of "mindful organizing" (Argote, 2006; Ashforth & Fried, 1988; Barton & Sutcliffe, 2009; Levinthal & Rerup, 2006; Louis & Sutton, 1991; Oliver & Roos, 2003; Weick, 2011; Weick & Sutcliffe, 2001; Weick, Sutcliffe, & Obstfeld, 1999). These studies define mindfulness in line with Ellen Langer and colleagues (Langer, 1989, 1997; Langer & Moldoveanu, 2000) as heightened awareness of context and alternative ways to deal with it, recognition of multiple perspectives, and the drawing of novel distinctions as opposed to overreliance on existing categories and routines.

Langer's own work has focused on individual mindfulness, but commenting on future leadership challenges, she has also formulated her own vision of *organizational* mindfulness. To promote mindfulness in their organizations, leaders

> would not only be mindful themselves; their most important responsibility would be to enable their followers to be mindful as well. One might argue that in an increasingly complex world—where work cuts across all types of institutional boundaries—the leader's only task may be to promote and harness "distributed" mindfulness. (Langer, 2010)

The Wiley Blackwell Handbook of Mindfulness, First Edition.
Edited by Amanda Ie, Christelle T. Ngnoumen, and Ellen J. Langer.
© 2014 John Wiley & Sons, Ltd. Published 2014 by John Wiley & Sons, Ltd.

Distributed mindfulness may work if organization members adopt two assumptions; that many challenges in contemporary organizations are unknown and unknowable, and that each actor's actions are sensible and reasonable from their own perspectives. The first assumption suggests that leadership means relating to new information and finding new answers, and the second may lead organization members to be curious, rather than judging of each other, and more tolerant of risk taking.

The literature on organizational mindfulness describes related ideas. Shared mental models and shared behavioural patterns are seen as factors that allow organizational members to act collectively in mindful ways. Here, mindfulness turns from a cognitive concept to an aspect of organizational culture (Bierly & Spender, 1995; Weick, 1987). Much of the theorizing developed while seeking explanations for reliability in organizations operating in complex and hazardous environments. In HROs such as nuclear power plants, air-traffic-control systems and medical-emergency units, processes of mindful organizing have been associated with recognizing early warning signals and coping resiliently with unexpected events (Faraj & Xiao, 2006; Weick & Roberts, 1993; Weick & Sutcliffe, 2001, 2007). In this perspective, resilience is achieved by a shared cultural mindset, as "there is variation in activity, but there is stability in the cognitive processes that make sense of this activity" (Weick et al., 1999, p. 87). Accordingly, Weick and Sutcliffe (2001, 2007) identified five characteristics of mindful organizing that make up a mindful organizational "infrastructure"; preoccupation with failure, reluctance to simplify interpretations, sensitivity to operations, commitment to resilience, and deference to expertise.[1] These five aspects of collective mindfulness are enacted both at the level of direct interactions in dyads or small groups, for example, in practices of mutual checking and questioning, and at the level of organization-wide practices such as heterogeneous team composition, job rotation, or review meetings on near misses (Jordan, 2010; Jordan, Messner, & Becker, 2009; Weick & Sutcliffe, 2001). These processes may help organization members keep more of their attention open to discrepancies, surprise, and continual learning. They counteract overconfidence, groupthink (Janis, 1982), and normalized deviance (Vaughan, 1996), as mindful attention "captures unique particulars, i.e., differences, nuances, discrepancies, and outliers that slow the speed with which details are normalized. These visible anomalies foreshadow potential problems and opportunities, and preclude incubation until events become unmanageable" (Weick & Sutcliffe, 2006, p. 518).

An understanding of collective mindfulness as a cultural phenomenon implies that organizations do not "possess" mindfulness once and for all but constantly need to enact and recreate a mindful culture. The odds and difficulties of maintaining a mindful organization culture *over time* have thus far been somewhat neglected in organizational mindfulness research (Nævestad, 2009; Maitlis & Sonenshein, 2010). To some extent, this is not surprising, as HRO studies form part of "positive organization research" (Vogus, 2011) that explicitly focuses on characteristics that make some exceptional organizations highly reliable despite complex and hazardous conditions. Since these explorations sought to explain the successful exceptions, the emphasis was on the positive. At the same time, some studies in this area have challenged and refined our understanding of collective mindfulness. Some authors have asked if less mindful processes under some conditions can be beneficial for organizations and live alongside more mindful practices (Levinthal & Rerup, 2006). Others have explored in more detail what may promote or undermine mindful practices in the first place (Busby, 2006; Dunbar & Garud, 2009; Snook, 2000; Vaughan, 1996; Weick, 1988, 1990, 1993, 2010; Weick & Sutcliffe, 2003). We aim to take this debate further by introducing perspectives on organizational reflection and defensiveness that help to systematically address a set of challenges to implement and maintain collective mindfulness. We build upon Jordan et al. (2009) who noticed that the literature on organizational mindfulness and critical reflection can be combined in useful ways, as they addressed similar phenomena from different perspectives. In particular, research on critical reflection can deepen our understanding of the challenges to organizational mindfulness by taking into consideration power dynamics, emotions, and pressures to conform to institutional demands.

Combining the concepts of organizational defenses and mindfulness, we argue that mindful organization cultures may be challenged by organizational actors' quests for avoiding social situations of embarrassment or threat. Organizational defensiveness can result from internal dynamics, for example, face-saving and mutual suspicions between superiors and subordinates, or between different areas of expertise such as "the accountants" and "the engineers," and may be aggravated in the course of managerial activities such as performance evaluation, budgeting, and quality control. Organizations do, however, not live in isolation. They seek to adapt to their wider context, such as conforming to dominant management ideals (e.g., "good corporate governance," "enterprise risk management"), cultivating a favorable image to external stakeholders, or responding to laws and regulations. Such adaptation can trigger defensive responses if and when the coping focus becomes one of avoiding potential embarrassment or threat.

We argue that more "micro" interactive and more "macro" institutional sources of defensiveness differ only in degree and not in principle. Concepts of organizational defenses thus help integrate insights from different literatures and enrich our understanding of organizational mindfulness. In the following, we first review factors that have been reported to reduce organizational mindfulness and go on to discuss how concepts of organizational defensiveness can help identify and understand challenges to sustain organizational mindfulness over time. We then go on to consider sources of defensiveness both within organizations and on a broader institutional level. We conclude by outlining areas for further investigation.

Impediments to Organizational Mindfulness

To explain variance in reliability, organizational mindfulness studies have looked closely at factors that concern the quality of collective attention and interaction, and how this may affect the ability to notice early warning signals or to mobilize resilience when an organization is hit by an unexpected event (Barton & Sutcliffe, 2009; Roberts, 2009; Weick, 1990, 1993; Weick & Sutcliffe, 2001, 2003; Weick et al., 1999). While several empirical and anecdotal accounts are drawn upon to describe and theorize on successful collective mindfulness (Weick & Sutcliffe, 2001, 2007; Weick et al., 1999), less systematic attention has been paid to *problems of practicing and maintaining* organizational mindfulness. From those studies that mention challenges to organizational mindfulness, we can identify a common theme: that mindful engagement may pose perceived threats to social actors in organized contexts. Such threats are mainly to do with (1) perceived risk of blame and loss of public credibility, (2) fear of interpersonal tensions caused by voicing critique, and (3) conflicts and uneasiness associated with deviating from accepted, institutionalized ways of working and organizing.

Risk of Blame and Loss of Public Credibility

In order to minimize personal risks facing critical events, organizational members may prefer sticking to standard interpretations and routines rather than exerting judgment and creating novel categories and action responses (Fiol & O'Connor, 2003). If people are afraid of being held accountable for mistakes, a strict work-to-rule may appear as the safer option (Ashforth & Lee, 1990). Based on the concept of behavioral commitment (Salancik & Pfeffer, 1978), Weick and colleagues argued that mindless behavior is likely to increase the more we commit ourselves publicly and irrevocably to a particular interpretation and course of action (Weick, 1988, 2006; Weick & Putnam, 2006; Weick & Sutcliffe, 2003). As actions become more public and irrevocable, they become harder to undo, and when actions are also volitional and related to professional autonomy, they become harder to disown. Publicity, irrevocability, and volition thus increase the tendency of selective attention, confident action, and self-confirmation, as illustrated by the case of "cultural entrapment" in the Bristol Royal Infirmary that led to failed recognition and amendment of enduring poor performance in pediatric cardiac surgeries (Weick & Sutcliffe, 2003).

Pluralistic Ignorance

Some studies have pointed out how the fear of interpersonal tensions and embarrassment associated with speaking up in front of others may hamper organizational mindfulness (Barton & Sutcliffe, 2009; Maitlis & Sonenshein, 2010; Rerup, 2009; Weick, 1990). Weick (1990, p. 588) used the term "pluralistic ignorance" to describe the tendency to refrain from publicly voicing concerns and cognitively framing the situation as "I am puzzled by what is going on, but I assume that no one else is." Lack of psychological safety (Edmondson, 1999, 2004; Edmondson, Bohmer, & Pisano, 2001), shared norms such as those promoted by "macho cultures" (Wicks, 2001), and deference to the "general," rather than situational, expertise of others (Barton & Sutcliffe, 2009) have been identified as factors that discourage voicing concerns in public. Low-status individuals may become overly reliant on "experts" and abdicate their own responsibility for contributing to the safety of the situation. In addition, pluralistic ignorance can be amplified if communication is disturbed by distance, noise, or smoke, or if team members are strangers (Ramanujam & Goodman, 2003; Vendelø & Rerup, 2011; Weick, 1993).

Institutional Work

Lastly, processes of mindful organizing have been reported to clash with accepted (e.g., hierarchical and centralized) ways of organizing in some contexts. In such institutional climates, it can be problematic to maintain mindful processes such as deference to expertise, as Madsen, Desai, and Roberts's (2006) account of a pediatric intensive care unit illustrates. Here, two leading physicians sought to implement a more democratic practice between doctors and nurses granting nurses more discretion, since they believed that this would make effective treatment easier. These decentralized structures met opposition from other departments. Madsen et al. (2006, 246) concluded, "Any organizational design that differs from an accepted, institutionalized model in its industry is necessarily fragile."

In a similar vein, other authors have argued that sensemaking in crises often serves to maintain institutions in which organizations are embedded. When coping with a crisis people tend to engage unwittingly in "institutional work" that maintains existing rules and norms, protects their professional identity, and legitimizes and restores trust in the social institution in question (Brown, 2005; Brown & Jones, 2000; Carroll, 1995; Wicks, 2001; cf. Pidgeon, 1997; Sagan, 1995).

As these case studies illustrate, perceived threats associated with emotions such as embarrassment, shame, and defensive feelings of pride may reduce the likelihood that people depart from set ways of thinking and acting, and voice critique in public. Maitlis and Sonenshein (2010) noticed that the role of such emotions has not been given much attention in mindfulness research thus far. Similarly, Weick (1995) had stressed the importance of power, politics, and institutional pressures for organizational sensemaking, but this has rarely been followed up in mindfulness research (Maitlis & Sonenshein, 2010; Weick, Sutcliffe, & Obstfeld, 2005). By contrast, related themes have been prominent in research on critical organizational reflection. For example, Jordan (2010) illustrated, using the case of novice nurses in anesthesiology, that not only is reflective practice (Schön, 1983) a matter of cognitive and interactive capacity, but also it requires the shared "willingness" to appear not-knowing or to question a superior's authority in public (cf., Yanow & Willmott, 1999, 2001). That willingness may depend on emotions such as fear, embarrassment, and shame as well as power relations between different professions or organizational functions (Reynolds & Vince, 2004; Vince, 2001, 2002; Vince & Saleem, 2004).

In what follows, we outline the relation between mindfulness and reflective practice, and we suggest that existing analyses of organizational defenses in relation to reflective practice may extend the organizational mindfulness debate.

Organizational Defenses and Mindfulness

The body of research on critical organizational reflection (Jordan, 2010; Nicolini, Sher, Childerstone, & Gorli, 2004; Raelin, 2001; Reynolds, 1998; Schipper, 1999; Vince, 2001, 2002; Vince & Saleem, 2004; Yanow & Tsoukas, 2009) has its main roots in Schön's and Argyris's work on the reflective practitioner (Schön, 1983, 1987) and the distinction between "single-loop" and "double loop" learning in organizations (Argyris, 1976; Argyris & Schön, 1978). Schön investigates how individual practitioners such as psychotherapists, architects, and managers engage in critical questioning of their own expectations, knowledge, and the adequacy of practiced routines while acting ("reflection-in-action"). Reflective practice involves paying heightened attention to the "objects" of one's practice, be it a technical construction, a plan, or a patient, and to have available multiple frames of reference beyond just applying textbook rules or standard operating procedures. In their joint work, Argyris and Schön focus more on reflective learning in the context of group and organizational dynamics. They particularly analyze defensive behavioral patterns that inhibit groups and organizations from challenging their assumptions and ways of operating when experiencing gaps between intention and outcome ("error"). Individuals and collectives, they argue, tend to respond to perceived errors by minor behavioral adjustments (single-loop learning) and tend to refrain from challenging the current practice and the underlying thinking and objectives more fundamentally (double-loop learning). Sticking to existing assumptions, interpretations, and routines, even in the face of major organizational crises, is particularly prevalent when social actors are faced with potential embarrassment and threat, and in response adopt more control-oriented defensive behavioral patterns (Argyris, 1990a). The defensive patterns described by Argyris and Schön may lead organizations to press mindlessly ahead on a set course, unimpressed by new information and deaf to warnings, whereas more mindful organizational practices involve the opposite (Barton & Sutcliffe, 2009).

We see the concept of organizational mindfulness as intimately linked to critical reflection. For example, a reflective practitioner's perception of surprise or a collective's recognition and framing of an error depend on individual and collective sensitivity to irregularities, deviances, and discriminatory detail, that is, mindfulness. Therefore, mindful awareness of multiple perspectives and discriminatory context details can be seen as a prerequisite for critical questioning of shared assumptions and routines. At the same time, Weick and Sutcliffe's (2007) processes of mindful organizing *comprise* reflective practices such as second-guessing and deference to expertise rather than authority. If mindfulness and critical reflection are related (and partly overlapping) concepts, then insights from each stream of literature can inform the other (Jordan et al., 2009).

In the literature on reflective practice, the idea that organizational defenses can get in the way of sensemaking and learning is important. We will argue that theories on organizational defenses can also expand our understanding of how organizational mindfulness can be challenged or undermined. In addition, concepts of organizational defenses can help make a connection between internal organizational processes and external contexts. We discuss defensiveness in internal organizational dynamics first, and second as a means to link those dynamics with wider institutional contexts.

Organizational Dynamics and Mindfulness

Defensive organizational dynamics have been discussed as major obstacles to critical organizational reflection and learning (Argyris & Schön, 1996; Ashforth & Lee, 1990; Bain, 1999; Beer & Eisenstat, 1996; McGivern & Ferlie, 2007; Vince, 2001).

Argyris and Schön observed in their experimental and interventionist studies an almost universal tendency for people to switch from a learning-oriented pattern to a control-oriented pattern when faced with potential embarrassment and threat (Argyris, 1986; Argyris & Schön, 1996). Faced with situations of conflict and disagreement, social actors tend to adopt defensive behavioral patterns that secure unilateral control and lead them to confirm, rather than challenge, preexisting assumptions (Argyris, 1994a). They also tend to be blind to the switch ("skilled unawareness"; Argyris, 1990a, pp. 21–23) *and* to be blind to the fact that they are blind. This dual unawareness Argyris and Schön saw as an integral part of the "algorithms" (theories-in-use) that humans follow in practice when facing difficult problems (Argyris & Schön, 1992). If we think of this in terms of mindfulness, we can say that the unawareness proposed in Argyris and Schön's perspective constitutes a form of mindlessness about mindlessness (Argyris, 1989).[2] In line with this observation, Langer has for decades argued that mindlessness is pervasive (e.g., Langer, 1978; Langer et al., 1978).

The automatic skills still often permit good communicators to succeed in defensive moves that avoid conflict and upsetting others and self. The cost is that difficult, yet important, issues become hard to address and to resolve. If this takes root in an organizational culture, it can be described as an organizational defensive routine (ODR): "Organizational defensive routines are actions or policies that prevent individuals or segments of the organization from experiencing embarrassment or threat. Simultaneously, they prevent people from identifying and getting rid of the causes of the potential embarrassment or threat" (Argyris, 1990a, p. 25). ODRs have been shown to develop in situations where potential organizational dilemmas need to be handled such as in performance reviews (Argyris, 1991), power relations between corporate and divisions (Argyris, 1990a), strategy implementation (Argyris, 1985; McLain Smith, 2002), the implementation of safety procedures (Bain, 1999), and management information systems (Argyris, 1977). Most of these examples involve managerial technologies that call for analytical rigor, but they also have the potential for making actors feel threatened. Under such conditions, actors tend to reason in defensive and self-sealing ways, often counter to the rigor that they espouse (Argyris, 1990b, p. 505).

ODRs can be set in motion by mixed messages that seek to tone down difficult underlying issues. For example, more elaborate accounting practices may be "sold" as assistance rather than control, for fear of triggering resistance. Line managers may still see it as control and hold back these concerns for fear of coming across as disloyal. Their dilemma is that they now don't have a way of addressing these concerns and finding solutions together with the accounting side and seek forms of covert adaptation instead. Right from the start of the process, the dilemmas surrounding controls have thus been made "undiscussable" (Argyris, 1990b).

A dilemma for the advocates of sound accounting practices may be that their methods cannot "account for the full complexity and uniqueness of a given context" (Argyris, 1990b, p. 503), and simultaneously, they feel committed to defending them as objective and rigorous. They may feel that admitting the dilemma would make them vulnerable. Denying it renders working out solutions with line managers difficult (Argyris, 1990b).

As defensive routines develop further from such first moves, parties begin to create explanations about each other's actions that take the shape of negative attributions that are very hard to test without causing upset. They are now in a double bind: to not raise the concerns will leave the dilemmas unresolved, whereas to raise them will easily set in motion a sequence of mutual blame. Gradually, parties become less able to act collectively and may begin to engage in activities such as budgeting games, or in stalling implementation of a joint strategy (Argyris, 1985). While people caught in defensive routines are mostly aware of the difficult issues not discussed, the full flow of the dynamic is usually outside of the players' awareness. In particular, parties may have developed a systemic blindness to how they have a share in the responsibility for perpetuating these routines (Johannessen, 2012).

Reflecting back over decades of research since 1974, Argyris and Schön (1992, p. xxii) reported that they had come to see organizational defensiveness as almost omnipresent.[3] In the meantime, other researchers have confirmed widespread defensive patterns (Ashforth & Lee, 1990; Vince & Saleem, 2004), and some have connected them to other types of avoidance than Argyris and Schön had described. For example, Vince (2001) joined calls for including unconscious emotions in the understanding of organizational defensiveness (Diamond, 1987) and also proposed directing more attention to politics, since any organization has a political power structure (an "establishment"). Organizational dynamics generated from the interplay of suppressed emotions and taken-for-granted power relations often undermine critical reflection. Established power relations and associated emotions such as fear of losing influence and control are often suppressed or denied in organizational discourses. With such defenses in operation, the emotions may continue to influence sequences of events and have ripple effects that escape the understanding of those involved (e.g., why well-intended initiatives run into the sand; Vince, 2001).

We have seen how defensiveness can imply individual mindlessness (e.g., skilled unawareness) and how organizational defenses can keep important issues out of collective awareness (e.g., denied dilemmas or suppressed emotions). We now return to the processes of mindful organizing (Weick et al., 1999; Weick & Sutcliffe, 2007) to look in more detail at how organizational defenses may have an impact on them. Out of the five processes of mindful organizing, we focus on preoccupation with failure, reluctance to simplify interpretations, and deference to expertise as examples.

Preoccupation with failure describes healthy ways by which an organization can stay vigilant and be sensitive to weak signals of impending trouble. Mindsets such as "I could be wrong, somehow" (Jordan, 2010) and institutionalized concerns with near misses (March, Sproull, & Tamuz, 1991) may, for example, promote learning from, and avoiding, mistakes (Weick & Sutcliffe, 2007). Organizational defenses may undermine such forms of organizational mindfulness if perceived risk of embarrassment is present, for example, when people are afraid of being held accountable and blamed for reported failures or near misses. Perceived threat can be related to how failure reports and performance appraisals are handled in a particular organization. Moreover, norms and behavioral patterns fostered by training, and by professional and organizational cultures, can influence the shared readiness to scrutinize one's own expertise and to openly discuss mistakes (Ashforth & Lee, 1990; Schön, 1983). Argyris (1991) investigated performance measurement practices of young employees in an international consulting firm. Since the "best and the brightest" had been selected for these jobs, he expected to find a group that would be particularly good at learning, but the group reacted to scrutiny with strong defensiveness. Argyris's interpretation of this is that the subjects had been trained and become very skilled at solving single-loop problems. They held themselves to unrealistically high standards of excellence and had a very low tolerance for error and failure (Argyris, 1991). Similarly, in an ethnographic study of an oil company, Bain (1999) pointed out that safety issues often are seen as threatening, and gave an example of how management bypassed operators when implementing a new redundancy. A recommendation to add an extra high-level alarm to an oil storage tank that overflowed was implemented instead of addressing the sensitive issue of why the operators ignored the existing alarm. By approving the redundant alarm, the local managers did not uncover any behavior patterns that might result in future incidents while at the same time claiming that they were doing everything possible to manage safety (Bain, 1999).

All organizing implies simplification at the risk of developing organizational blind spots, but HROs have been reported to counterbalance this "because they make fewer assumptions and socialize people to notice more" (Weick et al., 1999, p. 42). They feature *reluctance to simplify interpretations* by creating "requisite variety" in perspectives (e.g., recruiting team members from different backgrounds and job rotation) and by institutionalizing skepticism (e.g., through adversarial reviews). Weick et al. (1999) cautioned that the presence of divergent perspectives alone is no guarantee against oversimplification and suggested that interpersonal skills are important to negotiate disagreements between divergent voices in a team. But those skills may not be sufficient if organizational defensive routines are present, such as Argyris (1990a) suggested in his critique of the Rogers's Commission's report of the Challenger disaster. Argyris (1990a) pointed out how several engineers warned against the Challenger launch, that key players heard the warnings, interpreted them differently, and failed to discuss this. In a teleconference leading up to the decision, the engineers repeatedly warned against launching. One engineer testified that the listeners at NASA were not pleased with this recommendation, but he did not test this assumption or explore what led management to be displeased. When management had decided to launch, the engineers were given a final opportunity to speak up, and remained silent. They later said that they held back their concerns so they would not appear to be challenging the management's right to make decisions (Argyris, 1990a, pp. 37–43).[4]

Weick and Sutcliffe (2007) characterized *deference to expertise* as an organizational capacity for containment once a critical event has taken place. It describes mechanisms whereby HROs allow the formation of spontaneous groups based on competence, rather than formal authority, and that leave enough resources uncommitted to make such reallocation possible (Weick & Sutcliffe, 2007). While HROs such as fire departments and aircraft carriers are often structured in a hierarchical way, hierarchy yields to expertise and experience under critical conditions, making flexible and rapid responses to surprise possible (Bigley & Roberts, 2001). As Weick et al. (1999, p. 49) put it, "effective HROs … loosen the designation of who is the 'important' decision maker in order to allow decision-making to migrate along with problems." This mechanism requires that hierarchically superior people recognize and openly admit lack of own expertise, and that those with more situational knowledge step forward and are given temporary decision-making responsibility. Since these moves can be associated with loss of control and uncomfortable confrontation, they have the potential of evoking fear of threat and embarrassment of the social actors involved. Furthermore, defensive routines may have developed between organizational subgroups, for example, subgroups related to different professional backgrounds or functional departments. In such cases, relaxing authority and functional divisions to permit decision-making to migrate may be severely hampered by mutual suspicion and unwillingness to engage more deeply with the expertise of others. Vince and Saleem (2004), for instance, illustrated how defensive patterns of caution and blame undermine the practice of communication between hierarchical layers and across subsystems. Arguably, if such interactions are limited, it becomes difficult to recognize situationally relevant expertise in the first place, and deference to expertise will be inhibited.

While Argyris's interests as an organizational psychologist are microfocused on the way people interact defensively and skillfully, his organizational learning theory relates in many ways to broader institutional and societal characteristics (Bokeno, 2003). Not only do Argyris and Schön see defensive attitudes preserving "face" for self and others and protecting unilateral control and images of rationality as dominating and ubiquitous, but also, importantly, they regard them as *socialized* orientations. Schön (1983, 1987) saw the educational system (in the 1970s) as being stuck in a simplistic "technical rationality" that failed to equip students to become reflective practitioners. Similarly, Argyris (1991) argued that, in the 1980s, the educational system trained smart students in solving single-loop problems combined with a perfectionism that made them vulnerable when facing double-loop challenges. In this way, taken-for-granted societal ideals or "ideologies" about what constitutes good professional expertise (e.g., calculative rationality and unilateral control) play a relevant part in maintaining microlevel defensive interactions within organizations (Bokeno, 2003). In the next section, we use defensiveness as a conceptual link to discuss in more detail how broader institutional dynamics may interact with organizational defenses and pose challenges to organizational mindfulness.

Institutional Dynamics and Mindfulness

As we saw in the previous section, refraining from engaging in public inquiry and open dialogue may be a matter of avoiding conflict and embarrassment, vis-à-vis other organizational members, and may also arise from anxiety of appearing irrational, unprofessional, or irresponsible in the eyes of external stakeholders. Organizations do not operate in an "empty space" but depend on and connect to various stakeholders within an institutionalized environment. Taken-for-granted ideals embedded in legal, regulatory, and societal contexts can thus have an impact on thinking and interacting within organizations. The organizational mindfulness literature has tended to look at organizational norms and practices somewhat detached from their broader social and institutional contexts. In contrast, studies that deal with regulatory regimes and the governance of risk investigate the emergence and rationales of supraorganizational ideals, rules, and regulations (Hood, Rothstein, & Baldwin, 2001; Miller, Kurunmäki & O'Leary, 2008; Power, 1996, 2004, 2007, 2009). In the following, we discuss how the concept of defensiveness can help link organizational processes with such broader institutional and societal dynamics.

Legal and regulatory requirements for accountability, often reinforced in the after-math of events such as corporate scandals and accidents, can put important external demands on the organization. Legal demands are often generalized and inherently ambiguous. Faced with uncertainties posed by such ambiguity, some organizations seem to overreact by creating excessive levels of formalization and standards of uniformity beyond what is mandated by the law. Characterized by institutionalist research as "legalization" and "litigation mentality," organizations may thus respond to enforced regulatory demands with overproceduralization and excessive documentation in an attempt to symbolically assure organizational legitimacy (Bies & Tyler, 1993; Meyer, 1983; Scott, 1994; Sitkin & Bies, 1993, 1994). Via the emphasis on overprocedural-ization and rigid work-to-rule, legalization is clearly opposed to Weick and Sutcliffe's (2001, 2007) processes of mindful organizing.

Argyris (1994b) argued that overrigid procedures are enacted, because organiza-tional actors generally strive to prevent the creation of embarrassment and threat of being caught violating laws. The root cause of legalization thus lies in general organizational tendencies to enact defensive routines, rather than in the laws them-selves (Argyris, 1994b). Attending to recent discursive shifts in regulatory climates, Power (1996, 2007) took a slightly different perspective in his analyses of similar phenomena. He argued that particular regulatory discourses and regimes *do* matter, with certain regimes being more prone to the enactment of defensive organizational responses than others. Power did not primarily see this as a matter of specific laws, but focused more on regulatory "climates" and discourses in which particular laws and regulations are embedded. In his analyses of the "audit society" (Power, 1997) and integrated "enterprise risk management" rationales (Power, 2007), Power inves-tigated how recent regulatory regimes and associated ideals of governance and man-agement have emerged and speculated on their impact on organizational practices. In this perspective, recent attempts of "enforced self-regulation" are seen as a combina-tion of neo-liberal ideals of entrepreneurship and increased concerns for auditability and transparency fuelled by centralist anxieties of control. Initiatives for auditable self-regulation are situated in the context of a shift from the welfare state to the regulatory state, the emergence of new public management, and the rise of quality-assurance models of organizational control (Power, 1997). Organizations are thus facing an audit "explosion" that, since the 1980s, have set diverse "rituals of verification" in motion in areas such as financial audit, value-for-money audit, environmental audit, and research assessment (Power, 1997). Since the 1990s, such ideals have been increas-ingly attached to the governance of risk (Power, 2007). Such regulatory regimes typically advocate the audit of system compliance, checking whether an accepted control system is in place, rather than directly inspecting organizational activities (Power, 1996).

In line with the legalization argument, producing generally accepted, auditable control systems may entail an exacerbated concern with documentation, measure-ment, and procedure so as to construct visible signs of "reasonable practice." Rather than fostering critical scrutiny and reflection, rituals of verification institutionalize the production of comfort and reassurance in the face of regulatory anxiety (Pentland, 1993; Power, 1996, 2003). Auditable, legitimate forms of standardized practice produce comfort for auditees as they ensure against potential blame. Moreover, they produce comfort for auditors and society in general by producing an illusion of control. Regulators are protected from the anxiety caused by conflict with professionals that more direct inspection of processes might entail (McGivern & Ferlie, 2007). In this way, audit and enterprise risk management programs and technologies reaffirm order rather than furthering practices of mindful critique of established patterns of thinking and acting. Creating auditable systems of control may thus work well for defensive reputation management, but potentially less so for effective internal control (Power, 2000).

At its best, internal control could mean mindful awareness of early warning signals and learning from failures or near misses, but the increasing emphasis on auditability, systems compliance, and reputational risk may involve more time and attention dedicated to the detailed documentation of audit trails. As a consequence, actual practice may become somewhat decoupled from formal procedures and documentation. Drawing on Power's (1996) "audit society" thesis, McGivern and Ferlie (2007) illustrated such dynamics with the example of medical appraisals that medical professionals use as a defensive box-ticking exercise, achieving compliance by presenting their practice as legitimate while continuing to practice as before. At worst, formal procedures are prioritized so highly that organizational members are led away from engaging in professional judgment and practice that is less amenable to standardization and measurement (Power, 2007). In this case, mindful interrelating and organizing would be more directly affected.

Conclusion

In this chapter, we have sought to explore the particular challenges that may arise when attempting to maintain mindful organizational cultures over time. Weick and Sutcliffe (2007) developed their framework of ideal processes of mindful organizing based on case studies on HROs that show examples of how teams and organizations interact in ways that permit a high degree of adaptive learning, and a high capacity for coping with critical events. As we have shown, some studies also report tensions and difficulties in establishing organizational mindfulness, but lack more systematic theorizing on these challenges. Many reported challenges relate to how defensive phenomena of various kinds may undermine or disturb the processes of organizational mindfulness that are thought to equip some organizations with a high degree of reliability. We argued that concepts of organizational defenses can help us make better sense of how individual instances of defensiveness may transform into features of an organizational culture, take on a life of their own, and prevent organizational members from engaging in processes of mindful organizing. The concept of defensiveness helps to theorize on different, albeit interconnected, challenges to organizational mindfulness. While we can learn from Argyris and Schön's analyses of the intricacies of defensive interactions within organizations, institutional theories add to our understanding of how ideologies and institutional logics—as "external" sources of defensiveness—come about and become reinforced within and between organizations. These two perspectives thus place different emphasis on agency and structure, but are not incompatible.

To conclude this chapter, we discuss how a more thorough concern with organizational defenses opens up several avenues for future research on organizational mindfulness. To start with institutional dynamics, we may ask how different regulatory regimes interact with organizational defenses. Examples of mindful practice in HROs often involve using professional discretion in deviating from standard procedures in exceptional situations, and informal micropractices of framing problems in nonstandard ways (Weick & Sutcliffe, 2001). In regulatory climates that idealize quantifiable and auditable work-to-rule, mindful professional practice may be avoided to minimize potential blame. Few empirical studies have investigated such dynamics, and repeated calls have been voiced for detailed accounts of the practices and effects of internal control systems in interaction with divergent regulatory regimes and institutional actors such as consultants, professional bodies, and the media (Hood et al., 2001; Power, 2000, 2007).

Regulatory action (and its chances of succeeding in its intentions) also depends on the accompanying managerial technologies and the way in which they are implemented. In the examples from Argyris, we see how some of these technologies in use (e.g., management information and accounting systems) may be caught up in defensive routines. Risk and safety are areas of great concern for society, and some technologies are explicitly designed to manage these areas. For instance, reports of failure and near-misses and risk-management devices such as risk matrixes, registers, and indicators seek to heighten mindful awareness of risk factors (see, e.g., Collier & Agyei-Ampomah, 2007; COSO, 2004). A closer study of the implementation and use of these technologies that also would explore their interaction with defensive organizational patterns would be welcome.

We have seen that organizational mindfulness can be undermined by organizational defenses. We have also seen that some regulatory climates and societal discourses may increase the propensity to engage in defensive proceduralization and work-to-rule (Power, 1997, 2007). But if we do take existing HRO accounts on organizational mindfulness seriously, the question arises as to how some organizations may succeed in preventing or effectively dealing with organizational defenses. We may then ask whether HROs create behavioral worlds that have less defensiveness than average, and, if so, how have they developed? To reduce organizational defenses, Argyris and Schön (1996) had suggested two interventions: (1) to do research that could bring specific defensive routines in the organization to the surface and make them discussable; and (2) to train organization members in learning-oriented ("Model 2") skills so they could successfully discuss and resolve the underlying issues. Other theorists, such as Vince (2001), had suggested creating spaces to legitimately discuss and effectively work through omnipresent power issues and emotional dynamics. The HROs reported to have high levels of organizational mindfulness have (to our knowledge) not gone through the cures prescribed by Argyris and Schön or by Vince. We may therefore want to look more closely at examples of mindfulness in HROs and ask two questions: (1) Although not trivial, do those examples after all constitute single-loop learning under conditions of low threat? (2) In the examples where the answer may be "no," what do these examples look like under closer scrutiny? Could it be that HROs somehow manage to create nondefensive lacunas (e.g., to routinely discuss nonroutine safety issues) but that they act more traditionally in other areas (e.g., in disagreements over pay)?

Mindful organizational practices developed in some exceptional HROs caught the attention of researchers at Berkeley, who studied, scrutinized, and conceptualized them. Later, some of the findings were popularized and offered as recommendations for those who might want to learn from the HROs (Weick & Sutcliffe, 2007). Some consulting companies (e.g., McKinsey) and regulatory bodies (e.g., nuclear power regulatory bodies in the US) are now taking up concepts from the HRO literature, and combine it with their own ideals of quantification, measurement, and top-down strategies for developing safety cultures (Levy, Lamarre, & Twining, 2010; United States Nuclear Regulatory Commission, 2012). Studying the journey of these ideas and their transformation may be interesting in several ways. One question is what happens along the way, and whether anything is lost in translation, for example, by the influence of regulatory regimes and managerial ideologies. Another is to identify conditions under which consultants and other professionals may succeed or fail in helping organizations develop any of the desired qualities. Finally, one may ask under what conditions espoused ideals of mindfulness can themselves fall victim to organizational defenses.

Acknowledgments

We would like to thank Philip McArthur, Ellen Langer, Iain Munro, and Michael Power for valuable advice. The research for this chapter has been partly financed through the Complexity Project at Stord Haugesund University College, Norway. Funding has come from the Research Council of Norway and companies in the petro-maritime industries in the Haugesund region.

Notes

1. Deference to expertise was labeled "underspecification of structures" in earlier versions of the framework (Weick et al., 1999).
2. When teaching people alternative, learning-oriented skills, the first level of change therefore is to become mindful of the mindlessness, a complicated process for any interventionist, since the accompanying pain and loss of control will trigger new defenses (Argyris, 1989).
3. Argyris (1990a, p. 30) argues that defensive routines are commonplace and can lead to a self-perpetuating cynicism, "Employees in industrialized societies appear as fatalistic about them as peasants do about poverty."
4. Focusing on a particular aspect of defensive interaction, Argyris's (1990a) discussion is complementary to Vaughan's (1996) later analysis of the Challenger disaster. Vaughan argued that deviance in O-ring performance became gradually normalized and seen as an "acceptable risk" in NASA's culture of production (managerial "can do" attitude) and a culture of structural secrecy (interaction patterns that systematically undermine transmission of detailed information and the "attempt to know").

References

Argote, L. (2006). Introduction to mindfulness. *Organization Science, 17*(4), 501.

Argyris, C. (1976). Single-loop and double-loop models in research on decision making. *Administrative Science Quarterly, 21*(3), 363–377.

Argyris, C. (1977). Organizational learning and management information systems. *Accounting, Organizations and Society, 2*(2), 113–123.

Argyris, C. (1985). *Strategy, change and defensive routines.* Marshfield, MA: Pitman.

Argyris, C. (1986). Skilled incompetence. *Harvard Business Review, 64*(5), 74–79.

Argyris, C. (1989). *Reasoning, learning and action—individual and organizational.* San Francisco, CA: Jossey-Bass.

Argyris, C. (1990a). *Overcoming organizational defenses.* Boston, MA: Allyn & Bacon.

Argyris, C. (1990b). The dilemma of implementing controls: The case of managerial accounting. *Accounting, Organizations and Society, 15*(6), 503–511.

Argyris, C. (1991). Teaching smart people how to learn. *Harvard Business Review, 69*(3), 99–109.

Argyris, C. (1994a). Good communication that blocks learning. *Harvard Business Review, 72*(4), 77–85.

Argyris, C. (1994b). Litigation mentality and organizational learning. In S. Sitkin & R. Bies (Eds.), *The legalistic organization* (pp. 347–358). Thousand Oaks, CA: Sage.

Argyris, C., & Schön, D. A. (1978). *Organizational learning: A theory of action perspective.* Reading, MA: Addison-Wesley.

Argyris, C., & Schön, D. (1992). *Theory in practice: Increasing professional effectiveness.* San Francisco, CA: Jossey-Bass Classics (reprint of the original published in 1974, with a new introduction).

Argyris, C., & Schön, D. (1996). *Organizational learning II.* Reading, MA: Addison-Wesley.

Ashforth, B. E., & Fried, Y. (1988). The mindlessness of organizational behaviors. *Human Relations, 41*(4), 305–329.

Ashforth, B. E., & Lee, R. T. (1990). Defensive behavior in organizations: A preliminary model. *Human Relations, 43*(7), 621–648.

Bain, W. A. (1999). Application of theory of action to safety management: Recasting the NAT/HRT debate. *Journal of Contingencies and Crisis Management, 7*(3), 129–140.

Barton, M. A., & Sutcliffe, K. M. (2009). Overcoming dysfunctional momentum: Organizational safety as a social achievement. *Human Relations, 62*(9), 1327–1356.

Beer, M., & Eisenstat, R. A. (1996). Developing an organization capable of implementing strategy and learning, *Human Relations, 49*(3), 571–595.

Bierly, P. E., & Spender, J.-C. (1995). Culture and high reliability organizations: The case of the nuclear submarine. *Journal of Management, 21*(4), 639–656.

Bies, R. J., & Tyler, T. R. (1993). The litigation mentality in organizations: A test of alternative psychological explanations. *Organization Science, 4*(3): 352–366.

Bigley, G. A., & Roberts, K. H. (2001). The incident command system: High-reliability organizing for complex and volatile task environments. *Academy of Management Journal, 44*(6), 1281–1299.

Bokeno, R. M. (2003). The work of Chris Argyris as critical organizational practice. *Journal of Organizational Change Management, 16*(6), 633–649.

Brown, A. D. (2005). Making sense of the collapse of Barings Bank. *Human Relations, 58*(12), 1579–1604.

Brown, A. D., & Jones, M. (2000). Honourable members and dishonourable deeds: sensemaking, impression management and legitimation in the "Arms to Iraq Affair." *Human Relations, 53*(5), 655–689.

Busby, J. S. (2006). Failure to mobilize in reliability-seeking organizations: Two cases from the UK railway. *Journal of Management Studies*, 43(6), 1375–1393.

Carroll, J. S. (1995). Incident reviews in high-hazard industries: Sense making and learning under ambiguity and accountability. *Industrial & Environmental Crisis Quarterly*, 9(2), 175–197.

Collier, P., & Agyei-Ampomah, S. (2007). *Management accounting—risk and control strategy. CIMA Official Learning System.* Oxford, UK: CIMA Publishing/Elsevier.

COSO. (2004). *Enterprise risk management—integrated framework. application techniques.* Jersey City, NJ: Committee of Sponsoring Organizations of the Treadway Commission.

Diamond, M. A. (1987). Reviewed work(s): Strategy, change and defensive routines by Chris Argyris. *Administrative Science Quarterly*, 32(1), 153–155.

Dunbar, R. L. M., & Garud, R. (2009). Distributed knowledge and indeterminate meaning: The case of the Columbia Shuttle Flight. *Organization Studies*, 30(4), 397–421.

Edmondson, A. C. (1999). Psychological safety and learning behavior in work teams. *Administrative Science Quarterly*, 44(2), 350–383.

Edmondson, A. C. (2004) Psychological safety, trust, and learning in organizations: A group-level lens. In R. M. Kramer & K. S. Cook (Eds.), *Trust and distrust in organizations: Dilemmas and approaches* (pp. 239–272). New York, NY: Russel Sage Foundation.

Edmondson, A. C., Bohmer, R. M., & Pisano, G. P. (2001). Disrupted routines: Team learning and new technology implementation in hospitals. *Administrative Science Quarterly*, 46(4), 685–716.

Faraj, S., & Xiao, Y. (2006). Coordination in fast-response organizations. *Management Science*, 52(8), 1155–1169.

Fiol, C. M., & O'Connor, E. J. (2003). Waking up! Mindfulness in the face of bandwagons. *Academy of Management Review*, 28(1), 54–70.

Hood, C., Rothstein, H., & Baldwin, R. (2001). *The government of risk: Understanding risk regulation regimes.* Oxford, UK: Oxford University Press.

Janis, I. L. (1982). *Groupthink: Psychological studies of policy decisions and fiascoes.* Boston, MA: Houghton Mifflin.

Johannessen, I. A. (2012). *Mindfulness and defensive routines.* Paper presented at the NEON Conference, Oslo, 2011.

Jordan, S. (2010). Learning to be surprised: How to foster reflective practice in a high-reliability context. *Management Learning*, 41(4), 391–413.

Jordan, S., Messner, M., & Becker, A. (2009). Reflection and mindfulness in organizations: Rationalities and possibilities for integration. *Management Learning*, 40(4), 465–473.

Langer, E. J. (1978). Rethinking the role of thought in social interaction. In J. Harvey, W. Ickes, & R. Kiss (Eds.), *New directions in attribution research* (Vol. 2, pp. 35–58). Englewood Cliffs, NJ: Lawrence Erlbaum Associates.

Langer, E. J. (1989). *Mindfulness.* Reading, MA: Addison-Wesley.

Langer, E. J. (1997). *The power of mindful learning.* Reading, MA: Addison-Wesley.

Langer, E. J. (2010, April 28) A call for mindful leadership (Web log post). Retrieved from http://blogs.hbr.org/imagining-the-future-of-leadership/2010/04/leaders-time-to-wake-up.html

Langer, E. J., Blank, A., & Chanowitz, B. (1978). The mindlessness of ostensibly thoughtful action: The role of "placebic" information in interpersonal interaction. *Journal of Personality and Social Psychology*, 36(6), 635–642.

Langer, E. J., & Moldoveanu, M. (2000). The construct of mindfulness. *Journal of Social Issues*, 56(1), 1–9.

Levinthal, D., & Rerup, C. (2006). Crossing an apparent chasm: Bridging mindful and less-mindful perspectives on organizational learning. *Organization Science*, 17(4), 502–513.

Levy, S., Lamarre, E., & Twining, J. (2010). Taking control of organizational risk culture. (McKinsey working papers on risk, No. 16, 2010). McKinsey & Company. Retrieved from http://www.mckinsey.com/client_service/risk/latest_thinking/working_papers_on_risk

Louis, M. R., & Sutton, R. I. (1991). Switching cognitive gears: From habits of mind to active thinking. *Human Relations, 44*(1), 55–76.

Madsen, P., Desai, V., & Roberts, K. H. (2006). Mitigating hazards through continuing design: The birth and evolution of a pediatric intensive care unit. *Organization Science, 17*(2), 239–248.

Maitlis, S., & Sonenshein, S. (2010). Sensemaking in crisis and change: Inspiration and insights from Weick (1988). *Journal of Management Studies, 47*(3), 551–580.

March, J. G., Sproull, L. S., & Tamuz, M. (1991) Learning from samples of one or fewer. *Organization Science, 2*(1), 1–13.

McGivern, G., & Ferlie, E. (2007). Playing tick-box games: Interrelating defenses in professional appraisal. *Human Relations, 60*(9), 1361–1385.

McLain Smith, D. (2002). Keeping a strategic dialogue moving. In P. S. Brønn & R. Wiig (Eds.), *Corporate communication: a strategic approach to building reputation*, pp. 151–175. Oslo, Norway: Gyldendal akademisk.

Meyer, J. W. (1983). Organizational factors affecting legalization in education. In J. Meyer & W. R. Scott (Eds.), *Organizational environments: Ritual and rationality* (pp. 217–232). San Francisco, CA: Jossey-Bass.

Miller, P., Kurunmäki, L., & O'Leary, T. (2008). Accounting, hybrids and the management of risk. *Accounting, Organizations and Society, 33*(7–8), 942–967.

Nævestad, T.-O. (2009). Mapping research on culture and safety in high-risk organizations: Arguments for a sociotechnical understanding of safety culture. *Journal of Contingencies and Crisis Management, 17*(2), 126–136.

Nicolini, D., Sher, M., Childerstone, S., & Gorli, M. (2004). In search of the "structure that reflects': Promoting organizational reflection practices in a UK health authority. In R. Vince & M. Reynolds (Eds.), *Organizing reflection* (pp. 81–104). Aldershot, UK: Ashgate.

Oliver, D., & Roos, J. (2003). Dealing with the unexpected: Critical incidents in the LEGO Mindstorms team. *Human Relations, 56*(9), 1057–1082.

Pentland, B. T. (1993). Getting comfortable with the numbers: Auditing and the micro production of macro order. *Accounting, Organizations and Society, 18*(7–8), 605–620.

Pidgeon, N. (1997). The limits to safety? Culture, politics, learning and man-made disasters. *Journal of Contingencies and Crisis Management, 5*(1), 1–14.

Power, M. (1996). Making things auditable. *Accounting, Organizations and Society, 21*(2–3), 289–315.

Power, M. (1997). *The audit society: Rituals of verification.* Oxford, UK: Oxford University Press.

Power, M. (2000). The audit society—second thoughts. *International Journal of Auditing, 4*(1), 111–119.

Power, M. (2003). Auditing and the production of legitimacy. *Accounting, Organizations and Society, 28*(4), 379–394.

Power, M. (2004). *The risk management of everything: Rethinking the politics of uncertainty.* London, UK: Demos.

Power, M. (2007). *Organized uncertainty: Designing a world of risk management.* Oxford, UK: Oxford University Press.

Power, M. (2009). The risk management of nothing. *Accounting, Organizations and Society, 34*(6–7), 849–855.

Raelin, J. A. (2001). Public reflection as the basis of learning. *Management Learning, 32*(1), 11–30.

Ramanujam, R., & Goodman, P. S. (2003). Latent errors and adverse organizational consequences: A conceptualization. *Journal of Organizational Behavior, 24,* 815–836.

Rerup, C. (2009). Attentional triangulation: Learning from unexpected rare crises. *Organization Science, 20*(5), 876–893.

Reynolds, M. (1998). Reflection and critical reflection in management learning. *Management Learning, 29*(2), 183–200.

Reynolds, M., & Vince, R. (Eds.). (2004). *Organising reflection.* Aldershot, UK: Ashgate Publishing

Roberts, K. H. (2009). Managing the unexpected: Six years of HRO-literature reviewed. *Journal of Contingencies and Crisis Management, 17*(1), 50–54.

Sagan, S. D. (1995). *The limits of safety: Organizations, accidents, and nuclear weapons.* Princeton, NJ: Princeton University Press.

Salancik, G. R., & Pfeffer, J. (1978). A social information processing approach to job attitude and task design. *Administrative Science Quarterly, 23*(2), 224–253.

Schipper, F. (1999). Phenomenology and the reflective practitioner. *Management Learning, 30*(4), 473–485.

Schön, D. A. (1983). *The reflective practitioner: How professionals think in action.* New York, NY: Basic Books.

Schön, D. A. (1987). *Educating the reflective practitioner. towards a new design for teaching and learning in the professions.* San Francisco, CA: Jossey-Bass.

Scott, W. R. (1994). Law and organizations. In S. B. Sitkin & R. J. Bies (Eds.), *The legalistic organization* (pp. 3–18). Thousand Oaks, CA: Sage.

Sitkin, S. B., & Bies, R. J. (1993). The legalistic organization: Definitions, dimensions, and dilemmas. *Organization Science 4*(3), 345–351.

Sitkin, S. B., & Bies, R. J. (1994). The legalization of organizations: a multitheoretical perspective. In S. B. Sitkin & R. J. Bies (Eds.), *The legalistic organization* (pp. 19–49). Thousand Oaks, CA: Sage.

Snook, S. A. (2000). *Friendly fire: The accidental shootdown of U.S. Black Hawks over Northern Iraq.* Princeton, NJ: Princeton University Press.

United States Nuclear Regulatory Commission (US.NRC). The Safety Culture Policy Statement. Retrieved from http://www.nrc.gov/about-nrc/regulatory/enforcement/safety-culture.html

Vaughan, D. (1996). *The Challenger launch decision: risky technology, culture, and deviance at NASA.* Chicago, IL: The University of Chicago Press.

Vendelø, M. T., & Rerup, C. (2011). *Sensegiving and crowd safety after the Pearl Jam concert accident.* Paper presented at the Annual Academy of Management Meeting, San Antonio, TX, August 12–16 (pp. 1–37).

Vince, R. (2001). Power and emotion in organizational learning. *Human Relations, 54*(10), 1325–1351.

Vince, R. (2002). Organizing reflection. *Management Learning, 33*(1), 63–78.

Vince, R., & Saleem, T. (2004). The impact of caution and blame on organizational learning. *Management Learning, 35*(2), 133–154.

Vogus, T. J. (2011). Mindful organizing: Establishing and extending the foundations of highly reliable performance. In K. S. Cameron & G. M. Spreitzer (Eds.), *The Oxford handbook of positive organizational scholarship* (pp. 664–676). Oxford, UK: Oxford University Press.

Weick, K. E. (1987). Organizational culture as a source of high reliability. *California Management Review, 29*(2), 112–127.

Weick, K. E. (1988). Enacted sensemaking in crisis situations. *Journal of Management Studies, 25*(4), 305–317.

Weick, K. E. (1990). The vulnerable system: an analysis of the Tenerife air disaster. *Journal of Management, 16*(3), 571–593.

Weick, K. E. (1993). The collapse of sensemaking in organizations: The Man Gulch Disaster. *Administrative Science Quarterly, 38*(4), 628–652.

Weick, K. E. (1995). *Sensemaking in organizations.* Thousand Oaks, CA: Sage.

Weick, K. E. (2006). Faith, evidence, and action: Better guesses in an unknowable world. *Organization Studies, 27*(11), 1723–1736.

Weick, K. E. (2010). Reflections on enacted sensemaking in the Bhopal disaster. *Journal of Management Studies, 47*(3), 537–550.

Weick, K. E. (2011). Organizing for transient reliability: The production of dynamic non-events. *Journal of Contingencies and Crisis Management, 19*(1), 21–27.

Weick, K. E., & Putnam, T. (2006). Organizing for mindfulness: Eastern wisdom and Western knowledge. *Journal of Management Inquiry, 15*(3), 275–287.

Weick, K. E., & Roberts, K. H. (1993). Collective mind in organizations: Heedful interrelating on flight decks. *Administrative Science Quarterly, 38*(3), 357–381.

Weick, K. E., & Sutcliffe, K. M. (2001). *Managing the unexpected: Assuring high performance in an age of complexity.* San Francisco, CA: Jossey-Bass.

Weick, K. E., & Sutcliffe, K. (2003). Hospitals as cultures of entrapment: A re-analysis of the Bristol Royal Infirmary. *California Management Review, 45*(2), 73–84.

Weick, K. E., & Sutcliffe, K. (2006). Mindfulness and the quality of organizational attention. *Organization Science, 17*(4), 514–524.

Weick, K. E., & Sutcliffe, K. M. (2007). *Managing the unexpected: Resilient performance in and age of uncertainty* (2nd ed.). San Francisco, CA: Jossey-Bass.

Weick, K. E., Sutcliffe, K. M., & Obstfeld, D. (1999). Organizing for high reliability: Processes of collective mindfulness. *Research in Organizational Behavior, 21*, 81–123.

Weick, K. E., Sutcliffe, K. M., & Obstfeld, D. (2005), Organizing and the process of sensemaking. *Organization Science, 16*(4), 409–421.

Wicks, D. (2001). Institutionalized mindsets of invulnerability: Differentiated institutional fields and the antecedents of organizational crisis. *Organization Studies, 22*(4), 659–692.

Yanow, D., & Tsoukas, H. (2009). What is reflection-in-action? A phenomenological account. *Journal of Management Studies, 46*(8), 1339–1364.

Yanow, D., & Willmott, H. (1999). Considering passionate humility. *Administrative Theory & Praxis, 21*(4), 440–454.

Yanow, D., & Willmott, H. (2001). Passionate humility: Toward a philosophy of ethical will. In C. Hockings & I. Moore (Eds.), *Rethinking administrative theory: The challenge of the next century* (pp. 131–140). Washington, DC: Georgetown University Press.

24

Mindful Leadership

James L. Ritchie-Dunham

"Why can't we develop much more comprehensive responses to our most challenging issues in Vermont?," asked the leadership of the Maverick Lloyd Foundation, a significant philanthropy in Vermont. They were a leading force in a network of hundreds of not-for-profit organizations working to address social, economic, and environmental challenges in the state. As the result of a myriad of independent initiatives undertaken by these hundreds of organizations, Vermont led the country—and the world—on many fronts, especially in next-generation responses to energy efficiency and renewable energy. For example, Vermont created the first energy-efficiency utility, paid for taking watts out of the system through increased efficiency.[1] Vermont also led the nation in the percentage of its electricity coming from renewable energy sources, supported by aggressive regulatory policies. And, while these relatively large steps moved Vermont ahead of the pack, the Foundation's leaders felt that much more was possible. To them it seemed that a small state like Vermont, with fewer than 700,000 inhabitants, should be able to undertake a more coordinated, collaborative effort aimed at more aggressive goals for more radical solutions. What would it take to make this happen?[2]

There are many elements of this story that could explain why such an innovative state had not been able to address such large issues in a more comprehensive manner. It could be that the people in Vermont lacked resources, experience, education, technology, or interest. Any one of these would be sufficient to explain the lack of comprehensive social change, but the state is rich in all of these. Instead of a lack of resources, the issue might be uncertainty in the economics, politics, and social dynamics of these large-scale issues. There are many seemingly conflicting perspectives to integrate, adding to the political complexity and uncertainty. Each perspective has its own incentives, making it difficult to see information available to other perspectives, which added to the economic complexity and uncertainty. Given partial and

The Wiley Blackwell Handbook of Mindfulness, First Edition.
Edited by Amanda Ie, Christelle T. Ngnoumen, and Ellen J. Langer.
© 2014 John Wiley & Sons, Ltd. Published 2014 by John Wiley & Sons, Ltd.

conflicting perspectives, people attempting comprehensive solutions could have mis-characterized the context for large-scale issues, thus misidentifying the problem and possible solutions, elements of uncertainty in the social dynamics.

Three different interpretations of these elements of uncertainty and complexity—thinking, relating, and intention—suggest very different approaches. The thinking school suggests it is a lack of systemic thinking and integration—it is a systems-level problem requiring a systems-level solution. This could be accurate, as the many efforts within Vermont tended to focus on symptomatic solutions addressing a small part of the system. While each solution might be important, to address specific needs, such as building solar panels, shutting down a nuclear facility, or passing a water-use bill, these solutions do not encompass the dynamics of the whole system. This school assumes a lack of clear, comprehensive reasoning, which it might fix with a cognitive approach like systems modeling. A few attempts had been made in the state to address the comprehensive nature of energy policy through systems modeling, without any significant, large-scale consequences.[3]

The relating school suggests the problem is a lack of relationship. This could be true: different perspectives conflict on what the context is, what the problem is, and what the solution is. Proponents of this school suggested relationship-building con-venings across the state, engaging tens of thousands of Vermonters in hundreds of meetings, coming up with summary findings and possibly better relationships among the individual citizens, without shifting statewide policies.[4]

The intention school suggests that the problem is a lack of collective will to act together. This could be so, as little was done collaboratively across the state, with most people taking up their own small-scale efforts with great vigor. The intention school's recommended approach tends to focus on leadership that builds a shared vision, iden-tifies strategic leverage points for action, and engages large-scale processes.[5]

Another possibility is that all three schools are needed, at the same time. This Hand-book provides two different organizational-level perspectives that integrate the think-ing, relating, and intention schools. Sutcliffe and Vogus looked to high-reliability organizations for the complex organizational structures and processes that support healthy human interactions (relating) and that support ongoing alertness (thinking) through clear incentives and action plans (intention). The focus is on understanding the organizational complexity that supports ongoing, ever-ready alertness. Taking a very different tack, Langer teases out very simple, highly efficient and effective mech-anisms of mindfulness to leverage a small amount of effort into large changes. This chapter applies Langer's high-leverage focus on mindfulness to new perspectives, cat-egories, and information to develop an approach that interweaves effective thinking, relating, and intention.

This chapter also takes up the perspective of the leader of the organizational effort. As a leader, the power to exploit organizational uncertainty resides in the mindfulness of everyone in the organization.[6] Enabling this distributed mindfulness is strategic to every aspect of the mindful leader's organization (Langer, 2010).

What is mindful leadership? Leadership focuses on building shared meaning for the purpose of enabling change to deal with contentious problems (Dunoon & Langer, 2011). Langer's mindfulness perspective focuses on noticing new things (Langer, 1989b). When you are mindful, you are looking for change, and you embrace it.

Things are always changing, whether you embrace the change or not, so you are better off understanding how to deal with it, versus believing that you can hold it still or run away from it. Putting these two concepts together, mindful leadership uses mindful processes in a mindful culture to see, name, and work with uncertainty.

Mindful leadership is about mindful process. Leaders use strategic processes to guide their organizations through uncertainty. These strategic processes attempt to engage large parts of the organization in recognizing *new categories* (business opportunities and threats), responding to the emergence of *new perspectives* (stakeholders), and processing *new information* (feedback from the marketplace), showing how to avoid the dangers not yet arisen. Nonetheless, leaders today tend to provide yesterday's solutions to today's problems, as if things remain static. Leaders need to be aware that things are always changing and that things look different from different perspectives—uncertainty is the rule not the exception (Langer, 2010). Once leaders understand this, they can exploit the power in uncertainty through mindful processes that surface new categories, perspectives, and information.

Mindful leadership is also about mindful culture. Langer's mindfulness research showed that when a leader values uncertainty, they are less likely to be authoritarian, and workers are more likely to admit to problems rather than hide them (Langer, 1989a). Mindful leaders respect their followers and realize that mindful solutions can come from anyone in the organization. Research also shows that the mindful leader is seen as more charismatic, authentic, and trustworthy (Langer, 1989a). An organization's mindfulness leaves its footprint in its products, making them more successful. Employees encouraged to be mindful will take fewer sick days, have fewer accidents, work harder, and be more productive (Langer, 1997). Thus, mindful leadership increases organizational innovation, efficiency, and effectiveness, the three gold standards of organizational performance.

Translating social psychological insights from the laboratory to the field is challenging, especially in the complex social settings and long time frames of most leaders. To show how these mindfulness insights were applied in the field, we use the case-study method. The rest of this chapter focuses the lens of Langer's mindfulness research on the context of mindful leadership through four case studies of leadership.[7] I use the mindfulness lens to diagnose each leadership situation and suggest a mindfulness solution. I translate the mindfulness solution into organization practices, which I use to resolve the four cases. These include the importance of *new perspectives* in an electric company, *new categories* in a school board, *new information* in a textile company, and the use of all three in a statewide project.

New Perspectives

An electric utility, with a monopoly serving 20 million consumers, found itself in a strategic crisis. The government was proposing to deregulate the retail part of its business. To better understand the complex reality they might face in a deregulated retail world, the company asked the author to help them take a systemic look at their strategy. As part of the process, the leaders were asked to describe the goals, objectives, and possible actions that each of their stakeholders would take. It became clear very quickly that the leaders had a very limited and dated understanding of the particular worldview of the different stakeholders. These stakeholders included their consumers, regulators, their own corporate board, managers of different areas of their business, local communities, and their competition. For example, when asked about their end user, they said, "She wants cheap energy." When asked, "How do you know?," it became clear that it had been many years since the last time they had talked to their end users. Basically, believing they already knew what their stakeholders wanted from them, the leaders paid little attention to them. While that might have worked in the past, in a very stable, heavily regulated environment, it was clear that now they needed to know.

Looking at this case through the mindfulness lens, the central theme is the openness to new perspectives. Langer has referred to this as a societal cognitive commitment to content, which means that people commit beforehand to see a social situation from a specific, predetermined cognitive context (Langer, 1994). Cognitive commitment means committing to or freezing what is processed cognitively and how it is processed (Chanowitz & Langer, 1981).

Two experiments highlight the openness to new perspectives. In one experiment, a subject was asked to write *ababab* as long as it was enjoyable (Karsten, 1928). The subject did until he was completely weary, physically and mentally, to the point that his hand was numb. The researcher then asked him to sign his name for another purpose, and he did so quite easily. She did the same with reading poetry until the subjects were hoarse, yet they were no longer hoarse when complaining about the exercise. Put into a new context, they seemed to find their "second wind"; a second later, they were no longer exhausted (Langer, 1989a, p. 136). In another set of experiments, children who were used to sitting still in class were asked to look at a map for 45 s. In condition 1, they sat still, while in condition 2, they walked, and in condition 3, they shuffled their feet while sitting. They were all then asked to identify as many landmarks as they could. The children placed in a new context, not sitting still, remembered significantly more than those who remained in the same sitting-still context (Carson, Shih, & Langer, 2001). By having their context shifted, from one place to another, they now experienced the activity from another place, another point of view, another perspective.

Translating this to the world of organizations, when a leader closes themself off to the perspective of others, they lose the opportunity to understand the richness of different dimensions that other perspectives bring. Additionally, they miss the chance to see how their organization's actions impact the lives of others. They might do this because they fail to see that what seems like an incorrect answer—one not aligned with their own—might actually be a correct answer when seen from another's perspective. People tend to believe that the two perspectives, mine and yours, are the same, but they are not. Summarizing Langer's findings about the mindfulness of new perspectives, an actor's behavior makes sense from their perspective (Langer & Brown, 1992). They do what they do for a reason. The leader's ability to perceive and understand this reason depends on their mindfulness, their openness to other perspectives. This openness leads to more possibilities to creatively choose from, and it increases the probability of success of the change.

This suggests a solution for the energy company's strategic challenge: recognize that the company's stakeholders have good reasons for their actions, and that these reasons, going forward in a deregulated world, will be different than they were before. By being open to these new perspectives, the company increases the number of possible actions it can take to satisfy the stakeholders' multiple needs, and it simultaneously increases the probability of successful change.

Various organizational practices have evolved in the past years to support leaders and their organizations in being more mindful of the evolving perspectives of their multiple stakeholders. We will focus on two here: the process of inquiry and the framework of multiple stakeholders. Inquiry, popularized in the 1990s by Peter Senge through organizational learning, differentiates the question from the answer, listening from talking, and wanting to understand the other from wanting to explain oneself (Senge, 1990). This simple process of asking or inquiry seems to be one of the most difficult for many leaders. If you want to know what someone else is thinking, ask and listen, with the intention of understanding her perspective.

The other organizational practice is the framework of multiple stakeholders (Freeman, 1984). Three key lessons, relevant to mindfulness, have been learned over the evolution of this framework. First, a stakeholder is anyone who has a stake in the actions of the organization—the organization's actions impact them, and their actions impact the organization. Second, not including a stakeholder's actual perspective is equivalent to saying that the impact of its response to the company's actions is zero. Since we just defined that the stakeholder's actions do impact the organization, the only value we know to be wrong is zero—they do impact the organization. Therefore, it is important to understand the stakeholder's current perspective. Third, if you think you know what someone else is thinking without asking, the probability that you are wrong approaches 100%. Given these three lessons, since stakeholders do impact the organization, and we do not know what they are thinking now without asking, we return to the first practice—we ask. Many texts have been written on these two practices that help leaders and their organizations be more mindful of new perspectives.

Coming back to the energy company, leadership decided it was important to understand the perspectives of the different stakeholders. They started with the desire to understand, to want to know what the stakeholders thought. What are their intentions, objectives, and motivations? How might they react to different actions the company might take? Once they wanted to know, it was relatively easy to find people within the company who had both a connection to a particular stakeholder and the capacity to inquire with them. The company quickly discovered two things. First, the cost of getting the information was far less than the cost of not knowing. Second, what they thought the stakeholder would say, beforehand, was completely wrong—they learned something new in every case. And, now they knew the stakeholder's perspective, in his and her own words. These perspectives were incorporated into the systemic overview of the company's strategy. As we finished the project, the company's president shared that he loved the exercise, and that from now on he would require his executives to describe the impact of their strategic proposals in terms of the different stakeholders. Whom does the strategy you propose affect? What do the different stakeholders want, relative to the strategy? How do you know? Did you ask them?

In this case, Langer's perspective on mindfulness to new perspectives admonishes leaders to remember that every person has a different experience, based in their own context. Mindfulness to the perspective of the other is necessary for seeing, understanding, and embracing that part of uncertainty that resides in the reaction of the other.

New Categories

The board of trustees for a private school is responsible for the stability of the school's finances. In the majority of private schools, tuition covers only two-thirds of the operating costs. To cover the other third of the costs, most schools typically have an annual fundraising campaign. Even with a sizable endowment, the board found it necessary to ask the school community for donations every year. Over the years, a pattern became clear: nobody liked asking families in the school to make a donation. A board member said why: "Tuition is already very high for most families. Asking them for more is painful."

Langer's mindfulness research highlights a critical dimension in this case—the creation of new categories (Langer, 1994). The individual tends to commit unconsciously to processing the information with only one predetermined filter. Over many studies, Langer's lab has demonstrated the ability to open this unconscious process with a very simple twist. Instead of stating that something "is" a certain way, when it is stated conditionally as "it could be" a certain way, another more mindful universe opens up. It seems simple, and it is. Dozens of experiments validate this cognitive key for opening the human mind to new categories (Langer, Bashner, & Chanowitz, 1985).

In one experiment, subjects were shown three objects and given a questionnaire about them (Langer & Piper, 1987). For half of the subjects, the first paragraph read, "Object A is a rubber dog's chew toy; Object B is a polygraph pen; and Object C is a hair dryer attachment." For the other half of the subjects, the first paragraph replaced "is" with "could be." As the subjects completed the questionnaire, the experimenter told the subjects that they had made a mistake and needed an eraser. With the half that read it "is" a chew toy, only one of 20 subjects thought of using the rubber toy as an eraser. With the half that read "could be" a chew toy, 40% saw that it could also be a rubber eraser. By only changing from "is" to "could be," the majority of the people were able to see that the rubber chew toy could be categorized in two different ways: as a chew toy and as an eraser.

This research on mindfulness to new categories proposes a solution to the school board's difficulty with fundraising. Putting one's attention on the situation and context, one can use conditional phrasing to open up to and name uncertainties. Two organizational practices support the mindfulness to new categories—scenario planning (Georgantzas & Acar, 1995; Godet, 1987; Wack, 1985) and double-loop learning (Argyris, 1977, 1993). Both practices conditionally surface underlying assumptions—is it this way, or could it be this other way? Scenario planning develops and explores alternative futures in uncertain environments, evaluating the system's future resiliency to these different possibilities (i.e., how would we do if this played out or that played out? Can we be resilient enough to thrive under both scenarios?). Double-loop learning seeks feedback about the consequences of one's actions, adjusting both the actions that cause the consequences (single-loop) and the assumptions guiding the actions taken (double-loop). This practice asks if the mental model of cause and effect is correct or could be recategorized more accurately.

Applying the practices of mindfulness of new categories to the school board, three fixed categories that the board members carried appeared: the assumption of scarcity; the lack of financial resources on the part of the families in the school; and the need to beg for more of what they did not have. Applying scenario planning and double-loop learning, the board members began to examine these three fixed categories. First, they saw that the reality in which they lived was one of abundance for most of the school's resources—excellent teachers, parents who were dedicated to the pedagogy, creative and engaged students, and a large, beautiful campus with a functional and architecturally extraordinary building. They realized that the only thing that seemed scarce in their experience was the money that they did not want to ask the families in the school to give. They were able to open the category of scarcity to the possibility of abundance—it could be abundant.

Exploring the second fixed category, the lack of money in the community, the board members saw that it could be that there was plenty of money. Many of the families had large houses and nice cars, and took summer vacations overseas every year. And these same families loved the school, which they expressed by being very involved in many aspects of the school's life. They began to see that the category of "not enough money" could be "they don't give their money to the school." Playing with different future scenarios for this category, board members saw the possibility that the families with ample financial resources did not make big donations to the school because nobody had expressed an interest in them. "We only asked them for their money. We did not try to understand what they valued. What do they give their money to? Why?" Opening the category from "there's no money" to "we have not asked them what their contribution could be," the board began to get excited about engaging these families in conversations about their passions. That would be a fun conversation to be in with them. What would they like to see come alive in our community? As the board's mindfulness about this second category opened, the third category began to open—the need to beg people for money they do not have. They now saw that it was not true that people did not have money, and they saw that they were very excited about the inquiry with these families. As they recognized this, the board opened the third category from "don't beg" to "engage people who can make a more significant contribution." With the opening of the board to these three new categories, the energy to grow the school's financial resources skyrocketed, and a new pathway for engaging the school community's creativity opened.

In summary, mindfulness research suggests the importance of having leaders and their organizations be open to new categories. Being mindful to new categories, leaders pay attention to the situation and the context, fitting the solution to the context. This mindful awareness brings in much greater creativity for embracing uncertainty, leading to much more efficient and effective solutions that satisfy the needs of many more groups.

New Information

The leaders in a textile company observed a behavior pattern—they were very good at finding data to support the idea-of-the-day that they were trying to sell to their employees and customers. "See? This information confirms my idea, therefore we should ... (insert the idea being sold)." As a consequence of the observed behavior, they saw that often the information they collected confirmed a mistaken idea, leading to unintended consequences, and thus lower efficiencies. Instead of facing uncertainty, they hid it, constantly surprised by the outcomes. As they began to recognize this pattern, they discovered another phenomenon. Often they had, right in front of them, the information that would have helped them avoid the unintended consequences; but they did not pay attention to it. They asked, "Why?"

Langer's research on mindfulness of new information observes that people tend to preprogram their heads for the information they want to see. Langer describes this phenomenon as a premature cognitive commitment to process—I know what information I want to find to confirm the reality I want to see, so I am closed to perceiving other information (Langer, 1994). This research suggests much better results when one is able to pay attention to what is directly observable and discernible in the situation, and not getting lost in inferences or premature conclusions.

In an experiment in a nursing home, half of the residents were asked to decide for themselves when to water a plant they were given, where to receive visitors, and whether to see a movie. This simple instruction engaged the residents in receiving new information—requiring them to process it to inform a decision they had to make. The nurses on staff made these three decisions for the rest of the residents, as they usually did. The transformation was huge, with the more mindfully engaged residents participating more, being happier, more alert, and more active, and living longer (Langer & Rodin, 1976; Rodin & Langer, 1977). These results came from simply "giving residents something new to look at" (Langer, 1989a).

Organizational practice in the past couple of decades has evolved the art of refutation—looking for information that disconfirms the hypothesis—observing that a hypothesis is stronger the harder it is to disconfirm (Popper, 1959). This is the antidote to the confirmation bias, where one looks for information to support the hypothesis. Thus, a more rigorous process tries to disconfirm the hypothesis. Two organizational technologies support refutation—the content of a well-designed scorecard and the process of storybusting. Scorecards, like the "balanced scorecard," provide information from different strategic areas of the organization in a systemic way, showing the status of each area, and the relationships among the areas (Kaplan & Norton, 1992). This scorecard helps the leaders see both the whole system and its parts, at the same time, keeping attention on all of the content and not getting lost in the weeds of one area (Ritchie-Dunham, Morrice, Anderson, & Dyer, 2007). The storybusting process starts with a leader's "story," her cause–effect hypothesis of the relationship between a strategic intervention and the systemic consequences of that intervention. As Langer's research demonstrates, people tend to believe the stories they create, closing themselves off to other possibilities. Storybusting changes the focus from defending a story to attacking the same story—the process of refutation. What information would help me bust the story I created?

The textile company applied both the scorecard and storybusting technologies. They designed a scorecard that included future-oriented indicators for overall, company-wide performance—the number of new consumers and free cash flow for investment—and past-oriented indicators for the local-level performance of processes that protected the integrity of the products, business systems, culture, and capital management (Leaf & Hulbert, 2010; Ritchie-Dunham, Throneburg, Leaf, & Hulbert, 2010; Throneburg, 2011). The scorecard gave them the content. Storybusting gave them the process. Every time leadership came together to review the strategy, they reminded themselves of their "stories," the hypotheses they proposed between interventions and expected consequences. Calling these stories, they used the information in the scorecard to try to bust their stories. For example, one director said:

> I thought that launching the new website and the advertising campaign simultaneously would increase traffic to the online store, increasing profits without impacting our manufacturing processes. A few things could bust my story. One, it could have cost us more than we increased revenues. Two, it could have taxed our business systems or our culture. So, normally I would look at the online sales information for an increase, proclaiming success if I found it. Now, I look at sales, the number of new users, the net financial impact on cash available for future investments, and the four integrities. This partially blows up my story; there are impacts in other areas. On the other hand, this process enriches my story, helping me see dimensions of the interactions of the parts that I did not see before. I learned something.

In this case, mindful processes supported leaders in being more open to new information. This mindful opening allowed more learning and greater creativity, strengthening leadership's ability to embrace the uncertainty it faced.

All Three Together

Revisiting the case with which this chapter opened, a small group of foundations in Vermont decided that it was time to shift gears. While Vermont had long been the home of groundbreaking innovations in energy efficiency, renewable electric energy, and regulatory protection of the environment, this group felt it was time to step up the game, taking on a much more audacious, statewide goal of shifting the whole energy sector in the state (electricity, heating, transportation, and efficiency) to renewable energy. When they looked across the hundreds of renewable-energy-related efforts in the state, they saw many great initiatives each pushing their own perspective, with very little collaboration among them. The result was incredible innovation on relatively small scales. They realized that previous processes in the state minimized the possibility of an audacious energy future, by minimizing perspectives, categories, and information. They wanted to see if large-scale social change was possible. I saw that this large-scale effort would require opening a large group of people to new perspectives, categories, and information, all at the same time. I looked to Langer's mindfulness research to see if all three had been worked on together at the same time, to see what lessons could be learned.

In a five-day experiment, 17 subjects between the ages of 70 and 75 years old were taken to a retreat where half of them were centered in the present reflecting on their experience 20 years earlier, and half of them were centered in the past (Langer, 2009). This experiment shifted the context/perspective, information, and categories

Figure 24.1   Mindful meeting process (Ritchie-Dunham, in press).

of the subjects. At the end of the retreat, both groups showed significant differences from when they started—they looked younger, their hearing improved, they ate more heartily and remembered more, and their hand strength increased. Additionally, the half centered in the past experienced greater physiological and psychological changes than the half centered in the present—they experienced significantly improved joint flexibility, sitting height, manual dexterity, near-point vision, and mental processing (Langer et al., 1990). This study was replicated in 2010 with six celebrities on the BBC program "The Young Ones."[8]

Translating this mindfulness research to the organizational development literature exhaustively describes the importance of a few key processes for large-scale social change, which we integrate and summarize here with the "mindful meeting" process, as depicted in Figure 24.1. Starting on the bottom-right of the circle, at the deepest shared purpose, leadership sets the context, the vision for why the group is coming together. This uniting purpose provides the vision for and defines the playing space in which everyone has been convened. It seeks alignment of higher purpose. This alignment of purpose is contrasted with the more common experience of not knowing the purpose of a meeting or effort, and being at cross-purposes in what the purpose should be.

The second element aligns people around the values and contributions each individual brings to the group. Why are you here? Why am I here? Making explicit and sharing the specific reason each person is involved both reminds each individual of the contribution they are being asked to make and what they can expect from the others. This alignment of contributions contrasts with the experience of not knowing why people are in the room and what unique perspectives they are specifically expected to contribute.

The third element explores the individual and group understanding of the possibilities that can be seen through the unique contributions of each person. This element aligns people around what can be seen in the rich possibilities opened collectively, painted by the differences in the rich textures pointed at by the light of each individual, contrasting with the more common experience of each person focusing at most on what can be seen from the partial perspective they bring.

This process seeks alignment within each element and amongst the three elements. While alignment within any one of the elements strengthens the group's process, alignment among them leverages this much further. It is within the shared deeper purpose that each individual can be invited to make their unique contribution, highlighting unique textures of the possibilities the group can begin to see.

The fourth, fifth, and sixth elements then convert the possibilities seen into the probabilities the group can choose to manifest. As each individual sees themself within the probabilities seen by the group, they find their commitment to actions that address the shared purpose. This aligns and integrates participants around their commitments to the group process, responsibilities they each take up for specific actions.

To this organizational development process, Scharmer (2007) highlights the work with mind, heart, and will within the process. In this process, the deeper shared purpose and action both address issues of intention in the will. The individual's contributions address issues of relatedness, the heart level. Possibilities and probabilities address issues of thinking in the mind.

Langer's mindfulness is interwoven throughout this mindful meeting process, clarifying what content is being processed (*new information*), how an individual's mental model is processing it (*new categories*), and how to inquire about how others are processing the information (*new perspectives*). From the lens of this mindful meeting process, an assessment of the Vermont case shows a lack of alignment statewide within each of the six elements in Figure 24.1 and among all six elements, suggesting a process that aligns within and across the elements.

To address the challenge in Vermont, a small group of foundations embraced a process that invited new perspectives, categories, and information, resulting in a statewide mandate for a radical new energy future. Pulling together many of the insights described in the three cases above, the process focused on: (1) agreeing across many stakeholder groups on the collective goal of Vermont's ability to determine its own energy future through affordable, renewable energy; (2) creating clear maps of each of the many perspectives that influence the supply of and demand for renewable energy, that each perspective felt accurately represented their perspective; (3) sharing these individual-perspective maps interactively with each other; (4) integrating the individual-perspectives into a collective-perspective story, in which each individual saw themself, and how the different perspectives interrelated; (5) identifying leverage points to mobilize the whole system towards the agreed-upon goal; and (6) proposing specific action plans for implementing the leverage points.

In this process, people who had been in conflict with each other for many years over the right action plans and right outcomes were able to see the authenticity in and value of each other's perspective and how they each contributed to the larger goal they all desired. This opened them to new perspectives, from each other and from the collective. They also opened to new categories through this process, from anti-this and anti-that, constantly disagreeing with each other, to agreeing that they all had different contributions to the same category of pro-Vermont energy sovereignty. They also opened the category of my-efforts-alone to my-efforts-and-our-efforts. Possibly the biggest category shift was from seeing thousands of small intervention points, each spearheaded by a small group, to seeing four leverage points that they all played into. And this process opened the people to new information. Halfway through the process, they stumbled upon a great surprise: experts in each of the energy sectors (electricity, heating, transportation, and efficiency) were completely convinced that they could make a shift to 100% renewable energy in 20 years. They were each equally convinced that it would be impossible to accomplish this in the other three sectors. When they opened themselves in the conversation to new information from each other, they were shocked that they each believed it was possible, for their sector, and thus they saw that they could do it across all four sectors. Another shift across the state in new information was the ability to see who would join the effort. From the beginning to the end, they were constantly told that nobody would sign up for such a process, and definitely not for such a goal. Everyone was completely convinced of this, as this is what they always saw in Vermont, until they saw who was already in the room. This happened all the way to the governor's office, which used the outcomes from the process to guide the formation of the state's new 10-year Comprehensive Energy Plan, enacted in 2011.[9] In summary, this process leveraged three key insights from Langer's mindfulness research about openness to new perspectives, new categories, and new information to support a statewide effort to embrace an uncertain energy future.

Summary

When leaders are able to recognize and embrace the uncertainty they face, they can see how they can control the situation, they can learn about new aspects of the situation, and they can find new ways to satisfy different perspectives within the system. This recognition of uncertainty allows the leader to grow, and it enables the leader to develop a dynamic, not static, relationship with their environment (Dunoon & Langer, 2011).

Through four cases, we saw leaders who consciously engaged in the uncertainty they faced. We saw how they were able to do that more mindfully through organizational practices (see Table 24.1), and the benefits they received from it. Increasing the mindfulness of leadership increases the quality of available knowledge, proposed solutions, organizational engagement, and outcomes. It also positively impacts the perception people have of the leader. We hope that through mindful leadership of the uncertainty your organization faces, you as a leader can now begin to unleash greater power within your organization.

Table 24.1 Translation of mindfulness insights into organizational practices.

Mindfulness attribute	Mindful suggestion	Organizational practice	Organizational processes/ frameworks
New perspectives	Ask	Stakeholder inquiry	Appreciative inquiry, multiple stakeholders
New categories	"Could be"	Situation/context	Scenario planning, double-loop learning
New information	Directly observable, discernible	Refutation	Scorecards, storybusting

Notes

1. For more on the nation's first statewide energy-efficiency utility, Efficiency Vermont, see efficiencyvermont.com
2. For more on the Vermont case, see ecosynomics.com
3. For an example of energy systems modeling done in Vermont, using mediated modeling, see Participatory Energy Planning in Vermont, Department of Public Service in Vermont (http://www.publicservice.vermont.gov/planning/mediatedmodeling.html).
4. An example of the relatedness school is the two-year statewide process of the Council on the Future of Vermont (futureofvermont.org).
5. An example of the vision school is the Vermont Governor's Commission on Climate Change (http://www.anr.state.vt.us/anr/climatechange/GovernorsCCCWebsite/index.html).
6. We presented an earlier version of this chapter in Langer and Ritchie-Dunham (2013).
7. For applications of Langer's mindfulness research to strategic processes with leaders in Europe, Latin America, and the USA, see Ritchie-Dunham and Puente (2008) and Ritchie-Dunham (in press).
8. You can see the experiment and its impact on "The Young Ones" at (http://www.bbc.co.uk/programmes/b00tq4d3). This program was also nominated for a BAFTA award (http://www.bafta.org/television/awards/winners-2011,2394,BA.html).
9. To see Vermont's new Comprehensive Energy Plan, which was heavily influenced by this process, visit http://publicservicedept.vermont.gov/publications/energy_plan or contact the Energy Action Network.

References

Argyris, C. (1977). Double loop learning in organizations. *Harvard Business Review, 55*, 115–125.

Argyris, C. (1993). *Knowledge for action: A guide to overcoming barriers to organizational change*. San Francisco, CA: Jossey-Bass.

Carson, S., Shih, M., & Langer, E. J. (2001). Sit still and pay attention? *Journal of Adult Development, 8*(3), 183–188.

Chanowitz, B., & Langer, E. J. (1981). Premature cognitive commitment. *Journal of Personality and Social Psychology, 41*, 1051–1063.

Dunoon, D., & Langer, E. J. (2011). Mindfulness and leadership: Opening up to possibilities. *Integral Leadership Review, 11*(5). Retrieved from http://integralleadershipreview.com/3729-mindfulness-and-leadership-opening-up-to-possibilities/

Freeman, R. E. (1984). *Strategic management: A stakeholder approach.* Boston, MA: Pitman.

Georgantzas, N. C., & Acar, W. (1995). *Scenario-driven planning: Learning to manage strategic uncertainty.* Westport, CT: Quorum.

Godet, M. (1987). *Scenarios and strategic management: Prospective et planification stratégique.* London, UK: Butterworths.

Kaplan, R. S., & Norton, D. P. (1992). The balanced scorecard: Measures that drive performance. *Harvard Business Review, 70*(1), 71–79.

Karsten, A. (1928). Mental satiation. In J. De Rivera (Ed.), *Field theory as human science.* New York, NY: Gardner Press.

Langer, E., & Piper, A. (1987). The prevention of mindlessness. *Journal of Personality & Social Psychology, 53*(2), 280–287.

Langer, E. J. (1989a). *Mindfulness.* Cambridge, MA: Perseus.

Langer, E. J. (1989b). Minding matters: The consequences of mindlessness–mindfulness. In L. Berkowitz (Ed.), *Advances in experimental social psychology* (Vol. 22, pp. 137–173). San Diego, CA: Academic Press.

Langer, E. J. (1994). The illusion of calculated decisions. In R. Schank & E. Langer (Eds.), *Beliefs, reasoning and decision making.* Hillsdale, NJ: Erlbaum.

Langer, E. J. (1997). *The power of mindful learning.* Reading, MA: Addison-Wesley.

Langer, E. J. (2009). *Counterclockwise: Mindful health and the power of possibility.* New York, Ballantine Books.

Langer, E. J. (2010). A call for mindful leadership. In *HBR blog network/imagining the future of leadership.* Boston, MA: H. B. Review.

Langer, E. J., Bashner, R. S., & Chanowitz, B. (1985). Decreasing prejudice by increasing discrimination. *Journal of Personality and Social Psychology, 49*(1), 113–120.

Langer, E. J., & Brown, J. P. (1992). Control from the actor's perspective. *Canadian Journal of Behavioural Science, 24*(2), 267–275.

Langer, E. J., Chanowitz, B., Palmerino, M., Jacobs, S., Rhodes, M., & Thayer, P. (1990). Nonsequential development and aging. In C. N. Alexander & E. J. Langer (Eds.), *Higher stages of human development: Perspectives on adult growth* (pp. 114–136). New York, NY: Oxford University Press.

Langer, E. J., & Ritchie-Dunham, J. L. (2013). El Liderazo con Mente Abierta. In C. Díaz-Carrera & A. Natera (Eds.), *El Coraje de Liderar en la Democracia del S. XXI*, Madrid.

Langer, E. J., & Rodin, J. (1976). The effects of choice and enhanced personal responsbility for the aged: A field experiment in an institutional setting. *Journal of Personality and Social Psychology, 34*(2), 191–198.

Leaf, A., & Hulbert, N. (2010). *An assessment of ecosynomics at THORLO, with implications and possibilities.* Harrisville, NH: Institute for Strategic Clarity.

Popper, K. R. (1959). *The logic of scientific discovery.* London, UK: Hutchinson.

Ritchie-Dunham, J. L. (in press). *Ecosynomics: The science of abundance.*

Ritchie-Dunham, J. L., Morrice, D. J., Anderson Jr., & Dyer, J. S. (2007). A simulation exercise to illustrate the impact of an enterprise system on a service supply chain. *INFORMS Transactions on Education, 7*(3). Retrieved from http://archive.ite.journal.informs.org/Vol7No3/Ritchie-DunhamMorriceAndersonDyer/

Ritchie-Dunham, J. L., & Puente, L. M. (2008). Strategic clarity: Actions for identifying and correcting gaps in mental models. *Long Range Planning, 41*(5), 509–529.

Ritchie-Dunham, J. L., Throneburg, J. L., Leaf, A., & Hulbert, N. (2010). *Brand stewardship: Living ecosynomics at THORLO.* Harrisville, NH: Institute for Strategic Clarity.

Rodin, J., & Langer, E. J. (1977). Long-term effects of a control-relevant intervention with the institutionalized aged. *Journal of Personality and Social Psychology, 35*(12), 897–902.

Scharmer, C. O. (2007). *Theory U: Leading from the future as it emerges.* Cambridge, MA: Society for Organizational Learning.

Senge, P. M. (1990). *The fifth discipline.* New York, NY: Doubleday Currency.

Throneburg, J. L. (2011). *THORLO leadership and employee handbook: The structure-process of integration.* Statesville, NC: Second Registry Leadership Academy Press.

Wack, P. (1985). Scenarios: Shooting the rapids. *Harvard Business Review, 63*(6), 139–150.

25

Mindfulness at Work

Michael Pirson

Introduction

Mindlessness at work has become a global touchstone of mockery, and entertainers have enchanted audiences worldwide with comedies featuring mindless managers (including *The Office* or *Office Space*). Steve Carell, playing the role of Michael Scott as Regional Manager of a Dunder-Mifflin branch in Scranton, PA, epitomizes mindless behavior, which is characterized by a reliance on old, often outdated categories and a reduced awareness of one's social and physical world. While some argue that mindlessness is a necessity in the work environment, a closer examination reveals that mindlessness is rarely, if ever, beneficial, because it closes us off to possibility, freezes our responses, and prevents needed change (Langer, 1989; Langer & Moldoveanu, 2000). In this chapter, I will outline how mindfulness can be beneficial in the work environment and in the organizational context. To do so, I will (1) give a brief overview of the mindfulness notions and their convergence; (2) provide perspectives on mindful management; and (3) highlight organizationally relevant impacts of mindfulness with regard to (a) organizational culture, (b) learning and innovation, and (c) decision-making.

Mindfulness Conceptions

Western-scientific tradition versus Eastern-Buddhist tradition

Mindfulness from a Western-scientific perspective is a construct pioneered by Ellen Langer (1989). Langer's conceptualization of mindfulness grew out of her work examining mindlessness, described as follows: "When in a mindless state, an individual operates much like a robot; thoughts, emotions, and behaviors (hereafter just

The Wiley Blackwell Handbook of Mindfulness, First Edition.
Edited by Amanda Ie, Christelle T. Ngnoumen, and Ellen J. Langer.
© 2014 John Wiley & Sons, Ltd. Published 2014 by John Wiley & Sons, Ltd.

behaviors) are determined by 'programmed' routines based on distinctions and associations learned in the past" (Bodner & Langer, 2001, p. 1). Langer theorizes that
mindlessness is often a consequence of premature cognitive commitments or the tendency to apply previously formed mindsets to current situations, which lock individuals
into a repetitive unelaborated approach to daily life. Langer argues that we develop
mindlessness in two very different ways, through repetition or through a single exposure to a piece of information.

In contrast, Langer's conceptualization of mindfulness, which was conceived
entirely within a cognitive information-processing framework, is defined "[a]s a general style or mode of functioning through which the individual actively engages in
reconstructing the environment through creating new categories or distinctions, thus
directing attention to new contextual cures that may be consciously controlled or
manipulated as appropriate (Langer, 1989, p. 4).

Mindfulness, alternatively, is often regarded as a secularized adaptation of Eastern
Buddhist tradition. Accordingly, mindfulness is commonly defined as moment-to-
moment awareness without judgment (Thera, 1962) or "paying attention in a particular way: on purpose, in the present moment, and nonjudgmentally" (Kabat-Zinn,
1994, p. 4). Clinical psychology has made significant advances in conceptualizing and
measuring mindfulness as a meditative concept focusing on attention, awareness and
absence of judgment. Kabat-Zinn and colleagues have even developed mindfulness-
based interventions that are designed to increase mindfulness in the span of several
weeks through intensive meditative trainings.

The Western-scientific approach to mindfulness differs from the meditative, Eastern
approach in that meditative approaches are usually aimed at the inner experience of
the participant and involve nonjudgmental observation (Yeganeh, 2006). Traditional
spiritual orientations of mindfulness maintain that clearing the mind and living in the
moment enable an individual to access objective truth in the world, a concept called
veridical perception, or seeing the world as it is (Yeganeh, 2006). Western-scientific
interventions in contrast, usually include the treatment of material external to the individual participants (Baer, 2003; Langer, 1989). It pursues a learning agenda, can be
very goal-oriented, and involves the use of mindfulness in enhancing problem solving and other cognitive exercises (Baer, 2003; Langer, 1989). Yeganeh (2006) suggested that meditative mindfulness assumes that without momentary experience, we
become overengaged in subjective thoughts of past and future, and hence stray from
the reality of our present experience. Langer and colleagues place less of an emphasis
on momentary experience and emphasize continually acquiring many perspectives that
can reflect the complex world around us and then being flexible with them in various
contexts. Accordingly, mindfulness can be more formally understood as an active state
of mind characterized by novel distinction-drawing that results in being (1) situated
in the present, (2) sensitive to context and perspective, and (3) guided (but not governed) by rules and routines (E. Langer, 2009; E. J. Langer, 1989, 1997). This social
psychological conceptualization of mindfulness reflects three interrelated components
(Pirson, Langer, Bodner, & Zilcha, 2012), including (1) novelty seeking, (2) novelty
producing, and (3) engagement.

Yeganeh (2006) suggested ways to integrate Western and Eastern perspectives
by adding a notion of awareness and attention to the above-mentioned three

components. Although similar, mindfulness in the Western tradition comes about in a different, more immediate, way. Mindfulness is thus easier to learn, which makes it appealing to those unwilling to sit still to meditate.

Individual and organizational perspectives

Mindfulness from both perspectives has been shown to affect a plethora of cognitive, affective, and behavioral outcomes on the individual level. Mindfulness has been shown to positively affect outcomes such as creativity, physical well-being, and psychological well-being. While originally developed as an individual concept, it was then transferred to the organizational level in the context of research into error-free, reliable performance in high-reliability organizations (Weick & Sutcliffe, 2006; Weick, Sutcliffe, & Obstfeld, 1999). Based on Langer's conceptualization of mindfulness organizational scholars have convincingly argued that it affects organizational outcomes, for example, organizational safety climates (Weick et al., 1999; Weick & Sutcliffe, 2007), organizational attention (Weick, & Sutcliffe, 2006), IT security (Butler & Gray, 2006), creativity (Langer, Pirson, & Delizonna, 2010), innovation and learning (Levinthal & Rerup, 2006), adaptation, and performance (Albert, 1990; Rerup, 2005; Senge, 2006; Sternberg, 2000). Albert (1990) argued that mindfulness is an organizationally relevant social psychological concept, which has yet to be fully explored. Mindfulness in the work context is still underresearched, but progress has been made.

Mindfulness as an individual level concept can be affected by social and organizational environments. Research related to mindfulness in organizational contexts most often refers to a decidedly Western-scientific notion of mindfulness, a sociocognitive approach. Weick and Sutcliffe (2006) suggested that in that literature, the "prevailing way to conceptualize mindfulness has been to borrow from Ellen Langer's (e.g., 1989) ideas" that center on cognitive aspects of mindfulness including novelty seeking, novelty producing, and engagement. Weick and Sutcliffe (2006; Weick, Sutcliffe, & Obstfeld, 1999) themselves were extensively drawing on Langer's conceptualizations and defined mindfulness as a rich awareness of discriminatory detail generated by organizational processes. In 2001, they refined Langer's perspective when describing mindfulness as "the combination of ongoing scrutiny of existing expectations, continuous refinement and differentiation of expectations based on newer experiences, willingness and capability to invent new expectations that make sense of unprecedented events."

Levinthal and Rerup (2006) similarly understood mindfulness in an organizational context as an extension of Langer's sociocognitive perspective of mindfulness when they described it as "high sensitivity of perception and high flexibility of behavior to respond to diverse, changing stimuli (p. 505). They further suggested that mindfulness represents a conversion of experience into reconfiguration of assumptions, frameworks and actions (p. 507).

Integrating both perspectives on mindfulness Jordan, Messner, and Becker (2009, p. 468) defined it as a "state of mind or mode of practice that permits the questioning of expectations, knowledge and the adequacy of routines in complex and not fully predictable social, technological, and physical settings." Resolving how mindfulness in organizations can exist, they posited that it is important to understand that mindfulness does not exclude or oppose the idea of routines, but may in fact build upon routinized action (Levinthal & Rerup, 2006; Rerup, 2005). Therefore, they argued it can be regarded as an *organizational* phenomenon that, while grounded in individual mindful behavior (Weick & Roberts, 1993), also builds upon organizational mechanisms. Accordingly, such *collective* mindfulness is realized on (1) the level of direct interaction in dyads or small groups and (2) a more general level that comprises the rules and routines that help organize mindfulness (Jordan et al., 2009, p. 468).

Mindfulness measurement

Growing interest in mindfulness as a way to enhance psychological and physiological treatment has led to several attempts to operationalize and measure mindfulness based on an Eastern-Buddhistic perspective. Whereas such scales can be easily applied in the clinical setting, they are less conducive to action-oriented Western settings, for example, within organizational contexts. Langer's Western-scientific approach allows for more consistent usage of mindfulness theory within social contexts. A new 14-item scale of Langer's Mindfulness conception can help assess such organizationally relevant effects of mindfulness (Pirson et al., 2012).

Mindful Management

In contrast to Michael Scott of "The Office," mindful managers are aware of the social, cultural, and historical contexts, and are able to free themselves of existing and outdated categories.

Diversity management

One area in which mindful management is increasingly relevant is the area of diversity management. In one episode of "The Office," Michael Scott is assembling a basketball team from among his colleagues to play against the Warehouse crew. After naming himself to be on the team, he also asks his favorite office mate (Ryan) to join, who turns out to be really unmotivated. He then selects an African-American colleague, who he believes to be a great basketball player, simply because of his heritage. He turns down others who eagerly want to join the team but are either Hispanic ("I will use your skills come baseball season"), overweight, or female. Unsurprisingly, his team can barely keep up with the other team and can only come up with a tie using unfair means of play. A more mindful manager certainly would have been able to draw novel distinctions beyond the stereotype and be able to understand that skillsets can vary within and beyond categories of demographics. Even though this is a very stark example of a mindless manager, the current trends towards more diversity from a legal as well as performance-oriented perspective requires managers to be more mindful about the strengths and weakness of each individual member of the team and the organization. Especially in the hiring process, mindful distinction-making can be helpful to hire the right candidate rather than a cookie-cutter graduate. As Stuart Albert already suggested in 1990, an increasingly heterogeneous and multiethnic work force and the growing globalization of the economy make understanding prejudice and overcoming a central managerial task. In one experiment by Langer, Bashner, and Chanowitz (1985), a mindfulness training resulted in less indiscriminate discrimination. The participants were encouraged to create new categories by supplying multiple responses (vs. one response) to slides of handicapped and nonhandicapped individuals. After this training, subjects indicated who they wanted on their team for activities such as checkers, soccer, and so on, for which a given handicap might or might not be relevant. The results indicated that those given training in making mindful distinctions learned that handicaps are function-specific and not people-specific; in short, they learned that disability depends on context (Langer et al., 1985). Such training may help incoming managers as well not only to deal with diversity but generally to be more mindful about individual strengths and weaknesses of potential team members.

Motivation

Mindful management could also help overcome motivational problems of coworkers. Routine-induced boredom is most often cited as a reason for low levels of employee engagement (Csikszentmihalyi, 1996, 2003). Through mindful management such routines can become part of mindful engagement, specifically when they are viewed as general guides but not fix rules. Langer and Piper (1987) showed how one of the most "mindless" activities, watching television, was successfully transformed into a mindful and engaging exercise. The experiment highlights that it is not necessarily the routine itself that renders our work-life boring but our mindless perspective of it. If there are ways to engage in the work from different perspectives (such as finance, marketing, or logistics, or from the perspective of a supplier, customer, or investor), we can easily see how such routine work can become more engaging relevant and meaningful (see also Grant, 2008).

Negotiation and conflict resolution

Mindful management can also be helpful in social situations in which different interests may provide potential for conflict (Riskin, 2002, 2010). As much as the general managerial rhetoric has embraced win–win (or even triple-win) solutions as negotiated outcomes, the more surprising is how pervasive standard negotiation tactics have become. A negotiation seems to be, a priori, a very context-sensitive situation in which many participants may not even know what potential options exist for either them or other parties involved. As such, there is a lot of room for mindful distinction making of the various and potential interests, wishes, and emotional longings as well as a lot of potential room for the creative production of novel outcomes. However, negotiation is often taught as if negotiation participants have a clear utility function, which can be identified (Malhotra & Bazerman, 2007). Consequently, the negotiation process merely constitutes the detection of a balance of such interests. It is a very outcome-oriented perspective, which leaves out the process of negotiating that very much seems to influence potential outcomes.

To highlight this problem, consider a negotiation exercise where parties are confronted with the information that one party wants 8 eggs and the other party 7 eggs, while there are only 10 eggs to go around. The usual negotiated outcome is a split of 5 and 5. With a bit of further probing, the parties could find out that one party is only interested in the egg white and the other in using the yolks, so that everyone could have easily been satisfied and granted their entire need. This shows in many ways that negotiation is an exercise in mindfulness. Mindful managers are aware of the context and question given information by being aware of the traps of unquestioned assumptions. Mindful managers view negotiation as a creative process that cannot be predicted based on prior notions of interest and outcomes. Negotiation is reflected in the various aspects of mindfulness including engagement, novelty seeking, and novelty producing.

Strategy

Mindful management is also characterized by a general process focus. In business, however, there is a strong tendency to focus on the outcomes such as the bottom line. Langer (1989) pointed out that such a focus on outcomes can prevent managers from understanding how such outcomes are achieved by blinding them to process aspects. That mindless approach can lead to suboptimal, and even unethical, practices. Studies find that 20% of quarterly reports are indeed manipulated at any given time (Radovsky, 2012). There are other dysfunctional aspects of outcome focus that result in a disregard for experimentation, learning, and innovation that are often viewed only as costs. Using that output perspective arguably leads to bandwagon effects in which managers copy practices of the leading companies (determined by outcomes such as market size, profitability, etc.). Langer (1989, p. 46) stated that "when we envy other people's assets, accomplishments, or characteristics, it is often because we are making a faulty comparison. We may be looking at the results of their efforts rather than the process they went through on the way." A mindful manager is able to understand processes and their context sensitivity. Some processes might work better in one cultural setting than in another. Mindful managers try to develop context-specific processes instead of trying to force, for example, American employees to become more like the Japanese to manage quality (as often happened in the 1980s).

Langer's research suggests that paradoxically, by focusing on process and not outcome, one may improve both. Mindful managers understand that and try to refrain from being forced to manage for outcomes such as shareholder value maximization. In fact, the main reason why Google set up a special structure for being listed publicly was to avoid the mindless pressure of analysts so that they could still focus on product development.

Mindfulness and Its Organizationally Relevant Impacts

Whereas the above description of mindful management is nonexhaustive, it simply highlights the relevance of mindfulness for management. In the following part,

I wish to outline several ways mindfulness can further be of organizational relevance. In general, mindfulness can be an aspect of a humanistic, high-performance organizational culture. It can impact and affect organizational learning, creativity and decision-making in organizational contexts. Mindful managers will be able to support all these aspects, but they exceed the realm of individual managerial influence and become part of the organizational setup and structure.

Organizational culture

Mindlessness can be part of the cultural makeup of an organization. Any bureaucracy is suspect to routine-oriented employees following the letter of the law, rule, and stipulation without reflecting on appropriateness for a given context. The character, Milton, in the movie "Office Space" exemplifies such a mindless bureaucrat, which can only function in a culture that values mindless behavior. The main character of this film, Peter, ultimately gets fed up by this mindless culture after three different bosses ask him whether he had read a memo that specified the use of a rather irrelevant TPS report. This story, although fictional, highlights how a culture of mindlessness can lead employees to unhappiness, or what Gallup calls active disengagement. Active disengagement occurs when employees start undermining the company by sabotaging its operations. In "Office Space," Peter and his two coworkers take revenge and plot to tweak the payment system so that small sums of customer payments will be transferred to their account.

Office Space has become a cult classic, similar to Dilbert, as it highlights the mindless business culture many people experience as employees. In such a workplace, categories of thinking are rarely revisited, context rarely matters, individual differences and strengths are irrelevant to the job, while the focus remains on the execution of routines with an outcome rather than process orientation. It seems almost unsurprising that such workplace cultures take their toll on the physical and mental well-being of employees (Harter, Schmidt, & Keyes, 2003). Csikszentmihalyi (2003) and others have shown that mindful business cultures also increase the well-being of employees, which most often contributes to a better performance of the company. Psychological well-being is heightened via mindfulness not only because of higher awareness levels but also because it can buffer against depression. The ability to draw novel distinctions allows for reappraisal of situations of suffering better than mindless behavior can. Higher levels of mindfulness are also leading to higher probabilities of flow experiences (Csikszentmihalyi, 1997, 2003) and meaningful personal engagement. Pirson et al. (2012) also find that mindfulness is correlated with higher mental-health scores, higher levels of self-esteem, higher subjective well-being measures, and lower negative emotional states. Furthermore, mindful individuals are viewed as more humorous than mindless counterparts, and finally, mindfulness also leads to higher levels of job and life satisfaction (Pirson et al., 2012).

Mindful organizational cultures can most likely also affect physical well-being of employees (Crum & Langer, 2007; E. J. Langer, 2009). Organizations that foster mindful engagement with a task, such as chamber maids viewing their work as exercise, have been shown to have a positive effect on various measures of physical well-being. These effects have been explained by the salience of the mind–body connection according to which the mind and the body are not separate entities but are indeed mutually reinforcing each others' reactions (Crum & Langer, 2007). Thus, a higher level of mindfulness influences the ability of people to lead a healthy life, enjoy physical activity more, and see themselves as physically capable until old age (Pirson et al., 2012). Pirson et al. (2012) also found that higher mindfulness individuals need less rest and relaxation, because they can see their work generating positive energy.

Furthermore, they found that organizational cultures that help increase mindfulness similarly benefit employee well-being. Such effects can occur because mindfulness can influence the quality of social relationships via the ability to draw novel distinctions. This ability allows individuals to constantly reassess and mindfully interpret social actions. Low-mindfulness individuals will stick to routine judgments and stereotyping of others often missing potential alternative explanations of behavior. High-mindfulness individuals will allow for alternative explanations and possibly give the benefit of the doubt to coworkers, as such increasing the likelihood for positive relations overall. Mindfulness is found to impact the individual level of job satisfaction not only because of the higher quality of social relationships but also because a mindful reinterpretation of job tasks can counteract boredom that may ensue from routine. Similarly, employee engagement is influenced by mindfulness because the creation of novel distinctions can lead to higher levels of joy at work, higher levels of dedication to the tasks, and higher perceived ability to have an impact.

Creativity and learning

As many scholars have suggested (Levinthal & Rerup, 2006), improvisation or innovation is a result of the recombination of existing knowledge. According to Jordan et al. (2009) and Levinthal and Rerup (2006), improvisation takes at least two things: experience and creativity. Miner et al. (2001) suggested that experiential learning prior to action provides the necessary experience as building blocks, whereas mindfulness in action brings together experience and creativity. The creative recombination of these sets of action repertoires is a mindful activity.

Pirson et al. (2012) found that higher mindfulness individuals also perform better on creativity tasks, such as identifying alternative uses for a brick or a pencil. Mindfulness interventions have been shown to support product development (Langer, 1989). 3M's experience with Post-It Notes is a case in point: A glue that did not stick became a huge success through mindful reinvention (Albert, 1990). Mindfulness interventions have also been shown to overcome perceived incompetence at the beginning of a novel task (Grant, Langer, Falk, & Capodilupo, 2004) thus supporting creative engagement of participants. Other mindfulness interventions have helped reduce the negative effects of social comparisons on creativity, by focusing on process perspectives rather than outcome perspectives (Langer et al., 2010).

Various studies have also shown that learning can be improved by mindfulness interventions. For example, Langer and Piper (1987) demonstrated that by presenting information in a conditional versus an unconditional mode ("could be" versus "is") can be used to increase the chances of creative innovation. Similarly, Anglin, Pirson, and Langer (2008) found that simple changes in conditionality of instructions when presenting a set of math problems can help increase the math performance of females over males.

Langer (1997) presented a wholly new approach on education based on mindful pedagogy. She suggested that education should mindfully establish routines and practices as guides but not as absolute governing rules. Such perspectives could easily help increase learning and creativity in the workplace. In work environments, the interplay between routines and innovation becomes critical. Following Levinthal and Rerup (2006), mindful organizations, especially high-reliability organizations (Weick et al., 1999), recognize the impossibility of anticipating all problems and events in advance. For example, during the Apollo 13 mission, NASA needed to innovate and learn very quickly because the spaceship was stalled in space due to an explosion on board. According to Lovell and Kluger (1994), the mission was accomplished without loss of life because NASA was able to improvise based on rehearsed simulations. Mindful learning embraces the fact that any action is local and situated, and involves spontaneous recombination of wisdom accumulated from prior experimental learning (Levinthal & Rerup, 2006). Mindfulness in organizations is often manifested by the recombination of well-rehearsed routines (Weick et al., 1999). This argument is further developed in Bigley and Roberts's (2001) study of highly formalized and bureaucratic systems such as the Incident Command System (ICS). They found that despite popular perception, bureaucracies can also be very flexible, as an ICS can rapidly recombine people, resources, and structures to deal with unexpected situations (Levinthal & Rerup, 2006). For example, the ICS is designed to "oscillate effectively between various preplanned solutions to the more predictable aspects of a disaster circumstance and improvised approaches for the unforeseen and novel complications that often arise in such situations" (Bigley & Roberts, 2001, p. 1282).

Such interrelation of routine and innovation is well expressed through the metaphor of grammars (Levinthal & Rerup, 2006; Miner et al., 2001; Pentland & Rueter, 1994). Just as fixed grammatical rules allow people to create a larger number of sentences, organizational routines similarly allow actors to produce a variety of outcomes (Pentland & Rueter, 1994, p. 490). However, all of the above examples require what Langer (1997) calls a mindful understanding of routines as guides but not as ultimate fixated rules.

To create such an understanding and achieve collective mindfulness at an organizational level, communication is central (Jordan et al., 2009). Weick and Roberts (1993) called it "heedful interrelation" and which may take place spontaneously, for example in reaction to an unexpected event. Often, however, it is supported by interactive routines, which agents carry out quite habitually. Following Levinthal and Rerup (2006), the mutual enactment of these habitual routines comprises, on the one hand, questioning one's own knowledge and actions, and, on the other hand, questioning the knowledge and action of others (Jordan et al., 2009; Weick & Roberts, 1993). Mindfulness cultures are therefore based on activities and routines that explicitly aim at providing opportunities to question expectations and behavioral routines, and to evoke awareness of context in interaction. For example, flight attendants, pilots, and mechanics vary their checklist order to keep the process surprising and engaging (E. Langer, 2009; E. J. Langer, 1989). Similarly, Schulman (1993) observed that operators at nuclear power plants deliberately change the structure of the required paper work to be filled out to guard against mindless processing of safety-related information (Levinthal & Rerup, 2006). Similar interactive routines occur during the mutual checking and questioning practices between nurses and doctors in anesthesiology departments (Hindmarsh & Pilnick, 2007; Jordan et al., 2009) or during bungee-jump preparations (buddy-systems).

Decision-making

A central field of management research has been decision-making. As an individual-level concept, it allows an understanding of the variance and conformity of organizational strategies, reactions, and behaviors. Mindfulness research has only begun to permeate the field, but interesting findings can already be highlighted.

In recent studies, Chow (2012) found that higher mindfulness individuals are less susceptible to priming, draw on several sources of information, and end up making more balanced, more profitable, and more socially responsible investment decisions. In a test of mindfulness intervention, Shenoy (2008) found that participants make more virtuous decisions the more they articulate different perspectives on a variety of choices. They also predict their own well-being more accurately and value moral choices more highly not only retrospectively but also prospectively. This aspect is interesting, as it bridges the puzzle of bridging System 1 and System 2 decision-making (Kahneman, 2011) and provides ways for how to forego hedonistically and impulse-driven decision-making pushed for by advertisers.

On a more managerial level, Fiol and O'Connor (2003) suggested that mindful managers are able to avoid the bandwagon effects that dominate in the business world. That means they are less likely to accept general perceptions and remedies without checking for context and applicability in a specific situation. They are therefore more likely to question trends of "how to manage" as propagated by managerial magazines, books, and consultants in the field. They rely on their own judgment of the situation and draw distinctions of their own to see whether a new tool (such as the Internet), a new management approach (such as Total Quality Management) or a new innovation strategy is relevant to their own organization. Being vigilant and remaining aware of the changing environment, mindful decision makers are able to adapt more swiftly and appropriately to situational shifts.

Fiol and O'Connor (2003) argued that mindful decision makers go beyond a superficial search for information based on current trends and past behaviors (such as that which occurred in the housing crisis) and generate novel distinctions and context-dependent interpretations. Such an information search entails the scanning of current data that may or may not support existing beliefs. In addition, mindful engagement with such data means that own interpretations are regularly checked and updated to ensure perspectives most relevant to the organization. Finally, mindful decision making involves discernment as to what choices best fit a firm's unique circumstances, rather than simply following so-called "best practices."

Traditionally, such mindful engagement with the decision-making process has been neglected in decision research (Fiol & O'Connor, 2003). So far, cognition research has mostly focused on underlying decision structures as a means to enhance perceptual accuracy. Fiol and O'Connor (2003) compared such efforts to replacing an old telescope lens with a new and more powerful one, which would be in vain if nobody were actually using it. As an example of mindful decision making, they highlighted leadership choices at Griffin Hospital, during the 1980s and 1990s. Facing competitive pressures, the leaders could have followed the common wisdom of the time, either finding an alliance partner or reducing costs by cutting back on services, staff, and space. Instead, they chose a very different path and developed a strategy that fit the specific situation of the hospital. Leaders were able to identify a new customer segment, understand their needs, and develop the organizational capabilities to meet those needs (Fiol & O'Connor, 2003). These decisions have helped to turn around the organization. Not only have economic results improved but employees have become galvanized, and the hospital has become an employer of choice, as evidenced by consistent recognition as one of the 100 best places to work in the United States (Fiol & O'Connor, 2003). Similarly, Google and SAS Institute are considered leaders in their industry not because management followed existing trends of management but because their leaders decidedly chose to create a culture that fit its founders and employees' needs. As such, they were able to create a distinctive culture that now most mindless business leaders try to emulate.

Conclusion

In this chapter, I outlined the relevance of mindfulness to the work context. After outlining the various notions of mindfulness, I extended findings from mindfulness research into the managerial context, by describing mindful management in some examples. Furthermore, I specified several findings in the literature on how individual-level insights of mindfulness can be applied and strengthened within an organizational context. In summarizing, organizations can try to hire mindful people and help keep people mindful through their structures and culture. However, it seems much harder to induce mindfulness throughout mindless organizations. That may mean that we will have to laugh at many more humorous descriptions of mindlessness in the workplace in the time to come. Yet, there is sufficient hope for those not wanting to be cynical that work environments can support individual mindfulness and derive the various well-being-related benefits from it.

References

Albert, S. (1990). Mindfulness, an important concept for organizations: A book review essay on the work of Ellen Langer. *Academy of Management Review*, 15(1), 154–159.

Anglin, L. P., Pirson, M., & Langer, E. (2008). Mindful learning: A moderator of gender differences in mathematics performance. *Journal of Adult Development*, 15(3–4), 132–139. doi:10.1007/s10804-008-9043-x

Baer, R. A. (2003). Mindfulness training as a clinical intervention: A conceptual and empirical review. *Clinical Psychology: Science and Practice*, 10(2), 125–143.

Bigley, G. A., & Roberts, K. H. (2001). The incident command system: High-reliability organizing for complex and volatile task environments. *Academy of Management Journal, 44*(6), 1281–1299.

Bodner, T., & Langer, E. (2001). *Individual differences in mindfulness: the mindfulness/mindlessness scale.* Paper presented at the 13th APA Annual Meeting, Toronto.

Butler, B. S., & Gray, P. H. (2006). Reliability, mindfulness and information systems. *MIS Quarterly, 30*(2), 211–224.

Chow, E. (2012). *Mind your money: Mindfulness in socially responsible investment decision-making.* Cambridge, MA: Harvard University.

Crum, A., & Langer, E. (2007). Mind-set matters—exercise and the placebo effect. *Psychological Science, 18*(2), 165–171.

Csikszentmihalyi, M. (1996). *Finding flow: The psychology of engagement with everyday life.* New York, NY: Basic Books.

Csikszentmihalyi, M. (1997). *Creativity: Flow and the psychology of discovery and invention.* New York, NY: Harper Collins.

Csikszentmihalyi, M. (2003). *Good business: Leadership, flow, and the making of meaning.* New York, NY: Penguin Group.

Fiol, M. C., & O'Connor, E. J. (2003). Waking up! Mindfulness in the face of bandwagons. *Academy of Management Review, 28*(1), 54–70.

Grant, A. M. (2008). The significance of task significance: Job performance effects, relational mechanisms, and boundary conditions. *Journal of Applied Psychology, 93*(1), 108.

Grant, A. M., Langer, E. J., Falk, E., & Capodilupo, C. (2004). Mindful creativity: Drawing to draw distinctions. *Creativity Research Journal, 16*(2–3), 261–265.

Harter, J. K., Schmidt, F. L., & Keyes, C. (2003). Well-being in the workplace and its relationships to business outcomes. In C. Keyes & J. Haidt (Eds.), *Flourishing: The positive person and the good life* (pp. 205–244). Washington, DC: American Psychological Association.

Hindmarsh, J., & Pilnick, A. (2007). Knowing bodies at work: Embodiment and ephemeral teamwork in anaesthesia. *Organization Studies, 28*(9), 1395–1416.

Jordan, S., Messner, M., & Becker, A. (2009). Reflection and mindfulness in organizations: Rationales and possibilities for integration. *Management Learning, 40*(4), 465–473.

Kabat-Zinn, J. (1994). *Wherever you go, there you are: Mindfulness meditation in everyday life.* New York, NY: Hyperion.

Kahneman, D. (2011). *Thinking fast and slow.* New York, NY: Farrar, Straus and Giroux.

Langer, E. (2009). *Counter clockwise.* New York, NY: Ballantine Books.

Langer, E., & Moldoveanu, M. (2000). The construct of mindfulness. *Journal of Social Issues, 56*(1), 1–9.

Langer, E., Pirson, M., & Delizonna, L. (2010). The mindlessness of social comparisons. *Psychology of Aesthetics Creativity and the Arts, 4*(2), 68–74. doi:10.1037/A0017318

Langer, E. J. (1989). *Mindfulness.* Reading, MA: Addison-Wesley.

Langer, E. J. (1997). *The power of mindful learning.* Reading, MA: Addison-Wesley.

Langer, E. J. (2009). *Counter clockwise: mindful health and the power of possibility* (1st ed.). New York, NY: Ballantine Books.

Langer, E. J., Bashner, R. S., & Chanowitz, B. (1985). Decreasing prejudice by increasing discrimination. *Journal of Personality and Social Psychology, 49*(1), 113.

Langer, E. J., & Piper, A. I. (1987). The prevention of mindlessness. *Journal of Personality and Social Psychology, 53*(2), 280.

Levinthal, D., & Rerup, C. (2006). Crossing an apparent chasm: Bridging mindful and less-mindful perspectives on organizational learning. *Organization Science, 17*(4), 502–513.

Lovell, J., & Kluger, J. (1994). *Apollo 13.* New York, NY: Pocket Books.

Malhotra, D., & Bazerman, M. H. (2007). Investigative negotiation. *Harvard Business Review*, *85*(9), 72.

Miner, A. S., Bassof, P., & Moorman, C. (2001). Organizational improvisation and learning: A field study. *Administrative Science Quarterly, 46*(2), 304–337.

Pentland, B. T., & Rueter, H. H. (1994). Organizational routines as grammars of action. *Administrative Science Quarterly, 39*, 484–510.

Pirson, M., Langer, E., Bodner, T., & Zilcha, S. (2012). The development and validation of the Langer Mindfulness Scale—enabling a socio-cognitive perspective of mindfulness in organizational contexts. *Harvard University Working Paper Series*.

Radovsky, D. (2012). America's CFOs admit: Lots of companies are fudging their numbers. *Daily Finance*. Retrieved from http://www.dailyfinance.com/2012/07/26/americas-cfos-admit-lots-of-companies-are-fudging-their-number/

Rerup, C. (2005). Learning from past experience: Footnotes on mindfulness and habitual entrepreneurship. *Scandinavian Journal of Management, 21*(4), 451–472.

Riskin, L. L. (2002). Contemplative lawyer: On the potential contributions of mindfulness meditation to law students, lawyers, and their clients. *The Harvard Negotiation Law Review, 7*(1), 1–66.

Riskin, L. L. (2010). Further beyond reason: mindfulness, emotions, and the core concerns in negotiation. *Nevada Law Journal, 10*, 289.

Schulman, P. A. (1993). The negotiated order of organizational reliability. *Administrative Science Quarterly, 25*, 353–372.

Senge, P. M. (2006). *The fifth discipline: the art and practice of the learning organization* (rev. and updated. ed.). New York, NY: Doubleday/Currency.

Shenoy, B. (2008). Are virtuous choices especially valued once possessed? (Dissertation). Harvard University.

Sternberg, R. J. (2000). Images of mindfulness. *Journal of Social Issues, 56*(1), 11–26.

Thera, N. (1962). *The heart of Buddhist meditation*. New York, NY: Weiser.

Weick, K. E., & Roberts, K. H. (1993). Collective mind in organizations. Heedful interrelating on flight decks. *Administrative Science Quarterly, 38*(3), 357–381.

Weick, K. E., & Sutcliffe, K. (2006). Mindfulness and the quality of organizational attention. *Organization Science, 17*(4), 514–524.

Weick, K. E., & Sutcliffe, K. M. (2007). Managing the unexpected resilient performance in an age of uncertainty, second ed. Retrieved from http://avoserv.library.fordham.edu/login?url=http://library.books24x7.com/library.asp?´B&bookid=22786

Weick, K. E., Sutcliffe, K., & Obstfeld, D. (1999). Organizing for high reliability: Processes of collective mindfulness. *Research in Organizational Behavior, 1*, 81–123.

Yeganeh, B. (2006). *Mindful experiential learning*. Cleveland, OH: Case Western Reserve.

26

Two (or More) Concepts of Mindfulness in Law and Conflict Resolution

Leonard L. Riskin

Introduction

In 1989, I began learning—and becoming confused—about two technical concepts of mindfulness. Ellen Langer's then-new book, *Mindfulness* (Langer, 1989), which came as a gift from a wise friend, captured my attention and imagination. So did mindfulness and mindfulness meditation in the Eastern tradition, which I had recently started to study and practice. I realized, gradually, that the two ideas—for the purposes of this chapter, Eastern-derived mindfulness (EDM) and Langerian mindfulness (LM)—were not exactly the same yet had more than a little in common, including some overlapping goals, strategies, and outcomes. Even 10 years later, however, when I began introducing EDM into my teaching and training in law and dispute resolution, I was unable to grasp or explain the commonalities and differences, though I made one (inadequate) attempt to do so (Riskin, 2010), and I found almost no help in the literature, until recently (Siegel, 2007).

The explicit use of "mindfulness" in law and dispute-resolution education, training, and practice began in the late 1990s and has grown quite rapidly (Mindfulness Symposium, 2012). The vast bulk of this work is grounded on EDM. But teachers and writers have incorporated—knowingly or unknowingly—some elements of LM. Many scholars, teachers, and trainers in the mindfulness in law and dispute resolution world have only a vague comprehension of LM, and frequently fail to mention or distinguish it from EDM. The reverse also may be true: Writings on Langer's mindfulness do not typically compare and contrast it with EDM. At least until publication of this Handbook, the relationship between the two concepts has been opaque, or at best translucent. This opacity has had unfortunate consequences. In addition to fostering conflation and confusion, it has prevented efforts to use the two approaches jointly, in order to reinforce one another.

The Wiley Blackwell Handbook of Mindfulness, First Edition.
Edited by Amanda Ie, Christelle T. Ngnoumen, and Ellen J. Langer.
© 2014 John Wiley & Sons, Ltd. Published 2014 by John Wiley & Sons, Ltd.

The first section of this chapter briefly explains the two technical concepts of mindfulness. The second section explores the roles of each form of mindfulness in law and dispute-resolution education, training, and practice. Finally, the third section suggests ways in which the two forms of mindfulness can reinforce and complement one another.

More Than Two Concepts of Mindfulness

The idea that there are just two concepts of mindfulness is a bit misleading. First, in addition to the two technical concepts, there is a more common meaning: to be "conscious or aware of something" (Oxford Dictionaries, Soanes, & Stevenson, 2010). When I was a child, my mother told me to "mind your manners when you visit Aunt Minnie." Likewise, if you are driving from Toronto to Toledo for the first time, you should be very mindful of the road signs—even, or especially, if you have a GPS. Restaurateurs should be aware of what belongs in their food; in this spirit, "A More Mindful Burger" graces the awnings of the Epic Burger restaurants in Chicago. The two technical ideas of mindfulness on which this Handbook focuses have something in common with this general meaning.

A second reason that it seems inaccurate to speak of two forms of mindfulness is that the literature about EDM contains countless definitions (Williams & Kabat-Zinn, 2012), some of which appear quite inconsistent with others (Riskin, 2010; Williams & Kabat-Zinn, 2012).

Given the plethora of meanings, and in view of space limitations for this chapter, I will not try to present both technical forms of mindfulness comprehensively. Instead, I will feature important parts of each that I think have potential for usefully interacting with aspects of the other; I leave for other writers, in this book and elsewhere, the task of more fully unpacking these two constructs and how they relate to one another.

EDM

EDM encompasses a variety of ideas and practices that derive, directly or indirectly, from teachings and practices of the Buddha, who lived some 2,500 years ago and who built upon even more ancient Hindu and other teachings and practices that were well known in the areas where he taught, in what is present-day India (see Chapter 4). As it is usually introduced in the West, EDM *emphasizes* nonjudgmental awareness, in contrast to—or at least ahead of—thinking or evaluation. However, the most ancient and basic teachings and practices involve a good deal of both evaluation and thinking (Anālayo, 2003; Austin, 2012), and in connection with law and dispute resolution, mindful awareness in practice seems almost inevitably *connected with* thinking.

Modern commentators who emphasize the awareness aspect of EDM have defined mindfulness in a variety of ways. Jon Kabat-Zinn, the creator of Mindfulness-Based Stress Reduction, tells us that "Mindfulness can be thought of as moment-to-moment, nonjudgmental awareness, cultivated by paying attention in a specific way, that is, in the present moment, and as nonreactively, as nonjudgmentally, and as openheartedly as possible." (Kabat-Zinn, 2005). Bhante Gunaratana explains that mindfulness goes hand in hand with concentration and that concentration requires forcing the mind to focus on something, but mindfulness decides upon what to focus (Gunaratana, 1991).

Some researchers have operationalized the Eastern idea of mindfulness, that is, turned it into a construct that they could use for research (Siegel, 2007). Bishop and colleagues, for instance, define mindfulness to include:

> the self-regulation of attention so that it is maintained on immediate experience, thereby allowing for increased recognition of mental events in the present moment...[and] a particular orientation toward one's experiences in the present moment, an orientation that is characterized by curiosity, openness, and acceptance. (Bishop et al., 2004, p. 232)

Building upon that definition, UCLA psychiatrist Daniel Siegel describes mindfulness as including an "awareness of awareness" and an attitude toward moment-to-moment experience based upon "curiosity, openness, acceptance, and love (COAL)" (Siegel, 2007, pp. 1–13).

It is important to distinguish between EDM and mindfulness meditation. A person cultivates the ability to be mindful primarily through silent meditation and then deploys it in everyday life or in performing certain tasks. The meditation practices themselves have demonstrated benefits, including: a lowered pulse rate; enhanced ability to concentrate; mental clarity; increased activity in the portion of the brain associated with happiness; and decreased activity in portions of the brain associated with unhappiness (Riskin, 2010). Mindfulness meditation grew from—and, in many presentations, remains intricately interconnected with—ancient Buddhist philosophy, psychology, ethics, and related meditative practices (Kuttner, 2010). The Buddha's principal goal in teaching was to reduce suffering, by leading a person to overcome the causes of suffering—craving, aversion, and the delusion of a continuous, separate self, from which craving and aversion spring (Olendzki, 2010). In other words, mindfulness can help a person see things as they actually are. In both ancient and modern times, some scholars and teachers emphasize certain kinds of outcomes, such as enhanced satisfaction, peace of mind, concern for others, ethical behavior, health, and performance.

A large number of studies have focused upon the impact of mindfulness on students (Shapiro, Brown, & Astin, 2011). A recent study found that two weeks of mindfulness training significantly improved the subjects' Graduate Record Examination scores (Mrazek, Franklin, Phillips, Baird, & Schooler, 2013). A current study, conducted by psychology professor, Kennon Sheldon, and law professor, Richard Reuben, will measure the impact of mindfulness meditation on first-year law students at the University of Missouri. And neuroscientist Emiliana Simon-Thomas has done preliminary research to measure the effects of mindfulness training on first-year and advanced law students at the University of California-Berkeley School of Law.

LM

Professor Ellen Langer's notion of mindfulness (see Chapter 1), which she has been developing at least since 1972, is

> an active state of mind characterized by novel distinction-drawing that results in being (1) situated in the present; (2) sensitive to context and perspective; and (3)

guided (but not governed) by rules and routines. The phenomenological experience of mindfulness is the felt experience of engagement. Noticing/creating novelty reveals inherent uncertainty. When we recognize that we don't know the person, object, or situation as well as we thought we did, our attention naturally goes to the target. (Langer, Chapter 1)

"When we are mindful," Langer tells us:

we implicitly or explicitly (1) view a situation from several perspectives, (2) see information presented in the situation as novel, (3) attend to the context in which we are perceiving the information, and eventually (4) create new categories through which this information may be understood. (Langer, 1997, p. 111; see also Langer, 1989, pp. 62–74).

This concept of mindfulness is the opposite of mindlessness, which is (again, from Chapter 1):

an inactive state of mind characterized by reliance on distinctions/categories drawn in the past. Here (1) the past overdetermines the present; (2) we are trapped in a single perspective but oblivious to that entrapment; (3) we're insensitive to context; and (4) rules and routines govern rather than guide our behavior. Moreover, mindlessness typically comes about by default not by design. When we accept information as if unconditionally true, we become trapped by the substantive implications of the information. Even if it is to our advantage in the future to question the information, if we mindlessly processed it, it will not occur to us to do so (Chanowitz & Langer, 1981). The same rigid relationship results from mindless repetition. (Langer & Imber, 1980)

The Two Concepts of Mindfulness in Law and Dispute Resolution

My understanding of mindfulness developments in law and dispute resolution is almost certainly molded by my own background and experience. So, I feel compelled to reveal something about those matters.

I have been practicing mindfulness meditation since about 1989 and, since about 1999, have been and teaching mindfulness to law students, lawyers, judges, and mediators. In 2002, I began writing about mindfulness in law and conflict resolution (Riskin, 2002). In all these activities, I have greatly emphasized EDM, as have most of the mindfulness writings and programs in law and dispute-resolution education, training, and practice. I have been heavily influenced by, and trained to teach, Mindfulness-Based Stress Reduction and the meditative practices associated with the Theravadan Buddhist tradition, and known as mindfulness, insight, or vipassana meditation. Many other lawyers who have been active in teaching mindfulness draw on these traditions, as well. Some rely more heavily on Zen or Tibetan Buddhist practices or other teachings.

Mindfulness programs for lawyers and dispute resolvers began in the US in the late 1980s, when Jon Kabat-Zinn offered mindfulness training for Massachusetts Judges

(Riskin, 2002). In 1998, he and Ferris Urbanowski taught Mindfulness-Based Stress Reduction to lawyers in the Boston law firm then known as Hale and Dorr (Id.). In 1999, attention to mindfulness made its premier in the first of several retreats for Yale Law School students (with mindfulness instruction by Joseph Goldstein and Sharon Salzberg; Riskin, 2002). Shortly thereafter, in 2002, a Symposium on Mindfulness in Law and Alternative Dispute Resolution (ADR) took place at Harvard Law School (Mindfulness in Law and ADR Symposium, 2002). In 2010, the Mindful Lawyer Conference (n.d.) drew some 165 participants from around the world to the University of California-Berkeley School of Law, which cosponsored the program with five other law schools (Mindful Lawyer Conference Website, n.d.; Mindfulness Symposium, 2012). In June 2013, a Workshop on Mindfulness in Legal Education, sponsored by the Berkeley Initiative for Mindfulness in Law, gathered 54 professors, most of whom had been teaching mindfulness in law schools for some time, from 31 law schools (Berkeley Initiative for Mindfulness in Law, n.d.).

About 30 U.S. law schools offer or recently have offered opportunities for mindfulness instruction and practice. These efforts range from noncredit courses, such as full-blown Mindfulness-Based Stress Reduction courses at the University of Missouri to specially created for-credit courses, including some with "Emotional Intelligence" in their titles, at the University of Miami and the University of Missouri; "Effective and Sustainable Law Practice: The Meditative Perspective," at the University of California-Berkeley; "Tools of Awareness for Lawyering" at the University of Florida and "Conflict Management in the Legal Profession" at Northwestern; the Inns of Court Program at George Washington University; and the Lawyer in Balance Program at Georgetown. Some faculty integrate mindfulness into more traditional courses, including Trial Practice (Zlotnick, 2012), Professional Responsibility (Rogers & Jacobowitz, 2012), Negotiation and Mediation at the University of Florida and Northwestern (Riskin, 2012); and an Intimate Partner Domestic Violence Clinic at the University of Florida. Major programs have developed at several law schools, including the University of California at Berkeley (Berkeley Initiative for Mindfulness in Law, n.d.), CUNY (CUNY Contemplative Law Program, n.d.), and the University of Miami (Miami Mindfulness in Law Program, n.d.; Rogers, 2012). At Northwestern, a full-time psychologist in the law school's student services office offers mindfulness meditation workshops, in class presentations on mindfulness and lawyering, and weekly sitting opportunities—as well as mindfulness-based psychotherapy. Vanderbilt includes mindfulness meditation in its orientation.

Mindfulness appears routinely at bar association and dispute-resolution conferences and training programs. Major symposia on mindfulness in law or dispute resolution have appeared in three academic journals—the *Harvard Negotiation Law Review* (Mindfulness in Law and ADR Symposium, 2002); the *Nevada Law Journal* (Mindfulness, Emotions, and Ethics in Law and Dispute Resolution Symposium, 2008); and the *Journal of Legal Education* (Mindfulness Symposium, 2012)—contributing to a total about 30 articles in academic law journals and many more in bar journals and popular publications. Several recent books have connected mindfulness and lawyering (Calloway, 2012; Halpern, 2008; Rogers, 2009a, 2009b; Rogers & Jacobowitz, 2012). Thousands of lawyers, law professors, judges, mediators, and law students have attended specially designed mindfulness retreats, training programs, or conferences, mostly in the US. Lawyers meet weekly for meditation sessions in places such as Denver, Portland, OR, and Seattle.

These efforts explicitly embrace or address a variety of potentially related goals, which range, at the extremes, from spiritual enlightenment to just lightening up, and include present-moment awareness; managing stress; enhancing concentration, satisfaction, and performance at work or school or in life; and improving one's ability to deal with emotions and with conflict.

Most of these programs emphasize roots in Eastern mindfulness, employ ideas and practices derived from that tradition, and generally offer little or no explanation or even acknowledgment of Langer's mindfulness. There certainly are many exceptions to this general statement. Law-school professors who teach mindfulness do so in a wide variety of ways; no widespread pattern has emerged. When I teach mindfulness, I rely very heavily on EDM. However, I generally explain LM. I also introduce Langer's definitions and examples of mindlessness, which help students notice their own mindlessness and spark a good deal of enthusiasm. Langer's wonderful explanation that, when someone is mindless, it is as if "the light's on, and nobody is at home" (Langer, 1989) helps students understand and develop insight, as do her compelling examples of mindless behavior. And I have long told my students that these stories illustrate mindlessness under both concepts, and that EDM can help foster LM. Still, along with most of my mindfulness-in-law colleagues, I emphasize EDM.

Ironically, however, since long before Langer's time, traditional legal reasoning and practice (at high levels) have required or sought many of the skills and behaviors that both characterize and produce Langer's mindfulness. In addition, new developments in legal and dispute-resolution education, theory, and practice both foster and require the qualities associated with Langer's mindfulness.

In what follows, I intend to show how the two forms of mindfulness can or do connect with education in law and dispute resolution, through two examples: legal reasoning, especially as it is taught in law schools; and working with broader perspectives, especially through alternative (or appropriate) dispute resolution.

The Lawyer's Standard Philosophical Map

A particular frame of mind or mindset has long dominated legal education and much of professional practice. I call it the Lawyer's Standard Philosophical Map:

> What appears on the map is determined largely by the power of two assumptions about matters that lawyers handle: (1) that disputants are adversaries—i.e., if one wins, the other must lose—and (2) that disputes may be resolved through application ... of some general rule of law....
>
> On the lawyer's standard philosophical map ... the client's situation is seen atomistically; many links are not printed. The duty to represent the client zealously within the bounds of the law discourages concern with both the opponent's situation and the overall social effect of a given result.
>
> Moreover, on the lawyer's standard philosophical map, quantities are bright and large while qualities appear dimly or not at all. When one party wins, in this vision, usually the other party loses, and, most often, the victory is reduced to a money judgment. This "reduction" of nonmaterial values—such as honor, respect, dignity, security and

love—to amounts of money, can have one of two effects. In some cases, these values are excluded from the decision maker's considerations, and thus from the consciousness of the lawyers, as irrelevant. In others, they are present but transmuted into something else—a justification for money damages....

...The lawyer's standard world view is based upon a cognitive and rational outlook. (Riskin, 1982)

The Lawyer's Standard Philosophical Map, and the kind of reasoning described above, dominates most law-school courses and much of law practice in certain substantive (and geographic) areas. Often, that is appropriate and necessary; for instance, in taking a traditional law-school essay examination, the students' goal is to display their ability to skillfully perform this kind of reasoning. The same is true during Socratic dialogue in the law-school classroom and, often, in practice—for instance, in understanding the legal position of a client or writing a brief to a court or a memorandum of law for your superior in a law firm. I explain legal reasoning in the next section.

Another stream also runs through parts of the curriculum at virtually all U.S. law schools. It complements the narrow focus of the Lawyer's Standard Philosophical Map by adding broader or deeper perspectives, but its influence is far weaker and less pervasive. I describe this stream in the section "Working with additional and broader perspectives on lawyering and dispute resolution."

Legal reasoning: Exemplar of the Lawyer's Standard Philosophical Map

Legal reasoning and analysis are the most distinctive and fundamental skills of a lawyer or judge. They constitute what is commonly known as "thinking like a lawyer" and have been widely accepted in common law, and perhaps Roman law, for centuries. As taught in U.S. law schools, and conducted by the most skillful lawyers, legal reasoning and legal analysis require (perhaps without mentioning them) most elements that Ellen Langer has identified with mindfulness—but principally within a bounded perspective.

The foundational tasks of legal analysis and reasoning involve identifying and working with rules of law and their application to the facts. One aspect of this work concerns identifying or distinguishing potential precedent—rules previously articulated by courts that might apply in a particular situation. If we put some of the most important ideas from Langer's mindfulness into the form of instructions or guidelines, they would read something like this:

- Be aware of context.
- Gather details, about whatever might be relevant (including other people and their situations).
- Draw distinctions (analyze).
- Look for similarities (synthesize).[1]
- Be aware of uncertainty—that facts, perceptions, and context can change and may have changed; that that they might be ambiguous; that your own views may be biased; that your information may be incomplete.
- Be aware of your own mindset or the perspective(s) through which you are viewing the situation.

- Consider the mindsets or perspectives of other concerned people, and try viewing the situation through such perspectives.
- Consider that perhaps rules need not govern the outcome but could, instead, provide guidance.

These guidelines closely resemble the basic requirements for doing competent legal analysis and reasoning, as U.S. law schools teach these skills, and not only in legal writing courses, but also in most basic courses. This method of legal reasoning has been part of the common law (and probably Roman law) for centuries (Bezemer, 1997; Kadens, 2009). When I figured this out, I realized that I (and my colleagues and predecessors) had, in a sense, been practicing Langer's mindfulness for a long time. I was as surprised as Molière's character M. Jordain, when he discovered that he had "been speaking prose without knowing anything about it" (Molière, 1670). Lawyers had been using these elements of Langer's mindfulness centuries before Langer proposed them; her great insight was that these very skills could be important in many other arenas of activity.

A traditional law school essay examination question presents a fact pattern and asks students to identify or propose, through analysis and synthesis, potentially applicable rules and how they might apply to the facts. When answering most traditional law-school essay-examination questions, the student must be fully aware of the contours of the appropriate perspective (e.g., the Lawyer's Standard Philosophical Map); draw distinctions; analogize; synthesize; and recognize ambiguities (or "issues") about the law, the facts, and their potential interactions (Llewellyn, 1930, chapter 3; Neumann, 2005; Shapo, Walter, & Fajans, 2003). The idea that "rules *guide*, but they do not *control* decision"—expressed by Llewellyn (1930, p. 180),[2] a leader of the American Legal Realism School of jurisprudence—resonates with similar language in Ellen Langer's explanation of mindfulness (see Chapter 1). The most creative work in legal reasoning involves constructing novel theories about what the law is or should be, and how it might apply to the facts, and persuading someone else—a judge or opposing lawyer, for instance—to agree with, or at least consider, that angle. The student also must grasp arguments that favor both sides.

Law students and lawyers display a very wide range of abilities in performing legal analysis and reasoning. Those who do it well are exhibiting high levels of Langer's mindfulness—or at least many of its important characteristics. And poor performance on these tasks generally results either from a failure to carry out processes associated with LM or from inadequate familiarity with potentially relevant rules of law. When Langer suggests that one can do anything mindfully or mindlessly (Chapter 1) she seems to imply that that LM has an either/or nature. If so, that would be one way in which it would differ from EDM. In the Eastern perspective, mindfulness arises and disappears moment to moment, and can function with various objects, levels, and ranges of attention

For many years, I taught basic law-school courses, such as Business Organizations and Torts, in which students take essay examinations of the sort I described above. Looking back, I think that the students who did not do well on these exams generally were less mindful (in Langer's sense) than other students. They did not adequately make distinctions and recognize commonalities; they did not sufficiently acknowledge and address uncertainties. Simply put, for students who are familiar with the potentially relevant rules of law, the major cause of poor grades is a failure to identify and address "issues"—which, in this context, are synonymous with uncertainties in the potentially relevant law, the facts, and their interaction.

Working with additional and broader perspectives on lawyering and dispute resolution

The Lawyer's Standard Philosophical Map—and the pinched perspective that characterizes the legal analysis and reasoning that operate in within its borders—offer great value and strength, in certain contexts and for certain purposes. The problem is that they also exercise control—sometimes too much of it—outside those contexts. Too often, this perspective crowds out other ways of viewing, understanding, and addressing situations—an example of Langer's "entrapment in old categories." This can interfere with common sense and otherwise impede good service to clients. Consider Professor Kenney Hegland's (1982) account of an incident in his class at the University of Arizona:

> In my first year Contracts class, I wished to review various doctrines we had recently studied. I put the following:
>
> In a long-term installment contract, Seller promises Buyer to deliver widgets at the rate of 1000 a month. The first two deliveries are perfect. However, in the third month Seller delivers only 999 widgets. Buyer becomes so incensed with this that he rejects the delivery, cancels the remaining deliveries and refuses to pay for the widgets already delivered. After stating the problem, I asked "If you were Seller, what would you say?" What I was looking for was a discussion of the various common law theories which would force the buyer to pay for the widgets delivered and those which would throw buyer into breach for cancelling the remaining deliveries. In short, I wanted the class to come up with the legal doctrines which would allow Seller to crush Buyer.
>
> After asking the question, I looked around the room for a volunteer. As is so often the case with the first year students, I found that they were all either writing in their notebooks or inspecting their shoes. There was, however, one eager face, that of an eight year old son of one of my students. It seems that he was suffering through Contracts due to his mother's sin of failing to find a sitter. Suddenly he raised his hand. Such behavior, even from an eight year old, must be rewarded.
>
> "OK," I said, "What would you say if you were the seller?"
>
> "I'd say 'I'm sorry.'"

This comment precipitated outbursts of laughter, because it was wholly outside the frame through which the class was operating—even though, in a real situation, it might have proven quite helpful.

Beginning in the 1980s, law-school and conflict-resolution education and practice have seen a huge growth in efforts to supplement this perspective with new, broader ideas. These include: selecting or building the most "appropriate" form of dispute resolution (Riskin et al., 2009); interest-based negotiation (Fisher, Ury, & Patton, 1991); the core concerns construct for working with emotions in negotiation (Fisher &

Shapiro, 2005); certain forms of mediation, such as Understanding-Based Mediation (Friedman & Himmelstein, 2008); dispute-resolution systems design (Rogers
et al., 2013); and new forms of lawyering, such as collaborative law (Tesler &
Thompson, 2007).

The most important member of this family of concepts is the distinction between
positions and interests—the foundation of interest-based negotiation, popularized by
Roger Fisher, William Ury, and Bruce Patton in *Getting to Yes* (Fisher et al., 1991). A
position is what someone says they want or are entitled to. An interest is the underlying goal, motive, or need that they seek to serve by asserting that position. To take
a simple example, Howard Aibel, when he was General Counsel of ITT, described
a dispute between an ITT subsidiary and a West Coast corporation. The two firms
had a contract under which ITT was to supply control devices to the other company, which would install them in certain appliances, which it would then sell. The
West Coast firm asserted that defects in the control devices caused it to suffer a large
loss in market share. It claimed quite a few million dollars in damages—its position.
ITT's defense, its position, was that the control devices were not defective, and in the
alternative, that even if they contained defects, the defects did not cause any legally
cognizable damage. The West Coast firm filed suit, and after years of pretrial discovery, which required extensive legal fees for both sides, the general counsels conducted
what was then called a minitrial but, for our purposes, was essentially a negotiation.
Through that process, ITT agreed to pay the full amount demanded, but it did so
through discounts on future deliveries of the control devices, in which the defects
had been corrected (Aibel, 1985). This agreement, which some would characterize
as "win–win," satisfied important interests of both companies. Both firms had major
interests in making profits. ITT had an interest in selling the corrected version of its
control device and a related interest in reputation. The West Coast firm had an interest
in a reliable supply of a well-functioning control device. The lawyer-negotiators had
converted a dispute that was based on positions into a transaction that was based on
interests.

The principal popularizers of interest-based negotiation developed these simple
guidelines for conducting it:

-Separate the people from the problem (and be soft on the people and hard on the
problem)
-Focus on interests, not positions
-Invent options for mutual gain
-Insist on using objective criteria. (Fisher et al., 1991)

By focusing on interests more than positions (which can happen in client counseling,
negotiation, and mediation), we often can develop more creative and better solutions
than if we are limited to the narrow, positional perspective discussed above.

This simple rubric for interest-based negotiation provides very useful advice. The
other new, broader or deeper ideas that I mentioned above offer similar (but not quite
so simple) templates. Although such models are very powerful, and students gain a
level of command over them, many lawyers, mediators, and others who have learned
these ideas and associated techniques and decide to use them in particular situations

sometimes fail to do so, and looking back, regret this because they think these models would have produced a better process and outcome.

The elements of Langer's mindfulness that I listed above in the form of guidelines or instructions (see section "Legal Reasoning: Exemplar of the Lawyer's Standard Philosophical Map" earlier in this chapter) would seem to be minimum requirements for working skillfully with concepts and tools related to conflict and conflict resolution. The "Appropriate Dispute Resolution" approach seeks to identify or construct the most suitable method for managing a conflict, considering all of the circumstances, including the parties' interests. This requires a good deal of analysis. Operating skillfully within each of these alternative frames also requires extensive attention to detail; legal analysis and synthesis and application of law to facts (sometimes); and deliberate employment of different perspectives, including the perspectives of others and various ways of looking at conflict. Using, or appropriately considering, interest-based processes also requires a refined understanding of context, as well as how interest and position-based approaches can interfere with each other, giving rise to the "negotiator's dilemma" (Lax & Sebenius, 1985) and the potential risks inherent in each approach.

Relationships and Interactions Between the Two Forms of Mindfulness in Law and Dispute Resolution

I have suggested above that Langer's Mindfulness would be almost essential for high-level performance in legal reasoning (in the traditional narrow frame) and in working skillfully with concepts about conflict resolution, including broader perspectives, such as those often associated with the quest for the most appropriate method of dispute resolution, management, or handling (Menkel-Meadow, 2013). In this section, I set forth some obstacles to the actual use of LM in the law and dispute-resolution areas and show how EDM can foster and reinforce LM, in part by helping overcome such obstacles. I also will suggest how LM can foster and reinforce elements of EDM.

How EDM can foster the use of LM

In both contexts that I have discussed—engaging in legal reasoning and working toward appropriate dispute resolution—students or professional who wish to use LM (for simplicity, let's say they wanted to observe details, draw distinctions, and stay anchored to the present moment) could face a number of interrelated obstacles to actually doing so, such as the following:

- An excessively self-centered orientation, which might contribute to strong negative emotions that could interfere with one's ability or willingness to look outside themselves and, for example, to draw distinctions, see things as novel, and be engaged.
- Strong negative emotions, which tend to interfere with one's ability, and willingness, to think clearly or to understand or care about other people's perspectives or interests.

- Habitual ways of thinking, feeling, and behaving. Negative emotions tend to foster "reactive" behavior, based upon habit. They also promote a self-centered focus, a lack of concern about others, and a narrow perspective.
- Inadequate skills. I refer to social skills in the context of conflict resolution and to writing skills in the context of legal reasoning.
- Insensitivity to emotions, especially those of others. In writing a legal brief or negotiating, insensitivity to the emotions of others could lead to a conduct that offended others, thus impairing one's ability to engage with them.
- Inability to focus or think clearly. A wandering mind can make it difficult to perform almost any task well (Riskin, 2010).

I realize that LM is designed to overcome some of these very problems. For instance, it suggests that a person can develop LM by drawing distinctions and observing details. At times, however, a person may not have the ability or present-moment awareness to actually do these things. They might lack a sufficient amount of a certain kind of strength. This is analogous to the situation I faced when I briefly considered trying out for my high-school football team. I believed that could I could learn all about how and when to execute a block or a tackle, but, unless I had sufficient strength and flexibility—which I might develop through training (though I probably lacked the necessary foundation)—I could not have actually performed well. EDM practice helps develop something like an emotional and cognitive muscle. And it offers specific suggestions for evoking EDM in the moment—such as the 3-Minute Breathing Space (Segal, Williams, & Teasdale, 2002, pp. 209–211) and the STOP exercise developed by the Stress Reduction Clinic at the University of Massachusetts Medical School.

More generally, EDM (through meditation and mindfulness in daily life or specific activities) can help an individual overcome these obstacles to developing and sustaining LM, in the context of law and dispute resolution, by

- diminishing attention to self-centered concerns and thereby enhancing attention and concern for others;
- reducing the strength of negative emotions and enhancing positive emotions, including compassion toward other and self;
- developing awareness of, and distance and freedom from thoughts, emotions, and habitual perceptions and behaviors;
- fostering sensitivity to the emotions of others;
- enhancing social skills; and
- strengthening concentration. (Riskin, 2010).

How LM can foster EDM

Langer's mindfulness, especially as expressed in the guidelines that I have suggested above, can help sustain EDM by providing anchors to the present moment and tools—specific suggestions for engaging with the (primarily outer) world. EDM is vulnerable to the very challenges that it is intended to address, in the same sense that the Star Wars Missile Defense System was vulnerable to a missile attack. LM can help a person surpass these challenges and to engage in the present moment.

Conclusion

Each form of mindfulness is both a path and a destination, and each includes tools that could reinforce the other. I hope that adherents and proponents of each form will try to draw on aspects of the other, rather than allowing these visions to reside primarily in separate academic and practice silos.

Acknowledgments

Many thanks to Rhonda Magee, Richard Reuben, Scott Rogers, and Helene Shapo, for helpful comments on drafts of this chapter, and to James Austin and Flint Sparks, for insightful discussions.

Notes

1. I am not certain that Langer specifically mentions synthesis, but I include it here because it seems to run in tandem with analysis.
2. There is much debate about this assertion within the legal profession.

References

Aibel, H. J. (1985). ITT mini-trial settles long-pending expensive damage suit for market share loss. *Alternatives to the High Cost of Litigation, 5*(1), 6.

Anālayo. (2003). *Sattipatthana: The direct path to realization.* Cambridge, UK: Windhorse.

Austin, J. H. (2012). *Meditating selflessly: Practical neural Zen.* Cambridge, MA: MIT Press.

Berkeley Initiative for Mindfulness in Law (n.d.). Retrieved from http://www.law.berkeley.edu/14864.htm

Bezemer, K. (1997). *What Jacques saw: Thirteenth century France through the eyes of Jacques de Revigny, Professor of Law at Orleans.* Frankfurt am Main, Germany: Klosterman.

Bishop, S. R., Lau, M., Shapiro, S., Carlson, L., Anderson, N. D., Carmody, J., ... Devins, G. (2004). Mindfulness: A proposed operational definition. *Clinical Psychology: Science & Practice, 11,* 230–241.

Calloway, D. (2012). *Becoming a joyful lawyer: Contemplative training in non-distraction, empathy, and emotional wisdom.* Hartford, CT: Deborah Calloway.

CUNY Contemplative Law Program (n.d.). Retrieved from http://mindfulnessandthelaw101.blogspot.com/p/cuny-contemplative-law-program.html

Fisher, R., & Shapiro, D. (2005). *Beyond reason: Using emotions as you negotiate.* New York, NY: Viking.

Fisher, R., Ury, W., & Patton, B. (1991). *Getting to yes; Negotiating agreement without giving in* (2nd ed.). New York, NY: Penguin Books.

Friedman, G., & Himmelstein, J. (2008). *Challenging conflict: Mediation through understanding.* Cambridge, MA; American Bar Association and Harvard PON.

Gunaratana, H. (1991). *Mindfulness in plain English.* Somerville, MA: Wisdom.

Halpern, C. (2008). *Making waves and riding the currents: Activism and the practice of wisdom.* San Francisco, CA: Berrett-Koehler.

Hegland, K. (1982). Why teach trial advocacy? An essay on never ask why, in humanistic education in law, Monograph III (pp. 68–69). Project for the Study and Application of Humanistic Education in Law. Reprinted in Riskin (1982, pp. 45–46).

Kabat-Zinn, J. (2005). *Coming to our senses*. New York, NY: Hyperion.

Kadens, E. (2009). Justice Blackstone's common law orthodoxy. *Northwestern University Law Review, 103*, 1553–1606.

Kuttner, R. (2010). What does it mean to do the *right* thing? *Nevada Law Journal, 10*(4), 407–432.

Langer, E. A. (1989). *Mindfulness*. Reading, MA: Addison-Wesley.

Langer, E. J. (1997). *The power of mindful learning*. Reading, MA: Perseus Books

Lax, D., & Sebenius, J. (1985). *The manager as negotiator*. New York, NY: Free Press.

Llewellyn, K. (1930). *The bramble bush*. New York, NY: Oceana.

Menkel-Meadow, C. (2013). The historical contingencies of conflict resolution. *International Journal of Conflict Engagement and Resolution, 1*, 32–55.

Mindfulness in Law and ADR Symposium. (2002). *Harvard Negotiation Law Review, 7*, 1–141.

Mindfulness in Law Program. (n.d.). University of Miami School of Law website. Retrieved from http://www.miamimindfulness.org

Mindful Lawyer Conference Website. (n.d.). Retrieved from http://www.mindfullawyer conference.org/

Mindfulness Symposium. (2012). *Journal of Legal Education, 61*, 684–682.

Mindfulness, Emotions, and Ethics in Law and Dispute Resolution Symposium. (2008). *Nevada Law Journal, 10*, 289–534.

Molière, J. B. P. (1670). The middle class gentleman, Act Two, Scene IV (year). Retrieved from http://www.classicreader.com/book/851/7/

Mrazek, M., Franklin, M. S., Phillips, D. T., Baird, B., & Schooler, J. W. (2013). Mindfulness training improves working memory capacity and GRE performance while reducing mind wandering. *Psychological Science, 24*, 776–781.

Olendzki, A. (2010). *Unlimiting mind: The radically experiential psychology of Buddhism*. Boston, MA: Wisdom Publications.

Oxford Dictionaries, Soanes, C., & Stevenson, A. (Eds.). (2010). *Oxford dictionary of the English language* [Kindle Edition version] (2nd ed.). Oxford, UK: Oxford University Press.

Neumann, R. (2005). *Legal reasoning and legal writing: Structure, strategy and style* (5th ed.). New York, NY: Aspen.

Riskin, L. L. (1982). Mediation and lawyers. *Ohio State Law Journal, 43*, 29–60.

Riskin, L. L. (2002). Contemplative lawyer: On the potential contributions of mindfulness meditation to law students, lawyers, and their clients. *Harvard Negotiation Law Review, 7*, 1–66.

Riskin, L. L. (2010). Annual Saltman Lecture: Further beyond reason: mindfulness, emotions, and the core concerns in negotiation. *Nevada Law Journal, 10*, 289–337.

Riskin, L. L. (2012). Awareness and the legal profession: An introduction to The Mindful Lawyer Symposium. *Journal of Legal Education, 61*(4), 634–640.

Riskin, L. L., Westbrook, J. E., Guthrie, C., Reuben, R., Robbennolt, J., & Welsh, N. (2009). *Dispute resolution and lawyers* (4th ed.). Eagan, MN: Thomson West.

Rogers, N., Bordone, R., Sander, F., & McEwen, C. (2013). *Designing systems and processes for managing disputes*. Alphen aan den Rijn, Netherlands: Wolters Kluwer.

Rogers, S. L. (2009a). *Mindfulness for law students: Using the power of mindful awareness to achieve balance and success in law school*. Miami Beach, FL: Mindful Living Press.

Rogers, S. L. (2009b). *The six-minute solution: A mindfulness primer for lawyers*. Miami Beach, FL: Mindful Living Press.

Rogers, S. L. (2012). The mindful law school: An integrative approach to transforming legal education. *Touro Law Review, 28*, 1189–1205.

Rogers, S. L., & Jacobowitz, J. (2012). *Mindfulness and professional responsibility*. Miami Beach, FL: Mindful Living Press.

Segal, Z. V., Williams, J. M. G., & Teasdale, J. D. (2002). *Mindfulness-based cognitive therapy for depression: A new approach to preventing relapse*. New York, NY: Guilford.

Shapiro, S. L., Brown, K. W., & Astin, J. (2011). Toward the integration of meditation into higher education: A review of research evidence. *Teacher's College Record, 113*(3), 493–528.

Shapo, H. S., Walter, M. R., & Fajans, E. (2003). *Writing and analysis in the law* (6th ed.). Mineola, NY: Foundation Press.

Siegel, D. J. (2007). *The mindful brain: Reflection and attunement in the cultivation of well-being*. New York, NY: W. W. Norton.

Tesler, P. H., & Thompson, P. (2007). *Collaborative divorce*. New York, NY: HarperCollins.

Williams, M., & Kabat-Zinn, J. (Eds.). (2012). *Mindfulness: Diverse perspectives on its meaning, origins and applications*. Oxford, UK: Routledge.

Zlotnick, D. M. (2012). Integrating mindfulness theory and practice into trial advocacy. *Journal of Legal Education, 61*(4), 654–664).

Further Reading

Harris, A. (2012). Toward lawyering as peacemaking: A seminar on mindfulness, morality and professional identity. *Journal of Legal Education, 61*(4), 647–653.

James, C. (2011). Law student well-being: Benefits of promoting psychological literacy and self-awareness using mindfulness, strengths theory and emotional intelligence. *Legal Education Review, 21*, 217–221.

Kabat-Zinn, J. (1994). *Wherever you go, there you are: Mindfulness meditation in everyday life*. New York, NY: Hyperion.

Kornfield, J. (2000). *After the ecstasy, the laundry: How the heart grows wise on the spiritual path*. New York, NY: Bantam.

Kornfield, J. (2009). *The wise heart*. New York, NY: Bantam.

Kruse, K. (2010). Lawyers in character and lawyers in role. *Nevada Law Journal, 10*(2), 393–406.

Langer, E. A. (1993). Mindful education. *Educational Psychology, 28*(1), 43–50.

Langer, E. A. (2005). *On becoming an artist*. New York, NY: Ballantine Books.

Langer, E. A. (2009). *Counterclockwise: Mindful health and the power of possibility*. New York, NY: Ballantine Books.

Larkin-Wong, K. (2012). A newbie's impression: One student's mindfulness lessons. *Journal of Legal Education, 61*(4), 665–673.

Magee, R. (2011). Educating lawyers to meditate? *University of Missouri-Kansas City Law Review, 79*, 535–593.

Reuben, R. C. (2011). Bringing mindfulness into the classroom. *Journal of Legal Education, 61*, 674–682.

Riskin, L. L. (2003). Decision-making in mediation: The new old grid and the new new grid system, *Notre Dame Law Review, 79*, 1–53.

Riskin, L. L. (2006). Knowing yourself: Mindfulness. In C. Honeyman & A. K. Schneider (Eds.), *The negotiator's fieldbook* (pp. 239–250). Washington, DC: American Bar Association.

Shapiro, S. L., & Carlson, L. E. (2009). *The art and science of mindfulness: Integrating mindfulness into psychology and the helping professions.* Washington, DC: American Psychological Association.

Tan, C. (2012). *Search inside yourself: The unexpected path to achieving success, happiness (and world peace).* New York, NY: HarperOne.

Tsering, T. (2005). *The four noble truths volume 1: The foundation of Buddhist thought.* Somerville, MA: Wisdom.

27

Mindfulness in Law

Scott L. Rogers

Introduction

In the past 25 years, a remarkable change has taken place within the legal profession as mindfulness has moved from esoteric concept to hot topic. In an environment known for moving with "all deliberate speed," (Woodward & Armstrong, 1979), where legal doctrine and precedent are slow to evolve, and its practitioners are paid for being cautious and certain, mindfulness is permeating the landscape and blossoming in ways and at rates that surprise even those who planted and nurtured its seeds. So barren was the field that its flourishing is causing a great many to take notice, and a surprising number to take part.

Because the law is an integral part of society, the constitutional makeup (i.e., cognitive capacity, emotional competence, and general health and well-being) of lawyers and judges affects a great many people and institutions. Accordingly, the alarming rates of depression, anxiety, and substance abuse found across the legal profession and legal education have prompted the American Bar Association and the Association of American Law Schools to spearhead efforts to better understand the causes for these concerns and to find solutions (Magee, 2011; Sullivan, Colby, Wegner, Bond, & Shulman, 2007). Mindfulness has emerged as one solution, and extensive press and media attention has helped it gain entry into a profession whose natural tendency might otherwise have been to "object, irrelevant!"

But in a profession as emotionally guarded as the law, where battles are waged daily, colleagues are adversaries, clients are bitter, jobs are scarce, hours are long, time is money, and the pressure is always on, the fact that the contemplative practice of mindfulness might not only be taken seriously but also take root is cause for its own contemplative moment. And indeed, the embrace of mindfulness within the law

The Wiley Blackwell Handbook of Mindfulness, First Edition.
Edited by Amanda Ie, Christelle T. Ngnoumen, and Ellen J. Langer.
© 2014 John Wiley & Sons, Ltd. Published 2014 by John Wiley & Sons, Ltd.

has benefitted from the wide-ranging efforts of a number of people from across the country who have persevered, over the course of many years, to develop meaningful and effective ways of sharing mindfulness practices with lawyers, law professors, law students, mediators, paralegals, and judges (Bush, 2011; Magee, 2011; Riskin, 2002; Rogers & Jacobowitz, 2012). Though the journey is still in its early stages, much can be learned from the patient and creative efforts of the many who are paving the path.

This chapter explores the inroads that have been made bringing mindfulness into the legal profession and the approaches that have helped bring it about. It looks to ways that mindfulness will benefit a profession that many see as broken, but too consequential to fail, in terms of both the personal lives of lawyers and the approaches to practicing law and resolving conflict. Attention is also given to aspects of legal culture that are at odds with a contemplative practice, while also exploring deeper elements of the law with which a contemplative practice resonates.

The first section, "Watering the Seeds of Mindfulness in Law," traces the evolution of mindfulness in the legal profession beginning in 1984, where it received brief mention in an obscure law-review article, to its formal entry in 2002 into the legal community at Harvard Law School, and to the flurry of activity that followed in the years leading up to the convening of The Mindful Lawyer Conference in Berkeley in 2010. The second section, "The Blossoming of Mindfulness in Law," looks at the impact of the 2010 Berkeley Law conference and explores the landscape of mindfulness in the law today, as law schools are institutionalizing mindfulness programs, state and local bar associations are forming mindfulness groups, law faculty and psychologists are researching the efficacy of mindfulness training on law student well-being and resilience, and lawyer conferences are flush with mindfulness programming. These observations suggest that much has taken place in the past 25 years, and indeed the legal profession has opened its eyes to the important role mindfulness can play in helping to stabilize, clarify, and transform. Still, given the vast number of attorneys licensed to practice in this country (more than one million) coupled with the extraordinary role of law in society, there is much more ground to cover, including consideration given to the skillful means by which this ground is to be traveled. The third section, "The Growth of Mindfulness in Law," focuses on some of the different approaches and methods that law faculty and lawyers are using to introduce mindfulness to legal professionals, and to facilitate the integration of mindfulness into legal education and law practice. Attention is given to Jurisight®, a program I developed specifically for introducing mindfulness to legal professionals and which forms the basis of a collection of lawyers workshops and law school classes.

As you read these words, it is likely that you have noticed a large elephant standing nearby. And indeed, a conversation that brings together mindfulness and the legal profession is prone to surprise some and baffle others. Yet leaders of the mindfulness in law movement have long regarded the integration of the two as not only fitting but necessary to the well-being of the legal profession, its members, and even society. The final section of this chapter concludes by noting this paradox—that "mindfulness" in the context of the law elicits such interesting reactions while at the same time expressing its fundamental nature. Because flora that thrive amid harsh environments can be especially hardy, instances where mindfulness is taking root in the law may offer helpful guidance to those interested in integrating mindfulness across many aspects of society.

A preliminary matter

At the outset, it is helpful to note that there are a variety of approaches to mindfulness that have been shared with members of the legal profession. As will be explored, these include those derived from various wisdom traditions, modern adaptations of these traditional approaches, and contemporary practices developed through the lens of psychological insight and experimental research. One might observe that they all involve "paying attention." But exactly what "paying attention" means, how it is to be accomplished, and whether there might not be something more than "paying attention" that is of crucial concern to the practice and its teaching are questions with overlapping, and sometimes conflicting, answers. This diversity of approaches, while at times a source of debate among those deeply committed to their particular practice, in the context of the law, serves well the challenge of making mindfulness available to large numbers of people with very different personalities, backgrounds, and interests. For example, attorneys with a strong interest in reducing their stress levels, or with insight into how a sitting practice may awaken a deeper understanding of who they are, or benefit their effectiveness as a lawyer, are often inclined toward a more meditative approach. Others, however, with less of a felt need to manage stress or for greater self-awareness, or who are not interested in developing a meditative practice, or feel unable to do so, are more likely to be interested in cognitive-oriented practices—which carry with them their own capacity to awaken self-wonder, sharpen focus, reduce stress, and enhance well-being.

One area of great importance to legal professionals for which different approaches to mindfulness offer insight and relief is working with uncertainty. Indeed, much of the distress experienced by lawyers can be traced to the uncertainty inherent in the objectives they pursue coupled with their desire for greater certainty. This is a theme that runs through this chapter, as it offers a subject matter that illuminates the larger conversation, and a few minutes' attention to the ways meditative and nonmeditative approaches address this issue may be instructive.

A traditional meditative mindfulness approach to working with uncertainty—and the stress, anxiety, and worry that it can engender—involves learning to sit and notice the thoughts, feelings, and body sensations that arise in relationship to the uncertainty (Chodron, 2003; Hanh, 1999). Doing so, and it is challenging to say the least, offers one the potential to recognize the cues that trigger the discomfort, sense the ways that they may be perceiving more of a threat than there actually is, and come to appreciate their capacity to bear the discomfort and move forward with optimism and courage (Kabat-Zinn, 1990, 2006; Salzberg, 2002). Through this process, one may well find oneself less reactive and better equipped to respond in ways that can be productive and helpful to oneself and those around. This practice, in its most classic form, invites one to sit in quiet space, pay attention to the breath, and, when, one notice one's mind moving off into distraction (i.e., away from the breath), to return attention to the breath. Because it is an experiential practice, a connection to its "benefits" is somewhat murky, and it is through the sitting itself that a direct connection to these objectives might be realized. Hence, if one is uninterested in the practice or finds oneself unable or unwilling to sit, this connection may be too elusive to inspire sustained interest.

An alternate approach to cultivating mindful awareness that does not involve meditation, per se, is found in the work of Ellen Langer and others, who looked to more cognitive oriented approaches of attending to present-moment experience (Langer, 1989, 1997, 2009; Langer & Piper, 1987). Having well researched the tendency to default to "mindlessness" (Langer & Abelson, 1972; Langer, Blank, & Chanowitz, 1978), Langer encourages lawyers to, for example, take a few moments and notice things in their present surroundings that they had not noticed before—the quirky grain of the wood on their desk, the shape of eye glasses being worn by a colleague, the leaves on trees swaying outside their window. While a meditative practice may lead one to appreciate these nuances more naturally and spontaneously, Langer approaches it as if from reverse and encourages a direct cognitive engagement. She invites lawyers to expand their judgments of self and others by looking to complementary interpretations that take into account that they are not stable and independent of context. "Obsessed" might be regarded as "Concerned," "Bull-Dog" can be seen as "Committed," and "Mean" is understood as "Afraid." Doing so allows one to free oneself from fixed conceptions, see the larger perspective found in each moment and interpersonal interaction, and create new categories for enriching arguments, writings, and collaboration. With regard to working with "uncertainty," Langer invites us to shift deliberately from a personal attribution of uncertainty to a universal attribution. In doing so, one appreciates that "uncertainty is the rule for all of us and not just for the individual" (Langer, 2005; Langer & Moldoveanu, 2000). Lawyers who don't have an answer to the question "will we win this motion?" but think it is "knowable" may, out of insecurity and fear, overreact to the inquiry by unnecessarily retreating or recklessly charging forward. In retreating, they miss opportunities, and charging forward, they can mislead, offer unsound advice, and feel undue stress as the future plays itself out, and the answers come to be known. In contrast, lawyers who adopt a universal attribution of uncertainty are more likely not to take personal those times when they do not know the answer, more comfortably acknowledge that such is the case, be freed to engage in more productive problem solving, and sleep better at night.

While these two approaches appear to be distinct, they share many overlapping qualities. It might be said that they offer different paths along the same journey. Out of a more contemplative approach, the world begins to be viewed much as Langer advocates. And through Langer's approach, one may gain an interest, and perhaps capacity, to engage in a more contemplative manner of paying attention. For example, Langer's discussion of a universal attribution of uncertainty connects to traditional mindfulness teachings of impermanence, and the invitation to "pay attention" whether to one's breath or to something new surely share a great deal in common. The biggest difference may be the question of whether mindfulness practice is intended as an end in itself or a means to a more "concrete" end. And ultimately, this distinction too may collapse on itself. With this backdrop in mind, let us turn back the clock 25 years to a time when mindfulness was very new to the law and many of its practitioners, and the stirrings of something important and powerful were being felt.

Watering the Seeds of Mindfulness in Law

The lush ivy gripping the towers that adorn Yale and Harvard law schools in the late 1990s welcomed the spouting of an ancient strain that would signal the arrival of a contemplative practice that shares its patient and hardy resilience. At Yale, it was a series of student retreats led by one of America's great mindfulness teachers; at Harvard, it was a law-review symposium revolving around an article that would come to define a movement, events that together mark the formal introduction of mindfulness in legal education and the legal profession (Halpern, 2008; Magee, 2011; Riskin, 2002).

While these events loom large, the seeds of mindfulness in law had begun sprouting at least 15 years earlier, breaking through the soil and appearing in law-review articles—the erudite academic treatments of new, unresolved, and important legal issues (Anderson, 1996; Burns, 1990; Elkins, 1984; McHugh, 1994). Though it is unclear what effect these writings had on the profession, we can infer that their authors are representative of a larger number of law faculty and lawyers then grappling with the role mindfulness might play in their personal and professional lives, and across the profession—considerations very much at play today. The landscape of these earlier writings emerges more as an open field, assorted flowers in various stages of bloom. Whether some of these flowers flourished or, absent progeny, dropped back into the field, leaving it slightly more fertile than it had been, is difficult to know. Their presence, however, is noteworthy for the telltale signs they offer of the ways in which mindfulness was influencing lawyers and the manner by which they sought to share it.

Early scholarly writings

The following discussion draws from the handful of law-review articles that appeared between 1984 and 1996, the various ways mindfulness was being considered and introduced to the legal profession. Not surprisingly, these early treatments—which draw upon the writings and works of Zen masters (Thich Nhat Hanh, Bernie Glassman, and Sunru Suzuki), modern-day teachers (Jon Kabat-Zinn), and social psychology researchers (Ellen Langer)—are generally restrained and in some cases limited to short passages contained within a much larger conversation on a separate topic. Because of limitations in the database technologies of the 1980s and 1990s, these articles do not reference one another and have received very little attention, even within the mindfulness-in-law community.

The manner by which the term "mindfulness" was perhaps first introduced into legal academia arose out of a law professor's desire to offer his students a richer relationship to their work as lawyers. In his 1984 article, "Ethics: Professionalism, Craft, and Failure" (Elkins, 1984), Professor James Elkins looks to mindfulness as a means to connecting more deeply to one's work with clients and to one's relationship to the practice of law. Reflecting on his piece 28 years after its publication, Elkins notes that his focus was not on mindfulness as the term is now in use (J. Elkins, personal communication, August 2012). Inspired by Robert Pirsig's classic *Zen and the Art of Motorcycle Maintenance* and Carla Needleman's *A Work of Craft*, Elkins sought to weave concepts from these writings into a deeper conversation on the topics he was teaching his students.

Elkins does not dive into a discussion of mindfulness (which appears 18 pages into his article); rather, he first aligns with legal giant, Karl Llewellyn, and his commentary on the inherent richness of law practice and its connection to the liberal arts: "The truth, the truth which cries out, is that the good work, the most effective work, of the lawyer in practice roots in and depends on vision, range, depth, balance, and rich humanity" (Elkins, 1984, quoting K. Llewellyn, 1962). Having tethered his argument to one of the law's most solid figures, Elkins makes the case for mindfulness as a means to achieve a higher quality work product, writing that "mindfulness is reflected in the craft as the skill of getting something done right and doing it well, opposed to the mere act of completion or just getting it done" (Elkins, 1984). Notwithstanding the influence of Pirsig's classic work, Elkins does not mention any contemplative practice or tradition. Nonetheless, he defines mindfulness in a way that conveys a sense of the term that bridges a contemplative Eastern perspective with more modern Western treatments:

> Mindfulness means care, awareness and thoughtfulness but it is not the same thing as purpose or competence. Purpose and competence suggest a linear dimension of work and life, purpose helps us get from one place to another, from one case and one client to another. Mindfulness gives feeling and depth to the client and case at hand. The state of mindfulness gives us presence in the very moment at which we engage the client, in the moment of our choice to employ our skill and our knowledge in one way rather than another.

While Elkins' contribution may have carved out a patch of land and planted the seeds of mindfulness into a new terrain, the next watering of these seeds would not take place until 6 years later when law professor, Michael Burns, shared the insights of Zen master, Thich Nhat Hanh, and the eloquent voice of contemplative elder, Ram Dass, to inform the debate on affirmative action in education (Burns, 1990). This integrated approach is one that will emerge more fully in legal scholarship and the practice of lawyers in the decades to follow.

Burns devotes a considerable portion of the piece to explaining how mindfulness practices may play a meaningful role in more fully assessing the value of controversial policies aimed at restoring social justice. In doing so, he offers readers a thoughtful discussion of the Buddhist teachings of dependent coarising and craving, and how such insights relate to challenges faced in the United States to the acceptance and implementation of affirmative action policies. The writings of Thich Nhat Hanh, Ram Dass, and Joanna Macy are offered to address how a spiritual practice can, on the one hand, enhance a sense of despair through a deeper felt sense of suffering in the world and our interconnectedness, but also serve as an antidote to the ways our "intellect can be used to protect our heart" (Burns, 1990, p. 454). Drawing on his experience in Sri Lanka where he was exposed to a Buddhist society that embraced affirmative action policies, Burns introduces readers to the practices of mindful walking and mindful sitting as a means for beginning this inquiry and practice.

Whereas Elkins found strength in the company he chose to keep, and Burns found it by centering the conversation around affirmative action, in *Zen and the Art of Lawyering* James McHugh found it in the invitation to speak at a law-school memorial lecture (McHugh, 1994). This approach will become a familiar refrain in the years to come, as lawyers and judges invited to participate in a law-review event or speak at a bar function will use the opportunity to introduce mindfulness. McHugh, who was then general counsel to the American Bar Association, elaborated on the American Bar Association's 1992 call for the development of fundamental lawyering skills and professional values in law school. Perhaps taking a cue from Burns, McHugh looks to the wisdom of Zen masters, Bernie Glassman ("Honor your work"), Peter Matthiesson ("Your life is whatever you are doing right now"), and Shunryu Suzuki ("With beginner's mind there are many possibilities"). It didn't hurt that Glassman had recently been quoted in the Wall Street Journal (Gupta, 1992).

Sensitive to the means by which such insights are introduced to the legal community and perhaps seeking a sense of balance, McHugh looks to the writings of Ellen Langer (1989), suggesting that Langer's social psychological orientation may communicate the subject matter "in terms that are perhaps more accessible by our western minds" (McHugh, 1994, p. 1301). In doing so, he offers a practical application of her writing in the context of legal practice:

> Langer describes mindfulness as being open to new information—willing to hear even the information we do not like. Another essence of mindfulness is being able to look at issues from different points of view—seeing the perspectives of opposing attorney, the judge, the jury, the layman, the public. Another is being able to create new categories and contexts—for example what we see as a problem will look entirely different if we can view it as an opportunity.

McHugh's reference to Langer marks an important moment in the evolution of mindfulness in law, as it looks to an approach that does not draw on traditional meditation practice to cultivate mindful awareness. In essence, he is saying that lawyers can become more mindful without having to meditate. In addition, it is noteworthy that McHugh does not focus on stress reduction but instead attends to the way mindfulness may enrich one's effectiveness as a lawyer, a message that will emerge more fully in the years to follow.

In a piece that further brings together East and West, attorney Warren Anderson claims mindfulness practice is "critical" in the practice of law (Anderson, 1996). Exploring a pragmatic role for mindfulness in legal practice, Anderson writes "when I meet with my client I want her to have my complete attention." For support, he quotes Shunryu Suzuki and Thich Nhat Hanh. Anderson bemoans "not doing an adequate job" helping his clients find long-term help dealing with physical and emotion pain and points to the work of Jon Kabat-Zinn and Mindfulness-Based Stress Reduction (MBSR) as a resource to share with them. MBSR, which Kabat-Zinn developed in 1979 to help hospital patients deal with pain, had received a lot of attention for helping people relate more effectively to a host of emotional and physical challenges. In 1993, a few years prior to the publication of Anderson's article, the Stress Reduction Clinic that Kabat-Zinn established at UMass Medical

School was featured in the Bill Moyer's 1993 public television series, "Healing and the Mind."

MBSR and the legal profession

Anderson's reference to MBSR is a harbinger to an event that would take place two years later, in 1998, when MBSR was introduced at the highest echelons of the law, and it harkens back to 1987, when MBSR was first introduced to a group of judges, an event that, while remarkable, has received little attention (Kabat-Zinn, 1990, 2006; Magee, 2011; Riskin, 2002). The passage of a decade between these two events and the dearth of other mindfulness offerings during this period offer strong circumstantial evidence of the approach–avoidant relationship between mindfulness and the legal profession and to the challenge of introducing mindfulness to the profession in a way that has traction. As will be discussed, this traction—which began to take hold in the early years of the 21st century—likely required the direct involvement of lawyers in the sharing of mindfulness, and to the skillful deployment of traditional mindfulness teachings and practices so as to facilitate its accessibility.

As the new century approached, the emergence of mindfulness in the context of law took a variety of forms, most notably as a means of stress reduction. The practice of law was becoming especially focused on the bottom line, leaving attorneys feeling increasingly stressed and burned out. Moreover, the anxiety provoked by the uncertainty inherent in so many aspects of law practice was only compounded by a culture that not only admired but demanded a continual attitude of certainty and showing of confidence. With a cadre of lawyers trained in MBSR, mindfulness began to be talked about and promoted as a stress-management tool for lawyers (Weiss, 1997). Though feeling "less stressed" is often regarded in mindfulness circles as a state that can emerge along with the cultivation of mindful awareness, and not as a primary "objective," the West has been quick to look to mindfulness as a means of stress reduction that was becoming a much needed salve to the increasingly stressful practice of law. The stressful aspects of legal education also were being addressed with greater vigor by legal educators and commentators concerned with the disturbing rates of anxiety, depression, and substance abuse among law students (Benjamin, Kaszniak, Sales, & Shanfield, 1986; Krieger, 2002; Schiltz, 1999; Sheldon & Krieger, 2004).

In 1998, Jon Kabat-Zinn and Ferris Urbanowski, a senior teacher at the Stress Reduction Clinic, took on the challenge of sharing mindfulness with lawyers in one of Boston's most prestigious law firms, the 450-attorney, Hale & Dorr. Sensitive to finding the skillful means with which to introduce mindfulness to lawyers, Urbanowski modified aspects of the MBSR curriculum to be responsive to the kinds of challenges attorneys faced in their daily lives. On two occasions between 1998 and 1999, Urbanowski worked for 8 weeks with more than 70 Hale & Dorr attorneys, meeting with them for 2 hr, once a week, and asking them to practice each day for 30 min. Self-report inventories administered before and after the 8-week program revealed positive findings in the areas of improved focus and well-being. To help facilitate conversation among the participants who were initially reserved (the groups of approximately 40 included senior partners on "down" to first-year associates), Urbanowski had them meet in smaller groups, which greatly facilitated dialogue and led to participants feeling a strong sense of connection (F. Urbanowski, personal communication, October 2012). The program, though, was discontinued when the law firm's managing partner retired from his position (J. Kabat-Zinn, personal communication, 2012).

As word began to spread about the mindfulness program at Hale & Dorr, lawyers, concerned about the growing epidemic of lawyer stress and the lack of civility in the profession, began contributing articles on mindfulness to lawyer journals, which are often distributed to large numbers of attorneys through their bar memberships. The Hale & Dorr experiment served as fertile ground for discussion. To buttress lawyer receptivity, authors were quick to point out the mindfulness work being done with the Chicago Bulls, the L.A. Lakers, and the U.S. Rowing Team to manage stress and build concentration (Friedman, 2001; Porter, 2001).

The journal articles went one step further than most of the earlier law-review articles by traipsing into the territory of describing mindfulness practices and offering tips for bringing mindfulness into the workday. Though a departure from the more rigorous MBSR regimen of practice for up to 45 min a day (which itself was a departure from the more rigid and time-consuming traditional practices upon which it was founded), these authors sought to ease entry into the practice by suggesting, for example, paying attention to the breath during the day "for five minutes or even five seconds" (Friedman, 2001), and finding mindfulness reminders to breathe upon hearing the ringing of a telephone or pressing the "start" button on a copier (Weiss, 1997). As will be explored later in this chapter, the tailoring of the mindfulness discussion, along with the variety and length of prescribed practices, is very much at play within the legal profession today. Accompanying this inquiry, the question of what constitutes mindfulness practice and what might dilute the practice, an issue that has been explored in traditional mindfulness circles, is also being addressed in the legal community, especially among those who view mindfulness as a spiritual practice (Magee, 2011; Porier, 2010). Also later in this chapter, examples are provided of contemporary mindfulness practices that are aimed at easing the suffering associated with the lawyer's chronic need to know the answers to questions that can only become known through the passage of time.

The MBSR training at Hale & Dorr, coinciding as it did with the publication of Steven Keeva's *Transforming Practices: Finding Joy and Satisfaction in the Legal Life* (Keeva, 1999), signaled a turning point in receptivity to mindfulness by members of the legal profession. That shift is marked by events taking place at two of America's finest law schools. But before we leave MBSR and turn our attention to New Haven in 1998 and Cambridge in 2002, it is worth traveling back in time to 1987 and to a rare instance in which mindfulness moved from contemplative practice to law practice— from cushion to bench.

Sitting on the bench

Much like the morning glory blooms beautifully and fades fast, mindfulness blossomed in Western Massachusetts, when Jon Kabat-Zinn introduced MBSR to a group of judges in 1987, and then faded quickly, as a similar event would not take place again for many years; yet it was significant enough to inspire a judge to share mindfulness with his courtroom and perhaps influence the turning of the wheels of justice (Kabat-Zinn, 2006). That the criminal trial involved the prosecution of Amy Carter and Abbe Hoffman, along with a cast of supporting characters that include Daniel Ellsberg, and ironically Kabat-Zinn's father-in-law, and namesake, Howard Zinn, begins a discussion best left for another day. But the high-profile nature of the matter and powerful integration of mindfulness into the law, through the weaving of a mindfulness instruction into a jury instruction, are part of the story worth telling now.

In 1987, Jon Kabat-Zinn taught an 8-week MBSR course to a group of trial judges from Western Massachusetts. One of the judges who attended the workshop was Richard Connon, who, later that same year, would preside over the criminal trial of Carter and Hoffman (Kabat-Zinn, 2006). Knowing that the trial would involve a great deal of testimony and evidence that would be difficult for the jury to keep straight, Connon thought it would be helpful to provide the jury with a mindfulness instruction (Richard Connon, personal communication, October, 2012). In the charge to the jury before the evidence was presented, Connon instructed:

> It is important that you understand the elements of the case. It is also important that you pay attention with the terminology that I became aware of some time ago of mindful meditation. Mindful meditation is a process by which you pay attention from moment to moment. It is also important that you maintain an open mind, that you make no determination on this case until all the evidence has been submitted for your consideration. (Kabat-Zinn, 2006; Trial Transcript, retrieved from www.themindfuljudge.com/charge.html)

Judge Connon went on to integrate elements of this mindfulness instruction in other trials, especially when he felt the volume of evidence and testimony might overwhelm the jury, and for which a reminder to slow down and take in the material "moment by moment by moment" would be important (Connon, personal communication, October, 2012). Connon and a group of his colleagues emerged from the MBSR training and another stress-reduction program, inspired to write a book on stress-reduction for judges (Scannell et al., 1994).

As fate would have it, one of the defense attorneys at the trial, Tom Lesser, was a longtime mindfulness practitioner who, as one might imagine, was pleasantly stunned when he heard the judge deliver the mindfulness-oriented jury instruction. It was Lesser who subsequently recounted the story to Kabat-Zinn, and a telling of the history of mindfulness in law would not be complete without acknowledging the quiet role played by the numerous and largely unnamed Tom Lessers of the legal community. As a young man during the late 1960s, Lesser had taken a year off from law school to travel abroad and spent time in India where he was first introduced to mindfulness. Tom returned to America, having become friends with Sharon Salzberg, Joseph Goldstein, and Jack Kornfield, and to law school, which would prepare him for a successful legal practice and the ability to do a great deal of good for many. His mindfulness practice is now going on 45 years, and he serves the mindfulness community at large by organizing an annual retreat at Garrison Institute (T. Lesser, personal communication, 2012). While this chapter largely focuses on the attorneys who are working directly with members of the legal profession, the indirect role of attorneys like Tom Lesser has an impact that cannot be underestimated and perhaps forms the bedrock for much that is happening today.

Vipassanā at Yale

In 1998, just as Hale & Dorr's attorneys were being introduced to MBSR, Yale Law Professor, Robert Burt, opened the doorway to a profoundly rich series of mindfulness experiences for Yale law students. Burt was not a mindfulness practitioner (though in my conversations with him, I am taken by his natural embodiment of many mindfulness traits), and when asked by his Yale Law School classmate from 25 years earlier, Charlie Halpern, to serve as academic sponsor to a mindfulness program, Burt agreed. Financially supported by the Cummings Foundation, a philanthropic organization that Halpern then ran, the program involved a once-a-year weeklong mindfulness retreat at a beautiful and peaceful center located not far from New Haven.

There are few today who would not be challenged to muster sympathetic joy at the knowledge that these small group gatherings were led by Joseph Goldstein (Boyce, 2010; Halpern, 2008). In addition to being one of the foremost mindfulness teachers in the west, Goldstein was an ideal choice, given his penetrating intellect and lucid and accessible communication of Buddhist teachings. The Vipassanā retreat included instruction in mindfulness meditation, group sittings, and discussions that applied Buddhist insights to the life of the law student and lawyer (Goldstein, video interview, 2012; G. Burnett, personal communication, October 2012; S. Salzberg, personal communication, 2012). Sensitive to context, Goldstein and Halpern sought to find a balance between a traditional Buddhist program and one that more explicitly raised the practical applications of mindfulness practice to the challenges of being a lawyer (J. Goldstein, personal communication, January 2013). With many in attendance finding the program to be a meaningful and resonant experience (White, 1999), the event marks an important moment in the history of secular Buddhism and serves as an instructive roadmap for those interested in offering mindfulness training to the legal profession.

At the conclusion of the retreat, Burt invited students to gather in his office one evening each week and practice the sitting meditation they learned at the retreat. As Burt recollects, one of the most powerful aspects of the sittings was listening to a guided meditation recorded by Goldstein, as it recalled for many the transformative power of the retreat (R. Burt, personal communication, 2012). These annual retreats and the weekly sittings continued for three years—with mindfulness luminaries like Sharon Salzberg leading portions—until 2001 when Yale declined to take on the funding of the program. The retreats, however, continued as the Center for Contemplative Mind in Society, which Charlie Halpern had cofounded in 1997, expanded the offering, inviting law students, law professors, and lawyers from across the country to gather for an annual event at Spirit Rock Meditation Center, known as the "Meditation Retreat for Law Professionals" (Magee, 2011; Rogers & Jacobowitz, 2012).

While the Yale program, which had centered on law students, had come to an end, the methodology employed—mindfulness training for students accompanied by an ongoing opportunity to practice mindfulness at the law school—serves as a model being implemented in law schools across the country today. As Yale's contribution to the garden flowered during these three fertile years, a nearby section of the garden was being tended to by a group of academics, writers, and practicing lawyers at Harvard Yard.

Mindfulness at Harvard

Charlie Halpern not only played a role in bringing about the Yale Law School program, and the lawyer's retreat at Spirit Rock, but, in his capacity as Chair of the Center for Contemplative Mind in Society, also set in motion the events that would result in a Harvard Law School symposium that focused on mindfulness and the law. The Center for Contemplative Mind in Society, through the American Council of Learned Societies, awarded a fellowship to University of Missouri-Columbia law professor, Leonard Riskin, who used the funds to integrate mindfulness into a course called "Understanding Conflict." Riskin drew upon his experience and growing concentration on mindfulness to produce an article that introduced readers to mindfulness and set forth the state of mindfulness in the law (Riskin, 2002).

Fortuitously, Riskin did not receive an offer to publish the piece at a primary law review before he was offered publication by the Harvard Negotiation Law Review. The article received extensive attention, partly because the law review also convened a live symposium and published a print symposium on mindfulness in law and alternative dispute resolution (ADR). Riskin's article served as the centerpiece with five contributing authors commenting on Riskin's thesis (that mindfulness practice would not only reduce stress of members of the legal profession but also offer a skillset that would improve one's effectiveness as a law student and attorney) and offering further discussion on the role of mindfulness in law practice (Harvard Negotiation Law Review Symposium Issue, 2002).

Riskin, who, as an experienced mediator and negotiator, is adept at choosing his words carefully, begins his introduction by asserting that lawyers and law students across the country "are meditating." So as to hone this observation around the particular kind of meditation Riskin practices and shares with others—mindfulness meditation—Riskin elaborates: "They observe their breath, their body sensations, their emotions, and their thoughts" (Riskin, 2002). With these opening remarks, Riskin unabashedly established mindfulness meditation, a method he notes was developed thousands of years earlier by the Buddha, as a worthwhile consideration within law study and practice. In the years to come, he would develop "Tools of Awareness for Lawyers," a class for introducing mindfulness to lawyers and law students (Riskin, 2010), and, along with his collaborator, Rachel Wohl, would conduct workshops and integrate creative approaches for teaching mindfulness to lawyers, judges, law students, mediators, and other legal professionals.

As any good lawyer making their case, Riskin followed this concise statement of fact by preemptively acknowledging the seeming incongruity of an inwardly oriented practice being embraced by an outwardly oriented group (Riskin, 2002, p. 3, fn. 1). He then offered compelling support for his argument by looking to other groups that have benefitted from mindfulness training, including the Chicago Bulls, the L.A. Lakers, Monsanto Corporation, and a unit of the Green Berets. Riskin articulated two primary problems lawyers and law students can expect to lessen through mindfulness practice: (1) high levels of unhappiness, stress, and depression; and (2) missed opportunities to excel in their work as lawyers. He asserted that these challenges are, in part, due to "narrow, adversarial mind-sets that tend to dominate the way lawyers think and most legal education is structured" (Riskin, 2002, p. 8). Riskin aimed to persuade readers that mindfulness meditation can reduce distress and loosen the mind-states that lead to missed opportunities. Interestingly, his insight that mindfulness practice can soften a lawyer's narrow "mind-set" found support in Ellen Langer's writings on mindfulness, which offered pragmatic and accessible ways of cultivating mindful awareness (Langer, 1989, 1997, 2009). Riskin was aware of Langer's work, acknowledging the substantial overlap between Eastern conceptions of mindfulness and her approach, along with significant differences (Riskin, 2002, n. 108).

Riskin included a general discussion of what mindfulness practice entails, drawing on Kabat-Zinn's definition of mindfulness as "paying attention in a particular way: on purpose and in the present moment, and nonjudgmentally." Rather than focusing on mindfulness instruction, as he will do in later years, Riskin traipsed into the experiential with personalized accounts of lawyers and law students of the benefits they received through their exposure to mindfulness. His scope was broad enough to allow for meaningful commentary across a range of subjects, and indeed, the five articles offered in reply to Riskin anticipated a great many of the issues that would be explored in the coming decade. William Blatt of Miami Law suggested that mindfulness could not be practiced separate and apart from spirituality (Blatt, 2002). Clark Freshman, also of the University of Miami School of Law ("Miami Law"), and colleagues, wrote on the scientific underpinnings of mindfulness practice (Freshman, Hayes, & Feldman, 2002). Douglas Codiga, from the University of Hawaii, commented on the future of mindfulness in the legal profession (Codiga, 2002). Steve Keeva, with the ABA, contributed a piece on lawyer well-being (Keeva, 2002). And Scott Peppet, of the University of Colorado Law School (Colorado Law), invited the provocative question "Can saints negotiate?" suggesting that the mindful lawyer might be at a disadvantage given the wide berth lawyers enjoy in the negotiation realm and the liberal rules governing it.

During this time frame, lawyers with a mindfulness practice began to participate in facilitating law-related events. Though mindfulness teachers, primarily of the Buddhist tradition, would continue to lead lawyer workshops and retreats organized by attorneys, the involvement of lawyers in teaching at these events marks an important change that, in time, would promote interest across the broader legal profession. For example, Mary Mocine, a lawyer turned Zen priest, taught mindfulness workshops for lawyers at bar associations, law firms, and even the San Francisco Zen Center. Attorney, Dennis Warren, collaborated with mindfulness teacher, James Baraz, and conducted a lawyer workshop at Spirit Rock. Professor Riskin collaborated with Ferris Urbanowski in teaching a series of workshops on mindfulness and negotiation. These courses taught mindfulness not only as a way of dealing with stress but also to develop insight and compassion, and to improve conflict-related practices and satisfaction (Riskin, 2002). Mindfulness was popping up at more law schools too, as law

professors, either by themselves or working with mindfulness teachers, began con-
ducting mindfulness workshops and offering mindfulness classes to students. Schools
such as University of Missouri-Columbia Law School (Missouri Law), UNC School
of Law, Harvard Law School (Harvard Law), Cardozo School of Law, Marquette
University Law School, Touro Law School (Touro Law), Miami Law, Stanford Law
School, Suffolk University Law School, University of Denver Sturm College of Law,
UC Hastings, University of San Francisco Law School, and CUNY School of Law
(CUNY Law) either had programs for students or were the venue for lawyer programs.
Importantly, while the number of lawyers with mindfulness practices was growing, the
heart of many of these programs made explicit the connection to Buddhist teachings,
and participation was often a self-selected group that represented a minority of stu-
dents and attorneys.

In the years to follow, insightful and focused academic treatments, legal symposia,
lawyer workshops, law school classes, and conferences would emerge not as isolated
events conducted by a small collection of committed individuals, but as repeated offerings facilitated and organized by a growing number of lawyer-practitioners.

Nourishing the field of mindfulness in law

The number of law-review and journal articles published before 2002 and the number
of lawyer and law-student workshops to have taken place by that time, though modest,
supported the decision to hold the Harvard Law symposium. Some likely envisioned
that the symposium and its national exposure would contribute to a rapid acceleration
of articles and mindfulness programs while others likely anticipated the event would
amount to little more than a flash in the pan. Yet less than a decade later, on the other
side of the country at UC Berkeley School of Law (Berkeley Law), hundreds of lawyers,
judges, law students, and law faculty would congregate on a beautiful fall weekend to
learn and practice mindfulness, and to discuss the ways it had been and can be infused
more fully into the landscape of the legal profession. This event was coordinated by
Douglas Chermak, then Law Program Director of the Center for Contemplative Mind
in Society, in collaboration with faculty from law schools across the country, including
Berkeley Law, University of Florida College of Law (Florida Law), University of San
Francisco School of Law (USF), University of Buffalo School of Law, and CUNY Law.
The following summarizes the events taking place during these intervening years so
that we might glimpse the evolving methods and approaches that coincided with an
accelerating pace of activity. This discussion is by no means exhaustive and serves to
highlight but a representative sample of such events.

Law-school symposia

Between 2002 and 2012, at least five law-school symposia directly addressed mindfulness or were oriented around a theme to which mindfulness is a natural compliment.
In 2004, Professor Marjorie Silver and colleagues and students organized the symposia: "Lawyering and its Discontents: Reclaiming Meaning in the Practice of Law"
at Touro Law School, during which mindfulness was discussed. Arising out of the

symposia, the Touro Law Review published articles on stress and burnout (Silver, 2004), the comprehensive law movement (Daicoff, 2004), and ways of finding meaning in the practice of law (Silver, 2004).

Following the formation in 2007 of the "Balance in Legal Education" section of the American Association of Law Schools amid growing concern for law-student and lawyer well-being, especially in the areas of anxiety and depression, Washburn University School of Law convened a 2007 "Humanizing Legal Education Symposium" that packed in an extraordinary collection of plenary and concurrent presentations addressing lawyer and law-student stress, happiness, and well-being (Schwartz, 2008). While mindfulness was not its primary focus, Professor Rhonda Magee, a leader in the area of mindfulness and law, spoke on "The Mindful Law Professor" and the value of law faculty teaching and modeling mindfulness (Magee, 2007, 2009, 2013b).

In 2010, with a growing number of mindfulness articles circulating in mainstream academia, University of Nevada-Las Vegas Law School held a "Mindfulness, Emotions and Ethics" symposium. As in 2002, Professor Leonard Riskin contributed a centerpiece article on mindfulness, emotion, and negotiation (Riskin, 2010), to which eight law faculty, psychologists, and lawyers fashioned replies containing fresh insights and more finely detailed applications of mindfulness in law (Calloway, 2010; Freshman, 2010; Kruse, 2010; Kuttner, 2010a; Reilly, 2010; Shapiro, 2010; Stempel, 2010; Waldman, 2010).

Law-review articles

Since 2002, numerous writers haven taken on the challenge of integrating mindfulness into one or more areas of the law and the relevance of mindfulness to the lives of lawyers. In addition to those pieces, discussed above, written as part of a law-school symposium, many other have emerged on their own, as law reviews began to recognize the importance of mindfulness and its applicability to numerous subject areas. These include: ethics in dispute resolution (Riskin, 2009); community lawyering (Alfieri, 2012; Harris, Lin, & Selbin, 2007); compassionate practices and lawyering (Cantrell, 2010a, 2010b); negotiation (Bader, 2010; Bowling, 2010; Izumi, 2010; Freshman, 2006, 2010; Pounds, 2004), mediation (Riskin, 2003, 2004; Rock, 2006); and judicial decision-making (Maroney, 2011; Ramirez, 2009; Seamone, 2002). While most of these articles do not focus on Buddhism, a handful explicitly discuss the role of Buddhist teachings in areas ranging from working with anger to the adversarial process and deception (Ellinghausen, 2006; Kuttner, 2010b; Sturgeon, 2011).

Law-magazine articles

As more and more lawyers are being introduced to mindfulness and becoming excited about its prospects for the profession, lawyers and judges increasingly are penning articles on mindfulness for lawyer journals and magazines. These articles grapple with issues of mindfulness and professional responsibility (McIntire, 2009); stress (Adcock, 2008; Cohen, 2012; Cormack, 2009; Starzynski, 2009, 2010); civility (Gold, 2012); trial practice (Jacobowitz, 2013; Tropin, 2012); communication (Bronstad, 2008);

mediation (Fisher, 2003); law practice (Hyman, 2007; Rhoads & Williams, 2011; Zeglovitch, 2006); productivity (West Allen, 2009); finding meaning in the practice of law (Williams, 2010); and the formation of mindfulness groups for lawyers (Masich, 2010; Rogers, 2011, 2012b). At the same time, reporters for national lawyer magazines are being asked to write articles on mindfulness in legal education and law practice (Gillespie, 2013; Sloan, 2012).

With the legal community taking note of the beneficial role mindfulness can play across many facets of a lawyer's professional life, this connection is being recognized in magazines directed toward a nonlawyer audience. For example, the May 2010 issue of the Buddhist publication, *Shambhala Sun*, included an article in its *Mindful Society* column titled, "The Law of Mindfulness," which looked to the work being done nationally by attorneys sharing mindfulness with members of the legal profession (Boyce, 2010). More recently, one of the first issues of the newly minted *Mindful* magazine included in its "In the Workplace" column Professor Rhonda Magee's observations on the role of mindfulness, and other forms of meditation, in working with bias (Magee, 2013a).

Scientific research

In 2005, neuroscientist, Sara Lazar, and colleagues reported that mindfulness practice was associated with a thickening of regions of the middle prefrontal cortex and inversely related to age-related thinning of the cortex (Lazar et al., 2005). These findings and the explosion of neuroscience research to follow examining the impact of mindfulness practice on changes to the brain's structure and function began to be discussed in mindfulness circles and included in many mindfulness presentations. Prior to this time, compelling research had found that mindfulness practices could be helpful to people working with a variety of health and emotional difficulties. But there was something about the tangible and viewable changes to the brain itself that many lawyers and judges found exceedingly compelling. Not surprisingly, to the long-term lawyer practitioner, these effects were neither surprising nor much of a cause for approaching the practice differently. But among those looking to mindfulness for the first time, or who had not yet developed a serious practice, these findings were especially noteworthy and inspiring. Earlier research by Lazar includes work she conducted with Herbert Benson, finding brain regions associated with attention and control of the autonomic nervous system activated during meditation (Lazar et al., 2000). And indeed, the groundbreaking work of Herbert Benson, who made popular the "relaxation response," set the stage for the public's receptiveness to meditation and to the widespread awareness of the health benefits of a simple and straightforward meditation practice (Benson & Klipper, 1975).

I had wanted to devote myself more fully in developing and offering mindfulness programs for lawyers as early as 2003. It wasn't until the neuroscience research began to appear in the popular press, however, that I felt the time was right. In 2007, I conducted the workshop "Mindfulness, Balance & The Lawyer's Brain," a Florida continuing legal education (CLE) approved program and among the first to integrate not only mindfulness and law, but also neuroscience (Rogers, 2007). While neuroscience research and its relationship to mindfulness and law practice comprised a modest portion of the 2-day, 10-hr program, the subject matter was of great interest to many, and several found it to be a compelling reason to practice. Today, many mindfulness programs for lawyers mention and elaborate on neuroscience research, both to educate and to inspire, and, at times, to appease the skeptic. In 2009, I, along with Judge Alan Gold and Professors Leonard Riskin and George Knox, conducted the CLE program "Mindfulness & Neuroscience: Enhancing Lawyer Effectiveness and Stress-Reduction—From the Inside Out" at the Florida Bar's Annual Convention (www.themindfullawyer.com). Neuroscience findings are also being incorporated into programs addressing conflict resolution and other areas for which insight into the brain and body might inform a better understanding the underlying processes at play in, for example, the courtroom or a negotiation. Though a limiting factor has been the speaker's comfort with the science, the burgeoning industry of science books written for the lay audience and news articles reporting on the scientific findings of leading researchers like Richard Davidson, Britta K. Hölzel, Amishi Jha, Matthew Lieberman, and Eileen Luders offers helpful secondary source material for lawyers with a penchant for science to more comfortably introduce it into their presentations. At the same time, just as lawyers began collaborating with contemplatives to develop and facilitate mindfulness programs, so too they have begun working with psychologists and physicians to offer this element with a greater credibility, which, in turn, is leading to exciting collaboration and research. For example, I have the great fortune to work with cognitive neuroscientist, Amishi Jha, both on projects that involve members of the legal profession and on research projects outside the law but that look at issues relevant to lawyers (Jha, Rogers & Morrison, forthcoming). Attorney, Stephanie West Allen, who collaborates with Jeffrey Schwartz bringing together neuroscience and conflict resolution, publishes the popular blog, "Brains on Purpose," found at www.brainsonpurpose.com. And Richard Reuben, a law professor at Missouri Law, has collaborated with psychologist, Kennon Sheldon, and been awarded a grant to look at the effects of an MBSR program tailored for legal professionals and delivered to law students (R. Reubene, personal communication, January 2013; Missouri Grant, 2012).

The Blossoming of Mindfulness in Law

The 2010 Mindful Lawyer Conference

With momentum building in the years following the 2002 conference, a group of lawyers, judges, and law professors, many of whom had been working together to introduce lawyers to mindfulness, decided the time had come for a national gathering. The 2010 "Mindful Lawyer Conference," took place at Berkeley Law, bringing together as many as 200 members of the legal profession and 35 speakers. A waitlist of equal proportion emerged due to space limitations. The program schedule and audio and video recordings can be found at the conference website: mindfullawyerconference.com (Halpern, 2012, n. 1). With neuroscience research into mindfulness coming into vogue, the conference kicked off with two science-focused plenaries conducted by Philippe Goldin, a neuroscientist at Stanford University, who discussed research on mindfulness and the brain, and Shauna Shapiro, a psychologist at Santa Clara

University, who addressed the role of mindfulness practices on a lawyer's well-being. The mainstay of the conference involved plenary, panel, and breakout sessions led by law faculty, lawyers, and judges addressing mindfulness in the context of the law as well as offering experiential group mindfulness exercises. In 2012, the *Journal of Legal Education* published a series of articles contributed by speakers from the conference, including an overview of the conference and collected pieces (Riskin, 2012); mindfulness in legal education (Halpern, 2012); mindfulness and teaching law (Reuben, 2012); mindfulness and trial practice (Zlotnick, 2012); and a student's perspective on a law school's mindfulness class (Larkin-Wong, 2012).

The conference created, perhaps for the first time, a sense of community among many lawyers who did not previously know each other or, for that, matter realized that there were so many others who shared their interest in mindfulness. Participants left the conference inspired to play a more active role in bringing mindfulness to the legal profession and, as the now too-numerous-to-mention list of mindfulness programs across the country attests, many have done just that, thereby furthering the noble aspirations of those who first began to water these seeds all those years ago. The rapidly growing number of mindfulness in law offerings today can be found in lawyer workshops and on law-school campuses across the country. Since the 2010 conference, at least three law schools have held mindfulness conferences of their own, including Seattle School of Law, which held a day-long "Mindfulness and the Law Conference," Phoenix Law, which convened a weekend event titled "Law as Peacemakers and Healers: New Directions in the Practice of Law," and Miami Law, which held a mindfulness workshop for members of the Dade County Bar Association and Federal Bar Association's Mindfulness in Law Joint Task Force, and a teacher training for members interested in sharing mindfulness with members of the South Florida community. Also at Miami Law, students convened at The Mindful Law Student Conference, a 2-day event where students in the seminar "Mindfulness in Law" presented on an area integrating mindfulness and law, including animal rights, negotiation, family law, ethics, music law, jury selection, e-discovery, mediation, and judicial decision-making.

The success of the 2010 Berkeley Law conference led to the 2013 "Mindfulness in Legal Education" workshop at Berkeley Law where approximately 50 law faculty from over 30 law schools across the country convened for 3 days to discuss the role of mindfulness in legal education, share innovative ideas for introducing law students and faculty to mindfulness practices, and together experience mindfulness and related practices.

Lawyer and judge workshops and organizations

With more lawyers familiar with mindfulness and developing their own mindfulness practices, the call for lawyer workshops and the number of lawyers who can play a role in them have resulted in a growing number of mindfulness programs taking place at bar conferences and legal organization events across the country. A cumulative listing of lawyer workshops can be found in Riskin's (2002) article and Professor Rhonda Magee's (2011) comprehensive law-review article, "Educating Lawyers to Meditate?," which is a must read for anyone interested in a deep understanding of the evolution of mindfulness in law and its transformative potential for legal education, law practice, and society. Magee is the present Chair of Contemplative Mind in Society.

In 2012 alone, dozens of mindfulness presentations and workshops have taken place across the country. A listing of some of these organizations along with program titles suggests just how diverse the application of mindfulness in law has become. No longer is discussion limited to mindfulness in mediation or to ways mindfulness can help reduce stress. Programs include: the Akron Bar Association's ("Mindful Mediation: Applying Mindfulness Mediation in Your Law Practice"); the Florida Association of Family and Conciliation Courts (Opening Plenary: "Mindfulness in Law," "Deepening Cooperation: Mindfulness in Collaborative Divorce," and "Mindfulness in Parenting Coordination,"); Externships 6's Field Placement Conference ("Collaboration with Colleagues across the Curriculum: Integrating Mindfulness, Ethics and Legal Writing into the Externship Seminar"), Florida Children's Legal Services Conference ("Mindfulness, Balance and the Lawyer's Brain: The Motion for Relief from Everyday Stress"); Washington Woman Lawyer's Conference ("Mindful Meditation for Legal Professionals: The Practice within the Practice"); the 19th Annual New Mexico Children's Law Institute Annual Conference ("Mindfulness, Stress-Reduction, and the Unintentional Infliction of Emotional Distress"); Florida Supreme Court Dispute Resolution Conference ("Mindfulness and Dispute Resolution: Moving Mountains with the Breath"); SE/SW People of Color Legal Scholarship Conference ("Teaching Mindful Ethics"); Federal Bar Association's Southern District's Biennial Bench and Bar Conference ("Mindful Lawyering and Judging: Effectiveness, Wellness & Civility"); Pensacola's American Inn of Court ("Mindfulness and Stress-Reduction: Learning to Bring Order to the Cortex"); South Carolina's James L. Petigru Inn of Court ("Mindfulness and Mindful Living"); and the Dade County Bar Association's Bench & Bar Conference ("Mindfulness in the Law").

As a testament to the interest in mindfulness across the profession, it is not uncommon for judges, lawyers, law professors, and law students to serve together on panels. For example, the 2012 Arizona State Bar Annual Convention conducted the mindfulness-focused program, "Beyond Burnout: The Search for Happiness and Satisfaction in the Practice of Law," which was chaired by Arizona state appellate, Judge Donn Kessler, with panelists, Professors Judi Cohen, Mary Delores Guerra, Nancy Levit, and Rhonda Magee, and former Utah Supreme Court Chief Justice and Zen priest, Michael Zimmerman. A similar program, titled "Mindfulness, Meditation and the Practice of Law" was held at its 2011 convention.

While state and federal court judges, such as Alan Gold, Ronald Greenberg, Donn Kessler, Chris McAliley, and Michael Zimmerman, have participated in mindfulness presentations and programs directed to a lawyer audience, there have thus far been very few mindfulness programs organized for judges. That trend is beginning to change as mindfulness makes its way further into the legal system, as the legal system becomes an increasingly uncomfortable work environment for everyone, and as practicing attorneys exposed to mindfulness become judges. The 2012 National Association of Women Judges annual conference in Miami Beach, Florida, included a mindfulness workshop led by two judges, an attorney, a physician, and a cognitive neuroscientist, all of whom have a personal interest in mindfulness. Also, in 2012, the Federal Judicial Center's Workshop for Judges of the Eleventh Circuit included a mindfulness program led by a law professor and physician, both of whom have a personal mindfulness practice.

As lawyers are becoming more familiar with mindfulness and interested in bringing it into their personal and professional lives, many are looking to do so in an organized setting among their colleagues. Presently, lawyers in Arizona, California, Colorado, Florida, Ohio, Massachusetts, New York, Vermont, Washington, DC, and Washington, have established mindfulness groups as part of their local bar organizations for the purpose of offering information on mindfulness, developing and organizing mindfulness programs, and sitting together in meditation.

Law-school offerings

Law schools across the country are offering classes that integrate mindfulness, as an introduction to the sitting practice, as a means to further one or more teaching objectives, and/or as a vehicle to enrich the legal conversation and perhaps even transform legal doctrine. Following this progression, many schools have faculty familiar with mindfulness who share the practice with their students (and sometimes colleagues). A growing number have wellness programs for which mindfulness plays an important role, and two law schools have institutionalized mindfulness programs (Sloan, 2012). So as to provide a sense of the variety of law-school offerings that have sprouted up and been influential across this developing landscape, a selection of these courses, workshops, and groups is identified below.

Miami Law offers three mindfulness courses as part of its law-school curriculum with "Mindful Ethics," a class that integrates mindfulness and professional responsibility; "Mindfulness in Law," a class that introduces mindfulness to students across specific areas of practice and concerns such as mediation, negotiation, trial practice, ethics, client services, and judicial decision-making, and "Mindful Leadership," which integrates mindfulness into a discussion of leadership, explicitly drawing on traditional mindfulness practice and the work of Ellen Langer and of William George, of the Harvard Business School. Mindful Ethics and Mindful Leadership were developed and taught in collaboration with my colleagues, Jan Jacobowitz and Raquel Matas, respectively, thus allowing for a more robust course content, and to facilitate the training of faculty in mindfulness and the teaching of mindfulness. Many other schools also offer mindfulness classes as part of the curriculum, including Berkeley Law, Colorado Law, Connecticut Law School, CUNY Law, Empire State, Florida International University School of Law, Florida Law, Golden Gate Law School (Golden Gate Law), Hastings Law, Missouri Law, Northwestern Law, Phoenix School of Law ("Phoenix Law"), Roger Williams School of Law, and USF Law. A cumulative and frequently updated listing can be found at www.themindfullawschool.com. Among those law schools that have the most robust collection of mindfulness offerings are found administrators who appreciate and support these endeavors. As examples, Miami Law's Dean, Patricia White, and its Dean of Students, Janet Stearns, have played pivotal roles in the formation and ongoing success of Miami Law's Mindfulness in Law Program, and Berkeley Law's Dean, Christopher Edley, played a key role in the formation of the Berkeley Initiative on Mindfulness in Law and of

Berkeley Law hosting "The Mindful Lawyer" and the "Mindfulness in Legal Education" conferences.

Law schools also offer a variety of workshops and classes that introduce students to mindfulness as part of a series of skills for managing stress and performing well academically. In 2011, Vanderbilt University Law School's Assistant Dean for Student Affairs, Julie Sandine, complemented a popular student program that had been in place for several years with a lecture series entitled "Building a Sustainable Law Practice—and Life." This series includes "Two Aspects of Mindful Lawyering: Personal Authenticity and Judgment v. Compassionate Insight," "Mindful Movement: The Benefits of the Age-Old Practice of Qi Gong," and "Mindful Lawyering: Balancing Passion and Perspective" (Silver, 2012). Other law schools that have offered programs oriented around student well-being include Georgetown Law School's Lawyer's in Balance Program, CUNY Law's Contemplative Urban Lawyering Program, Miami Law's Mindfulness in Law Program, Berkeley Law's Initiative on Mindfulness in Law, and George Washington University Law School's "Breaths for Success" program (Rogers & Jacobowitz, 2012; Rosen et al., 2013; Silver, 2012). Northwestern Law has a full-time psychologist working for the Office of Student Services who offers drop-in mindfulness sittings and mindfulness-based psychotherapy.

Faculty exposed to mindfulness through traditional practices are especially inclined to offer mindfulness sitting opportunities to students, and a growing number of faculty and students exposed to mindful sitting groups are interested in developing and participating in them. Perhaps the first formal group was the "Law and Mindfulness Practice Group" at Berkeley Law. Begun in 2003, this group continues to this day, and a room has been set aside for Berkeley Law students to practice on their own anytime during the day. Other schools with student sitting groups include: USF Law, Missouri Law, Miami Law, Seton Hall School of Law, Florida State University School of Law, Phoenix Law, Harvard Law, Golden Gate Law, and Georgetown Law. Students at a few schools, including Missouri Law and Miami Law, have formed organizations to explore and practice mindfulness, and relate it to the study and practice of law (Rogers, 2012a). Law schools are also beginning to offer mindfulness trainings and workshops to faculty interested in learning more about mindfulness and better understanding the programs being developed and offered at their schools and others around the country. At Miami Law, for example, "The Faculty of Attention," is a 4-week training offered to faculty members.

The Growth of Mindfulness in Law

When the profession is ready: Modern treatment of an ancient tradition

The maxim "When the student is ready, the teacher will appear," speaks to one of the sensitivities and challenges inherent in introducing a contemplative practice to the legal profession. Given the depth of suffering taking place, and explicit calls from bar leaders, law schools, and national and state law organizations, it seems clear to many that any effort to introduce to the profession a means to reduce stress, relieve anxiety and depression, attenuate substance abuse, and facilitate a less unkind adversarial landscape would be most welcome. At the same time, the contemplative aspect to a mindfulness practice coupled with its strong Buddhist roots harkens to the maxim's ancient insight to be responsive to another's request for help but not to presume it. This is all the more so when introducing a form that is associated with a religious or spiritual practice (Blatt, 2002; Cantrell, 2010a).

Nonetheless, the scientific findings and health benefits of mindfulness seem to have lifted it out of its contemplative pigeon hole and are facilitating a more active willing-ness of bar leaders, law faculty, judges, and others to look to mindfulness as an effective means to help accomplish a hugely important objective. Hence, the coming together of East and West is making for an interesting opportunity and conversation. The fol-lowing discussion identifies different forms that mindfulness practices often take when shared with lawyers and examines an approach I developed to share mindfulness with lawyers, law students, and judges.

At the outset, it will be helpful to consider three primary methods that have evolved for introducing mindfulness to members of the legal profession.

1   The initial foray of mindfulness in law often involved short mindfulness discussion and/or exercises at the beginning or ending of programs and classes to help bring about calm, sharpen focus, or enhance a deeper engagement with the material.
2   In time, these conversations and exercises were woven more comprehensively into the context of legal practice with direct ties made to the ways a mindfulness practice might benefit one's law studies and practice. One such benefit, as noted earlier, is how mindfulness might be helpful in dealing with stress and working with clients. As the conversation evolved, creative means were developed to establish greater relevance to the practice of law.
3   As lawyers with mindfulness practices became more involved in the teaching of mindfulness, the infusion of mindfulness into the legal landscape took on a more integrated structure, as evidenced in articles and workshops directed to specific groups (e.g., judges, mediators, litigators), specific practice areas (e.g., family law, negotiation, litigation) and law-school classes that endeavor to weave mindfulness insights and practices into the very substance of the material (e.g., criminal law, race relations, ethics).

These three approaches, termed (1) "mindfulness moments," (2) "mindfulness infusions," and (3) "mindfulness integrations," are treated for the purpose of discus-sion as if they were conceptually distinct. In fact, however, they very much flow in and around each other, and their expression is not necessarily linear. A fourth approach, which we might term, "mindfulness transformation," speaks to the ways that legal analysis and doctrine may become increasingly influenced and molded by the applica-tion of mindful awareness and insight.

An interesting evolution in the area of mindfulness in law that dovetails with the development of these approaches is the role lawyers play in the process. Not sur-prisingly, many of the early programs and events introducing lawyers, law students, and judges to mindfulness involve instruction by teachers with long-term mindfulness practices, mainly from within the Buddhist tradition, who are not attorneys. The 1987 introduction to judges was by Jon Kabat-Zinn, and the 1998 introduction to lawyers at Hale & Dorr was by Kabat-Zinn and Ferris Urbanowski. The 1998–2001 Yale Law School mindfulness retreats, which were conducted primarily by Joseph Goldstein (with involvement by Sharon Salzberg and Mirabai Bush), are noteworthy because of the collaborative involvement of attorneys and law professors, including Charlie Halpern, Grove Burnett, and Steven Schwartz, in the development of their structure. As lawyers and law professors introduced to mindfulness became serious practitioners, they have begun leading mindfulness programs on their own, or in collaboration with other attorneys. Not surprisingly, this has led to greater lawyer participation and interest along with the approval of more programs for a larger number of CLE credits.

Still, the breadth of mindfulness offerings remains robust. Attorneys like Grove Burnett, a respected teacher at Spirit Rock, lead lawyer retreats oriented around more tradition forms of practice and conversation. Others like Robert Zeglovitch, trained in the Zen tradition as well as in MBSR, lead MBSR workshops for attorneys. While I am a student in the Zen tradition also trained in MBSR, as I discuss in more detail below, much of the work I do involves sharing mindfulness in more modern forms. Other attorneys, like Judi Cohen, formed "Warrior One," and developed "Essential Mindfulness for Lawyers," where she coaches lawyers in mindfulness training and leads mindfulness programs, often employing more modern approaches that are crafted specifically for legal professionals.

Jurisight: A mindfulness offering crafted for members of the legal profession

In 1999, I introduced a group of lawyers to the mindful practice of law. Filling in for a presenter who had been slated to speak on professionalism, I focused on mindfulness, an area of increasing relevance for me and my legal practice. By that time, I had been discussing mindfulness with colleagues who, it struck me, were quite interested in the topic but less so in practicing it. As discussed more fully elsewhere (Rogers, 2012a), this presentation and those that followed led to the development of Jurisight, an approach that grew out of a similar method I had developed for sharing mindfulness with parents (Rogers, 2005), using the language and culture of the law to share fundamental mindfulness insights and exercises with law students, lawyers, and judges (Rogers, 2007, 2009a, 2009c; www.jurisight.com). Jurisight has been the foundation for many CLE programs across the country, is being used to help teach mindfulness to law students at several law schools, and is an integral part of the Mindfulness in Law Program at Miami Law, where I have the good fortune to teach. Below, I describe a collection of Jurisight demonstrations and exercises to provide a glimpse of methods that have been found to be successful for sharing mindfulness with members of the legal profession.

Along with Jurisight, there are a growing number of other approaches, developed and taught by creative and inspiring lawyers, judges, and law faculty (Cohen, 2012; Magee, 2009, 2011; Zlotnick, 2012). Because these more modern approaches share features, discussion of Jurisight may offer an insight into the ways that the larger collection of approaches resonates and has gained traction in the law. The following discussion refers to all members of the legal profession as "students," both for the sake of brevity and as a reminder of the shared experience mindfulness offers law students, lawyers, and judges.

Whereas much mindfulness training centers around formal practices, and in particular a sitting practice, out of which flows insight and a deeper appreciation of one's true nature, Jurisight works, in large part, the other way around. Based on the premise that most judges, attorneys, and law students are not actively in search of a contemplative practice to integrate into their lives (even though they may be quite stressed, anxious, or depressed), and many who are so inclined do not believe they have the time, patience, or ability to cultivate a sitting practice, Jurisight begins by introducing legal professionals to mindfulness insights and short mindfulness practices. A key element to Jurisight is that the insights and exercises resonate with lawyers and law students because they are integrated into the language and culture in which the lawyers and law students are already immersed. Moreover, by sharing insights and exercises in a contextually contoured manner, everyday events are likely to generate mindful awareness, and the generation of mindful awareness will motivate and inspire practice (Rogers, 2008, 2009c). That is to say, Jurisight seeks to meet students where they are and invites them to integrate mindfulness into their lives, law-school experience, and careers in ways that make sense to them and feel right.

Jurisight entails a grafting together of Eastern and Western approaches to mindfulness as a means of offering mindfulness instruction that is responsive to the interests and needs of the legal profession. The manner in which these mindfulness insights and exercises are presented in a legal context offers a sense of the ways in which traditional Eastern practice is melded together with Western approaches to teaching and learning. Each class or program segment orients around a fundamental mindfulness concept dressed in legal garb that is then connected to the context in which students find themselves. Discussion of the concept in relation to their circumstance—coupled with experiential practice—facilitates absorption of the insight and its applicability to everyday moments. The end result is a conceptual understanding of mindfulness as well as the capacity to engage mindful awareness moment by moment, both as a spontaneous arising and out of deliberate intent. In this regard, mindfulness is *the noticing and experiencing of the richness of the moment, cultivated by intentionally paying attention to present-moment phenomena as well as through a spontaneous shift of consciousness, occasioned by something in particular or by nothing at all.*

So that this approach may be more clearly presented, the following discussion looks at three methodologies used to capture attention, effect a more profound absorption of mindfulness insights, and inspire practice. These include (1) surprise, (2) humor, and (3) prompts.

Surprise

Surprise can be a powerful vehicle for engaging present-moment awareness. The study and practice of law is a largely conceptual enterprise, driven by language and precision. Legal doctrine is oriented, in large measure, by the need for certainty, and legal principles are often fit into rigid categories. As Ellen Langer notes, in her early treatments of mindfulness, the rigid reliance on a category can lead to suffering, as it limits our potential to see the present moment as it is, and we cling to preconceived beliefs that have little relevance to the moment at hand (Langer, 1989). This is akin to Riskin's reference to lawyers being trapped by narrow "mind-sets" (Riskin, 2002). Mindful practice can help free us to make new categories, dissolve old categories that no longer pertain, and perhaps even come to relate to life (and legal practice) without being bound by categories (Hanh, 1999). Similarly, as we create new categories, we naturally attend more directly to situation and context, which brings about a greater awareness of present-moment experience (Langer, 1989, 1997). Surprise is one method Jurisight draws upon, as illuminated in the following discussion of the legal phrase "pain and suffering" and the term, "justice."

Pain and suffering   In a legal action arising out of personal injuries, money damages are often sought for "pain and suffering." Students are asked to consider the relationship between pain and suffering, and it is generally agreed that the more pain there is, the more suffering there will be, and hence the greater the award for damages. Once this intuitive, mathematical relationship is established, a *mindfulness* discussion of pain and suffering introduces the possibility that the more one embraces their pain, the less they will suffer (Joko Beck, 1989; Smalley & Winston, 2010; Zeidan et al., 2011). This counterintuitive proposition is one that registers as a keen insight into the human condition. As a result, in juxtaposition to the way the topic is introduced, the mindfulness piece often provokes an "ah-ha" moment that naturally interests the student to further explore the concept and its practical implications. As such, the conversation introduces an insight regarding relief from suffering that proposes a means of experiencing this relief, that is, a mindfulness practice, which becomes of interest, both as a practical matter and as a means of satisfying the curious mind that wonders, "Can this be true? And, if so, how do I do it?"

Through the element of "surprise," Jurisight facilitates the absorption of mindfulness insights by creating new categories. The conditional aspect of this teaching simultaneously arouses in students a freedom from fixed conceptions (in this case, "suffering"), offers them a memorable insight—owing in part to its having been associated with a familiar legal concept—and engages their interest in learning more (Langer, 1989, 1997, 2000; Rogers, 2009a).

Justice   Another example of the way Jurisight uses the language of the law to help dissolve categories and, at the same time, offer insight is through the use of the word "Justice." When presented to students, the term is first discussed in its legal sense and then split into the two-word phrase, "Just Is," noting the mindfulness insight that if we are interested in bringing about justice, and in participating in processes that lead to just outcomes and wise and compassionate decisions, it is crucial that we see that world as it "Just Is." A fuller conversation explores what it means to notice the moment as it "Just Is *Changing*." The work of Ellen Langer on mindlessness and how states of mindful awareness can be established by noticing "what is new" dovetail with this approach. The discussion concludes with a "bare attention" exercise that invites students to notice what "just is" arising and changing, facilitating a state of mind that "notices new things, and is sensitive to context" (Langer, 2000, 2005).

It may well be that much lawyer dissatisfaction stems in part from the belief that "justice" is seldom realized. A profound realization for students presented with this perspective is that *resisting* a past injustice, rather than noticing it as an event that "just is," depletes their energy and passion, and gets in the way of their contributing to a more just tomorrow. Students appreciate that what they are resisting is ... *reality.* This awareness frees them from preconception and allows for a greater receptivity to new information (Langer, 1997) or changed circumstances—and to making a difference in moments to come.

Humor

Related to the above discussion, one's mindset, especially when contemplating serious subject matter, can elicit suffering, limit creativity, and foreclose possibilities. Humor serves as a catalyst for learning new information and enhances well-being. Lawyers, charged with a larger responsibility to society and to the service of justice, can become less effective and experience emotional distress when they feel ineffective or become convinced that the system is unfair. Through clever wordplay, often eliciting a smile and laughter, Jurisight allows students to break free of limiting mindsets surrounding their own narrow views as well as the legal system at large.

Just Is Holmes   Several mindfulness exercises incorporate the phrase "Just Is" in conjunction with the name of a famous legal figure. For example, Supreme Court Justice Oliver Wendell Holmes, Jr. coined the famous phrase "stop, look, and listen" in a decision prescribing appropriate conduct when approaching train tracks. In the Jurisight exercise known as the "Just Is Holmes," students are instructed to "stop, look, and listen" as an informal practice when approaching a stop sign, when sitting at a traffic light, or anytime for that matter, and as a formal 3-min practice (Rogers, 2011), which dovetails with the "Three-Minute Breathing Space" developed as part of the MBCT program (Segal, Williams, & Teasdale, 2002). One application that bridges Eastern conceptions with Western approaches to mindfulness invites students to close or lower their eyes and "stop, look, and listen" as a bare awareness practice and, upon opening their eyes, to identify something "new" in the field of their awareness (Langer, 1989, 1997; Rogers & Jacobowitz, 2012). Other exercises include the "Just Is Story," named after Justice Joseph Story. Students learn of Marcus Aurelius's "Our life is what our thoughts make it" and are invited, when agitated, to listen to the "story" they are telling themselves, cultivating the ability to notice the thought as an event that "just is" (Rogers, 2009a; Tolle, 2004). At Miami Law, two weekly sittings are known as the "Just Is Holmes" sitting (10 min) and the "Just Is Story" sitting (30 min; www.miamimindfulness.com)

Motion for relief from judgment   Many lawyers spend a great deal of time drafting and responding to motions, and all law students learn the craft of developing motions to help advance a client's cause. A popular pleading is the "Motion for Relief from Judgment" in which an attorney asks the court to relieve their client from being bound by an adverse judgment, F.R.Civ. P. 60(b)(5). The "Motion for Relief from Judgment" mindfulness exercise is one that defies the adage that lawyers who represent themselves have fools for clients. Attorneys who have been introduced to the mindfulness notion that judgments, of self and others, can be a source of suffering elicit a knowing smile as they read the motion (see Figure 27.1). This "intellectual" exercise stimulates a greater attentiveness to the arising of judgments (and hence awareness of their arising) and may encourage students who have been introduced to mindfulness as a sitting practice to do so. This additional perspective on what constitutes a "judgment" is expanded upon and reinforced in the "Judge-Mint" mindfulness cue discussed below.

Prompts

It is rare to participate in a mindfulness program that does not make some reference to how we "spend so much time in our heads." This is especially the case in discussions with lawyers. The title of Kabat-Zinn's "Coming to Our Senses," along with the body of this work, makes explicit how sensory experience naturally aids us in emerging from automatic pilot (Moffitt, 2007). Sensory experience can also be helpful when grappling with abstract concepts. The insight of "impermanence" flows out of mindfulness practice and alleviates the suffering that can arise when undesirable circumstances are regarded as static and permanent. In the life of a lawyer and law student, agitated emotional states often arise out of, for example, resistance to an uncertain outcome, the belief that there is "not enough time," or the momentary arising of judgments. As elaborated on below, Jurisight uses "prompts" to make more tangible abstract concepts such as "uncertainty," "time," and "judgments"—as well as the distracted mind. It does so drawing on different sense modalities. These prompts, in turn, can be used as mindfulness cues, both eliciting a recollection of various mindfulness insights and inspiring experiential practice.

The motion to embrace life's uncertain-tees The mind's tendency to move into future and anticipate worse-case scenarios is often discussed in mindfulness programs and readily acknowledged by many through direct experience. For lawyers, it is a double-edged sword, as anticipating and guarding against undesirable scenarios are part of the job description. This Jurisight demonstration, which falls also within the "surprise" category, transforms worrisome future events into a small piece of wood, thereby reminding students that it is not so much the troubling event but its "uncertainty" that is causing them to suffer.

The exercise begins as a demonstration with students handed a box of raisins. The students are surprised to find that the box does not contain raisins and, upon further investigation, learn that though it feels and they assume it to be empty, it contains a snugly fitted golf tee with "One of Life's Uncertain-Tees" embossed on it. Along with the laughter this exercise elicits, a discussion of the series of erroneous assumptions they made ("the box contains raisins," to "he's giving us a snack to eat") and the various fleeting feelings they experienced ("excitement," "disappointment," or "relief") allows for a rich conversation across a variety of mindfulness areas. This exercise is completed when students read a 6 × 8 card with an illustration on one side that helps reinforce these insights, and a legal motion on the other that, along with the tee, serves as a mindfulness cue for working with uncertainty (see Figure 27.2). The "Motion to Embrace Life's Uncertain-Tees" is filed in the "Neural Circuit Court" and concludes with a mindfulness insight that we can bear (literally) the uncertain-tee.

IN THE NEURAL CIRCUIT COURT IN AND FOR THE GREAT AND HEALTHY STATE OF MIND

YOU, aka "ME"

         Petitioner,

     vs.

REALITY

         Respondent.

MOTION FOR RELIEF FROM JUDGMENT

Pursuant to the laws of the great and healthy State of Mind, Petitioner respectfully moves for relief from the unnecessary pain and suffering caused by the never-ending judgments that arise in the mind.

1. Petitioner has been blessed with an intellect and capacity to reason, analyze, judge, and make decisions.

2. Much of Petitioner's prior experience has positively reinforced these skills, especially the ability to make judgments about facts, events, other persons, and Petitioner.

3. Petitioner has survived all prior obstacles and challenges and unconsciously attributes this survival to a panoply of skills, especially the making of judgments. This attribution is in and of itself a judgment.

4. Due to the enormous volume of judgments generated by Petitioner's mind, coupled with there having been positive reinforcement by virtue of Petitioner's survival, it has become impossible to efficiently discern judgments based on law and fact and admitted as credible evidence from those not based on law and fact, or that constitute hearsay.

5. As a result, the incessant flow of judgments has led to circumstances where Petitioner overreacts to circumstances; prejudges; misjudges; criticizes people ans events; and interacts with people and treats oneself in a manner that is biased and based on erroneous assumptions – all of which causes undue pain and suffering.

WHEREFORE, Petitioner seeks relief from the unnecessary pain and suffering occasioned by this always-judging nature.

Respectfully submitted,

YOU, Esq.
Counsel for Petitioner

IN THE NEURAL CIRCUIT COURT IN AND FOR THE GREAT AND HEALTHY STATE OF MIND

YOU, aka "ME"

         Petitioner,

     vs.

REALITY

         Respondent.

ORDER GRANTING RELIEF FROM JUDGMENT

Before this Neural Circuit Court is Petitioner's Motion for Relief from Judgment. For the reasons set forth below, Petitioner's Motion is GRANTED.

1. This Court finds that Petitioner is continually making judgments about everything that arises in Petitioner's mind.

2. This Court also finds that the enormous quantity of thoughts continuously arising in Petitioner's mind, along with Petitioner's prior conditioning, makes it exceptionally challenging to efficiently discern judgments based on facts admitted into evidence from those not in evidence.

3. This Court also finds that as a result, Petitioner will, from time to time and often without awareness, overreact to circumstances; prejudge people and outcomes; and interact with people and treat oneself in a manner that is biased and based on erroneous assumptions—all of which is likely to cause undue pain and suffering.

ACCORDINGLY, Petitioner's Motion for Relief from Judgment is GRANTED. This Order will be SELF-enforcing. Although this Court, being a Neural Circuit Court, is mindful of the challenges (and paradox) inherent in looking to the self to enforce this order, it believes that such collaboration in necessary in order to ensure the long-term relief that is sought.

Done and ordered in Chambers this _____ day of _____.

_____
The Honorable You
Neural Circuit Court Judge

Figure 27.1   Motion for relief from judgment. Copyright 2008. Institute for Mindfulness Studies. All Rights Reserved.

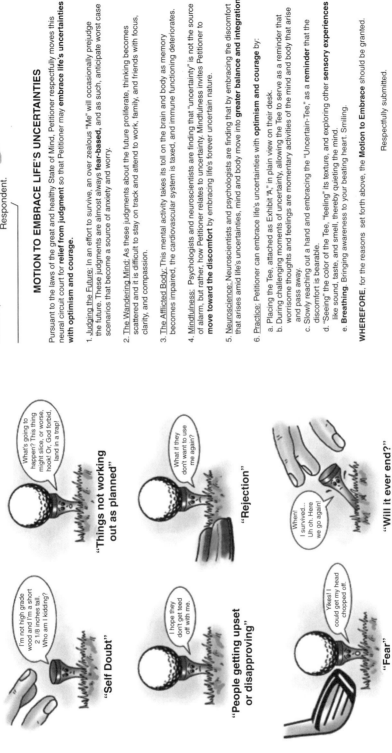

Figure 27.2 Motion to embrace life's uncertain-tees. Copyright 2008. Institute for Mindfulness Studies. All Rights Reserved.

When this exercise is included in a multiweek class or workshop, I'll often conduct the MBSR "raisin" exercise (Kabat-Zinn, 1990; Segal et al., 2002) a few weeks earlier to facilitate greater surprise and humor. Interestingly, the instructions of Kabat-Zinn's now-classic exercise are very much aligned with Langer's approach of learning to pay attention and notice new things. As such, it highlights the interrelated and overlapping aspects of the various approaches to teaching mindfulness and cultivating mindful awareness.

Motion for extension of thyme   Feelings of not having enough time are common, given the law's highly stressful and adversarial climate. As these feelings take hold, they can result in greater emotional reactivity and impair decision-making. Sometimes, these feelings of urgency and thoughts of "not enough time" can be overreactions, and it can be challenging to discern the difference when one is overwhelmed. In legal practice, time concerns can be assuaged through the often-used and frequently abused "Motion for an Extension of Time." A mindfulness demonstration involves having students fill in the blanks of a "Motion for an Extension of Time" (see Figure 27.3) that asks them to identify the areas in which they find themselves short on time and their accompanying thoughts, feelings, and body sensations. The motion is granted as an "Order Granting Extension of *Thyme*" where students are handed a sprig (or "extension") of thyme and guided in a mindfulness exercises that incorporates aroma and a "coming to our senses." Students are reminded that they can keep some thyme handy and practice the simple exercise when they find themselves feeling a sense of urgency or stressed for time (Rogers & Jacobowitz, 2012).

Judge-mints   A mindfulness prompt that, along with the "uncertain-tee" and "extension of thyme," helps make elusive mindfulness insights more memorable and accessible is the "Judge-Mint" (see Figure 27.4). This edible mint provides on the wrapper, "Look Inside to Find Refreshing Judgments," helping to make tangible the concept of a "judgment" along with the insight that we can experience relief when the judgment is "noticed" and "observed" as opposed to identified with and believed to be the truth.

Landscape of the distracted mind   The final Jurisight exercise that we'll consider typifies Jurisight's contextually contoured approach. It is one thing to note the distractibility of our minds and the ways it leads to suffering, and another to connect visually with that insight.

The legal doctrine of the "Attractive Nuisance," one that most lawyers and law students long remember, allows for this insight to be made tangible, and perhaps facilitate greater awareness of mental reactivity. The doctrine arises from a series of 19th-century cases in which someone died in a seemingly safe environment that, despite appearances, proved deadly. In the classic "poison pool" cases, young boys, playing in an open field on a hot day, came across an inviting pool of cool water and took a swim. Sadly, the water was toxic, and the boys succumbed shortly after jumping in. The legal issue explores the question of liability—the owner of the land who did not have adequate warnings in place or the young trespassers. After recollecting the facts of this legal case, a mindfulness discussion explores the sometimes-toxic places

IN THE NEURAL CIRCUIT COURT IN AND FOR THE GREAT AND HEALTHY STATE OF MIND

YOU, aka "ME"

Petitioner,

vs.

REALITY

Respondent.

MOTION FOR EXTENSION OF TIME

Pursuant to the laws of the great and healthy State of Mind, Petitioner respectfully moves for an order extending the amount of time available to focus on law school studies and related tasks and projects.

1. Petitioner is enrolled in law school, known far and wide as a grueling experience where time is short and the workload is heavy.

2. From time to time, Petitioner finds that there is not enough time to get everything done. Such times include:

3. During such times, Petitioner begins to think that:

4. Petitioner feels:

5. Petitioner also experiences sensations in the body that include:

6. As a result, Petitioner occasionally feels a sense of urgency that increases stress, undermines Petitioner's ability to perform optimally, and adversely affects Petitioner's relationship with:

WHEREFORE, Petitioner respectfully requests that this Court enter an order extending the amount of time petitioner has to study for class, prepare for exams, finish projects, exercise, eat, relax, sleep, and spend time with friends and family.

Respectfully submitted,

_____
YOU, Esq.

IN THE NEURAL CIRCUIT COURT IN AND FOR THE GREAT AND HEALTHY STATE OF MIND

YOU, aka "ME"

Petitioner,

vs.

REALITY

Respondent.

ORDER GRANTING EXTENSION OF THYME

Before this Neural Circuit Court is Petitioner's Motion for Extension of Time. For the reasons set forth below, Petitioner's Motion is GRANTED.

1. This Court finds that Petitioner is enrolled in law school, which can be a grueling experience in which there is limited time to accomplish a great deal. This Court also finds that there are moments when Petitioner believes that there is not enough time to get everything done. During moments such as these, Petitioner can experience worrisome thoughts, distressing feelings, and uncomfortable sensations in the body.

2. This Court finds that owing to these uncomfortable thoughts, feelings, and sensations, Petitioner tends to impulsively react with conduct that can be unproductive and waste time.

3. This Court finds that die growing sense of urgency and procrastination can increase stress, undermine Petitioner's ability to perform optimally, and adversely affect Petitioner's relationship with others.

4. This Court is inclined to deny Petitioner's motion on the basis that additional time will, after a short period of relief, likely result in a similar pattern of conduct, leading once again to distress and procrastination.

5. However, this Court, being a Neural Circuit Court in and fat the Great and Healthy State of Mind, has decided to grant Petitioner an Extension of Thyme with which to come to their senses.

ACCORDINGLY, Petitioner's Motion for Extension of Thyme is GRANTED. Petitioner is instructed to, close their eyes, place the extension of thyme underneath their nose, gently notice its aroma, and pay attention to the rise and fall of the breath.

Done and ordered in Chambers this _____ day of _____.

_____
The Honorable "You"
Neural Circuit Court Judge

Figure 27.3 Motion for extension of thyme. Copyright 2008. Institute for Mindfulness Studies. All Rights Reserved.

Figure 27.4 Refreshing judge-mints. Copyright 2008. Institute for Mindfulness Studies. All Rights Reserved.

our attention wanders. The "Landscape of the Mind" illustration (see Figure 27.5) sets in motion a lively, entertaining, and serious conversation as students give voice to familiar places and ponder why their thoughts wander there, again and again. Jack Kornfield's metaphor of attention as a puppy dog we place by our feet and instruct to "stay" is apropos. This illustration has been found to be useful in a variety of contexts extending beyond the law.

Closing Thoughts

The introduction of mindfulness into the legal profession generally regards mindfulness as a means of bringing stability, clarity, and compassion to a challenging profession whose members are suffering. This understanding is one that applies to a great many contexts across our culture in which mindfulness is being introduced. The law, however, stands in a fairly unique position as a societal structure that emerged, in the first instance, to bring stability, clarity, and compassion to a "state of nature" in which a great many were subjected to unnecessary pain and a great deal of suffering (Hobbes, 2010). Most law students learn early in their law school careers that legal systems evolved to bring order out of chaos. Humans lived in a "state of nature" that was, in the words of Thomas Hobbes, "nasty, brutish, and short," and presumably one filled with an inordinate amount of pain. The rule of law evolved as a "social compact" whereby one forfeited a slice of personal autonomy to the sovereign in exchange for rules and an enforcement mechanism that would stabilize the chaotic and allow for the further evolution of society. And so the emergence of the law of property rights, criminal law, contracts, and torts offered a structure to understand and predict outcomes, to limit physical and emotional distress, and to enable individuals and groups to create and accomplish.

Today, however, the very system that emerged to establish predictability and order is becoming increasingly unstable. And indeed, many lawyers and judges regard the

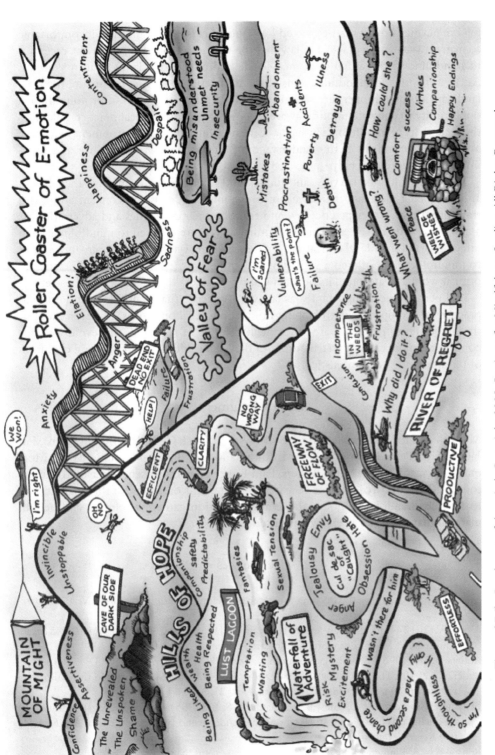

Figure 27.5 Landscape of the mind. Copyright 2008. Institute for Mindfulness Studies. All Rights Reserved.

environment in which they work as "nasty and brutish," and sadly, a disturbing number are having shorter-than-expected lives and careers. So hostile and uncomfortable to many lawyers is the practice of law that the very idea that a lawyer may be receptive to mindfulness is regarded by some—inside and outside the law—as an oxymoron. At the same time, as mindfulness insights and practices continue to nurture the legal landscape, its practitioners are sensing that law practice itself offers a profoundly rich opportunity to cultivate mindful awareness—a form of "reciprocal practice." Perhaps the receptivity of mindfulness in such a seemingly inhospitable environment may serve as a fertile ground for better understanding effective ways to introduce and teach mindfulness more generally.

Many law students, lawyers, and judges find mindfulness to improve their health and well-being, decrease their levels of stress, improve focus and concentration, and transform the way they practice law and relate to their colleagues and adversaries. As a new generation of law students and future lawyers are exposed to mindfulness as an integral part of their legal education, and practicing lawyers and judges are introduced to mindfulness and offered a variety of authentic and meaningful ways of practicing, both at work and at home, its benefits will ripple across the profession and society.

And perhaps most importantly, as lawyers appreciate that mindfulness insights and practices are compatible with helping bring about legal objectives, but even more so that mindfulness principles are inherent in the rule of law itself, this evolution may contribute to the current restructuring of the legal profession and ongoing evolution of our laws and system of justice.

Acknowledgments

Many thanks to William Blatt, Andrew Dawson, Patrick Gudridge, Betsy Havens, Jan Jacobowitz, Peter Lederer, Lily Levi, Rhonda Magee, Elliott Manning, Milica Mormann, Leonard Riskin, Millie Rogers, Pam Rogers, Robert Rosen, Karen Throckmorton, and Kunihiko Yoshida, for very helpful comments on a draft of this chapter, and to Barbara Brandon, for going above and beyond in gathering relevant and helpful material that I had not been aware existed.

References

Adcock, T. (2008, July 30). Become a better counselor through meditation. *New York Law Journal.*

Alfieri, A. (2012). Educating lawyers for community (January 24, 2012). *Wisconsin Law Review*, University of Miami Legal Studies Research Paper No. 2012-02.

Anderson, W. (1996). Ecumenical cosmology. *Texas Tech Law Review, 27,* 983.

Bader, E. (2010). The psychology of meditation: Issues of self and identity and the IDR cycle. *Pepperdine Dispute Resolution Law Journal, 10*(2), Article 1.

Benjamin, G., Kaszniak, A., Sales, B., & Shanfield, S. B. (1986). The role of legal education in producing psychological distress among law students and lawyers. *American Bar Foundation Research Journal,* 225.

Benson, H., & Klipper, M. (1975). *The relaxation response.* New York, NY: Avon.

Blatt, W. (2002). What's special about meditation? Contemplative practice for American lawyers. *Harvard Negotiation Law Review, 7*, 109.

Bowling, D. (2010). *Mindfulness meditation and mediation: Where the transcendent meets the familiar, in bringing peace into the room: How the personal qualities of the mediator and their impact on the mediation.* Chichester, UK: John Wiley & Sons.

Boyce, B. (2010). The law of mindfulness. *Shambhala Sun.*

Bronstad, A. (2008, October 24). Try a course in meditation after other law school classes. *National Law Journal.* Retrieved from http://www.lawjobs.com/newsandviews/LawArticle.jsp?id=1202425505639&slreturn=20130914160912

Burns, M. (1990). Lessons from the Third World: Spirituality as the source of commitment to affirmative action. *Vermont Law Review, 14*, 401.

Bush, M. (2011). Mindfulness in contemporary education. In *Contemporary Buddhism.* New York, NY: Routledge.

Calloway, D. (2010). Using mindfulness practice to work with emotions. *Nevada Law Journal, 10*, 338.

Cantrell, D. (2010a). Can compassionate practice also be good legal practice? Answers from the lives of Buddhist lawyers. *Rutgers Journal of Law & Religion, 12*, 12.

Cantrell, D. (2010b). What's love got to do with it? Contemporary lessons on lawyerly advocacy from the preacher Martin Luther King, Jr. *St. Thomas Law Review, 22*, 296.

Chodron, P. (2003). *Comfortable with uncertainty: 108 teaching on cultivating fearlessness and compassion.* Boston, MA: Shambhala.

Codiga, D. (2002). Reflections on the potential growth of mindfulness meditation in the law. *Harvard Negotiation Law Review, 7*, 109.

Cohen, J. (2012, May 15). Mindfulness and stress. *The Recorder.* Retrieved from http://www.law.com/jsp/ca/PubArticleCA.jsp?id=1202553739638&Mindfulness_and_Stress

Cormak, C. (2009, March). Lawyers turn to meditation to fight stress and improve performance. *Canadian Lawyer.* Retrieved from http://www.canadianlawyermag.com/Lawyers-turn-to-meditation-to-fight-stress-and-improve-performance.html

Daicoff, S. S. (2004). *Lawyer, know thyself: A psychological analysis of personality strengths and weaknesses.* Washington, DC: American Psychological Association.

Elkins, J. (1984). Ethics: Professionalism, craft, and failure. *Kentucky Law Journal, 73*, 937–965.

Ellinghausen Jr., D. (2006). Venting or Vipassanā? Mindfulness meditation's potential for reducing anger's role in mediation. *Cardozo Journal of Conflict Resolution, 8*, 63.

Fisher, T. (2003). Who's minding the mediator? Mindfulness in mediation. *ADR Bulletin, 5*(10), 165.

Freshman, C. (2006). After basic mindfulness mediation: External mindfulness, emotional truthfulness and lie detection in dispute resolution. *Journal of Dispute Resolution,* 511.

Freshman, C. (2010). Yes, and: Core concerns, internal mindfulness, and external mindfulness for emotional balance, lie detection, and successful negotiation. *Nevada Law Journal, 10*, 365.

Freshman, C., Hayes, A., & Feldman, G. (2002). Adapting meditation to promote negotiation success: A guide to varieties and scientific support. *Harvard Negotiation Law Review, 7*, 67.

Friedman, W. (2001). The mind has a mind of its own and you can use it to reduce stress. *Lawyers Journal, 3*, 7.

Gillespie, B. (February 1, 2013). Mindfulness in legal practice is going mainstream. *ABA Journal.* Retrieved from http://www.abajournal.com/magazine/article/mindfulness_in_legal_practice_is_going_mainstream/

Gold, A. (2012, May). Mindfulness: A challenge for our times. *Dade County Bar Association Bulletin*. Retrieved from http://www.dadecountybar.org/media/bulletin/May2012 Final.pdf

Gupta, U. (January 2, 1992). Blending Zen and the art of philanthropic pastry chefs—Buddhist monk puts the poor to work, and houses them with the profit. *Wall Street Journal*.

Halpern, C. (2008). *Making waves and riding the currents: Activism and the practice of wisdom.* San Francisco, CA: Berrett-Koehler.

Halpern, C. (2012). The mindful lawyer: Why contemporary lawyers are practicing meditation. *Journal of Legal Education*, 4, 641.

Hanh, T. N. (1999). *The miracle of mindfulness: An introduction to the practice of meditation.* Boston, MA: Beacon.

Harris, A., Lin, M., & Selbin, J. (2007). From the art of war to being peace: Mindfulness and community lawyering in a neoliberal age. *California Law Review*, 95, 2073.

Harvard Negotiation Law Review Symposium Issue. (2002). Mindfulness in the law and ADR Symposium. *Harvard Negotiation Law Review*, 7.

Hobbes, T. (2010). *Leviathan* (rev. ed., A. P. Martinich & B. Battiste, Eds.). New Haven, CT: Broadview Press.

Hyman, J. P. (2007). The mindful lawyer: Mindfulness meditation and law practice. *Vermont Bar Journal*, 33, 40.

Izumi, C. (2010). Implicit bias and the illusion of mediator neutrality. *Washington University Journal of Law & Policy*, 34, 71.

Jacobowitz, J. (2013). The benefits of mindfulness for litigators. *ABA Journal*. Retrieved from http://www.americanbar.org/publications/litigation_journal/2012_13/spring/benefits-mindfulness.html

Jha, A., Rogers, S., & Morrison, A (forthcoming). Mindfulness training in high stress professions: Strengthening attention & resilience. In R. Baer (Ed.), *Mindfulness-based treatment approaches: A clinician's guide* (2nd ed.). San Diego, CA: Elsevier.

Joko Beck, C. (1989). *Everyday zen: Love and work.* New York: HarperOne.

Kabat-Zinn, J. (1990). *Full catastrophe living: Using the wisdom of your body and mind to face stress, pain, and illness.* Delta.

Kabat-Zinn, J. (2006). *Coming to our senses.* New York, NY: Hyperion.

Keeva, S. (1999). *Transforming practices: Finding joy and satisfaction in the legal life.* Chicago, IL: Contemporary Books.

Keeva, S. (2002). Practicing from the inside out. *Harvard Negotiation Law Review*, 7, 97.

Krieger, L. (2002). Institutional denial about the dark side of law school, and fresh empirical guidance for constructively breaking the silence. *Journal of Legal Education*, 52, 112.

Kruse, K. (2010). Lawyers in character and lawyers in role. *Nevada Law Journal*, 10, 393.

Kuttner, R. (2010a). What does it mean to do the right thing? *Nevada Law Journal*, 10, 407.

Kuttner, R. (2010b). From adversity to relationality: A Buddhist-oriented relational view of integrative negotiation and mediation. *Ohio State Journal of Dispute Resolution*, 25, 931.

Langer, E. J. (1989). *Mindfulness.* Cambridge, MA: Da Capo Press.

Langer, E. J. (1997). *The power of mindful learning.* Cambridge, MA: Da Capo Press.

Langer, E. J. (2000). Mindful learning. *Current Directions in Psychological Science*, 9(6), 220–223.

Langer, E. J. (2005). *On becoming an artist.* New York, NY: Ballantine Books.

Langer, E. J. (2009). *Counterclockwise: Mindful health and the power of possibility.* New York, NY: Ballantine Books.

Langer, E. J., & Abelson, R. (1972). The semantics of asking a favor: How to succeed in getting help without really trying. *Journal of Personality and Social Psychology*, 24, 26–32.

Langer, E. J., Blank, A., & Chanowitz, B. (1978). The mindlessness of ostensibly thoughtful action: The role of "placebic" information in interpersonal interaction. *Journal of Personality and Social Psychology, 37,* 2014–2024.

Langer, E. J., & Moldoveanu, M. (2000). Mindfulness research and the future. *Journal of Social Issues, 56,* 129–139.

Langer, E., & Piper, A. (1987). The prevention of mindfulness. *Journal of Personality and Social Psychology, 53,* 280.

Larkin-Wong, K. (2012). A newbie's impression: One student's mindfulness lesson. *Journal of Legal Education, 4,* 665.

Lazar, S., Bush, G., Gollub, R., Fricchione, L., Khalsa, G., & Benson, H. (2000). Functional brain mapping of the relaxation response and meditation. *Neuroreport, 11,* 1581.

Lazar, S. W., Kerr, C. E., Wasserman, R. H., Gray, J. R., Greve, D. N., Treadway, M. T., ... & Fischl, B. (2005). Meditation experience is associated with increased cortical thickness. *Neuroreport, 16*(17), 1893.

Llewellyn, K. (1962). *Jurisprudence: Realism in theory and practice.* Chicago, IL: University of Chicago Press.

Magee, R. (2007). *The mindful law professor.* Unpublished manuscript.

Magee, R. (2009). *The mindful law professor interview* [Audio recording]. Retrieved from http://themindfullawprofessor.com/podcast/magee2009.html

Magee, R. (2011). *Educating lawyers to meditate? UMKC Law Review, 79,* 535.

Magee, R. (2013a). Paying attention to diversity. *Mindful Magazine.*

Magee, R. (2013b). Mindfulness and the renewal of legal education. In *New directions for teaching and learning: Contemplative studies in higher education, no. 134* (p. 31). San Francisco, CA: Jossey-Bass.

Maroney, T. (2011). Emotional regulation and judicial behavior. *California Law Review, 99,* 1485.

Masich, M. (April 1, 2010). Meditating lawyer group going strong one year later. *Law Week Colorado.* Retrieved from http://www.lawweekonline.com/2010/04/meditating-lawyer-group-going-strong-one-year-later/

McHugh, J. L. (1994). Zen and the art of lawyering. *Villanova Law Review, 39,* 1295.

McIntire, E. (2009). President's message: A call for mindfulness in our profession. *Massachusetts Bar Journal, 16*(7), 1.

Moffitt, P. (2007, September). Awakening in the body. *Shambhala Sun.* Retrieved from http://www.shambhalasun.com/index.php?option=com_content&task=view&id=3126

Porier, M. (2010). *Is Buddhism a religion: Should this matter to legal professionals.* Paper presented at the Annual Meeting of the The Law and Society Association. Retrieved from http://www.allacademic.com/meta/p406701_index.html

Porter, N. (2001). Stress-reduction: The mountain comes to Mohammed. *Pennsylvania Lawyer, 23,* 14.

Pounds, V. (2004). Promoting truthfulness in negotiation: A mindful approach. *Willamette Law Review, 40,* 181.

Ramirez, M. K. (2009). Into the twilight zone: Informing judicial discretion in federal sentencing. *Drake Law Review, 57,* 591.

Reilly, P. (2010). Mindfulness, emotions, and mental models; theory that leads to more effective dispute resolution. *Nevada Law Journal, 10,* 433.

Reuben, R. (2012). Bringing mindfulness into the classroom: A personal journey. *Journal of Legal Education, 4,* 674.

Rhoads, S., & Williams, S. (2011). Paying attention: Integrating mindfulness into your practice. *Washington State Bar News, 65*(7), 27.

Riskin, L. (2002). The contemplative lawyer: On the potential contributions of mindfulness meditation to law students, lawyers, and their clients. *Harvard Negotiation Law Review*, 7, 1.

Riskin, L (2003). Decision-making in mediation: The new old grid and the new new grid system. *Notre Dame Law Review*, 79(1). Retrieved from http://papers.ssrn.com/sol3/papers.cfm?abstract_id=1465214

Riskin, L (2004). Mindfulness: Foundational training for dispute resolution. *Journal of Legal Education*, 54, 79.

Riskin, L. (2009). Awareness and ethics in dispute resolution and law: Why mindfulness tends to foster ethical behavior. *South Texas Law Review*, 50, 494.

Riskin, L. (2010). Annual Saltman Lecture: Further beyond reason: Emotions, the core concerns, and mindfulness in negotiation. *Nevada Law Journal*, 10, 289.

Riskin, L. (2012). Awareness and the legal profession: An introduction to the Mindful Lawyer Symposium. *Journal of Legal Education*, 4, 634.

Rock, E. (2006). Mindfulness meditation, the cultivation of awarenes, mediator neutrality, and the possibility of justice. *Cardozo Law Conflict Resolution*, 6, 347.

Rogers, S. (2005). *Mindful parenting: Meditations, verses and visualizations for a more joyful life.* Miami Beach, FL: Mindful Living Press.

Rogers, S. L. (2007). *Mindfulness, balance & the lawyer's brain* [Florida CLE approved CD set and handbook].

Rogers, S. L. (2008). *The hand-dial: An interpersonal neurobiology application for teaching mindfulness to lawyers, 2008 Interpersonal Neurobiology Session with Daniel Siegel's Mindsight Institute* [Paper on file with author/audio podcast available on iTunes].

Rogers, S. L. (2009a). *The six-minute solution: A mindfulness primer for lawyers.* Miami Beach, FL: Mindful Living Press.

Rogers, S. L. (2009b). *Mindfulness for law students: Using the power of mindful awareness to achieve balance and success in law school.* Miami Beach, FL: Mindful Living Press.

Rogers, S. L. (2009c). *A context-contoured approach to mindfulness training: Enhancing accessibility by "speaking their language."* Presentation at Center for Mindfulness 7th Annual International Scientific Conference for Clinicians, researchers, and Educators [Audio-recording on file].

Rogers, S. (2011). Stop, look & listen—regain your focus through mindfulness. *The Young Lawyer*, 15 (4).

Rogers, S. L. (2012a). The mindful law school: An integrative approach to transforming legal education. *Touro Law Review*, 28, 1189.

Rogers, S. L. (2012b, March) Mindfulness matters. *Dade County Bar Association Bulletin*. Retrieved from http://www.dadecountybar.org/media/PDF%20Web%20Files/March%20Bulletin%20-%20FINAL%20HIGH%20RES.pdf

Rogers, S. L., & Jacobowitz, J. L. (2012). *Mindfulness and professional responsibility: A guide book for integrating mindfulness into the law school curriculum.* Miami Beach, FL: Mindful Living Press.

Rosen, R., Parker, C., Nielsen, V., Rogers, S., Kipnis, R., & Saeed, A. (2013). *Lawyers are followers and the poetry of resilience.* Unpublished manuscript.

Salzberg, S. (2002). *Faith: Trusting your own deepest experience.* New York, NY: Riverhead.

Scannell, W., Connon, R., Gibbons, A., Graham, R. M., Killam, J., & Richardson, M. (1994). *Judicial wellness: A stress management guide for and by judges.* Reno, NV: The National Judicial College.

Schiltz, P. J. (1999). On being a happy, healthy, and ethical member of an unhappy and unethical profession. *Vanderbilt Law Review*, 52, 871.

Schwartz, M. (2008). Humanizing legal education: An introduction to a symposium whose time came. *Washburn Law Journal*, 47, 235.

Seamone, E (2002). Judicial mindfulness. *University of Cincinnati Law Review*, 70, 1023.

Segal, Z. V., Williams, J. M. G., & Teasdale, J. D. (2002). *Mindfulness-based cognitive therapy for depression: a new approach to preventing relapse*. New York, NY: The Guilford Press.

Shapiro, D. (2010). From signal to semantic: Uncovering the emotional dimension of negotiation. *Nevada Law Journal*, 10, 461.

Sheldon, K. M., & Krieger, L. (2004). Does law school undermine law students? Examining changes in goals, values, and well-being. *Behavioral Sciences and the Law*, 22, 261–286.

Silver, M. (2004). Stress, burnout, vicarious trauma, and other emotional realities in the lawyer/client relationship. *Touro Law Review*, 19, 847.

Silver, M. (2012). Symposium introduction: Humanism goes to law school. *Touro Law Review*, 28, 1141.

Sloan, K. (2012, September 17). How to learn the law without losing your mind. *The National Law Journal*. Retrieved from http://www.law.com/jsp/nlj/PubArticleNLJ.jsp?id=1202571280345&thepage=3

Smalley, S., & Winston, D. (2010). *Fully present: The science, art and practice of mindfulness*. Boston, MA: De Capo Press.

Starzynski, J. (2009, July 3). Meditation great way to ease stress. *The Lawyers Weekly*. Retrieved from http://www.lawyersweekly.ca/index.php?section=article&volume=29&number=9&article=5

Starzynski, J. (2010, January 29). Teaching lawyers to be in the now. *The Lawyers Weekly*, 23. Retrieved from http://www.olap.ca/starzynski/23_V1_LAW_Jan29.pdf

Stempel, J. (2010). Feeding the right wolf: A Niebuhrian perspective on the opportunities and limits of mindful core concerns. *Nevada Law Journal*, 10, 472.

Sturgeon, A. (2011). The truth shall set you free: A distinctively Christian approach to deception in the negotiation process. *Pepperdine Dispute Resolution Law Journal*, 11, 395.

Sullivan, W., Colby, A., Wegner, J., Bond, L., & Shulman, L. (2007). *Educating lawyers: Preparation for the profession of law*. San Francisco, CA: Jossey-Bass.

Tolle, E. (2004). *The power of now*. Novato, CA: New World Library.

Tropin, H. (2012, June). Meditation and controlling the inner-mongo. *Dade County Bar Association Bulletin*. Retrieved from http://mindfulnessinlaw.com/mil_information_files/Harley_Tropin_Inner_Mongo_120901.pdf

Waldman, E. (2010). Mindfulness, ethics & emotions: The right stuff? *Nevada Law Journal*, 10, 513.

Weiss, A. (1997). Under pressure: Deal with your (and your employees') stress right at your desk. *Law Management*

West Allen, S. (2009). Exercise mind hygiene on a daily basis. *The Complete Lawyer*, 4(3). Retrieved from http://westallen.typepad.com/files/exercise-mind-hygiene.pdf

White, M. (1999). *Report on the contemplative law program and the Yale law contemplative practice retreat* (Fetzer Institute and Center for Contemplative Mind in Society).

Williams, D. (2010, March). Mastering stress and finding meaning as a lawyer. *Bench & Bar of Minnesota*, 67(3). Retrieved from http://www.mnbar.org/benchandbar/2010/mar10/practice.html

Woodward, B., & Armstrong, S. (1979). *The Brethren: Inside the Supreme Court*. New York, NY: Simon & Schuster

Zeglovitch, R. (2006). The mindful lawyer. *GPSolo*, 23, 7.

Zeidan, F., Martucci, K., Kraft, R., Gordon, N., McHaffie, J., & Coghill, R. (2011). Brain mechanisms supporting the modulation of pain by mindfulness meditation. *The Journal of Neuroscience*, 31(14), 5540–5548.

Zlotnick, D. M. (2012). Integrating mindfulness theory and practice into trial advocacy. *Journal of Legal Education*, 4, 654.